Odd Fellowship

Also from Westphalia Press

westphaliapress.org

Odd Fellowship

Its History and Manual

by Theo. A. Ross

WESTPHALIA PRESS
An imprint of Policy Studies Organization

Westphalia Press
An imprint of Policy Studies Organization
1527 New Hampshire Ave., NW
Washington, D.C. 20036
info@ipsonet.org

ISBN-13: 978-1-63391-223-6
ISBN-10: 163391223X

Cover design by Taillefer Long at Illuminated Stories:
www.illuminatedstories.com

Daniel Gutierrez-Sandoval, Executive Director
PSO and Westphalia Press

Updated material and comments on this edition
can be found at the Westphalia Press website:
www.westphaliapress.org

Thomas Wildey

ODD FELLOWSHIP:

ITS HISTORY AND MANUAL.

BY

THEO. A. ROSS,

GRAND SECRETARY OF THE SOVEREIGN GRAND LODGE.

CONTRIBUTORS:

HENRY L. STILLSON, *Past Grand Master,* - - OF VERMONT.
J. FLETCHER WILLIAMS, *Past Grand Master,* - - OF MINNESOTA.
GEO. COBURN, *Past Grand,* - - - - OF MARYLAND.
MRS. L. B. HALL, - - - - - OF INDIANA.

With an Introduction by

JOHN H. WHITE, *Grand Sire.*

TO THE MEMBERS OF THE

INDEPENDENT ORDER OF ODD FELLOWS

THROUGHOUT THE WORLD :

THAT GREAT AND UNIVERSAL BROTHERHOOD,

BOUND WITH THE CHAIN OF THE TRIPLE LINKS,

FRIENDSHIP, LOVE, TRUTH,

IN AN ESPECIAL COVENANT

TO PROTECT THE WIDOWS AND ORPHANS ; TO BURY THE DEAD :
TO HELP EACH OTHER IN WANT ; TO COUNSEL EACH OTHER
IN DIFFICULTY ; TO IMPROVE AND ELEVATE THE CHAR-
ACTER OF MAN ; TO ENLIGHTEN HIS MIND ; TO
ENLARGE THE SPHERE OF HIS AFFECTIONS ;
WHOSE FIELD OF ACTION IS BOUNDLESS AS THE EARTH,
AND WHOSE OFFERINGS UPON THE ALTAR OF HUMANITY
AGGREGATE NOT LESS THAN

ONE HUNDRED MILLIONS OF DOLLARS

IN THIS, THE NINETEENTH CENTURY,

THIS VOLUME,

A WORK OF LABOR, AND OF LOVE,

IS AFFECTIONATELY DEDICATED.

PREFACE.

THIS book was written to satisfy a want long felt in Odd Fellowship. Notwithstanding the existence of this Society since 1819, its history, aims, objects, and its extraordinary success in its peculiar work, are little understood by the community at large.

The membership itself is not as well informed upon these subjects as their great importance demands. For the first time access to this knowledge is rendered easy and it is hoped pleasant.

The plan of the present work differs in many respects from that of any other on the same subject. In its preparation, the aim has been to produce a convenient, compact and complete book of reference to everything connected with Odd Fellowship, that will instruct and enlighten the reader, lay or otherwise, and furnish him with a comprehensive exposition of its teachings, duties, objects and the wonderful results already attained. In order to accomplish this, and at the same time confine the work within reasonable limits, great care has been given to the condensation of the subject matter.

An Organization, consisting of 550,000 members, laboring faithfully for the amelioration of the human race—which has expended for that purpose more than forty-three millions of dollars—whose field of labor is co-extensive with the globe, presents to the world a unique spectacle that commands and deserves the earnest and most critical examination and consideration of all those who have, at heart, the welfare of their fellow man.

To all Grand Officers, officers and members generally, the work will be a *Vade-mecum*, a ready reference book for daily consultation. When the Sovereign Grand Lodge shall determine to establish under its guidance and control something in the nature of a National Endowment or Insurance Association, the Tables of Progress presented in this work will furnish the necessary basis whereon to erect a proper and well matured structure, wherein none will fear to enter, as each for himself can demonstrate its stability.

The numerous tables herein given, a work of infinite patience and labor, are of the utmost and far-reaching importance, and nothing, so graphically and succinctly, presents to our comprehension the mighty work done throughout the Order. It is only after a careful study of the results here presented, in compact form, that anything like a just appreciation of the grandeur of our past efforts can be gained. One is surprised and delighted, at every step, with the new sensations developed in their study. We know, in a general, hazy way that much has been done, but here we see who did it, and when and how it was done. We have, in them, the history of the Order crystallized and in shape for every day use. It is believed they will be of infinite use to the Order, and of great practical value, to every member, in its propagation.

The work enlarges the horizon of the reader. He is enabled to take in, at one sweeping glance, the panorama before him. As in Nature we observe that the beauty of the landscape consists in the harmony of its outlines, so here, in this work, where the object is to unfold the laws and workings of the Order, there is found a similar harmony of construction, which is calculated to impress one with a sense of its fitness and originality.

The Order is everywhere growing in usefulness and popularity. It has passed its season of infancy and now enjoys the lusty vigor and energy of ripe manhood. It everywhere faithfully performs its sacred mission, "to relieve the distressed, bury the dead, comfort the widow and educate the orphan."

There are now 8,334 Subordinate Lodges, contending with each other in their laudable efforts for supremacy in good works. Subordinate Encampments, to the number of

2,016, are daily depriving the pilgrimage of life of many of its terrors to the weak and oppressed.

The gentle sex has been enlisted under its banner, to assist in the fight against poverty, vice and the innumerable woes incident to life. Their labors have been crowned with unqualified success. They now number over forty thousand, and their ranks are daily increasing in numbers, power for good, and unlimited usefulness.

Nothing more clearly shows the marvelous and rapid increase of the Order than the unprecedented growth of the Patriarchs Militant. On September 24th, 1885, the status of this Branch was as follows: 1 Canton and 30 Chevaliers; on September 1st, 1887, 462 Cantons and 18,000 Chevaliers.

Every member in Odd Fellowship should know its history, duties and doctrines, in order the more effectually to proclaim its many victories in its chosen realm of warfare. He is enabled, from this storehouse of facts, to show that the results already attained are of such surpassing grandeur as to rival, in effectiveness, any and every other human agency devised for the relief of suffering humanity.

Let every brother and well-wisher of humanity, seriously and with calm deliberation, study the labors of our puissant army of workers, in the domain of Friendship, Love and Truth, that they may have a reason for their faith in our continued and unbounded success, and for encouragement in scattering broadcast the good seed, that our future harvests may embrace mankind in one harmonious whole.

INTRODUCTION.

BY JOHN H. WHITE, Grand Sire.

The object of the following pages is to give information to the general public, of the character, objects and import- ance of an institution in their midst but little known to them, as well as to make the members of it, better acquainted with themselves and the organization to which they belong, the second oldest fraternal institution in the world. The opera- tions and work of the Independent Order of Odd Fellows, are so quiet and unostentatious, that there is a lamentable ignorance, even upon the part of a vast number of those who take a most active interest in the work of their Lodges, and in ministering to the necessities of those members with whom they are directly associated. The Order has been in existence comparatively but a few years, not exceeding two hundred at most, yet in that short period of time, it has at- tained to an importance which is truly surprising. The first recorded evidence we have of its existence, is in the first half of the eighteenth century, but tradition, that lying jade, carries it back to a much earlier period. The place of its birth was England, and it seems to have been an organiza- tion of mechanics and laboring men, united for social pur- poses and to aid its members to obtain employment, as well as to assist them pecuniarily, when in need. So popular was the institution that it increased rapidly, and in 1887, from actual returns, the number of adult male members belonging to the Manchester Unity of Odd Fellows was 617,587, being an increase of 11,665 during the year, and the number of juveniles, young men from sixteen to twenty-one years of age, was 31,375, making a grand total of 648,962. Other Orders of Odd Fellows exist. (*See Chapter XIII.*)

As rapid as was the increase of the Order in England, it was very slow compared with the growth of the great American Branch of the Order. This Branch, self constituted in Baltimore, in the State of Maryland, April 26th, 1819, by five English Odd Fellows, with Thomas Wildey at the head, has during the sixty-eight years of its existence, increased so that on January 1st, 1887, from actual returns, its adult male members numbered 547,303, and the number of female members of the Rebekah Degree was 33,958. Surely there must be something true, and good, and noble, in an institution which takes such a hold upon the popular feeling, in an enlightened and civilized community, as to cause such an increase in so short a time. Remember that these numbers are mostly adult males, and largely men of families, who exert an influence not only upon their immediate connections, but, as well, in the communities in which they reside. It is sometimes said that Odd Fellowship is the offspring of Masonry, but this is in no sense true and the writer of this knows whereof he speaks. While occasionally a similarity of expression can be traced in a few of the unimportant part of the ceremonials, in the fundamentals they are essentially different. Masonry is a noble institution, but is as unlike Odd Fellowship, as two institutions, organized by human beings can well be. The one is theoretical, the other practical; the one is ancient, the other modern; the government of the one is autocratic, the other democratic; the one deals out charity and assists its needy members, but only to a limited extent and only *as* a charity; the other assists its members, not only from charity, but because it is their due, and this assistance is afforded in large measure. American Odd Fellowship is composed of the great middle, industrial classes almost exclusively; Masonry, of all grades of society, from the titled and wealthy of this and foreign lands, to the humblest laborer in our midst. In England, when Odd Fellowship arose, we are told that Masonry was composed almost exclusively of the titled and the proud, and not of the mechanics and working men who organized the more modern institution. Masonry has been long in achieving its present standing. Odd Fellowship in less than two centuries has outstripped it in numbers and importance, and is to-day the grandest fraternal organization of the world. The two great Orders of Odd Fellows, the Manchester Unity, and the American Order, from actual returns, number 1,164,890 adult males, scattered throughout the habitable globe. Masonry, according to partial returns and from *estimates* made by the Masonic Token, from all jurisdictions, numbers among its devotees throughout the world 1,082,992 persons, or 81,898 less than the two branches of Odd Fellows above mentioned. How nearly correct these estimates may be, is of course, much a matter of speculation, as there are no returns accessible, for unlike Odd Fellowship, it has no grand central head to which its various Grand Bodies hold allegiance and to which they send annual reports.

The Order of Odd Fellows was the first to establish, as auxiliaries to the regular Lodges, Mutual Aid and Benefit Associations, which granted stipulated sums, on the death of members, in addition to the regular weekly and funeral benefits granted by the Lodges themselves. All the numerous Aid and Benefit Associations which have sprung up in the country, in the last few years, are but offshoots of our great Order, and have been copied after it.

The main objects of Odd Fellowship are, to afford mutual relief and protection to its members in times of want, distress, danger or difficulty; to cultivate social relations among its members, teach them to be industrious and frugal, inculcate correct moral principles and increase, by the practice of charity, their love for their fellow men.

In its government the Order is popular. Its legislative bodies are purely representative. First we have the Subordinate Lodges and Encampments, chartered, by the Sovereign Grand Lodge, then, when a sufficient number of these Lodges or Encampments are instituted in any particular State, Colony or Country, they are organized and formed into State or Colonial Grand Lodges or Grand Encampments, which receive their Charters from the Sovereign Grand Lodge. The membership of these Bodies is composed of past presiding officers of Lodges or Encampments, or Representatives of them, or both, and certain legislative powers are granted to them by the supreme head of the Order. This supreme head is called the Sovereign Grand Lodge. It has original jurisdiction in Odd Fellowship the world over, and is composed of Representatives from these several State and Colonial Grand Bodies, and the officers elected by it to preside over its deliberations and manage its affairs in the recess of the sessions of the Supreme Body. These Officers and Representatives hold office for two years and the Body meets annually at such place as it shall have selected at the preceding annual session. In its inception, the Order was composed only of the Subordinate Lodges and when a few of them had been chartered by the original one, a Grand Lodge was organized. Subsequently the Encampment Branch was added, the members of which were all members of the Subordinate Lodges. Then Rebekah Lodges, composed of Lodge members and their wives, were organized, and lastly the military Degree, known as " Patriarchs Militant," all the members of which must be members of Subordinate Encampments.

This work is compiled for the purpose of more fully explaining and amplifying the Order, and especially the American Branch of it. It gives us, in detail, its history, tells us of its origin, shows the various and gradual steps it has taken in arriving at its present magnificent proportions and, in this connection, is given, from the records of the Sovereign Grand Lodge, a synopsis of the yearly legislation of the supreme head, with statistical tables showing its regular and steady increase in numbers and importance, the amount of its receipts and expenditures, and the money paid for the relief of its members. In a large sense, it is a documentary history of the Order. It also contains a Manual; a chapter illustrating and explaining the Emblems of the Order, the principles and precepts they inculcate etc. In short, it tells the whole story of the origin, rise and progress of the institution, and, as such, is invaluable to every Odd Fellow who seeks to know to what manner of organization he is attached.

CONTENTS.

CHAPTER VIII.

CHAPTER IX.

CHAPTER X.

CHAPTER XI.

CHAPTER XII.

CHAPTER XIII.

CHAPTER XIV.

CHAPTER XV.

CHAPTER XVI.

PORTRAITS.

GENERAL ILLUSTRATIONS.

CHAPTER I.

HISTORY OF THE ORDER.

OUR Order is now everywhere known as a benefactor of the human race. Our flag proudly floats in the breeze of every clime, as a beacon to the pilgrims of life's fitful journey, and a welcome guide to the tempest-driven mariner across the troubled waves of human woe to its calm haven of rest.

It exists in response to the cravings of the soul for a domain of brotherhood, a fraternity wherein sweet and congenial companionships and mutual offices of kindness and regard would soften the asperities of life and remove the evils of prejudice, bigotry and intolerance. An Order that teaches a higher ideal of life, that gives men a new faith in virtue, charity and love, assuredly deserves a considerate study by all those who are interested in the welfare of the human race. As a means to an end, it has become one of the most powerful weapons in the warfare upon ignorance, vice and the host of evils that beset man at every step in his earthly career.

It does not seek a veiled origin in the misty shades of the past to surround it with the false glamour that arises from the belief in the doctrine of *omne ignotum pro magnifico.* This age of enlightenment has emancipated us from the gross credulity of the past. Antiquity bears with it no passport of truth or goodness.

The Order of Odd Fellows originated in England in the Eighteenth Century. In the early part of that century the celebrated Daniel De Foe mentions the Society of Odd Fellows, and in the *Gentlemen's Magazine* for 1745, the Odd

Fellows' Lodge is mentioned as "a place where very pleasant and recreative evenings are spent." The poet James Montgomery, in 1788, wrote a song for a Body of Odd Fellows. The *Odd Fellows' Keepsake* states that the early English Lodges were supported and their members relieved by each member and visitor paying a penny to the Secretary on entering the Lodge. These allusions are sufficient proof of the existence of the Order at the time, but they tell us nothing of its aims, objects and characteristics.

From other sources it is known that the Lodges were originally formed by workingmen for social purposes, and for giving the brethren aid and assisting them to obtain employment when out of work. When a brother could not obtain work he was given a Card and funds enough to carry him to the next Lodge, and if unsuccessful there, that Lodge facilitated his farther progress in the same way.

Where he found employment, there he deposited his Card.

At first there was little or no Ritual, and no formal method of conducting the business of the Lodge. These were matters of gradual and slow growth. The English are and were very conservative, and do not readily yield to innovations. Time, however, works wonders, so that in the end many radical and necessary changes were made in the Order. Even to this day some of the original and characteristic features of the Order are still practiced in the English branch of the fraternity. In the early days of the institution, after the formal business was transacted, conviviality and good fellowship became the order of the night, and the brethren, glass and pipe in hand, made the welkin ring with the melody of their favorite songs :

> " When Friendship, Love and Truth abound
> Among a Band of Brothers,
> The cup of joy goes gaily round
> Each shares the bliss of others."

Or

> "Then let us be social, be generous, be kind,
> And let each take his glass and be mellow,
> Then we'll join heart and hand, leave dissensions behind,
> And we'll each prove a hearty Odd Fellow."

It is said that the titles of the officers of the Lodge were taken from the "Order of Gregorianus," which met at St. Albans, in May, 1736. In the early history of the Order each Lodge was the arbiter of its own fate and practically supreme. The doctrine of self-institution prevailed then, as it did afterwards, in the establishment of the Order in the United States. Secessions from Lodges were frequent and rendered the Lodges less able to fulfill the object of their being. The brethren were slow to learn that "in union there is strength." They finally learned this wholesome truth and with it came, in 1809, the formation of the Manchester Unity, the most gigantic beneficial society in the world, the history of the birth and growth of which will be found in a subsequent chapter.

Wildey, the father and founder of American Odd Fellowship, brought with him to this country the seed, which carefully sown and nurtured, has grown to such a mighty tree that, in the shade produced by its wide-spreading branches, the brethren may seek and obtain solace and security from most of the storms incident to human life.

> " Ours is no sapling, chance-sown by the fountain,
>   Blooming in summer, in winter to fade;
> And when every leaf is stripped from the mountain,
>   The more shall our brethren exult in its shade.
>   Moored in the rifted rock,
>   Proof to the tempest's shock,
>   The firmer 'tis rooted, the ruder 't may blow;
>   Heaven send it happy dew,
>   Earth lend it sap anew,
>   Greenly to bourgeon and broadly to grow."

Its perennial growth is now well assured, for the grateful tears of the widow and orphan have watered the tender plant, and it has been warmed and vivified by the sunny smile of approving heaven.

The natal day of American Odd Fellowship was the 26th of April, 1819. The attempts made, prior to this date, to establish the Order here, failed, or the sickly and sporadic growth became absorbed in the more vigorous family

planted by Wildey. The circumstances attending this historic event are here briefly presented.

Thomas Wildey was born in London on the 15th day
of January, 1782. On reaching manhood he was initiated
into an Odd Fellow's Lodge in which he distinguished himself by his zeal and integrity.

This was prior to the formation of the Manchester
Unity, so that the body to which he belonged, existed and
worked according to the early mode of self-institution.

Desirous of spreading the Order to which he was so
ardently attached, he, with others, started a new Lodge,
styled Morning Star Lodge, No. 38, located in London.

Until 1817, he continued to be actively interested in
the work of the Order and more than once passed through
the chairs. The cheering news and the favorable reports
received by him from countrymen here, decided him to
seek, in this new and highly favored land, a fairer fortune.
He possessed hope, health and industry, sure passports to
prosperity anywhere. The exigencies of commerce had
greatly mollified the hatred and animosities engendered by
the late war, so that he had every reason to expect the full
fruition of his hopes.

As was natural to a stranger in a strange land, he immediately sought to make the acquaintance of his fellow countrymen residing in the City of Baltimore. Among the first
of these whom he met was John Welch, an Odd Fellow.
Animated by his former zeal for the Order, and feeling the
loss of his wonted field of labor and its allied social pleasures and advantages, he at once took steps to form a Lodge.
The requisite number was five, so that with three the way
to success would be clear. They advertised for the lacking
number in the *Baltimore American*, at first with partial success. They inserted the following in the same paper on the
27th of March, 1819, and met with complete success :

NOTICE TO ODD FELLOWS.

" A few members of the Society of Odd Fellows will be glad to meet
their brethren for the purpose of forming a Lodge, on Friday evening, 2d
April, at the Seven Stars, Second street, at the hour of seven P. M."

"THE SEVEN STARS," SECOND STREET, BALTIMORE, 1819.

This last advertisement brought to the rendezvous a certain Richard Rushworth, who, with John Duncan and John Cheatham, whom they had met a month before, completed the charmed number. They all had been initiated into the Order in England, and so far their qualifications were correct. On that memorable 26th day of April, they, in accordance with the ancient custom, self-instituted themselves a Lodge, which they named " Washington Lodge of Odd Fellows."

Thus their frail bark was launched upon a wide and unknown sea. How would the voyage end and to what haven go? Still their buoyant spirits and energetic natures augured well for their ultimate success. They presented the Order to the world—God's problem awaiting man's solution. The seed that was to grow into such a mighty oak was this day planted. They could not foresee the result, the soil to them was unknown, untried ; they contributed their all to success, patient labor and constant vigilance, and that, too, in the face of bitter opposition.

They met at the public house of Thomas Lupton, the place designated in the above advertisement, and after the formal opening of the Lodge, Thomas Wildey was installed, Noble Grand, and John Welch, Vice Grand. The other offices were distributed among the rest of the brethren.

The Order was now started on its mission to fraternize the world and disseminate everywhere its peculiar doctrines of Friendship, Love and Truth. In 1817, the Manchester Unity made a number of radical changes in the Work of the Order. In fact for several years prior to this date, the Unity was engaged in evolving order out of chaos, in constructing a suitable Ritual and a practical Code of Laws for its better regulation. As these changes and additions were unknown to Wildey and his brethren, the work performed by them was necessarily not in harmony with that of the Unity. They learned this fact from a Henry M. Jackson, who arrived in Baltimore shortly after the institution of the Lodge. It appears that Mr. Jackson came to America with the prime object of introducing Odd Fellowship. He was ignorant of the fact that the Order already existed here. He visited the Lodge at the "Seven Stars" and obligingly instructed the brethren aright in the Work and placed them in possession of all the information necessary to work in conformity with the regulations of the Unity. In September, 1819, the Lodge numbered nineteen members. This incident showed them the necessity of fraternal union with that rapidly growing branch of the Order in England, the Manchester Unity. At this time and while the brethren were in this frame of mind, P. G. Crowder, of Preston, England, visited Baltimore. Brother Crowder, at their request, promised that on his return he would present to the proper authorities their petition for a Charter and for future fellowship. Upon his return he presented the petition to his own Lodge, which promptly granted the ORIGINAL CHARTER FOR WASHINGTON LODGE. (*Engraved on opposite page.*)

This Charter was not received by the Lodge until October. On the 23d of that month it was accepted, and the Lodge was then considered to be legally established. At the election in this month, Noble Grand Wildey was re-elected, but not without opposition. Washington Lodge was not altogether a happy family at this time ; discord and dissensions had arisen and the consequent result of disintegration was going on, to end at length in the withdrawal of the dissatisfied.

Those who withdrew desired to form a new Lodge to be called " Franklin Lodge," and to work under a Charter to be obtained, if possible, from the Manchester Unity.

Their application to the Unity for a Charter of course failed, as Washington Lodge under its Charter was the Supreme Mother Lodge, with untrammeled and sole jurisdiction in respect to the granting of Charters. After the forma tion of the Grand Lodge of Maryland and the United States, Franklin Lodge received a Charter from that Body on August 22d, 1821. The Lodge was instituted on the 5th of September, 1821, and is still earnestly at work promulgating and practicing the principles of the Order.

WASHINGTON'S LODGE.

Pluribus Unum.

THE GRAND
LODGE OF MARYLAND,
AND OF THE
United States of America,
OF THE
INDEPENDENT ORDER
OF
ODDFELLOWSHIP.

TO all whom it may concern this *Warrant* or *Dispensation*, is a free gift from the DUKE of YORK's LODGE, of the Independent Order of ODDFELLOWSHIP, holden at Preston, in the County of Lancaster, in Old England, to a number of Brothers residing in the City of Baltimore, to establish a Lodge, at the House of Brother THOMAS WOODWARD, in South Frederick Street in the said City; Hall'd by the Title of "No. 1, WASHINGTON'S LODGE, the GRAND LODGE of Maryland, and of the United States of America" that the said Lodge being the first established in the United States, hath power to grant a *Warrant* or *Dispensation* to a number of Brothers of the Independant Order of ODDFELLOWSHIP, into any State of the Union, for the encouragement and support of Brothers of the said Order, when on Travel or otherwise.——And be it further observed that the said Lodge be not removed from the House of Brother THOMAS WOODWARD so long as five Brothers are agreeable to hold the same——In testimony hereof we have subjoined our Names and affixed the Seal of our Lodge this the First Day of February One Thousand Eight Hundred and Twenty.

James Mawdsley	G.M	*John Crowder*	P.G	*Geo Ward*	P.G
John Cottam	N.G	*Wm Topping*	P.G	*John Walmsley*	P.G
Geo Naylor	V.G	*Saml Pemberton*	P.G	*Geo Bell*	P.G
John Eccles	S..y				

FAC-SIMILE OF ORIGINAL CHARTER OF ODDFELLOWSHIP.

COLORS.

 PURPLE    BLUE

RED   MAROON. (SEAL)

For more than two years and a half after the establishment of the Order, Washington Lodge was the sole exponent and custodian of the rites and mysteries of Odd Fellowship.

It was a long night of labor to firmly lay the foundation of the present magnificent superstructure. The weary toiler had but little rest, until the bright sun of success appeared at last, and dispelled at once the darkness of doubt, and the clouds of despair.

The long-looked for day was near at hand.

In 1820, the " Committee of Past Grands " was constituted. " This Body does not appear to have been in possession of any established powers, extent of jurisdiction, or permanent officers, and in convention was destitute of all regulation other than such as was reflected by the dim light of ' ancient usage.' Matters of grievance was the principal business submitted to it ; but its decisions were in no case final or operative, being merely recommendatory to the Lodge, and were adopted or rejected at option."

The condition of the Order at this time was quite anomalous compared with the existing order of affairs.

Washington Lodge was both a Subordinate and a Grand Body. It stood alone, for Franklin as yet had no legitimate existence.

The membership perceived that something should be done to remove the legislative from the operative Body. On February 7th, 1821, a meeting of the Committee of Past Grands was held, to take into consideration the propriety of establishing a Grand Lodge of legislative capacity, separate and distinct from Working Lodges. After a careful consideration of the subject, it was unanimously decided that it was necessary to make the above separation, and as a concomitant thereto, Washington Lodge was invited to surrender to the Grand Lodge to be formed, the sole possession of the Charter received by the said Lodge from England. To all this the Lodge formally agreed, and on February 22d, 1821, the Charter of Washington Lodge, received from the Duke of York's Lodge, was surrendered with all its powers into the hands of the Past Grands who were then to constitute the Grand Lodge. The Grand Lodge of Maryland and the United States was organized, and the following officers installed :

Thomas Wildey, Grand Master; John P. Entwisle, Deputy Grand Master; Wm. S. Couth, Grand Warden; John Welch, Grand Secretary; John Boyd, Grand Guardian ; Wm. Larkam, Grand Conductor.

Washington Lodge having surrendered its Charter, the Grand Lodge organized and proceeded forthwith to present it with a Charter. The document, however, was not prepared until the 9th of February, 1822.

CHARTER OF WASHINGTON LODGE, No. 1, O. I. O. F.

ORDER OF INDEPENDENT ODD FELLOWS.

To Whom It May Concern :

The Grand Lodge of Maryland, by authority of a Grand Charter granted from the Grand Lodge of the United States held in the City of Baltimore, State of Maryland, doth hereby grant

This Warrant or Dispensation

To a number of brothers of the Order of Independent Odd Fellows, residing in the City of Baltimore, State of Maryland, to establish a Lodge in any convenient place, to be hailed by the title of THE WASHINGTON LODGE, No. 1, for the encouragement and support of brothers of the said Order when on travel, or otherwise. And the said Washington Lodge being duly formed, is hereby authorized and empowered to initiate into the mysteries of said Order, any person or persons duly proposed and approved according to the law of Odd Fellows, and to administer to these Brothers all the privileges and benefits arising therefrom, and to enact By-Laws for the government of their Lodge ; *Provided always*, that The Washington Lodge, No. 1, do act according to the order and in conjunction with and obedience to the Grand Lodge, adhering to and supporting the Articles, Charges and Degrees delivered with this Dispensation ; and in default thereof, this Warrant or Dispensation may be suspended or taken away, at the discretion of the Grand Lodge ; and further, the Grand Lodge (in consideration of the due performance of the above) do bind themselves to repair all damage or destruction of the Dispensation, Charges or Degrees, whether by fire or other accident ; provided, sufficient proof be given, and there is no illegal concealment or wilful destruction of the same. And the Grand Lodge will support The Washington Lodge, No. 1, in the exercise of their duty, and in the privileges and honors of the Order.

IN WITNESS WHEREOF, we have displayed the colors and subscribed our names, and affixed the Seal of the Grand Lodge of Maryland and of the

United States, this 22d day of February, Anno Domini, one thousand eight hundred and twenty-one.

[SEAL.] THOS. WILDEY, G. M.   JOHN WELCH, G. S.
          J. P. ENTWISLE, D. G. M.   JOHN BOYD, G. G.
          WM. S. COUTH, G. W.   EZEKIEL WILSON, G. C.

At this meeting, on February 22d, 1821, the Grand Lodge provided means for its support as follows :-

Resolved, That *ten per centum* be paid by the Subordinate Lodges on their receipts, for the support of the Grand Lodge.

Resolved, That each member pay to the Grand Lodge *seventy-five cents* for the Golden Rule Degree.

Resolved, That thirty dollars be charged for Dispensations for opening Lodges, *viz. :*

Ten dollars for the Dispensation.

Ten dollars for the White, Blue and Scarlet Degrees, and Books of Charges, and

Ten dollars for the Intermediate Degrees, called the Covenant and Remembrance.

The Covenant and Remembrance Degrees were prepared by John P. Entwisle, P. G., and adopted by the Committee of Past Grands in 1820. The Golden Rule Degree was at this time conferred only upon Past Grands.

In the proceedings of August 22d, 1821, there is reference made to the " Grand Committee." This term is used to distinguish the officers and members of the Grand Lodge when acting in other than the regular sessions of that Body. Business transacted by the Grand Committee was not clothed with all the authority of law until approved by the Grand Lodge at a regular session.

In 1822 Grand Guardian Boyd presented two-eighths of tickets of the Washington Monument Lottery, purchased for the use of the Grand Lodge. The numbers were 12,594 and 15. There is no report of their having drawn prizes. At the same session, in order to have punctuality and a better attendance, the following resolutions were adopted :

Resolved, That any member of the Grand Lodge having been regularly summoned to attend said meeting, without sending an apology in writing, shall be fined 50 cents ; and at a Grand Committee meeting, 25 cents ; and that any brother leaving the room at any meeting without the consent of the Grand Master, or presiding officer, shall be fined one dollar.

Resolved, That every member of the Grand Lodge not being present within fifteen minutes after the specified time, shall be subject to the fine affixed to such offence.

The Grand Committee met pursuant to call, on April 13th, 1823, to consider an application from Massachusetts Lodge, No. 1, at Boston, for a Charter with Grand Lodge powers.

Massachusetts Lodge, No. 1, was organized, at Boston, Mass., on the self-institution principle, on the 26th of March, 1820. It continued to work under the impression that it was the only Lodge in the country, until February, 1822, when correspondence took place between the Baltimore and Boston brethren. When they were informed that the Grand Lodge of Maryland and of the United States was working under a Charter and was possessed of the powers therein set forth, they immediately acknowledged the Grand Lodge to be the supreme authority, and at once asked for a Charter for a Grand Lodge, with authority to grant Charters to Lodges that might be formed in that State. Their request was immediately complied with, and a Charter was granted to Massachusetts Lodge, No. 1, and a Dispensation for a Grand Lodge to issue Charters for other Lodges in the State. Grand Master Wildey was appointed to convey the Charter to Boston, which he did, and on the 9th day of June, 1823, he instituted Massachusetts Lodge, No. 1, and on the 11th, the Grand Lodge of Massachusetts. The following Grand Officers were installed :

Daniel Hersey, Grand Master; Henry Solomon, Deputy Grand Master; James B. Barnes, Grand Warden; William Bishop, Grand Secretary; John Snowden, Grand Guardian; James B. Eaton, Grand Conductor.

The application from Massachusetts imparted new life to the members of the Grand Lodge of Maryland, as they were at this time in correspondence with members of the Order in New York, who, like the Boston brethren, were ignorant of the existence of the Order elsewhere. The New York Lodge was finally brought to acknowledge the authority of the Grand Lodge of Maryland and of the United

States, and the Grand Committee met on June 15th, 1823, to consider the following application for a Dispensation for a Grand Charter :

To the Grand Lodge of Maryland and of the United States:

We, the undersigned, for and in behalf of Columbia Lodge, No. 1, of I. O. F., held at Brother Lovett's, 279 Grand street, having received a legal Dispensation from the Loyal Beneficent Duke of Sussex Lodge, No. 2, Liverpool, for the Subordinate Lodge, do further petition for a Dispensation from your Lodge, to form a Grand Lodge of the State of New York. We trust you will forward us the necessary documents early as possible, as G. M. Wildey intends installing our officers on his return from Boston. Wishing the Grand Lodge of Maryland and of the United States every prosperity, we remain yours in the bonds of F. L. and T.,

P. G. JOHN B. ROBINSON,	P. G. R. WATTS,
P. G. JAMES SIMISTER,	M. N. G. THOS. TURNBULL,
P. G. JAMES CLARIDGE,	V. G. JOS. BARTON,
P. G. JOHN GRANT,	SEC'Y T. BALL.

It appears that Grand Master Wildey, on his way to Boston, visited the Lodge and set forth so earnestly and satisfactorily the advantages to accrue from a union with the Maryland Order, that the New York brethren became fully persuaded and lost no time in forwarding the above application.

The Dispensation was at once granted, and on June 24th, 1823, G. M. Wildey instituted that Body and installed the following Grand Officers :

John B. Robinson, Grand Master ; James Simister, Deputy Grand Master ; John Grant, Grand Warden ; James Claridge, Grand Secretary.

After the Grand Committee had considered and acted upon the application of Columbia Lodge, New York, a petition was presented from William Matthews, N. G., and other officers and members of Pennsylvania Lodge, at Philadelphia, for a Charter for said Lodge. This Lodge was self-instituted on the 26th of December, 1821. It first met at the house of John Upton, at No. 66 Dock street. In a short time it was removed to Broad street, and afterwards to the corner of Chestnut and Seventh streets.

The following brothers composed the Lodge at its institution :

John Pearce, Noble Grand ; James Day, Vice Grand ; John B. Robinson, Secretary ; John Upton, Treasurer ; Samuel Croucher, Guardian.

Thomas Hepworth, who was the first member admitted, was immediately elected Secretary in place of John B. Robinson. Grand Master Wildey, on his way to Boston, visited Pennsylvania Lodge and found that the members were desirous of obtaining a Charter from Columbia Lodge of New York. His visit to Boston was providential in all respects. He brought New York into fellowship and perforce Pennsylvania also.

The following letter to P. G. Entwisle from the officers of the Lodge in Philadelphia is self-explanatory :

PHILADELPHIA, June 6th, 1823.

Respected Brother—We have the pleasure to inform you that G. M. Wildey arrived in Philadelphia on Sunday, in good health. We assembled a few brothers by two o'clock. The information we received from our worthy brother was pleasing and instructive. This Lodge had come to a determination to take a Dispensation, Charter and Degrees, and hearing that a Lodge in New York received a Dispensation from England, we had applied for one from them before the arrival of Brother Wildey. Brother Wildey wrote us a letter from New York which we received this morning. He gives us such information as to enable us to apply to the Grand Lodge of Maryland and the United States for a Charter, etc., and he says he will, on his return, provide us with other documents.

Wishing you every blessing this world can afford, we remain in the bonds of F. L. and T.,

WM. MATTHEWS, N. G.   JNO. STURGIS, V. G.
THOS. HEPWORTH, P. G.   AARON NICHOLS, P. G.
NATH'L LONGMIRE, SEC'Y.

P. G. ENTWISLE, ESQ.

The Charter for the Lodge, as prayed for, was granted, as well as a Grand Charter for a Grand Lodge. Grand Master Wildey, on his return from Boston, presented the Charter to Pennsylvania Lodge, No. 1, and instituted the Grand Lodge of Pennsylvania, on the 27th of June, 1823, and installed the following Grand Officers :

Aaron Nichols, Grand Master ; Thomas Small, Deputy Grand Master ; Benjamin Richardson, Grand Warden ; Benjamin Daffin, Grand Secretary ; Joseph Richardson, Grand Treasurer.

The position of the Grand Lodge of Maryland and the United States was now more anomalous than ever since the admission of the jurisdictions of Massachusetts, New York and Pennsylvania.

To obviate all difficulties, it was proposed to form a Grand Lodge of the United States, to be composed of the Representatives and Proxies of the several Grand Lodges, and that the Grand Lodge of Maryland should have jurisdiction over the Subordinate Lodges in Maryland, and that the Grand Lodge of Maryland and the United States should surrender its Charter and powers to the Grand Lodge of the United States, to be thus formed. This scheme had been submitted to the several Grand Bodies, and the result was, that at the annual session, held February 22d, 1824, the Grand Master announced that Proxies had been appointed to organize a separate Grand Lodge of the United States, *viz.*: Massachusetts, Grand Master Wildey; New York, P. G. Scotchburn; and Pennsylvania, Grand Guardian Boyd. Maryland was represented by Grand Secretary Entwisle, who was elected for that purpose at this session. Grand Master Wildey declined to act as Proxy for Massachusetts, on account of his position as Grand Master, but appointed Maurice Fennel, who had been elected Assistant Grand Secretary, August 22d, 1823, to act in his place. The Grand Lodge took a recess to give an opportunity to the Grand Committee to make arrangements for the organization of the Grand Lodge of the United States.

The Grand Committee met and organized, by inviting Grand Master Wildey to preside. The following resolutions were then unanimously adopted:

Resolved, As the opinion of the Representatives assembled, that it is essentially necessary to the success of a Grand Lodge, that it should be established on the most undoubted basis; and to which end, it is advisable to obtain from the Grand Lodge of Maryland and of the United States, the Charter under which the said Grand Lodge now operates.

Resolved, That the Grand Lodge of Maryland and of the United States be invited to convey the Charter, obtained from England, to the Grand Lodge of the United States, in a separate and distinct capacity, for the exclusive use of that Body.

Resolved, That the Representatives of each Grand Lodge be directed to communicate with their constituents, on the propriety of obtaining the original Charter, as provided for in the foregoing resolutions ; and that the Grand Master call the Representatives together, within the shortest possible time, for the purpose of ascertaining the views of the several Grand Lodges.

At a called session of the Grand Committee, April 15th, 1824, pursuant to the last resolution, Grand Secretary Entwisle reported that the above resolutions in reference to the organization of the Grand Lodge of the United States, had been approved by the several Grand Lodges. The subject was referred to a committee, who submitted certain pertinent resolutions and the following preamble, which were unanimously adopted :

Whereas, It is expedient, in sound policy, that the Grand Lodges of the Order of I. O. F. in the United States should hold a close adherence, and a regular correspondence with each other, and it is imperative, in strict justice, to render the several Grand Lodges in the Union, independent of each other, and equally represented in the Grand Lodge of the United States, either by Representatives or Proxies ; and that it is inexpedient, as well as invidious, that the Grand Lodge of Maryland, and the Grand Lodge of the United States, should act under the same Charter, and be presided over by the same Grand Master, whereby the office of Grand Master would be confined to the State of Maryland, to the preference of one State, and possibly to the injury of the whole.

The Charter of the Grand Lodge of Maryland and of the United States, was to be invested in the Past Grands of the Grand Lodge of the United States.

The next thing in order was the preparation and adoption of a Constitution. The committee, to whom the duty of preparing the Constitution was assigned, reported August 23d, 1824; the result of their labors was adopted, and a copy ordered to be forwarded to each of the Grand Lodges for concurrence. The next meeting of the Grand Lodge of Maryland and of the United States, held November 22d, 1824, was the last in its dual state. After this session the Grand Lodge of Maryland acted in its capacity of a State Grand Lodge.

A preliminary meeting for the organization of the Grand Lodge of the United States was held January 15th, 1825, at which the following Constitution, referred to the several Grand Lodges for concurrence, was presented and accepted :

THE FIRST CONSTITUTION OF THE GRAND LODGE OF THE UNITED STATES.

THE GRAND CONSTITUTION OF THE GRAND LODGE OF THE UNITED STATES, OF THE INDEPENDENT ORDER OF ODD FELLOWS—FORMING AND COMMENCING 22ND OF FEBRUARY, 1825.

§ 1. ART. 1. The Grand Lodge of the United shall be composed of a G. M., D. G. M., G. S., G. G., and a Representative or Proxy of each Grand Lodge in the United States, acting under a legal Charter.

ART. 2. Every State Grand Lodge shall be equally represented in the Grand Lodge of the United States, especially on every subject of importance, as also on alterations, repeals, or amendments, etc., in any of the laws or Constitution.

ART. 3. Any motion for an alteration, repeal or amendment to the Constitution, must be communicated in writing, and sent to the Grand Master of the Grand Lodge of the United States, or his Deputy, six months previous to the annual meeting, in order that the Grand Lodge may communicate the same to the Representatives of each Grand Lodge in the United States, in order that they may send Deputies or appoint Proxies to vote on the same ; and a majority of two-thirds will be necessary to decide.

ART. 4. The Grand Lodge of the United States shall meet annually on the 22nd of February, on general business, and the G. M., or his Deputy, shall have discretionary power to call a Special Committee on extraordinary business.

ART. 5. That the City of Baltimore, in the State of Maryland, be the permanent seat of the Grand Lodge of the United States, being senior in order, as well as central in situation.

ART. 6. That the Representative or Proxy of each Grand Lodge, in order to be regularly admitted into the Grand Lodge of the United States, must be in possession of a Certificate signed by the G. M., D. G. M., and G. S., with the Seal of the said Grand Lodge affixed. Should the Representative not be known to any member of the Grand Lodge of the United States, he shall be put on his oath and solemn obligations, that the Certificate that he is in possession of, is genuine ; and on entering the Grand Lodge, he must work his way by the Golden Rule of the Fourth Degree.

ART. 7. That no Representative or Proxy leave the Lodge during its session, without permission of the G. M., or presiding officer, and Password from the D. G. M.

ART. 8. That every Representative or Proxy, being regularly summoned by the G. S. to attend an annual meeting, and neglecting to attend such meeting, shall be fined five dollars, as no apology will be sufficient, except sickness, or beyond ten miles from where the Grand Lodge of the United States is held ; and likewise neglecting a summons to attend a committee, will be fined one dollar.

ART. 9. That each State Grand Lodge shall pay equal proportion toward defraying the expenses that shall occur in the Grand Lodge of the United

States ; and also, each Grand Lodge to bear the expenses of their Representative.

ART. 10. That at the annual session of the Grand Lodge of the United States, the Constitution and By-Laws will be read, and the members of the different Grand Lodges be admitted to hear any business that may be transacted.

ART. 11. That the Grand Lodge of the United States enact By-Laws for the government of their meetings, and for the regulation of their pecuniary affairs, provided, they do not interfere with the Constitution.

§ 2. ART. 12. The Officers of the Grand Lodge of the United States are : The M. W. Grand Master, R. W. D. Grand Master, R. W. Grand Secretary, W. Grand Guardian, and W. Representatives or Proxies.

That each State Grand Lodge may nominate a candidate for the office of G. M. of the Grand Lodge of the United States ; the said candidate must be a P. G. M. of a State Grand Lodge, and on being seconded after three times calling, the nominated candidate shall be put to the ballot ; and the G. M. shall be elected by a majority of tickets. That the G. M., so elected, shall nominate and choose a D. G. M. residing in the State of Maryland, where the Grand Lodge of the United States is held. And also, each Grand Lodge nominating a candidate, must communicate the same to the Grand Lodge six months previous to the G. M. of the Grand Lodge of the United States leaving his seat. The G. S. shall be elected by the members in session. The G. G. shall be appointed by the G. M.

ART. 13. That the G. M. shall hold his office four years, and shall be eligible for a candidate for three years longer—after the expiration of which, he shall not be eligible as a candidate until the expiration of four years after ; but provided it should so happen that a candidate nominated should not be qualified to fill that important station, that he remain elected until a suitable person is brought forward to take the seat ; and further, that the G. M. shall not be in possession of the title of P. G. M. of the Grand Lodge of the United States, unless he serves the specified term, and that the G. M. of the Grand Lodge of the United States cannot hold the office of G. M. of any State Grand Lodge.

The D. G. M. shall likewise hold his office for the space of four years—at the expiration of which, he may be continued without limited time to fill that office ; and unless he serves his four years, he cannot hold the title of P. D. G. M. of the Grand Lodge of the United States.

The G. S. shall hold his office for the space of four years, and may be continued without limited time ; and unless he serves his four years, he cannot hold the title of P. G. S. of the Grand Lodge of the United States. Also, a reasonable compensation must be appropriated for his services.

The G. G. shall also hold his office for four years to qualify him as a P. G. G. of the Grand Lodge of the United States.

ART. 14. The duty of the G. M. is to preside during the session, preserving order and due observance of the laws—impartially put to the vote all propositions, and in case of equal votes, to give the casting vote.

The duty of the D. G. M. is to open and close the Lodge meetings ; to support the G. M. by his assistance and to take his seat during his absence ; he must also read all petitions, propositions, reports and communications laid before the Grand Lodge of the United States, and on elections or votes, to report the statement thereof to the G. S.

The G. S. must record a just and true account of the proceedings of the Grand Lodge, and likewise communications from the Grand Lodges throughout the United States, and to transact all the writing of the Grand Lodge.

The G. G. is to prove every member before he admits him ; to allow none to depart or enter without a Password, and to prevent the admission or departure of any during actual transaction of business, without the permission of the G. M.

The Representatives or Proxies are to weigh attentively every transaction that may come before them, and to represent their State Grand Lodge to the best of their judgment, and to the full extent of their power.

In case of occasionable absence of the G. M., when the D. G. M. takes the highest situation he shall immediately appoint a Deputy *pro tem.*, as that important office must never be left vacant. In case of the death of the G. M., the D. G. M. shall take his chair until some other candidate is nominated and elected.

ART. 15. After an election has taken place, the candidate in whose favor it has resulted, will be duly informed of the same, and it shall be communicated to all the Grand Lodges throughout the United States by the G. S.; and the candidate so elected will be notified to attend and be present to take his seat, otherwise the election will be annulled. Also, he must be present when he resigns his seat ; and in the interim, the D. G. M. may act in his stead.

The G. M., D. G. M., G. S. and G. G., as officers, shall not vote on any occasion whatever, as the same solely devolves on the Representatives or their Proxies ; but when the votes are equal, the G. M. shall give the casting vote, as before mentioned.

All letters or communications must be directed to the G. M., or his Deputy ; and the postage of all letters to and from the Grand Lodge of the United States, must be paid by the Grand Lodge of every State, as communications may require.

§ 3. ART. 16. In case five brothers of the Independent Order of Odd Fellows wish to start a Lodge in another State, not already chartered, application must be made to the Grand Lodge of the United States to obtain a Charter, and the G. M., or his Deputy, must communicate the same to the Representatives of each Grand Lodge, and they or their Proxies must decide on the same ; if the majority decide unfavorably, the G. M., if a motion be made and seconded, shall refer the petition to a second consideration, and afterwards put it to vote, and decide accordingly.

ART. 17. The Charter, with the Charges and Lectures of the First or White, Second or Blue, Third or Scarlet, together with the Covenant and Remembrance Degrees, shall be charged at thirty dollars, to defray the expenses thereof—the money to be paid immediately on the delivery of the same ; but provided that the Lodge so forming have not the means to pay that amount, the Degree Books will be detained, until they can comply with the whole charge. They must also defray all traveling expenses. The Lodge so forming in a new State will have to act under the Grand Lodge of the United States, until they have five Past Grands attached to them.

ART. 18. When a Charter is granted, a member of the Grand Lodge must be deputed to deliver the same, to open the new Lodge, and to give instructions such as he finds them prepared to receive, and are necessary for them to have.

ART. 19. Every State Grand Lodge acting under the Grand Lodge of the United States, shall send, three months previous to the annual meeting of the Grand Lodge of the United States, their statement of expulsions or suspensions, if any—the names and reasons thereof—and any other circumstances of general importance ; all of which the Grand Lodge of the United States will cause to be circulated to all the Grand Lodges throughout the United States.

ART. 20. Every State Grand Lodge must give a proof impression of their Seal, to be deposited in the Grand Lodge of the United States ; and all their communications must be sealed therewith.

ART. 21. The Grand Lodge of the United States shall forward a yearly Password for traveling members, to each State Grand Lodge.

Maryland and Massachusetts approved. New York approved, except the words "*residing in the State of Maryland, where the Grand Lodge of the United States is held,*" in the 12th Article. Pennsylvania excepted to the word "*permanent,*" in the 5th Article. Subsequently New York joined with Pennsylvania at a special meeting of the Grand Committee, September 25th, 1825, as reported by Grand Master Wildey, in the request "that the Constitution of the Grand Lodge of the United States should be amended by striking out the word 'permanent' and insert 'present,'" and "the subject of the proposed amendment to the Constitution, *viz.:* strike out the word 'permanent,' and insert 'present,' was considered, and after mature deliberation it was adopted, by the following vote—the yeas and nays being ordered : Yeas—Reps. Common, of Maryland ; Fennell, of Massachusetts ; Scotchburn, of New York ; and Boyd, of Pennsylvania," all residents of Baltimore. At a regular session of the Grand Lodge of the United States, April 25th, 1826, this action of the Grand Committee was approved.

At the preliminary meeting, January 15th, 1825, the Representatives elected the following Grand Officers:

Thomas Wildey, P. G. M., Grand Master; John Welch, P. D. G. M., Deputy Grand Master; William Williams, P. G., Grand Secretary; all of Maryland.

The Grand Master-elect appointed Thomas Mitchell, P. G. W., Grand Guardian. The Grand Officers were not installed until March 30th, 1825. According to Article XIII. of the Constitution they were to hold office for four years, or until the installation of their successors.

At the annual communication held April 25th, 1826, the titles of " Grand Sire " and " Deputy Grand Sire " seem to have been used by general consent. Section IV., consisting of the following articles, was added to the Constitution :

ART. 22. All Lodges acting under the Grand Lodge of the United States, when having five Past Grands, are at liberty to petition the Grand Lodge for a Grand Charter, with the different Degrees belonging to a Grand Lodge, the same not before granted to a Subordinate Lodge, so as to enable them to have a State Grand Lodge, for the government of such State as the same may require.

ART. 23. That a State Grand Charter, together with the Golden Rule and Royal Purple or Fifth Degrees, be charged at twenty dollars, to be paid for on delivery, and all necessary expenses incurred shall be paid by such State as shall apply for the same.

The Patriarchal Degree was received from England after the adoption of the Constitution, and the charge for the same was now fixed at two dollars and fifty cents. The following shows the condition of the Order at the commencement of the career of the Grand Lodge of the United States and at the close of its first year :

FOR THE YEAR ENDING FEBRUARY, 1825.

GRAND LODGES.	WHERE HELD.	NO. OF LODGES.
Maryland.	Baltimore.	3
Massachusetts.	Boston.	2
New York.	New York.	1
Pennsylvania.	Philadelphia.	3

FOR THE YEAR ENDING APRIL, 1826.

GRAND LODGES.	WHERE HELD.	NO. OF LODGES.
Maryland.	Baltimore.	3
Massachusetts.	Boston.	2
New York.	New York.	3
Pennsylvania.	Philadelphia.	4

In the year 1826, Grand Sire Wildey visited England in order to obtain all the information possible from the officers and members of the Manchester Unity that might in any way be useful to the Order here. How well and hospitably he was received the following farewell address to him, delivered by Corresponding Secretary Wardle, of the Manchester Unity, fully attests:

Most Worthy and Respected Sire.

In the name and on behalf of the Independent Order of Odd Fellows in England, I rise to address you.

This task, Worthy Grand Master, should have been in the hands of a more able man than myself, but the lot has fallen upon me, and I will do it all the justice I can.

Permit me first to congratulate you on your safe arrival in your native country, for, however ardently you may be attached to the country of your adoption, however much circumstances may have endeared it to you, yet there is a feeling in the human breast never to be forgotten, never to be entirely suppressed, however far we roam, and that feeling is a love for our native land !

"——— dear the schoolboy spot,
We ne'er forget tho' there we are forgot !

Hence, Sire, I congratulate you on your safe arrival, and sincerely hope that all those views, and objects, and wishes, which induced you to cross the Atlantic, have been amply and happily realized.

As an Odd Fellow, Worthy Grand Master, in the name of the Order, I give you their best thanks. To you and to you only, the United States of America are indebted for the existence of the inestimable blessing of Odd Fellowship ! But for you, that truly great country would have been, at this hour, without one of the most social, moral and benevolent institutions ever formed by man. To you belongs, distinctly and unequivocally, the glorious title of " Founder and Father of American Odd Fellowship."

This title, Most Worthy Sire, none can dispute with you—it is clearly, plainly yours—and your name will be revered by future ages, when the memory of heroes and conquerors will have been forgotten. I ought not here, perhaps, to pass over the names of two or three of your early and worthy coadjutors—to Brothers Welch, Boyd and Crowder, if they be yet with you, we wish to convey the best thanks of the Independent Order in England. Should they have left this for "another and a better world," their friends will have the consolation of knowing that their names are on record, and that they will be handed down to posterity as fellow-laborers in this great work of love, as friends and brothers of the Founder and Father of American Odd Fellowship.

The existence of a press among us, both here and in Baltimore, renders it unnecessary for me to recapitulate the particulars of the rise and progress of your undertaking. The magazines now put every brother in possession of all the leading facts connected with the Order, which were formerly necessarily confined to a few. To those magazines I triumphantly refer them for an account of the almost miraculous marches which you have made for the good and welfare of your infant institution—exertions which none but a mind most determinedly bent on benevolence could have performed—exertions, I firmly believe, unequalled in the history of any other society—exertions never heard of before, if we except, perhaps, those of the great philanthropist, the immortal Howard !

Faith, we read, Sire, will remove mountains—but what will not Charity achieve! After traversing the various extensive States of the truly great country of your adoption, and rendering all their Lodges as one, you bend your pilgrimage hitherwise—you join them to those of England—removing, as it were, the vast Atlantic, extending and perpetuating the principles of benevolence, and bringing thousands, at an immense distance from each other, under the standard of Friendship, Love and Truth.

To you, Sire, we are indebted for all this—you laid the plan—you formed the whole design—you have now the happiness of seeing a new creation rising up around you. I say a new creation, Sire, because no man can become a genuine Odd Fellow without becoming at the same time a better man.

However good he may have been before, the duties of an Odd Fellow will point out to him many sources for the exercise of his goodness which before were unknown to him. He will necessarily become more useful. The facilities that our beloved Order affords, I may say makes, for the display of that first of virtues, CHARITY—(without which all pretentions to goodness are mere mummery)—these facilities, I say, will give him an opportunity of putting his goodness in *full* practice.

I do not mean to confine myself, Sire, to that Charity which giveth only, but to that principle of universal benevolence which embraces ALL the wants of ALL mankind. I do not mean alone their physical necessities—I mean to include their moral inabilities. A really charitable man will feel a greater desire to remove the latter than to relieve the former; because he knows if a man be not morally right he cannot be physically happy.

Worthy Grand Master, a few words more on this subject: It is the principal pillar of our Order ; we have a high authority for the fact—"the first of these is charity." I know of no delight equal to the luxury of doing good ; but the first delight is to find out, succor and relieve the uncom-plaining, the heart-broken, yet proud spirit, that cannot dig, and will not beg. Believe me, Sire,

> " Full many a stoic eye and aspect stern,
> Hide hearts where grief has little left to learn."

I have now, Sire, done with this part of my subject. I will not presume to point out to this assembly the many opportunities that present themselves for the exercise of these virtues ; the active and the benevolent will readily perceive them, and to such only can they be of any service.

In your address, Sire, on your arrival among us, you told us that you had " now more than ever cause to bless the happy hour in which you became an Odd Fellow." We shall not soon forget the compliment. Long may you live to enjoy such feeling, and may every hour increase its felicity !

I shall not here particularize the many valuable communications received from you. They shall be cherished among us, and communicated in due time to the respective Lodges throughout the Order ; and we are satisfied that what you have received from us will be laid out to the best advantage among your children when you return home.

It now becomes my painful duty to bid you, Most Worthy Grand Master, officially, at least, farewell ! A young world of your own creation is now anxiously awaiting your arrival. May the waves and winds of the Atlantic speedily waft you safely home, and may you find " all well." You have the wishes and prayers of thousands for your welfare. This lecture will bear with me, I am sure, when I exclaim, " Hail, Odd Fellowship ! all hail Columbia ! Long life and happiness to the Founder and Father of American Odd Fellow-ship !"

As soon as the Grand Sire returned home a Special Committee meeting was called, October 3d, 1826, to hear his report :

Officers and Representatives :

The Grand Sire respectfully reports : That after a passage of twenty-one days he arrived at Liverpool, and visited the Lodges, but being desirous of reaching Manchester, he took leave of the brethren there, and proceeded on his journey. On arriving at Manchester, he was received with open arms by a few of the brothers.

The Corresponding Secretary was ordered to prepare notices for the assembling of the Order on the following day, at 4 o'clock P. M., and at the appointed time he met about six or seven hundred of the brethren, and all seemed overjoyed at his arrival. After some preliminary business had been gone through with, the Grand Sire delivered an address, which was received with approbation. It will appear in the next number of the *English Magazine.*

For six successive nights during his stay among them, he frequently vis-ited two Lodges of an evening ; a conveyance was in attendance to take him from place to place, and at all of the Lodges he explained to them the plan on which the Lodges worked in the United States.

Several committee meetings were held for the transaction of business with him during his stay in Manchester.

The Grand Sire attended several public dinners, at which much good humor prevailed, and the healths of the Grand Masters of Maryland, Massachusetts, New York and Pennsylvania, were severally drank, confirmed by the honors of the Order.

Several alterations have taken place in the Work of the Order, which the Grand Sire is of the opinion may be productive of service to the Order.

The Grand Sire presented the Committee of the Manchester Unity with the Covenant, Remembrance, and Grand Lodge Degrees, which were approved of by them, and were left for their adoption.

Before leaving Manchester, the brethren being desirous of bestowing a mark of respect on the Grand Sire, but considering the subject of a delicate nature, they resolved that the same should be intimated to him by the Grand Treasurer, privately, which was accordingly done, by suggesting a gold medal as suitable.

The Grand Sire replied, that if it was their wish to present him with a token of their esteem, he would prefer, to anything else, a Charter for the Grand Lodge of the United States, confirming the one granted by the Duke of York's Lodge, Preston. To this suggestion they instantly promised compliance, and on his return from London he was presented with a Charter, splendidly executed on parchment, through the hands of G. M. Thomas, Derbyshire, in a suitable manner ; when the Corresponding Secretary of the District accompanied the delivery with a highly complimentary address. (*A fac-simile of this Charter is engraved on the preceding page.*)

From Manchester the Grand Sire proceeded to London, where he was received in a highly gratifying manner.

While visiting the Lodges, there, he observed an Emblem representing the foundation-stone laid by our forefather Adam, and procured one, which he now presents to the Grand Lodge.

After leaving London he returned to Manchester, and visited the country Lodges, where he was met by a very numerous body of the Order, who congratulated him in a highly gratifying manner.

The Charter was at once accepted, and by its acceptance the position of the Grand Lodge was placed upon a better foundation. The original Charter from the Duke of York's Lodge had been made to do duty twice, and its authority was somewhat impaired in the estimation of many of the members, and only the exigencies of the occasion compelled them to accept the transfer of the old Charter from the Grand Lodge of Maryland and the United States to the Grand Lodge of the United States. Now this Charter from the Manchester Unity, a competent Body, removed forever all the difficulties. Of this matter Grand Sire Wildey spoke as follows :

This change of government produced a slight innovation upon the powers of the original Charter, but the necessity was so evident that it could not be avoided ; and to remove all source of cavil, I crossed the Atlantic to obtain a Grand Charter for the Grand Lodge of the United States, confirming every act that had been performed, arising from events that human foresight could not control, and giving the Grand Lodge of the United States entire jurisdiction to act in its sovereign capacity, in whatsoever things that may be required, not inconsistent with the principles of the Order.

At the May session of 1827, Representative Scotchburn, of Maryland, reported that the Grand Lodge of Maryland was about to have a copper-plate engraved for Traveling Certificates, so as to suit any State or Lodge and prevent imposition. It is proper here to state that the Grand Lodge of Maryland, for many years after the establishment of the Grand Lodge of the United States, furnished that Grand Body with what are now termed " supplies." It was some time before the Grand Lodge of the United States ascertained that the control and sale of these articles could be made a source of revenue.

(*The fac-simile of the Traveling Certificate above mentioned will be found on the following page.*)

Washington Lodge, No. 1, used a Certificate or Card three by five inches, of which the following is a copy :

TO ALL WHOM IT MAY CONCERN.

THE

WASHINGTON LODGE, NO. 1,

OF

INDEPENDENT ODD FELLOWS.

Instituted at Baltimore, 26th Day of April, 1819.

Held at the ....

....

....Baltimore.

These are to Certify that our well-beloved Brother................................
aged............Years being well recommended to us was..........................into
this our Lodge. We therefore recommend him to your Friendship and Protection and to admit him into all regular Lodges throughout the Universe. In testimony whereof we have subscribed our Names and affixed the Seal of our Lodge aforesaid the ....Day..................................in the Year of our Lord ....

                              _____N. G.

                              _____V. G.

                              _____Sec'y.

"TO ALL WHOM IT MAY CONCERN"

BENEVOLENCE

ESTOTE — FIDELES

FRIENDSHIP — LOVE — AND TRUTH

Independent Order of Odd Fellows.

Lodge No. ═══ of the State of ═══
═══ Instituted at ═══
the ═══ 18══ now held at the ═══

These are to Certify, that our well beloved Brother ═══
═══ was regularly admitted a Member of our
Lodge on the ═══ Day of ═══ 18══ and has paid
all demands up to this Day, we therefore recommend him
to your friendship and protection and to admit him into
all regular Lodges in the Universe. In Witness whereof,
we have subscribed our Hands and affixed the Seal of
our Lodge aforesaid the ═══ Day of ═══ in the
Year of our Lord 18══

N.B. The Brother that holds this Certificate, will have to deposit the same in a
Lodge after getting employment, provided he is within five Miles where a
legal Lodge is held.

═══ N. G.

═══ Sec. y

THE FIRST VISITING CARD.

November 12th, 1827, the Grand Committee, on a petition for a Charter for a Lodge to be located at Washington, D. C., from Thomas M. Abbett, Robert Boyd, John Cragg, Thomas Smith and Samuel Knapp, granted the Charter, and it was decided to open the Lodge (Central Lodge, No. 1) on the 26th of November. In the following January, Georgetown Lodge, No. 2, at Georgetown, was instituted. In the same month the expulsion of Stranger's Refuge Lodge, No. 4, by the Grand Lodge of New York, was approved. It appears that the members of this Lodge, accustomed to the mode of government prescribed by the Manchester Unity, refused to pay the fees for Degrees and dues to the Grand Lodge, so that Body was compelled, in order to sustain its authority and dignity, to use its extreme powers. The Lodge was subsequently reinstated.

At the annual communication, held May 1st, 1828, the following very important resolutions were passed :

Resolved, That at each annual meeting of the Grand Lodge, it shall be the duty of the Representatives or Proxies of each State to estimate the current expenses of the ensuing year, and draw on each Grand Lodge for the same, which must be immediately paid, to enable the Grand Sire to pay the necessary and essential expenses that may occur, and that he keep a regular account of the same, and present it to the Grand Lodge at the annual communication. That the Grand Secretary draw out a blank report, for the use of State Grand Lodges, in order for them to give a correct statement of their financial affairs, with their annual communications, and that the Grand Secretary have fifty copies of the same printed. That a list of regular Lodges be published in these minutes for the information and satisfaction of the different States.

The first resolution informs us how the Grand Lodge at this time was supported, and needs no comment. As far as the history of the Order is concerned, no resolution of greater importance than the second was ever passed. It did much to spread the Order and show its power and necessary usefulness. It is well, too, that it was enacted as early as 1828. Some time, however, elapsed before the full scope and object of the resolution was perceived and carried out.

The third resolution was no doubt commendable at the time, when the Lodges were few ; but to do so now, when they number more than 8,000, would be a serious and costly work. The resolution was complied with at once and the following list was appended to the minutes of the session :

LIST OF GRAND AND SUBORDINATE LODGES UNDER THE
JURISDICTION OF THE GRAND LODGE OF THE
UNITED STATES.

THE GRAND LODGE OF MARYLAND, BALTIMORE, HAVING UNDER ITS JURIS-
DICTION :
Washington Lodge, No. 1, Baltimore ; meets every other Monday.
Franklin Lodge, No. 2, Baltimore ; meets every other Thursday.
Columbia Lodge, No. 3, Baltimore ; meets every other Wednesday.
William Tell Lodge, No. 4, Baltimore ; meets every Tuesday.
The Encampment of Patriarchs meets the first Friday in every month.

THE GRAND LODGE OF MASSACHUSETTS, BOSTON, HAVING UNDER ITS JURIS-
DICTION :
Massachusetts Lodge, No. 1, Boston ; meets every second Friday.
Siloam Lodge, No. 2, Boston ; meets every second Friday.
Good Samaritan Lodge, No. 3, Taunton ; meeting not reported.
New England Lodge, No. 4, Cragie's Point ; meeting not reported.

THE GRAND LODGE OF NEW YORK, NEW YORK CITY, HAVING UNDER ITS
JURISDICTION :
Columbia Lodge, No. 1, New York ; meets every Monday.
Friendship Lodge, No. 2, Pleasant Valley ; meets every Saturday.
Hope Lodge No. 3, Albany ; meets every Tuesday
Philanthropic Lodge, No. 5, Albany ; meeting not reported.

THE GRAND LODGE OF PENNSYLVANIA, PHILADELPHIA, HAVING UNDER ITS
JURISDICTION :
Pennsylvania Lodge, No. 1, Philadelphia ; meets every Wednesday.
Washington Lodge, No. 2, Philadelphia ; meets every Tuesday.
Morning Star Lodge, No. 4, Kensington ; meets every Thursday.
Franklin Lodge, No. 5, Philadelphia ; meets every Thursday.
General Marion Lodge, No. 6, Philadelphia ; meets every Monday.

THE FOLLOWING WERE UNDER THE IMMEDIATE JURISDICTION OF THE GRAND
LODGE OF THE UNITED STATES :
Central Lodge, No. 1, Washington, D. C. ; meets every Tuesday.
Georgetown Lodge, No. 2, Georgetown, D. C. ; meets every Friday.

On September 28th, 1828, there was presented to the Grand Committee a petition from Thomas M. Abbett and John Wells, Past Grands of Lodge No. 1, and Robert Boyd, James Gettys and James Ashton, Past Grands of Lodge No. 2, praying for a Charter for a Grand Lodge, to be located at Washington, D. C. The Charter was granted and the Grand Lodge was instituted on the 24th of November, 1828.

March 30th, 1829, the Grand Committee granted a Charter for New Jersey Lodge, No. 1, at Camden, New Jersey, and at a meeting, April 10th, authorized a Charter for Benevolent Lodge, No. 2, at Paterson, New Jersey. These proceedings were approved at the annual communication held May 4th, 1829. At this session the Constitution was amended so that the annual meeting of the Grand Lodge of the United States should be held on the first Monday in September thereafter.

The resolution adopted at the previous session, for the appointment of a Movable Committee, was amended by striking out the words " Representative or Proxy," and inserting " a Past Grand of any State, District, or Territorial Grand Lodge."

The result of the election for Grand Sire, for the term of four years, was the re-elevation of Grand Sire Wildey to the highest position in the Order. Augustus Mathiot, P. G., was elected Grand Secretary for two years. The Grand Sire nominated Thomas Scotchburn, P. G. M., for Deputy Grand Sire, and Robert Gott, P. G., for Grand Guardian, and they were approved.

A Constitution and a Code of Rules of Order were adopted at this session. The following preamble to the Constitution was also adopted :

WHEREAS, It has been found expedient and of the greatest importance to mankind to perpetuate those institutions which confer on them great and essential benefit :

Therefore, We do for the more effectual purpose of binding each other in the bonds of one common union, by which we will be enabled to ensure a co-operation of action, and of providing for the best interests of our beloved Order, based as it is upon the permanent principles of universal benevolence, friendship and philanthropy, and to secure unto ourselves and posterity the more effectually the blessings which are to be derived from so valuable and beneficial an institution, ordain and establish this Constitution.

A committee was appointed to draft a blank report for the use of the Grand Lodges, to enable them to communicate such information to the Grand Lodge of the United States as is required by the Constitution.

CONDITION OF THE ORDER MAY, 1829.—(*Eighth Annual Report.*)

Grand Lodge of Maryland, Baltimore, Maryland, 4 Lodges.
Grand Lodge of Massachusetts, Boston, Mass., 6 Lodges.
Grand Lodge of New York, Albany, N. Y., 6 Lodges, 1 expulsion.
Grand Lodge of Pennsylvania, Philadelphia, Pa., 13 Lodges, 4 expulsions, 1,009 members.
Grand Lodge of the District of Columbia, Washington, D. C., 2 Lodges.
Total 31 Lodges.

The first reports on record were made to February, 1822, and simply state the name and number and location of the Lodges, *viz.:* Washington, No. 1, Franklin, No. 2, Baltimore. In the second, to February, 1823, the information as above, the revenue of No. 1, $275,80, No. 2, $167.10, and the time of meeting are stated. The third, to February, 1824, has in addition the names and location of the Grand Lodges of Massachusetts, New York and Pennsylvania, and Columbia Lodge, No. 3, Baltimore. There was an increase in the revenue, No. 1 reporting $322.50 and No. 2, $520.60. These were previous to the organization of the Grand Lodge of the United States. The fourth, to February, 1825, has only the names of the four Grand Lodges and number of Subordinates under each, the grand total being nine. The fifth report was to April, 1826, when the number of Subordinates was increased to twelve; the sixth to May, 1827, showing fourteen Lodges; the seventh to May, 1828, nineteen Lodges, twenty expulsions, and 568 members in Pennsylvania. The ninth report, to May, 1830, includes two Lodges in New Jersey, one in Rhode Island—a total of fifty-eight; initiations reported by Maryland, Pennsylvania and District of Columbia numbered 1,598, three suspensions, fourteen expulsions; revenue of Maryland, $2,427.00; Pennsylvania, $12,905.20; District of Columbia, $395.28; total, $15,727.48. Members in Maryland, 709; Pennsylvania, 2,247; District of Columbia, 80; total, 3,036.

1830.

The Order had now passed its period of probation, the child had grown into a promising youth, and gave every expectation of a lusty and vigorous manhood.

From this time it made such rapid strides in the path of progress that the wildest dreams of the fathers of the Order were more than exceeded. Already an army had been enlisted in the service of the cause of Friendship, Love and Truth ; there remained but to drill and regulate these raw recruits so as to make them prepared for every emergency. This willing body of eager workers was as the plastic clay in the hands of the modeler awaiting the exercise of his genius and skill to evolve therefrom the thing of beauty we now know it to be. Henceforth, the Grand Lodge of the United States was principally occupied in legislating for the growing wants and ever changing conditions of the Order. The reader will obtain its history from this time in the continuous and tentative efforts of the Grand Lodge to remove every impediment in the way to our present condition of success. The road was an untraveled one ; many a time there were wanderings from the correct path, but perseverance and unremitting diligence, with a determination to succeed, finally overcame all obstacles. In the remaining portion of this chapter it is not proposed to dwell upon the extensive and marvelous growth of the Order, (for all the information desired on this subject can be obtained from the chapter on Grand Jurisdictions and from the Tables of Progress), but upon the wise and prudent legislation of the Grand Lodge, to which more than anything else, we owe our present unparalleled success.

At the regular annual communication held in the City of Baltimore, in September, 1830, it was

Resolved, That the several Grand Lodges instruct the officers of the Subordinate Lodges under their jurisdiction to cause all Traveling Certificates to be endorsed in the proper handwriting of the brother applying for the same, for the purpose of identity.

The following preamble and resolution were adopted :

WHEREAS, A Constitution and By-Laws have recently appeared, purporting to be the "Constitution and By-Laws of the Grand Lodge of Pennsylvania, of the Independent Order of Odd Fellows, established by authority of the Grand Lodge of Maryland and of the United States, revised and adopted at their new hall, North Fifth street, Philadelphia, February 23d, 1830," which Constitution and By-Laws are calculated to mislead, inasmuch as the said Grand Lodge of Maryland and of the United States had dissolved, and became extinct on the 22d of February, 1825, and no Charter has ever been granted to the said self-styled Grand Lodge ; therefore—

Resolved, That said Lodge claiming to be established by authority above stated, is spurious and unauthorized by any competent jurisdiction.

At a special session held February 22d, 1831, the following propositions were submitted for consideration at the next annual communication :

1st. That a Grand Treasurer be elected.

2d. That all communications for the Grand Lodge be addressed through the medium of the Grand Secretary, and not through the Grand Sire, as heretofore.

1831.

At the regular annual communication held in the City of Baltimore, on the 5th of September, the above propositions were adopted, and William Hall, P. G., of Maryland, was elected Grand Treasurer. Until this time the duties of Grand Treasurer had been performed by the Grand Sire.

The following resolutions were adopted :

That each State Grand Lodge furnish, annually, the name of the street and number of the house wherein their respective Subordinate Lodges hold their meetings.

That the Royal Purple Degree shall be a necessary qualification for the Representatives in the Grand Lodge of the United States.

That the Grand Lodge of the United States is the only legitimate authority for granting Charters to open Lodges and Encampments in Foreign States, and in the Districts or Territories of America.

That the Grand Secretary be directed to forward a copy of the resolutions passed May 1st, 1828, respecting the Working S's of the Order. (It is not stated to whom this information was to be sent.)

The present Grand Sire shall discharge the duties of that office from the expiration of his present term until the ensuing annual meeting of this Grand Lodge.

That when this Grand Lodge adjourns, it will adjourn to meet on the first Monday in March.

A committee was appointed to remodel the Funeral Ceremony and report at the adjourned session in March.

The Grand Sire was authorized to procure a sufficient number of the *English Magazine* and distribute them among the Grand Lodges.

The Grand Lodge of Delaware, for want of five Past Grands to continue work, was directed to return its Charter.

A petition from five Past Grands of Cincinnati for a Grand Lodge was granted, on satisfactory information being furnished that the applicants had passed the chairs.

The Grand Lodge of Pennsylvania, through Representative Birkey, presented to John Boyd, late Proxy of that Grand Body, a handsome medal in recognition of services rendered.

At this session the Grand Lodge for the first time granted a Charter for a Grand Encampment, *viz.*: The Grand Encampment of Maryland.

The Grand Sire presented communications from the Manchester Unity Committee and others, which represented the Order as increasing in members and respectability, equaling its progress on this side of the Atlantic.

At the close of September, 1831, the Order had sixty-nine Lodges.

At the adjourned session, March 5th, 1832, a Charter was authorized for Wildey Encampment, No. 1, New Orleans; also for the Grand Lodge of Louisiana.

1832.

The regular annual session, held in the City of Baltimore, was brief, owing to the prevalence of Asiatic cholera throughout the country. The Grand Body adjourned, without electing its officers, until the first Monday in March (4th), 1833.

The Grand Lodge met from day to day, but unwilling to transact business without the presence of the Representative of Pennsylvania, on March 6th, adopted the following:

Resolved, That in consequence of the continued disappointment in the non-arrival of the Representative of Pennsylvania, this Grand Lodge, ever anxious to consult the wishes of so great a Body as work under the jurisdiction of that Grand Lodge, deem it proper to adjourn until Monday, the 18th inst., at ten o'clock, A. M., unless the Representative from Pennsylvania should sooner arrive; in which case the Grand Sire has the power to convene the Grand Lodge.

Prior to this adjourned session the record shows that the credentials of the Representatives were presented, examined and found correct. On March 4th the following communication was received:

I do hereby empower Robert Neilson, D. G. M., to act for me in the Grand Lodge of the United States, as Representative of Louisiana, during my sickness.　　　　　　　　SAMUEL LUCAS, *Proxy Rep. of Louisiana.*

Rep. Ridgely, of Ohio, submitted the following, which was adopted:

Resolved, That the deputation presented by the Representative of Louisiana to P. G. Neilson be referred to a Special Committee, with instructions to report forthwith.

The Grand Sire appointed Reps. Ridgely, of Ohio; Keyser, of Maryland; and Gettys, of the District of Columbia, the committee. This committee was the first to act as a Committee on Credentials, and no doubt suggested to Rep. Hopkins the presentation of the following, which was adopted March 18th, 1833, and is still in force:

Resolved, That when the credentials of a Representative be presented to the Grand Lodge of the United States, before he can be acknowledged as such, his Certificate shall be referred to a committee, whose duty shall be to examine its authenticity and also the qualifications of the Representative.

The following composed the first "Committee on Credentials:" Reps. Hopkins, of Pennsylvania; Neilson, of Louisiana; and Brannan, of the District of Columbia.

At the adjourned session of the Grand Lodge, held in Philadelphia, June 7th, 1833, the following was adopted:

Resolved, That all brothers, members of Grand Lodges and in possession of the Royal Purple Degree, if recommended by the Representative of the State from which they hail, be admitted to witness the proceedings of this Grand Lodge.

1833.

At the regular annual communication held in the City of Baltimore, September, 2d, 1833, James Gettys, P. G. M., was elected and installed Grand Sire; Robert Neilson, D. G. M., Deputy Grand Sire; Samuel Pryor, P. G. M., Grand Secretary; Augustus Mathiot, P. D. G. M., Grand Treasurer. Thomas Morse, P. G., was appointed and installed Grand

Guardian. At this session there was a new Constitution adopted. The Grand Body was awakening to a better comprehension of its duties and requirements. This Constitution was more elaborate and contained many new provisions. The more notable are the following:

ART. 1. This Lodge shall be known by the name, style and title of "The Grand Lodge of the Independent Order of Odd Fellows of the United States of America," and possesses original and exclusive jurisdiction in Odd Fellowship over the Territories comprising the Federal Government of the United States. It is the source of all true and legitimate authority in Odd Fellowship in the United States of America. All State, District and Territorial Grand Lodges and Encampments assemble under its Warrant, and derive their authority from it. With it is placed the power to enact such laws and regulations as shall be for the good of the Order in general. It is the ultimate tribunal to which all matters of general importance to the State, District and Territorial Grand Lodges and Encampments are to be referred, and its decisions thereon shall be final and conclusive—and with the consent of the Grand Lodge or Encampment of a State, District or Territory, may receive an appeal of a Subordinate Lodge from the decision of its State Grand Lodge. To it belongs the power to regulate and control the Work of the Order, and the several Degrees belonging thereto; to fix and determine the customs and usages in regard to all things which concern Odd Fellowship. This Grand Lodge has inherent power to establish Lodges in Foreign Countries where no Grand Lodge exists. Such Lodges shall work by virtue of a Warrant granted by this Grand Lodge.

Past Grand Sires are provided for in:

ART. 8. Past Grand Sires shall be admitted to seats in this Grand Lodge, and be entitled to one vote on all questions coming before this Grand Lodge.

The following article contains new matter:

ART. 10. Representatives or Proxies from Grand Lodges must be Past Grands in good standing who have received the Royal Purple Degree; they must have been elected or appointed by the Grand Lodge they represent, and be furnished with a Certificate as follows:

To the Grand Lodge of United States, I. O. of O. F.

F. L. T.

This Certifies that P. G. .... has been duly elected (or appointed) Representative (or Proxy) from the Grand Lodge of .... to the Grand Lodge of the United States, for the period of one year from the date hereof.

WITNESS our hands and Seal of Grand Lodge, this .... day of ...., 18 , A. D.

[SEAL.] .... *Grand Master.*

.... *Grand Secretary.*

Each Representative, or in his absence, the Proxy, shall be entitled to vote on all questions before the Grand Lodge, in manner following, to wit : Each Grand Lodge having less than one thousand members, one vote, and each Grand Lodge having more than one thousand members, one additional vote ; the annual returns of the several Grand Lodges to determine the number of votes each Grand Lodge is entitled to. No officer of the Grand Lodge, unless he be a Representative, shall be permitted to vote, except in the case of the Grand Sire, or Past Grand Sires, as hereinbefore provided, and no Representative, or Proxy, shall represent more than one Grand Lodge at the same time.

As provided in Article XI., the annual communication is hereafter to be held on the first Monday in October.

Two or more Subordinate Lodges or Encampments having seven Past Grands or Patriarchs in good standing may petition for a Charter for a Grand Lodge or Grand Encampment.

The reports for the year ending September, 1833, exhibited eight Grand and 100 Subordinate Lodges.

The Grand Lodge held an adjourned session in Washington, D. C., January 8th, 1834. The following was adopted :

Resolved, That all necessary traveling expenses of the officers of the Grand Lodge shall be paid out of the funds of the Grand Lodge.

The Grand Lodge at the adjourned session in New York, August 16th, 1834, adopted the Seal reported by the committee appointed September 3d, 1833. The device is the same as on the present Seal of the Sovereign Grand Lodge, which, it will be noticed, bears the date 1834.

1834.

At the regular annual session, held in the City of Baltimore, October 6th, a form of petition for a Grand Lodge, or Grand Encampment, was adopted, and it was provided: " That all applications for Charters for a Grand Lodge, or Grand Encampment, must be by vote of the several Subordinate Lodges, or Encampments, in the State, District or Territory."

George Keyser, P. G. M., of Maryland, was elected Grand Sire ; Daniel P. Marshall, P. G. M., of New York,

Deputy Grand Sire; Robert Neilson, D. G. S., of Maryland, Grand Secretary; Charles Mowatt, P. G., of New York, Grand Treasurer.

In October, 1834, there were two Grand Encampments, one in Maryland, the other in Pennsylvania, and nine Subordinate Encampments located in various places. The Lodges numbered ninety-five.

There was a special session of the Grand Lodge held September 1st, 1835, to consider petitions for Charters for Grand and Subordinate Lodges.

1835.

At the regular annual session, October 5th, held in the City of Baltimore, the Grand Lodge presented Past Grand Sire Wildey an elegant service of plate valued at five hundred dollars.

The report of the Committee on Revision of the Work of the Order was, at this session, considered, amended and adopted.

The following, offered by Representative Ridgely, of Maryland, was adopted :

Resolved, That the Committee on Correspondence of this Grand Lodge be directed to address a congratulatory letter to our brethren in Great Britain upon the state of the Order in that country, and respectfully to suggest to them the propriety of discontinuing all convivial practices in their Lodges, and to solicit from them a detailed historical account of the origin, rise and progress of the Order, and to transmit to them a copy (neatly bound) of the Constitution, and proceedings up to this session, inclusive, of the Grand Lodge of the United States, and the revised Work of the Order as adopted at this session ; and most especially to request them to make no alteration whatever in the general features of the Order, without a mutual consultation on the subject, as uniformity of actions and principle is essentially necessary to the welfare of the Order.

The letter was written in the spirit and tenor of the above resolution. The committee, among other things, said :

Next to religion, we believe Odd Fellowship the best institution which Providence has given to man for the amelioration of his moral and social relations. Prizing it thus sacredly, a pious regard to the purity of its purposes has been most religiously inculcated with us ; and in the attainment of this desideratum, anxious efforts have been made from time to time to lop from it every excrescence and disembarrass it from all extraneous habits and customs which were not strictly auxiliary to its benevolent purposes, and more particularly to divest it of all practices which were at war with its first principles, and were calculated to bring it into disrepute and odium. Among the first of the improvements to the Order in America, required by duty and a decent respect for the opinions of mankind, was the abolition of all social and convivial practices at Lodge meetings ; since when it has riveted the respect and esteem of the virtuous of all classes and augmented our numbers almost incredibly.

The Grand Sire was authorized to appoint a qualified Past Grand, as District Deputy Grand Sire, in each State, District and Territory, to visit each Lodge working under Warrant of this Grand Lodge in said State, District or Territory, and communicate all information and instructions which may be by this Grand Lodge directed to be made ; also to open Lodges and Encampments when Charters are granted, and perform the Ceremony of Installation. His expenses whilst so engaged to be charged to the Lodge he may be required to visit.

The following preamble and resolution were also adopted :

WHEREAS, By the Constitution of this Grand Lodge, Past Grand Sires are admitted to seats in this Grand Lodge and are entitled to one vote on all questions coming before this Grand Lodge ; therefore—

Resolved, That this clause of the Constitution does not make a Past Grand Sire an officer of this Grand Lodge.

On motion of Past Grand Sire Wildey the following was adopted :

Resolved, That a committee be appointed to draft and superintend the engraving of a general Traveling Certificate, to be used by all Grand and Subordinate Lodges working under Warrant from this Grand Lodge.

The Deputy Grand Sire elect not having presented himself for installation, John Pearce, P. G. M., of New Jersey, was elected for the ensuing term.

In the list of officers installed we find that of Grand Chaplain mentioned for the first time.

At this session there was also adopted a Form of Funeral Obsequies.

The following was adopted:

That from and after the 31st day of December, 1836, each and every Lodge and Encampment working by authority derived from this Grand Lodge, shall charge the candidates or brothers the following fees:

For Initiation, not less than $5; White Degree, $5; Covenant Degree, $4; Royal Blue Degree, $3; Remembrance Degree, $2; Scarlet Degree, $1; Patriarchal and Encampment Degrees, $5; Golden Rule Degree, $4; Royal Purple Degree, $3.

Provided, A majority of Grand Lodges shall, on or before the next annual session of this Grand Lodge, certify their willingness to the establishment of the above fees.

A Certificate or Diploma, to be issued to members in good standing, was ordered to be prepared.

The number of Lodges, at the close of October, 1835, was ninety-six. There were eight Grand Lodges, two Grand and ten Subordinate Encampments.

There was a special session called for November 30th, 1835, to consider petitions for Charters for Lodges; but as a quorum was not present the Grand Sire declared the Grand Lodge adjourned until December 14th, when for want of a quorum the special session was declared closed, *sine die.*

1836.

The Grand Lodge met in regular annual session, in the City of Baltimore, October 3d.

The Grand Treasurer, Charles Mowatt, of New York, on account of ill health, resigned his office, and Andrew E. Warner, P. G., of Maryland, was elected to fill the vacancy, and was duly installed.

The following was adopted:

That a Special Committee be appointed to take into consideration the propriety of having a Corresponding Secretary of this Grand Lodge, and to report at the present communication.

The following Grand Officers were elected:

James L. Ridgely, P. G. M., of Maryland, Grand Sire; Frederick Leise, P. G. M., of New York, Deputy Grand Sire; Robert Neilson, P. D. G. Sire, of Maryland, Grand

Secretary; Andrew E. Warner, P. G., of Maryland, Grand Treasurer.

Five hundred copies of the Work of the Order, including the Degrees, and one hundred copies of the Funeral Obsequies were ordered to be printed in German.

The Grand Sire, Deputy Grand Sire and Grand Secretary were empowered to grant Charters to Subordinate Lodges during the recess of the Grand Lodge.

The Grand Lodge adjourned to meet on the third Monday in May, 1837.

The Special Committee on the situation of affairs in the State of New York reported that it was not in their power to adjust the differences and restore harmony between the members of the City of New York and those of the City of Albany.

As the result of this report and another from a Special Committee on the subject, the following were adopted :

Resolved by the Grand Lodge of the United States,

That the Grand Charter of the Grand Lodge of the I. O. O. F., in the State of New York, is hereby forfeited and annulled ; and the Grand Secretary is directed to demand the surrender of the said Charter, books, funds, and all documents connected with the Order in said State.

That the Committee on the State of New York be authorized to restore the original Charter, on satisfactory evidence of a restoration of order in that State, with such remarks on its face as shall show its having been annulled this day and restored by the committee.

The Charter was restored November 23d, 1837, and the Grand Lodge located in New York City.

The Grand Sire elect, James L. Ridgely, on the 17th of May, declined the office, and Samuel H. Perkins, P. G. M., of Pennsylvania, was unanimously elected Grand Sire.

At the close of the year, ending October, 1836, there were nine Grand and one hundred and fourteen Subordinate Lodges, with a membership of 6,819 ; two Grand and thirteen Subordinate Encampments.

1837.

At the regular annual session, held in the City of Baltimore, October, 2d, a committee was appointed to prepare resolutions expressive of the profound regret felt for the loss of George Keyser, Grand Sire, who died on the 19th of September, 1837, during the recess of the Grand Lodge.

The following officers were installed :

Samuel H. Perkins, P. G. M., of Pennsylvania, Grand Sire ; Frederick Leise, P. G. M., of New York, Deputy Grand Sire; Robert Neilson, P. D. G. Sire, of Maryland, Grand Secretary ; Andrew E. Warner, P. G., of Maryland, Grand Treasurer.

The Grand Sire made the following appointments ;

Sater T. Walker, P. G. C., Grand Chaplain ; Gotleib F. Buhre, P. G., Grand Guardian ; John E. Chamberlain, P. G., Grand Messenger.

At this session the office of Corresponding Secretary of the Grand Lodge was created. It was this officer's duty to conduct the correspondence of the Grand Lodge, except so far as it related to the financial concerns thereof. The salary provided for him was *fifty* dollars per annum.

The following was adopted :

That the Encampment Regalia cannot be worn in any other department of the Order except in the body of an Encampment of Patriarchs.

Past Grand Sire Wildey was appointed Traveling Agent for the Order throughout the United States. He was invested with special powers " to organize Lodges whenever proper and constitutional applications shall be made for the same." He was required to report all his acts and doings to the next annual session of the Grand Lodge.

At the close of the year ending October, 1837, there were two Grand and eleven Subordinate Encampments; eight Grand and one hundred and ten Subordinate Lodges. The number of contributing members in the Lodges was 6,833.

1838.

At the annual session, held in the City of Baltimore, October 1st, the following Grand Officers were elected:

Zenas B. Glazier, P. G. M., of Delaware, Grand Sire; A. Mondelli, P. G. M., of Louisiana, Deputy Grand Sire; William G. Cook, P. D. G. M., of Maryland, Grand Secretary; Andrew E. Warner, P. G., of Maryland, Grand Treasurer.

The Work of the Order for Subordinate Lodges was authorized to be translated and printed in the French language, without expense to the Grand Lodge.

It was resolved that the resolution adopted at last session on the subject of Encampment Regalia does not contain anything intended to forbid the wearing of the colors of the Encampment, in a Grand Lodge, by brothers entitled to those colors.

Grand and Subordinate Bodies were requested to transmit to the Grand Lodge proof impressions, in wax, of their respective Seals.

It was decided: That it is irregular to admit any brother into a Subordinate Lodge, from a Lodge under the jurisdiction of another Grand Lodge, as a member or visitor, unless he presents a Certificate under the signature of the officers and the Seal of the Lodge, and the counter-signature of the Grand Secretary of the Grand Lodge of the State in which he was a member; and prove himself in the T. P. W. and the Degree in which the Lodge is open. The above has been modified to require the counter-signature of the Grand Secretary of the Sovereign Grand Lodge, instead of that of the State Grand Secretary.

The following was unanimously adopted:

Resolved, That no brother can at the same time hold office or membership in two distinct State Grand Lodges or Subordinate Lodges under the jurisdiction of this Grand Lodge.

At the close of the year ending October, 1838, there were eleven Grand Lodges, two Grand, nineteen Subordinate Encampments and one hundred and fourteen Subordinate Lodges, with a membership of 8,175 and a reported revenue of $46,764.27.

1839.

The Grand Lodge met in Philadelphia, October 7th, to hold its annual session, but for want of a quorum adjourned to meet in Baltimore, April 21st, 1840, when the Grand Sire elect, Zenas B. Glazier, offered his resignation, which was unanimously declined. The officers elected in 1838, except the Deputy Grand Sire, (who was absent,) were duly installed, and the Grand Sire appointed the following :

George M. Bain, P. G. M., of Virginia, Grand Chaplain ; Gotleib F. Buhre, P. G., of Maryland, Grand Guardian ; John E. Chamberlain, P. G., of Maryland, Grand Messenger.

A new Standing Committee, entitled a Standing Committee on the State of the Order at Large, was, for the first time, appointed.

Forms for Dispensations to open Lodges and Encampments were adopted.

At this session James L. Ridgely, P. G. M., was elected Grand Corresponding Secretary.

At the close of the year ending October, 1839, there were two Grand and twenty-two Subordinate Encampments, with 565 members; fourteen Grand and one hundred and thirty Subordinate Lodges · 9,381 members ; revenue for the year, $58,412.22.

1840.

At the annual session October 5th, it was decided that a Past Grand Sire has not the right to vote as Past Grand Sire and also as a Representative, and that a Representative is entitled to two votes when his colleague is absent.

The following was adopted :

Resolved, That the Secretary of this Grand Lodge be ordered, after having had the proceedings of its session printed, to forward to each State Grand Lodge as many copies as it has Subordinate Lodges working under its jurisdiction, one copy being ordered to each Subordinate Lodge; and for the use of the State Grand Lodge one copy for each Subordinate Lodge under its jurisdiction; to each Subordinate Encampment one copy; and for the use of the Grand Encampment as many copies as it may have Subordinate Encampments working under its jurisdiction; also, to each Subordinate Lodge or Encampment working under the jurisdiction of this Grand Lodge, one copy.

The requirement of the signature of the Grand Secretary on a Traveling Certificate was rescinded, and it was—

Resolved, That no individual claiming to visit or deposit his Card in a Lodge of these United States shall be admitted, unless he presents a regular Card, signed by the Noble Grand and attested by the Secretary, under the Seal of the Lodge, and the name of the individual holding said Card be indorsed thereon, in his own proper handwriting.

Regalia for officers and Representatives was ordered.

The Constitution was amended so as to cause annual sessions to be held on *the third Monday of September*.

William W. Moore, P. G. M., of the District of Columbia, was elected Deputy Grand Sire for the residue of the term, *vice* A. Mondelli, who was not present at the adjourned session, April 23d, 1840, to be installed.

Grand Lodges and Encampments, Subordinate Lodges and Encampments, were required to embody in their reports, in addition to the information required by existing regulation, detailed information in relation to the subjects embraced under the following heads: Name of Lodge, Number of Initiations, Rejections, Admitted by Card, Withdrawn by Card, Suspensions and Cause, Expulsions and Cause, Deaths, Amount expended for Relief of Brothers, for Relief of Widows and Orphans, for Education of Orphans, Number of Contributing Members, Whole Amount of Receipts.

The Committee on Diploma reported their labor completed, and that one thousand copies were printed, and, with the plate, delivered to the Grand Sire.

It was ordered that a new Seal, to be made of steel, be procured by the next annual session.

A Form of Diploma, or Certificate for Representatives, was adopted, and the Grand Sire was directed to have the same executed in handsome style of penmanship during the present session.

The following is the Form:

In Grand Lodge assembled, present a Representation from Maryland, New York, Pennsylvania, etc., we have unanimously presented to our well-beloved Brother, ..., the R. W. G. Representative of the Grand Lodge of ...., this Diploma, as an evidence of his regular communion and fellowship with the Independent Order of Odd Fellows, and in appreciation of his zeal and devotion to the welfare of our beloved Order.

Done at the City of Baltimore, on the .... day of ...., in the year of our Order in the United States................, of our Lord................

This Diploma was to be signed by the Grand Officers and Representatives.

State Grand Lodges were informed that the Degrees are numbered and named as follows: First, or White; Second, or Covenant; Third, or Blue; Fourth, or Remembrance; Fifth, or Scarlet.

A number of Past Grands in the Republic of Texas made application for a Charter for a Grand Lodge, but it was refused because that jurisdiction did not have two Subordinate Lodges at that time.

At this session James L. Ridgely, P. G. M., was, for the second time, elected Grand Sire.

The following list of grievances submitted, at this session, by the Grand Lodge of Ohio, will give the present generation of Odd Fellows some idea of the difficulties that have since been overcome. It took a long time before matters were made to travel smoothly in their proper path. Age and experience were the twin factors at work in bringing order out of chaos:

1st. The Traveling Password of the United States is unnecessarily delayed, or transmitted in a questionable manner.

2d. The Annual Proceedings of the Grand Lodge of the United States are transmitted with the same irregularity as the yearly Password.

3d. Letters to the Grand Secretary of the Grand Lodge of the United States are unanswered, or answered by persons to whom they were not addressed. In this there is a great want of regularity.

4th. The importance of immediate information of amendments to, or alterations in the Work of the Order. By the proceedings of 1838, it will be seen that a resolution was offered declaring it illegal to admit a brother from a Lodge in another State, unless his Card is countersigned by the Grand Secretary of the Grand Lodge of said State. Appended to this, is a resolution requiring the Grand Secretary to inform all Grand Lodges of the passage of the above resolution.   Is this to be done officially by him, or are the printed proceedings considered a sufficient notification ?

5th. What is the proper construction of the resolution referred to, and also the amendment reported by the Committee on the Work of the Order, at April session, 1840?   Is the Grand Lodge of Ohio, by her Secretary, to indorse all Cards in blank, or after they have been filled by Subordinate Lodges ?   If in blank, what use can be made by those countersigned by one Grand Secretary when another has been elected, the year having expired ?   If, after being filled, how can the law be complied with, when Lodges are three hundred or four hundred miles distant from each other in the same State ?

6th. Admission of members of Manchester Unity.   The brethren from England claim admission into our Lodges, as they suppose, under sanction of the Grand Lodge of the United States, but without any of the requisites.

7th. Regalia.   Much difference of opinion exists among the brethren in relation to Regalia.   Particular information is desired on this subject.   Is a member without Degrees entitled to a rosette or silver trimmings ?   If so, what is the distinctive mark of the First Degree or of the Grand Lodge?

8th. Want of uniformity in the Work of the Order.   There is much difference in the mode of working in the several Lodges in the United States, and that of the Manchester Unity possesses not even the semblance of Odd Fellowship as known to us.

9th. The Installation and Charges to the officers are entirely changed.   All officers are required by the Constitutions of their respective Lodges to perform their duties in accordance with the Charges given them.   The books now in use contain no Charges.

10th. Innovations by Grand Lodges sanctioned.   By the printed proceedings of 1840, it appears that the Grand Lodge of Pennsylvania, without the authority of the Grand Lodge of the United States, caused to be translated into the German and French languages the Charges and Degrees of the Order.   The Grand Lodge of the United States adopted them as its own, without reproof for exercising an authority not vested in a State Grand Lodge.

Some of the above grievances were owing to the fact that most of the State Grand Lodges were represented by Proxies, who generally resided in Baltimore.   Proxy representation was subsequently abandoned, and the Representatives were expected and required to keep their jurisdictions informed as to the legislation and requirements in the Work of the Order, and thus insure the necessary uniformity.

A full length oil painting of Past Grand Sire Wildey was ordered.   This was the first one of the handsome collection on the walls of the hall of the Sovereign Grand Lodge.

At the close of the year ending September, 1840, there were four Grand, and thirty-six Subordinate Encampments, fourteen Grand and one hundred and fifty-five Subordinate Lodges reported. The statistics of membership, etc., are incomplete.

1841.

With the regular annual session this year, held in the City of Baltimore, in September, Grand Corresponding Secretary Ridgely began his series of elaborate reports, which were continued from year to year without intermission until his death.

As there was much difficulty encountered by visiting brethren of the Manchester Unity in obtaining admission and recognition in our Lodges, the Grand Secretary zealously endeavored to correct this evil, which was mainly brought about in consequence of the changes made in the Work in England. In relation to this subject, he wrote to the officers of the Unity as follows:

What necessity, if any, led to such important alterations in Great Britain, we have never had the good fortune to learn. We respectfully ask to be informed of the extent of these changes in the Work, and the circumstances under which they have been made. It will be obvious, that unless great uniformity is maintained in this particular, our members will be respectively excluded from each other's Lodge rooms, and one of the brightest characteristics of the Order, to wit: its faculty of succoring a distressed brother in a strange land, will be frequently unexerted by reason of the difficulty of understanding "that peculiar language" by which Odd Fellows should be readily known in every clime throughout the habitable earth.

His efforts, as we shall see later, were without effect, and the estrangement became greater until all relations between the Manchester Unity and the Grand Lodge of the United States were terminated.

An Index of the Grand Lodge Journal, from 1827 to 1840 inclusive, and a Digest of the Laws, prepared by Brother Isaac D. Williamson, were approved and adopted.

The following amendment to the Constitution was adopted by a vote of ten yeas to four nays:

That State Grand Encampments be admitted to a representation in the Grand Lodge of the United States, on the same terms that the State Grand Lodges are represented.

It was provided that a brother may visit a Lodge if introduced by a Grand Representative, or other elective officer of
the Grand Lodge under whose jurisdiction he wishes to
visit.

At this session the first step was taken in the matter of
requiring the business of the Subordinate Lodges to be transacted in the Scarlet Degree. Rep. Cook, of New York,
offered the following resolution, which was read, and on his
motion its consideration was postponed until the next annual
session:

> That the Work of the Order be, and the same is hereby so altered, as to
> make it imperative that the business proceedings of Subordinate Lodges be
> transacted in the Scarlet Degree.

The correspondence had so increased that the Grand
Lodge directed that

> A suitable copying press, copying books, writing trough and such neces-
> sary articles as may be required for taking and preserving copies of said cor-
> respondence, and for such other documents as may be deemed necessary,
> shall be procured.

It was decided on appeal, and subsequently by the adoption of a resolution, that

> No member of the Grand Lodge but a Representative or Past Grand Sire
> can address the Grand Lodge, except upon leave first asked and obtained.

The Committee on Reports and Returns presented a
lengthy document detailing the errors in the reports of Grand
and Subordinate Bodies, stating that "the blanks passed
upon at the last communication have been wholly unattended
to," and submitting four distinct Forms for reports, *viz.:*
State Grand Lodges to the G. L. U. S.; Subordinates to
State Grand Lodges; Subordinates under the G. L. U. S.;
Grand Encampments to the G. L. U. S.

The report of the Committee was adopted.

The Grand Sire elect, James L. Ridgely, resigned that
office, and John A. Kennedy, P. G. M., of New York, was
elected Grand Sire for the ensuing term of two years.
James L. Ridgely, P. G. M., was elected Grand Recording
Secretary for the same period.

The Covenant was made the Official Magazine of the Grand Lodge of the United States. It was to be published monthly. James L. Ridgely, Grand Secretary, was elected the editor. It proved unprofitable from the first, and in 1845 ceased to be the official organ.

The Grand Officers elect were duly installed.

The Grand Sire, by and with the advice and consent of the Grand Lodge, appointed the following Grand Officers:

Isaac Hefley, P. G. M., of Ohio, Grand Marshal; Rev. Isaac D. Williamson, P. G., of New York, Grand Chaplain; William Warren, P. G., of Maryland, Grand Guardian; John E. Chamberlain, P. G., of Maryland, Grand Messenger.

The following was adopted:

Resolved, That the yearly Password, to be forwarded by the Grand Sire, go into use on the 1st day of January, annually; and in the contingency that no communication of this Grand Lodge be held in the interim, the Grand Sire shall, nevertheless, forward a Password as in the above case made and provided.

At this session a commission to proceed to England to confer with the Manchester Unity was authorized.

The difficulties existing in Louisiana, for which the brotherhood were held blameless, excited considerable attention and the sympathy and assistance of the Grand Lodge were tendered.

The following was adopted:

Resolved, That the Grand Sire be authorized, upon proper application made for that purpose in the recess, to issue his Dispensation for the formation of State Grand Lodges or Encampments.

At the close of the year ending September, 1841, there were five Grand, thirty-four Subordinate Encampments, eighteen Grand and one hundred and ninety-nine Subordinate Lodges.

1842.

At the annual communication held in the City of Baltimore, September 19th, the following Grand Officers were present:

John A. Kennedy, Grand Sire; Horn R. Kneass, Deputy Grand Sire; James L. Ridgely, Grand Corresponding and

Recording Secretary; Andrew E.Warner, Grand Treasurer; William Warren, Grand Guardian; John E. Chamberlain, Grand Messenger.

At this session Grand Encampments appear to have been represented for the first time, the Journal showing the names of Representatives from the Grand Encampments of Maryland and New York.

Grand Secretary James L. Ridgely and Grand Chaplain Isaac D. Williamson having been commissioned to visit Eng-' land to reconcile all difficulties and bring about a closer union, made a lengthy report to the effect that all their efforts had been unavailing. Uniformity of the work in both Grand jurisdictions was the great desideratum. These Represent- atives of the Grand Lodge of the United States proposed to the Manchester Unity the adoption of the following:

1. The Grand A. M. C. of the Manchester Unity and the Grand Lodge of the United States shall each adopt and practice throughout the entire jurisdic- tion the Ancient Work of the Order.

The sub-committee of the Grand Annual Movable Com- mittee having declared it impossible to determine "the Ancient Work of the Order," the Commissioners subsequently modified the proposition by substituting "the Five Degrees of Odd Fellowship, with their respective colors, S. T. P. W. and G's, as agreed upon in the year 1826," etc.

2. No change shall ever be made in the Work so adopted, by either party, without the consent and concurrence of the other.

The sub-committee in their report to the Deputies of the G. A. M. C., submitted nine propositions, the first and third embracing the above, presented by the American Commis- sioners. The eighth, however, "That our American breth- ren do agree on their part to admit the English brethren, who are in possession of legal Cards, to full membership into their Lodges, on payment of a sum not to exceed ten shillings and six pence of the money of Great Britain," the Commissioners could not accede to, and stated very fully the reasons why the resolution was dissented from. The explanation, however, had no effect, and on the 4th of June a circular was issued by the Corresponding Secretary of the M. U., informing the Order in Great Britain "that a rupture has taken place between our American brethren and the Independent Order in England," etc.

The Committee on the English Mission made a report and submitted three resolutions :

1st. Thanking Brothers Ridgely and Williamson for their services.

2d. That until the A. M. C. shall restore the Work of the Order to its ancient form, and rescind the resolution to establish Lodges in America, all intercourse shall cease between the two Bodies.

3d. That all Grand and Subordinate Lodges and Encampments working under a Charter from this Grand Lodge, be instructed by a circular, to be addressed to them by the Grand Corresponding Secretary, that they are hereafter required to refuse admission into their Lodges to all persons who claim admission by virtue of a Card granted by a Lodge in connection with the Manchester Unity.

The rupture became complete in 1843 by formal resolution.

At this same session the Work and Degree for Grand Encampments were accepted as reported by the committee, to whom the subject had been referred.

Up to this time there was no regular period for making the returns from State Grand Lodges and Encampments, and Subordinate Lodges and Encampments working under the jurisdiction of the Grand Lodge of the United States. The time was counted from the institution of the Lodge or Encampment and produced much confusion in the accounts. The following were adopted to remedy this evil :

Resolved, That the various Lodges and Encampments working under this immediate jurisdiction be, and they are hereby directed so to make up their respective reports and returns as to embrace the following periods of time, *viz. :* Annual reports from July 1st to June 30th, inclusive; semi-annual reports (if any) from July 1st to December 30th, inclusive ; and quarterly reports to be made up for the corresponding periods, commencing respectively on the first days of July, October, January and April of each year.

Resolved, That in order to enable the Subordinate Lodges to fulfill the requirements of the foregoing resolution, they be, and are hereby authorized, in all cases where the longest part of their terms (seven weeks or more) under present regulations shall have expired, to make one short term, so as to end the quarter at one of the above specified dates, and the officers for said short term, shall be deemed to have served during the regular Constitutional period, and be entitled to all the rights and privileges accruing therefrom ; and where less than seven weeks of a quarter shall have expired, they are hereby directed to extend the term, so as to require the officers, for the time being, to serve for such an additional number of nights as will enable the Lodge to make up its returns in compliance with the spirit and intent of the foregoing regulation.

Resolved, That the terms of Encampments be either diminished or extended, in accordance with the principles herein laid down for Subordinate Lodges, so as to enable those Bodies also to prepare their returns agreeably to the above instruction.

Grand Lodges and Grand Encampments were recommended to conform, as far as practicable, to the above regulations.

The next important subject that engaged the attention of the Grand Lodge was the abolition of Proxy representation. In order to accomplish this object, it was seen that the revenue of the Grand Lodge must be, in some way, increased to defray the expenses of Representatives.

The Grand Recording Secretary was instructed to ascertain the views of the State Grand Lodges as to the propriety of the abolishment of the Proxy system and also as to their disposition to contribute to the funds of the Grand Lodge for the purpose of securing a *bona fide* representation from all the States.

The Grand Sire was authorized, during the recess, to receive a petition from seven Scarlet Degree members, for the purpose of instituting an Encampment in a place where no Encampment was organized.

The following was deemed advisable at this time:

Resolved, That the several Grand Lodges under the jurisdiction of this Grand Lodge, be and they are hereby empowered to confer the Honorary Degrees of P. V. G. and P. Sec'y on all brethren who have served as N. G. of a Lodge during the first and second quarters after its organization, although they have not filled the said offices of Vice Grand and Secretary.

The Grand Lodge was incorporated under the laws of the State of Maryland, and the act of incorporation was formally accepted.

As the most effectual method of replying to many inquiries on the subject, the term "good standing," was now defined. (*See Manual.*)

The Grand Secretary was appointed to revise and cause to be printed a correct Journal of the Proceedings of the Grand Lodge of the United States from its formation.

The following Grand Officers were elected for the ensuing term:

Howell Hopkins, P. G. M., of Pennsylvania, Grand Sire; George M. Bain, P. G. M., of Virginia, Deputy Grand Sire; Jas. L. Ridgely, P. G. M., of Maryland, Grand Corresponding and Recording Secretary; Andrew E. Warner, P. G. M., of Maryland, Grand Treasurer.

1843.

The Grand Lodge met in regular annual session, in the City of Baltimore, on Septmber 18th.

Grand Sire Kennedy, in his report, said:

Nearly all parts of the jurisdiction give forth, by a unity of expression, their exultation on the prosperity which has resulted from our labors, and at present we are enabled to ascertain the highly gratifying fact, that but two States, of the entire extent of our wide domain, now remain, in which Odd Fellowship has not been successfully established; and in each of these we have satisfactory evidence that progress is making, which will, within a few months, include them also in our social compact; when will be presented the pleasing spectacle of every portion of a great nation having united in rendering a benefaction to humanity, unsurpassed by any former moral effort.

At this session George M. Bain declined the office of Deputy Grand Sire, and William S. Stewart, P. G. M., of Missouri, was elected in his stead. He, with the other officers, elected in 1842, was duly installed September 19th, 1843.

The following were appointed by the Grand Sire:

William Curtis, P. G. Sec'y, of Pennsylvania, Grand Marshal; Albert Case, P. G. M., of South Carolina, Grand Chaplain; Richard Brandt, P. G., of New Jersey, Grand Guardian; John E. Chamberlain, P. G., of Maryland, Grand Messenger.

At this session a Daily Journal was printed, and it was the first occasion the members had the opportunity of reading the transactions of the previous day.

An informal petition was presented for a Lodge at Hamburg, Germany, and a Charter was authorized on receipt of a formal application.

The following were adopted:

As the opinion of this Grand Lodge, no brother can represent a Grand Lodge or Grand Encampment in this Grand Lodge, unless he resides in the State, District or Territory where the Grand Lodge or Grand Encampment, of which he offers himself as a Representative, is located.

State Grand Lodges are prohibited from conferring the Grand Lodge Degree for a pecuniary consideration, with a view to increasing their revenue, or for any other consideration, except the regular performance of the duties of the N. G.'s chair; the said Degree having been designed as a reward for faithful service in the Subordinate Lodges, and cannot legally be reached by any other means.

State Grand Lodges and Grand Encampments are required to provide laws to protect their brethren in adjoining or distant States, by prohibiting the Lodges under their jurisdiction from initiating persons at places remote from their permanent residence, while Lodges or Encampments are known to be located in their immediate neighborhood.

The Grand Lodge cannot recognize the right of any State Grand Lodge or Encampment to print any portion of the Work of the Order, and the system of honorary membership as provided for in some of the By-Laws for the government of Subordinate Lodges is inconsistent with the nature and true interests of the Order, and should be abolished.

Past Officers of every description, and members in possession of the Encampment Degrees, and all other members of the Order, when visiting Grand or Subordinate Lodges under this jurisdiction, are entitled to wear the Regalia and Jewels pertaining to the highest Degrees which they may have taken, if they think proper to appear in such Regalia.

A Grand Lodge or Grand Encampment is not entitled to representation until its Warrant be confirmed, nor liable for Representative Tax; and the dues from its Subordinates must be paid to the Grand Lodge of the United States until the Warrant be confirmed.

1844.

The Grand Lodge met in regular annual session, in the City of Baltimore, September 16th.

The following Grand Officers were elected for the ensuing term:

Thomas Sherlock, P. G. M., of Ohio, Grand Sire; George W. Churchill, P. G, M., of Maine, Deputy Grand Sire; James L. Ridgely, P. G. M., of Maryland, Grand Corresponding and Recording Secretary; Andrew E. Warner, P. G. M., of Maryland, Grand Treasurer.

The Grand Lodge declared "the A. T. P. W. to be for the use of brethren who are traveling beyond the limits of the jurisdiction to which they belong, and that it is confided to the two highest elective officers of a Lodge at the time of their installation." (*See Manual.*)

A committee of five, consisting of Representatives Chapin, of Massachusetts; McCabe, of Virginia; Moore, of the District of Columbia; Grand Secretary Ridgely and P. G. Sire Kennedy, were elected to revise the Work of the Order.

The Grand Lodge expressed its opinion that it should be the duty of Subordinate Lodges to determine upon the practicability of opening and closing with prayer, and that they should be the judges of what form they should adopt.

A form for examining visiting brethren was adopted. (*See Manual.*)

The final steps for the disposition of the Official Magazine (*Covenant*) were taken at this session. Three resolutions were adopted, *viz.*:

That the Finance Committee be directed to audit the accounts of the Official Magazine up to the close of the present volume, and to provide that unsettled claims against that department be liquidated.

That the Grand Lodge entertains a profound sense of the lasting obligations which James L. Ridgely, P. G. M., has imposed upon the Order at large by the faithful, energetic, and distinguished manner in which he has, during the existence of the *Covenant* and Official Magazine, edited and managed the same, and that the Grand Sire and the Past Grand Sires in attendance be a committee to have prepared, at the most convenient season, a suitable gold medal, for presentation to the said meritorious brother, as a feeble tribute of the Order's affectionate regard for him.

That the committee appointed to dispose of the Official Magazine be instructed to give the preference to Brother P. G. M. Neilson in the sale of said work, if the terms of his offer are as favorable as those of any other bidder.

The following, of questionable utility, was adopted:

That the printing of the tables of returns of State Grand Lodges and Encampments be hereafter discontinued, and the reports of the D. D. Grand Sires be printed as an appendix to the Journal in lieu thereof.

The importance of defining the position of a Grand Lodge in a foreign country, was the subject of a report by

Representative Torre, of South Carolina, from a special committee, submitting a resolution:

> That upon the creation of a Grand Lodge in a Foreign Country, such organization will be considered by this Grand Lodge as a distinct Sovereignty in the Order, and as exercising independent powers.

The measure, however, failed to secure the approval of the Grand Lodge; the report and resolution being laid on the table.

The following was adopted by a vote of twenty-three to twelve:

> That so much of the action of this Grand Lodge, at the September session of 1842 as relates to the adoption of the Honorary or Side Degrees of P. C. P. and P. H. P. be and the same is hereby repealed.

The Constitution of the Grand Lodge of New Hampshire was amended by striking out a provision authorizing the initiation of "the son of an Odd Fellow, who may be admitted at the age of twenty."

The Grand Secretary was authorized to procure one thousand copies of the Journal of Proceedings of this session, and five hundred copies of the Constitution and By-Laws of the Grand Lodge.

A Form of Visiting Card; also Form of Withdrawal Card, submitted by the Committee on the State of the Order, received the sanction of the Body, and the documents are practically of the same tenor as the Cards now in use.

A special session was held in Baltimore, commencing September 9th, 1845, to consider the report of the Committee on Revision. The committee stated that they had completed the revision of all those portions which appertain to the Work and Degrees of Subordinate Lodges and the Forms for the Installation of Grand and Subordinate Officers, and for constituting new Lodges. The committee proposed to make another and a special report on the subject of the Patriarchal Work.

The report of the committee was adopted.

1845.

The Grand Lodge met in annual session, in Baltimore, September 15th.

Grand Secretary Ridgely in his report speaks of the progress of the Order as follows:

> Odd Fellowship has submitted its claims and capacity as a minister of good among men, and has been approved by the intelligence of the age, as is clearly witnessed in the number of initiates in every grade and class of society which it has gathered within its Lodge rooms. It has nothing to apprehend from external causes. From within alone we may fear evil. By cherishing a deep love and veneration for the laws and ordinances of the Order, by a strict adherence to the relations of subordination which its discipline provides, by an elevated example reflected from its highest department, this apprehension may be wholly dissipated. The Order contains within itself, perhaps to a greater extent than most other federations for benevolent objects, the true elements of self-conservation, arising out of the liberality of its principles, the comprehensiveness of its character and the perfect equality of its form of government ; these, in a very great measure, independently of its own inherent excellence, will serve to free it from the common evil of internal decay, which for the most part follows close after rapid and premature prosperity.

Weighty words of warning, as applicable to-day as for the period in which they were written.

The elective Grand Officers were duly installed, and the Grand Sire appointed the following:

Rev. James D. McCabe, P. G., of Virginia, Grand Chaplain; John G. Treadwell, P. D. G. M., of New York, Grand Marshal; Levin Jones, D. G. M., of the District of Columbia, Grand Guardian; John E. Chamberlain, P. G., of Maryland, Grand Messenger.

The Committee on Revision reported the Patriarchal, Golden Rule and Royal Purple Degrees as revised, and also Forms for Opening and Closing an Encampment.

The Degrees and Forms were adopted as reported.

The committee appointed to revise the Work were instructed to write out in cipher, and illustrate with diagrams, all the * * * and * * * belonging to the Order, and place the same in the hands of the Grand Corresponding Secretary on or before the first day of January, 1846; also to have the revised Lectures and Charges of the

Order translated into the French, German and Welsh languages.

The Grand Lodge, believing that it would be of immense importance in preparing any statistical tables that might thereafter be required, adopted the following :

Resolved, That every Grand Lodge and Grand Encampment under the jurisdiction of this Grand Lodge, be requested to furnish this Grand Lodge with an entire copy of the Journal of their Proceedings, (as printed). And that hereafter a copy of their Quarterly Proceedings be regularly transmitted to the office of the Grand Corresponding Secretary of the Grand Lodge of the United States, to be there preserved as a valuable part of the progressive history of the Order.

This was wise and valuable legislation and the resolution has been faithfully complied with, as the annual reports of the Grand Secretary show.

To correct certain irregularities the following were adopted :

Resolved, That the regular quarterly term known to the Order under this jurisdiction is thirteen weeks, and is to end either with the month of March, June, September or December ; and that, whenever a Lodge is not instituted at least seven weeks before the termination of a regular quarter, it will be necessary for the officers first elected to hold their respective stations for and during the remnant of the first part of a quarter, and to the end of the next ensuing quarter ; and that any division of service by which one full term and part of another term may be made to give two terms of more than seven weeks each, be and is hereby prohibited.

Resolved further, That Encampments be, and they are hereby directed strictly to observe the spirit of the rule above prescribed for Subordinate Lodges—that is, that they interpret the law according to the same principles, making due allowance for the difference which exists in the length of their respective terms.

The Lodge and Encampment terms have since been made of uniform length. (*See Terms, in Manual.*)

The first legislation on behalf of the wives and widows of Odd Fellows was as follows :

Resolved, That each Subordinate Lodge may, by a vote of two-thirds of its members voting, grant a Card to the wife of any member who may apply for it, signed by the officers of the Lodge, and countersigned by the recipient on the margin, and to remain in force not more than one year, and that similar Cards may be granted to the widows of Odd Fellows, to remain in force as long as they may remain such.

A Form of Card for a wife or widow was also provided. It is instructive to learn that this legislation was adopted by a vote of twenty-three yeas to twenty-one nays.

In order to increase the revenue the following were adopted :

Resolved, That from and after the 1st of January, 1846, all Cards, Visiting and Clearance, issued by Subordinate Lodges and Encampments, shall be countersigned by the Grand Corresponding and Recording Secretary of the Grand Lodge of the United States, and that the price ($5.00 per 100) recommended in the report of the Committee on Finance be approved.

Resolved, That in case any Lodge or Encampment shall have on hand at the time specified in the above resolution, Cards not signed, that the Grand Secretary, on their delivery at his office, be directed to furnish proper Cards in their place.

The following was adopted to protect the Representatives while in the performance of their duties as such :

Resolved, That the absence of a member of any State Grand Lodge, on duty as a Representative in this Body, is a sufficient reason for releasing him from any disqualification that he may have incurred by reason of absence from his seat in any other office that he may hold in his Grand Lodge.

Under the provisions of the Constitution, nominations for Grand Sire and Deputy Grand Sire were confined to the Representatives from State Grand Lodges. An amendment, proposed in 1844, to add after "Grand Lodge" the words "and each Grand Encampment," was adopted by a unanimous vote. Another amendment giving the right of appeal to a Subordinate, (when its effects had been surrendered,) without the consent of the State Grand Body, was adopted.

The Grand Secretary reported that steel plate engravings of Final and Visiting Cards had been procured; impressions were ready January 1st, 1845, and fifty-eight thousand and seventy-six Cards had been received from the printers, and sold from January 1st to September 15th.

Certain Grand Lodges were requested "to forward the necessary information to complete a Numerical Registry, as provided for at the annual session of 1843."

Authority was given to Brothers James W. Hale and Thomas Colburn, P. G's, to institute Oriental Lodge, No. 2, at Liverpool, England, but although the Warrant, books, etc., were sent to Liverpool, the Lodge was not established.

The vexed question of the "Official Magazine" was settled for all time by the unanimous adoption of the report of the Special Committee on the subject, which declared, in effect, that the Grand Lodge had not transferred its title in the Magazine; that "the Magazine had been a losing concern to the Grand Lodge for the time it was published;" that Brother Neilson had offered fifty dollars for the publication, but the sale was not consummated; that the committee doubted "whether the Magazine was at that time worth the fifty dollars offered by Brother Neilson," and the committee recommended the formal relinquishment of all rights, etc., of the Grand Lodge in "*The Covenant*" to Catherine Neilson, widow of Brother Robert Neilson. A resolution to that effect was submitted, and also one:

That all magazines, periodicals or other publications purporting to treat upon Odd Fellowship are solely and entirely upon the responsibility of the individuals publishing and editing the same, and have no sanction or authority from this Grand Lodge of the United States for anything that may appear therein.

An important action was the adoption of Article XVIII., By-Laws, providing for the appointment of District Deputy Grand Sires and prescribing their duties.

An unsuccessful effort was made to establish at Louisville, Kentucky, a Western Depot for the distribution of Books, Cards, etc.

It was ordered that Diplomas shall be signed by the Recording Secretary of the Grand Lodge of the United States and the Grand Master of the State Grand Lodge to which the recipient belongs.

It was again declared:

That honorary membership shall under no circumstances be allowed under this Jurisdiction. That full membership in a Subordinate Lodge is essential to membership in an Encampment.

1846.

The Grand Lodge met in annual session, in the City of Baltimore, on Monday, September 21st.

A Special Committee of three was appointed by the Grand Sire, for the purpose of reporting a Form and

Regulations for Regalia and Jewels for Officers of Grand and Subordinate Encampments.

The Committee on the State of the Order was instructed to make a report defining the position and privileges of a member of the Order, under penalty pending an appeal in his case to the Grand Lodge of the United States.

The following Grand Officers were elected for the ensuing term:

Horn R. Kneass, P. D. G. S., of Pennsylvania, Grand Sire; Newell A. Thompson, P. G. M., of Massachusetts, Deputy Grand Sire; James L. Ridgely, P. G. M., of Maryland, Grand Corresponding and Recording Secretary; Andrew E. Warner, P. G. M., of Maryland, Grand Treasurer.

The Grand Encampment of the District of Columbia, instituted at Alexandria, June 6th, 1846, was represented by Edwin S. Hough, and the Grand Encampment of Canada, instituted at Montreal, September 3d, 1846, was represented by Christopher Dunkin.

Grand Sire Sherlock, in his report, represented the Order as having continued its peaceful march, triumphing over the opposition of ignorance and bigotry. The truth of its principles, the beauty of its Work, and the eminently practical nature of its operations secured to it the affections of those who bow at its altars. He pointed to the spectacle of 90,000 men banded together, by the most enduring ties, acting under one common head, performing their labors of love, and an expenditure of $190,000 for these objects.

The Grand Secretary in his report called attention to the fact that all the Odes and Charges had been printed in card form by Subordinate Lodges and Encampments, and in some instances by individuals. He stated that the authorization of this practice will materially divert the revenue of the Grand Lodge.

On account of the inability to procure from Grand Secretaries and Grand Scribes lists of Lodges and Encampments as instituted, the Grand Secretary recommended the repeal of the Registry law, and the Grand Lodge accepted the suggestion. He also stated that after attaching his signature to twenty-one thousand Cards to comply with the law of 1845, he found that every other duty of his office must be abandoned to strictly conform to the requirements, and therefore obtained the "approbation of the Grand Sire to a substitution of the *fac-simile* for the proper signature of the Grand Corresponding Secretary." He regretted that the direction to the Committee on Revision to write out, in cipher, the Unwritten Work of the Order, and place the same in the hands of the Corresponding Secretary, on or before July 1, 1846, had not been complied with. No argument is required "to maintain the value of such a work, to be preserved in the archives of the Order, and to be transmitted to posterity as the true and only standard of precision in the unwritten language of the Order."

The terms of official service in Subordinate Lodges was extended to six months, as a longer term in office would secure to the Order the benefit of riper experience and more extensive knowledge of the affairs of the Order.

An unsuccessful effort was made to extend the terms of Officers of Encampments to one year.

The position and privileges of a member of the Order under penalty, pending an appeal to the Grand Lodge of the United States, were defined to be nothing different from those he enjoys and occupies under the laws of his State Grand Lodge.

An Odd Fellow applying for and obtaining relief from a Lodge of which he is not a member, must have the amount of the benefit granted endorsed on his Card, and the Lodge, to which he belongs, notified by the Secretary of the Lodge granting the benefit, of the amount so granted.

When a Lodge grants a Withdrawal Card to a brother applying therefor, it severs his connection with the Order, and relieves the Lodge granting it from all liability for benefits, whether the Card is actually taken or not. But if the Card be taken, the brother receiving it is entitled to the A. T. P. W. in use at the time, and retains the right to visit for the period specified in such Withdrawal Card.

An effort was made to require the Subordinate Lodges to work in the Fifth Degree, but it was defeated. The minority report in favor of the rejection of the proposition was adopted by the vote of forty yeas to sixteen nays.

A Digest of the Laws was needed, and to afford the required relief, a committee of five, Brothers Ridgely, Hopkins, Griffin, Seymour and Parmenter, was appointed to revise and analyze the laws and decisions at present in force and report to the Grand Lodge, at its next session, a complete Digest; also a Funeral Service.

The following was adopted :

That the Grand Secretary be instructed to make out an alphabetical list of the Representatives, and have the same printed, to be used in calling the yeas and nays. That the Grand Secretary be requested to prepare and have printed with each Journal of Proceedings of this Grand Lodge, a correct Index, and also an Index for the Journals from 1843 to the present session, and that a suitable compensation be granted him for the work.

A Special Committee reported in favor of the establishment, by the Order, of an Institution of Learning. The State Grand Lodges were earnestly requested to consider the expediency thereof and to devise plans for the accomplishment of the object, should they deem it expedient to undertake the work.

Upon an appeal to a State Grand Lodge by a member of a Subordinate Lodge, charged with violating a known law of the Order, if the decision of his Lodge be reversed, he may be reinstated without the consent of his Subordinate Lodge.

The right to print or publish the Lectures, Charges or Odes adopted by the Grand Lodge of the United States for the use of the Grand and Subordinate Lodges and Encampments under its jurisdiction, or any portion thereof, or any Form of Diploma now used by the G. L. U. S., is exclusively the property of the G. L. U. S., and any violation of this right by Grand or Subordinate Bodies or individuals, is in opposition to the laws, rights and privileges of the G. L. U. S.

The issuing of Circulars by Subordinates, applying for pecuniary aid having become very prevalent, in order to prevent imposition, the following was adopted :

Any Lodge, asking pecuniary aid, in consequence of loss by fire, or for any other cause, shall, in the first instance, make application to the Grand Lodge of the State in which such Lodge may be located, and if not in the power of the Grand Lodge to render the aid required, such Grand Lodge may, if deemed expedient, ask the assistance of Grand Lodges in adjacent States, or of all Grand Lodges in the Union through the Grand Masters of the same, who shall have power to issue Circulars to their Subordinates, stating circumstances, etc., to make such appeal available. The following is the form of Circular to be issued :

Whereas, ...Lodge, No..................., of the State (Territory, District or Province), of..is under the necessity of appealing to her sister Lodges for pecuniary aid, in consequence of... .

The Grand Lodge of.., recommends to her Subordinate Lodges, to contribute to the aid of said Lodge.

....*Grand Master.*

A Special Committee on the subject submitted an amendment to Article XXIV., By-Laws, containing Forms of Prayer for Opening a Grand Lodge or Grand Encampment; Closing a Grand Lodge or Grand Encampment; Opening a Subordinate Lodge and Closing a Subordinate Lodge. The report was accepted by a vote of thirty-two yeas, twenty-two nays; but, failing to receive the affirmative votes of two-thirds of the Representatives, the amendment was laid on the table.

The Order in Canada having applied for an independent Charter for the Body to be known as the "Grand Chapter of British North America," the committee on the subject submitted a favorable report constituting the Grand Lodge and Grand Encampment of Canada an Independent Jurisdiction to be known as "The Grand Lodge of British North America." The action was approved by a vote of forty-seven yeas, nine nays.

On Thursday, September 24th, at four o'clock P. M., Howell Hopkins, Past Grand Sire, chairman of the Special Committee on the subject, presented to James L. Ridgely, G. C. and R. Secretary, a splendid Hunting Case Gold

Watch and Chain, "as a feeble tribute of the Order's affectionate regard for him." The eloquent addresses upon the occasion will be found on pages 939, 940 and 941 of the Journal of the Grand Lodge.

Regalia and Jewels were prescribed for Officers of Grand and Subordinate Encampments.

It was ordered that immediate steps be taken for the return of the Charters and Books granted to Pioneer and Oriental Lodges in England, and

That the Grand Corresponding Secretary be instructed to communicate to the R. W. Australian Grand Lodge, I. O. O. F., the acknowledgement of their courteous letter, and to tender the assurance of the high respect of this Grand Lodge, and of our warm and abiding interest in their welfare and prosperity.

A report on Encampment membership elicited an earnest debate, which resulted in the rejection of five of the six resolutions of the Committee. The law was finally determined as follows:

That to acquire or retain membership in an Encampment, full membership in a Subordinate Lodge is indispensably necessary.

That the granting of a Withdrawal Card by a Subordinate Lodge to one of its members, who is also a member of an Encampment, has the effect of severing at once, his connection with his Encampment, but on the renewal of his membership in a Subordinate Lodge, his membership in his Encampment is thereby renewed; *provided*, such renewal shall occur within one month from the date of such Withdrawal Card.

A report authorizing Degree Lodges, naming the officers, providing for conferring Degrees, etc., was indefinitely postponed.

A Regalia to be worn at the funeral of a deceased brother was prescribed; also a Form of Procession, and general directions to be observed on such an occasion.

The Book of Diagrams presented by Brother Kennedy, Past Grand Sire, was declared the Unwritten Work of the Order, and subsequently the following resolutions were adopted:

That the Grand Secretary be instructed to copy in the Book of Diagrams of the Unwritten Work of the Order, the explanation of the same contained in the old Book of Illustrations, and that the said old Book of Illustrations be by him immediately thereafter destroyed.

That the Unwritten Work of the Order shall in no wise be altered or amended except by a unanimous vote of this Grand Lodge, and that the Written Work of the Order shall in no wise be altered or amended except with the concurrence of four-fifths of the members of this Grand Lodge.

Three thousand copies of the Proceedings of the Session, were ordered printed.

The following was adopted :

That the Grand Secretary be, and he is hereby authorized to procure a sufficient number of desks and chairs for the use of this Grand Lodge, and that the sum of five hundred dollars be appropriated to purchase the same.

In 1844 a quarter of a century had passed, and in striking contrast with the feeble beginning of the Order on the 26th of April, 1819, was the record September, 1844 : 26 Grand, 457 Subordinate Lodges ; 11,192 Initiations during the year ; 97 Past Grand Masters ; 4,485 Past Grands ; 40,238 Members ; $283,132.50 Revenue ; $72,113.81 Relief expenditure ; 10 Grand, 102 Subordinate Encampments ; 1,258 Initiations ; 3,536 Members ; $20,663.85 Revenue. In the succeeding year the initiations were 22,894, the membership had increased to 61,853, the revenue to $455,977.24, the relief to $125,361.27, the Subordinate Lodges to 686. The reports for the year ending June 30th, 1846, exhibited 28 Grand, 992 Subordinate Lodges ; 32,316 Initiations ; 144 Past Grand Masters ; 8,500 Past Grands ; 90,753 Members ; 11,349 Brothers and 817 Widowed Families relieved ; 485 Brothers buried ; $197,317.06 expended for Relief ; $708,205.40 Revenue ; 15 Grand, 237 Subordinate Encampments ; 3,331 Initiations ; 9,409 Members ; $53,999.03 Revenue.

1847.

The Grand Lodge met in annual session, in the City of Baltimore, on the 20th of September. Twenty-six State Grand Lodges and eighteen Grand Encampments were represented. The membership of the Order now aggregated 118,961 in number ; the amount expended in relief for the year ending June 30th, 1847, by Lodges and Encampments was $310,209.06 ; the receipts of Subordinates were $970,-769.17.

Grand Sire Sherlock, in his report, stated that a Charter had been prepared and forwarded to " The Grand Lodge of British North America," by which that Body was " erected into a distinct sovereignty, with power, in all matters relating to Odd Fellowship within British North America, independent of this Grand Lodge," with certain reservations.

On the subject of newspapers in the interest of the Order, he said:

The discussion of the internal affairs of our institution, by a portion of the public press, claiming to be the organs of Odd Fellowship, will, I fear, be seriously detrimental to its best interests. Whilst I cheerfully accord to the brothers who have so zealously labored to extend the field of its influence, the purest motives, and freely acknowledge that they have accomplished much good, yet I am constrained by a sense of duty to say, that many erroneous constructions of law and usage have been made the subject of comment and controversy; paper has warred against paper, each enlisting in its support a portion of the Order; and discord has been fostered, if not created, where peace and harmony previously existed.

The attentive reader of the Journal of the Sovereign Grand Lodge will not fail to find that after the lapse of forty years " history repeats itself."

On the subject of establishing " a general system of education," the Grand Secretary regretted to announce that very few responses had been made by Grand Bodies to his circular, and those were generally opposed to the project. He said:

Notwithstanding the present position, he remained firm in his conviction of the practicability and expediency of the measure, and unshaken in the confidence, that although the Order may not now be prepared to concentrate its energies in the cause of education, the time is not distant when a different sentiment will prevail.

He also reported the appropriation for desks and chairs for Representatives insufficient, stating:

The sum appropriated was expended in the purchase of desks constructed of walnut, suited to the dignity of the office for which they were designed, made after the model of those in use for the Senators in the Congress of the United States. A similar appropriation will be necessary to supply a chair for each Representative corresponding in style and convenience with the desks already provided.

The plates of the Journal to the end of the session of 1845, and the copyrights, were held by a party in New York, and of 1846 by a party in Baltimore, and the Grand Secretary urged that the Grand Lodge acquire the ownership, which was eventually accomplished.

The Patriarchal Work in German had been furnished; but no part of the Revised Work had been translated into the French language.

Complaint was made that the law prohibiting the printing of Odes was still violated.

The irregular organization of Excelsior Lodge, No. 1, and the self institution of Pacific Lodge at Honolulu, Sandwich Islands, the Grand Secretary commended to the special attention of Representatives.

Certain changes in the fundamental laws of the Order were agitated; the principal one was the organization of State Grand Lodges upon the representative system, representation to be in proportion to numbers. In some jurisdictions a Representative casts the vote of his Lodge and the other Past Grands are disfranchised, as under the law every Past Grand in good standing is entitled to a seat in his Grand Lodge. The reader will learn in due time the result of this struggle.

The revenue of the Grand Lodge the past year was $3,402.45 less than that of the previous year.

A Digest of the Laws of the Order containing every law, decision and usage, arranged so that the members may see and know their rights and duties, was adopted, and this was the first Digest published, an 18mo. book of 100 pages.

The following was the principal legislation enacted at this session:

All amendments to the Constitutions of Grand Lodges and Grand Encampments must be submitted to the Grand Lodge of the United States for examination, and if approved they become organic law. If error be found it must be corrected.

The practice of accompanying a Visiting Card, when forwarded to an absent brother, by a letter from the N. G. of the Lodge granting it, to the N. G. of some Lodge in the place where the absent brother is temporarily resident, conveying a request that the A. T. P. W. should be communicated. was sanctioned.

It is permitted a member of a Lodge who changes his residence to another State, to join an Encampment in the place of his new abode, while continuing his Lodge membership in his former residence.

The Grand Secretary was directed to keep a Secret Journal of the Proceedings of this Body, in which shall be recorded such matters as in the judgment of the Grand Lodge should not be made public.

The following was adopted :

> That the Past Grand Sires and Grand Secretary be a committee to prepare and report to the next session full and complete instructions in the whole Work of the Order, and that the Grand Secretary shall keep a secret record of such instructions, and of all alterations or changes that may hereafter be made in the same.

The Grand Lodge appropriated five hundred dollars for the purchase of chairs for the members.

The Grand Sire and Grand Secretary were authorized to acquire the copyright and plates of the bound volumes of the Journal.

Charters were authorized for Excelsior Lodge, No. 1, Honolulu, Sandwich Islands, and Venezuela Lodge, No. 1, Caracas, Venezuela, South America ; and were refused to Pacific Lodge, No. 1, Honolulu, and a Lodge at Pelotas, Brazil.

The amendment to Article X. of the Constitution, providing for the election of Representatives for two years, proposed at the session of 1846, was adopted.

Article XXV., By-Laws, was amended so as to provide Regalia and Jewels for Grand Representatives, Officers and Past Officers and Representatives.

It was ordered " that a Special Grand Representative be accredited by this Grand Lodge to the Right Worthy Grand Lodge of British North America, for its next annual communication in Montreal," and James L. Ridgely, Grand Secretary, was appointed by the Grand Sire such Special Representative, and unanimously confirmed.

A Funeral Service, submitted by the Committee on Digest, was adopted.

The Grand Secretary was directed to sell the Digest at thirty-seven cents per copy, or $25.00 per 100 copies.

It was decided that—

A test O. B. N. is no part of the method of examining visitors, and a Lodge or Encampment introducing such mode would deserve severe censure.

Persons who have withdrawn from the Manchester Unity can come into our Order only by initiation, as other initiates. The Clearance Cards issued by the Manchester Unity are not to be recognized.

A State Grand Lodge has power to expel a member from its own Body, but it possesses no power to expel a member altogether from the Order. It may order a Subordinate to try a member, and the direction must be obeyed.

On appeals to the Grand Lodge of the United States the parties appellant shall be required to present a sufficient number of printed statements of their case to furnish one copy to each member of this Grand Lodge.

The Grand Encampment Degree can regularly be given only during the session and in the room in which the Grand Encampment is assembled ; but by special permission it may be conferred in some contiguous room. A similar rule applies to the Grand Lodge Degree.

Under the law as it now stands, it is discretionary with the Encampments to use prayer or not, *at the opening and closing. In the conferring of the Degrees*, the prayers are an integral part of the Work and cannot be abandoned without destroying its symmetry.

The Grand Secretary be directed to furnish Certificates in the nature of Withdrawal Cards to all members of Subordinate Lodges or Encampments immediately under the jurisdiction of the Grand Lodge of the United States, which are now or may hereafter become extinct ; said Certificates to be signed by the Grand Secretary, to be attested by the Seal of this Grand Lodge, to entitle the holder to all the privileges exercised under Withdrawal Cards, and only to be issued after the presentation by the applicant of satisfactory evidence of membership and good standing.

The above, last resolution, was specially to cover the cases of Brother George Bolsover, P. G. M., of Pioneer Lodge, England, and others of that country, the Grand Sire reporting that there was no "authority or precedent to warrant the Grand Officers in furnishing the facilities to enable brethren so situated to become members of other Lodges," and the law was made general in its application.

It was ordered that the Subordinate Work be translated into the French and Spanish languages and two hundred copies printed in each language.

A proposition intended to authorize the admission to membership of "civilized Indians who are of mature age and of good moral character," was rejected.

In accordance with a resolution on the subject, the Committee on the State of the Order reported the following, which was adopted :

That the provision of the Constitution (Art. XI.) is, that the meetings of the Grand Lodge shall be held at such place as may from time to time be determined. No amendment would be necessary, therefore, to change the location. A simple law would effect the object.

The committee are convinced that the proposed change (that the meetings of the Grand Lodge of the United States shall be hereafter held at the City of Cincinnati, Ohio,) would not be beneficial. The position of Baltimore presents peculiar advantages which no other city could offer. It is midway between the North and the South, on the great highway of trade and travel, and easily accessible from all sections of the country. The selection originally was fortuitous, but the committee consider it one of the happiest accidents in our career. Under any circumstances the change should be made with reluctance, as the Grand Lodge has been chartered by the State of Maryland ; but, after a careful estimate of its merits, the committee are satisfied that there is no sound reason for deserting the cradle of the Order.

At this session the Grand Lodge of British North America was represented by L. B. Campbell, Provincial Deputy Grand Sire for the Province of Toronto. This was the first Foreign Grand Body of the Order erected into a distinct Sovereignty.

William Tell Lodge, No. 4, of Baltimore, Maryland, for seventeen years, by the special permission of the Grand Lodge of Maryland, worked alternately in the English and German languages. For this purpose two sets of officers were elected, but each set served *twenty-six nights*. The propriety of this mode of working having been called in question, the Grand Lodge, under all the circumstances, decided that the privilege in the instance of this particular Lodge should not be withdrawn.

A Lodge working in a foreign language may keep a record of its proceedings in the language in which it works, but it is bound to keep a record in the English language also. Subsequent legislation has changed this.

The Grand Officers elected at the session of 1846 were installed, and the Grand Sire appointed the following :

Rev. James D. McCabe, P. G., of Virginia, Grand Chaplain; Smith Skinner, P. G., of Pennsylvania, Grand

Marshal; Samuel L. Harris, P. G., of the District of Columbia, Grand Guardian; John E. Chamberlain, P. G., of Maryland, Grand Messenger.

1848.

The Grand Lodge met in annual session, in the City of Baltimore, on the 18th of September. Twenty-six State Grand Lodges and eighteen Grand Encampments were represented. Two sets of Representatives from the State of New York presented their credentials. It resulted from what is designated as the New York controversy.

The Order now numbered about 123,000, with a revenue for the past year of about $874,000. The Subordinate Lodges numbered 1,713, and the Subordinate Encampments, 338.

Grand Sire Kneass, in his report, said:

I cannot forbear the expression of my profound gratitude to the Author of all good for the increased strength, almost universal harmony and enhanced usefulness by which our progress, during the last year, has been distinguished, and, at the same time, to tender to the other officers, Representatives and other members, my most cordial congratulations upon the happy manifestation of the various healthful influences of our fraternity, which, ramifying through every condition of life, give encouragement, comfort and peace wherever they are felt, and confirm the institution in the intelligence and regard of the people by whom they are either witnessed or enjoyed. Occupying so large a space in the public eye as does this Order, to whose advancement we have contributed our sleepless energies, and whose prosperity is promotive of and inseparable from the improvement of the moral condition of every community where its maxims are promulgated, it cannot be but gratifying to those engaged in the development of its mild yet effective power, to find, upon each successive annual return, the general expectation satisfied, and a still more extended usefulness ensured.

He presented his views of the difficulties in the State of New York and his decisions on the several vexatious questions submitted, in an able and forcible manner. He said:

Convinced, however, as I was, that the view I entertained of the law of the case was correct, I nevertheless, in a sincere desire to adjust the entire controversy in as effectual a manner as it could be accomplished, and entertaining for my own opinion, (although maturely formed after the most thorough and deliberate examination of the subject,) no tenacity that should not yield to the force of additional and more enlightened argument, I determined to call to my assistance such aid as might remove any misimpression I might have received, and guide me to a sound conclusion in case I had erred. Although unwilling to resile from any legitimate duty, yet I was not disposed to refuse such helps as I could invite in its discharge. Feeling upon this subject an anxiety of no ordinary character, and cherishing the hope that it could be settled and disposed of in consonance with that justice which should ever be our admiration and an unshakable bond of union alike, I resolved upon the issuing of a Commission for the purpose of ascertaining the whole facts in the case, and to report to me the same as well as the law that was applicable to them.

The elaborate report of the Commission (James L. Ridgely, Howell Hopkins, Zenas B. Glazier, Wm. R. Smith and E. M. P. Wells) will be found on pages 1162 to 1189 of the Journal. This was referred to the Special Committee of five that had been elected by ballot to consider "the New York controversy," *viz.:* Reps. Parmenter, of Massachusetts; Marshall, of Kentucky; Ramsdell, of Michigan; Baker, of Pennsylvania; Smith, of Maine.

The Grand Secretary reported that

The chairs, corresponding in style and convenience with the desks already provided for the use of the Grand Representatives, for which the appropriation was made in the eleventh resolution, have been procured, and are now present for the accommodation of the Representatives. The appropriation authorized has been unavoidably exceeded by the sum of sixty-four dollars, for which your approbation is asked.

Soon after the adjournment of last session, the Corresponding Secretary closed the contract authorized in the twelfth resolution with Messrs. McGowan and Treadwell, for the copyright and stereotype plates of the Journal of the Grand Lodge of the United States, in so far as these brethren were the proprietors of the same. The terms and stipulations indicated in the resolution were conformed to on the part of the proprietors, and the certificate of the Grand Representatives of the State of New York evidencing their examination of the plates, and their perfect condition and state of preservation is now on file in this office. In consideration of which the undersigned delivered to Messrs. McGowan and Treadwell the corporate notes of the Grand Lodge of the United States at one, two and three years, for five hundred dollars each, bearing date 17th January, 1848. The plates have been safely delivered, the copyright assigned and the value of two hundred dollars worth of bound copies of the Journal of the Grand Lodge of the United States has also been received. This purchase not having entirely extinguished individual proprietorship in the Journal, the undersigned in pursuance of a contract made last year with James Young, the printer of the Journal for September session, 1847, obtained from him, accompanied with a

certificate from the Grand Representatives of Maryland, of the proper condition of the plates, a surrender to the Grand Lodge of the United States of all
his interest in the copyright and stereotype plates by the proper assignments,
upon the payment to him of the sum of one hundred and sixty-one dollars and
eighty-seven cents—being the cost of the stereotype plates. The absolute
right of property in the Journal is, therefore, fully vested in the Grand Lodge
of the United States, and two volumes being now completed, with an index
to the whole, it will be proper for you to fix the price per volume at which the
work shall be sold, and to provide by law for its revision in the event of a
reprint of the same.

He stated that a supplement to the Digest was prepared,
which, together with the original Digest, was copyrighted
in the name of the Grand Lodge of the United States, and
that ten thousand copies were printed and bound at the
aggregate cost of $1,100. The sales having nearly exhausted
this edition, a new one of five hundred copies upon the same
terms was contracted for.

An application was received for the institution of Hope
Lodge, No. 1, Vera Cruz, Mexico, which was declined on
account of the absence of a Card of one of the applicants.

He reported the finances of the Grand Lodge in a good
condition, and said:

With a large property on hand, a respectable permanent investment, and
a considerable outstanding indebtedness to her, she is comparatively free from
debt. It may, therefore, in view of this exhibit of the finances of the Grand
Lodge of the United States, be supposed that a reduction in the revenue ought
to be made. I deem it my duty on this subject to remark, for the information
of the Representatives, that the permanent fund of the Grand Lodge of the
United States has arisen principally from the sales of the Revised Work and
the Digest of Laws, and not from the ordinary sources of revenue; that the
Charter and percentage fees from Subordinates to this jurisdiction, which
have heretofore formed a large source of revenue, will soon entirely cease.

During the recess Warrants were issued for the institution of two Grand Lodges, five Grand Encampments, seven
Subordinate Lodges and twenty-one Subordinate Encampments. The receipts of the Grand Lodge for the past year
were $9,903.42. During the year there was an increase of
321 Subordinate Lodges and 3,733 members.

Peter Allan Brinsmade, P. G., of Excelsior Lodge, No.
1, Honolulu, was admitted to the floor of the Grand Lodge

in consideration of his representing the Order in that distant region of the world.

Past Grands from several jurisdictions were also, by special resolutions, authorized to be present at the session.

A Legislative Committee, to have charge of all questions of new legislation, was for the first time constituted.

A plan for the classification and a mode of drawing for terms of Representatives were adopted. From this time the Body could not consist of entirely new members. The entire Body was now divided into two classes, the first class to serve for one year and the other for two years, and thereafter the Representatives to be elected for two years. The terms of service of the present Representatives were determined by ballot; those who drew number two were declared members of the session of 1849.

In reference to qualifications for membership, it was decided that while no peculiar religious persuasion is requisite for admission into the Order, so also none disqualifies.

The following legislation was had :

An officer who voluntarily withdraws from the duties of a station, before the expiration of his term, forfeits the honors thereof, and his successor who discharges the duties for the unexpired term becomes entitled to said honors.

While the Grand Lodge recognizes the right of State Grand Lodges and Encampments to instruct their Representatives in matters pertaining particularly to said Lodges and Encampments, it also deems the doctrine of instruction in matters of interest to the entire Order throughout this jurisdiction as highly inexpedient.

It shall be the duty of the Scribe of each Subordinate Encampment to furnish to the Secretary of each Subordinate Lodge a list of members of said Lodge, who are also members of said Encampment, and that it shall be the duty of each Secretary to advise each Scribe, within a reasonable time, of the granting of a Withdrawal Card to any member of his Lodge, who is also a member of such Encampment ; and also of the suspension, expulsion or reinstatement of any such member.

It is the duty of the Representatives to the Grand Lodge of the United States to correctly instruct the respective Grand Bodies which they represent in the actual Work of the Order.

The dues of a Lodge accrue weekly ; are paid at stated periods, and only for the convenience of the Lodge. It is, therefore, at any time the right of a brother to pay his dues ; but in case a brother has neglected to pay his dues for such length of time as to be debarred by the rules of his Lodge from drawing benefits while sick, he cannot be permitted while he continues sick to come in and pay his dues so as to entitle himself to benefits, since an injury would thereby be inflicted on such members of the Lodge as are regular in payment of their dues. The brother by his own act has committed the wrong, and it would be improper to permit him to derive benefit from his own negligence.

The propriety of requiring the Work of the Order throughout the United States to be transacted in the English language was considered, but deemed inexpedient.

A resolution was submitted abolishing the Past Official Degrees. This action was also deemed inexpedient.

Renewed efforts were made to return to the three months, term of Subordinate Lodges. The quietus of inexpediency was again administered.

The Grand Lodge again refused to recognize the existence of movable Grand Lodges and Grand Encampments; they must hold their sessions in the places designated in their Charters.

The Grand Lodge refused to allow the names and numbers of defunct Lodges to be given to others at the expiration of three years, and thus continued the existing law.

As to the power of a Subordinate Lodge to remit initiation fees, the Grand Lodge decided that this subject belongs to State Grand Bodies to legislate thereon, and as each is supreme within its own jurisdiction, their decisions, however contradictory, must be binding upon themselves and their Subordinates.

The following were adopted:

Since the right of leaving the Order is well established, and one so retiring has no claim upon the Order for benefit or protection, it would be inexpedient to amend the existing law so as to render him liable to penalty, whilst he experienced no corresponding good. By the existing law a Withdrawal Card may be declared void for good cause, existing at the time of granting the Card, but not discovered until after it has been delivered. In regard to the competency of a C. P. or N. G. to officiate at the installation of his successor, the necessities of the case may sometimes require a C. P. or N. G. to install his successor; he is therefore competent to do so in the absence of the Grand Master or his Deputy, and of all Past Grands.

The law governing benefits to members depositing their Cards, and taken sick or dying before the period prescribed for becoming entitled to sick benefits, is that of the Lodge in which the Card has been deposited.

The amount and character of the evidence which should be required by State Grand Lodges before conferring the several Degrees, is a matter of legislation which can properly be decided by the State Grand Lodges alone.

The granting of Cards during the recess of a Subordinate Lodge is highly inexpedient and in conflict with a decision of the Grand Lodge on page 1085 of the Journal.

As to whether a brother desirous of resuming membership in the Order should deposit his Card in the Lodge *nearest* his residence, "there is no direct law on the subject, but from the analogy of the case, the Card should be deposited in the Lodge nearest his place of residence, but should there be several Lodges at equal or nearly equal distances from his residence, the option, in which to deposit his Card, would undoubtedly remain with him."

Every Constitution submitted to this Grand Lodge shall be a fair and legibly written or printed copy of the Constitution adopted by the Grand or Subordinate Lodge submitting the same.

The report of the Committee on the Unwritten Work shall be copied on parchment, and inserted in the Secret Journal, and the original report preserved.

By virtue of service in the N. G's chair, an officer becomes entitled to the rank of Past Grand, and right to a seat in the Grand Lodge; he (a Junior P. G.) can, therefore, be elected Representative.

State Grand and Subordinate Lodges are forbidden to print Odes; the several Grand Bodies to be notified, and on failure to comply with the direction, the Grand Secretary is instructed to report at the next session, in what jurisdiction such violations of the law continue.

No Forms of Prayer, besides those laid down in the Charge Books, have been adopted by this Grand Lodge, with the single exception of a Form of Prayer for Funeral Services, and the use of this Form is left optional, the only requisite being, that if any Form is used, the one suggested shall be used.

A Grand Master has the right to examine the books of a Subordinate; to make extracts himself, or by one appointed by him for that purpose; but the Grand Lodge alone should have power to require copies of the proceedings.

Past Grands, being by the fundamental laws of the Order entitled to certain privileges, and having certain rights in them, cannot surrender these privileges and rights to any Body in the Order; they may fail to use them, but the right remains so long as they are members in good standing in the Order.

The name of a candidate for initiation and membership, after being referred to a committee, may be withdrawn before the report of that committee is presented, but not subsequently. If the report is recommitted it is then too late to withdraw the name.

A Special Committee was appointed to report at next session a Form for Laying Corner-stones; also for Dedication of Odd Fellows' Halls.

By a unanimous vote, a Special Diploma was ordered to

be prepared and presented to James W. Hale, Grand Representative of New York, in consideration of his services as Special D. D. Grand Sire for the American Lodges in England in 1845.

The Special Committee on the Work of the Order submitted a report (which was adopted), that they had prepared full and complete instructions in the whole Work of the Order.

A Special Committee on obtaining portraits of Past Grand Sires and the Grand Secretary reported:

- The committee accepted the likenesses of Past Grand Sires Gettys, Keyser, Perkins, Hopkins and Sherlock. The likenesses of P. G. Sires Glazier and Kennedy, also that of the Grand Secretary, are in progress, and will be ready for presentation at the next session.

The above completed the gallery of oil paintings to this date.

The provision relating to the alteration of the Work of the Order, heretofore adopted, was a simple resolution subject to change (as decided at session of 1847), by a majority of the Body ; therefore, an amendment to Article I. of the Constitution, proposed in 1847, was adopted, viz. :

That the Unwritten Work of the Order shall in no wise be altered or amended, except by a unanimous vote of this Grand Lodge, and the Written Work of the Order shall in no wise be altered or amended, except with the concurrence of four-fifths of the members of the Grand Lodge.

This important addition to the Constitution was sanctioned by a unanimous vote of 64 yeas.

On the subject of Jewels for officers, the following was adopted :

That it is as imperative upon all Grand and Subordinate Lodges and Encampments to furnish the officers of their respective Lodges and Encampments with the Jewels appertaining to their rank and station, as laid down in the Work of the Order, as it is for members thereof to be clothed in suitable Regalia.

A committee was appointed to report at next session a Form of Constitution for all Grand Lodges; also for all Grand Encampments.

The Special Committee to whom was referred the subject of the pecuniary distress of Past Grand Sire Wildey reported, in effect, as follows:

> They recommend to this Grand Lodge to appropriate out of its uninvested funds, if possible, a sufficient amount to pay off the incumbrances on Past Grand Sire Wildey's property. If the uninvested funds be not sufficient for the purpose indicated, the committee further recommend that the deficit be supplied from the invested funds. The committee desire to be understood as recommending, not an absolute gift of this amount, but only a temporary dedication thereof. They advise the Grand Lodge to accept formal assignments of the judgments, mortgages and other claims, and to hold the same as a kind of collateral security for its reimbursement.
>
> The committee think that the Grand Lodge should not bear the whole brunt of the project of relief, but that the entire brotherhood should be allowed the privilege of participating, and to that end they recommend that the Grand Corresponding Secretary address a circular letter to the several Grand Masters and Grand Patriarchs requesting them to call on their Subordinates for such contributions as they may think fit to bestow. The fund to be thus raised is to be designated the "Wildey Fund." They also recommend that the same circular letter shall include a request for the Subordinates to bestow upon the P. G. Sire a small annuity to be called the "Wildey Annuity."

Nine resolutions were submitted which, with the report, were adopted, sixty-eight voting in the affirmative and eight in the negative.

The Grand Secretary was instructed to issue, as soon as practicable, a circular to all the Subordinate Lodges within this jurisdiction, soliciting contributions for the purpose of erecting an Odd Fellows' Hall in the town of Honolulu, Sandwich Islands, and requested to receive such contributions, and, so soon as a sufficient amount shall have been received, authorized, in conjunction with a committee of two, to purchase the materials and procure the work necessary for the erection of said hall, in conformity with a plan to be approved by them; and forthwith to ship the same for the use of Excelsior Lodge, No. 1, in Honolulu.

Grand Secretary Ridgely, of Maryland, Special Representative to the Grand Lodge of British North America, made a report, in which he says: "The Representatives in attendance greeted me in the most cordial manner, and the attention then paid me was followed by unremitting kindness during the entire period of my sojourn among them. * * * * The idea of an interchange of Representatives was fortunately conceived, and so long as the system shall prevail, the strong bonds which already unite the Odd Fellows of Canada and the United States will remain unimpaired."

Grand Sire Kneass made the following decision which was approved by the Committee on the State of the Order, but the report was laid on the table :

By a usage of the Order, well recognized and based upon sound considerations, a vote by ballot is conclusive, and no one, after it has been taken, has a right to move for a reconsideration, or to proceed to ballot anew. To submit a question a second time to a Lodge after she has decided it in the most deliberate manner known, not merely to our institution, but to civilized men, is utterly inconsistent with this usage.

The following was adopted on the fifth day of the session :

That the Secret Journal and Book of Diagrams be placed in the hands of the Deputy Grand Sire, during the remainder of the session and that he be authorized to instruct Representatives in the Work of the Order.

The Grand Lodge again refused to extend the terms of Subordinate Encampments to one year.

A By-Law was adopted providing for the appointment of a Standing Committee at the commencement of every session, to open and decide upon proposals for printing the Journal, etc., and report the decision to the Grand Lodge.

The majority of the Committee on the New York case submitted their report, accompanied with the following resolutions :

That John J. Davies and James W. Hale are the legal Representatives from the Grand Lodge of New York, and Joseph D. Stewart and W. W. Dibblee are the legal Representatives from the Grand Encampment of New York, and that they be admitted to seats in this Grand Lodge.

That the Grand Bodies by whom the foregoing Representatives are elected or appointed, are hereby recognized as having a legal existence under the authority of the Grand Lodge of the United States.

After considerable discussion the report and both the above resolutions were adopted. Robert H. Griffin, the Grand Sire elect, at his request, was excused from voting, for the reason assigned by him, that he considered it "improper for him to take part in the final decision of a question directly bearing upon the privileges of the station which he is expected hereafter to fill."

Representative Marshall, of Kentucky, submitted a minority report accompanied with the following resolutions, which were not adopted:

That the Constitution submitted by the Grand Lodge of the United States to the Grand Lodge of New York, was taken up by that Body at its November session, 1847, as directed by the Grand Lodge of the United States, and amended and adopted, and as amended and adopted forthwith became the Constitution of the Grand Lodge of New York.

That John W. Dwinelle and Theodore Dimon, having been duly elected members of the Grand Lodge of the United States from the Grand Lodge of New York, are entitled to seats in this Body.

The evidence, in this New York case, taken by the committee will be found in the Appendix of the Journal, pp. 1355-1381.

Sixteen Representatives of Grand Bodies protested against the decision of the Grand Lodge in adopting the majority report of the Committee on the New York case in the following words:

They believe such decision utterly destructive to all the powers heretofore vested in State Grand Lodges, to all the rights of the State jurisdictions, and that it vests in a single hand the entire prerogative of this Body. They, therefore, feel it their duty solemnly to protest against it.

The following Grand Officers were elected:

Robert H. Griffin, P. G. M., of Georgia, Grand Sire; A. S. Kellogg, P. G. M., of Michigan, Deputy Grand Sire; James L. Ridgely, P. G. M., of Maryland, Grand Corresponding and Recording Secretary; Andrew E. Warner, P. G. M., of Maryland, Grand Treasurer.

1849.

The Grand Lodge met in annual session, in the City of Baltimore, on the 17th of September. Twenty-six Grand Lodges and sixteen Grand Encampments were represented.

This was the first session under the new arrangement, and on calling the roll, a quorum of the Representatives, designated in 1848 to serve two years, was declared present.

Hugh Edmonstone Montgomerie, P. G. M., was acknowledged as Special Grand Representative from the Grand Lodge of British North America.

In his report Grand Sire Kneass said :

Fresh not merely from the State and District tribunals within our jurisdictions, but also from the working Lodges, familiar not merely with the legislative departments of our institution, but with the minute details of Subordinate Lodge duty, you have brought with you to this more elevated stage of honorable and enlarged action, funds of valuable information, which your zeal in behalf of the objects of our common affiliation will prompt you so advantageously to employ as to tighten the bonds of our union—supply the diversified wants of the various sections over which our healthful influences sweep ; and, in short, to contribute to the melioration of our common race, wherever our emblematic chain is furbished by society's sure attrition.

To you, then, will all eyes be turned as the Representatives of a constituency composed of no common share of the intelligence, virtue and worth of the nation in which we reside, and extending not only from ocean to ocean and from the lake frontier to the Rio Del Norte, but beyond the borders of our country to people just emerged from barbaric darkness, and spreading there the light of civilization and Odd Fellowship. Full and warm-gushing will be the general aspirations that your deliberations may secure universal harmony and undisturbed peace within our limits—maintain our time-honored customs and rules, which have thus far led to our general prosperity ; save unbroken and unimpaired our integrity, in order that our labors in Friendship, Love and Truth may be best prosecuted, and redound to the glory of our beloved institution.

The Grand Secretary reported : " The resolution of last session, page 1317, Journal, directing the Unwritten Work to be engrossed and inserted in the Secret Journal, has been complied with." The receipts from Lodges and Encampments for account of Excelsior Lodge, No. 1, Honolulu, pursuant to the resolution of last session amounted to $75. The contributions from the same sources for the Wildey Fund and Annuity aggregated respectively $1,113.50 and $136.90.

The Grand Secretary said, in conclusion:

I beg to felicitate the Grand Lodge upon the continued prosperity of the vast jurisdiction which now acknowledges her as its supreme head, stretching from the Lakes upon the North to the Gulf, from the Atlantic to the Pacific shores, and to invoke in behalf of the preservation of so sublime a spectacle and the maintenance of its unity the most profound concern.

The following were adopted :

Five hundred copies of the Journal of Proceedings of this Grand Lodge shall be printed, from day to day, for the use of the members.

The Book of Diagrams and all matters connected with the private Work of the Order shall be placed in the official keeping of the R. W. Deputy Grand Sire, during the present session, and Representatives shall be allowed to consult with him in relation to the Work of the Order, and to examine said Work.

It is competent for a Subordinate Lodge to receive, on deposit, a Card of Clearance from a Lodge that became defunct after issuing it, if, at the *time it was granted*, the Lodge labored under no disability, a Card of Clearance relating alone to the past. The rule must be otherwise as to Visiting Cards, which speak in the *present* of the connection of the bearer, whose right undoubtedly expires with his Lodge.

A brother has the right to withdraw his application for a Final Card at any time previous to a vote thereon.

It is the duty of the Vice Grand, while occupying the chair of the Noble Grand, to wear the Regalia of the Noble Grand.

Unworthy members can be expelled only after a proper trial, upon charges duly preferred and investigated.

After a Grand Lodge has acquitted a brother who has been expelled by his Subordinate Lodge, the Grand Lodge may reconsider such vote and pass a resolution confirming the decision of the Lodge. It is in accordance with the parliamentary law which generally prevails in the Grand Bodies.

A State Grand Lodge may appoint such officers, additional to those required by the law of the Digest, as its wants and convenience may require.

It is not expedient to confer any title or honorary distinction on Past Degree Masters.

A Subordinate Lodge has no jurisdiction or power over the holder of an expired Withdrawal Card.

The clause, "Nor can they (Subordinate Lodges) lawfully enter into correspondence with each other without the consent and approval of their Grand Lodges," in Sec. 3, Art. III., Division 3 of the Digest, be and it is hereby repealed.

The following amendment to the Rules of Order was adopted :

ART. 44. The report of no committee shall be acted upon on the day of its presentation, except the Committee on Credentials.

Forms for uniform Constitutions for Grand Lodges and Grand Encampments were submitted by the Special Committee on that subject, but their consideration was indefinitely postponed.

A Select Committee of three was appointed to obtain for the Grand Lodge the portrait of Past Grand Sire Horn R. Kneass.

A Special Committee of three was appointed to take into consideration the state of the Order in New York.

The following was ordered to be spread upon the Journal:

The Representatives in this Body from the State of New York respectfully protest against the action of the Grand Lodge of the United States in ordering and appointing a committee " to take into consideration the state of the Order in New York," inasmuch as neither the Grand Lodge nor Grand Encampment of the State of New York, or their Representatives, have brought any subject before this R. W. Body requiring the action of this Grand Lodge, or of a committee thereof ; such action being utterly destructive to all the powers vested in State Grand Lodges, to all the rights of State jurisdictions, and an interference with the rights guaranteed by their Constitutions, approved by this R. W. Body, and by their valid and unreclaimed Charters.

One thousand copies of the reports of the Grand Sire and Grand Secretary were ordered to be printed for distribution.

It was ordered that the future legislation of the Grand Lodge be by bill, in the manner pursued in the Congress of the United States, so far as the different organization of the Grand Lodge will allow.

The Special Committee of three, appointed to take into consideration the state of the Order in New York, submitted with their report eight resolutions for the consideration of the Grand Lodge. In the first resolution, the New Constitution Grand Lodge of the State of New York was recognized as having legal existence under the Grand Lodge of the United States, upon and after the passage of this resolution, with jurisdiction over the Northern Judicial District of the State, and with the title of *The Grand Lodge of Northern New York*. The second resolution provides that the Grand Lodge of New York, under the title of *The Grand Lodge of Southern New York* shall have jurisdiction over the Southern Judicial District. The third resolution provides that each of the Grand Lodges shall have exclusive jurisdiction in its own District, with the proviso that the Subordinates now in one District, but working under the Grand Body in the other, may elect, prior to the 1st of January, 1850, to which Body they shall be attached. They may so elect, after that date, with the consent of both Grand Lodges, provided that Lodges that are in allegiance out of their District shall not receive less than the minimum rates for Initiation, Degrees, etc., which are received by Lodges in the same Districts and attached thereto. The fourth resolution confirms all Charters granted by the Grand Lodge of Northern New York. The fifth resolution confers jurisdiction over the Southern Judicial District upon the Grand Encampment of New York, which is to be known as *The Grand Encampment of Southern New York*. The sixth resolution confers jurisdiction over the Northern District upon and after the passage of this resolution, upon the New Constitution Grand Encampment, which is to be known as *The Grand Encampment of Northern New York*. In the other resolutions the provisions above, applicable to Subordinate Lodges, are made to apply to Subordinate Encampments, and Article VIII. of the By-Laws, was amended to provide for representation in the Grand Lodge of the United States from the four Grand Bodies in New York.

The Representatives of the Grand Lodge and Grand Encampment of Northern New York were not admitted to seats in the Grand Lodge, on account of the informality of their credentials.

The Constitution of the Grand Lodge of Northern New York was presented and referred to the Committee on Constitutions. This reference was resisted, it being contended that, as the act creating the said Grand Lodge had passed only last night, the alleged Constitution could not have been adopted by that Body, since it had not been as yet instituted.

The Grand Sire was authorized, so soon as he sha'l have been advised officially by the Grand Lodge and Grand Encampment of Northern New York, respectively, of the selection by these Bodies of their location, to issue a Charter in proper form of law, to the officers and members of said Bodies, respectively, and either in person or by deputation to deliver the same formally.

The Congressional Manual of Judge Sutherland, of Pennsylvania, was adopted for the government of the proceedings and debates of the Grand Lodge, so far as the same is applicable and does not conflict with any of its special rules. The manual was recommended to the Grand and Subordinate Lodges of the different States and Territories.

The Grand Lodge decided that when it shall have passed upon the business brought and to be brought before it, instead of closing the present session, it shall adjourn to the second Monday of September, 1850, to meet in the City of Cincinnati, then and there to take into consideration the present Constitution of the Grand Lodge of the United States, and to digest and agree to report the same with such alterations or amendments as may be deemed advisable, to be considered at the next annual session of the Grand Lodge. At such adjourned session, the Grand Lodge of the United States will not entertain any motion for, or transact, any business, except that mentioned in the above resolution.

In answer to the query, whether infidels can be proposed as members, it was decided, that propositions for membership must be subject to the laws and regulations of the Order. And since no peculiar religious views, which do not affect the belief of the person asking admission into the Order " in a Supreme Being, the Creator and Preserver of the Universe," can disqualify him for membership, neither can those views be allowed to interfere with the privilege of members in respect to propositions for admission.

There was ordered to be published a new edition of five hundred copies of the Journal of the Grand Lodge, including its proceedings up to the close of the present session.

A Special Committee of nine was appointed to inquire into the expediency of procuring a suitable block of marble, granite, or other stone, to be contributed on behalf of this Body towards the monument now erecting in the City of Washington in honor of the Father of his Country.

The Chair decided that the term of Representatives commences with the annual session of the Grand Lodge of the United States, next succeeding their election or appointment.

The Grand Officers elect were duly installed on the second day of the session, and the following were appointed by the Grand Sire:

Rev. E. M. P. Wells, P. G. M., of Massachusetts, Grand Chaplain ; John R. Johnson, P. G., of Georgia, Grand Marshal ; S. H. Lewyt, P. G., of Maryland, Grand Guardian ; John E. Chamberlain, P. G., of Maryland, Grand Messenger.

The time for installation of Grand Officers was changed so that the ceremony shall take place after the reading of the Journal on the first day of the session.

A Special Committee of three was appointed to prepare and report at the next annual session of the Grand Lodge of the United States a Form for Opening and Closing Degree Lodges, and for the installation of the officers of such Bodies, and was instructed to prepare and report at the next annual session of the Grand Lodge of the United States, appropriate Lectures to be given on the conferring of the Past Official Degrees.

The gold excitement in California, alluring many members of the Order to the Pacific, induced the Grand Sire to grant a Warrant for opening California Lodge, No. 1.

During the past year Warrants were issued for one Grand Lodge, two Grand Encampments, three Subordinate Lodges and three Subordinate Encampments. The total receipts for the year were $14,106.31. The invested funds of the Grand Lodge now amounted to $12,817, which sum accrued, to a great extent, from the sale of the Revised Work. The membership increased 16,545 in the Subordinate Lodges, and 197 in the Subordinate Encampments.

The amount of mileage and per diem for Representatives and officers attending sessions of the Grand Lodge was fixed ; and to meet the payment thereof it was decided to annually assess each Grand Body—said assessment to be estimated *pro rata* upon the number of members of the Subordinate Lodges and Encampments of such State Grand Bodies respectively.

The following legislation was had :

The expenses of Representatives and Officers (excepting those to whom stated salaries are given) attending the sessions of the Grand Lodge of the United States, shall be paid by the Grand Lodge.

This was an amendment to Art. XII. of the Constitution. It was adopted by the vote of 53 ayes to 25 nays.

The Representative Tax assessed by Art. XII., Sec. 4, is hereby ordered to be hereafter appropriated towards the payment of expenses of Representatives, as provided for in the amendment to Article XII., adopted at this session.

The officers of this Lodge in making an assessment, in conformity with the resolutions adopted at this session, shall make an assessment merely for such sums as may be necessary, in addition to the Representative Tax.

There shall be made a uniform translation of the Work of the Order, for the use of the French and Spanish Lodges of this jurisdiction ; provided, that all such Subordinate Lodges shall continue to keep one copy of their minutes in the English language.

No Representative can be recognized upon the floor of this Grand Lodge, at any future session, unless clothed in the full Regalia of a Grand Representative.

A Grand Master has the right to take part in the proceedings of his own Subordinate Lodge ; vote for officers, membership, and on motions which come before it.

A brother holding a Withdrawal Card has no right to join a procession of the Order, without the consent of the Lodge by which the procession is formed.

State Grand Bodies have the option to change the Password quarterly, instead of semi-annually, when in their opinion it shall be for the interest of the Order in their respective jurisdictions.

A wife divorced *a vinculo matrimonii* can testify, upon the trial of her former husband under charges, but if the divorce be merely *a mensa et thoro*, the separation of the parties is not complete, and the wife cannot testify.

A written resignation severs the connection of a brother, finally and entirely with the Order, provided he be in good standing in his Lodge at the time of such resignation. When a brother has so separated himself from the Order, he is no longer, in any respect, subject to its jurisdiction.

The manner of electing or appointing Grand Representatives to the Grand Lodge of the United States has been left to State legislation, and the State Grand Lodges may, in the event of a vacancy, vest the power of appointing their Grand Representatives in their Officers at their discretion.

Under no circumstances is it expedient to initiate into the Order any member deprived of the senses of sight, hearing, or the power of speech.

A Grand Lodge has the right to grant permission to a Subordinate to have semi-monthly meetings, but twenty-six night's service is necessary to complete a term.

The refusal or willful neglect of a member of a Subordinate Lodge to appear and answer charges preferred against him, constitutes " contempt."

A brother under suspension is still a member of his Lodge, although deprived of certain rights and privileges, and is subject to its laws in relation to discipline for unworthy conduct.

The Order does not regulate the beverages of its members. While temperance is a cardinal principle of its teachings, it will not attempt to enforce total abstinence.

The Grand Lodge held an adjourned session in Cincinnati, Ohio, September 9th, 1850, to revise the Constitution of the Grand Lodge in accordance with the action at the annual session of 1849.

On account of a quorum not appearing, the Body adjourned from day to day until Friday, September 13th, when a Constitutional quorum was reported present.

The Grand Marshal having resigned, the Grand Sire appointed H. A. Crane, P. G., of Georgia, to fill the vacancy.

Representatives from the Grand Lodge and Grand Encampment of Northern New York were present and their terms of service determined.

The business of the session was rapidly proceeded with, and numerous amendments to the Constitution were submitted and laid on the table for action at the annual session.

Sixteen Representatives whose terms expired with the adjourned session received $1,705.56 for mileage and per diem, and seven officers and forty-three Representatives accredited to the annual session to commence September 16th, were allowed $3,347.76, making the total expenses of the adjourned session $5,053.32.

1850.

The regular annual session was held in Cincinnati commencing September 16th.

In his report, Grand Sire Griffin, said :

So far as my information goes, few relics now remain of the excited contest which for so long a time paralyzed the energies of the Order in New York and caused apprehension of great danger to our institution in the minds of nearly all the brotherhood.   *   *   *   *   *   *   *   *

I submit to you the proceedings of the adjourned communication, and refer you to the amendments there reported ; but I trust you will excuse me for adding, that in my judgment the spirit of your Constitution would be violated by taking action upon amendments thus proposed. It is true that this Grand Lodge is the judge of the necessity of alterations in her own laws; but I consider it to be only proper that where the fundamental law is to be altered, the Order at large should have an opportunity of examining the proposed alterations. We have lived long and grown great under our present Constitution, and I can see no reason for sudden or violent change.

The Grand Secretary in his report said:

During a series of years the undersigned has importuned the Grand Lodge to relieve the office of Corresponding Secretary from the responsibility which, under existing circumstances, devolves upon it of entering into contracts, during the recess, for supplies. To some extent this appeal has been recognized by the law of the last session, authorizing the appointment of a committee to contract for the public printing ; but there remains yet a large amount of responsibility with the Corresponding Secretary, in the purchase of indispensable necessaries during the recess, which involves an expenditure of some thousands of dollars, such as printing Cards, upwards of sixty thousand of which have been printed and sold during the past fiscal year ; also the printing of Diplomas, Charge and Installation Books, and the Encampment Work. The undersigned is not desirous of shrinking from any just responsibility, yet he respectfully suggests that no expense should be incurred without authority of law, and provision should be made for appropriations to meet the wants of the office, and nothing should be left to the discretion or responsibility of the incumbent.

The surplus, together with the accruing receipts of the year, have been, so far as was necessary, employed in the payment of the note of the Grand Lodge of the United States for $4,000, given by the Grand Officers in discharge of the appropriation made for the relief of P. G. S. Wildey, which note has been retired, and will accompany the vouchers of the Grand Treasurer. The Grand Lodge of the United States has thus been enabled to extend to this worthy brother the most substantial relief in the hour of his need, without the necessity of disturbing the invested funds, and at the same time without, in the slightest degree, embarrassing its fiscal operations. This act of commendable liberality and gratitude will pass to our posterity in the Order, as one among the many ennobling characteristics of the present generation of Odd Fellows, and as an enduring monument of the due appreciation on the part of the Grand Lodge of 1848, of the benefaction conferred upon us by the founder of the Order.

The assessment levied to pay the mileage and per diem amounted to $11,278.50. The lowest amount levied was $8.68 on Texas, and the highest $2,079.12 on Pennsylvania. It was calculated that sixteen hundred miles was the average distance traveled by each member, going to and returning from the session. The assessment was made on the basis of one hundred and eighty thousand four hundred and fifty-seven members of Subordinates.

During the year Warrants were issued for one Grand Encampment, three Subordinate Lodges, and four Subordinate Encampments.

The total receipts for the year were $12,169.12. The invested funds of the Grand Lodge now amounted to $16,817. The Subordinate Encampments increased 90 in number, and the Subordinate Lodges, 627. There were now 31 Grand Lodges and 27 Grand Encampments.

The resolution providing for levying an annual assessment for the payment of mileage and per diem was repealed.

The following was submitted and referred to the Committee on the State of the Order, but the Legislative Committee reported on the subject:

That the Committee on the State of the Order inquire into the propriety of instituting appropriate Honorary Degrees as follows: One for the wives and daughters of age of Scarlet Degree members; also one for the wives and daughters of Past Officers.

From this resolution resulted, in time, the Degree of Rebekah. The victory was not won at once; many sessions passed before the Degree attained its present condition. Representatives J. C. Larue and J. A. Kennedy, a majority of the Legislative Committee, reported that the institution of such Degrees was unadvised and inappropriate. Representative Schuyler Colfax, of Indiana, made the following minority report: (It is quoted at length in view of the present position of this Degree.)

That he agrees with the majority of the Committee in reporting against a special Degree for the wives and daughters of Past Officers, as distinguished from the wives and daughters of Scarlet Degree members.

But in regard to the main question, that of instituting a Lady's Degree for the wives of Scarlet members, he is compelled to differ widely from his associates.

He presents the following reasons for the views he entertains:

1. It would tend to increase the resources of Subordinate Lodges by the advance of members in the Degrees. The experience of other Orders which have adopted kindred systems has proved this. It affords an additional incentive for brethren, and an additional argument for those allied to them, to induce them to progress upwards in the Order.

2. It would complete the present imperfect system in force in most of the jurisdictions, by which wives' and widows' Cards are now authorized.

3. It would lessen and ultimately destroy the prejudice felt against the Order, by many of the fairer sex in various portions of the Union, and which undeniably often tends to prevent accessions of members in Subordinate Lodges. We appear to exhibit a distrust of them, which other prominent Orders do not. In many of the States the Masonic Lodges are authorized to confer a similar Degree upon those ladies connected with their members. The Sons of Temperance have a kindred branch of their Order, called the Daughters of Temperance, and the Rechabites have also their Daughters of Rechab. Others in addition might be named. It would seem to require no argument to prove that ladies becoming connected with the two latter Temperance organizations, knowing that Odd Fellowship apparently exhibits no confidence, reposes no trust in them, would endeavor to induce those related to them to join the other more courteous Orders, while a different number, who are not connected with such, and do not desire to participate in the details and labor of business incidental to such organization, but who would prefer simply to have a tie in common with the Order of which their companions are members, would strive to incline the undecided mind of sucb husbands to this argument, tending of course decidedly against the increase of our Order.

4. Such a Degree could be made to assist Odd Fellowship in peculiar and difficult cases of brothers' sickness. In many such, the kindly nursing of woman is needed far more than the assiduous and constant attendance of man, for she was formed to minister at the couch of affliction ; and in the watching, which our laws so strictly and properly provide for, we only strive to compel the observance, by laws and penalties of what in her is Instinct, the promptings of Nature, the impulse of the Heart. By making such assistance in cases of peculiar exigency, at the crisis of a tedious or dangerous disease, a *duty* known to be expected by the Order, as well as due in like cases to those of their own sex thus associated with them—a valuable and systematic aid will be secured. The promotion by this association of warm Friendships between the lady members, thus afflicted, is not in addition, an unimportant consideration.

He presents for adoption the following resolution, which is intended simply to prepare the way for the definite consideration of such a Degree at the next session.

Resolved, That a Special Committee of three members be appointed to prepare an appropriate Honorary Degree, with an accompanying Sign or Signs and Passwords, to be conferred upon the wives of Scarlet Degree members who are in good standing in the Order, and that such Committee report such Degree for consideration at the next communication of this Grand Lodge.

This, the minority report, was adopted.

At this session the following resolutions were adopted :

The Finance Committee are hereby instructed to report to the Grand Lodge the probable amount of expenses, including mileage and per diem of members for the current year, and also to report on the practicability of raising revenue sufficient to meet the same, by the sale of supplies, etc., furnished by this Body.

A suspended member arraigned for trial and punishment must be temporarily admitted to his Lodge for the purpose of making his defence.

The suspension of a brother for non-payment of dues is intended as a means of punishment.

The Grand Lodge of the United States will neither entertain nor consider any inquiry as to what are the laws or usages of the Order, unless the same be brought before the Body by an appeal from the decision of a Grand Lodge or Grand Encampment, or unless the same be presented by a Grand Lodge or Grand Encampment.

The pay of Representatives to, and officers of, this Body (excepting those to whom stated salaries are allowed), shall be three dollars per diem during their attendance upon the sessions of the Grand Lodge of the United States. In addition to the above, the said Representatives and officers shall also receive five cents for each mile traveled from their respective residences to the place of meeting of the Grand Lodge of the United States, and back again; the said mileage to be computed by the nearest mail route between said points. The said per diem allowance and mileage shall be paid by the Grand Treasurer on the Certificate of the Grand Secretary, and these resolutions shall go into effect from and after the close of this communication; all laws inconsistent therewith shall be thenceforth repealed.

The Grand Secretary is directed to require cash payments for all orders from State Grand Lodges and State Grand Encampments for Books, Odes, Diplomas, Cards, etc.; and no Representative from such State Grand Body shall be allowed or permitted to occupy a seat as a Representative upon this floor on and after the present communication of the Grand Lodge of the United States, whose State Grand Lodge or Grand Encampment has not first paid all amounts due by said Grand Body to this Grand Lodge.

No Representative shall be permitted to occupy a seat on the floor of this Grand Lodge, after the present communication of this Grand Lodge, whose State Grand Lodge or Grand Encampment shall not have paid the Representative tax levied by the Constitution of this Right Worthy Body.

Article VIII. of the Constitution was amended to read:

Past Grand Sires shall be admitted to seats in this Grand Lodge, with the power of debating and making motions, but shall not have the privilege of voting unless they be Representatives.

The action of the Grand Lodge of the United States in levying assessments upon Subordinates to pay the mileage and per diem of Grand Representatives was a legitimate exercise of its powers. The various Subordinates which had refused to pay such assessments had virtually asserted a right to nullify the acts of the Grand Lodge of the United

States, which could not be recognized. The payment of said assessment was required.

The question of depriving recusant Grand Bodies of representation in the event they persisted in refusing to pay said assessment, was referred to the Grand Lodge at its next annual communication, when its consideration would more properly arise.

It was deemed inexpedient to translate the Work of the Order into the Welsh language, as there was no demand for it except from the jurisdiction of Pennsylvania.

The consent of the Grand Lodge of the United States was given to the Grand Lodge of Illinois to remove the seat of the Grand Lodge of that State from Peoria to Springfield, in the same State.

It was decided inexpedient for the Grand Lodge to legislate on the subject of uniform prices for Degrees, as the several Grand Lodges and Grand Encampments were the best judges of the rates that ought to be charged, within their limits, for Degrees, as well as initiations, dues, etc.

The Chair decided that the call for the yeas and nays opened the debate, and made any motion admissible.

A protest was received from the Grand Lodge of Maryland against the legality and constitutionality of the meeting of the Grand Lodge of the United States out of Maryland, and also against the mileage and per diem law.

In reference to the above protest, as to meeting out of Maryland, the Committee on the State of the Order, to whom the subject was referred, said :

In 1824, the Grand Lodge of Maryland, conceiving the importance and propriety of forming a Grand Lodge of the United States, a committee being formed for that purpose, passed resolutions and formed a Constitution, to be submitted to the Grand Lodges of Massachusetts, New York, and Pennsylvania, which went to fix the seat of government permanently in the City of Baltimore ; this feature was objected to by New York, and Pennsylvania absolutely refused to consent, unless the word permanent was first stricken out and present inserted ; and you find that on the 25th of September, 1825, after Grand Master Wildey had returned from a visit to these Grand Bodies, for the express purpose of inducing them to accept it, it was unanimously stricken out by Maryland herself, and you will see that at the next meeting, Pennsylvania did appear in the person of a Representative ; so that it is clearly shown when and how the compact was established, and that it only existed in the imagination of Maryland herself.

In the Constitution of 1829 this matter was settled beyond all doubt, the word present at Baltimore being inserted ; and again in 1833, when the present Constitution was adopted, it was provided that they should meet at such place as the Grand Lodge should from time to time determine, and this view has, until now, been quietly acquiesced in by those Grand Bodies, as will be shown by the session held in Philadelphia, 1833 ; Washington City, January, 1834 ; New York, August, 1834, and again in Philadelphia, 1839, at all of which places their Representatives were present, without protest.

In this connection the following was adopted :

The claim set up by the R. W. Grand Lodge and Grand Encampment of Maryland to the permanent seat of government of this Grand Lodge is unfounded, and is not sustained by law or fact.

The following protest by the Grand Lodge of Pennsylvania was presented :

We protest sternly and solemnly against the assessment made by order of the Grand Lodge of the United States, as being unconstitutional in every portion of the mode by which the law therefor was passed, and consequently in the operation of the law itself.

The Grand Lodge of Ohio having asked to be allowed to remove from Cincinnati to Columbus, the following was adopted :

That the whole subject be referred back to the Grand Lodge of Ohio to determine at her next annual session whether she will hold her session in Cincinnati or Columbus.

The consent of the Grand Lodge was given to the amendment of the Constitution of the Grand Lodge of Georgia, changing the location of the Grand Lodge from Savannah to Macon, in said State.

Permission was refused the Grand Lodge of New Jersey to change the location of said Grand Lodge, from Trenton, to Newark and Camden, alternately.

The Constitutions of the Grand Lodge and the Grand Encampment of Northern New York were presented for approval, but as their provisions made them movable Bodies, and did not recognize the continuance of certain Subordinates in that jurisdiction, under the supervision of Southern New York, the following was adopted :

The articles in the Constitutions of the Grand Lodge and Grand Encampment of Northern New York, relating to places of meeting are hereby stricken out, and the Constitutions adopted, together with the recommendation of the committee regarding certain Subordinate Lodges.

The Finance Committee to whom was referred the matter of devising ways and means of raising sufficient revenue to meet the current expenses of the year, including mileage and per diem, reported that the probable expenses of the ensuing year would amount to $16,000, and estimated the receipts as follows:

Sale of Visiting and Clearance Cards, 70,000, 10 cents each, $7,000; Work and Degree Books, 1,500, $2 each, $3,000; Installation Books, 500, $1 each, $500; Odes, 15,000, 3 cents each, $450; Encampment Work Books, 300, $2 each, $600; Diplomas, 150, $1 each, $150; Representative tax of 90 Representatives at $50 each, $4,500. Total, $16,200.

A Special Committee of three was appointed to prepare and report to the next session of the Grand Lodge Forms of Ceremony to be used at the Laying of Corner-stones, and at the Dedication of Odd Fellows' Halls.

Representatives Colfax, of Indiana, Martın, of Mississippi, and Steele, of Tennessee, were appointed the Special Committee provided for in the resolution of the minority report of the Legislative Committee, to prepare an appropriate Honorary Degree, to be conferred on the wives and daughters of members of the Scarlet Degree.

Several amendments to the Constitution were adopted.

1851.

The Grand Lodge met in annual session, in Baltimore, on the 15th of September.

The following Grand Officers elected at the session of 1850, were duly installed on the first day of the session:

William W. Moore, P. D. G. Sire, of the District of Columbia, Grand Sire; H. L. Page, P. G. M., of Wisconsin, Deputy Grand Sire; James L. Ridgely, P. G. M., of Maryland, Grand Corresponding and Recording Secretary; Andrew E. Warner, P. G. M., of Maryland, Grand Treasurer.

The following were appointed by the Grand Sire:

Junius M. Willey, P. G. M., of Connecticut, Grand Chaplain; John Sessford, P. G. M., of the District of Columbia, Grand Marshal; John E. Chamberlain, P. G., of Maryland, Grand Messenger; S. H. Lewyt, P. G., of Maryland, Grand Guardian.

Grand Sire Griffin, in his report, congratulated the Grand Lodge on the continued progress of the Order, and said:

One generation ago a prophet's eye might have pierced the dark and heavy folds of the curtain which separated the pioneers of the Order from the days in which we live; but a prophet's voice, revealing, in the glow of inspiration, the enacted history of that intervening time, would have fallen upon mocking ears. From the pinnacle upon which we stand, the retreating shadows of events which prophecy would have predicted are dimly visible. The bubbling spring has expanded into the rushing river. The pigmy company has swollen into the giant army. The bending sapling has flourished into the anchored oak. * * * * I put off the harness of office with my heart brimming full of friendship for all whom I have ever met under the shadow of this great tent, and overflowing with gratitude to this exalted Body for the confidence it has so often manifested, and the honors it has so plentifully bestowed. And in the portion of my life which is yet to come, be that portion long or short, my aspirations for the prosperity and increasing usefulness of my well-beloved Order shall ascend in unbroken succession to that Eternal Source whence we have borrowed the great principles of our brotherhood.

I cannot take leave of you without a few words of paternal counsel. The times in which we act are times of restless motion. The age to which we belong is the transition age. The foundations of society are heaving upwards. Science is peopling the earth with new creations. Art is disinterring her old renown. Grim antiquity is giving up her buried lore. The fair features of the youthful present are wrinkling with struggles to bring back all the conquests of the ancient past. The old law of progress has been re-enacted, and is sweeping the world. The glorious contagion you yourselves have caught, my brothers. Your honorable ambition stimulates you to advance, farther and yet farther, the standard of our Order. God speed you in the good work! But, I beseech you, "make haste slowly." Make your fires glow with sevenfold heat, and submit all proffered gold to the fierce trial of the crucible. Remember in your heart of hearts that all changes are not reforms, and that all movement is not progress. Chain down with adamant that portion of your legacy which has passed the ordeal. Scatter to the winds whatever your judgment, deliberately, yes, even painfully matured, shall report to you as worthless. But, in all coming time, guard well those great features of our time-consecrated institution which have preserved their beauty and integrity through all mutations of circumstance and fortune. And, as the parting admonition of one whose counsels derive importance chiefly from the position which you have assigned to their author, but in the solemn language of the inspired King, I charge you, "Remove not the ancient landmarks which your fathers have set."

In his report the Grand Secretary said:

At no time since the undersigned has had the honor of occupying the office has he had greater pleasure in presenting his Annual Report, in view of the universal harmony and general prosperity which prevail throughout the jurisdiction, the evidence of which will abundantly appear from the details herewith submitted. * * * * It is a source of great pleasure to report that most, if not all, of the State Grand Bodies which withheld, at the last session, payment of the assessment levied under the per diem and mileage law, upon the ground of its unconstitutionality, have, although under protest, made payment into the treasury of the respective sums due by them.

The Grand Secretary expressed his regret that the failure to conform to the law, in proper time, caused a loss of about one thousand dollars to the Grand Lodge, as it was necessary to dispose, at a forced sale, of valuable securities in the treasury to pay the mileage and per diem due to the Representatives.

The Finance Committee's hopes, that the sales of supplies at the increased prices would furnish sufficient amounts for the wants of the treasury, proved fallacious.

During the year Warrants were issued for one Grand Lodge, one Subordinate Lodge and four Subordinate Encampments.

The receipts for the year were $23,670.16. The invested fund of the Grand Lodge was $9,461.50. The Subordinate Lodges increased in number 293. There was added to the Lodge membership 14,875. There were expended for the education of orphans $7,348.44, and for the relief of widowed families $42,410.23.

The roll of jurisdictions showed thirty-two Grand Lodges and twenty-seven Grand Encampments.

An effort was made, at this session, to abolish Grand and Subordinate Encampments, and to merge the latter into the Subordinate Lodges.

Article X., of the Constitution, was amended to read as follows:

All vacancies occurring in the office of Representatives of a Grand Lodge or Grand Encampment during a recess, may be filled in such manner as the State or District Grand Bodies may prescribe by law.

The same Article was further amended to require a Representative to be a contributing member of a Subordinate Encampment.

At every session of the Grand Lodge persistent efforts were made to return to the *three* months' term of office. To every appeal to this end, the Grand Lodge turned a deaf ear. At this session the subject came up again, and the committee to whom the matter was referred said in their report:

It could hardly be believed that after such repeated and decisive rejection by this Grand Body, its stability of legislation could have been so little respected as the infliction upon it again of the consideration of this subject necessarily proves. The committee cannot reconcile the pertinacity with which this matter is pressed upon our deliberations, with the deference justly due to the grave character of this Grand Lodge. It cuts off the hope that should be so reasonably anticipated of a settled acquiescence of the Order at large, in its deliberate resolves.

A subject three times referred to the Committee on the State of the Order, differently and ably constituted, twice to the Legislative Committee, and by each unanimously disapproved, and at each several time likewise rejected by the Lodge, ought, one would suppose, be suffered to rest in peace. It should, at least, raise a doubt as to its acceptability to the Order at large. Your committee, therefore, dare entertain the hope that this is the last communication, for several years to come, that we shall be disturbed by the restless wanderings of the ghost of the three months' term. *Requiescat in pace.*

It was resolved that, at the commencement of each session hereafter, the desks of the several States shall be numbered, and the Representatives shall proceed to draw lots therefor by States, and shall occupy, during the session, the desks corresponding to the drawn numbers.

The Committee on the "Female Degree" reported a Degree which, after an animated debate, was adopted by the vote of 46 yeas to 37 nays.

During the debate on this subject the Chair made the following ruling:

That, in his judgment, as the pending proposition contemplated introducing into the Order a new and distinct feature, which neither made nor involved the change of a single letter or word of the existing Work, the vote of a majority of the members present was competent to pass it.

That the provision incorporated in the Constitution at the session of 1848 was designed to protect the existing Work of the Order; that the said Work would not be in any way changed or affected by the pending proposition; that this proposition had in view a special object, without having any necessary or inseparable connection with the existing Written or Unwritten Work; that the Degree for women, now proposed, simply conferred a privilege, and did not necessarily affect the brethren now in possession of the Work, because they were not required to avail themselves of this privilege. Therefore, the pending proposition being in fact merely to adopt a side Degree, the decision of the Chair is, that it can be now adopted by a majority vote, and, in the same manner, if it shall be adopted, it can hereafter be expunged by a majority vote.

The yea and nay vote on the ruling of the Chair being a tie, the Chair sustained its own decision, by giving the casting vote.

The Chair ruled that the Grand Lodge could not recognize a mere printed pamphlet, purporting to be the proceedings of the Grand Encampment of New Jersey, without any authentication by the Seal or Signatures of the Grand Officers of that Body.

A Special Committee of three was appointed to inquire into the amount of revenue and expenditures of the various Subordinate Lodges attached to the several State Grand Lodges subordinate to the Grand Lodge, with reference to establishing the same upon some solvent and stable basis, to report thereon, and upon the expediency of uniform rates of fees and benefits, at the next regular communication of the Grand Lodge.

The jurisdiction of the Grand Lodge of the State of Arkansas was extended over the Indian country, west of the State of Arkansas, embraced in the jurisdiction of the United States District Court for the District of Arkansas.

The following were adopted:

All Grand Lodges and Grand Encampments shall have the power and privilege to determine, in their Constitutions and By-Laws, where their sessions shall be held.

A member expelled in one jurisdiction can be neither legally nor honorably reinstated in another jurisdiction, except by consent of the Lodge expelling ; and if reinstated, except by consent, is a member neither of the Lodge expelling nor of the Order.

Good standing in the Order is defined in the Digest, and the freedom from any disability by reason of non-payment of dues of every kind is one of its requisites. No member is in good standing while his note is held for dues ; the indebtedness by note is a new form, not a discharge of the debt.

A Withdrawal Card may be annulled for good cause existing at the time of granting it, at any time between its granting and expiration. After the expiration of twelve months the Card becomes utterly null, and by the decision of this Body, all jurisdiction over the holder ceases. Time definite appearing on the face of the Card, it would be impolitic to extend the power of the Lodge to annul after that time has expired. It is proper for a Lodge to report to the Lodge granting the Card any conduct on the part of the holder calculated to injure the Order in the eyes of the community at large. The State Grand Lodges, as declared legislative heads of the Order in their respective jurisdictions, have the right of pointing out to their Subordinates their duty in this respect, but it would be far better to leave the general direction of this matter to the legislation of the Grand Lodge of the United States, which can alone govern the whole Order.

A Subordinate Lodge has no right to refuse admission to one who has a regular Card, on the ground of his improper initiation. One having proper credentials should be received as a visiting brother, and his conduct, if improper, be reported to the Lodge granting the Card.

A Subordinate Lodge has no right to refuse its members Visiting Cards, to decline accepting their dues, or refuse to pay them benefits, when they purpose a temporary residence in California, or anywhere else, when the Lodge believes the change in occupation would increase the risk of life and health.

State Grand Bodies are perfectly competent to decide whether it is necessary to obtain permission from a Lodge to withdraw an application for membership prior to the report of the committee.

The Grand Masters of the various Grand Lodges of this jurisdiction are requested, immediately after the receipt by them of this resolution, to issue notice to the various Subordinate Lodges, soliciting, for the relief of Excelsior Lodge, No. 1, Sandwich Islands, the contribution of a sum not exceeding $1 from each Subordinate Lodge, and transmit the same directly to the Grand Secretary of the Grand Lodge, at Baltimore, at their earliest convenient time, to be appropriated by him to the payment of the debts due by Excelsior Lodge, No. 1, Sandwich Islands, and for the erection of a hall to an amount not to exceed $2,000 ; the surplus, if any, to be remitted to said Lodge, as Trustee, for the sole and exclusive purpose of establishing a fund for the relief of traveling brothers in those far distant islands of the sea, and to be used for no other purpose.

The members of this Body are respectfully urged, at as early a date as possible, to endeavor to obtain from the respective Grand Lodges of which they are members, an annual appropriation of $40, to continue during the life of Past Grand Sire Wildey, and to be applied to his support.

The committee that presented the above, said :

We have sought information relative to the pecuniary affairs of Past Grand Sire Wildey, and find his condition indeed deplorable. By his confidence in his brethren of the Order, and by his devotion to and exertions in the cause of Odd Fellowship, the little accumulations of his lifetime have disappeared, and in his old age he is found by us almost penniless. The policy, the interest, the character of the Order as a benevolent institution, imperatively demand that the founder of the Order should not be permitted, in his declining days, to become an object for the cold charities of the world, while a numerous, youthful and vigorous band—his offspring—possesses the ability to provide for his necessities.

State Grand Secretaries and Grand Scribes were required to prepay postage on letters to the Grand Secretary.

The Chair ruled that an amendment having been regularly proposed at the last session agreeably to the provisions of the Constitution, although it might be substantially the same as another proposition of amendment, properly came up for consideration at the present session, and that it would not be right for the Chair to suppress it.

So much of a resolution of the Grand Lodge, passed at its session of 1849, and found on page 1492 of the Journal, as adopted the Congressional Manual of Judge Sutherland for the government of the proceedings and debates of the Grand Lodge of the United States, was repealed, and it was ordered that the Manual of Luther S. Cushing be adopted in the place thereof ; and that the resolution go into effect at the next session of the Grand Lodge.

It was decided that a brother holding a Final Card from a Subordinate Lodge or Encampment under the jurisdiction of the Grand Lodge of British North America, and having our A. T. P. W., might deposit the same in a Subordinate Lodge or Encampment, as the case might be, as though the same had been granted by a Subordinate Lodge or Encampment under the jurisdiction of the Grand Lodge of the United States.

A block of marble at a cost of $450 was contributed by the Grand Lodge for the Washington Monument, at Washington, D. C. The block was embellished with the

Seal of the Grand Lodge of the United States, and a suitable inscription.

It was determined that it was not consistent with the rules of the Order for any one to make, or use, any writing relating to the Degrees or rank of the Order, unless the same be done under the authority of the Grand Lodge.

State Grand Lodges were directed to prohibit Subordinate Lodges under their jurisdiction from assembling in convention for the purpose of legislating on any subject without having first obtained the consent of their Grand Body.

It was decided that the enactment of general laws for the government of Subordinates belonged appropriately to the several State Grand Bodies. As legislative heads within their jurisdictions, the local wants of their Subordinates should be their guide upon the subject. In the language of the Digest, Subordinates "have no legislative power whatever, except to make By-Laws for their own internal government."

The Grand Lodge assented to the removal of the place of meeting of the Grand Lodge of North Carolina, from Raleigh to Wilmington, in that State.

The Grand Secretary was authorized to procure Regalia for the Grand Officers of the Grand Lodge; to procure desks and chairs for the hall, for the use of such of the Representatives from State Grand Lodges and Encampments as are now without them, and to have all pending amendments to the Constitution arranged and printed in the same form as those used at this session, and ready for use at the opening of the session of 1852.

The Grand Lodge of Pennsylvania was authorized to provide, at its semi-annual session in November, By-Laws for the election of its officers at its annual session in the following May.

The price of the bound volume of the Ladies' Degree, to be printed under the direction of the Grand Secretary, was fixed at one dollar, and the Grand Secretary was instructed to furnish them, as soon as printed and bound, to Grand Lodges at that price.

State Grand Lodges and Grand Encampments were directed hereafter to state in their annual returns to the Grand Lodge, the total amounts of invested funds in the treasuries, and widow and orphans' funds, and investments, of their Subordinates.

The Grand Lodge approved the action of the Grand Lodge of Ohio, in changing the location of said Grand Lodge from Cincinnati to Columbus, and directed that the Charter of said Grand Lodge be altered accordingly.

The Corresponding and Recording Secretary was instructed to have the drawing of the Seal designed for the block of marble for the Washington Monument, etc., placed in a suitable frame, and draw on the Grand Treasurer for the cost of the same.

1852.

The Grand Lodge met in regular annual session, in the City of Baltimore, on September 20th.

The Grand Lodge opened with Representatives from thirty-one State Grand Lodges and twenty-six Grand Encampments, and seats were allotted to ninety-six Representatives. Five States were each entitled to four, and New York (Northern and Southern), to eight Representatives.

A Committee was appointed to superintend the drawing of seats which now took place for the first time. The Committee consisted of Schuyler Colfax, John A. Kennedy and James M. Cassady.

They recommended the following method which was adopted.

That ballots from No. 1 to 32, corresponding with the number of States and jurisdictions represented in this Body, be placed in a hat, and that the senior member of each State or jurisdiction draw one of these numbers, commencing with the senior Representative from Maryland. The State that draws No. 1 shall be entitled to as many seats, commencing at desk numbered one, as the Grand Lodge and Grand Encampment of that State are entitled to; the State drawing No. 2 shall occupy the desks numbered consecutive to those occupied by No. 1, and so on to No. 32, who will consequently occupy the highest numbered seats. This plan, the committee think, will avoid confusion, and at the same time enable the members from each State or jurisdiction to be seated together, as they now are, for convenience of consultation.

Grand Sire Moore, in his report, said :

Being again convened in annual session, pursuant to the fraternal compact which binds together our great and flourishing institution, to survey its present condition, and unite our counsels for its future welfare, it reverently becomes us, before entering upon the business upon which we have assembled, to acknowledge, with gratitude, the infinite wisdom and goodness of an all-wise Providence, to whose protecting care we are so greatly indebted for the many blessings we enjoy. Both as citizens of a common country, and as members of an association whose beneficent operations extend to every part of its inhabited Territories, we have had, during the past year, abundant cause of felicitation, in the evidences of increasing prosperity and happiness which have marked its progress. Blessed with peace in all our borders, preserved from pestilence, favored with plentiful harvests, and witnessing in active and successful operation all the appliances of industry, science, and art, cold indeed must be the heart that does not glow with a sense of devout thankfulness to the Giver of all good for His benignant dispensations towards us. It would be supererogation for me to enter upon the details, whilst informing the Representatives here congregated, from all parts of our widely-expanded jurisdiction, that the institution of Odd Fellowship has shared largely in the general prosperity and advancement of our age and country. Its Lodges and membership have been greatly increased ; its wealth and power proportionally augmented, and its business affairs, in all their extensive ramifications, distinguished by a harmony the most auspicious and encouraging. In short, in its noble career of beneficence, it continues to disarm prejudice, to silence slander, and calm the swells of sectarian bigotry, at the same time that it more securely fortifies itself against successful opposition, and more widely and firmly establishes its proud claim to pre-eminence amongst the most benevolent institutions of the age. Grand Lodges having been established in all the States (except California), and Grand Encampments in nearly all of them, there now remains but little Territory in which it is the province of this Grand Lodge to organize Lodges or Encampments.

The Grand Secretary, in his report, said:

It is a source of the most unfeigned gratification to the undersigned to report that the appeal made in behalf of our distant brethren of Excelsior Lodge, No. 1, of the Sandwich Islands, for the purpose of enabling our brethren of that jurisdiction to erect an "Odd Fellows' Hall," has been responded to with a liberality and promptitude characteristic of the true principles of Odd Fellowship, and in the highest degree creditable to the Order at large. The amount received has been carried to the credit of a fund denominated the "Honolulu Hall Fund," and amounts to the sum of $1,121.50 up to September 1, 1852. * * * * He begs to be permitted to say that the preparation of the Index, as he advised the Grand Lodge at the last session, was committed to the hands of the M. W. Grand Sire, William W. Moore, and that the magnitude of the work, in view of the precision and great accuracy necessary to render it a valuable production, has caused, not-withstanding the diligent labor of the author, a very considerable delay.

A communication, dated London, April 30th, 1852, and signed "on behalf of the Central Corresponding Delegate Committee of England," by P. G. M., L. M. Clogg ; P. G. M., P. L. Mair, and P. G. P., L. M. F. Wood, Corresponding Secretary, has been received at this office, addressed to the Grand Lodge of the United States, which earnestly advocates a union of that Order with this jurisdiction. This paper purports to be the act of a Committee authorized by a Delegate Meeting of the Independent Order of Odd Fellows of England, which meeting, it is alleged, represented two hundred and thirty-three thousand Odd Fellows. * * * * This organization is known in that country as the "London Order of Odd Fellows," and is wholly independent of the Manchester Unity, the only Body of Odd Fellows in England, with which the Grand Lodge of the United States ever held fellow-ship.

The Grand Sire, Grand Secretary and Grand Lodge, thought the union not at all desirable unless the London Order would adopt the entire Work of the Order as practiced in the jurisdiction of the Grand Lodge of the United States.

Application was made at this session for a Charter for a Grand Lodge for the State of California.

The Grand Sire called attention to some imperfections in the laws; the most remarkable being the absence of legislation regulating the terms of the officers of State Grand Bodies. There are also no provisions prescribing the mode in which membership may be renewed by brothers holding expired Withdrawal Cards, or for the replacing of Cards that have been lost or destroyed.

During the year, Warrants were issued for one Grand Encampment, three Subordinate Lodges and one Subordinate Encampment.

The total receipts were $16,589.55. The profit on the sale of supplies amounted to $9,705.19.

The Subordinate Lodges increased in number 82; $10,750.85 were paid for education of orphans, $52,230.75 for relief of widowed families, $172,442.79 for burying the dead, and $372,384.92 for relief of brothers, by the Subordinate Lodges.

Representatives De Saussure, Colfax, Barnard, Ellison, and Past Grand Sire Griffin were elected a committee to report such amendments to the Constitution, By-Laws and Rules of Order as they shall deem required by the Order.

Rule of Order, No. 16, was amended to read as follows:

On a call of Representatives of three States, Districts or Territories, a majority of the Lodge may demand that the previous question shall be put, which shall always be in this form : *" Shall the main question be now put?"* and, until decided, no further debate shall take place, and the vote shall be taken first, on any amendments that may be pending, and next, on the final question.

The following was added to the Rules of Order :

No more than two amendments to a proposition shall be entertained at the same time : that is, an amendment, and an amendment to the amendment, and the question shall be first taken on the latter.

Rule 37, that " The previous question cuts off all amendments," was struck out.

This action, with the amended Rule of Order, No. 16, changed the practice of the Grand Lodge under the previous question.

The Grand Lodge refused to pass a law requiring Subordinate Lodges to pay benefits to sick stranger brethren. The committee to whom the subject was referred, said :

It will be more advantageous to the Order that no change should be made in the construction put upon the law governing benefits, but that the matter should be left to the comity now existing between Lodges, and to that spirit which never turns a deserving brother empty away. Upon the expiration of a Card, it is the duty of the brother to return it to his Lodge, and if relief has been granted, such relief should be endorsed upon the Card, and is almost universally returned by the Lodge granting the Card, to the Lodge affording relief.

The following were adopted :

A brother having proper credentials should be received as a visiting brother, for a Lodge has no right to decline admitting a visiting brother, if he is correct in the usual forms required.

A Subordinate Lodge has no power to adjourn, but must close in due form. If an extra meeting is required, it can be called in the manner pointed out by the By-Laws of the Lodge.

The subject of dues in Subordinate Lodges is one peculiarly for the legislation of State Grand Bodies, and any interference therewith, on the part of this Body, is objectionable.

If a brother who has honorably withdrawn by Card from his Subordinate Lodge, and has remained out of the Order for a period of twelve months, his

Card thereupon becomes invalid for the purpose of visiting, but remains effective as evidence of previous good standing in the Order, when application is made for a renewal of membership.

A brother who has so withdrawn his Card, and which Card may have been lost or destroyed, on satisfactory proof thereof, may be readmitted to membership as an Ancient Odd Fellow, and will be entitled to the rank he may prove himself as having attained.

When a Card of Withdrawal may have been lost or destroyed, the Lodge which issued the same, may grant a Certificate under Seal, setting forth the fact of such original issue ; and the Certificate so granted may be used in lieu of a Card as evidence of previous good standing.

Persons claiming to have been members of the Order, but who are unable to establish satisfactorily their claims, can be readmitted only by initiation. Any such person shall be required to set forth, in his petition for membership, that he has never been suspended or expelled from any Lodge, and that he is unable to obtain evidence of his former connection with the Order.

A Card of Withdrawal is the absolute property of the holder, and is an evidence of his former membership, and when he offers to deposit it, and thus gain admission into a Lodge, if rejected the Lodge, or its officers, have not the right to mutilate the Card by endorsing "rejected" thereon.

Suspension from membership works no suspension from arrears. It is a mode of punishment, and the punishment would often be deprived of its force should the arrears cease to run. Upon a reinstatement, the full amount accruing before and after suspension, is that which should be paid.

But one course is open for members to regain admission into the Order who have lost connection therewith by disuse. It is to apply to the Lodge with which they were formerly connected for reinstatement. It is within the power of the Lodge to make such arrangement in regard to the accumulated arrears as will enable this reinstatement. But no Lodge can receive into membership one who has ceased to be a member of the Order from disuse of his privilege, since such person is unable to answer satisfactorily the questions propounded to every applicant relative to former connection with the Order.

Under the existing law, Visiting Cards cannot be granted by the Noble Grand or Secretary, or in any other manner than by the action of the Lodge.

As a Subordinate Lodge has no right to refuse a Card to a member because of his intention to visit a more dangerous climate than that in which the Lodge is located, by parity of reasoning, a Lodge would have no right to refuse benefits accruing from sickness in such climate. If the disease has been contracted from immoral living, the members would generally be excluded from benefits, by the laws of the several Lodges. But unless contracted by such immoral conduct, the hazard of the climate appears to be one of the risks insured against, and the member would be entitled to benefits.

A Subordinate Lodge cannot grant to an officer leave of absence for a majority of the nights of a term, without a forfeiture of the honors of the term to the officer to whom the leave is granted.

A ballot cannot, under any circumstances, be reconsidered, but must stand as a final judgment. If fraud is charged, the ballot could certainly be scrutinized ; and if fraud is established, a new ballot should be ordered, but a reconsideration of a ballot is inadmissible.

There is no law which prevents the delivery of the Past Grand's charge by the Noble Grand. And although the charge should be given by a Past Grand, if present, yet circumstances may often require that this duty be intrusted to the Noble Grand. Under no circumstances, however, should this charge be given by the Vice Grand.

The duty of preparing a Form of Dedicating Halls of Grand and Subordinate Lodges is referred to a Special Committee of three, to report thereon at the next annual communication.

It is inexpedient to make any change in the existing law upon the subject of contemporaneous membership in the two branches of the Order. While the representation in this Body continues to legislate for both branches, it is but proper to preserve the law unchanged.

It would be highly inexpedient to make a change in the existing law requiring the German Lodges to keep their minutes in the English language. Its effect would be to place the Lodges, to a great extent, beyond the supervision of their respective State Grand Bodies.

State Grand Bodies have the right to establish a system whereby their legislation is restricted to a Representative basis, and are the proper Legislatures whence this system should emanate.

The Encampment Branch has usually been considered as more exalted than the Subordinate, and that precedence is generally given to the Patriarchal Degrees. This, however, may be controlled by circumstances ; as for example, where the procession is organized under and in behalf of a single Subordinate Lodge. In this case, precedence is usually given to the Body under and on whose behalf the procession is organized.

By the present Form of Card it is in the power of the officers of the Lodge to express the Degree or rank of a brother at the time of filling it up.

The Grand Treasurer elect is hereby required to enter into bonds with the Grand Sire and Grand Secretary in the penal sum of ten thousand dollars, and the said bond shall be presented to this Body previous to his installation.

The Grand Secretary, with the approbation of the Grand Sire, is hereby authorized to procure a new Seal and press for the use of his office.

The Degree of Rebekah was adopted on the 20th of September, 1851. The wives of Odd Fellows in good standing throughout the Union, acquired at that time, to a certain extent, a vested right to receive that Degree, whenever conferred by the Lodges of which their husbands were members. The wives of Odd Fellows were of course not responsible for the delay in the printing and distribution of the books, and should not be prejudiced thereby ; therefore, though their husbands may have deceased since that date, they may, if they still remain widows, receive the Degree in the Lodges of which their husbands were members, the assent of the Lodge thereto being first obtained, and other ladies being present at the same time with their husbands for initiation in the Degree.

The Grand Secretary was authorized, in making up the revised Journal, to enter as blanks all votes cast at the late election of Grand Officers for persons not in nomination.

A Ceremony for Opening and Closing Degree Lodges was adopted, and ordered to be printed and distributed to Grand Lodges.

In reference to the preparation of a plate for Cards for wives or widows of members of the Order, it was decided that under the existing law the preparation and distribution of such Cards should be left with the several Subordinate Lodges.

In reference to the mergement of the Encampment Branch the committee said :

We regard the time unpropitious for the introduction of a change so important. The proper period for the introduction of that qualification was when the Order was in its youth, when but few persons would have been affected by the operation of change. At this time, it might work great evil, in being regarded as oppressive to a large number of individuals, who have attained membership in Grand Lodges ; and this Grand Lodge should adopt no new measure which would have the effect of creating undue excitement in the Order, or which would give encouragement to any wide extended dissatisfaction.

The block of marble ordered at last session, was presented, in the name of, and in behalf of, the Grand Lodge of the United States, to the Washington National Association, as a testimonial of the veneration of our Order for the memory of America's most distinguished citizen. It was presented on the 17th of April, 1852, and the President of the United States, in his letter accepting it on behalf of the Association, spoke of it as worthy of the Association, and doing equal honor to the donors and to him to whose undying fame it is intended, in part, to commemorate.

The Committee on Petitions, in relation to granting a Charter for a Grand Lodge for California, said:

Whilst your committee do not feel authorized to recommend the granting of a Charter for a Grand Lodge upon the evidence now before them, they are convinced that the interference of this Grand Lodge offers the only efficacious means of establishing system and bringing about that certainty of organization which will insure to us, at all times, the means of prompt supervision over the Order in that distant region, and the perfection of those bonds which shall make us, with them, united in the government as we are now united in feeling and purpose, for the advancement of the common objects of our beloved Order. The efforts of our brothers in California, associated as Lodges, and individually, to relieve human suffering, and to stay the torrent of selfishness and depravity which, at times, seemed to obscure the moral atmosphere of California, will ever present an era for proud reference in the history of the influences of our fraternity, and must ever ensure the undivided support of the whole Order, in the furtherance of such measures as shall lead to the permanent establishment of an organization whose labors have been productive of so great good.

The subject of the condition of the Order in California was referred to the Grand Sire, with power to act, and appoint, in his discretion, a well qualified member of the Order to attend to its interests in that District. In making this appointment a preference was to be given to permanent residents of California.

The Grand Lodge of Georgia petitioned for a return to the " Old Work " for initiation.

The Grand Lodge refused to furnish a Book of Diagrams of the Unwritten Work to each Grand Lodge and Grand Encampment.

The following decisions of Grand Sire Moore were approved:

A Grand Master has no power summarily to remove an officer of a Subordinate Lodge, as his official relations are not with the officers of Lodges, but with the Lodges themselves in their Lodge capacity ; and, therefore, if a Noble Grand persists in permitting improper Work in violation of his instructions, it is the duty of the Grand Master to inform the Lodge that, unless it shall require its officers to conform to the Work, it will be dealt with for insubordination.

Past Grands deputized to install the officers of Subordinates, are charged with a special duty, clearly prescribed by law, and are entitled to all the respect due to the officer whom they represent, but they have no authority summarily to deprive a Lodge of its Charter, nor any right to assume the rank of elective officers, and introduce strangers without Card or Password into a Lodge

On a regular night of meeting when, in the absence of the two principal officers, a Lodge had been opened for business with a Past Grand in the Noble Grand's chair and a Scarlet member in the Vice Grand's chair, the proceedings of said meeting could not be pronounced illegal on the ground that there was present no Past Grand to occupy the chair if the acting Noble Grand had been required temporarily to vacate it, because, if the chair had been thus temporarily vacated, it would have been the duty of the R. S. to occupy it.

The N. G. of a Lodge has not the right to admit a member belonging to another Lodge in his State jurisdiction, without the term Password, but he may admit members of his own Lodge without said word, if they be not in arrears to an amount that would disqualify them from receiving it.

A Secretary has no right to withhold a Card which has been granted by a Lodge, and for doing so he is liable to arraignment, even if the responsibility be assumed on the alleged discovery of crime on the part of the intended recipient.

A brother who has lost or been dispossessed of a Withdrawal Card, for no cause which should impeach his own conduct, may obtain a new Card, bearing the same date, from the Lodge which had granted the original one, the said Lodge being the judge as to the propriety of granting the new issue ; and, if granted, expressing on its face that it is a duplicate.

A brother holding a Withdrawal Card which has run out of date, may be recognized as an Ancient Odd Fellow, and be allowed to renew his membership by the deposit of said Card, in a Lodge at the place of his residence, upon the payment of such fee as the laws of said Lodge may require.

It is not necessary or proper to reconsider or rescind a vote granting a Withdrawal Card, in order to arraign the brother to whom such Card may have been given, because the Card having been voted the membership of the brother ceases, and he has a legal right to the Card, which, if he desires to renew his membership, he can deposit in the usual mode, or if it shall have been indiscreetly granted to an unworthy brother, the Lodge may annul it, taking care to allow the brother implicated a fair and impartial trial, as in the case of suspended members against whom charges are preferred.

A brother who is a member in good standing in a Subordinate Lodge in one State, and at the same time a resident in another State, is a proper candidate for initiation into an Encampment at the place of his residence.

The Degree of Rebekah is an honorary Degree to be conferred under the regulations adopted at the last session, upon such Scarlet members and their wives as may desire to receive it ; but the officers of all Lodges which are in possession of the Work ought to be in regular possession of the Degree, upon the same principle that they are required to assume other obligations belonging to their official stations.

1853.

The Grand Lodge assembled in regular annual session, in the City of Philadelphia, on September 5th, in accordance with the amended Constitution.

The following Grand Officers elected at the last session were duly installed:

Wilmot G. De Saussure, P. G. M., of South Carolina, Grand Sire; Horace A. Manchester, P. G. M., of Rhode Island, Deputy Grand Sire; James L. Ridgely, P. G. M., of Maryland, Grand Corresponding and Recording Secretary; Joshua Vansant, P. G., of Maryland, Grand Treasurer.

The following were appointed by the Grand Sire: .

Junius M. Willey, P. G. M., of Connecticut, Grand Chaplain; James M. Cassady, G. M., of New Jersey, Grand Marshal; Solomon H. Lewyt, P. G., of Maryland, Grand Guardian; John E. Chamberlain, P. G., of Maryland, Grand Messenger.

Grand Sire Moore, in his report, said:

Since the last meeting of this Grand Lodge, the experience of another year has further developed the popularity, resources, and efficiency of our beloved Order ; and the results are the most gratifying, in enabling me to state, what has been substantially expressed on so many similar occasions, that the area of Odd Fellowship continues to expand as well in territorial jurisdictions as in the enlargement of its membership and the increase of its revenue. With the accessions of the past year, our Lodges must now have enrolled but little less than two hundred and thirty thousand contributing members, and have under their control, applicable to beneficent purposes, an annual income approximating a million and a half of dollars. But, flattering as are these evidences of uninterrupted prosperity, they are even less impressive, as a source of mutual congratulation, than the all-pervading influence among the brotherhood of those ennobling sentiments upon which our Order was founded, and the unceasing predominance of which, during a series of so many years, gives the strongest assurance of the stability of our institution and the wisdom of its organization. In the encouraging success thus bestowed upon our labors, we have abundant cause for a renewed expression of our gratitude to that Supreme Being to whom we are indebted for all earthly good.

During the year, the Order in California had received new life and vigor through the active efforts of D. D. G. Sire Samuel H. Parker.

The establishment of the Grand Lodge of California was the first on the Pacific.

The Grand Secretary, in his report, said:

I regret to report that the Grand Lodge of British North America has virtually ceased to exist. Information to this effect first reached this office

through several of the Subordinates of that jurisdiction, from whom an application was received to be restored to the United States jurisdiction. It
appears that the demise of this Grand Body was not superinduced by any
want of health or prosperity on the part of the Subordinates, many of which,
notwithstanding the neglect, and total apathy of the Grand Lodge, have for
a long time continued to flourish, and still maintain a prosperous existence.
The circumstances of the dissolution of this Grand Body, as far as they have
reached the undersigned, indicate an entire abandonment of the obligations
which the Charter received from the Grand Lodge of the United States, and
the Charges and general Work of the Order imposed upon the constituted
authority of that jurisdiction.

The Grand Secretary reported the amount of the
Honolulu Hall Fund, received from September 22d, 1852, to
September 6th, 1853, to be $374.91. The receipts for the
Wildey Annuity Fund, from September 25th, 1852, to Sep-
tember 22d, 1853, were $456.

The total receipts of the Grand Lodge for the year
were $17,528.87.

The Territory of Oregon was added to the domain of
the Order, and the Grand Lodge of Minnesota had been instituted. At this time the Grand Lodge of British North
America had virtually ceased to exist, but many of its Subordinates were still in a healthy and flourishing condition.
For the outcome of this condition of affairs the reader is
referred to the Grand Jurisdiction of Canada.

During the preceding year, Warrants were issued for two
Grand Lodges, two Subordinate Lodges and seven Subordinate Encampments. The profit on the sales of supplies
amounted to $7,981.47. The increase in the number of
Subordinate Lodges was 212; in Encampments, 33; amount
paid by Subordinate Lodges for education of orphans was
$11,800.52; for relief of widowed families, $55,314; for
burying the dead, $70,123.85; for relief of brothers, $351,-
437.87.

The committee to whom were referred the Constitution,
By-Laws and Rules of Order of the Grand Lodge submitted
an entirely new Constitution, as an amendment to the old
one, as they believed it would be a more symmetrical
instrument. It, together with the By-Laws, etc., was spread
upon the Journal, and will be found on pages 2029–2042.

An elaborate report, illustrated by tables constructed upon the established principles of life and health insurance, was made upon the true relations that should subsist between dues and benefits. It will be found on pages 2043–2101 of the Journal.

At the invitation of the Mayor of Philadelphia, the Grand Lodge moved in procession and in Regalia to visit the Hall of Independence.

The various State Grand Bodies were authorized to permit Lodges and Encampments under their jurisdiction, which worked in foreign languages, to dispense with an English copy of their records. But it was determined that it was competent for said Grand Bodies, or their proper Executive Officers having jurisdiction over said Lodges and Encampments, to compel them, when required, to furnish extracts from their minutes, translated into the English language.

It was decided that Lodges must extend to lunatics the same benefits as are given to those who suffer from bodily infirmity.

The following resolution was not adopted:

That a committee be appointed to report to this Grand Lodge at its next session a suitable point for the permanent location of a place of meeting for this Grand Lodge.

It was decided that:

Upon the issuing of a Visiting Card by a Subordinate Lodge or Encampment, the Secretary or Scribe thereof shall endorse upon it the amount of weekly and funeral benefits allowed by the Constitution and By-Laws of said Lodge or Encampment, and it shall be bound for any relief extended to a brother holding such a Card to the extent of the benefits so rendered.

Where a Subordinate Lodge, Encampment or General Relief Committee is applied to for relief, by a brother holding a Card, such Lodge, Encampment, or General Relief Committee shall require the Certificate of a respectable physician, showing the time that the brother has been sick, and shall take a draft upon his Lodge or Encampment for whatever amount he may have received, which, with the Certificate, shall be forwarded for payment: *Provided*, that in the event of the death of a brother, and his being buried by a Lodge, Encampment, or General Relief Committee, it shall be necessary to forward only the physician's Certificate, or that of some other respectable citizen, together with his Card and a proper voucher for the amount so advanced. Payment of the same shall, in all cases, be promptly made.

The Grand Secretary was instructed to transmit to the several Grand Bodies under this jurisdiction, as early as practicable after the adjournment of the session, a copy of the foregoing.

The Form of Certificate referred to above, is as follows:

This certifies that the Constitution and By-Laws of the within named Lodge (or Encampment) allow for weekly benefits the sum of .... dollars per week, and for funeral benefits the sum of .... dollars ; and that Brother .... is entitled to the said benefits from the date of the within Card until the expiration of the same.

The following were adopted :

Hereafter in cases of contested claims to seats in the Grand Lodge, mileage and per diem shall be allowed to him only who shall be admitted to the seat.

All propositions to amend the Constitution or Laws of this Grand Lodge shall be written out in full, in the precise words in which it is proposed that the amendment shall read, if adopted.

The effect of annulling a Withdrawal Card, (which can only be done during the twelve months in which such a Card has vitality), would be to revoke it, and instead of expelling the brother from the Order, it brings him back into the Lodge, where, after due notice of the charges against him, which have induced the Lodge to abrogate his Card, and a fair and impartial trial thereof, he may be expelled or acquitted.

Grand Lodges do not have the *exclusive* right to adopt laws regulating the manner in which Withdrawal Cards shall be annulled ; but they do possess the right to enact laws relative thereto, provided they do not conflict with the legislation and decisions of this Body.

A brother who has received only the Patriarchal, or the Patriarchal and Golden Rule Degrees, is certainly entitled to the Semi-annual Password to enable him to work his way in.

A Noble Grand cannot refuse to confer the T. P. W. upon a brother who presents his Traveling Card, with a letter of request to that effect from his Lodge, both under Seal and in due form of law.

If a person has been irregularly elected, through fraud or error, (and by the word irregularly is understood illegally or fraudulently), a majority of the Lodge can, previous to the applicant's initiation, order a new ballot. After initiation, if the applicant is innocent of any misrepresentation, and the illegality has been confined to the Lodge, he shall be protected in his membership, the same as if legally admitted. If he has been guilty of fraud his initiation cannot be declared void, as this might be construed as releasing him from his obligation, which perhaps would also be considered void, if the whole initiation was ; but in such a case he can be expelled therefor after proper trial.

The Grand Lodge deem it inexpedient to admit the wives of brothers who have taken the Degree of Rebekah, to witness the installation of the officers of Subordinate Lodges.

The question as to the greatest length of time to which a Lodge can extend a suspension for cause, is one to be decided by the legislation of Subordinate Lodges ; the Grand Lodge not having made any enactment on this point, except that *indefinite* suspension of members for non-payment of dues may be terminated by a Grand Lodge without the consent of its Subordinates.

Any brother occupying, either permanently or temporarily, a subordinate station in a Lodge, should wear the Regalia of the office he thus occupies. A brother is not justified in refusing to give the Password to a Past Grand, acting temporarily as Warden, who had not assumed the proper Regalia of the Chair. If the presiding officer of the Lodge recognized him as the Warden, and gave him orders accordingly, the brothers of the Lodge should follow his example by acknowledging his authority in that office. If they desire to question his right to act, while improperly clothed, they should raise the objection in some other way than by refusing to give him the Password.

A Book of Diagrams was again refused to Grand Lodges and Grand Encampments.

A Special Committee was appointed to report, at next session, a Form of Ceremony for Installing the Officers of the Grand Lodge of the United States.

The Grand Lodge refused to require, from the members who take Withdrawal Cards, the payment of dues accruing for one year afterwards, and giving them benefits for the same length of time.

The sum of five hundred dollars was appropriated by the Grand Lodge in aid of the sufferers by yellow fever in New Orleans, and the sum of two hundred and fifty dollars was donated to the General Relief Committee of the I. O. O. F. of Mobile, for the relief of sick and distressed brethren of Mobile, during the prevalence of the epidemic in that city.

The Grand Secretary was directed to have the Degree of Rebekah translated and printed in the German language, and furnish the said Work to Lodges at the same rate as the English Edition.

The following decisions of the Grand Sire were approved :

A Grand Representative, duly elected and commissioned, who fails to take his seat in this Body at the first session of his term, does not, for that reason, under the laws of this Grand Lodge, forfeit his right to a seat at a subsequent session, his credentials being good for two years. He may, nevertheless, be arraigned and removed for neglect, by his own Grand Lodge, if its penal laws shall so provide.

The Grand Officers of State Grand Lodges, when visiting the Subordinate Lodges under their own jurisdiction, should give at the outside door the same Password that is required of other brothers. Our laws make no distinction in this respect, nor could any distinction be made with propriety, for the reason that it is impossible for the Grand Officers to become personally known to the entire brotherhood of any State jurisdiction.

A District Deputy Grand Sire, in absenting himself temporarily from his jurisdiction, has authority to appoint a qualified brother or brothers to install the officers of Lodges and Encampments during his necessary absence ; but if the officers of any Lodge or Encampment should be regularly installed by any qualified brother who had not been thus appointed by the District Deputy Grand Sire, such installation would be legal and valid. Installations may be legally made by other persons than District Deputy Grand Sires, and no legal installation can be vitiated. If a brother, deputed to install officers, should fail to attend, the ceremony, rather than be deferred, should be performed by a qualified member in attendance. If the brother deputed should present himself, and his authority be disregarded by a Lodge, then the District Deputy Grand Sire has his remedy in arraigning the Lodge for misconduct.

Pending the decision on granting a Withdrawal Card, charges may be preferred against the brother making application therefor ; and, under such circumstances, the vote on granting the Card should not be taken until the charges be withdrawn or a trial be had upon them.

Any person who, being at the time in good standing, shall have withdrawn from the Order by a written resignation, may be readmitted as an Ancient Odd Fellow, provided he first pass a satisfactory examination in the Work ; and if he fail to pass a thorough examination, then he can be readmitted only by initiation.

1854.

The Grand Lodge met in regular annual session, in the City of Baltimore, on the 4th of September.

In his report, Grand Sire De Saussure said:

The remeeting of my brethren, Representatives of our widely extended charity throughout this vast continent, affords me an opportunity of imparting to them the gladsome tidings that our work goes bravely on. The returns from the various jurisdictions and Bodies under the jurisdiction of this Grand Lodge, show a healthful condition of the Order, both in numerical strength and in financial prosperity. But most of all do they exhibit the liberal handed charity with which the distressed of our fraternity have been aided. The last annual report exhibited a total of 2,941 Lodges, a membership of 193,000, and a revenue of $1,209,228.90, of which $491,322.12 were expended for the relief of the sick, the burial of the dead, the aid of the widowed and the education of orphans. The report to be presented at this communication will show about 3,110 Lodges; 204,000 members; $1,375,000 revenue, and $530,000 of expenditures for the benevolent purposes of our organization. Penetrating deep into the recesses of the North, and stretching toward the frozen regions of the Arctic Circle, as if emulous of the philanthropic efforts which science is making for the release of the bold navigator, Sir John Franklin, and his gallant companions, from their icy prison, Charity, too, is seeking in those far-off lands to relieve and comfort suffering humanity. Following the axe of the hardy pioneer, and bearing the best principles of civilization within its bosom, Charity seeketh in the westward the opportunities of proclaiming good will towards men. Wafted by the wings of the wind to the Isles of the South, even there Charity raiseth her standard, proclaiming to the tempest-tossed mariner rest from his labor and community with his brethren.

The Grand Sire in October, 1853, visited the brethren in Canada with a view to resuscitate the Grand Lodge of British North America. His mission failed in that respect, but the brethren were received again under the jurisdiction of the Grand Lodge of the United States. At the time of the Grand Sire's visit to Montreal there were but six Lodges working, but at the date of the present session there were fifteen.

The Grand Secretary, in his report, said :

The information relating to vital statistics, required from the Subordinate Lodges embrace much matter of which the Lodges have no record whatever, and the obtaining of which necessarily imposes a considerable amount of labor upon each Lodge, and some expense. This labor is devolved upon the Secretary, an officer whose duties are already arduous, and, although for the most part unrequited, are cheerfully performed in view of the incumbent's just expectation of advancement in his Lodge. * * * * * If the subject shall continue to receive the favorable consideration of the Grand Lodge, it is respectfully suggested that legislation, of a more practical character, is necessary to render it effective.

By a resolution of the session of 1852, the Corresponding Secretary was authorized to obtain a new Seal and press for the use of his office. I have to report that they have been received and are now in use. A copy of the impression of the Seal is herewith annexed. The seal cannot be surpassed, if equalled, by any work of the character in this country.

The total receipts of the Grand Lodge were $15,536.17, and the profit realized from the sale of supplies $7,379.27.

The money received for the Wildey Annuity Fund from September 22d, 1853, to September 2d, 1854, amounted to $245.

The following amounts were expended by the Subordinate Lodges : For relief of brothers, $350,502.40 ; for relief of widowed families, $58,916.17 ; for education of orphans, $11,721.51 ; for burying the dead, $76,815.31.

During the year, the Lodges increased in number 188, and the Encampments, 72.

The Manchester Unity made a proposition for inter-communion between it and our Order. A treaty was refused unless the Unity agreed to return to the ancient land-marks, assume our obligations and conform to our Work.

Warrants were issued during the year, for six Lodges in Canada, two in Nova Scotia, two in Oregon, one in the Sandwich Islands, and for one Subordinate Encampment in the Sandwich Islands.

The Constitution, By-Laws and Rules of Order, sub-mitted at the session of 1853, were considered, amended and adopted.

The following decisions of the Grand Sire were approved :

A Grand Representative to the G. L. U. S. is an officer of his State Grand Body, and in a procession organized within his State, will occupy such posi-tion as the laws of such State point out for officers. If the procession were organized by the G. L. U. S., a Grand Representative would take position with that Body, and *ipso facto*, one of precedence over the officers and mem-bers of State Bodies.

There is no general law of the Grand Lodge, regulating the time which the holder of a Card that has been rejected, must lay off before he can again offer it for deposit in the same State. As a general rule, the matter is left to the local laws of the several State Grand Bodies.

Applicants for Degrees must be balloted for by the Lodge open in the particular Degree applied for, and the proceedings had by Lodges when open in particular Degrees for the purpose of ballot or conferring Degrees, are wholly distinct from the ordinary Lodge proceedings, and are to be recorded in a distinct minute or record book.

Whether a member can be expelled for non-payment of dues, depends upon the local law, and a Lodge cannot publish, (the word publish being used in its popular acceptation), such fact of expulsion, as it would be in violation of the secrecy enjoined in respect to the dealings of the members one with another.

The Noble Grand and Vice Grand of a Lodge should receive the Degree of Rebekah, before installation into their respective offices.

A Grand Patriarch can issue a Dispensation for a more remote Encamp-ment to elevate to the Patriarchal Degrees an applicant, the only Encamp-ment near the residence of the applicant having assented thereto.

If the Chinese believe in a Supreme Being, the Creator and Preserver of the Universe, they may be received into the Order, and if Lodges were estab.. lished among them, such Lodges would work on the conditions the law now requires of Lodges working in German, French, etc.

A convention, held by Past Grands, intended to redress some alleged local grievance, is illegal. (*See page* 1076 *of the Journal.*)

There is no law of the Grand Lodge ot the United States forbidding the imposition of fines for non-attendance of members in Subordinate Lodges. The spirit of the Order appears to be opposed to the policy of such fines.

Where no local law provides therefor, an installed officer does not vacate his office by non-attendance. If an officer elect is not present upon the installation night, and no sufficient reason be given for his non-attendance, the installing officer can require the Lodge immediately to elect an officer.

If a Noble Grand should fail to appear for installation for some time after the regular time, his duties would devolve upon the Vice Grand. If the local law provides for the vacation of office for non-attendance, the Lodge can treat the officer as installed and vacate his office.

The following were adopted :

The Grand Secretary is instructed to have printed upon all Visiting Cards which may hereafter be issued from his office, the blank Form of Certificate relative to benefits, as passed by this Grand Body at its last session.

In all cases where a candidate for membership in a Subordinate Lodge has been elected, but subsequent to his election, and prior to his initiation, the Lodge shall become satisfied that he is unworthy, it shall be competent for the Lodge to annul such election, and declare it void, by a majority of two-thirds of the members present.

A brother is eligible to the chair of Noble Grand, who, in consequence of sickness, was unable to perform the duties of Vice Grand for a majority of the nights of the term for which he was elected, and who was excused from time to time by his Lodge. It is otherwise where the absence is voluntary, even though he should have the leave of the Lodge.

The fact of a member of a Grand Lodge being an appointed officer, a Past Grand Master, or a Grand Representative, confers upon him no peculiar privilege in respect to voting. When his Grand Lodge is composed of all the Past Grands in good standing within its jurisdiction, such a member votes as every other Past Grand does, and simply because he is a Past Grand. Where his Grand Lodge has adopted a representative system, unless he has been elected and is duly accredited as a member, he is not entitled to vote at all, except in the election of Grand Officers, when all Past Grands in good standing in the jurisdiction are *ex-officio* entitled to vote. His privilege of voting arises altogether from the fact of his being a Past Grand in good standing in his jurisdiction, in the one case, and in the other because he has been elected and credited, and not because he may chance to occupy any or either of the stations mentioned.

No matter how many members present Withdrawal Cards to the Grand Officers and receive a Dispensation creating a new Lodge, it shall be composed of only those who, pursuant to that authority, appear and assume before the instituting officer, the obligations required by the laws. The absentee applicants can gain admittance only by withdrawing their Cards from the hands of the Grand Officers, and applying in the usual mode for admission to membership by Card.

A Grand Master of one State cannot, on the written request of the acting Grand Master of another State, confer on a qualified Past Grand the Grand Lodge and Past Official Degrees. His Grand Lodge may do so, provided it has the consent contemplated by law.

The Grand Sire was directed to appoint a committee of five members of the Order, whose duty it should be to prepare and report to the next session of the Grand Lodge a plan merging the Subordinate Lodges and Encampments. The committee was directed to inquire into the expediency of so amending the Written Work of the Order as to restore to the Initiatory Degree some of the effective ceremonies of the old Work ; and if said committee deemed it expedient, they were directed to report at the next session of the Grand Lodge the Initiatory Degree in a new form, embracing the proposed amendments.

The Chair ruled that all reports of committees were the subject of amendment at the pleasure of the Lodge.

1855.

The Grand Lodge met in regular annual session, in the City of Baltimore, on the 17th of September, the time fixed by the amended Constitution adopted in 1854.

The Grand Lodges and Encampments were at this time entitled to one hundred and four Representatives.

The following Grand Officers, elected at last session, were duly installed :

William Ellison, P. G. M., of Massachusetts, Grand Sire ; George W. Race, P. G. P., of Louisiana, Deputy Grand Sire ; James L. Ridgely, P. G. M., of Maryland, Grand Corresponding and Recording Secretary ; Joshua Vansant, P. G., of Maryland, Grand Treasurer.

The following were appointed by the Grand Sire :

Rev. Reuben Jones, P. G., of Arkansas, Grand Chaplain ; James W. Hale, P. G. Rep., of Southern New York,

Grand Marshal; Solomon Lewyt, P. G., of Maryland, Grand Guardian; John E. Chamberlain, P. G., of Maryland, Grand Messenger.

Grand Sire De Saussure, in his report, said:

A beautiful and happy coincidence fixes the time of your assemblage in the harvest period of the year, and you are now met to inquire what fruits have been reaped from our vast fields, what stores garnered into our granary, and to consult together in what manner the blessings thus granted to our brotherhood's labor may be best redistributed in the cause of humanity. The cycle which brings you again into consultation, proclaims that another year has been harvested to eternity. Whether the labors performed during its revolution have been for weal, or woe, is now to be considered by you. In the theocratic government established of old, it is taught that man's necessities required, not alone fixed periods for rest, but also fixed times for reflection. You, Representatives, as the stewards of a great and exalted charity, are now invited to review the work already done; if well done, to continue the culture heretofore successful; if illy and unprofitably performed, so to remodel the system as will best insure abundant returns for the labor expended.

Yet, even while gladdened by the general prosperity with which we are blessed, the wail of sorrow and anguish falls upon our ears; the cry of despair reaches us from our afflicted brethren of Norfolk and Portsmouth. Desolation such as theirs, rarely is permitted to visit mankind; the human heart, harrowed by the tales of human misery, gladly turns to that charity which strives to ameliorate the suffering, and we, as Odd Fellows, may regard, with mournful satisfaction, the evidences of sympathy and fraternal feeling exhibited towards the afflicted, by the liberal contributions made by the Subordinate Lodges of our land.

The following decisions of the Grand Sire were approved:

If a member commits suicide his family are not thereby debarred from benefits.

A Grand Representative elect, taking a Withdrawal Card, thereby forfeits his office, although he afterwards deposits the Card in another Lodge.

A Subordinate Lodge violating the laws laid down by the Grand Lodge of the United States, and refusing to observe such laws, may be expelled therefor, and the Grand Master, during the recess, may demand its Charter.

When visiting for installation purposes, a Grand Master is entitled to take the chair of the Noble Grand, but when otherwise visiting, he is not entitled to that chair as a matter of right.

A reconsideration of a ballot is inadmissible.

A Noble Grand elect, having failed to appear for installation and forfeited, (under the local laws), his office, the member elected and installed in his place is the Noble Grand of the Lodge.

The correctness of giving two of the Patriarchal Degrees upon the same evening, is to be determined by the local law.

It is improper to confer an Encampment Degree upon one holding a Withdrawal Card from a Subordinate Lodge.

At the request of the Grand Sire, Grand Secretary Ridgely visited the various Lodges under the jurisdiction of the Grand Lodge of the United States in British North America. Of his reception in Quebec, he said:

In this ancient and remarkable city I found the warm heart and cordial grasp of the Odd Fellow, prompt to welcome and greet me upon my arrival. Although a stranger, and in a distant land, the mystic language which I spoke, the generous and noble mission with which I was charged, and the lofty name of that vast brotherhood whose humble minister and Representative I was, opened wide the heart and hospitalities of the Canadian brethren, who lavished upon the undersigned, during his sojourn in their midst, one uninterrupted and continuous stream of kindness, courtesy, and attention. Never did I feel prouder in my life, in my character as an Odd Fellow, than on this occasion. I felt that our beloved Order had already achieved its own full-grown and matured fame; had indeed constructed for itself a monument more enduring than iron or brass; a monument engraven upon the tablets of the human heart, and destined to perpetuate Odd Fellowship, its virtues and its offices of benefaction, to the latest posterity.

The Order in the Lower Provinces and Canada West was reported in a healthy condition.

The Grand Secretary, in his report, said:

It is respectfully suggested that the Committee on Returns be required to analyze carefully the annual reports, as accurate opinions on this subject are highly desirable. The Report of the Committee on Returns now merely embraces an inquiry into the form of the returns; if found in accordance with the forms prescribed by law, they are approved. The opportunity is now afforded of carrying inquiries into the substance of the annual reports, to an analysis of their details, by which light may be had upon the important subject of the health of the Lodges and of the proper ratio of dues and benefits.

Two Grand Lodges were established in British North America during the year; one in the Lower Provinces, and the other in Canada West. In addition thereto, Warrants were issued for three Subordinate Lodges and one Subordinate Encampment.

The amount received for the Wildey Annuity Fund from September 2d, 1854, to September 18th, 1855, was $231.

The total receipts were $14,412.54, and the profit from the sale of supplies, $6,800.52.

The number of Lodges increased during the year 184, there was also a gain of seventy-two Encampments.

The following amounts were paid out by Subordinate Lodges: For relief of brothers, $373,385.12; relief of widowed families, $69,913.41; education of orphans, $12,-465.73, and for burying the dead, $92,650.50.

From the reports from Lodges aggregating a constituency of over one hundred thousand, the following table was compiled. It shows opposite each age, from twenty-one to seventy, the number of members reported, the number of weeks' sickness at each age, and the average rate of sickness per member expressed in weeks and decimals.

Age.	Number of Members.	Weeks Sick.	Rate of Sickness.	Age.	Number of Members.	Weeks Sick.	Rate of Sickness.
21	*	*	*	46	1,125	1,024	.911
22	1,265	548	.454	47	967	931	.963
23	1,732	797	.460	48	1,057	1,082	1.024
24	2,135	999	.468	49	595	652	1.097
25	2,458	1,190	.476	50	948	1,093	1.154
26	2,700	1,306	.484	51	393	475	1.209
27	2,760	1,358	.496	52	472	542	1.215
28	3,085	1,570	.590	53	384	470	1.236
29	2,996	1,575	.529	54	412	517	1.257
30	3,631	1,956	.536	55	323	421	1.304
31	2,986	1,552	.552	56	248	339	1.369
32	2,910	1,633	.561	57	160	236	1.481
33	2,964	1,680	.567	58	130	216	1.665
34	3,071	1,753	.570	59	88	162	1.953
35	3,215	1,861	.579	60	115	253	2.201
36	2,619	1,537	.587	61	58	141	2.438
37	2,440	1,488	.610	62	38	103	2.735
38	2,466	1,590	.949	63	27	96	3.561
39	2,085	1,442	.692	64	21	92	4.400
40	2,632	1,895	.720	65	50	246	4.938
41	1,671	1,249	.748	66	13	71	5.478
42	1,776	1,383	.779	67	12	73	6.017
43	1,673	1,358	.812	68	7	45	6.465
44	1,549	1,312	.847	69	5	34	6.973
45	1,597	1,403	.879	70	12	88	7.381

Seventeen hundred copies of the Daily Journal were ordered to be printed.

A proposition requiring all legislative business of Subordinate Lodges to be transacted in the Scarlet Degree, was declared inexpedient, and was not adopted,

It was decided that the appellation of *Representative* and not that of gentleman, is recognizable by this Grand Lodge.

The following were adopted :

All appeal papers, on appeals brought before this Grand Lodge, must be furnished by the appealing parties, printed in pamphlet form, on a page of the same size as that of the printed Journal of Proceedings of this Grand Lodge, and in default thereof, the respective appeal, shall be liable to be referred back for informality.

In case of a vacancy in the office of Noble Grand, or Vice Grand of a Subordinate Lodge, and all qualified members refusing to accept the office, the Lodge may elect a Scarlet member to the office ; provided, however, that a Dispensation for the purpose, be first obtained from the proper authority in the jurisdiction to which the Lodge belongs.

The right to charge for Visiting or Withdrawal Cards is to be regulated by the local jurisdiction. Where the local law requires payment for a Card, the Lodge, or the officer whose duty it is to issue it, has the right to require payment therefor before delivering it.

Where the applicant for membership is a citizen or a subject of a foreign power, and only a *temporary* resident within the jurisdiction of the Grand Lodge of the United States, he cannot be initiated into the Order. Residence is an elementary qualification for membership. An individual can have only one legal residence, and where such residence is under a foreign power, a *temporary* residence within the jurisdiction of the Grand Lodge of the United States can confer no new rights.

A State Grand Body, after admitting a Past Grand or Past Chief Patriarch to membership, upon a Certificate, made in due form, as having served the regular term entitling him to said favor, can go behind said Certificate and rescind the consent given to his admission, and refuse him a seat, when it ascertains that the facts asserted in the Certificate are incorrectly stated. The Certificate is merely *prima facie* evidence of qualification. Where the fundamental regulation does not otherwise provide, every representative Body must judge for itself of the qualifications of its members.

As the Grand Lodge refused to consent to the admission of the *daughters* of Odd Fellows to the Degree of Rebekah, still less would *adopted* daughters be entitled to this privilege.

If a member wilfully absents himself, with the evident purpose of avoiding the service of notice of charges, he may be expelled for contempt.

Whether a member of a Subordinate Lodge must have his account settled up to the last day of the past term to entitle him to receive the Password of the current term, and whether a brother, thus in arrears, has the right to sit in his own Lodge without the Password, prior to suspension, are questions to be determined by the proper authorities, and according to the laws of the State jurisdictions in which they arise, and not by this Grand Lodge.

The law passed at the session of 1853, requiring certain statistical returns in connection with dues and benefits, is hereby repealed.

In cases when charges are preferred against a brother of the Order in any Lodge or Encampment to which he may belong, but from having absconded, or from his permanent absence or concealment, he cannot be found, so that the charges preferred or notice of trial cannot be personally served upon him, the respective Lodge or Encampment may regularly proceed with the trial, upon proof of the fact rendering such personal service impracticable, and that a copy of the charges and notice of trial has been deposited in the post office nearest the last known residence of such brother, directed to him at such place of residence, post-paid, and that a like copy of the charges and notice of trial was left at his last place of residence, if the same be known ; *provided*, that such papers shall be deemed to have been served upon the brother, only from the date when the constructive service above described is complete ; and provided, further, that in case such brother returns after the conclusion of the trial, not having appeared on such trial either in person or by counsel, and asks for a new trial, the same shall be granted him.

Hereafter it shall be the duty of the Grand Secretary to open an account in his books with each specific appropriation, charging to such appropriations severally, the amount reported by the Finance Committee, and placing to the credit of such account all payments made on account thereof ; and in no case shall such payments exceed the amount of the specific appropriation on account of which they are made, nor shall any transfer of appropriations be allowed without the consent of the Grand Lodge.

A Lodge has no right to refuse to grant a Card to a brother who is under no legal disqualification at the period of application. If a Lodge should refuse a Card, the brother may have redress upon appeal to the local Grand Lodge.

From and after the adjournment of this annual session of the Grand Lodge of the United States for 1855, the pay of Representatives to, and officers of this Body, (excepting those to whom stated salaries are allowed), shall be two dollars per diem during their actual attendance upon the sessions of this Body, and four cents per mile for each mile traveled from their respective residences to the place of meeting of the Grand Lodge and back again ; said mileage to be computed by the nearest mail route between said points.

It shall be the duty of the Grand Secretary, at the opening of every annual communication of this Grand Lodge, to place in the hands of the Grand Sire a written statement, showing the name or names of any Grand Lodge or Grand Encampment which may be indebted to this Grand Lodge, with the amount of such indebtedness, which statement shall be placed by the Grand Sire in the hands of the Committee on Credentials, immediately upon the appointment of said committee, so that the said committee may be able to make their report in conformity to the eleventh Article of the By-Laws of this Grand Body.

It was deemed inexpedient to authorize the admission into the Order of one who, from advanced age, sickness, or constitutional infirmity, was incapable of being received into membership in a Subordinate Lodge, with the full benefits of the Order, on his own proposition to renounce all pecuniary benefits.

The Grand Lodge decided that it had no power to pass

a law permitting brethren to join the Order in California without the usual deposit of Clearance Cards, and without their making any efforts to settle their accounts with the Lodges they had left, upon their making certain to the Lodge they propose to join that they had been suspended for non-payment of dues and for no other cause.

The Grand Sire was authorized to call the next annual session of the Grand Lodge at such place as he deemed most practicable, in case he was satisfied that the health of the city determined upon by this Grand Lodge for its meeting rendered such a change necessary.

1856.

The Grand Lodge met in regular annual session, in the City of Baltimore, on the 15th of September.

Grand Sire Ellison, owing to long continued indisposition, was unable to attend the session. The Deputy Grand Sire, George W. Race, presided.

E. C. Robinson, P. G. M., of Virginia, was appointed Deputy Grand Sire *pro tem.*

Grand Sire Ellison, in his report, said :

Representatives and Brethren : Assembled as you are, at this moment, upon the threshold of another and a new communication, it affords me much pleasure to assure you that no disturbing element has arisen during the past year, to interrupt that peace and harmony and prosperity so beautifully pervading our entire jurisdiction at the close of the official labors of my esteemed predecessor. The fair field of the past has been so fragrant with the blossoms of love, and the flowers of obedience, that I should scarce find it necessary to address you at this time, were it not a constitutional requirement. The first impulse of grateful hearts, my brethren, is to render our united thanks to the Supreme Ruler of Heaven and Earth, without whose watchful care and parental love our institution would never have so steadily increased from weakness into strength ; from a small and feeble beginning to its present magnitude and moral influence. In pouring forth our thank-offerings, gushing warm from the heart, let us not forget to invoke the blessings of our Heavenly Father, that His protecting arm may be at all times over us, guiding us by His spirit, so that the influences of our institution may hasten that period when the high and impassable barriers that separate man from his fellow-man shall be forever removed ; when the spear of the warrior shall be broken, and the sword of the conqueror shall lay rusting in its scabbard, and discord and contention shall be known no more.

The iron wheels of time, in their never-ending revolutions, find you again, my brethren, at this post of honorable duty, forsaking for a time the cares of business and the comforts of home, to give such direction to our united labors as will continue to strengthen the bonds and increase the usefulness of our beloved fraternity. Coming, as you do, from the Subordinate tribunals and working Lodges of our jurisdiction, familiar with all the details of our organization, knowing each throb and pulsation of the great heart of our Order, animated by the spirit of love and fraternity, the result of your official labors must, of necessity, continue to strengthen the bonds that unite us together as one happy family. And God grant that your labors may not be in vain! The conflicting and discordant elements of society can find repose and safety, only in the conservative spirit of philan-thropic institutions which have in themselves no inherent element of discord, but whose mission it is to teach us that "no one liveth to himself," but that we are created and placed here to labor for our fellow-men, to improve our social condition, to strengthen the bonds of our union, to elevate our country, and to advance our race in all the essential elements of a healthy civilization. In aristocratical governments, where freedom and civilization rest with oligarchies, forging fetters for both mind and body, instead of paving the way for individual amelioration, the influence of philanthropic institutions is lost in an atmosphere where freedom of opinion exists only in name. But in this young republic, the home of liberty, where freedom of opinion, and freedom of speech, and freedom of the press are the natural and inalienable rights of all, our association has a great and important work to perform. It can never soil its spotless robes in the dust and discord of the political arena. We have no fears of its ever being converted into a political or sectarian engine, for it ranks among its members men of all parties, and creeds and opinions, eminent for intellect and piety, and love of country, whose nationality knows no geographical lines, but is as broad and universal as humanity itself.

We cannot shut our eyes to the fact that in our own country events are ever on the wing, which, like the storm cloud, when meeting an opposing force, sends forth its messenger of destruction, leaving only a withering and blighted footprint to mark its career. When sectional hatred is intensifying itself; when men's minds are darkened by strong passions and fierce conflicts ; when the spirit of disaffection is growing stronger, and the bonds of our social compact correspondingly weaker, it is then that our institution may go forth in its robes of universal love, with its diadem of friendship and its cincture of truth, going behind the distinctions of sect, and party, and nation, teaching man that his own comfort and welfare are interwoven with the well-being of his race. It is true, as our beautiful Ritual teaches us, that our Order holds no fellowship with the divisions and classifications of human society. Of local ideas we may be, at times, tenacious, but when they seal our vision to other and more comprehensive truths, we should remember that our relations and duties are exceedingly broad and far-reaching. We should not forget that all men are of one family ; that to the Odd Fellow there is but one country—the Earth ; but one nation—the human race. Let these great truths make our institution a solid landmark, amid the waves of faction, the storms of passion, and the conflicts of error. Thus will it become the palladium of our liberties, the ark of our national safety ; and on the rainbow of Hope, which encircles us, let there be inscribed, in golden characters, Union, which shall be the crowning beauty and safeguard of the whole.

The following decisions of the Grand Sire were approved :

A brother or Patriarch residing in one State, is not entitled to admission as a member, nor can his proposition for membership upon a Final Card be received in a Subordinate Lodge or Encampment of another State, he remaining a resident and a citizen in the State from which his Card was issued, unless the previous consent of the Grand Lodge or Grand Encampment, or Grand Master or Grand Patriarch is first had and obtained.

A brother holding a Withdrawal Card from one State is entitled to the Annual Traveling Password in use at the time, and retains the right to visit in another State with the same Password for a year.

A brother holding a Withdrawal Card which has run out of date, may be recognized as an Ancient Odd Fellow, and be allowed to renew his member-ship by the deposit of said Card in a Lodge at the place of his residence, subject to the payment of such fee as the local law may require.

It is not competent for a Lodge, after its first term, to elect a Scarlet member to the office of Noble Grand when brothers who have served as Vice Grand are in nomination, except in cases where all qualified members refuse to accept the office of Noble Grand ; then the Lodge may elect a Scarlet member, provided, however, a Dispensation for the purpose be first obtained from the proper authority in the jurisdiction to which the Lodge belongs.

There is no general law of the Order limiting or regulating the number of times a candidate can be proposed after rejection ; the inquiry is a matter for local law.

A brother suspended from membership in his Lodge is thereby cut off from all benefits and privileges, and in case of his death during such suspension, the Lodge incurs no new liability on account of his decease.

A brother holding an unexpired Withdrawal Card, retains a right to prefer charges for unworthy conduct against a member of his Lodge during the year for which said Card extends.

It is the right of a Lodge to examine a visiting brother every night he may present himself for admission, and he must be introduced by the examin-ing committee.

A Grand Master, when visiting a Subordinate in his official capacity, is entitled to the Honors of the Order, but a Grand Master may visit in his indi-vidual capacity as a member of the Order, and upon such visits he should not expect to be received with the Honors. It is only when he announces himself as Grand Master, that the visit becomes official.

A brother suspended for a definite period for non-payment of dues, when that time expires, is placed precisely in the same position in which he was previous to his suspension, with the additional amount of dues accruing dur-ing his suspension ; and, if the Lodge wish to discipline him further, his case must be taken up again ; but a brother suspended for a definite period, as a punishment for some specific offense, upon the expiration of his term of suspension is *ipso facto* restored to membership.

The Grand Secretary, in his report, said :

I am gratified to report, that although the actual receipts will fall short of the amount estimated by the committee, and the expenditure estimated has been exceeded by the appropriation for publishing the fourth volume of the Journal, authorized after the adoption of the Finance Report, yet the estimated deficit will not actually occur. On the contrary, it is believed there will be a considerable less deficit, arising from the fact that the actual expenditure for mileage and per diem, and for printing, has fallen short of the specific appropriations for those objects in the sum of fifteen hundred dollars.

The amount received for the Wildey Annuity Fund from September 18th, 1855, to September 15th, 1856, was $190.

Thirteen Lodges were reported in good working order under the Grand Lodge of Canada West. The jurisdiction of California now comprised sixty Lodges with a membership of more than two thousand four hundred. During the year, two Subordinate Lodges were established in Nebraska Territory.

The total receipts of the Grand Lodge for the past year amounted to $15,072.93. The profit on the sale of supplies was $6,463.32.

The Subordinate Lodges increased in number 84, while the Subordinate Encampments suffered a loss in number compared with the previous year.

The Subordinate Lodges expended for relief of brothers, $335,834.23 ; for relief of widowed families, $71,715.99 ; for education of orphans, $10,663.33 ; for burying the dead, $74,572.66. The Subordinate Encampment reports were very imperfect and were lacking in many important details.

The proposed amendment to the Constitution, to abolish representation of Grand Encampments in the Grand Lodge was indefinitely postponed.

The Committee on the State of the Order was requested to inquire into the expediency of consolidating the Order on the Pacific Coast and the Islands of the Pacific into one Grand Lodge and one Grand Encampment; provided, that the Grand Bodies of Oregon and California assent thereto.

The brotherhood of the City of Norfolk, Virginia, invited the Grand Lodge to participate in the ceremony of dedicating a new Odd Fellows' Hall in that city. The invitation was accepted and the Grand Lodge participated in the dedication.

Permission for ladies, having the Rebekah Degree, to be present at the installation of the officers of Subordinate Lodges was again refused.

The following were adopted:

There is nothing in our present laws preventing the members of the Degree of Rebekah from organizing for the purpose of promoting the cause of benevolence. (This resulted in the establishment of numerous associations of members of the Degree throughout the country, most of which eventually became Degree Lodges of the Daughters of Rebekah.)

All Visiting and Final Cards shall hereafter be signed by the holders thereof in the presence of the officer by whom the Annual Password is communicated to such holders.

The Grand Sire possesses the power of appointment of the Standing Committees of this Body, only when he is the actual presiding officer of the session; and in case of his not so actually presiding, from absence or other inability, the appointment of those committees devolves, with the other duties of the Grand Sire, as presiding officer, upon the officer who shall, pursuant to the provisions of the Constitution, be actually presiding over the session at the time that order of business is reached.

Grand Patriarchs and their Deputies are empowered to confer the Degrees of a Subordinate Encampment upon Scarlet Degree members of Subordinate Lodges for the purpose of organizing new 'Encampments, provided, no Subordinate Encampment is located within thirty miles of such new Encampment.

WHEREAS, There are in the hands of the Grand Secretary several hundred copies (unbound) of " *The Covenant*," which are of no more value to this Grand Lodge than so much waste paper ; therefore,

Resolved, That the Grand Secretary be authorized to present one copy thereof to each member of this Grand Lodge, who may apply for the same.

The Grand Secretary is directed not to fill any orders for supplies, from Lodges or individuals, unless the cash accompany such order in bankable par funds.

The officers of Subordinate Lodges and Encampments shall not be installed, nor furnished with the Semi-annual Password, unless the reports, returns, and moneys due from such Lodges and Encampments to their respective superior jurisdictions be actually made and placed in the hands of the proper officer, or be actually in transit to the proper destination.

The system of specific appropriations, adopted at the last session, shall be so far modified as to authorize and permit the transfer from one appropriation to another, when the wants of any appropriation may demand it, of such sums as the Grand Sire may direct.

Subordinate Lodges and Encampments, in reinstating members suspended for non-payment of dues, shall have power to remit, in whole or part, the dues accruing during the suspension of such members.

When a report of the Committee of Appeals, or a resolution accompanying the same, is regularly before the Lodge and action is being had thereon, the statement of facts contained in the report of the committee, and in the record of appeal, shall be deemed conclusive, and it shall not be in order to make any statement in debate thereon, inconsistent with the facts so stated in such record or report. This rule shall not apply when action is had upon a motion to recommit such report with instructions.

The laws of the Grand Lodge require the Noble Grand of a Lodge, when present at its meetings, always to preside, and the Vice Grand to act as Noble Grand in the absence of that officer; and that a Noble Grand, or Vice Grand acting as Noble Grand, has not the right or power to waive his right, and place a Past Grand in the Noble Grand's chair during the presence in the Lodge room of either of the first two officers above named ; provided, that this decision is not to be considered as applicable to a *temporary* absence during a portion of a Lodge meeting of those officers, in which case the chair must be filled as provided in the Charge Book.

Any Subordinate Lodge or Encampment admitting a citizen of another jurisdiction to membership, without the previous consent of the proper officer or Body in such jurisdiction, upon conviction thereof before its Grand Body, shall forfeit and pay to its Grand Lodge or Grand Encampment, as the case may be, all Initiation and Degree Charges received from such person up to the date of such conviction.

1857.

The Grand Lodge met in regular annual session, in the City of Baltimore, on the 21st of September.

The State Grand Bodies were entitled to 103 Representatives.

The following Grand Officers elect were duly installed :

George W. Race, P. G. M., of Louisiana, Grand Sire ; Timothy G. Senter, P. G. M., of New Hampshire, Deputy Grand Sire ; James L. Ridgely, P. G. M., of Maryland, Grand Corresponding and Recording Secretary ; Joshua Vansant, P. G., of Maryland, Grand Treasurer.

The following were appointed by the Grand Sire :

Rev. J. D. McCabe, P. G., of Virginia, Grand Chaplain ; A. M. Foute, P. G., of Tennessee, Grand Marshal ; Solomon Lewyt, P. G., of Maryland, Grand Guardian ; John E. Chamberlain, P. G., of Maryland, Grand Messenger.

Grand Sire Ellison, in his report, said:

It is again my agreeable duty to inform you, Representatives, as you may learn by the annual returns from the several Subordinate jurisdictions and by the reports of the D. D. Grand Sires, that our Order still continues to hold an onward course. From the correspondence of the executive department may be gleaned the agreeable information that the remote extremes of our jurisdiction continue to exhibit a healthy progress and a never-tiring activity. It is in new States and Territories, remote from a dense population, that the blessings and the benefits of an institution like ours, are so intimately interwoven with the stability and advancement of the social compact. It is in new fields of enterprise, where the spirit of adventure has carried man far from home and friends, and the easy facilities of frequent social intercommunion, that he finds a necessity for some union with his fellow-man that will lift him above the toils and cares of every day life, that will permit him to breathe a purer atmosphere than can be found in the turmoil of business or the hot strife of political or polemical discussion. An institution that will bring men together under such circumstances, upon the broad platform of equality, forgetting for a time the distinctions of sect, and party, and creed, must of necessity separate the alloy from the pure gold of our existence, fill us with higher and nobler thoughts of our own duty and destiny, and give us a clearer conception of those ennobling virtues, whose primitive simplicity and purity breathe the spirit and the essence of universal love.

It is not in those far-off islands of the sea, where the standard of Odd Fellowship waves in triumph, nor by the rivers of Oregon, whose tumbling waters give voice to desolation, nor in the far-distant Territorial possessions of the West that we must look for a decline in interest or numerical strength, but in the populous States, where it is an easy matter to be an Odd Fellow; where social life and social pleasures, in their never ending variety, the natural concomitants of a crowded population, draw us almost imperceptibly from the quiet retreat of the Lodge room and its healthy influences, until indifference and neglect, like base rust which consumes solid iron, will contract our resources and our means for doing good, and may one day undermine the structure itself. * * * * Oh, in this world of unrest, where fate weaves its wild contrasts and civilization multiplies its varieties, where substantial comforts are bartered for false theories of human happiness, and friendship and love are sold for an inheritance of sin, when the mental powers become paralyzed and dark, it is well for us that there are institutions, philanthropic and religious, containing "that Promethean spark that can again man's former light relume." Be it your duty, my brethren, to watch with a Vestal care, the fair flower of Odd Fellowship, which, in the fullness of time, will pass from the germ to a matured and noble fruition. It is in the stillness of the night, and by the pillow of the suffering one, that its vigils are kept and its offices of love are freely administered. A kind word spoken, a single sorrow relieved, when the rude storms of adversity are assailing us, will lay up for us treasures which, in that last hour, will prove a trophy imperishable and deathless, still living and speaking while the earth and the stars are fading away.

The following decisions of the Grand Sire were approved :

There is no provision of law to furnish a Subordinate Body with two Charters, except in a case where the original one has become mutilated or destroyed.

A duplicate Charter should be signed by the officers of the Body granting it, with an endorsement stating that the Charter was issued in place of one granted at such a time, and which had become mutilated or destroyed.

No brother is entitled to enter or leave the Lodge room unless clothed in Regalia. If an officer, and his Regalia be in his chair in the Lodge room, he must enter in Scarlet Regalia, if of that Degree, and there exchange it for official Regalia.

It is a question for local law, whether a Grand Patriarch has the power, during the recess of a Grand Encampment, to suspend a Subordinate Encampment.

It is improper, by general law and usage, to ballot collectively on a number of applications for membership by deposit of Card. Every member of a Lodge has a right to deposit his ballot upon each individual application for membership, and a collective ballot would be an infringement of this right.

A brother cannot become in arrears so as to disqualify him from receiving benefits during sickness or disability, if he is beneficial at the commencement of such sickness or disability. It is the duty of the Lodge to retain so much of his benefits as would keep him in good standing during his sickness or disability.

The Grand Secretary reported that several of the jurisdictions had complied with the request contained in the circular issued by him in reference to the bound Journals of the several Grand Bodies. He acknowledged the receipt of quite a number, mentioned in detail on page 2711 of the Journal. He said:

The annual returns of the State Grand Lodges have, I am gratified to say, been generally received in time for this report ; but the non-receipt of several of these returns, renders it impossible, at this time, to present an accurate table of the progress of the Order during the past year. * * * * I regret to report that the Order has gone down in Canada East, notwithstanding the manly exertions of a few devoted members to sustain it. The only Lodge in that jurisdiction, which survived after the demise of the former Grand Lodge of British North America, viz., Albion, No. 4, located at Quebec, was dissolved during the past year by a vote of the membership. * * * * I have great pleasure in reporting that the condition of the Order in the Lower Provinces of British North America is progressive and improving.

The amount received from September 15th, 1856, to September 22d, 1857, for the Wildey Annuity Fund, was $292.

During the year, Warrants were issued for five Subordinate Lodges and three Subordinate Encampments.

Total receipts for the year, $17,654.40; profit on the
sale of supplies, $9,271.93.

There was an increase of 108 in the number of Subordinate Lodges, and in Encampments, 18.

The following amounts were expended by Subordinate
Lodges: For relief of brothers, $287,972.74; for relief of
widowed families, $61,082.11; for education of orphans,
$13,469.33; for burying the dead, $75,887.15.

The following were adopted:

In cases of indefinite suspension for the non-payment of dues, the matter
of reinstatement shall be left to the discretion of the respective State jurisdictions in which such suspensions may take place, and as the local law may
determine.

Whenever a Lodge or Encampment, or a member of either, when under a
charge, shall desire to take the testimony of a witness whose personal presence cannot be had before the tribunal trying such charge, his deposition may
be taken in the following manner: The party desiring to take the deposition
shall file with the Secretary of the Lodge, or the Scribe of the Encampment,
the interrogatories he wishes to be propounded to the witness or witnesses,
naming them. The Secretary or Scribe shall immediately deliver, or cause to
be delivered, to the opposite party a copy of the interrogatories. The latter
party, within one week from such service, may file counter interrogatories
with the Secretary or Scribe, if he or they think proper. At the expiration of
the week, or sooner, if counter interrogatories be sooner filed, the Secretary
or Scribe shall forthwith forward them to the Noble Grand of a Lodge near
the witness, with a communication requesting him to take the deposition of
the witness or witnesses named. Upon receipt of the same, the Noble Grand
shall, as soon as possible, take or cause the depositions to be taken, by some
competent member of the Order, causing every interrogatory to be propounded
to the witness, and the answer to each reduced to writing in the presence of
the witness; and when the deposition is completed, shall cause the witness to
sign the same, and then the Noble Grand, or person taking the same, shall
certify the same to be duly taken, and such Certificate shall be verified by the
Seal of the Lodge, and the deposition shall then be sealed in an envelope
and transmitted by mail, to the Lodge or Encampment before which the trial is
pending. The depositions thus taken and certified may be read in evidence
in the cause to which it relates.

Neither a Grand Master nor a Grand Lodge can grant a Dispensation to a
Subordinate Lodge to dispense with its regular meetings. Twenty-six meetings of the Subordinate Lodge, whether held weekly or at longer periods, are
required to constitute a full term; but if circumstances over which the Lodge
can exercise no control shall occur, by which the meetings cannot be held, the

Junior Past Grand should not, from that fact alone, be disqualified from admission into his Grand Lodge. If, however, the meetings of a Lodge are suspended by its own seeking or application, for causes over which it could exercise control, and the Lodge fails to comply with the requisites of the law, the officers of the Lodge, for the term, would therefore properly be deprived of their Past Official Degrees. The Dispensation of the Grand Lodge or Grand Master, could have no effect on the result.

Where all the brothers who may cast black balls against an applicant for membership, voluntarily make a motion for a reconsideration of the ballot, the same may be reconsidered, and in such case the vote on the reconsideration shall be taken by ball ballots, and if all the ballots cast be in favor of it, the reconsideration shall be had ; whereupon the application shall lie over till the succeeding meeting, when another ballot shall be had with ball ballots, and if the same be unanimously in favor of the applicant, he shall thereby be elected ; but if one or more black balls appear in either ballot, the applicant shall be rejected, and in no case shall a reconsideration be had, except upon the voluntary motion of all those who cast the black balls, and never more than one motion for a reconsideration in the same case shall be allowed.

The Seal of a Lodge or Encampment, to be authentic, must be printed or impressed upon the paper or instrument it authenticates, and not affixed thereto. This shall take effect on the first day of January, 1858.

It is not competent for a State Grand Lodge to change the terms of Subordinate Lodges in its jurisdiction, so as to begin and end at periods different from those established by this Grand Body.

Subordinate Bodies, by existing regulations, possess an inherent right to protect themselves from disorder, the want of decorum, and violations of the ordinary proprieties of life.

A *candidate* for the office of Grand Representative to this Body should possess, *at the time of his election, all* the qualifications prescribed by the Constitution.

It is a question for local legislation, whether Subordinate Lodges can discriminate against suspended members by charging them an increased amount of arrears during the time of suspension.

Until his credentials are recognized by the Grand Lodge of the United States, the person elected or appointed is a Representative *elect* and not a Representative. He *may* be held disqualified and refused his seat. Until his credentials are submitted, and he is declared entitled to his seat, he is not entitled to wear the Regalia of a Grand Representative.

Immediately after the election of a Grand Representative, it shall be the duty of the Grand Scribe or Grand Secretary of the Body which he is to represent, to forward to the Grand Secretary of the Grand Lodge a duplicate copy of said Representative's Certificate of election.

The propriety of extending funeral honors to brothers in arrears, but against whom no charges for unworthy conduct are pending at the time of death, is a matter for regulation by local law.

A member of the Order who resides in one jurisdiction, and is a contributing member of a Lodge in an adjoining jurisdiction, (he having been initiated in the Lodge nearest to his residence, by the consent of the Grand Lodge or Grand Master of the State or jurisdiction in which he resides), is entitled to the same privileges and honors to which members are entitled who belong to Lodges located in the State or jurisdiction in which they reside.

It is improper for a Grand Lodge or Grand Master, to grant a Dispensation to a Subordinate Lodge to enable it to suspend the payment of its weekly benefits.

As to the vote required by Subordinate Lodges to make investments of its funds, it is a matter exclusively for local legislation.

Any brother who acquires the Semi-annual Password improperly, and by making use thereof obtains relief from a Lodge of which he is not a member, is guilty of a double fraud on the Order, and should be required to refund the amount received, to the Lodge from which he received it, and be punished by his own Lodge for the offense. It would not be proper to hold a Lodge responsible for funds obtained under such circumstances.

A Certificate from the Secretary of a State Grand Lodge, who becomes the custodian of the Charter, books, papers, etc., of extinct Subordinates, setting forth the actual standing of a member of a Lodge at the time of its demise, is competent evidence for Subordinates, in their action upon the application of a member of a defunct Lodge for admission into the Order.

In case of the extinction of a Subordinate Encampment or Lodge, in which an officer or member of the Grand Lodge of the United States holds membership, the seat of such officer or Representative shall not be vacated thereby, provided, that within one month after such extinction he shall connect himself with some other Subordinate Encampment or Lodge.

The jurisdiction of Oregon Territory and the Subordinate Lodges in Washington Territory were authorized to consolidate into one jurisdiction, to be hailed as " *The Grand Lodge of Oregon and Washington;* " provided, the assent of the Grand Lodge of Oregon and of the Subordinate Lodges in Washington Terrritory be first had and obtained.

Two important amendments to the Constitution were adopted; first, changing the dues of State Grand Bodies from fifty dollars to seventy-five dollars for each vote they are entitled to; and second, providing for the installation of officers at the conclusion of the session at which they are elected.

1858.

The Grand Lodge met in annual session, in the City of Baltimore, on the 20th of September.

Grand Sire Race, in his report, said:

Although this year's harvest may not be so abundant as that of some former years, yet there is no less cause for congratulation and thank-offerings.

True prosperity is not always evidenced by increased numbers. The refining and purifying process—the trying of the metal in the crucible and the separating of the dross from the pure gold, is as necessary in Odd Fellowship as in any other human institution. History will characterize the nineteenth century as "The Age of Associations," or "The Age of Societies;" and yet out of the hundred and one "societies" that are now putting forth pretensions to public favor, there are but few worthy of the name of *Charity*, and entitled to the aid and sympathy of *humanity*. As in popular governments, the masses follow a phantom for a time, but soon right themselves; so in these mushroom societies that have filled this country during the last few years. Even good Odd Fellows have been attracted thither by their *ignis fatuus*, but must soon leave their bacchanalian halls and obscene representations in disgust, to again become co-laborers in this great cause of humanity. But these bacchanalian revelries and kindred mock associations have a still more baneful influence upon the minds of those dupes, who are not Odd Fellows or Free Masons, by leading them to believe that all "secret societies" are similar in character, and are alike unworthy of their admiration and support. This erroneous view is confirmed by seeing around them known members of our Order, actively engaged in demonstrating the rare qualities of the "*Maltese*," or pleased spectators and enthusiastic congratulators of the persons "sold." That man who continues to co-operate with such associations after the baneful influences have been pointed out to him, ceases to be an Odd Fellow in spirit and in truth. Whilst we have our Forms and Ceremonies, our Signs and Pass-words, whereby we recognize each other, ours is no fancy association with gewgaws to attract and catch the silly and the thoughtless. But it addresses itself at once, unto the nobler and higher attributes of our nature. It is the high, if not the distinguishing characteristic of an Odd Fellow, to believe that among the most acceptable services which man can render his God, is relief to his fellow-man. And the exercise of this unselfish philanthropy is emphatically his mission.

It appears that the two jurisdictions of "Oregon" and "California," with but *four* Representatives, have cost this Grand Lodge in *two* years the sum of $3,389 more than their contributions; and within the next two years, instead of *four* Representatives from these two jurisdictions, they will send *eight* Representatives, and cost this Grand Lodge as much annually as they have during the past two years. These examples are sufficient to demonstrate that in proportion as our Order expands, under the present system, so will the finances of the Grand Lodge fall short the more to meet its expenses.

The following decisions of the Grand Sire were approved:

Upon principle, a Grand Master should not hold office in his Subordinate Lodge, or in a Degree Lodge.

The place designated in the Charter or Constitution for the meetings of a Grand Encampment, can be changed by a vote of that Body, with the same facility that a By-Law or Rule of Order can be altered, provided it be done in conformity with the rules laid down in its Constitution for such change.

An "Ancient Odd Fellow" is one who has been regularly initiated into the Order and retired therefrom in good standing, either by taking his "Permanent" or "Withdrawal Card," or by "resignation." If done by resignation he at once becomes an "Ancient Odd Fellow," and if by taking a Permanent Card he becomes so at the expiration of one year from the date of the Card.

A District Deputy Grand Master has not the right to introduce visitors whose Cards are out of date. That power being restricted by law to "Elective Grand Officers."

Where the By-Laws of a Subordinate Lodge read "that every member, etc., against whom there is no charge shall be entitled to benefits," a brother who is not entitled to sick benefits, by reason of the non-payment of his dues, cannot, during his sickness, by the payment of all arrearages, reinstate himself in good standing in his Lodge, so as to be entitled to benefits during that illness.

A Lodge in surrendering its Charter and effects should also relinquish into the control and custody of the Grand Lodge its available and unavailable assets.

The Grand Secretary, in his report, said :

The annual returns of the State Grand Bodies, I have great pleasure in saying, have been generally received in time for this report. It is, however, to be regretted that, notwithstanding the repeated appeals that have been made on this subject, for a compliance with the law requiring them to be in hand thirty days previous to the annual session, several reports are yet outstanding, the absence of which prevents me from presenting an accurate tabular statement of the condition of the Order.

The Grand Lodges of Nebraska and Kansas were organized during the year, and each had five Lodges under its jurisdiction.

At the close of the last session, after the payment of the necessary expenses, there was a deficiency in the treasury of about $3,500.

The amount received for the Wildey Annuity Fund, from September 22d, 1857, to September, 1858, was $160.00.

The total receipts during the past year were $16,943.72, and the profit on supplies, $6,965.34.

The following amounts were expended by Subordinate Lodges: For relief of brothers, $294,992.91 ; for relief of widowed families, $66,614.55 ; for education of orphans, $11,287.06 ; for burying the dead, $67,364.70.

A communication from William F. Langley, Grand Secretary of the "Victoria Grand Lodge of the Australian

Independent Order of Odd Fellows," to the Grand Secretary of the Grand Lodge of California, and dated at Melbourne, May 5th, 1858, had two objects: First, to inform the officers and members of our Order in California of the existence and condition of the Order in Australia; and secondly, to obtain supplies of Certificates, etc.

The Grand Lodge of Victoria had, at this time, under its jurisdiction six Subordinate Lodges, *viz :* The Duke of York Lodge, Melbourne; The Fitzroy Lodge, Melbourne; The Australia Lodge, Collingwood; The Prince Albert Lodge, Strachxan; The Ashby Lodge, Geelong; The Loyal Brothers Lodge, Geelong. None of the above Lodges held Charters from any Grand Body authorizing them to work according to the Ritual and usage of the Independent Order of Odd Fellows of the United States. The Grand Secretary was authorized to correspond with the Australian Grand Lodge and ask them their wishes as to recognition by our Order. This correspondence, thus commenced, finally resulted in bringing the Order there, into full communion with ours, as will appear in a subsequent chapter.

The following were adopted :

The several Grand Bodies in this jurisdiction, are hereby authorized to confer upon their Subordinates, the right to install their officers in public; provided that the ceremony be conducted by one or more of the Elective Officers of such Grand Body, or a District Deputy Grand Master, and provided that they use the Form prescribed by this Grand Lodge.

A brother holding an expired Withdrawal Card, is not competent to be a petitioner for a new Lodge.

A Lodge or Encampment may visit a sister Lodge or Encampment in a Body, when accompanied by one of its first two officers, who may introduce the brothers in the manner provided for the introduction of visitors by the elective Grand Officers.

Subordinate Lodges and Encampments have clearly the right to examine a visitor whenever he presents himself, and, when examined, he must be introduced by the committee. But it was never supposed that after a first regular examination it was *imperative* to pursue the same formalities, in the same Lodge or Encampment, on each subsequent visit. After the visitor has been once recognized, the examination and introduction, in form, *may* be subsequently dispensed with, if the Lodge or Encampment is so minded, provided the presiding officer shall find the Card of the visiting brother to be in date.

It is inexpedient, and adverse to the best interests of the Order, to grant in the future, any Warrant or Charter for the establishment of a Grand Body, unless there shall be under the jurisdiction of the proposed Body, at least one thousand contributing members at the date of the application.

Whenever a Lodge, Encampment, or member of the Order, authorized by existing laws to introduce testimony in any proceeding, may desire the testimony of a non-resident witness, such Lodge, Encampment, or member, may take the deposition of such witness in the mode prescribed by the resolution of the Grand Lodge passed at the session of 1857, and to be found on page 2,738 of the Journal.

The granting of Withdrawal Cards, to members of defunct Lodges and Encampments, is more appropriately a subject for local legislation.

None but those properly qualified for membership in their Grand Lodge, can be allowed to vote for the officers thereof.

A Past Grand cannot be deprived of his right to vote for the officers of his Grand Lodge ; but after the right has been exercised, a constitutional provision limiting this right to Representatives of Lodges in the Grand Lodge, when such Grand Lodge is composed of Representatives and all other Past Grands, is entirely legal and equitable, and does not infringe upon the original right of a Past Grand to vote at such elections.

That further legislation upon the length of terms and periods of official service in Subordinate Lodges is inexpedient. (The committee, in reporting this resolution, said : For years the subject of the alterations of the terms of Subordinates has been one of most persistent and distressing agitation in this Body, returning like an annual epidemic, and stalking through our halls like an unquiet ghost in a haunted mansion. The Grand Lodge tolerated the afflictive visits of this unwelcome guest with the most fearful patience until the session of 1851, when a Representative from North Carolina, distinguished alike by generous qualities of head and heart, a noble devotion to the Order, and a courage worthy of the cause, undertook to "lay the spirit " of this ghostly visitor and consign it to a lasting tomb. It appears, by page 1,758 of our Journal, that this pious task was solemnly accomplished ; the sepulchre was constructed and the unwelcome wanderer wrapped in the cerements of the grave, its troubled spirit no more to stalk before us like Banquo's ghost "to fright the souls of fearful " Representatives. The "restless wanderer " was finally laid at rest ; its catholic burial performed, and the requiem "Requiescat in pace" mournfully dirged forth to a solemn air ! After some years of quiet, during which the Grand Lodge had become perfectly reconciled to the absence of its departed intimate, the air suddenly grows cold about us with a deathly chill, and we are aware that our ghostly visitor has returned to his former haunts. We look around for an explanation of the unwelcome phenomenon and are appalled to find that North Carolina, who consigned the intruder to the tomb, and volunteered to stand, herself, as a sentinel at its portals ; that North Carolina has herself broken the seal of the sepulchre and permitted the restless spirit to escape and resume its wanderings and its persistent annoyances. We recommend its exorcism by the passage of this resolution).

The terms "free white males," in Article XVI., Section 3, of the Constitution, are descriptive of the pure Caucasian race, and exclude all other races and colors from membership in our Order, and, therefore, Chinese and Polynesians are not eligible to membership.

It is inexpedient to inquire into the propriety of abolishing the custom of wearing aprons, by members of the Order. (This appears to have been the first effort in this direction ; repeated attempts succeeded in abolishing them).

Grand Lodges and Grand Encampments, and Subordinate Lodges and Encampments working under the jurisdiction of this Grand Lodge, having revised or amended Constitutions or By-Laws to submit for the examination and approval of this Grand Body, are hereby instructed to furnish their documents in such form as to distinguish, by marginal memoranda, or otherwise, such parts of the revised instrument as have not already received the sanction of the Grand Lodge of the United States.

An officer of this Grand Lodge, or a Representative thereto, or an officer of a State Grand Body, taking a Withdrawal Card does not vacate his office thereby, if the same be immediately deposited in his State Grand Body accompanying an application for a new Charter, or if, on occasion of change of residence, the Card be, within one month, deposited in a Subordinate at his new residence ; provided that while holding such Withdrawal Card, and until such new Lodge or Encampment be instituted, such person can discharge no official act.

The following amendment to the Constitution was adopted :

The elective officers shall have the power of debating and making motions, but shall not have the privilege of voting, unless they be Grand Representatives. The appointed officers, unless they be Representatives, shall not be allowed to take part in the proceedings and debates of the Grand Lodge, except by a vote of the majority thereof.

Encampment members were refused permission to retain their membership in that Branch of the Order, after having honorably withdrawn from their Subordinate Lodges.

Arrangements were made for a grand celebration of the fortieth anniversary of the Order, in the City of New York, on the 26th of April, 1859.

The following was unanimously adopted in 1857 :

That a suitable testimonial be and is hereby voted to Representative Stuart for his invaluable services in digesting and arranging the Secret Work of the Order. (The Grand Sire, at the session of 1858, reported in reference to this resolution : Your committee have performed that pleasant duty, by procuring and presenting to Brother F. D. Stuart, a beautiful silver "tea set," engraved on one side of the urn : "Presented to P. G. Master F. D. Stuart, by the Grand Lodge of the United States, I. O. O. F., for meritorious services. September session, 1857," and on the converse : " M. W. G. Sire, G. W. Race ; R. W. D. G. Sire, T. G. Senter ; R. W. G. C. and R. Secretary, J. L. Ridgely ; R. W. G. Treasurer, J. Vansant, Committee.")

The following Grand Officers were elected, and installed at the close of the session :

Samuel Craighead, P. G. M., of Ohio, Grand Sire ; Edward H. Fitzhugh, P. G. M., of Virginia, Deputy Grand Sire; James L. Ridgely, P. G. M., of Maryland, Grand Corresponding and Recording Secretary ; Joshua Vansant, P. G. M., of Maryland, Grand Treasurer.

The following were appointed by the Grand Sire :

A. Paul Repiton, P. G., of North Carolina, Grand Chaplain; Isaac M. Tucker, P. G., of New Jersey, Grand Marshal; Solomon H. Lewyt, P. G., of Maryland, Grand Guardian ; John E. Chamberlain, P. G., of Maryland, Grand Messenger.

1859.

The Grand Lodge met in annual session, in the City of Baltimore, on the 19th of September.

Grand Sire Craighead, in his report, said :

Representatives: We have again come together from every part of the broad land over which our jurisdiction extends, for the purpose of reviewing and revising the labors of the past, and maturing such measures for the future as shall best advance the interest and honor of our organization. Entering thus anew upon the discharge of important trusts in behalf of our great cause, it behoves us, as intelligent and responsible creatures, humbly to return our grateful acknowledgments to the Dispenser of all Good, for the manifold blessings which have attended our past efforts, and to implore His mercy and favor for the future.

The pleasure I have in meeting with you upon this occasion, is increased by the satisfaction and hope which the present condition and prospects of the Order are so well calculated to create. During the past year, as citizens and Odd Fellows, we have been highly favored indeed. Health, peace and plenty have abounded in the land ; industry, enterprise and skill, in every department of human effort, have been honored and rewarded ; the dark cloud of pecuniary embarrassment, which for a time depressed the energies of our people and retarded the progress of our Order, is fast passing away, and the future is full of brightness and promise. It is true that in some fields of our vast vineyard, the tidings that reach us are not so cheering as I could wish to report. That there are, here and there, fallings off in numerical strength and financial condition, is not to be disguised. * * * In the immature days of Odd Fellowship—when it was less careful and circumspect than at present —many, out of mere thoughtlessness, more from idle curiosity, and some from purely selfish motives, sought and obtained admission to our fold. But, never having been imbued with the ennobling principles of brotherhood, which constitute the life of our fraternity, they have proved unworthy, and have, to a large extent, and in various ways, during the last few years, gone out from among us. But current events indicate that the *winnowing period* is approaching its end, and that our Order, sharing in the returning prosperity of the country, is moving forward, on its high and holy mission, with a new and confident impulse. Be it our duty to see that it is so directed, that the great interests of humanity shall be advanced through its instrumentalities.

The following decisions of the Grand Sire were approved :

When the holder of a Withdrawal Card has, within a few months after its issue, deposited the same in, and thereby become a member of another Lodge, the Lodge issuing such Card has no power to annul it.

It is competent for a State Grand Lodge to prescribe, by law, that all applications for Visiting or Withdrawal Cards must be in person or in writing.

It is not competent for a Lodge, or Encampment, to try a deceased member, or deprive his widow of the benefits allowed by the laws—her husband having been beneficial, and not under any charges at the time of his decease.

If, under the law authorizing public installations, any controversy arises between an elective Grand Officer and a District Deputy Grand Master, as to which shall conduct such installation, the elective Grand Officer, being superior in rank, shall have precedence.

The Grand Secretary, in his report, said :

The Corresponding Secretary, early after the close of the last session, set on foot measures to carry out, in the most effective manner, the direction given to him touching the celebration of the fortieth anniversary of American Odd Fellowship. * * * * The great moral spectacle was exhibited on the 26th of April, 1859, of thousands and tens of thousands of men banded in the cause of human benefaction, united around one common altar, in humble thanksgiving for the rich favor of Heaven already vouchsafed to their labors, and in fervent prayer for the continuance of the Divine Blessing. In every quarter of the jurisdiction, remote from the place appointed for the general celebration, the greatest enthusiasm was displayed, and the day was celebrated by processions, orations, and other appropriate ceremonies. * * * * The undersigned will not entrench upon the prerogative of the committee, by any reference to the character of the celebration at the city of New York, further than to remark that truly an avalanche of Odd Fellows was there, at the head of which was the M. W. Grand Sire, Samuel Craighead, from his distant home in the State of Ohio. It was, indeed, a mighty gathering in a noble cause. With but one exception, the display made on that occasion, was the greatest pageant of the Order which has ever been witnessed in the United States. It

was estimated that five thousand brethren, at the least, were in the line of procession, and that a gathering of ten thousand was assembled in the public
park, in whose presence Grand Representative Boylston, of South Carolina,
pronounced an address replete with literary beauty, eloquence, and historical
interest.

During the past year, the Grand Encampment of
Delaware voluntarily surrendered its Charter.

A petition was received from the Victoria Grand Lodge
of Australian Odd Fellows, praying for intercommunion, and
a Charter upon the same terms as that issued to "the Grand
Lodge of British North America." The Australian Branch
of the Order was organized by the Grand Lodge of
England, I. O. O. F., under a Charter for the formation of a
Grand Lodge at Sydney, New South Wales.

The amount received for the Wildey Annuity Fund,
from September, 1858, to September, 1859, was $120.

The total receipts of the Grand Lodge for the past year
were $17,373.70. The profit on the sale of supplies
amounted to $7,501.32.

The following sums were paid by Subordinate Lodges:
For relief of brothers, $300,389.15; for relief of widowed
families, $61,454; for education of orphans, $13,888.72; for
burying the dead, $65,227.75.

A Warrant was issued during the recess, for Far West
Encampment, No. 1, Leavenworth, Kansas.

An application was received for a Charter for Paradise
Lodge, No. 1, Santa Fe, New Mexico.

The following were the principal enactments of this
session :

A State, District, or Territorial Grand Lodge or Grand Encampment, has a
right to declare *vacant* the seat of a Grand Representative who does not return
to his jurisdiction on, or before, the first day of January following the annual
session of this Grand Lodge, at which he shall represent such State, District,
or Territorial Grand Body, unless he be prevented by sickness or other
unavoidable accident, of which the Grand Body he represents shall be judge.

When a brother without the Term Password, shall apply for admission to
his own Lodge, it shall be the duty of the Noble Grand, after he has ascertained from the proper financial officer that such brother is not disqualified
from receiving such Password, to *direct* the admittance of the said brother.

It is inexpedient to legislate on the subject of employing a Lecturer to
visit the various Grand Bodies, as it is the special business of the Represent-

atives to this Grand Lodge to instruct their various Grand Bodies in the Work of the Order

On and after the first day of January next, the rank or Degree of all members to whom Withdrawal or Visiting Cards may be granted by Subordinate Lodges or Encampments, shall be expressed on the face of the Card.

An appellant should bring his appeal and record to the session of this Grand Lodge *next* after the granting of it, and where the appellant has failed to do this, it is for the State Grand Body to determine, in the first instance, whether they will renew the permission to take the appeal, if satisfied that the delay was without fault or negligence.

A Subordinate Encampment has jurisdiction to try, and punish a member for words spoken (which are offensive in themselves, and evidence conduct unbecoming an Odd Fellow), in a Subordinate Lodge, when open, and during its regular proceedings.

When a Subordinate Lodge or Encampment becomes extinct, any member of such Subordinate shall, upon payment of such dues as may appear against him, be entitled to receive from the Grand Master and Grand Secretary, or the Grand Patriarch and Grand Scribe, or the Grand Sire and Grand Corresponding and Recording Secretary, as the case may be, or from such other authority as may be prescribed by the laws of the respective jurisdictions, a Card of Withdrawal, which shall have the same force and effect, and shall entitle him to the same privileges, as a Card of Withdrawal issued to him by an existing Subordinate in good standing ; provided, that the officers to whom the application is made, shall require satisfactory evidence that the applicant is, at the time, worthy of recommendation to the "friendship and protection" of the brotherhood. And provided further, that the Charter, books, etc., of said defunct Lodge or Encampment shall have been surrendered to the proper officer.

This Grand Lodge deems the establishment or publication of a monthly periodical, devoted to the interests of the Order, under the auspices or direction of the Grand Lodge, inexpedient and impracticable.

When a Subordinate Lodge disregards the law of its own Grand Lodge, or a provision of its own Constitution, and yet acts in accordance with the laws of this Grand Lodge, it is not subject to punishment by the State Grand Body. But a Subordinate would violate a law of its Grand Body at its peril, and, of course, the State Grand Body would be the proper tribunal to judge of such violation ; but if such Subordinate had acted in accordance with the laws of this Grand Lodge, this Grand Body would, on an appeal being properly taken, protect such Subordinate.

All State Grand Officers, and officers of all Subordinate Lodges and Encampments, are prohibited from signing any Diploma, Certificate, or Card, not issued by the authority of this R. W. Grand Body, to brothers of the Order, and properly authenticated by the signature of the R. W. Grand Corresponding Secretary, written or engraved on the margin thereof.

Article IV. of the By-Laws, was amended to read :

Ten or more Subordinate Lodges, or five or more Subordinate Encampments, located in any State, District or Territory, (where a Grand Lodge or

Grand Encampment has not been established), having seven Past Grands or Past Chief Patriarchs, in good standing, may petition the Grand Lodge of the United States, in writing, praying for the Charter of a Grand Lodge or Grand Encampment, in such State, District or Territory, which, if approved of by a majority of the votes given, shall be granted ; and such Grand Lodge or Grand Encampment shall be opened by the Grand Sire, or some qualified brother or Patriarch, whom he shall deputize for that purpose.

1860.

The Grand Lodge met in annual session, in the City of Nashville, Tennessee, on the 17th of September.

The Grand Sire, Samuel Craighead, was not present at the session, and his chair was filled by Deputy Grand Sire, Edward H. Fitzhugh. This was the second time in twenty-three years, in which the Grand Lodge was organized with the Deputy Grand Sire in the chair of its presiding officer.

The Hall of the House of Representatives of the State of Tennessee, was tendered to the Grand Lodge for its use during the session, and the Grand Lodge proceeded in a body to the Hall, where they were addressed by Brother E. D. Hancock, P. G., on behalf of the Order in Nashville, and afterwards welcomed and tendered the hospitality of the city, by its Mayor, Brother S. N. Hollingsworth. The Deputy Grand Sire made a suitable response.

Grand Sire Craighead, in his report, said :

I am happy to be able to report that, so far as I have learned upon diligent inquiry, the Order is generally prosperous. Founded as it is on the best impulses of human nature, it can decline only with the decadence of the race. The past year of its existence has exhibited a steady and healthful, although not rapid, increase in members, resources and influence. The benign results which must always follow the faithful observance and practice of the precepts and principles of Odd Fellowship cannot fail, in every intelligent and virtuous community, to obtain for it popular sympathy and support. Whilst we should not arrogate an influence superior to every other organization, we have a right to claim that, as an association springing out of the principles of Christian civilization, Odd Fellowship is entitled to a high rank amongst the instrumentalities now in operation throughout the world, not only to relieve the calamities and distresses incident to human life, but to promote the elevation and happiness of mankind. So long as we remain faithful to its principles, and so long as that fidelity is preserved by those who succeed us, so long, it is my confident hope and belief, will that healthful prosperity continue, which it is now my agreeable duty and privilege to report.

It is a fact, worthy of special notice, that amidst the convulsions and distractions which, at times, disturb our political systems, and, that while other organizations have been rent asunder, the integrity of our Order remains unimpaired and unthreatened. A fact which at once displays a continued fidelity to its high mission, and the extent and solidity of the foundations upon which it is based.

His views were prophetic, the civil war, so near at hand at this time, proved the truth of his remarks.

The following decisions of the Grand Sire were approved:

A Grand Sire has the constitutional power to restore a Charter, in vacation.

After an Encampment has been regularly opened, members, except the Junior Warden and the candidate for initiation, cannot enter or leave the room before the Encampment is closed, without observing the usual formalities.

Where the Degrees are conferred by a regular Degree Lodge, separate from the Subordinates, the application of the brother desiring the Degree must be acted upon in his Subordinate Lodge, by such members only, as have taken the Degree applied for. If the application is granted, a Certificate of the fact is given to the applicant, which Certificate being presented to the Degree Lodge, authorizes it to confer the Degree.

Subordinate Encampments may, with the consent of their Grand Encampments, (and where there is no Grand Encampment, then with the consent of the Grand Lodge of the United States), hold but one meeting per month instead of two, but if the number of meetings be thus reduced, the official term of the officers should be extended to twelve months, as provided by law.

It is not within the power of a Grand Patriarch to authorize the removal of a Subordinate Encampment from one town or city to another.

The Grand Sire cannot authorize a Grand Body to do anything in violation of its organic law.

It is not competent for a Subordinate Encampment or Lodge to insert, in its Constitution, a provision that a member who may draw a Final Card shall have the privilege of depositing the same in said Lodge, within a *specified time*, by a simple vote of the Lodge, instead of a ballot vote, as in the case of initiating members.

The Grand Secretary, in his report, said:

At the present session there will be but two complete sets of the entire Journal of the Grand Lodge of the United States available for use, and about one dozen copies of the Digest. Under these circumstances, it is worthy the deliberation of the Grand Lodge, whether some means should not be devised for preserving this valuable work, and keeping up the legislative history and progress of the Order in a permanent, enduring and accessible form. Should the financial condition of the Grand Lodge still interpose an insurmountable

obstacle to the accomplishment of this measure, it is suggested, very respectfully, that the subject be submitted to the competition of private enterprise,
with the privilege of the use of the stereotype plates, upon such terms as might
be deemed advantageous.   It is indispensably necessary that the work should
be republished, and the continuous legislation of the Body be preserved in
some more enduring form than the pamphlet edition known as the Revised
Journal.

Upon a review of the operations of our beloved Order during the past
year, in the vast field of labor which employs its energies, there is the most
abundant cause for the outpouring of gratitude to Almighty God for the continued favor which he vouchsafes to our ministrations, not the less signally displayed by the great prosperity which crowns our institutions in behalf of
humanity, than in that profound spirit of peace and harmony which charac-
terizes the internal government of the Order in all its details, and hallows the
relation of brotherhood which binds us together.

The financial condition of the Grand Lodge had slightly
improved during the past year.   The total receipts amounted
to \$18,082.90; profit on the sale of supplies, \$8,935.03.
The receipts for the Wildey Annuity Fund were \$220.

The following amounts were paid by Subordinate
Lodges: For relief of brothers, \$349,698.35 ; for relief of
widowed families, \$62,342.79 ; for education of orphans, \$12,-
682.07 ; for burying the dead, \$55,016.06.

The Grand Lodge visited " The Hermitage," (the tomb
of ex-President Jackson,) where a Hickory Arm Chair was
presented by Dr. J. M. Lawrence, the custodian of the
grounds.   The Grand Lodge adopted the following :

Resolved, That the Hickory Arm Chair, presented through the Grand Sire
be accepted, and that the Grand Corresponding and Recording Secretary
be instructed to have the following inscription placed, in permanent form,
on the chair: "Presented at The Hermitage to the Grand Lodge of the
United States, I. O. O. F., by Grand Representative H. K. Walker, of
Tennessee, on behalf of Dr. John Marshall Lawrence, a member of the
family of the late Andrew Jackson, who constructed the chair with hickory
withes grown upon the Hermitage estate.   Nashville, September 20th, 1860."
(See Journal, pages 3263, 3272, 3316.)

The chair, with the above inscription on a silver plate is
at present in the Grand Secretary's office in Columbus,
Ohio.

It was enacted that :

The presiding Noble Grand of a Subordinate Lodge has no right to sign
an annual or semi-annual report returning himself as a Past Grand, he not
having previously passed the Noble Grand's chair.   The return is to be made

of the proceedings of the term *then* expiring, and must be signed by the officers in the capacity they then fill. In a separate schedule a return is made of the officers elect. These latter officers cannot be installed until such returns have been dispatched, and until this be done, the officer who signs the return thus forwarded, is Noble Grand, and not Past Grand.

The Certificate of either the Recording Secretary, or the Permanent, or Financial Secretary of a Subordinate Lodge, under the Seal of the Lodge, is sufficient evidence for Encampments, to show the standing in the Subordinate Lodge, of members seeking admission into the Encampment Branch of the Order.

An appropriate obituary tablet shall be prepared, and placed in the Journal, upon which shall be recorded, in a fitting manner, the decease of such members and ex-members of this Grand Lodge, as shall be announced at each session of this Body. Such record upon the obituary tablet, shall be in lieu of resolutions relative to the death of members and ex-members of this Grand Lodge, excepting Past Grand Sires and elective officers.

The resolution adopted by this Grand Lodge, to be found on page 3134 of the annual session of 1859, having reference to the authentication of all Certificates and Cards issued by State Grand Officers, and officers of all Subordinate Lodges and Encampments, shall not be construed to apply to Certificates signed by Grand Officers of State jurisdictions to members of defunct Lodges and Encampments, as heretofore provided.

The Form, adopted by this Grand Lodge, for public Dedication of Halls and Laying Corner-stones shall be published in the appendix to the proceedings of this Grand Lodge, and these Forms, and no other, shall be used by the Order.

The Grand Secretary is authorized to employ a competent person to prepare an entire new index to the Journal, to be published with the new edition of the Journal, authorized at this session.

Officers of Subordinate Lodges may confer the Degree of Rebekah upon the widows of deceased Odd Fellows, who were in good standing at the time of death, after application in open Lodge.

Any propositions offered for reference to any Standing Committee of this Body, which shall require an entry in full upon the Journal, shall be submitted in duplicate, either in print or manuscript ; and if in writing, they shall be on paper not less in size than half a page of foolscap. (This is now Rule of Order, 44).

This Grand Lodge hereby express the great pleasure derived from our visit to Mrs. James K. Polk, and tender that estimable lady our unfeigned thanks for her very elegant, courteous and hospitable reception. (Pending the question upon the resolution, Representative Walker, of Tennessee, said : "Most Worthy Grand Sire : On behalf of Mrs. Polk, I am requested to return her sincere thanks to the members of this Lodge, for what she is pleased to consider, the distinguished honor paid her by them in their visit to her mansion this morning, and to assure them that she will cherish the recollection of the event as one of the pleasantest and most agreeable of her life.")

The thanks of this Grand Lodge are due, and they are hereby tendered to R. W. Deputy Grand Sire Fitzhugh, for the very able, courteous, dignified and impartial manner in which he has discharged the unusually arduous duties of Grand Sire during the present session. In consideration of these services, and of the services heretofore rendered this Grand Lodge, in all the departments of duty which he has been called upon to discharge and fill, the Grand Lodge recognize a debt of obligation which they propose, in part, to discharge, by tendering this acknowledgment, and the additional request that he consent to sit for his portrait to embellish our Grand Lodge, and that an engraved likeness be made, to be inserted in the bound Journal, and that the Grand Secretary have the same carried into effect.

The following Past Grand Sires were present during the session and participated in the deliberations of the Grand Body: Thomas Wildey, of Maryland, Grand Sire from 1825 to 1833; John A. Kennedy, of New York, Grand Sire in 1841 and 1842; Geo. W. Race, of Louisiana, Grand Sire in 1857 and 1858.

The following Grand Officers were elected and installed: Robert B. Boylston, P. G., of South Carolina, Grand Sire; Milton Herndon, P. G. M., of Indiana, Deputy Grand Sire; James L. Ridgely, P. G. M., of Maryland, Grand Corresponding and Recording Secretary; Joshua Vansant, P. G. M., of Maryland, Grand Treasurer.

The following were appointed by the Grand Sire: Rev. E. M. P. Wells, P. G. M., of Massachusetts, Grand Chaplain; E. D. Farnsworth, P. G. M., of Tennessee, Grand Marshal; Solomon H. Lewyt, P. G., of Maryland, Grand Guardian; John E. Chamberlain, P. G., of Maryland, Grand Messenger.

1861.

The Grand Lodge met in annual session, in the City of Baltimore, on the 16th of September.

Six officers and sixty-six Representatives were present. The thirty seats allotted to the Representatives from Tennessee, Virginia, Mississippi, North Carolina, Texas, South Carolina, Florida, Arkansas, Alabama, Louisiana and Georgia were vacant. In the absence of Grand Sire Boylston, of South Carolina, Deputy Grand Sire Herndon, of Indiana, presided. He addressed the Grand Lodge as follows :

Representatives and Brothers : The circumstances that surround us at this time are unparalleled in our history. Heretofore, the Representatives of our beloved Order have annually convened, always under the most favorable auspices. Heretofore, Representatives when they met, uniformly congratulated each other upon the great success and growth of Odd Fellowship.

What a terrible change a few months have wrought! Civil war with all its attendant evils has been inaugurated in our once happy country. While we act the part of good citizens we may pour oil upon the troubled waters, and alleviate, in some degree, the suffering incident to this unnatural strife.

It will not be expected that I should give a detailed statement of the workings of our Order ; or that I should speak of the financial condition of the Grand Lodge. The unhappy condition of the country, the utter impossibility of corresponding with all the jurisdictions, coupled with the fact that another should have presided over your deliberations, and made to you a report in due form, preclude me from doing so. For a statement of the condition of our Order, financially and otherwise, I refer you to the reports of the R. W. Grand Corresponding and Recording Secretary, and the R. W. Grand Treasurer. Nor will I presume to make any suggestions as to the steps which should be taken by this Grand Lodge in view of the distracted condition of the country. Grave questions must arise, requiring much and serious consideration, and your known devotion to the principles of Odd Fellowship is a sufficient guaranty that you will give them that thought and deliberation which their importance demand, having a due regard to the perpetuity of our organization, and its cherished principles.

In conclusion, permit me to express the hope that your deliberations may be characterized by that dignity and decorum which the great and important trusts confided to your care seem to demand. And may He who holds in His hands the destinies of all human institutions, aid you to come to correct conclusions, and smile upon every well directed effort to ameliorate the condition of our race.

The Grand Secretary, in his report, said :

In presenting to the Grand Lodge the usual summary of the condition and progress of the Order, the Corresponding Secretary has to regret the paucity of material at hand out of which to construct his report. From the jurisdictions south and southwest of Maryland, no annual returns have been received, and but little correspondence has been had in that direction during the past year ; the reason for which state of things is well known to the Grand Representatives, and it is therefore unnecessary to make any special reference to that subject. From such material, however, as is within my reach, I present a general statement of the condition of the Order in the entire jurisdiction.

The ordinary plan of shifting the deficiency of one year to the next by borrowing, in anticipation of accruing receipts, is now wholly impracticable, and the assessment of new taxes on the Order, in any form, could not, at this time, for a moment be considered. Upon the causes of the falling off of the revenue, it is unnecessary to dwell, but I may be permitted to say that the Grand Lodge may congratulate itself, when it surveys the general prostration and wreck which prevail, that it is in the power of the Representatives at so small a sacrifice, (a reduction of the rate of mileage from five to three cents,) to sustain its credit, not only by the prompt payment of the current debt of the year, but by freeing it entirely from a continuous deficit, which it has been carrying forward, from session to session, for several years. * * Upon a review of the condition of the Order, presented by the reports from various jurisdictions, the heart is gladdened that amid the terrible scenes which now pervade the land, its glorious mission of mercy, blessed and prospered of God, has been unchecked, and its great office of benefaction to man continues to be exerted with an eye single to its high calling—yet, in the midst of our gratulations and thanksgiving to a beneficent Providence for the especial favor vouchsafed to our Order, we have not escaped the withering influences inseparable, in the nature of things, from so all permeating a calamity as that which now afflicts our country.

The Grand Secretary retained the services of Edward H. Fitzhugh, Past Deputy Grand Sire, to prepare an entire new index to the Journal. It was not completed at this session, the work was subsequently done by Representative Ellis, of Maryland.

The Order in Canada West was reported to be in a gratifying condition. Union Encampment, No. 1, at St. Catherine's was instituted. In the Lower Provinces the good work was progressing favorably. The success of the Order in California was reported as phenomenal. The invested capital of the Lodges in this young jurisdiction, amounted to over $300,000. There was an active membership of nearly six thousand, distributed among one hundred and one Lodges. Reports for the year ending June 30th, 1861, were not received from Virginia, South Carolina, Georgia, North Carolina, Mississippi, Louisiana, Alabama, Texas, Tennessee, Arkansas and Florida.

The total receipts of the Grand Lodge for the past year were $10,590,11. The profit on the sale of supplies was $4,887.85.

The following amounts were paid by the Subordinate Lodges: For relief of brothers, $257,902.48; for relief of widowed families, $60,815.29; for education of orphans, $94,707.23; for burying the dead, $56,660.61.

The amounts paid out by Subordinate Encampments were: For relief of members, $31,448.79; for relief of widowed families, $3,177.58; for education of orphans, $160; for burying the dead, $5,601.47.

These amounts would have been much greater had reports been received from all the jurisdictions.

Owing to the illness of Grand Secretary Ridgely, the Grand Sire appointed Representative Lucius A. Thomas, of Connecticut, Grand Secretary, *pro tem.*

The following legislation was enacted:

A brother who has been suspended for non-payment of dues in a Lodge which has, since his suspension, surrendered its Charter, may be admitted to membership in a Lodge upon such terms, and upon such evidence, as the proper State, Territorial or District Grand Lodge may, by law, prescribe.

The Territory of Nevada be and the same is hereby attached to the jurisdiction of the Grand Lodge of California.

Should circumstances justify the Grand Secretary, and if in his opinion the safety and security of the archives and books of the Grand Lodge may require it, he is authorized to remove the same to Philadelphia or New York, and in the event of an interruption of the meeting in Baltimore in 1862, the Deputy Grand Sire is authorized to convene the Grand Lodge at some central and convenient place.

Rep. Escavaille, of Maryland, offered the following preamble and resolutions, which were adopted:

WHEREAS, The very spirit of Odd Fellowship, the life it breathes over all the world, the profession it makes everywhere, and at all times recognizes but one nation—the earth; but one family—the race of man. This is one of its boasts—one pillar of its strength; and *whereas*, its universal adaptation to the wants of man appears in the demonstration that its principles are inspired, its doctrines divine; and *whereas*, the trouble, discord and faction, that so often and so fiercely prevail in and between the various associations of the day, enter not the portals of Odd Fellowship; and *whereas*, the bickerings, the jealousies, the strifes for place and power, the spirit of aggrandizement, the thoughts of self, the contests of sections and of party, which pervade society, embitter friendships, and occasionally even desecrate the sanctuary, have cast no shadow within our Lodges; and *whereas*, to cement more strongly the ties that bind us together, and to renew our vows and devotions upon the sacred altar of Odd Fellowship; be it

Resolved, That the perpetuity of Odd Fellowship, and its beneficial influence, can only be maintained and exercised by a rigid adherence to its Ritual and fundamental laws.

That the members of this Grand Lodge will employ every means, and will endeavor to impress upon the minds of their constituents, the necessity of so doing, to cultivate and practice those sentiments and principles, which will be best calculated to preserve our beloved Order intact, wherever its benign influence has spread, wherever the banner of Odd Fellowship has been unfurled.

That it is the duty of every good Odd Fellow, at all times, so to act, and so to speak, that his words and deeds may give no just cause of offense to those whom circumstances have, for the time being, cut off from friendly and social intercourse with us.

That this Grand Lodge hopes, and will continue to hope, that the trying difficulties now existing, and which have shaken our common country to its very foundation, causing distrust and estrangement between brothers and friends, may be speedily and amicably settled, and that the storm which is now raging in the hearts of the people of this once peaceful and happy land, may be assuaged, and the clouds which have darkened the hopes and blighted the prospects of a whole nation, may be swept away, giving place to a cloudless sky, a bright and genial sunshine, shedding peace, harmony and joy over and throughout this widespread land.

The session was attended by Past Grand Sires Thomas Wildey, of Maryland, (his last appearance in the Grand Lodge of the United States), and John A. Kennedy, of New York.

1862.

The Grand Lodge met in annual session, in the City of Baltimore, on the 15th of September, with six officers and sixty Representatives present.

Deputy Grand Sire Herndon, in his report, said:

On entering upon the responsible duties intrusted to us, our first obligation and heartfelt gratitude are due to the God whom we all worship, and from whom cometh every good and perfect gift. Although our beloved country has been distracted by fratricidal strife, and the blood-red cloud of war still darkens our horizon, yet, as an Order, we have been signally favored in the last year throughout the jurisdictions from which reports have been received. Absorbing as have been the troubles in the land, our brotherhood have not been unmindful of the leading office in our affiliation—our sick have been visited, the distressed relieved, orphans educated, and our dead buried ; and there has been no abatement in the efforts of past years to propagate a knowledge and inspire the practice of the more intrinsic virtues of our beloved Order. Besides the special favors bestowed upon our peculiar labors, as a people we have been blessed with general health, and an abundant harvest has rewarded the toil of the husbandman, which alike demand, and should receive, the acknowledgment of our hearts.

Of the unhappy condition of our beloved country it will not be considered expedient that I speak in this report ; but I may be permitted to express the hope that the gentle influences of peace will soon be vouchsafed us, and the period of which prophets have spoken and poets have sung is not far distant, when "the God of Jacob shall judge among the people and rebuke strong nations ; and they shall beat their swords into ploughshares and their spears into pruning hooks ; nation shall not lift up a sword against nation, neither shall they learn war any more."

He announced the death of Past Grand Sire Thomas Wildey, who died in Baltimore, on the 19th day of October, 1861, in the eightieth year of his age, and also the death of Past Grand Sire Horn R. Kneass, who died in Philadelphia, December 12th, 1861.

Bro. T. Rogers Johnson, Grand Secretary of the Jurisdiction of California, was commissioned to proceed to Australia, or send a suitable brother, and ascertain the condition of Odd Fellowship there, and if found favorable, to institute the Order in that far off land as an independent jurisdiction.

The following decisions of the Deputy Grand Sire were approved :

The functions of the Grand Master and Grand Patriarch are separate and distinct, not co-ordinate, and the good standing of a Lodge, and its members therein, are absolutely essential to maintain like good standing in an Encampment.

The Grand Patriarch, whose province it is to appoint District Deputy Grand Patriarchs to install the officers of a Subordinate, is responsible to the Grand Encampment if he tolerates, or recognizes as right, an illegal act of his Deputy or of a Subordinate. The Grand Scribe must recognize as legal, all officers of Subordinates officially reported to him, until all doubts about the matter shall have been settled by the Grand Encampment.

The Grand Master, or Grand Patriarch, has the power to suspend a Subordinate for any act of insubordination. Said suspension, however, is but temporary, until the meeting of the Grand Body, which must try the case.

When the Constitution and By-Laws of a Subordinate conflict with the laws and decisions of the State Grand Lodge, or of the Grand Lodge of the United States, the laws of the latter Bodies must be conformed to.

The Grand Secretary, in his report, said :

It is a source of great pleasure to the undersigned, to present so gratifying an exhibit of the finances of the Lodge, especially in view of the fact that, at the last session, on account of a deficit, it became necessary to retrench expenditures, when the Representatives magnanimously voted a sufficient reduction of their mileage to meet the emergency.

We have occasion to be grateful to a beneficent Providence, that He has, in a great measure, kept our beloved Order aloof from the troubles and excitements which have, more or less, disturbed many of the associated organizations in the country. This blessing is the fruit of a faithful adherence to the principles of our Order, which sternly ignore all extraneous influences and command an undivided heart in the cause of human benefaction. Let us continue to labor with an eye single and steady to our sacred mission, turning neither to the right nor to the left, and the same Providence which hath hitherto so signally prospered our Order, will deliver it from all peril.

The receipts of the Grand Lodge for the past year were $10,642.65; profit on the sale of supplies, $3,879.97.

The following sums were expended by the Subordinate Lodges: For relief of brothers, $239,973.74; for relief of widowed families, $51,729.21; for education of orphans, $8,524.64; for burying the dead, $55,132.36.

The Subordinate Encampments expended: For the relief of Patriarchs, $29,293.82; for relief of widowed families, $1,875.50; for burying the dead, $4,764.07.

The following letter was received by the Grand Secretary during the session of the Grand Lodge and accepted by the Body with great gratification:

I. O. O. F.

OFFICE OF THE M. W. GRAND MASTER OF THE R. W. GRAND LODGE OF VIRGINIA.

NORFOLK, September 17, 1862.

James L. Ridgely, Esq., Grand Secretary :
 DEAR SIR AND BROTHER :
 Permit me to remind you that our mail facilities are open between us, notwithstanding the difficulties of this causeless war, and it will afford me much pleasure to receive your daily printed proceedings.
 I am, dear sir, yours respectfully,
 A. L. HILL, *Grand Master.*

All the jurisdictions were represented except South Carolina, North Carolina, Louisiana, Virginia, Alabama, Vermont, Georgia, Tennessee, Mississippi, Texas, Florida and Arkansas.

The Grand Secretary was directed to send to the absent Representatives of Grand Bodies, the same number of copies of the proceedings of the Grand Lodge, and other documents, as were furnished to the Representatives present.

The following report was adopted:

The Special Committee to whom was referred so much of the Report of the Grand Sire as relates to the death of Past Grand Sire Wildey, ask leave to report that they have had that subject under consideration, and respectfully submit to the judgment of the Grand Lodge the following memorial :

When, in the providence of God, we are called upon to mourn the loss of one who, after a long pilgrimage and an eventful career in life, has sunk at last into his rest, it is eminently proper that we pause to contemplate the scene thus presenting itself to our consideration, to commemorate the virtues of the departed Patriarch, and to give expression to those peculiar emotions which such an event is calculated to inspire.

The Grand Lodge of the United States, of the Independent Order of Odd Fellows, having assembled in annual communication for the transaction of business appertaining to the great cause of human brotherhood, is met, at the threshold of its duties, by the official announcement of the death of that distinguished Patriarch and Founder of the Order in America, Past Grand Sire Thomas Wildey, of Baltimore.

This solemn and affecting dispensation, while it calls upon us to humble ourselves before that Great Being who is too wise to err, too just to do wrong, too good to be unkind, imposes upon this Grand Body a duty which may not be postponed, and which demands the earliest attention of the Grand Officers and Grand Representatives now assembled, in placing upon the records of the Grand Lodge, an appropriate and becoming tribute to the memory of the distinguished dead.

To the world at large, proud of its attainments in science and art, and absorbed by its untiring exertions after wealth and distinction, Past Grand Sire Wildey may have been a plain old man ; unlettered, untitled, unpretending, and almost unknown ; but to his children, the tens of thousands of Odd Fellows scattered over the vast Territory covered by THE JURISDICTION OF THIS GRAND LODGE, HE WAS A GREAT AND GOOD MAN.

"Great, not like Cæsar stained with blood," but great in the accomplishment of great good ; in the building up of one of the most magnificent charities the world has ever known—practical, comprehensive, and far-reaching in its influence ; having its foundation laid in the best feelings of the heart, and its superstructure continually progressing in the development of those higher and nobler qualities of the soul that ally man to his God ; a charity that seeks not alone the relief of those distresses that are incident to humanity, but aims also at the elevation of the character of man, and labors to imbue him with just conceptions of his capabilities for good ; to enlarge the sphere of his affections, to still the storm and soothe the spirit of passion, and to bring into subjection to the higher purposes of his being all those powers and capacities "which it has pleased an all-wise Providence to confer upon him."

Standing at the grave of our departed Grand Sire, and reviewing the past while we contemplate the future of this great charity, we are constrained to ask, Who was Thomas Wildey and what the part he has borne in this vast scheme of benevolence and love ? And the answer comes back to us in the language of one of Maryland's most eloquent advocates as applied to a bad man and a bad cause : "He was its author, its projector, its active executor ; bold, ardent, faithful, and untiring—his brain conceived it, his hand brought it into action."

Beginning his labors in this, the city of his choice, and devoting to the accomplishment of his great purpose the activity and energy of his earlier manhood, no obstacle discouraged, no temporary failure defeated him. Regarding with equal indifference "the world's dread frown" or "its scornful smile," and armed with that faith in the success of his mission which conscious rectitude of purpose inspired, he recrossed the ocean to the land of his nativity in search of material aid in his great enterprise, and returned in triumph to the land of his adoption, bearing with him, not only the power and authority he sought, but the prayers and benedictions of the brotherhood beyond the waves.

Such energy in the prosecution of his purpose, such zeal in the success of the cause he had espoused, it was impossible should escape the attentive criticism of an observing and progressive people. The practical effect was to bring to his aid, in the cause of human benefaction, the energies and activities of other and perhaps more cultivated minds, and in a few years we find the peaceful banner of Odd Fellowship floating in triumph over a territory broader even than our national domain, and gathering beneath its folds a brotherhood of hearts which no political distinctions, no national prejudices, have yet been able entirely to separate.

True it is, that in consequence of the disturbed condition of the country, fraternal intercourse between different sections of this jurisdiction is for a season suspended ; but we are proud in the anticipation that when a return of better days comes—as come they must, we fondly hope—it will be found that the spirit and offices of Odd Fellowship have borne no insignificant part in the restoration of peace and unity to our now distracted land.

But here we pause to inquire, Did Past Grand Sire Wildey, under the weight of years, grow weary of his labor and suffer his zeal for the success of Odd Fellowship to languish and die? Did he, like too many of his followers, having enjoyed all the honors and emoluments of the Order, forsake its altars and abandon its temples, to seek distinction in other fields of more ambitious enterprise? We answer emphatically, he did not, but, yielding to the impulses which ever actuated him, he undertook and accomplished long journeys, in the feebleness of age, to mingle his sympathies with the brethren of other and distant jurisdictions. Clinging with the tenacity of early love to the pillars of the great temple he had reared, he watched with affectionate solicitude over its developing beauty, and grandeur, to the latest hour of his life, and although the words may not, in fact, have fallen from his lips, yet, as the ruling passion is always strong in death, we are warranted in the assumption that the earnest desire of his heart, in the last moments of expiring nature, is best and fully expressed in the Apostolic injunction, so touching in its simplicity, so comprehensive in its beauty :

"My little children, love one another."

Venerating the memory of our departed Grand Sire, and emulating the virtues which he, in his long and eventful pilgrimage, illustrated, we, the Grand Officers and Grand Representatives, in the Grand Lodge of the United States assembled, hereby solemnly renew upon the altar of Odd Fellowship, all the vows we have hitherto taken, mutually pledging to each other, and to the Grand Jurisdictions we respectively represent, the best energies of the remnant of our days to the cause in which we are engaged.

AND WHEREAS, The Grand Lodge of Maryland has kindly tendered to this Grand Body an invitation to be present at the delivery of a eulogy upon the life and character of the deceased, by our distinguished brother, Past Grand Master James L. Ridgely, and the Grand Lodge has already accepted the invitation and resolved to attend the contemplated ceremonies :

Resolved, That the Most Worthy Grand Sire be requested to solicit a copy of the proposed eulogy, when delivered, for the purpose of having the same spread upon the Journal of this Grand Lodge.

The following proceeding of the Grand Lodge of Maryland was referred to a Special Commitee of one Representative from each jurisdiction represented :

The Grand Representatives of this Grand Lodge in the Grand Lodge of the United States, be and they are hereby instructed, to bring before that Grand Body, at its next annual session, the fitness, propriety and justice of the erection of such a monument to the memory of Past Grand Sire Wildey, as shall be alike worthy of his eminent character, as the Father and Founder of American Odd Fellowship, and becoming the supreme legislative head of the Order, over whose deliberations he so long and ably presided ; and, in further-ance of this object, that the co-operation of all sister jurisdictions be invited, to the end that the offering may be the spontaneous and united tribute of the brotherhood at large.

This initial step resulted in the erection of the present monument in Broadway, in the City of Baltimore.

The following report was adopted:

The committee to whom was referred the official announcement of the death of Past Grand Sire Horn R. Kneass, of Pennsylvania, respectfully beg leave to report, that this Grand Lodge has heard with deep regret of the loss which the brotherhood has sustained in the decease of this worthy and dis-tinguished brother.

Past Grand Sire Horn R. Kneass was a man whom to know was to love ; courteous in his manners, refined and dignified in his deportment, his suavity, and sensibility to the kindly intercourse of our fraternity, won the hearts and commanded the respect of all who approached him. His intellectual acquire-ments were of a high order, and were fully evinced during his administration of the executive duties of the principal chair in this R. W. Grand Body. His history as an Odd Fellow, is written in the Journals of the Order, whilst his memory will be cherished by the members of the Grand Lodge, and by the brethren of the Order, among whom his life was spent, and who have profited by his example.

The committee respectfully submit the following for the consideration of the Grand Lodge :

Resolved, That this Grand Lodge entertains a kindly and grateful recollection of the valuable services rendered to the Order by Past Grand Sire Horn R. Kneass, and directs that the foregoing be entered upon the Journal, as a tribute of respect for his memory.

The following were adopted :

Grand Bodies, whose territorial jurisdiction is contiguous or adjacent, are hereby empowered to pass laws, permitting Encampments and Lodges in other jurisdictions, to initiate or admit to membership, persons whose residence, though not actually in said jurisdiction, is nearest to the place of location of such Encampment or Lodge.

A brother should be in possession of the A. T. P. W. when depositing a Withdrawal Card in a Lodge, in order to acquire membership therein. Lodges when giving Withdrawal Cards to members, should therefore impart to them the A. T. P. W., which it is the duty of the brothers to remember. Should they fail to do so, or should the officers of the Lodge have neglected their duty, or should the Card be an expired one, the brother may be admitted to membership as an Ancient Odd Fellow.

All term reports which may hereafter be made to Grand Bodies, by their Subordinates, shall contain, in their own handwriting, the signatures of the elective officers thereof, and shall be carefully preserved by the Grand Scribes and Grand Secretaries.

Grand Scribes and Grand Secretaries are hereby prohibited from delivering, or transmitting Visiting or Withdrawal Cards, to any person whatever, or to any Encampment or Lodge, excepting upon the order in writing, of an Encampment or Lodge, signed by its Scribe, or Secretary, as the case may be, and authenticated by the official Seal of the Encampment or Lodge.

The Grand Secretary is requested, after each session, to insert at the end of the Journal of Proceedings of the Grand Lodge, in the form of an appendix, all resolutions which properly come under the denomination of " *Standing Resolutions,*" so that the same be readily accessible, when reference thereto is desired.

All Grand Bodies are hereby empowered to pass such laws, as to them may seem expedient, changing the commencement and ending of the terms of their Subordinates, so that the same may commence and end with October and April instead of July and January.

Should circumstances justify the Grand Secretary, and if in his opinion the safety and security of the archives and books of the Grand Lodge may require it, he is authorized to remove the same to Philadelphia or New York.

In the event of a probable interruption of the meeting of this Body in 1863, the M. W. Grand Sire is authorized to convene the Grand Lodge at some central and convenient place, sufficient notice to be given to the different jurisdictions.

WHEREAS, The acting, Grand Sire, Brother Herndon, having, during the past two sessions of this Body, presided over its deliberations with credit to himself, and fidelity to the Order, and during the recess of this Body performed the arduous and responsible duties. appertaining to the station of M. W. Grand Sire, therefore,

Resolved, That the thanks of this Body be and are hereby tendered to him, for his faithfulness and devotion to the Order during the past two years, and, as an appreciation of his services, he be requested to sit for his portrait, the same to be placed among the portraits of the Past Grand Sires.

The following Grand Officers were elected and installed:

James B. Nicholson, P. G. M., of Pennsylvania, Grand Sire; William H. Young, P. G. M., of Maryland, Deputy Grand Sire; James L. Ridgely, P. G. M., of Maryland, Grand Corresponding and Recording Secretary; Joshua Vansant, P. G. M., of Maryland, Grand Treasurer.

The following were appointed by the Grand Sire:

Rev. I. D. Williamson, P. G. M., of Ohio, Grand Chaplain; B. W. Dennis, P. G. M., of Michigan, Grand Marshal; Augustus Pfaff, P. G., of Pennsylvania, Grand Guardian; John E. Chamberlain, P. G., of Maryland, Grand Messenger.

1863.

The Grand Lodge met in annual session, in the City of Baltimore, on the 21st of September. The Deputy Grand Sire, on account of severe illness, was absent, but all the other officers and seventy-three Representatives were present. The State of Tennessee, for the first time since 1860, was represented, the full complement (three) being present.

Grand Sire Nicholson, in his report, said:

Grand Representatives: The first duty of Odd Fellows has been appropriately performed by the Worthy Grand Chaplain, in expressing our thanks to Almighty God for His fatherly care over us and our beloved Order during the past year, and in invoking the continuance of His divine favor in the future. We have, amid our sorrow, many causes of thankfulness—to enumerate them would be to recite the history of our lives ; but we feel to-day that there is one crowning joy that, in itself, should cause our souls to swell with gratitude and thanksgiving to God. Our Order still maintains its vantage ground in the cause of humanity. Tried as human institutions seldom are, it still stands comparatively unharmed by the whirlwinds of men's passions that have swept around it. The reports that come up from the different jurisdictions, although naturally showing somewhat diminished numbers, yet exhibit a great brotherhood firmly united for purposes of human benefaction, and carrying out with a zeal and activity never surpassed, the simple yet sublime objects of our fraternity. So conspicuous have been the efforts of the brotherhood in ministering to the wants and soothing the sufferings of others in these calamitous times, that already, in some jurisdictions, has a reaction from the recent depression commenced. Many who have witnessed the kindly ministrations of the Order have sought and obtained admission to our councils. Becoming partakers of our labors, they now rejoice in their affiliation. If we are faithful this will undoubtedly continue, and our ranks will be swollen beyond their former proportions. When the losses and gains of the Order are finally summed up, it will no doubt be found that what at one time seemed to threaten the Order with destruction has, on the contrary, added to its strength, power, and usefulness. The fierce winds have only sent its roots deeper into the soil of the affectionate hearts that have loved and cherished it, and will add to the number of the partakers of its heavenly fruit. Grateful for the past, God guiding us in the present, we can go forth fearlessly into the cloudy future, knowing that success must eventually crown the efforts of those engaged in the cause of God and humanity.

Permit me, Representatives, to congratulate you upon the recurrence of the annual session of the Grand Lodge of the United States. To many of you it is not novel, but none the less delightful, to exchange fraternal greetings with brothers from remote jurisdictions, whom you have met and loved in years gone by. Others clasp here, for the first time, friendly hands that have been separated by rivers, lakes, mountains, and plains. Material agencies have done their work and brought you together. Odd Fellowship unites you at once in affection, interest, and inclination. The lessons that you have learned at your widely scattered and far distant altars, you have brought with you to this common centre, and in a moment, at the first flash of recognition, the teachings of the Order have banished the feeling of strangeness, and you meet as friends and brothers, animated by the same hopes and fears, and having a common object in view, the spread and triumph of Odd Fellowship. I sincerely trust the present annual communication will have the effect of still further strengthening the bonds of our Fraternity—of renewing and increasing the sympathetic ties by which the brothers are held in unity.

Having no policy to define, or course of legislation to recommend, I leave with you, in consonance with our laws, the entire responsibility of the supreme legislature, well satisfied that the power is well placed and will be worthily employed. The wishes and wants of your immediate constituents will doubtless be faithfully represented, and your resolves be equally beneficial and acceptable to the entire brotherhood. Duty requires the submission to your review of my official acts during the past year. Their nature and rarity indicate unmistakably, not only the absence of serious difficulties, but the existence of harmony in the Order, so far as my correspondence can lead to a determinate conclusion.

The following decisions of the Grand Sire were approved:

The Junior Past Grand is not strictly an officer of the Lodge; but it is his duty to occupy the chair of the Past Grand for one term, and deliver the Past

Grand's charge to candidates at initiation. It is therefore improper to elect him to any office in the Lodge.

A Grand Master has no right to take the chair of a Noble Grand to prevent that officer submitting an illegal motion. If the Noble Grand persists, in violation of law and his obligations, it is the duty of the Grand Master to inform the Lodge, that unless it shall require its officers to conform to the law he will proceed against it for insubordination. The official relations of a Grand Master are not with the Noble Grand, but with the Subordinate Lodge itself, in its Lodge capacity.

The Grand Sire has no legal right to authorize a Grand Master to communicate the A. T. P. W. to a brother holding a Withdrawal Card, to enable him to visit a Subordinate Lodge. A Grand Master, or other elective officer of a Grand Lodge may, if properly satisfied, vouch for and introduce a brother holding an unexpired Withdrawal Card, into any Subordinate Lodge in the jurisdiction to which the Grand Officer is attached.

A member in good standing in a Lodge or Encampment may be elected to, and installed into office in the Grand Lodge, or Grand Encampment, to which his Lodge or Encampment is subordinate, although he does not reside in the State in which the Grand Body is located, *provided*, there be no prohibition in the local law.

An Encampment that "works" in the German and English languages may have two sets of Charge Books, one set in each language.

The Grand Secretary, in his report, said :

Under the difficult circumstances in which the business concerns of the country have been involved for the last two years, we have reason to be gratified at the exhibit of our finances.

Upon a review of our annual reports, it will be found that the general condition of the Order is better than at the last annual session.

Since we last met, there has been no substantial change in the condition of our country ; notwithstanding, our Order is still preserved unscathed amid the storm and perils which environ it. How grateful should we be to the Almighty Disposer of human events, that by His mercy and providence we are still clinging to our altars and cherishing our great mission of love. Amid the riot of human passion, Odd Fellowship still lifts its voice of peace and good will among men, feeble though it may be, yet nevertheless persistent and earnest, and, like the oasis of the desert, presenting one green spot upon which men of all opinions may meet and mingle in sacred fellowship.

Let us, brethren, remember, in view of the great blessing vouchsafed to us of perfect freedom from the desolations which prevail, that "in God we trust," and that from Him "proceedeth every good and perfect gift."

The Order in Vermont was reported to be in a feeble condition, while in Canada its success was steady. Satisfactory reports were received from Tennessee, and the Grand Lodge remitted the Representative tax for 1861 and

1862, and authorized supplies to be furnished, free of cost, to its Representatives present, to enable the Subordinates to work.

The total receipts of the Grand Lodge for the past year were $10,040, and the profit on supplies, $3,753.41.

The Subordinate Lodges expended the following sums: For relief of brothers, $268,464.54; for relief of widowed families, $50,849.53; for education of orphans, $8,048.06; for burying the dead, $66,615.88. The Subordinate Encampments expended for relief of Patriarchs, $32,599.30; for relief of widowed families, $2,537.17; for education of orphans, $60.90; for burying the dead, $5,219.90.

The following were adopted:

In all cases of appeal which may hereafter be presented to the Grand Lodge of the United States, the Subordinate Grand Body from whose action any appeal is taken, shall be required to settle definitely all questions of fact in such appeal, and shall duly certify the same, under its Seal, and the signatures of its executive officer and Grand Scribe, or Secretary, as the case may be, so that the sole and only business of this Grand Lodge shall be to determine the law applicable to the facts thus certified.

This Grand Lodge will entertain no appeal unless the facts involved be settled and certified in the manner prescribed in the preceding resolution, by the Grand Body from whose decision or action the appeal is taken.

This Grand Lodge has uniformly adhered to, and recognized, the right and duty of the Subordinate Lodges and Encampments to tax their members, in order that they may be enabled to grant stipulated weekly benefits to sick members.

All proceedings had by Lodges in reference to balloting or conferring Degrees must be recorded in a book kept exclusively for that purpose.

Grand or Subordinate Lodges under the jurisdiction of the Grand Lodge of the United States, be and they are hereby empowered to receive into their membership, by initiation, persons who retain membership in the Manchester Unity of Odd Fellows.

A Noble Grand is permitted to invite a Past Grand to occupy his chair during initiation, or the conferring of Degrees.

Where the books of an extinct Lodge or Encampment have been lost or destroyed, the Grand Master and Grand Secretary, or the Grand Patriarch and Grand Scribe, or the Grand Sire and Grand Corresponding and Recording Secretary, as the case may be, on being satisfied of the good standing of any member of such extinct Lodge or Encampment, may issue to him a Card of Withdrawal, which shall have the same force and effect and shall entitle him to the same privileges as a Card of Withdrawal issued by an existing Subordinate.

If a brother, applying for a Visiting Card, be absent from the location of his Lodge or Encampment, so that he cannot obtain the A. T. P. W., with his Card in person, it shall be the duty of the proper officers, upon the granting of such Card, to transmit the same to the brother, and also send therewith a letter in the following form, to wit :

.... Lodge, (or Encampment), No. ....,

Of ...., State of ....,

.... day of .... , 18

To the Noble Grand of any Lodge of the I. O. O. F.:

(or Chief Patriarch of any Encampment.)

The bearer, Brother (or Patriarch) .... , holding a legal Card from this ...., dated this .... day of .... , 18   for the period of .... months, is entitled to the A. T. P. W., for the current year, which please communicate to him after due examination, whereupon you will retain or destroy this letter.

[SEAL.]   ...., N. Grand (or C. P.)

Attest :   ...., Secretary (or Scribe.)

The Grand Corresponding and Recording Secretary shall forward to the Representatives of Grand Bodies subordinate to this Grand Lodge, who are absent from this session, the same number of copies of the proceedings of this Grand Lodge, and other documents as are furnished to the Representatives of this Grand Body, and shall also furnish the Grand Secretary of each Grand Body not here represented, the same number of copies of proceedings and other documents as are furnished to the Grand Secretaries of those Grand Bodies represented here this day, whenever he shall be satisfied that they will reach safely the persons and Bodies to whom he sent.

The proper construction of the clause of the Constitution, which reads : " Appeals may also be heard from a member or members of a State, District or Territorial Grand Lodge or Grand Encampment from a decision thereof," confines such right of appeal to questions affecting the general interests of the entire Order or to the general interests of the Order in the particular jurisdiction from which the appeal comes, and does not extend it to questions of grievance of individual members or Lodges.

The Grand Lodge authorized the Grand Lodge and Grand Encampment of California to institute Lodges and Encampments in the Colony of British Columbia, on receipt of the proper applications, and the Colony was attached to the jurisdiction of California, *pro tem.*

The State of Oregon and the Territories of Washington and Idaho were attached to the jurisdiction of the Grand Encampment of California, with authority to organize Subordinate Encampments therein. The Territory of Idaho, for the institution and control of Subordinate Lodges therein, was attached to the Grand Lodge of Oregon.

Article XIII., of the By-Laws, was amended by adding :

Provided, however, that any Subordinate Lodge or Encampment working under the immediate jurisdiction of the Grand Lodge of the United States, in any State, District, or Territory, may, at its own request, be made subordinate to any contiguous State Grand Lodge or Grand Encampment.

A committee was appointed to procure a bust of Past Grand Sire Wildey, from the model in possession of Grand Representative Escavaille, or otherwise, and have moulds made therefrom, so that Lodges or members of the Order can procure bronze or plaster copies of the bust, on the payment of such sum as the committee may determine.

1864.

The Grand Lodge met in annual session, in the City of Boston, on the 19th of September.

The Grand Lodge and Grand Encampment of Tennessee were fully represented.

The Grand Lodge of the United States was presented to the Grand Lodge of Massachussetts by William Ellison, Past Grand Sire, after which an address of welcome was made by Grand Master Ford, and responded to by Grand Sire Nicholson. Invitations to visit the Cochituate Water Works, to receptions, etc., were presented and accepted.

The death of Deputy Grand Sire, William H. Young, was announced. He was accidentally killed on the 22d of June, 1864, while on his way to Philadelphia to attend a meeting of the Wildey Monument Committee.

Grand Sire Nicholson, in his report, said :

My heart swells with joy and gratitude as I take a commanding view of the present condition of the Order. No halting nor hesitation in its progress is visible, but firm, confident, and hopeful, it continues to advance with noiseless, yet triumphant steps. A revived interest is being manifested in almost every jurisdiction. In some, large accessions have been made to the membership, more than compensating for heavy, but inevitable losses. The indications everywhere are, that the greatest triumphs that the Order has yet achieved will be eclipsed by those that await us. Like an angel, with love stamped upon its brow, Odd Fellowship daily wins its way to the affections of those who were strangers to its beauty; who listen thenceforth to its heaven-born teachings, and taste of unselfish, ennobling joys. The faith of the brethren is being increased by the daily accumulating evidences of the entire adaptability of Odd Fellowship to all the exigencies of human existence. A future, radiant with promise, seems to be opening before the Order. Years of trial have proved its inestimable value, and it needs but blue skies over our heads, and peaceful valleys beneath our feet, to enable Odd Fellowship to accomplish its great mission of love and benefaction to the human race. Our beloved Order, born in darkness, nurtured in sunshine, rocked amid storms, still lives and flourishes, giving greater reasons than ever before for believing that it will live forever.

The following decisions of the Grand Sire were approved:

The customs and usages of the Order, prohibit the initiation of a person whose physical deformity prevents a compliance with the requirements of the laws of the Order. The decision of the question as to the applicability of the general principle to special cases of partial deformity, rests with the local authorities, and especially with the Subordinate Lodge, to which admission is asked.

Until Cards suited for the purpose are issued by the Grand Lodge of the United States, State, District, or Territorial Grand Lodges may have prepared and issue a Certificate or Card to members of extinct or suspended Subordinate Lodges in their respective jurisdictions, said Certificate to set forth, on its face, the circumstances of the case ; to be signed by the Grand Master, attested by the Grand Secretary, under Seal, and to have the same force and effect as a regular Withdrawal Card.

An "Ancient Odd Fellow," who can satisfactorily establish his claim to be so considered, and can prove himself in the Initiatory Work, is not required to be re-initiated into the Order. His rank or standing in the Lodge to which he may be admitted, will be determined by the Lodge, upon the report of the committee appointed to make the necessary examination.

"One principal purpose to be subserved by the office of Grand Representative being the communication of the A. T. P. W. to the Executive of his respective jurisdiction," before the first day of January following the session of the Grand Lodge of the United States, a State Grand Body has the right to instruct its Grand Representative as to *the mode* by which the A. T. P. W. shall be communicated to the Grand Master or Grand Secretary, whether personally or otherwise, due regard being had to safety.

A member of an extinct Lodge, who did not regularly withdraw therefrom prior to its extinction, can be admitted to membership *only* upon the presentation of a Card from the officers of the Grand Lodge under which the defunct Lodge formerly existed.

The Grand Secretary, in his report, said:

From every quarter of our vast jurisdiction within the Federal lines, there comes up to the Supreme Grand Lodge a common voice, eloquently sublime, proclaiming in gentle tones, Peace, Harmony, Brotherly Love and Unity predominant, cheering and soul-stirring; the fruit of this Gospel is increased strength and power for good, and its high moral is active incentive to yet nobler efforts in the path of duty. May that incentive awaken a cordial response in the honest heart of every true Odd Fellow, everywhere, and may it nerve his arm with a stalwart purpose " to weary not in well doing ! " It is true that without these lines, this picture, bright as it is with us, has its shade; that there hangs cloud and gloom in the far distance, and that amid the sad and desolating work which has been, and is now enacting, Odd Fellowship has, by the pressure around it, been whelmed beneath conflicting elements; yet, although prostrate and inanimate to the natural eye, it is not dead, it but slumbers; the spirit survives in its shattered but precious casket; the undying principle hath not, will not perish, but will again, when halcyon peace, with healing upon its wing, shall descend in mercy among the children of men, lift its fraternal voice to awaken a kindred and sympathetic pulse in the great heart of the Order. This shade may not, therefore, though deep and sombre and sad as its contemplation now is, detract from the present moral grandeur of our Order, but it lends the more sublimity and eloquence to its mission, in the fact that it illustrates its tenacity of life and its capability of endurance, amid trials and conflicts such as the world has heretofore never known.

Brother Henry Bier, the Grand Secretary of the Grand Lodge of Louisiana, reported the Order flourishing to an unprecedented extent in the City of New Orleans.

No reports were received from Louisiana, Virginia, Mississippi, Texas, South Carolina, Alabama, North Carolina, Georgia, Arkansas, Florida, Lower Provinces and New Mexico.

The total receipts of the Grand Lodge for the past year were $11,738.40; profit on supplies, $4,960.36.

The following amounts were expended by Subordinate Lodges : For relief of brothers, $288,460.95 ; for relief of widowed families, $59,970.81 ; for education of orphans, $3,296.54 ; for burying the dead, $68,485.75. By Subordinate Encampments : For relief of Patriarchs, $32,514.36 ; for relief of widowed families, $2,875.88 ; for education of orphans, $20.45 ; for burying the dead, $6,572.25.

The amount, at this time, subscribed for the Wildey Monument Fund was $12,077.49.

The subject of life membership was considered, but it was deemed inexpedient to legislate thereon.

The appointment of Past Grand Master Steele, as Commissioner for West Virginia, was approved and confirmed.

The principal legislation of this session was as follows:

Any fraudulent misrepresentation of his age, by a party seeking admission into either Branch of this Order, whereby membership therein is illegally obtained, or obtained for a less consideration than the law of the Lodge or Encampment requires, shall discharge the Lodge or Encampment, as the case may be, from any and all responsibilities growing out of the initiation of the party in question, from and after the time such fraud shall be discovered and proved or determined, upon a fair investigation and upon competent testimony.

In the payment of sick and funeral benefits and funeral expenses, the Subordinate Lodges and Encampments are sovereign, both as to the amount of such benefits and in the disposition of the same, so long as the benevolent and charitable features that underlie the institution of Odd Fellowship are complied with, and the enactments of their respective State jurisdictions in that connection are obeyed.

All refreshments in the way of edibles, or beverages (except water), shall be strictly excluded from all Lodge rooms, or ante-rooms, or halls, connected with or adjoining thereto, under the control of any Subordinate, or Degree Lodge, or Encampment of this Order.

No Subordinate Lodge or Encampment of this Order shall hold any anniversary or other celebration, ball or party, where the Regalia of the Order may be worn, or the name of the Order assumed, without the consent of the Grand Master or Grand Patriarch of the jurisdiction first obtained in writing—such permission to be predicated only upon the direct promise, through the officers of the Subordinate seeking the permission, that no intoxicating beverages of any kind shall be offered by them to the members or guests present.

This Grand Lodge does hereby declare all attempts to divert the funds or property of a Lodge or Encampment from the objects and purposes for which they were, in the name of our Order, collected, by dividing or appropriating them to some other object or purpose before breaking up or surrendering its Charter, to be wrong and dishonorable, and in direct violation of the *trust* which they have voluntarily assumed. The funds and property collected under, and by authority of a Charter duly granted to a Lodge or Encampment of the Independent Order of Odd Fellows, are *trust funds*, and can be applied only to the objects for which they were collected, and when a Lodge or Encampment shall fail from any cause to continue as a working Body, and yield up its Charter, the money and property, of whatsoever kind, of which it may be possessed, and belonging thereto, must be surrendered up and paid over to the State Grand Body from which it derived its authority, and no division of the funds or property or other disposition of it, except for the legitimate objects of the Order, can or will be recognized, or tolerated by this Grand Lodge. State Grand Bodies are directed to enact such laws as will most effectually put a stop to all such practices, and affix such penalties to the acts as will prevent any member participating therein, from ever again uniting with the Order, without first making due reparation therefor. When the laws of the Order shall be ineffectual for the purpose, the State Grand Bodies shall be justified in invoking the laws of the country to compel a a surrender of the *trust funds* to the proper parties and objects. All State Grand Bodies, which have not heretofore legislated on this subject, are hereby directed to enact suitable and appropriate laws and regulations for the care of the funds and the property of defunct Lodges and Encampments, which shall thereafter become a separate *trust* or fund, to be employed and used under the direction of such Grand Body or committee duly constituted by them, in aiding and assisting working Lodges and Encampments when in need of funds to sustain them in their organization. For the purpose of enabling Grand Bodies the more effectually to avail themselves of the means to obtain redress in the matter referred to, said Grand Bodies are hereby advised to obtain for themselves legislative acts of incorporation.

The right to print or publish the Lectures, Charges or Odes adopted by the Grand Lodge of the United States for the use of the Grand and Subordinate Bodies under its jurisdiction, or any portion thereof, or any Form of Diploma now used by the Grand Lodge of the United States, is exclusively the property of this Grand Lodge, and any violation of this right by Grand or Subordinate Lodges or individuals is in opposition to the laws, rights, and privileges of this Grand Body.

In any case where an appeal is taken from the decision of any State Grand Lodge, or Grand Encampment, and the Subordinate Grand Body shall fail to settle the question, of fact, or the Executive Officer and Grand Scribe, or Secretary shall neglect or refuse to certify them, as required by the resolution adopted at last session (Journal, pp. 3532, 3533), such neglect or failure to certify, shall be deemed a sufficient reason to reverse the decision of such Grand Body, unless some satisfactory reason shall be given for such neglect or refusal.

A committee was appointed to wait upon the President of the United States, or other proper authority, on the subject of injury done to the halls and other property of the Order by military power.

The following Grand Officers were elected and installed :

Isaac M. Veitch, P. G. M., of Missouri, Grand Sire; James P. Sanders, P. G. M., of Northern New York, Deputy Grand Sire; James L. Ridgely, P. G. M., of Maryland, Grand Corresponding and Recording Secretary; Joshua Vansant, P. G. M., of Maryland, Grand Treasurer.

The following were appointed by the Grand Sire:

Rev. I. D. Williamson, P. G. M., of Ohio, Grand Chaplain; Joseph Kidder, P. G M., of New Hampshire, Grand

Marshal; Augustus Pfaff, P. G., of Pennsylvania, Grand Guardian; John E. Chamberlain, P. G., of Maryland, Grand Messenger.

1865.

The Grand Lodge met in annual session, in the City of Baltimore, on the 18th of September.

The war had then ceased and the Representatives from the Southern jurisdictions returned to the seats that, at every session, had been set apart and designed for them. The eight officers and eighty-seven Representatives were present.

Grand Sire Veitch, in his report, said :

Since the adjournment of your last session the dark cloud of war, which had so long overspread a large portion of our paternal domain, has been dispelled ; the night of gloom has ended ; light has come forth from the womb of morning ; a better and kindlier day has dawned upon humanity ; the apprehension and fear for the safety and stability of our beloved Order have given place to a joyful assurance of its unity, inspiring us with hopes for its perpetuity ; and peace, concord, and love reign triumphant over the whole extent of our field of philanthropic enterprise.   *   *   *   *   It is a source of the highest gratification and rejoicing, that we are permitted to meet again the Representatives of nearly all the jurisdictions, who have been precluded from fellowship and communion with us for the last four years. Their absence from our annual councils we have long deplored and regretted, ever entertaining for them an affectionate regard, which has been heightened and intensified by their sufferings. Our hearts are this day gladdened by their presence, and, acknowledging them as brethren of the same household, we cordially welcome them to the renewal of those relations which unite us in fraternal sympathy, which knows no distinction of country, party or sect, and which seeks to embrace within the scope of its influence the entire family of man.

The following decisions of the Grand Sire were approved :

Where the laws of a Grand Lodge or Grand Encampment provide that a Grand Representative is an elective Grand Officer thereof, he is to be recognized as such, and entitled to the Honors of the Order when visiting a Subordinate officially.

It is the duty of a Subordinate to obey the decisions of its Grand Lodge, which are final and conclusive, until reversed by the Grand Lodge of the United States, upon proper appeal thereto. Pending such appeal, the Subordinate Lodge is not entitled to any privileges other than those accorded to it by its Grand Lodge, which may enforce its decisions by demanding the Charter and effects of the Subordinate, for non-compliance with the decision appealed from.

A number of Subordinate Lodges cannot legally establish a Union Degree of Rebekah Lodge, and hold regular meetings thereof, for conferring and working that Degree.

As it is the duty of a Grand Representative, on his return to his jurisdiction, to instruct his constituent Grand Body in the Work of the Order, a Grand Master or Grand Patriarch is charged with the duty of requiring of Lodges and Encampments, as well as of members, a strict compliance with the instructions received by him from the Grand Representative.

A candidate for membership in the Order, who has been elected in a Lodge where he resides, cannot be initiated in a Lodge located where he may have a temporary residence, upon the request of the Lodge electing him, but all initiations must take place in the Lodge in which the applicant is elected.

The annual reports from the various jurisdictions showed that the membership had largely increased, and the horizon of the future was bright and promising.

On the 26th of April the corner-stone of the Wildey Monument was laid with appropriate ceremonies.

The Grand Sire had issued a proclamation appointing the 20th day of September, 1865, as the time for the reception and dedication of the monument, and directing that a grand National celebration of the Order be held on the occasion. The sum contributed for the monument to this date exceeded $16,600.00.

The procession on the 20th of September, excelled anything of the kind ever before seen in the city, and the event was long remembered with pride and pleasure, by the thousands of spectators, and by those participating in the grand parade.

The President of the United States and his Cabinet were invited to be present at the unveiling of the statue of Charity and the dedication of the Monument.

Numerous invitations were extended to the Grand Lodge to visit theatres and places of interest in the city, amongst them an invitation from Artemus Ward to visit Concordia Opera House and hear his humorous entertainment " Among the Mormons."

Banquets were given to the Grand Lodge by the city corporation and merchants of Baltimore.

An important event of the session was the consideration of the report of the Committee on Finance (page 3,806,

WILDEY MONUMENT, BROADWAY, BALTIMORE, 1865.

Journal) on Tuesday the 19th of September. The resolutions submitted were " that the Grand Lodge of the United States hereby remits the tax of the Grand Lodges and Grand Encampments of Virginia, North Carolina, South Carolina, Georgia, Alabama, Mississippi, Louisiana, Texas, and of the Grand Lodges of Florida, Arkansas and Vermont, for the years 1861, 1862, 1863, 1864," and " that the Grand Secretary be, and hereby is, authorized to furnish, upon reasonable credit to such institutions, whatever supplies he may deem necessary, during the current year." The rule on reports was suspended, and after eloquent addresses by several eminent members of the Order, the report was unanimously adopted. A scene of rejoicing, such as was never before and has never since been witnessed in the Grand Lodge, followed this action. It was a glad reunion of long separated brethren, and tears of joy filled many manly eyes that were unused to weeping. Further business was abandoned, and the Body immediately adjourned.

The Grand Secretary, in his report, said:

Information of the most reliable and soul-stirring character has been presented to you from every jurisdiction within our federation as an Order, without exception ; this fact of itself is unprecedented in our history, and may be regarded as auspicious. Our beloved institution lives, preserved and rescued from the desolation which has sundered and scattered into fragments every other organization of a national character, whether moral, religious or secular. The reports from every quarter, however remote, greet us with messages of love and pledges of unextinguishable devotion to the unity and prosperity of the Order. From the eminent standpoint which it is my province, by your favor, officially to occupy, the field lies as it were before me in perspective ; its surface is dotted all over with colors of varied hue, which vie in interest and attraction ; the scene grows in beauty as it advances upon the delighted vision, diffusing all around an electric glow, until at length the ideal culminates in the real, and the rescued genius of Odd Fellowship, lifting its head above the conflict, looms pre-eminent in the foreground. There it stands, no longer a myth, but the living Temple of Humanity, which, unaided and opposed, our hands builded upon a rock so firm as to assure to it an inherent life and power, which time nor trial hereafter may imperil. There it stands, towering heavenward in grandeur ; the storms have beat about its base, the winds have howled their requiem through its granite fissures and archways ; the tempest ocean of human passion has surged and tossed to its topmost peak ; yet it stands and survives, and will survive. To-day come forth, like a mighty avalanche, her sons from every hill and valley, from every mountain and every plain, from North and South, from East and West, from the uttermost limits of the nation's domain, as pilgrims to her sacred shrine. Here, around her common altar, the scattered tribes re-unite. Upon one broad and comprehensive platform congenial spirits meet, invoked by her divine voice of tolerance, "which gathers within its orbit antagonist natures, controls the elements of discord, stills the storms and soothes the spirit of passion, and directs in harmony man's united efforts to fraternize the world."

Charters were authorized for the Grand Lodge and Grand Encampment of West Virginia, and the Warrants issued during the recess, for Hesperian Encampment, No. 2, Nebraska; Utah Lodge, No. 1, Utah; Greble Lodge, No. 1, Fortress Monroe, Virginia; Liberty Lodge, West Virginia, and Rocky Mountain Lodge, No. 2, Colorado, and the restoration of the Charter of the Grand Encampment of Delaware were confirmed.

The Order in Canada West was reported to be progressing very favorably, while that of the Lower Provinces was not in so prosperous a condition.

Upon the breaking out of the war the Order in New Mexico was wholly disorganized, but on the 14th of June, 1865, Paradise Lodge, No. 2, was revived.

The total receipts of the Grand Lodge for the past year were $19,167.03; profit on supplies, $10,756.43.

The following amounts were expended by the Subordinate Lodges and Encampments, respectively:

	LODGES.	ENCAMPMENTS.
For relief of members	$332,405.02	$36,892.41
For relief of widowed families	74,292.73	3,489.71
For education of orphans	11,695.48	23.40
For burying the dead	83,861.08	7,292.71

Article XVI., Section 4, of the Constitution was amended as follows:

By striking out all after the words "*provided, however,*" and adding: That when it shall be satisfactorily represented to the Grand Lodge of the United States that the necessities of a State, District or Territorial Grand Jurisdiction require it, a resolution may be passed by a vote of three-fourths of the Representatives present at any meeting, granting to the particular State, District or Territorial Grand Jurisdiction applying therefor, the right to readmit to membership within its jurisdiction, upon such terms as it may prescribe, suspended members of the Order residing in the same, who may have been suspended for non-payment of dues, and who have not been under suspension for less than three years; and also the right to admit members of defunct Lodges not able to get a Card, it being distinctly understood that so soon as the necessity requiring it shall have passed away, this privilege shall be yielded up by the jurisdiction receiving it.

Representatives of twenty-eight jurisdictions applied for permission to admit suspended members under the above amendment; but the privilege was refused to all except Kansas.

The following were adopted:

Officers and members of Subordinate Lodges and Encampments, when visiting another Lodge or Encampment in a Body, and introduced by their own officers, are *not* entitled to be received with "the Honors of the Order."

From and after this date, expired Withdrawal Cards may be received on deposit for applications for Charters of Subordinate Lodges; and for Charters for Subordinate Encampments, where the holders of such Cards are contributing members of Subordinate Lodges.

Visiting and Withdrawal Cards heretofore issued by any Southern jurisdiction, countersigned by the Grand Secretary, and attested by the Seal of the Grand Body issuing the same, shall be taken and deemed to be as effectual as if the same had borne the counter-signature, or a *fac-simile* thereof, of the Grand Secretary of the Grand Lodge of the United States.

A brother who has been expelled for non-payment of dues, or crime, from a Lodge which subsequently became extinct, can regain membership in the Order only through the Grand Lodge to which the Lodge he belonged was subordinate; and this rule applies to the Patriarchal Branch of the Order.

Subordinate Lodges and Encampments shall vote by ballot upon all applications for Final Cards, made in accordance with existing laws; and the affirmative vote of a majority of the members present shall be necessary to the granting of such Cards. Should, upon such ballot, a majority of the members present refuse their assent to the granting of a Final Card to an applicant therefor, such applicant, upon the payment of all dues, and tendering a written resignation of his membership, and not being otherwise disqualified, shall be entitled to receive from the Secretary or Scribe, under Seal, a Certificate that he has resigned his membership; and such Certificate shall be sufficient evidence that the brother was in good standing at the time of his resignation, *Provided,* That upon the refusal of a Lodge or Encampment to grant such Withdrawal Card, the member applying for the same shall have the right to appeal to the Grand Lodge or Grand Encampment of his jurisdiction.

In all cases, when privilege is asked to re-admit to membership, members of defunct Lodges, or members suspended for non-payment of dues, under authority of the Constitutional Amendment (Article XVI., Section 4), adopted in reference thereto at this session, the application shall be accompanied by the action had by the Grand Body seeking the privilege, setting forth the reasons and necessity for such legislation, and requesting the action of this Grand Lodge upon the subject.

A bust of Past Grand Sire Thomas Wildey was presented to the Grand Lodge by Brother James Fryer, of Iris Lodge, No. 48, of Baltimore.

Appropriate legislation was enacted for the consolidation of the two Grand Lodges and the two Grand Encampments of New York. The new Grand Lodge was to be known and hailed as " *The Grand Lodge I. O. O. F. of the State of New York*," and the new Grand Encampment as " *The Grand Encampment of Patriarchs of the I. O. O. F. of the State of New York*."

The Grand Sire was directed to issue his proclamation making known the union and consolidation of the above respective Grand Lodges and Grand Encampments.

The following resolutions were unanimously adopted:

Resolved, That in the death of the Most Worthy Past Grand Sire, Robert B. Boylston, of South Carolina, this Grand Body has lost one of its most honored and esteemed members; the nation a valued and patriotic citizen; and Odd Fellowship one of its most devoted, earnest and truthful champions.

Resolved, That the Grand Secretary be, and he is hereby directed, to procure a portrait of Past Grand Sire Boylston from such source as he may be able, and have the same placed in the Hall of this Grand Lodge.

Resolved, That this Grand Lodge deeply sympathize with the bereaved and afflicted wife of our lamented brother, and his orphaned children, in this their night of sadness and gloom; and, while we know how feeble and inadequate our ministrations of consolation must appear to their lacerated spirits, overwhelmed with so great a grief, we would earnestly point to One abundantly able to protect the widow and shield the orphan.

1866.

The Grand Lodge met in annual session, in the City of Baltimore, on the 17th of September.

Grand Sire Veitch, in his report, said:

It affords me pleasure to state, that the general condition of the Order is highly gratifying. At no former period of its history, on this continent, has it exhibited greater vigor and prosperity than at the present time, especially in that portion of the general jurisdiction which was exempt from the depressing effects of the late civil contest, and which has enjoyed uninterrupted fraternal intercourse. The meeting of the Representatives from the various sections of the country, at your last session, after so long a separation, and the cordial and happy reunion of the brotherhood which then took place, gave to the entire Order a fresh impetus, and imparted to it a renewed zeal, which in the main continues unabated.

I avail myself of the occasion to congratulate you, not only upon the elevated condition of prosperity the Order has attained, but also upon the unity which has ever distinguished it amid the discordant elements that have surrounded it on every hand. In contrast with the disorganizing spirit so prevalent in our times, Odd Fellowship has everywhere maintained, by the inherent power of a broad charity, its noble and sublime unity. While nearly every other organization has been sundered by the repelling forces of conflicting interests, our Order has preserved unbroken its organic and national bond of affinity, and is unitedly and faithfully engaged in its great work of benevolence and love.

The following decisions of the Grand Sire were approved :

When the Constitution of a Grand Body designates and fixes the place of its meetings, and that instrument is amended so as to permit the Grand Body to determine by resolution, or otherwise, where its sessions shall be held, such amendment must be approved by the Grand Lodge of the United States, and until approved, the Grand Body must continue to meet at the place required by its Constitution prior to the adoption of the amendment.

The A. T. P. W. required of a brother to prove himself in possession of, when he offers to visit a Subordinate on a Visiting, or unexpired Withdrawal Card, or is an applicant for membership by deposit of a proper Card, is the A. T. P. W. of the year in which the Card was issued and bears date.

The Grand Secretary, in his report, said :

From a candid review of the situation, as deduced from the annual reports received, and the general correspondence of this office, it will be apparent, that as an Order, we owe largely accumulated obligations to the Supreme Disposer of human events ; not only that from the ruin which has rioted as the inseparable effect of war and its train of evil He has graciously rescued the genius of Odd Fellowship, but for the unmistakable prosperity which has crowned its labors during the year now just closed ; for the splendid progress which it has made throughout the vast moral field in which its efforts have been employed ; for the unexampled strength of its national finance ; for the heroism which challenges our admiration and love, with which He has inspired our prostrate brethren in the South, who, gathering up the scattered and desolate fragments, have reconstructed the material, and again uplifted and unfurled the banner of " Peace on earth and good will to men." For these and countless other favors of Heaven, a positive recognition, on our part, of the unerring hand of God, eminently becomes us, and a general thanksgiving, with anthems of praise, should ascend from our altars everywhere " to *Him* from whom all blessings flow."

The Grand Lodges and Grand Encampments of Northern and Southern New York were consolidated during the year, as the Grand Lodge of New York and the Grand Encampment of New York, respectively.

The Grand Lodge and Grand Encampment of West Virginia were organized at the City of Wheeling.

Two Encampments were instituted in Canada West.

The Order in California was very flourishing. The total amount of property belonging to it was, at the date of the last report, $579,963.26.

Warrants were issued, during the recess, for two Subordinate Lodges and six Subordinate Encampments.

The total receipts of the Grand Lodge for the past year, were $27,693.67, and the profit on the sale of supplies $14,911.36.

The following amounts were expended by the Subordinate Lodges and Encampments, respectively:

	LODGES.	ENCAMPMENTS.
For relief of members.........................$364,149.78		$41,587.92
For relief of widowed families.................. 83,086.98		2,465.86
For education of orphans 11,417.75		89.00
For burying the dead......................... 83,592.33		7,533.32

The Grand Sire was directed to appoint a Day of Thanksgiving, to be observed throughout the Order, for the unmistakable prosperity which crowned its labors of the past year.

The following was the important legislation of the session :

No Lodge or Encampment, or any one of the members thereof, shall, in the name of the Order, resort to any scheme of raffles, lotteries or gift enterprises, or schemes of hazard or chance of any kind, as a means to raise funds for any purpose of relief to such Subordinate, or to individual members.

No Lodge or Encampment, shall entertain any application for pecuniary aid or assistance, under whatsoever scheme it may be presented, unless the same be authorized by the Grand Body, or its principal Grand Officer, of the jurisdiction in which such aid is solicited, and in accordance with the form prescribed for such purpose by this Grand Lodge.

The question of the right of any Subordinate to appropriate its funds to pay the expenses of celebrating the Anniversary of the introduction of our Order into America, rests exclusively with the members of said Subordinate.

All acts of incorporation obtained by Subordinate Lodges or Encampments, must be submitted to their several State Grand Bodies for approval before the same can be accepted and acted upon by such Subordinates, and it shall be the duty of such State Grand Bodies to see that such Charters contain no provision inconsistent with the laws of this Order, and that the rights of the property of the State Grand Bodies, and of the said Subordinate Lodges and Encampments, are as fully protected as the legislative proceedings of the several States will permit.

A Card stating the rank of the holder thereof, is not sufficient or conclusive evidence to entitle him to the privilege such rank confers ; he must be proved in the Work of the Degree expressed on the Card. *Provided*, however, if the Card states the holder thereof to be a Past Grand, and he shall not be able to prove himself in the Work of that Degree, from not having received it, the fact set forth in the Card shall be sufficient evidence to entitle him to the privileges such rank confers.

A temporary abeyance from benefits in a Lodge, under the law thereof, and when there has been no action of the Lodge in suspending therefrom, does not work a forfeiture of benefits in an Encampment, when the brother is free from indebtedness therein.

The Grand Sire is authorized and directed to appoint and commission a Special Commissioner to visit the Lower Provinces and Canada East, and said Special Commissioner shall, in the exercise of a sound discretion, have ample and full authority to restore the Charters of extinct Lodges and institute new ones, whenever, in said jurisdiction, a Grand Lodge does not exercise authority, and generally to take such steps and resort to such measures as, in his judgment, will be most likely to revive our Order in those jurisdictions.

In all cases of application for membership in Subordinate Lodges and Encampments *under the immediate jurisdiction* of the Grand Lodge of the United States, three black balls shall be necessary to reject the candidate ; but if the application shall be by Card, a majority only of the members present, on ballot, shall be necessary to elect.

"Satisfactory evidence of former connection with the Order," within the meaning of the law, must come from the Lodge of which the brother was formerly a member, or, in the event of such evidence being inaccessible by reason of its being defunct, or otherwise, then from the Grand Body under whose jurisdiction the Subordinate existed. And should neither of these be accessible or obtainable, then such evidence shall be regulated for each of the State Grand jurisdictions by the Grand Bodies thereof. Should the applicant fail to meet these requirements, he may then make petition for admission into the Order by initiation, as prescribed by existing law.

Hereafter all Grand and Subordinate Lodges and Encampments under the jurisdiction of this Grand Lodge, shall make a summary of the report submitted, in the following form :

Number of members per last report...........................

Initiated during the year..

Admitted by Card during the year.............................

Reinstated during the year.....................................

                    Total...

Expelled.....................................

Withdrawn by Card..................... ....

Suspended.................................... ..

Deceased...

　　　　　Total...................... ....

Now in membership........................ ....
　　The Form of Annual Returns, hereafter printed, shall contain the above addition.
　　All State Grand Bodies shall require their Subordinates to make their returns in a similar manner.

The attention of State Grand Lodges, was again earnestly called to the instructions and laws of the Grand Lodge of the United States in relation to Union Rebekah Degree Lodges, and to the fact that all societies purporting to be connected with the Order, under the name of " Rebekah," in whatever form they might be, could not be countenanced or permitted. It was decided that the Degree could be conferred, or worked, only in open Lodge, with the regular Lodge officers presiding, and any departure from that plan of working in the Degree was irregular and forbidden.

The Grand Secretary was requested to attach the proper name, in large letters, to each portrait in possession of the Grand Lodge.

The Grand Lodge remitted the Representative tax of the Grand Lodges of North Carolina, South Carolina, Arkansas and Florida, and the Grand Encampment of North Carolina, for the year 1865.

It was recommended that a memorial be prepared by the Grand Officers, and laid before the proper authorities at Washington, setting forth the claims of the Order for Lodge property destroyed during the war.

A revised Form of Funeral Procession was adopted.

A Committee, composed of the Grand Sire, the Grand Corresponding and Recording Secretary and three other members of the Grand Lodge, was appointed to prepare a tract or pamphlet, presenting the teachings, principles and operations of the Order.

The benefit of Section 4, Article XVI of the Constitution, as amended in 1865, permitting Grand Bodies to provide for the admission of members suspended for non-payment of dues in other jurisdictions, was given to the jurisdictions of Virginia, Indiana, Michigan, Wisconsin, Tennessee, Iowa, Alabama, California, Oregon, Missouri, West Virginia and South Carolina.

The cost of the Wildey Monument and improvements was reported to be $17,035.02 (Journal, page 4033).

The Grand Lodge directed that a circular be issued, calling upon the jurisdictions not subjected to the ravages of the late civil war, to contribute aid to the Order in the South, and the Body appropriated, for this purpose, $1,000.

The following Grand Officers were elected and installed:

James P. Sanders, Past Deputy Grand Sire, of New York, Grand Sire; E. D. Farnsworth, P. G. M., of Tennessee, Deputy Grand Sire; James L. Ridgely, P. G. M., of Maryland, Grand Corresponding and Recording Secretary; Joshua Vansant, P. G. M., of Maryland, Grand Treasurer.

The following were appointed by the Grand Sire:

Rev. I. D. Williamson, P. G. M., of Ohio, Grand Chaplain; John S. Heiss, P. G., of Pennsylvania, Grand Marshal; John P. Foss, P. D. G. M., of Illinois, Grand Guardian; John E. Chamberlain, P. G., of Maryland, Grand Messenger.

1867.

The Grand Lodge met in annual session, in the City of New York, on the 16th of September.

Seats were drawn for one hundred and ten Representatives.

The Grand Lodge was invited by the Park Commissioners to visit Central Park, and many other invitations were presented.

Grand Sire Sanders, in his report, said:

Representatives: In the discharge of the various duties intrusted to our respective care, we again assemble in annual communication, and, under the careful guardianship of the Great Creator, we meet under auspices of the most cheering and favorable character. The past year has indeed been a fruitful

one to our great family. Throughout our entire jurisdiction have our Lodges
and Encampments prospered and become strong ; the weak have been strengthened, and the strong become more fully developed, in the greatness of our
principles. Peace and tranquility reign triumphant, and we have, more than
ever, especial cause for thanksgiving and praise to the Most High. That
He has watched over us as an Order during the past year, and that so
few of our number have been called hence to be with us no more ; that He has
vouchsafed to us, as an institution, unexampled health and prosperity ; for
these, and the manifold blessings we have received in the past from His
hands, we should acknowledge our obligations with grateful hearts and
cheerful voices, and beseech from Him a continuance of these great favors to
us, not only as individuals, but as members of a great and growing fraternity,
having for our foundation stone the happiness and welfare of the great human
family.

The appeal made to the Order soliciting contributions
for the benefit of our Southern brethren, on September 2d,
1867, amounted to $5,366.42, and it was expected to reach
not less than $12,000.

Fred. D. Stuart, Past Grand Master and Past Grand
Representative, was sent by the Grand Sire, as a Special
Commissioner to the Lower Provinces and Canada East, to
resuscitate defunct Lodges, to institute new ones, to take such
steps and to resort to such measures as would be likely to
revive the Order in those jurisdictions; to enter into correspondence with the officers of the Order under the Manchester Unity, wherever he should find them, for the purpose
of effecting a union of the entire Order of North America
under our authority, etc. Brother Stuart first went to St.
John, N. B., where he was unable to do anything; he then
proceeded to Halifax, thence to Pictou, the home of live Odd
Fellowship, where Eastern Star Lodge, No. 2, was flourishing. The Special Commissioner stated that the brethren in
Nova Scotia not only preached, but practiced to the fullest
extent, the great and ennobling principles of our beloved
Order, and cited some charitable acts to the poor not members of the institution. He attended the Grand Lodge, and
thoroughly instructed the Body in the Secret Work. At this
time there was no Encampment in Nova Scotia, so, having
obtained the requisite number of petitioners, he instituted
Stuart Encampment, at Pictou. One result of his mission

was the appearance of a Representative at the session, the first in four years.

The report of Brother Stuart detailed the result of inquiries concerning the Manchester Unity, and the conclusion reached by him was that a union of the two Orders was not advisable. The document, pages 4108–4117 Journal, is quite lengthy and very interesting.

The following decisions of the Grand Sire were approved:

Public Installations cannot be held, unless the State Grand Body has given consent to its Subordinates to have the same ; and where the Grand Master of the jurisdiction has forbidden the same, the Grand Sire has no power to interfere with his decision.

The Noble Grand of a Lodge has no power to set aside any part of the Constitution of his Lodge. The objectionable section must be repealed, or amended, in the manner provided for in said Constitution, which is binding on him and his Lodge until so repealed or amended.

A Grand Lodge has no right to grant more than *one ballot* and *one reconsideration* of the same, to a candidate for membership in a Subordinate Lodge.

A Grand Lodge has no right to require a residence for any definite period, before a brother can deposit a Withdrawal Card from a sister jurisdiction. A law of such a character is in direct violation of our principles.

The Grand Lodge of the United States, having decided, by its Constitution, the necessary qualifications for membership in the Order, no Grand Body has the right to change the same.

A person who has lost *an arm* is not eligible for membership into the Order by initiation.

The Grand Secretary, in his report, said :

In closing this report, I beg to ask the special attention of the Representatives to the condition of the Order, relatively in the North, East, West, and in the South. On the one hand, in every quarter of the former jurisdictions, the eye rests upon a scene of moral grandeur which justly awakens our delight. A vast brotherhood, inspired by the purest philanthropy, toils in generous rivalry, and wearies not in its conflict for the vindication of a higher and holier humanity among men. With a liberal and generous hand it has scattered its blessings ; not only promptly meeting just demands upon its treasure, but often moving outside of its legitimate sphere to expend its beneficence upon other meritorious subjects, when properly presented. Splendid rewards have, in consequence, crowned its labors, supplying abundant resources for future ministrations, and for the further advancement of the area of its usefulness. On the other hand, how different appears the field of its labor. Our brethren of the South, members of our household, speaking the same common language, worshipping around the same altars, laboring in the same good cause, are cheered and encouraged by no such inspiring scenes. Difficulties of unparalleled magnitude, trials which no other institution could have survived, have comparatively overwhelmed them ; their zeal, although unabated, has been unnerved ; their devotion to the great principles of the Order, although cherished in their innermost heart, is powerless for active effort. They have the will, but, without essential and substantial aid, their progress to recuperation must be slow, if not of doubtful success. Why or how calamity has overtaken them, is not now the inquiry ; a pure and elevated humanity does not pause to analyze or moralize in the presence of misfortune, especially when that misfortune invades the family circle ; rather does it uplift the fallen, and rescue the sinking subject. At the last session the Grand Lodge entered upon this subject with fraternal sympathy and alacrity, and the means devised failed of accomplishment, only by reason of delays and hindrances already fully explained. The necessity has been made the more apparent by the delay which has intervened ; the delay itself has not been prejudicial to the efficient interposition of our good offices, for supplying, as it does, fuller information as to the extent of the need, it presents the opportunity for a larger liberality, and a more deliberate legislation upon the subject. Peace, Concord, Fraternity, are the cardinal elements of our power ; Friendship, Love, Truth, chastened by a high moral culture, the single idea of our great mission. Under this standard, uplifted, its march has been onward, until it has gathered within its ranks the good and the wise in every State, District and Territory of our country, of the adjacent Provinces, and of the Islands contiguous, and will, by the Divine aid, at no distant future, penetrate wherever civilization has found a home on earth.

During the year, the Grand Lodge of Nevada and the Grand Encampment of Kansas were instituted.

Warrants were issued for the institution of one Subordinate Lodge and four Subordinate Encampments.

The total receipts of the Grand Lodge during the year, were $28,547.89. The profit on the sale of supplies was $16,203.90.

The following amounts were paid out by the Subordinate Lodges and Encampments, respectively :

	LODGES.	ENCAMPMENTS.
For relief of members	$410,431.13	$51,035.67.
For relief of widowed families	97,378.68	3,756.20.
For education of orphans	15,863.94	———
For burying the dead	102,688.87	9,568.77.

The principal legislation enacted was the following :

Whenever, in the judgment of a State Grand Body, it may be expedient, it shall be lawful to allow a Lodge or Encampment to be resuscitated upon the application of five of the former members of the Lodge, or seven of the former members of the Encampment, as the case may be, and to give the name, Charter and effects of such defunct Subordinates to such applicants, *Provided*, that the petitioners, at the time of their application, shall not be connected with any other Subordinate Lodge or Encampment.

The right of Subordinate Lodges and Encampments to re-elect their officers, is under the control of the several State, District and Territorial Grand Bodies.

The name of the Grand Lodge of Canada West, be and the same is hereby changed, and that jurisdiction shall hereafter be known and hailed as the " Grand Lodge of Ontario," and the Charter, Constitution and By-Laws of that jurisdiction shall conform to the change of name hereby made.

State Grand Bodies are hereby required to expel from their own membership, and Subordinate Lodges and Encampments to expel from the Order, any member thereof who shall attach to any Chart, Certificate, Diploma, or other document, any copy or impression of the Seal of this Grand Lodge, or of the Seal of any Grand or Subordinate Lodge, of which he has not the official use and custody. The above-named Bodies shall inflict the same penalty upon any member knowingly publishing or circulating any Diploma or Certificate, purporting to be by authority of the Order, which is not authorized by law.

The " Tract " on Odd Fellowship, prepared by the Grand Secretary, entitled " Odd Fellowship—What Is It ? " is hereby adopted.

The 26th of April, be and the same is hereby established as the Anniversary of this Order, and all Grand Lodges and Encampments are requested to urge their Subordinates to observe the day in some appropriate manner.

Grand Encampments have the right to approve the Constitution and By-Laws of a Subordinate Encampment, in which previous service as a High Priest, is made a necessary qualification to eligibility as a candidate for Chief Patriarch.

The Grand Secretary is instructed to forward to each member of this Grand Lodge, ten copies of the Revised Journal. (This is now a *Standing* Resolution.)

The expediency of dispensing entirely with the Charge and Degree Books in Subordinate Lodges, and making the entire Work unwritten, is a subject for the legislation òf State Grand Bodies.

The right of a Past Grand, in good standing, to vote for Grand Officers is an inherent vested right, of which he cannot be deprived.

Article IV., of the By-Laws, was amended by adding to the concluding sentence the following :

Provided, That nothing contained in this article shall operate to prevent the Grand Lodge from entertaining and granting, or instructing the Grand Sire to grant in the recess, the application for a Grand Charter to any less number of Lodges or Encampments, who may regularly petition therefor, and accompany the petition with reasons which shall be deemed satisfactory for such grant by two-thirds of the members of the Grand Lodge at any regular session.

The Grand Sire was requested to issue a Charter for a Grand Lodge in Colorado, whenever a petition in proper form, and accompanied by the proper fee may be presented to him. This action resulted from a memorial, presented by the four Lodges in Colorado, in which they promised to pay the expenses of their Representative to the Grand Lodge, until such time as they may have the regular number of Lodges to entitle them to a Grand Lodge.

It was ordered that on all blank Forms for "Annual Returns," hereafter issued, there shall be printed the following:

INSTRUCTIONS TO GRAND SECRETARIES AND GRAND SCRIBES.

When Subordinates fail to report, you will consider them, in making your report to this Grand Lodge, as returning the same number of members as in their last report.

When a Subordinate is expelled, you will enter the number of members they last reported as "*expelled.*"

When a Subordinate forfeits its Charter, or becomes extinct by failing to report, you will (unless Cards are issued to any of the members by Officers of the Grand Body) enter the number of members last reported as "*suspended.*"

When a Subordinate has its Charter returned, the number of members receiving the Charter are to be entered as "*reinstated,*" unless they hold Withdrawal Cards or Certificates, in which case, all holders of Cards or Certificates are to be entered as "*admitted by Card.*"

When Withdrawal Cards (or Certificates having the same effect) are issued by Officers of Grand Bodies to members of defunct Subordinates, who have been previously entered as "*suspended*" or "*expelled,*" you will enter them as "*reinstated,*" and "*withdrawn by Card.*"

In the first return from a newly organized Grand Body, the number of members in the Subordinates should be entered as "*admitted by Card,*" and the Body to which they were previously attached should enter them as "*withdrawn by Card.*"

All members reported by Subordinates as "*dropped,*" should be entered as "*suspended,*" and those reported as "*resigned*" should be entered as "*withdrawn by Card.*"

The names of those expelled and suspended "*for offense*" should be entered and "*numbered.*"

The particular attention of Grand Secretaries and Grand Scribes; the Secretaries of Subordinate Lodges, and the Scribes of Subordinate Encampments under the jurisdiction of the Grand Lodge of the United States, was directed to the importance of using their best efforts to procure correct reports of the work of Subordinates.

The lithograph portrait of P. G. Sire Wildey, from the chirographic production of Brother R. Morris Swander, of Pennsylvania, containing the eulogy of Grand Corresponding and Recording Secretary James L. Ridgely, and presented to the Grand Lodge, was accepted by the Body, and its thanks cordially tendered to the author for the preparation of such a remarkable work. (The above-mentioned portrait is in the Grand Secretary's office in Columbus, Ohio.)

Preliminary steps were taken on the subject of a change in the name of the Grand Lodge. The following were proposed: "The Grand Lodge of the Independent Order of Odd Fellows," and "The Supreme Lodge."

1868.

The Grand Lodge met in annual session, in the City of Baltimore, on the 21st of September.

Grand Sire Sanders, in his report, said:

The past year has more fully developed our greatness. From nearly every jurisdiction comes up the sounds of rejoicing. Our altars burn brightly, and the incense therefrom is scattered abroad so profusely as to excite the appreciative interest of the good and virtuous, who are compelled to take cognizance of the great benefits resulting to mankind from our united efforts to promulgate our great principles. Acknowledged everywhere as an established Order, our cause has taken deep root in the human heart, and we have but for the future to reap the fruits planted by the early pioneers of our Order. Surely we have great cause for congratulation to ourselves ; and especially should we, at the commencement of our annual session, render devout thanks to the ever living God for the many blessings that we, as an Order, have received at His hands, and beseech Him that His face may not be turned from us. From the reports of the Grand Secretary and Treasurer it will be perceived that never since our existence as an Order, have we received, in one year, so numerous a body of members into our fold. Nor is this increase confined to any particular jurisdiction ; all seem to have enjoyed the fruits of prosperity, and from nearly every jurisdiction comes up the glad sounds of victory. The number of members received the past year into our Subordinate Lodges exceeds forty thousand. Nor should we be ashamed of the men who have been received among us. From numerous visitations made the past few years, I have been forcibly impressed that we are adding such strength to our numbers that they will be felt in time to come. Men who have learnt our principles, who have seen our work in the world, and are convinced that Odd

Fellowship is a reality, and thus being convinced, they have given us the bene-fit of their counsel, help and countenance. The growth is a healthy one, and will, I am sure, endure to the end. The finances of our Order, not only in this Grand Lodge, but in our Subordinates, never were in a better condition. Our treasuries are augmenting, and everywhere, peace and prosperity in our Order are the standing words.

The 26th day of April, 1869, will be the semi-centennial anniversary of our Order in the United States. It would seem necessary and proper that the day should be celebrated rather more than on ordinary occasions, and I trust you may take some action in the premises. Let there be rejoicings wherever a Lodge of the Order can be found. Let the world, as far as possible, know what Odd Fellowship is. If we have faith in our principles, let the people know them, and the result must be good. I believe the time has come when we should proclaim our mission to the world.

The following decisions of the Grand Sire were approved :

The Seal of a Lodge or Encampment is in the official care of the Secretary or Scribe. They have no right to use the same, except as authorized by their Lodge or Encampment, or in the legitimate business of the Lodge or Encamp-ment, where it may be necessary to use the Seal.

A brother in possession of a Traveling or Visiting Card, is not thereby deprived of holding office, or of his rights as a member of his Lodge.

Traveling or Visiting Cards are only intended to be used by a brother when traveling or visiting beyond his State jurisdiction. The A. T. P. W. cannot be used by a brother while visiting a Lodge within his own State, and a N. G. of a Lodge within the same jurisdiction would be justified in refus-ing to admit the brother unless he has the P. W. of the term.

The R. S. of the N. G. temporarily occupying the N. G's. chair has no right to authorize a brother to confer the Term word upon another brother of the same Lodge to enable him to visit other Lodges.

There is no such rule in the Order "as to change the place of trial of the brother." He must be tried in the Lodge or Encampment where he is a mem-ber, and where the charges are preferred. No other Lodge or Encampment has jurisdiction in the matter, except in Subordinate Lodges, under the jurisdiction of State, District or Territorial Grand Lodges, whose By-Laws make provisions for change of venue.

A District D. Grand Sire has no right, by virtue of his office, to take the C. P's chair in an Encampment. He can take such chair only when surrendered to him for installation of the officers.

A brother holding a Traveling or Visiting Card is entitled in visiting to use the A. T. P. W. in force at the time his Card was granted.

A Special Deputy, appointed to institute a Lodge or Encampment, fulfils his duty when such Lodge or Encampment is instituted, and he has made his report of the same.

All members of the Order are in duty bound, while in their Lodge or En-campment, to be governed by the well-known usages of the Order, and in case

of their refusal, it is proper to prefer charges against them for conduct unbecoming an Odd Fellow. No member can claim indulgence on account of his
official position in the Order.

The Grand Secretary, in his report, said :

In 1819 Odd Fellowship set on foot its mission under the auspices of five
plain and unpretending citizens ; with feeble voice it uttered its proclamation
of peace and good will to men on earth ; its banner was flung to the breeze of
heaven, with its noble motto inscribed upon its folds, Friendship, Love and
Truth, the Fatherhood of God over all, and the universal brotherhood of man.
Moving forward from this noble standpoint, in half a century it has enrolled in
its army over half a million of votaries, most of which, this day, are at active
labor. To a single Lodge of five members it has added thousands upon
thousands, scattered over all the wide earth where civilization prevails, and
still its stately tread is onward among the islands of the sea. This mighty
host has pursued a single idea, continuously, unremittingly, and with invio-
lable fidelity, turning neither to the right nor to the left, no matter how grave,
exciting or momentous the collateral issue—always ignoring self, and conse-
crating its massive energies and resources to the cause of humanity.

Thus have we built, upon the foundations laid in 1819, a superstructure
whose lofty dome towers heavenward, opens wide its portals to the weary and
careworn, and cordially invites the good and the true to co-operative labor
in aid of suffering man. While our hearts swell with just pride in the review
of our labors and their fruits in fifty years, and our imagination, taking
wings and vaulting into the great future, fifty years hence, looks out upon the
scene then existant, let us not be led to exultation ; let us never forget that it
is God who hath given us the victory; that it is His wisdom which has guided
our counsels ; His providence which has shielded us from external danger,
and saved us from internal dissensions, by the inspiration of a unity and
concord which challenge comparison in the affairs of men. Let us thank Him
earnestly for an enlightenment which has lifted us often in advance of the age
in which we have acted, and which has supplied us with nerve and energy so
effective as to enable us to counteract ignorance and prejudice, and to overcome the vexatious delays and hindrances which these weapons have often
interposed in our path, and above all, let us thank Him for the magnitude
and value of our offering upon the great altar of humanity.

During the recess, Warrants were issued for the institution of the Grand Lodge of Colorado, Cheyenne Lodge, No.
1, Dakota Territory, (now Wyoming), Arizona Lodge, No.
1, Arizona Territory, and two Subordinate Encampments.

A. D. Meacham, P. G. Rep., of California, who accepted
the mission of introducing our Work into Australia, reported
that on the 22d of February, 1868, he instituted the Grand
Lodge of Australia, installed the officers, and instructed
all present in the Unwritten Work. The Order in Aus-

tralasia at this time consisted of 69 Lodges and 4,208 members distributed among the colonies of Victoria, New Zealand, South Australia and Tasmania. (*See Australasia, in a subsequent Chapter.*)

The receipts of the Grand Lodge for the past year were $29,630.86. The profit on the sale of supplies was $18,353.02. The gross assets of the Grand Lodge were $29,400.82.

The following amounts were expended by the Subordinate Lodges and Encampments, respectively:

	LODGES.	ENCAMPMENTS.
For relief of members	$458,538.48	$56,146.58
For relief of widowed families	113,275.02	4,047.25
For education of orphans	19,957.26	59.90
For burying the dead	103,847.50	10,184.22

Article XXII. of the By-Laws, in reference to the Regalia of the Order, was amended.

The elective Grand Officers of the Grand Lodge reported that they had distributed the funds placed in their charge, amounting to $13,678.95, amongst the respective Southern jurisdictions interested, as in their judgment appeared to be just and equitable.

The Grand Lodge, on the evening of the 21st of September, visited Washington Lodge, No. 1, the "Common Parent" of all Lodges.

The following were adopted :

When a financial officer of a Subordinate Lodge refuses to settle his accounts and deliver all moneys, books, and papers belonging to the same over to the Lodge, he cannot of right demand a Card of Clearance, and a Lodge may refuse to grant such Card until the brother's accounts are adjusted, and the Lodge is satisfied that he is clear of the books, and free from all charges of whatsoever kind.

Hereafter the names of *suspended* members are not to be returned to this Grand Lodge.

State jurisdictions are directed to so amend their laws that brothers shall not be *expelled* for non-payment of dues.

Any State Grand Lodge is authorized to confer the Grand Lodge and Past Official Degrees, upon Past Grands of another State jurisdiction upon the presentation of a Visiting Card, from their own Lodge, and also a Certificate executed by the Grand Master and Grand Secretary, under the Seal of the Grand Lodge to whose jurisdiction such Past Grands belong, that they are eligible and entitled to the same.

When a brother who holds a current Visiting Card, wishes to visit a Lodge or Encampment in the jurisdiction to which he belongs, but is without the Term Password, or Check word, the presentation of his Visiting Card shall make it the duty of the presiding officer of the Lodge or Encampment to communicate to him the Pass or Check of the jurisdiction, after ascertaining that the person presenting it is the legal holder of the Card.

Grand Patriarchs, and their duly commissioned Special Deputies, are hereby empowered, under such rules and regulations as may be prescribed by the Grand Encampments, respectively, to confer the Subordinate Encampment Degrees upon a sufficient number of Scarlet Degree members of a Subordinate Lodge, for the purpose of qualifying them as proper petitioners for a Warrant or Charter for an Encampment within their jurisdiction, at a place where none exists.

When a member of an Encampment, in good standing, takes a Withdrawal Card from the Subordinate Lodge of which he may be a member, his membership in his Encampment shall not be affected thereby, for a year from the date of his said Withdrawal Card.   He shall be considered in good standing in his Encampment, if he deposits his Withdrawal Card in a Subordinate Lodge, and becomes a member thereof, at any time within a year from the date of his said Withdrawal Card, provided he shall keep his dues paid up in the Encampment, during that time.

Hereafter, in the designation of the name and rank of brethren of the Order, the title or rank of the brother shall be placed after, instead of before the name, as has hitherto been practiced.

A brother, who has lost his right hand, or whose right hand has been so injured that its natural use has been seriously impaired, is qualified and eligible for the chair of N. G.

A Grand National Celebration of the occasion, (the fiftieth Anniversary of the Order), under the auspices of the Grand Lodge of the United States shall take place in the City of Philadelphia, in connection with the local observance of the day at that place.

The widow of an Odd Fellow who had not attained the Scarlet Degree, but who was in good standing at the time of his death, may receive the Degree of Rebekah, at the option of the Lodge of which her husband was a member at the time of his death.

Grand Lodges are authorized to institute Degree Lodges of the Daughters of Rebekah (*See Journal, pages* 4383, 4384, 4416.)

All officers of Subordinate Lodges and Encampments, shall wear the Jewels of their offices during the transaction of business.

The question of eligibility to membership in the Order, by initiation, of persons who have lost a limb be, and the same is hereby remitted to the jurisdiction and disposal of the Subordinate Lodge to which admission is asked.

A design for an Odd Fellow's Flag as described page 4305 Journal, was adopted; also a Collar and Jewel for a Past Grand Patriarch.

The Order in California invited the Grand Lodge to

hold the next session in San Francisco, and Rep. A. J. Gunnison, of California, received and submitted the following telegram.

SAN FRANCISCO, Cal., Sept. 24, 1868.

A. J. Gunnison, Grand Representative:

Templar Lodge has unanimously agreed to secure expenses of Representatives, amounting to ten thousand dollars. Invite Grand Lodge.

T. RODGERS JOHNSON, *Grand Secretary.*

This invitation resulted in the adoption of the following:

Resolved, That the next annual communication of this Grand Lodge be held in the city of San Francisco, in the State of California, and that the officers and members of this R. W. Grand Lodge be requested to assemble at Omaha, Nebraska, on the 10th day of September, 1869, to be conveyed thence, by the Great Pacific Railroad across the continent, to the said city of San Francisco, and that the mileage to be paid to the Representatives by this R. W. Grand Lodge, on that occasion, shall be computed from their respective homes to and from the said city of Omaha, excepting the Representatives from jurisdictions on the Pacific slope, whose mileage shall be computed to and from San Francisco. Provided, That if the said Pacific Railroad shall not be completed and running regular trains through, between Omaha and Sacramento City, by the first day of August, 1869, so that the Representatives can be conveyed through without change of cars or detention, then, and in that case, the M. W. Grand Sire shall, on that date, issue his proclamation calling the Grand Lodge to assemble in annual communication in the City of Baltimore, in the State of Maryland.

Article XV., of the By-Laws, was amended, so as to give the Grand Sire authority to fill vacancies occurring in offices during the recess.

There was further legislation on the readmission of non-affiliated members into the Order. (*See Journal, pages* 4354, 4355, 4400, 4415, 4421.)

The following Grand Officers were elected and installed: E. D. Farnsworth, P. D. G. Sire, of Tennessee, Grand Sire; Fred. D. Stuart, P. G. M., of the District of Columbia, Deputy Grand Sire; James L. Ridgely, P. G. M., of Maryland, Grand Corresponding and Recording Secretary; Joshua Vansant, P. G. M., of Maryland, Grand Treasurer.

The following were appointed by the Grand Sire: Rev. J. W. Venable, P. G. Rep., of Kentucky, Grand Chaplain; John W. Orr, P. G. M., of New Jersey, Grand Marshal; J. W. Smith, P. G., of Connecticut, Grand Guardian; John E. Chamberlain, P. G., of Maryland, Grand Messenger.

1869.

The Grand Lodge met in annual session, in the City of San Francisco, on the 20th of September.

This session was made memorable by crossing the continent to the Pacific by rail, the Grand Lodge being the first organized body so to do, and by the overwhelming attentions paid to the Representatives and ladies by the Odd Fellows of the States and Territories on the route.

According to arrangement, the officers, members and accompaying visitors met at Omaha on the 10th of September, 1869, where they were heartily received and accorded a lavish hospitality. Before reaching Sacramento, they were met by a committee from the Lodges of that city, who, on their arrival, took the party in carriages to hotels where accommodations had been secured.

The next day a procession of the Subordinate Lodges and Encampments of the city and surrounding country was formed, and marched through the streets to the site of the Odd Fellows' Temple, where its corner-stone was formally laid by the Grand Sire. In the evening, the entire body was sumptuously entertained at a grand banquet. On the afternoon of the 16th the members reached Alameda, where they were entertained at the residence of Nathan Porter, P. G. Rep., and they arrived in San Francisco at 3:30 P. M. They were welcomed by the Order in California, and under the escort of the National Guard, and a procession of several thousand Odd Fellows, passed through some of the principal streets to the California Theatre, where several addresses were made. The next day, the entire party made an enjoyable trip through the Golden Gate and on the Pacific Ocean. The time of their sojourn in San Francisco was one continued round of pleasure; the brethren and people of California were unstinted in their efforts to promote the comfort and happiness of their visitors. The financial panic of "Black Friday" occurred while the Grand Lodge was in session, causing embarrassment to the Grand Treasurer and others.

Grand Sire Farnsworth, in his report, said:

On this occasion our meeting is characterized by more than ordinary interest; an uncommon energy has distinguished all the jurisdictions during the recess, in order that each should be present here to-day, however remotely situated from the seat of legislation. Among the many very remarkable and extraordinary incidents connected with the history of Odd Fellowship, and which have by their distinctive character been regarded as epochs in its career, there is, I venture to say, not one which will surpass that which is now transpiring. The Grand Lodge of the United States, representing a constituency diffused over this continent and beyond it, is this day assembled in annual session on the Pacific Coast, at the splendid city of San Francisco, the metropolis of one of the greatest commonwealths of the American Federal Union. For the most part, the Representatives present are distant thousands of miles from their homes, transported hither as if on the wings of the morning, whirled across a vast continent, over a highway which is not only the wonder of our people, but the marvel of the world. Nor is the character of the incident, extraordinary as it is, more transcendent for its illustration of daring genius and enterprise, than is the field itself upon which it has been enacted, remarkable and pre-eminently the subject of wonder. Here, in this distant part of the Republic, about a quarter of a century ago, the wilderness reigned; on this spot, a few isolated men, in ignorance and indolence, then herded in perhaps squalid hovels and the rudest tenements; this beautiful bay of world-wide renown, now glistening all over with fluttering canvas, knew then only the hardy whaler, chased hither for shelter by the storm king of the ocean. Civilization, if any, was primitive, and only reflected from the dim light of missionary zeal; the foot prints of the Anglo-Saxon had not pressed this earth, nor had his adventurous spirit yet been free to wing its way hitherward. In the order of Providence, and in the fullness of time, our countrymen came; ignorance and indolence and superstition retired from their presence, as if withered by the contact; the wilderness smiled and blossomed; thrift and enterprise and intellect constructed out of this material an Empire, such as we behold California to-day. Great and remarkable as these facts are, which exhibit the grandeur of a mighty State, rising as it were by magic out of comparative chaos, they appear, if possible, still more wonderful, if the moral elevation of the commonwealth be regarded. With improved civilization, came, as inseparable from it, general enlightenment and the broad spirit of humanity; in this train was Odd Fellowship. Planted by the pioneer spirit of our countrymen, and cherished by the love and devotion of a faithful brotherhood, it has kept pace with all other institutions of the State, manifesting as extraordinary a career of success and prosperity as does the body politic itself. Although a comparatively young jurisdiction, California already ranks among the strongest of our State organizations, and is destined, under a future administration correspondent to that which has characterized it in the past, to outstrip most of its older sisters. The truth of this remark is supplied, not so much in the number as in the zeal and activity of her Lodges; in their stability, strength and resources; in the extent and efficiency of their work; the large amount of relief afforded; in the great interest displayed to advance the

usefulness of the Order, by supplying the means of a high moral and intellectual culture to the membership, and in that grand and noble spirit of fraternity,
which has rendered her name a synonym with munificence and liberality
throughout the Order; but beyond all these, in that earnest love and devotion
of our brethren, which is so distinctive in the invitation extended to this
Grand Lodge, to come to this, the city of their just pride, to witness their
marvelous growth, to partake of their splendid hospitalities, and to do them
good by our example, our influence, and our fraternal counsels. All hail to
the Grand Lodge of California and its membership. In your behalf I render
them your sincere acknowledgments, and invoke for them a largely increased
prosperity in the future, as a just reward for their unparalleled devotion to
our cause.

The Grand Sire visited such of the Southern jurisdictions as his time would permit, "with a view to a revival of
interest and materially to increase the membership in those
jurisdictions." He reported "the condition of the Order
generally, in the interior of the Southern States pecuniarily
bad."

The semi-centennial Anniversary of Odd Fellowship was
celebrated in the City of Philadelphia, April 26th, "with appropriate ceremonies at the Academy of Music, and by a
most imposing procession of the brotherhood, numbering
not less than thirty thousand souls, and forming a continuous line not less than ten miles in length."

Bro. John W. Orr, P. G. M., of New Jersey, who was
appointed Grand Marshal, at the last session, resigned and
Brother J. Griswold, P. G. Rep., of New Jersey, was appointed in his stead.

The Grand Sire suggested that the time had now
arrived when the Degree of Rebekah should be placed on
a footing with the rest of the Work, and be so equalized in
authority, that Lodges of the Daughters of Rebekah, should
be established in every jurisdiction.

The following decisions of the Grand Sire were approved:

The costumes worn in the G. R. D. cannot be used on public occasions.

A brother of the Patriarchal Degree is entitled to receive the Semi-annual
word.

Voting in a Lodge is by the usual sign of an Odd Fellow, except on
ballot for membership, and is prescribed by the Work.

It is unlawful for the Charge Books, or others containing or relating to the Secret Work of the Order, to be taken from the Lodge room.   The N. G. of a Lodge, being the proper custodian of such books, may entrust them to his subordinate officers for the purpose of qualification, while in the Lodge room.

The laws of the Order prohibit the writing of the Initiatory Charges, as well as all other parts of the Secret Work.

Grand Officers should address the Chairs as other members do ; Grand Honors should be given them immediately after their recognition by the officers of the Lodge.

Suspensions for cause, cannot be indefinite, nor for any unreasonable length of time.

A member visiting a Subordinate Lodge, on a Card, shall be examined in the A. T. P. W., and also in the Degree in which the Lodge is open.

The Grand Secretary, in his report, said :

The fiftieth anniversary of American Odd Fellowship was observed as a day of thanksgiving and rejoicing, almost universally, throughout the entire jurisdiction, as recommended by the Grand Lodge, and from the accounts received, was celebrated with marked and fervid enthusiasm at every point.   It is a source of congratulation to the brotherhood to witness the abiding love and veneration for our noble institution, which this memorable occasion has, on every hand, and in every quarter of our wide-spread domain, so profoundly evoked ; what volumes of encouragement does the incident supply to stimulate our efforts for the general diffusion of its blessings throughout the world ! and what sincere gratitude to the Author of all good should it inspire in our hearts !   May we measure up, as a brotherhood, to a full appreciation of the value of this experience.

As an Order, we have a net capital invested of over nine and a half millions of dollars, above the legitimate demands of our present need.   The question arises, whether we measure up to our full ability as philanthropists and humanitarians.   Do we occupy the field which lies open before us, earnestly inviting laborers to its golden harvest, commensurately with our whole ability ?   We have done much within the last forty years, and the offering has gone up like "the alms and the prayers" of the good old centurion, "for a memorial before God," but there is yet work to be done, and ever will be whilst the world and humanity survive.   We began our career simply as assurers of each other against sickness and death ; beyond ourselves, our next aim was to care for those "in whom we live again," our second selves, our families ; to material support to these, we super-added, in time, moral aid ; the area of our ministrations has continued to amplify and enlarge, comprehending as it now does, many collateral auxiliaries to the general object.   In all these we have eminently prospered, and shall we, resting upon this reward, be content "with our laurels," or shall we go forward for further triumphs under the broad banner of Odd Fellowship?   The world moves, and shall we, in active sympathy with its fruitful genius, onward "pitch our moving tent," or passively lag behind ?   That we have accomplished our original mission, and nobly, is very true ; all our obligations have been met, yet resources remain.   Can we not avail of these and of the propitious fortune which smiles upon our labors, to enlarge their value to our membership, to our widows, to our orphaned ones, to humanity at large ? Let us diligently inquire into this subject. There is no organization of men in the world in which abound greater elements of material power, and whose combined energy, harmoniously directed, is capable of producing a larger influence for good within its legitimate scope. Let us invoke His counsels and favor, who has ever been our friend and support, let us learn our whole duty as men and brethren, and under His guidance enter with alacrity and wisdom upon its performance.

During the recess, Warrants were issued for the Grand Encampment of Victoria, Australia; the Grand Encampment of Ontario, and eight Subordinate Encampments.

B. W. Dennis, Grand Representative of the Grand Encampment of Michigan, the Special Commissioner appointed to visit the jurisdiction of Vermont, reported that he devoted three months in the service ; " received three petitions for new Lodges, and set two of them at work ; received five petitions for the revival of defunct Lodges, and set three at work ; " also instituted three Rebekah Lodges, and had imparted thorough instruction in the Work.

The Order in Australia was progressing rapidly. The Grand Lodge of New Zealand was instituted March 11th, 1869, with a jurisdiction of six Subordinates. Two Subordinate Encampments, Victoria, No. 1, Melbourne, and Corio, No. 2, Geelong, were also instituted.

The number of initiates for the following decades, presents, at a glance, the continued growth of Odd Fellowship :

From 1830 to 1839 inclusive.. 18,000
From 1840 to 1849 " 179,754
From 1850 to 1859 " 234,252
From 1860 to 1869 " 228,193

The gross assets of the Grand Lodge now amounted to $35,686.55. The total receipts for the past year were $33,769.50. The profit on the sale of supplies was $19,086.14.

The following amounts were expended by the Subordinate Lodges and Encampments, respectively :

	LODGES.	ENCAMPMENTS.
For relief of members	$496,874,97	$63,719.15
For relief of widowed families	114,287.36	5,148.45
For education of orphans	17,531.18	355.90
For burying the dead	120,395.24	13,506.95

The following were adopted :

The Grand Patriarch of a Grand Encampment, has no authority to suspend the Constitution of a Subordinate Encampment ; and any Dispensation of a Grand Patriarch in conflict with such Constitution is void.

Upon proper application from a sufficient number of brethren in Germany, for authority to organize a Lodge or Lodges, the Grand Sire be, and he is hereby, authorized and instructed to issue a Dispensation, or Dispensations, for such Lodge or Lodges, and to appoint and commission a Special Deputy, if, in his opinion, the good of the Order requires it, with full power and instructions, to institute the Independent Order of Odd Fellows, in Germany, with such restrictions thereon, as our laws and the necessities of the case may require ; and he may, in like manner, establish the same in other civilized countries, upon proper application for the same. *Provided*, nevertheless, that no expense attending the same shall be borne by this Grand Lodge.

No resolution, order, or other action of the Grand Lodge of the United States, shall operate to change, alter, or amend any of its By-Laws, unless said resolution, order, or other action, shall, upon its face, and by its terms, assume to make such change, alteration, or amendment, and shall state distinctly the particular By-Law to be affected.

Each jurisdiction is authorized to prepare and adopt a suitable Form of Charter for Rebekah Degree Lodges.

The organization of a Rebekah Degree Lodge, in a given District, does not supersede or interfere with a Subordinate Lodge to confer said Degree within the same District.

The Grand Corresponding and Recording Secretary is authorized to alter the steel plates of Visiting and Withdrawal Cards, by having conspicuously engraved on the former the word "Visiting," and on the latter the word "Withdrawal."

The Grand Corresponding and Recording Secretary is directed to have the "Flag" belonging to this Grand Body, present, and displayed in some conspicuous place, on all occasions, when this Grand Lodge shall hold a regular or special session.

Until further ordered by this Grand Lodge, the Grand Lodge of Australia and the Grand Lodge of New Zealand have leave to print their own Odes.

A Ceremony for instituting Degree Lodges of the Daughters of Rebekah, and installing the officers thereof, presented by the Special Committee on the subject, was adopted.

On the fifth day of the session, Past Grand Representative Porter, on behalf of the Order in California, presented to Grand Secretary Ridgely a magnificent California laurel wood cane, with a massive gold head, studded with precious stones.

Seven Past Grand Sires were present at the session.

1870.

The Grand Lodge met in annual session, in the City of Baltimore, on the 19th of September.

Grand Sire Farnsworth, in his report, said:

Never was the development of our work more characteristic of its noble principles, or its fruits more practical and abundant. Peace, brotherly love, and concord, which are the very life of Odd Fellowship, and inseparable from its well-being, prevail throughout our borders, and not a ripple disturbs the serene surface of our moral field. The divine spirit of fraternity, inspired by our cardinal idea of tolerance; the mutuality of human obligations and sympathies, elaborately embodied as generic truths in our code, and the happy illustration of these virtues in the details of practice, have justly commended the Order to all good men, and secured their zealous co-operation in its general diffusion. In addition to this excellence, which underlies our moral temple as its solid substratum, we have perfected a form of government and laws, so admirably adapted to the harmonious working of the system, and protective of the Subordinates, that universal acquiescence in the law, as ex pounded and administered, has ever prevailed, and no instance of serious conflict between the large number of the Lodges and their respective State jurisdictions, or between the State Grand Bodies and the Supreme Grand Body, has transpired during the half century of our existence. It is also our good fortune, to have trained the great army enrolled under our banner, so to love and venerate our Order, and so to appreciate its blessings, that intensity of affection for it grows with the growth and strengthens with the strength of the constituency, ever generating among them a spirit of emulation and rivalry "to weary not in well-doing." The natural and inevitable fruit of these combined elements has been great prosperity. This prosperity, however, from the necessity of things, although manifest to us, has not been so generally known or felt by the outside world. It is true that the public witness our continuous increase in numbers, the accumulation of our resources, our thorough occupation of cities, towns, villages and counties, and our acquisition of new fields of labor abroad; these, although pregnant evidences of our power for good, present but a superficial view of the effective value of the institution, either to its own household, upon which it immediately acts, or to the outside community, where it exists. To look upon the mission of Odd Fellowship in its real character, to understand its influence as an agent of benefaction, to witness its practical and personal aids and humanitarian offices, a standpoint must be occupied upon a higher elevation.

The Grand Sire presented a very interesting statement of his mission to Germany in pursuance of the action at the session of 1869; his visit to California on business, the generous act of Templar Lodge, No. 17, despite the protest of the Grand Sire, in appropriating twelve hundred dollars for the purpose of establishing the Order in Germany ; the reasons which induced him to undertake the mission instead of delegating the authority to establish the Order in Germany to others ; the failure of the object at that time on account of the commencement of hostilities beween France and Germany, etc.

Of his disappointment he said :

When within a few hours of Southampton, a pilot came on board, whose story of war fell like a bolt of thunder upon our startled ears, rendering it too certain that our mission was now at an end. It is impossible for me to represent, in language, any adequate idea of the severity of this disastrous blow, and of the profound emotions of sorrow and disappointment which it awakened. Anticipations of complete success had been daily strengthened as our journey progressed, and not a shadow of doubt lingered upon my mind.

He recited his successful efforts, on his arrival in London, to communicate by mail and telegraph with Brother John F. Morse, P. G. M., of California, who "succeeded with great difficulty, and at great sacrifice of personal comfort," in reaching London, when a plan of operations was presented by the Grand Sire, and Brother Morse was duly authorized to establish the Order, as contemplated by the Grand Lodge. The reader is referred to pages 4,706 to 4,711, and 4,725 to 4,740, Journal of 1870,for complete details of the proceedings of Grand Sire Farnsworth, in his efforts to introduce American Odd Fellowship into Germany and Switzerland.

The Grand Sire suggested that the name of the Grand Lodge should be changed—that " no territorial limit should define our jurisdiction, but, measuring up to the full scope of our ambition, should harmonize, by the adoption of an appropriate style and title, our profession and practice."

The subject of suspension for non-payment of dues was adverted to, and the attention of the Grand Lodge was called to the question. The importance of the matter was shown by the fact that although last year nearly fifty thousand were initiated the net gain in membership was less than thirty thousand.

On the 5th day of July, 1870, the following circular was issued by the Grand Sire:

DEAR SIR AND BROTHER: It has been represented to me that in some of the State jurisdictions, thoughtless and inconsiderate brethren have used the Subordinate Lodge rooms for the purpose of conferring *Degrees, so called*, having no connection whatever with the Order, and, if not positively indecent and contrary to good morals, certainly of an unbecoming and discreditable character, one of which is known as the Degree of "The Oriental Order of Humility."

As such practices are in gross violation of our laws, and calculated to bring our Order into disrepute, you are hereby required to suppress them promptly within your jurisdiction, if any such exist, and to take such measures as may be proper and necessary to give to this circular general publicity.

This action was endorsed by the Grand Lodge.

The following decisions of the Grand Sire were approved:

When a brother renounces Odd Fellowship, such so-called renunciation of the Order has no effect whatever upon his membership or standing in his Lodge.

Immemorial custom and usage has assigned particular places for all the officers of a Subordinate Lodge; which, in the absence of written law to the contrary, is binding, and under this assignment the Warden's position is in front of the Right Supporter of the Noble Grand.

No Regalia is legitimate, except that prescribed by law.

Final Cards are granted only by vote of the Lodge; the vote to be had by ball ballot.

When charges are to be preferred against the Noble Grand of a Lodge, they are properly placed in the hands of the Vice Grand, to be brought before the Lodge; but there is no reason why any brother may not prefer such charges.

The vote by which a Withdrawal Card was authorized, cannot be reconsidered or rescinded.

A Grand Master, when visiting *as such*, in his own jurisdiction, should wear the Regalia and Jewel of his office.

The Grand Secretary, in his report, said:

The subjoined table will show the progress of the past year, as compared with that immediately preceding; it is full of interest and encouragement to every thoughtful Odd Fellow, and its lesson should stimulate the whole brotherhood to renewed efforts in the future.

Lodges in 1869, 3,473; in 1870, 3,867; increase, 394. Initiations in 1869, 41,183; in 1870, 46,309; increase, 5,126. Revenue in 1869, $2,347,073.86; in 1870, $2,724,419.46; increase, $377,345.60. Relief in 1869, $760,429.54; in 1870, $860,343.86; increase, $99,914.32. Members in 1869, 268,608; in 1870, 298,637; increase, 30,029.

The exhibit is truly cheering, and justly awakens our honest pride and mutual gratulations. True, although it may be, that the splendid humanities and benevolence to which these large sums have been applied, are primarily absorbed within our own family, in obedience to a fundamental idea which we cherish as the great heart from which the life-current of Odd Fellowship flows, yet their effects reach far beyond this limit ; they permeate thoroughly the surroundings ; they diffuse their benign influence outside the immediate recipient, to his wife, to his children, his parents, brothers, sisters, kindred, attendants of the sick chamber, physicians, neighbors, and through these, ultimately find their way to the great public, warming every heart which they touch in their course, with congenial ardor and love for the Order. Hence this paramount idea in our Order, so far from being exclusive, as has been sometimes intimated, is as well, the true source of its value to the outside world as to its household. The greater its capacity and effectiveness to its own, the greater the radius of its external benevolence and usefulness ; action and reaction are educed and made reciprocal between the two instrumentalities ; our humanity, wherever and whenever displayed, challenges the public confidence and respect, and wins its kindred sympathy. Thus do we conquer prejudice and draw within our fold, "by the cords of love," large accessions of members and resources, from the ranks of the good and generous.

The Order in Vermont had much improved. There were now twelve Lodges at work, with a membership of five hundred and thirty.

Warrants were issued, during the recess, for the institution of four Subordinate Encampments and one Subordinate Lodge, viz.; Dakota, No. 1, Yankton, Dakota.

The assets of the Grand Lodge were $30,014.07, the total receipts for the year, $33,178.71, and the profit on the sale of supplies, $21,874.07.

The following amounts were paid out by the Subordinate Lodges and Encampments, respectively :

	LODGES.	ENCAMPMENTS.
For relief of members......................	$579,043.81	$75,734.02
For relief of widowed families..............	122,043.65	4,848.53
For education of orphans...................	19,444.16	138.00
For burying the dead......................	132,659.21	12,454.76

The following were adopted :

Representatives may present to this Grand Lodge the instructions that they have received ; but, in order to have the subject matter referred to a committee, or acted upon by the Grand Lodge, the Grand Representatives must submit the same in the form of a resolution or amendment, as the nature of the subject may require.

Grand Lodges are requested to take action, at as early a day as possible, and, where practicable, to provide for the establishment of suitable places where the orphan children of the members of the Order in their several jurisdictions, may be supported and educated. Also for the establishment, at suitable localities, of asylums for the use and benefit of valetudinary members of the Order, where they may be comfortably supported during the remnant of their days. In cases where Grand Lodges may omit to take action in relation to either of these objects, any Lodge, or number of Lodges in such jurisdictions, are authorized to raise the funds necessary, and to apply the same in the establishment and support of such institutions or asylums.

A member of the Order who becomes in arrears for dues for the period of one year, may be suspended, or dropped from membership, but he cannot be expelled from the Order on account of being in arrears for dues.

After one year from the date of suspension, a member dropped or suspended for non-payment of dues, may be reinstated upon the payment of the fee charged for an initiate of the same age, as prescribed by the By-Laws.

A member suspended or dropped for non-payment of dues, wishing to regain membership in another jurisdiction than that in which he was suspended or dropped, shall be entitled to receive, and the Lodge or Encampment to which he belonged shall grant, upon proper application, a Dismissal Certificate, upon the receipt of one dollar.

In all cases wherein a Lodge or Encampment has refused to reinstate a member suspended or dropped for non-payment of dues, he shall be entitled to receive, and the Lodge shall, upon proper application, grant a Dismissal Certificate, upon the receipt of one dollar.

A member suspended or dropped for non-payment of dues, after five years' suspension, wishing to join a Lodge or Encampment in the same jurisdiction, shall be entitled to receive, and the Lodge or Encampment shall grant, upon proper application, a Dismissal Certificate upon the receipt of one dollar. The form of Certificate shall be as follows:

INDEPENDENT ORDER OF ODD FELLOWS.

To all whom it may concern,
Fraternally greeting.

THIS CERTIFIES that .... was admitted to membership in................................, No...................., at................................ in the Jurisdiction of................................, on the .... day of ...., 18......, and by ...., and that he retained his membership in said .... until the .... day of ...., 18 ......, when he was suspended for non-payment of dues, and he is entirely dismissed from membership in said ....

In Witness whereof, we have hereunto subscribed our names and affixed the Seal of the .... this .... day of................................, A. D., 18.......

[SEAL.]

The Noble Grand and Recording Secretary, or the Chief Patriarch and Scribe, as the case may be, shall issue such Certificate, upon proper application, in open Lodge or Encampment, and payment of the fee, without a vote of the Lodge or Encampment.

A member of a Subordinate Lodge, (who is also a Grand Lodge officer), has a right to vote at an election of officers in his own Lodge, clothed in his official Regalia.

A decision of the Grand Sire, approved by the Grand Lodge, cannot supersede or set aside a By-Law of the Grand Lodge.

Non-affiliated Odd Fellows, who have been regularly initiated in the Order, and have retained membership therein for at least ten consecutive years, and who, at the time of making application for reinstatement or membership, shall be over fifty years of age, may be admitted to membership in any Lodge or Encampment, as non-beneficial members, upon such terms as the local law may prescribe.

It is not imperative on Subordinate Lodges, to have the duties of Chaplain regularly performed in the opening and closing ceremonies.

In the opinion of this Grand Lodge, the establishment of Odd Fellows' libraries, in every place where the same can be done successfully, is calculated to promote the best interests of the Order, and such action is earnestly recommended.

When a brother applies for membership, on deposit of Card, and is elected, and signs the Constitution, his Card should remain in the Lodge. So, also, if the local law date membership from the time of the applicant's *election*, the Card should then remain in the Lodge after election; and the applicant cannot demand its return, whether he sign the Constitution or not. But, if the local law date membership from the time of signing the Constitution, the brother elect who fails to appear and sign the same, may demand the return of his Card, because, until he signs the Constitution, he is not a member of the Lodge.

No Lodge, Encampment or Degree Lodge, shall hold any meeting for Work or business upon Sunday, except for funeral purposes.

No Lodge room within the jurisdiction of this Grand Body shall be used for the conferring of any Degrees or Secret Work not provided for by the existing laws of the Order; and any officer of a Subordinate or other Lodge or Lodges, who may aid or permit such Degrees to be conferred in such Lodge rooms, shall be guilty of a violation of the laws of the Order. Provided that this resolution shall not be interpreted so as to affect any such proceedings as may be had in such Lodge rooms by other secret associations not under the color of Odd Fellowship.

Subordinate Encampments, when they appear in public, may wear such uniform style of head dress as may be approved by the Grand Patriarch of the jurisdiction.

A new Digest prepared by Bro. John H. White, Representative from New York, was submitted and referred to a committee who approved it, and presented resolutions authorizing the compiler to complete the Digest, so as to embrace the legislation of 1870, and providing for printing the book, etc.

The Grand Lodge refused to print its proceedings in the German language.

An important action was the authority given to Grand Lodges and Grand Encampments to "return surrendered Charters that have remained unclaimed for not less than five years, upon the petition of the requisite number of qualified brothers, although only one of the petitioners may have been a member of said defunct Lodge or Encampment."

The Grand Lodge refused to "allow the several Grand and Subordinate Lodges to use the yeas and nays in voting, as the various Grand and Subordinate Lodges may direct."

On the occasion of official visits of District Deputies, Subordinates were directed to award them the same Honors that are given to Grand Masters and Grand Patriarchs.

The following Grand Officers were elected and installed:

Frederick D. Stuart, P. D. G. Sire, of the District of Columbia, Grand Sire; Cornelius A. Logan, P. G. M., of Kansas, Deputy Grand Sire; James L. Ridgely, P. G. M., of Maryland, Grand Corresponding and Recording Secretary; Joshua Vansant, P. G. M., of Maryland, Grand Treasurer.

The following were appointed by the Grand Sire:

Rev. J. W. Venable, P. G. Rep., of Kentucky, Grand Chaplain; Stuart W. Case, P. G. P., of Alabama, Grand Marshal; James Smith, P. G. M., of Ontario, Grand Guardian; John E. Chamberlain, P. G., of Maryland, Grand Messenger.

1871.

The Grand Lodge met in annual session, in the City of Chicago, on the 18th of September. It was welcomed by the Grand Lodge of Illinois, in Metropolitan Hall, where interesting and appropriate addresses were made. The brethren of Illinois had planned a public procession in Regalia, to take place on the morning of the 19th. The brotherhood of Chicago and the adjacent States were well represented.

The officers of the Grand Lodge and Grand Encampment of Illinois, and the officers and members of the Grand Lodge of the United States filled about one hundred carriages, while not less than five thousand Odd Fellows were in the ranks. This grand procession called forth the most flattering encomiums from all observers, and no doubt contributed to the future growth and welfare of the jurisdiction of Illinois.

The Grand Lodge was overwhelmed with invitations from the brethren and the community.

Grand Sire Stuart, in his report, said :

We are assembled to-day upon a wonderful spot of ground ; in the metropolitan city of an empire State, a city born as it were of yesterday, and to-day displaying a colossal growth, not only of numbers, but of every other element of power which commands admiration. We stand to-day in the presence of an unparalleled civilization, and behold around and about us, on every side, the substantial fruits of the all-conquering power of capital, genius and enterprise, guided by wisdom in developing advantages of position and general surroundings. The history of the world does not furnish a grander, if a parallel progress, unless it be in the fabulous stories invented for the amusement of the young. Here, less than half a century ago, reigned in solitude the primitive forest and the virgin prairie, as God vouchsafed them on the morning of creation. Dominion here was disputed only by the wild beasts and the untutored savage ; now, behold, arisen as it were by talismanic power, a city, the third in wealth of the great Republic, outranking hundreds of the old world, which date back to the Cæsars ; lifting its proud head erectly to the heavens, inspired by the rewards of its past energy and by the bright promise which gilds its future horizon, to struggle on to further greatness and renown ; here dwell a people, many of them our brother Odd Fellows, all of them our fellow citizens, who have built an empire ; denizens of a glorious commonwealth, a community abounding in wealth, of material, moral, political and social, attainments ; inferior to none on the earth in refinement, intellect, industry, energy, genius and its rewards, having an unconquerable determination to reach pre-eminence, a goal very clearly indicated in their near future. We are here, in this great city, by the special request of the Grand Lodge of the State, to whose noble and generous invitation we have promptly responded. By that distinguished Body, and thousands of its membership, and invited brethren from adjoining jurisdictions, have we been met upon our arrival at this beautiful city, and welcomed to their hospitality and their homes. What a grand and sublime moral ; how commandingly does the scene display the benign and fraternal character of Odd Fellowship ! Strangers to each other but a few days ago, in person, in name, in character, and position in life, yet kindred in *Friendship* and *Love*, and in the practical illustration of that grand *Truth* which proclaims the brotherhood of man, and the Fatherhood of God over all. In your name, Representatives, and as your chief officer, I tender to our brethren of Illinois profound and heartfelt acknowledgments for this mark of high respect ; I thank them most sincerely for this noble demonstration, the influence of which will awaken in the bosom of every Odd Fellow throughout the world, renewed affection for our beloved Order, and esteem for the brotherhood of Illinois, who have this day so grandly illustrated its splendid morale.

Standing here as representative men, occupying so elevated a platform, we cannot fail to see by the transcendent career of Illinois and Chicago, a mirror which, in fact, vividly reflects our own progressive history as an Order. Let us recognize in the lesson, which is so instructive, that by just such a spirit of energy and unconquerable devotion, sustained by the favor and blessing of God, have we grown Odd Fellowship from a feeble germ to a great tree, whose branches now reach the ends of the earth. If we would be worthy of the noble men from whom we received it, let our highest aspirations be to transmit it, not only in the beauty and excellence which now adorn it, but to go on adding to it grace and virtue and comeliness, so that henceforth everywhere, and from all men, it shall be hailed as a blessing to our age and race.

It is my privilege to report to you, that unexampled prosperity has rewarded our labors during the past year, in every section of the general jurisdiction.

Peace and concord, which have from our infancy characterized the institution, amid all the external conflicts and tumults of the world, continue unbroken within our borders, and a general spirit of emulation and rivalry, prevails among the brethren to excel in the great cause of human benefaction. In no period of our history, whether we consider our numbers, our finances, or our work of benevolence, have we had greater reason for gratification.

He reported the institution of four Lodges in Europe, (three in Germany, and one in Switzerland,) and an Encampment at Berlin.

Wurttemberg Lodge, No. 1, was instituted at Stuttgart, December 1, 1870, by Bro. J. F. Morse, P. G. M., Special Commissioner, assisted by Brothers Austin and Meyer, of California; Kohlas, of Pennsylvania; and Pretchmer, of Delaware. The organizers of the Lodge were Bros. M. Bernheim, P. D. D. G. M., of California; Otto Schaettle, of Pennsylvania ; E. Klauprecht, of Ohio ; Kohlas, of Pennsylvania ; and H. Woernle. The Special Commissioner furnished a very interesting statement of his experience in the work, which, with documents on the subject, may be found in the Journal, on pages 5,005 to 5,038, inclusive. Of the

German Mission, Grand Sire Stuart in his report, page 4983 Journal, said:

"Bro. Morse had incurred large expense in responding to the telegram of the Grand Sire, by his presence, at London, and was forced to assume personal responsibility at every step of progress which he made in the discharge of his office, and had actually advanced from his private resources considerable sums of money. I was pained to know that the mission was languishing for want of funds. You may well imagine that I was very seriously embarrassed by this condition of things. Bro. Morse had been duly commissioned as an officer of the Grand Lodge of the United States—the appointment had been approved and confirmed by the highest authority in the Order—he had entered upon his important duties, incurred pecuniary responsibilities, and needed, indispensably to success, considerable resources. There was no power to approach the Treasury of the Grand Lodge of the United States ; on the contrary, a positive inhibition had been made against such attempt. The splendid and generous appropriation of Templar Lodge having, as I learned, been expended in the attempt of the Grand Sire to reach Germany—for the purpose of giving his personal efforts to the work—no portion thereof having reached the hands of Bro. Morse, the alternative stared me in the face of abandonment of the great enterprise, or of a manly and earnest effort to meet the crisis. Accordingly, I did not hesitate as to my duty after consultation with safe counsellors, on whom the Grand Lodge had long been accustomed to rely. I at once addressed a letter to several of the larger and more wealthy State Grand Jurisdictions, through their respective Grand Secretaries, invoking their generous aid. To this appeal a prompt and liberal response was returned, and several thousand dollars were contributed, and transmitted directly by them to Bro. Morse, S. D. G. Sire, by whom it was duly received and most promptly and efficiently applied."

About three thousand dollars were received from Subordinates in Tennessee, California, New York, District of Columbia, New Jersey, Indiana, Pennsylvania and Missouri.

The following decisions of the Grand Sire were approved :

A Grand Lodge of a State, has no power to appoint a committee of the Grand Lodge, to try a brother of a Subordinate Lodge. It may, however, order a Subordinate Lodge to try a member, and to the order, the Subordinate Lodge must yield obedience.

Any brother who has retired, and wishes to re-enter the Lodge the same evening, *may* use the Vice Grand's P. W. or the explanation of the P. W. of the current term for that purpose.

Members holding expired Withdrawal Cards, are competent applicants for Charters for new Lodges, and there is no limit to the age of the Card.

There is no law preventing members holding Dismissal Certificates from being applicants for Charters for new Lodges.

A Noble Grand has no right to refuse to put any legitimate question to the Lodge—his differing with the Lodge has nothing to do with the matter.

Every brother present, in a Lodge or Encampment, is obliged to vote on all questions, unless excused by the Lodge or Encampment; and no particular number of votes is necessary, so long as a quorum is present.

There is no reason why persons akin to each other, no matter how close the relation, should not hold office, at the same time, in the same Lodge.

A Subordinate Lodge is the proper tribunal to try all cases of delinquency, when the charge is cognizable under the laws.

Officers elect, having been examined in the ante-room, when they enter for installation do not address the chairs.

There is no law against installing officers of Subordinate Lodges in any suitable hall outside the Lodge room, provided the Form of Public Installation is used.

A brother withdrawing from his Lodge, for the purpose of establishing (with others) a new Lodge, and failing to appear when the Lodge is instituted, cannot be considered as one of the Charter members. If he wishes to join that, or any other Lodge, his Card must be presented regularly, and he must be balloted for according to law.

No brother can visit the Grand Lodge of the United States, except upon a voucher of a Representative of the State from which he hails; and no Representative is authorized to vouch for any visitor, unless he is in good standing in his Lodge and Encampment, is a Past Grand, and in possession of the Royal Purple Degree, and by being a Past Grand is meant having the Grand Lodge Degree—inasmuch as it would be absurd to admit a visitor to the Grand Lodge of the United States, who was not qualified to visit a State Grand Body.

A Lodge may appoint or elect a Chaplain, and he would be called an officer, because he holds an office; but holding that office would not make him eligible for an elective office.

The Warden's position is in front of the R. S. of the N. G., and he cannot deliver his charge from any other place without a violation of law.

There is no authority for an elective officer of a State Grand Body, to introduce into a Subordinate Lodge, a brother holding an expired Withdrawal Card—it cannot legally be done.

The Grand Secretary, in his report, said:

The experience, as well in this office, as of the Grand Secretaries generally, in jurisdictions where the annual sessions of the State Grand Bodies are held in the late spring or during the summer, renders it absolutely necessary, that the fiscal year, which now terminates 30th June, should be changed. In some instances, the annual sessions are held in July, and in others in August, rendering the preparation of reports from these Grand Bodies, by reason of the brief period which intervenes before the meeting of the Grand Lodge of the United States, unavoidably much hurried and liable to inaccuracy; in addition to which I may say, that the annual report of the Grand Corresponding and Recording Secretary is often thus delayed, to so late a period, that it is only got to press a day or two in advance of the annual session. I recommend that the fiscal year of the Grand Lodge of the United States terminate hereafter, on the 31st of December, in each and every year, and that suitable provision be made to *enforce* reports from State Grand Bodies prior to 30th June of the succeeding year.

We have abundant cause for congratulation in the present splendid exhibit of the treasury, indicative, as it most unmistakably is, of the general prosperity.

In closing this report, it is again my great pleasure to rejoice with the Representatives at the magnificent reward which has been vouchsafed to our united labors during the last year. Nearly thirty thousand members have been added to our fold, and more than a million of dollars have been applied in aid of suffering humanity. Thus do we go on, from year to year, in our noble office of benefaction, adding lustre, and glory, and renown to our beloved institution, and vindicating, by our works, our fealty to that great and good law which commands us to "visit the sick, relieve the distressed, bury the dead, and educate the orphan."

The Order in the South was reported to have greatly improved. During the recess, Warrants were issued for the Grand Encampments of Minnesota and Vermont, eight Subordinate Encampments, and three Subordinate Lodges, besides those in Germany and Switzerland.

An application was received from Lima, Peru, South America, for a Charter for a Subordinate Lodge.

Mt. Royal Lodge, No. 1, Montreal, in the Province of Quebec, Canada, was instituted, during the recess, by the Grand Sire.

The total receipts of the Grand Lodge for the past year were $42,830.79; profit on the sale of supplies $24,866.90; assets of the Grand Lodge $40,652.40.

There was an increase of 415 Lodges, and 29,240 members during the year.

The following amounts were expended by the Subordinate Lodges and Encampments, respectively:

	LODGES.	ENCAMPMENTS.
For relief of members	$664,569.40	$93,563.03
For relief of widowed families	135,742.99	5,160.25
For education of orphans	18,848.16	25.50
For burying the dead	158.400.82	15,785.27

The following important legislation was enacted:

No member of the Order shall, either directly or indirectly, use, or sanction the use, of any of the Emblems, the name, or any of the titles, or the mottoes, or the initials thereof, of this Order, in the prosecution of any private business or enterprise.

No member or officer of any Lodge or Encampment of this Order shall, either directly or indirectly, use, or permit the use of his name, as such member or officer, in any private business or enterprise.

The thanks of this Grand Lodge are extended to Baron Gerolt and Prince Bismarck, of the German Empire ; to the generous governments of Wurttemberg, Prussia, Saxony, and Switzerland ; to our Minister, George Bancroft, of Berlin, and Horace Rublee, of Switzerland; to our Consuls, O. H. Irish, at Dresden, and S. H. M. Byers, at Zurich, for their aid in securing the privilege of establishing our Order in Germanic nations.

A member of the Order shall not use any of its Emblems, its name, or any of its titles, its mottoes, or the initials thereof, in any advertisement or public display, not authorized by some law of the Order.

After one year from the date of suspension, a member dropped or suspended for non-payment of dues, may be reinstated upon the payment of the fee charged for an initiate of the same age, as prescribed by the By-Laws, or such lesser sum as may be fixed by the By-Laws of the Lodge to which such application is made ; provided such sum be not less than the amount of one year's dues of said Lodge.

Hereafter the name of any person, while living, shall not be used as the chartered name or title for any Lodge or Encampment to be instituted under the immediate jurisdiction of this Grand Lodge, or under that of any jurisdiction subordinate thereto.

Degree Lodges of the Daughters of Rebekah, are authorized to ballot on all applications for membership in such Lodges, and a majority vote of all members present, and voting, shall be necessary for an election to membership, except in such jurisdictions as may otherwise provide.

The time in which rejected applicants may renew their application in a Degree Lodge of the Daughters of Rebekah, is left to the jurisdictions subordinate to this Grand Lodge.

Art. XXVI. of the By-Laws, was amended to read :

The Fiscal Year of this Grand Lodge shall commence on the first day of January and terminate on the thirty-first day of December, and all Grand and Subordinate Lodges and Encampments shall make their annual reports, as required by Article X, to correspond with the Fiscal Year.

Distinctive Regalia, and Stations for appointed officers of Subordinate Encampments, were adopted.

Grand Secretary Ridgely, on behalf of the brotherhood of California, presented to Bro. John F. Morse, Special Deputy Grand Sire for Germanic Europe and the Republic of Switzerland, a Grand Representative's Jewel. Its artistic maker ingeniously blended, in symbolic union, the nationality of the United States and Germany and the Emblems of Odd Fellowship, while the American Eagle in solid gold, and in full relief, surmounted the whole. The Jewel weighed seven ounces, and was of eighteen carat gold. Thirty diamonds, fourteen rubies, one garnet and forty-five pearls embellished it. On the reverse of the medal were engraved the following words: " Presented to Jno. F. Morse, S. D. G. Sire, G. Rep., and P. G. Master of California, I. O. O. F., by the Lodges of San Francisco, commemorating the successful establishment of the Order in Germany and Switzerland, under his auspices. September, 1871."

1872.

The Grand Lodge met in annual session, in the City of Baltimore, on the 16th of September.

Grand Sire Stuart, in his report, said:

Grateful to Almighty God that my life has been graciously preserved to meet you again in council, that it is my privilege to share with you in the duties and pleasures of another of our accustomed re-unions, and to mingle my heartfelt congratulations with yours at our continued prosperity, I render, pursuant to law, my second annual report.

It is a source of profound gratification, that I am permitted to greet you with the gladsome salutation, that "all is well within our borders," that by the mercy of that good Providence, whose kind favor has been always our chief support, our labors during the past year have been rewarded with an abundant yield, and that unbroken harmony and concord, throughout the entire brotherhood, combine to illustrate, as well our fidelity and devotion to our principles, as our unwearied energy and zeal for the advancement of the general welfare.

The correspondence with Australasia, that distant part of our jurisdiction, has been extremely limited during the past year; yet, enough has been learned from Special Deputy Grand Sire, Henry Vine, to assure us of the continued prosperity of our beloved Order in each of the jurisdictions of Australia and New Zealand, of the profound respect the members in that region have for this Right Worthy Body, and of the warm fraternal feeling which they entertain for their brethren on this continent.

It is a source of inexpressible pleasure to me to be able to report that Odd Fellowship in Europe is already in a highly prosperous condition. The reports, and correspondence from the District Deputy Grand Sires, Hugo Wollheim for Prussia, M. Bernheim for Wurttemberg, O. Arnoux for Saxony, and C. Heinrich for Switzerland, give abundant evidence of the fact that our relations with our trans-Atlantic brethren are of the most friendly and fraternal character; and that they are fully imbued with the pure and ennobling principles of our institution. The progress, considering all things, has been fully equal to what was expected. At the last session, there were five Lodges and one Encampment, now there are eleven Subordinate Lodges, one Degree Lodge, one Rebekah Degree Lodge, and one Encampment, with a flattering prospect of largely increasing the number of Lodges and extending the area of our field of labor.

The official term for which, by your partiality, I was elected, is drawing to a close, and in looking back upon my administration, I am cheered by the consciousness of having left unemployed, no effort within my power to promote the general welfare.

Doubtless, I have left undone much that ought to have been done, and it may be that I have done some things which I ought not to have done; nevertheless, I feel assured that our beloved Order has not suffered from any error of judgment on my part, but, on the contrary, has advanced upward and onward, moving forward proudly, conquering every obstacle in its path, and fulfilling grandly its high mission. I tender my sincere thanks to the brotherhood at large, for their fraternal courtesies and hospitalities wherever it has been my duty and my pleasure to appear among them. I thank this distinguished Grand Body, for the kind and generous spirit of indulgence which it has ever extended to me, the memory of which I shall long cherish. I thank my associate Grand Officers, for their hearty co-operation and wise counsels. Especially am I indebted to my much esteemed friend and brother, the R. W. Grand Corresponding and Recording Secretary, not only for the valuable aid he has given me in the performance of the varied and responsible duties incident to my office, but for the brotherly love and delicate consideration, for which he has ever, and more particularly during the past two years, evinced towards me; and now, when I am about to retire from my high office, I desire to commend our beloved Order to the favor of Him who has ever been our " strength and shield," and to whom we owe our splendid fortune, invoking in its behalf His further succor and support.

The Order was introduced into Peru, South America, by the institution of Lima Lodge, No. 1, at Lima.

Soon after the session of 1871, the great Chicago fire occurred, and the appeal made to the brethren for relief for the sufferers, resulted in the reception, for that purpose, of the magnificent sum of $131,000.00.

The following decisions of the Grand Sire were submitted, but by inadvertence were not approved until the session of 1873:

The Grand Lodge of the United States has not said how many black balls shall reject a candidate, except so far as applies to Subordinate Lodges under its immediate jurisdiction—that says, three black balls reject, etc.

An application for membership, may be withdrawn without permission of the Lodge, before the report of the committee thereon is read to the Lodge, but not afterwards.

Any brother of the Order, suspended *indefinitely* for cause, no matter when, should, under the existing general law, be at once reinstated or restored to membership.

No Subordinate Lodge can reinstate an expelled member of its own motion. The consent of the Grand Lodge to which the Lodge is subordinate, or of the Grand Master, by its authority, is absolutely necessary to authorize the restoration.

The Grand Secretary, in his report, said :

It is almost a third of a century since, when comparatively a youth in years and experience, I entered upon the office of Grand Secretary of this august Grand Body. By your unreserved confidence and favor, I have continued its incumbent up to this day. The record will better contrast the position in 1841 and 1872 than any words which I could employ, and with more propriety. During that protracted incumbency, it would, indeed, be extraordinary if I had not committed errors, and if, with the best intentions otherwise, I had not sometimes counselled unwisely ; yet, our beloved Order has suffered no detriment thereby, for its career has been always onward and upward, scattering with generous love, the richest blessings in its pathway. The highest ambition of my life has been to prove myself worthy of your confidence. In this endeavor I have, in part at least, succeeded, since your faith in me as an officer, has been unbounded, has never wavered, and has been the most cherished treasure of my life. To measure up to the vast responsibility, which such a confidence inevitably challenges from a just man, has occupied my deepest solicitude, and my most constant efforts. To know and feel that I have conciliated your approval, have won your love and your marked appreciation, gives me the assurance, that in your judgment, the trust has not been misplaced. How then, after the lapse of so many years of life, in so delightful a moral atmosphere, could this occasion give rise to other than fragrant memories ! The retrospect of every one of those succeeding years, laden with such precious freight, is before me at this moment, and with overwhelming volume. The emotions which struggle within me, under such a train of thought, who can idealize—by what moral alchemist may they be analyzed ? The past, the beautiful past, lies before me in grand perspective. Odd Fellowship, from its tender years to its maturity, may be traced ; its lights and shadows, ups and downs, and varied experiences, may be progressively discerned, beginning far away in the distant horizon, following along its glorious pathway to its meridian sun. Of this we are sure, but what of the future, the great future ? Echo says what ! and reverberation, to use the beautiful idea of my brother Morse, answers echo.

True, my brethren, no oracle will reach us from that future ; true, no lesson nor instruction can it impart ; yet, with unerring certainty the past will pronounce upon its performances ; that past will be the voice of God, for it will be the law of cause and effect. The same labor, the same wisdom, the same devotion, the same fidelity, will produce in the future, like fruits, yet richer and grander, in proportion to the light and resources which experience will supply.

To realize this possession, will be the heritage of our descendants, perhaps the privilege of some of this generation. The aged Patriarch, as advancing years cast their shadows upon his waning disc of life, may, like the captain of Israel's host, look out upon the distant promised land. In the presence of this pregnant moral, let us thank a beneficent God, who has lengthened our span of life, " To the sere and yellow leaf," for the splendor of the vision.

For myself, I pray that my eyes may rest upon it to the end, as the sweetest solace of declining years.

The total receipts of the Grand Lodge, for the year, were $41,832.30; profit on supplies, $21,735.34.

The following amounts were expended by the Subordinate Lodges and Encampments, respectively:

	LODGES.	ENCAMPMENTS.
For relief of members	$526,945.51	$77,352.06
For relief of widowed families	87,373.09	3,695.92
For education of orphans	9,784.65	77.16
For burying the dead	125,819.72	12,873.72

The membership of the Subordinate Lodges was now 348,898, and of the Subordinate Encampments, 67,813.

The following were adopted :

That there be added to the Standing Committees of this Grand Lodge, a "Committee on the Degree of Rebekah," a "Committee on Printing Supplies," and a "Committee on Foreign Relations," each to consist of seven members.

In cases in which a Subordinate Lodge has suspended a member for cause, other than non-payment of dues, the Lodge may commute or remit such portion of his accumulated dues (if unpaid), as it may determine, upon the reinstatement of such brother, such matters being properly the subject of local legislation.

It is not lawful to pass a local law whereby a Subordinate Lodge or Encampment may receive a fixed sum as dues, and, as a consideration therefor, relieve the member, so paying, from further obligation to be charged with dues during his membership.

Encampments are permitted to wear such style of Street Uniform, on parade, as may be sanctioned by the Grand Encampments of their respective jurisdictions ; but under no circumstances shall the funds of an Encampment be appropriated to meet any expense incurred thereby.

This Grand Lodge respectfully requests all State Grand Jurisdictions, to make such returns of Rebekah Degree Lodges, as will enable this Grand Lodge, at its next session, to fully estimate the claims of the Rebekah Degree Branch of our Order for a radical change in their membership relations to Odd Fellowship.

The Grand Corresponding and Recording Secretary be, and he hereby is, authorized and empowered to appoint a subordinate in his office, to be called the "Assistant of the Grand Secretary," who shall perform such duties as may, from time to time, be assigned to him by that officer. The said Assistant shall be removable at the pleasure of the Grand Secretary, and shall receive such compensation as shall be prescribed by law.

In addition to the said Assistant, it shall be lawful for the Grand Secretary, from time to time, as he shall find it necessary to do so, to appoint and remove at his pleasure, such temporary assistants, clerical, or other aid, as may be required for the satisfactory discharge of the duties of his office. Such additional force shall receive a compensation, not to exceed a maximum to be prescribed by law.

Representatives who have eulogies to pronounce upon deceased brothers, are permitted to prepare them in writing and lay them on the Secretary's desk, and have them printed in the Journal.

Constitutions of Grand Lodges and Grand Encampments, and all amendments thereto, upon approval by this Grand Lodge, immediately become in force, and do not depend for validity upon any further action whatever.

It is not competent for a Subordinate Lodge to enact a By-Law restricting membership to persons not over a certain age.

It is not the right of a Subordinate Lodge, under the existing laws, to require any member in good standing, to retire from the Lodge room while such Lodge is open in the Initiatory Degree.

If the successor of the retiring Noble Grand has been duly installed, and if said past officer possesses all other requisite qualifications at the time of his election, he is then eligible to the office of Grand Representative to the Grand Lodge of the United States.

A Charter was granted to the ten Subordinate Lodges in Germany, for the " Grand Lodge of the German Empire," to be located at Berlin, Prussia. The committee, in their report on the subject, said :

Let us now establish a principle, upon which our relations to the Order in foreign countries can rest secure. Let us now give Germany a Charter, the great feature of which shall be freedom in Odd Fellowship. Let us dedicate all Germany as a Temple of the Order, and then our German brothers can proclaim, in the language of our dedicatory service, Odd Fellowship hath here a home.

The Grand Sire was authorized to establish the Order in the British Isles, on proper application, if he shall be of the opinion that it is judicious to take that step.

Suitable Regalia (usually called " a combination Collar,") was adopted for a Past Grand, who is also a Past Chief Patriarch.

The use of trust funds and property of defunct Lodges and Encampments, was extended so as to be applied to the assistance of the widows and orphans of such defunct Bodies, etc.

A Diagram of a Lodge room, to show the relative positions of the various officers of a Subordinate Lodge, was adopted.

The following Grand Officers were elected and installed: Cornelius A. Logan, P. D. G. Sire, of Kansas, Grand Sire; M. J. Durham, P. G. M., of Kentucky, Deputy Grand Sire; James L. Ridgely, P. G. M., of Maryland, Grand Corresponding and Recording Secretary; Joshua Vansant, P. G. M., of Maryland, Grand Treasurer.

The following were appointed by the Grand Sire: Rev. J. W. Venable, P. G. Rep., of Kentucky, Grand Chaplain; Caleb Rand, P. G. M., of Massachusetts, Grand Marshal; A. Cohen, P. G. M., of Arkansas, Grand Guardian; J. W. Hudson, P. G. Rep., of Wisconsin, Grand Messenger.

1873.

The Grand Lodge met in annual session, in the City of Baltimore, on the 15th of September.

Grand Sire Logan, who at this time was United States Minister to Chile, was not present at the session, and Deputy Grand Sire Durham presided.

The report of Grand Sire Logan, received on the 17th, contained the following:

Since this Grand Body last convened in regular session, the plastic hand of time has moulded twelve fleeting months into a completed year, and has notched another mark upon the tally-stick of all our lives; another click has been heard in the machinery of the universe; another step has been taken toward the goal to which we are inevitably tending; thirteen moons have fulled and waned, and another sun going down in untarnished glory, has lengthened the shadow of the world, another measure of distance toward the eternity, when "the wrecks of matter and the crush of worlds" shall announce the birth of the millennial man. "The year that's awa," has been pregnant with events, not alone in the world at large, but also in that portion of it, which we, as Odd Fellows, represent.

GERMANY.—As soon as practicable after the adjournment of the last session, the Charter for *The Grand Lodge of the German Empire*, was prepared in accordance with the special grant, and duly forwarded to BRO. Hugo Wollhelm, D. D. Grand Sire for Prussia, with a Special Commission, authorizing him, or such proper person as he might appoint, to institute the same. The papers reached their destination in good season, and "The Grand Lodge of the German Empire" was formally instituted at Frankfort-on-the-Main, pursuant to previous notice to each District or Jurisdiction, on the twenty-eighth day of December, 1872. The following brothers were duly chosen Grand Officers: Hugo Wollheim, M. W. Grand Sire; M. Bernheim, R. W. Deputy Grand Sire; Otto Schaettle, R. W. Grand Secretary; Wm. Altvater, R. W. Grand Marshal; E. Wenzel, R. W. Grand Chaplain; S. Spiro, R. W. Grand Guardian; G. Berlin, R. W. Grand Messenger.

SWITZERLAND.—Three Lodges have been instituted in this historic Republic: Helvetia Lodge, No. 1, Zurich; Pestalozzi, No. 2, Baden; Fellenberg, No. 3, Berne. The jurisdiction is at this time under the charge of D. D. Grand Sire Altenhoffer, and the Lodges named, are in a highly prosperous condition. BRO. Heinrich, the former D. D. Grand Sire, has proven himself one of the most efficient workers in the cause of Odd Fellowship in Europe, and the success of the Order in Switzerland, is largely due to his energy and ability. A public dedication of the Odd Fellows' Hall in Zurich, was held on October 1st, and was a most gratifying success. Believing we have struck the true policy of propagandism, in the organization of parent Bodies in foreign countries, when circumstances and sufficient numbers warrant it, I recommend that proper measures be taken for the organization of a Grand Lodge for Switzerland.

I had hoped to have been with you in person, at your present session, up to a recent moment; but the lateness of my arrival in Chile, and the many claims upon my time, will prevent it, greatly to my disappointment and sorrow. I have the promise to make, however, that no effort shall be spared on my part, to advance the interests of the Order, and no duty neglected, whereby its well-being may suffer. Should my life and health be spared, I shall enjoy the pleasure, (to me, a most genuine one), of meeting you again at our next session. Let me then bid you adieu until that time, with the expression of the hope, that you may enjoy a pleasant and profitable session, and that the good work in which you are engaged—now become part of the history of the epoch in which we live—may continue to grow in proportion, until its spread shall comprehend every people of the globe, and its happy influence be everywhere recognized among the dwellers of earth,

> "As the rainbow to the storms of life;
> The evening beam, that smiles the clouds away,
> And tints to-morrow with prophetic ray."

The following decisions of the Grand Sire were approved:

The official term of Grand Officers, is twelve months, and they must serve for a major period of the term, or they are not entitled to the past Honors.

The Constitution of a State Grand Body can be amended only in the manner prescribed by the Constitution itself.

Neither a Grand Lodge, nor any Body subordinate to the Grand Lodge of the United States, can change the terms of officers.

It is not a compliance with the law requiring that officers shall wear *Jewels* to have them *wrought* in the Regalia.

The Grand Secretary, in his report, said :

We are building up an improved civilization, in fact, a great moral empire. In co-operation with the noble spirit of benevolence which marks the age, we are adding our rich contributions to the general welfare. As the world moves, and its needs expand, there must be a corresponding supply. This supply is met by the progress of society, by the progress of individuals, by the elevation and amelioration of men and women, in the continuous development of mind, and in the application of its reward to the ever-shifting drama of life. Odd Fellowship has been, during fifty years, in this great field. What are its fruits ? If we cast our eyes upon the broad and beautiful expanse of our happy country we are greeted on every hand by a response to this inquiry, which comes ringing from afar off, with electric power. Wherever our people have penetrated, in whatever distant or perilous quarter, even to the remotest frontier, do our temples lift their spires and our workmen toil. As the wilderness passes from chaos to order, and system follows in the footsteps of civilization, does Odd Fellowship supply its aid to the great transition. Nor do these offerings limit their sphere to home, to country, or nationality. Wide as the world is our scope, and free as the air is our welcome to the children of men. Scattered far away, distant thousands of miles from the birth-place of Odd Fellowship, do its conquests extend, and does its broad catholic spirit seek larger fields and more distant climes. A work of such magnitude, is not the reward of a day or generation, but is for all time, for all peoples, and for humanity. Time is the great regulator, the balance-wheel which adjusts the moral as well as the material world ; it is the stern winnower which separates the chaff from the wheat. By its authority, virtue survives and vice falls. To it, analysis and philosophical processes, systems, doctrines, dogmas, and theories of every kind must stand. As it rolls on, its tests are in motion, evolving and resolving, until in its own fulness, truth is delivered from error. To this ordeal do we confidently submit. Thus is civilization advanced. In this struggle we have gallantly toiled, as a band of brothers, impelled only by the instinctive law of love. We have covered every habitable part of our own happy land with laborers in this great cause ; have carried our system to Germanic Europe, to Switzerland, to the islands of the Pacific Ocean, to the continents of South America and Australia, and it is simply a question of time when Odd Fellowship shall dwell all over the world. Considering the relation of human events with each other, in all the past, this sentiment is natural as well as logical. From this standpoint, our system of human beneficence is but in its childhood, and however great the distance which our fathers may have advanced it, the prize which is before us, if we labor on, is immeasurably beyond.

During the recess, the Grand Encampment of Colorado was instituted, and Warrants were issued for four Subordinate Encampments, (one of which was located in Dresden, Saxony,) and seven Subordinate Lodges, (one in Saxony, two in Switzerland, one in Peru and one in Montreal.)

The Charter of one Encampment was restored, and duplicate Charters were issued to one Lodge and one Encampment.

The receipts of the Grand Lodge were $50,156.93; profit on supplies, $23,471.55.

The following amounts were expended by the Subordinate Lodges and Encampments, respectively :

	LODGES.	ENCAMPMENTS.
For relief of members....................	$927,428.06	$129,782.91
For relief of widowed families.............	163,207.91	8,392.17
For education of orphans....	19,126.72	218.00
For burying the dead....................	233,127.39	22,256.86

The following were adopted :

Dismissal Certificates shall be authenticated by the signature of the Grand Corresponding and Recording Secretary, as in the case of Withdrawal and Visiting Cards.

This Grand Lodge will not interfere with the right of State Grand Encampments to determine the question, as to whether Past High Priests shall, or shall not, be members of its Body.

A member of any Grand Encampment, under the jurisdiction of this Grand Lodge, shall, if in good standing, on due proof of such membership, under existing laws, be entitled to visit any other of the Grand Encampments of the Order, anything to the contrary in any local law, notwithstanding.

Grand Encampments, in their several jurisdictions, are hereby authorized to allow Subordinate Encampments to elect Financial Scribes.

Grand Lodges, having Degree Lodges of the Daughters of Rebekah, under their jurisdiction, shall require such Lodges to report annually, on the thirty-first of December, the information necessary to complete the returns required by this Grand Lodge.

The Grand Corresponding and Recording Secretary is instructed to procure Visiting Cards for use of sisters of the Rebekah Degree ; the same to be printed in a neat manner, on paper similar to the Visiting Cards for brothers of the Order, and to be furnished State jurisdictions at the same price as other Visiting Cards.

The application to print and issue Visiting and Withdrawal Cards in the German language, to be issued exclusively by the Grand Lodge of the German Empire, is granted ; said Cards to be printed only on the backs of our Visiting and Withdrawal Cards, in accordance with the form submitted with the petition, except that the initials I. O. O. F., being emblematical characters of the Order, are to be substituted in place of U. O. S. B.

Any Grand Lodge, or Grand Encampment, may regulate the matter of the numbers of extinct Subordinate Lodges, or Encampments, in their respective jurisdictions, that have been extinct more than twenty years, and any law that conflicts with this resolution is hereby repealed.

It is lawful for a Lodge, under some circumstances, to refuse to pay a brother's benefits during a disability because of immoral conduct, without charges, trial and conviction, under the penal provisions of the Constitution.

The Grand Corresponding and Recording Secretary be, and he is hereby authorized and empowered, to appoint a subordinate in his office, to be called the " Assistant Grand Secretary," who shall be a competent book-keeper ; who shall have charge of all supplies furnished by this Grand Lodge, receiving and disbursing the same. The said officer to be under the control of, and removable by the Grand Secretary ; and, in addition to the above services, he shall perform generally, such duties as the Grand Secretary may direct.

No member or members of any Subordinate Lodge or Encampment, shall vote upon any question in which he or they may be interested, or in which he or they intend to become interested, by reason of his or their connection, or intended connection, with any Lodge or Encampment of this Order, then existing or about to exist, or with any other organization. And, should a member, or members so vote, he or they shall, upon the discovery and proof of the fact, be considered guilty of unbecoming conduct, for which he or they may be suspended from the Order. And the Lodge or Encampment in which the offense was committed, may, in case said member has joined some other Lodge or Encampment of this Order, institute charges for said offense, in said other jurisdiction, with the right to appeal from its decision, should the brother be acquitted of the charge.

When a member of an Encampment, in good standing, is sick or disabled and under the care of, and receiving benefits from the Encampment, his membership therein, shall not be affected during the continuation of said sickness or disability, although the Subordinate Lodge of which he was a member, may have ceased to exist, by reason of a surrender or forfeiture of its Charter.

Hereafter there shall he no forfeiture of membership in Degree Lodges of the Daughters of Rebekah, except by such rules and usages as apply to brothers in Subordinate Lodges.

Hereafter no printed, or written communications, from Grand or Subordinate Lodges, under the immediate jurisdiction of this Grand Lodge, will be considered, unless the same shall be presented before the close of the third day of each annual session.

A Form for Reports of Grand Lodges concerning Degree Lodges of the Daughters of Rebekah was adopted, and also an " Order of Business," to be printed in future editions of the Degree of Rebekah Charge Book.

The Special Committee on Dues and Benefits and Mutual Aid Associations made an elaborate report, full of useful information. (*See Journal, pages* 5906—5615.)

Appropriate resolutions were adopted, eulogistic of the life and character of John A. Kennedy, P. G. Sire whose decease was announced. The remarks of Grand Secretary

Ridgely, Past Grand Sire Ellison, Representatives Medole and Fitzhugh, on the life, ability and invaluable services of this beloved and lamented brother, are worthy of perusal. (*See Journal, pages* 5863—5871.)

A few hours before the close of the session, Rep. Washburn, on behalf of Bro. Sehorn, Rep., and Bro. Danbury Past Grand Representative, presented to Grand Secretary Ridgely a very odd and emblematic cane, combining the history of the Grand Secretary and the Order. (*See Journal, pages* 5962—5964.)

The Grand Secretary was requested to act as Historiographer of the Grand Lodge, and supervise and direct the preparation of a history of Odd Fellowship for publication, under the direction of the Grand Lodge of the United States, and an appropriation of three thousand dollars was made to defray expenses.

1874.

The Grand Lodge met in annual session, in the City of Atlanta, on the 21st of September, and was heartily welcomed and hospitably entertained by the brethren and citizens of Georgia.

Grand Sire Logan was at his position in Chile, as United States Minister, and, on account of ill-health and pressing public duties, was unable to attend the session. Deputy Grand Sire Durham presided.

Grand Sire Logan, in his report, said:

Modern science tells us that no atom of matter is ever lost in the economy of the universe; but that dissolution simply implies reconstruction, and the formerly supposed annihilation of death, a new, and perhaps, more complex life. In the great laboratory of nature's moral forces, however, there are elements as unchangeable as the property of matter called gravitation, which, when it shall cease to act, or change its form, all things terrestrial shall be

    *   *   "Melted into air, into thin air;
And, like the baseless fabric of this vision,
The cloud-capp'd towers, the gorgeous palaces,
The solemn temples, the great globe itself,
Yea, all which it inherit, shall dissolve,
And like this insubstantial pageant faded,
Leave not a rack behind."

Among these elemental moral forces, insusceptible to change without absolute destruction to man, as a living being, is the feeling of association with his brother man ; the feeling which stamps the brand of *humanity* upon his species ; the feeling which it is the design of this Order to culture and perpetuate ; the feeling which expresses itself in the sentiment of *brotherhood*, and draws the sharp line of separation between man as an animal, and the baser creations disputing the conditions of organic life with him. Such a moral force as this, is intrinsically and radically a principle precedent of human existence ; it is an elemental unit in which neither time nor circumstance, can move the breadth of a hair. Antiquity cannot measure it—space cannot gauge it. It lives through the independency of its own creation, and is perpetuated as one of the factors of a higher vitality.

Dealing with such a force, founded upon such a basis, the great work of Odd Fellowship must roll on through all ages of man's career, and cease only when his mission is fulfilled. While dealing with man in the aggregate, as the *summum bonum* of its aspiration toward man in the individual, the unit is but an atom of the mass, and the work of a single hand can be duplicated by a million others. Who built the Pyramids, which for forty centuries have watched the fretful changing of the Libyan sands, beneath the burning sun of Egypt ? The answer comes from a myriad of artisans, not one of whom was of more importance to the completed structure as a whole, than a single granule in the composition of their rocky masses.

This being true of a mere mechanical work, how much more apposite the observation to a work which deals, not with man in his material form, but with his higher, intellectual life, intimately associated as it is, and trenching upon the borders of his spiritual and immaterial aspects. The voice of brotherhood is the voice of God, out of the mouth of man ; and will resound through the labyrinths of Time, until the echo is swallowed up in the chasms of Eternity.

Hence, while all may give their best energies to a good work, with the assurance that something has been added to the common store, though but a particle of sand upon the shores of the sea, let no one vainly imagine his efforts to be indispensable—his little span to compass the orbit of a universe ; but rather let him, while drawing comfort from the tribute of his mite, remember the song of the brook : " For men may come, and men may go ; But I flow on forever."

He reported the Order, at home and abroad, to be in a flourishing condition. He instituted Valparaiso Lodge, No. 1, at Valparaiso, Chile, April 14th, 1874, with seven petitioners, three of whom held regular Cards and four he "made" Odd Fellows for the purpose.

The Grand Secretary announced the selection, by the Committee on Printing Supplies, of Theodore A. Ross, Grand Representative of the Grand Lodge of New Jersey, as Assistant Grand Secretary, who was formally invited,

by the Grand Secretary, to the position, and entered upon
the discharge of the duties December 1st, 1873.

In his report, the Grand Secretary said :

It is my pleasure and privilege to rejoice with you, my brethren, that we
have been permitted, in the providence of God, once more to assemble in
annual council. We are gathered from all quarters of our beloved country,
and from the neighboring nationalities, with one heart in the great cause which
unites us. No mandate from Government, no summons from civil or eccle-
siastical authority, no political shibboleth, no tocsin of war, no cry of sect
reform, which in the same breath professes virtue and practices intolerance ;
yea, no personal or individual aspiration of any kind draws us together.

Our presence in this beautiful city of the Empire State of the South,
among its generous people, is by special invitation from our noble brethren,
to mingle with them at their homes and firesides, and to grasp their hands
with true fraternal warmth. Our mission is one of love, pure and disinterested. In that cause only, are we here as temporary exiles from our families,
our business and our private interests. How morally grand such a spectacle,
how sublime the sentiment which impels the offering !

This cause we have pursued, through good report and through evil report, in the furtherance of which we have expended many long years of precious time, many millions of treasure, and many heroic laborers have fallen by
the way, without the slightest worldly expectation or desire ; a cause which
our fathers, in the goodness of their hearts, set on foot and actively advanced,
in their day and generation, and which they bequeathed to us as a precious
legacy ; which we have cherished and venerated as a sacred heritage, and
which, by the blessing of God, we mean to transmit, as an " improved talent,"
" to our children's children, and to their descendants."

Warrants for five Grand Lodges, (Switzerland, British
Columbia, Wyoming, Montana and Utah,) eight Subordinate Lodges, and eight Subordinate Encampments, were
issued during the recess.

The receipts of the Grand Lodge were $44,266.13 ;
profit on supplies $25,397.92.

The following amounts were paid by the Subordinate
Lodges and Encampments, respectively :

	LODGES.	ENCAMPMENTS.
For relief of members..................	$926,211.24	$122,349.67
For relief of widowed families.............	153,216.93	5,911.00
For education of orphans..................	17,891.38	45.00
For burying the dead.....................	231,275.06	22,238.39

The members of Degree Lodges of the Daughters of
Rebekah numbered 15,213. They paid out for relief of

brothers, $313.00; sisters, $2,140.05; widowed families, $452.50; orphans, $269.88, and for burying the dead, $374.90. Total relief $3,550.33. Nineteen jurisdictions reported 512 Lodges.

A new Funeral Ceremony was adopted; also a Ceremony to be observed at the celebration of the Anniversary of the Order. (*See Journal, pages* 6173, 6174, 6175, 6181, 6182, 6183, 6184, 6185).

The following were adopted:

Past High Priests, who are Past Grands, and members of a Grand Encampment, may wear the combined Regalia now authorized to be worn by Past Chief Patriarchs.

In *no case* can a Lodge adopt a By-Law for the admission of members by deposit of Card, in any different way from that pointed out by the general law, viz., by an application referred to a committee, and ballot, as in case of an original application for membership.

The Grand Sire be, and he is hereby authorized, to adopt such measures in relation to the establishment of the Order in Austria, as shall seem to him most judicious, for obtaining the permission of the Austrian Government to establish the Order in Austria, and of establishing it there if such permission be obtained.

Hereafter, no vote shall be taken on any motion or resolution required to be submitted in writing, until the same has been read in full from the desk of the Grand Secretary.

Each officer and member of this Grand Lodge, is requested to furnish the Committee on Mileage and Per Diem, with the name of the State, or country of his nativity, to be printed in the table prepared by them.

Every brother present in a Lodge or Encampment, if qualified to vote, is obliged to vote on all questions, unless excused by the Lodge or Encampment, and no particular number of votes is necessary so long as a quorum is present.

The manner in which expelled members shall be received back into the Order, is and has always been left to local legislation.

None but members of the R. P. Degree shall be permitted to wear the street Uniform described in the report on pages 6242, 6243, 6317, 6318, 6319, Journal.

Another Standing Committe be, and is hereby constituted, to consist of seven members, and to be known as the "Committee on Miscellaneous Business."

All spirituous vinous, and malt liquors shall be excluded from the Lodge rooms and ante-rooms, or halls connected with, or adjoining thereto, when under the control of any Subordinate or Degree Lodge or Encampment of this Order.

"The sole right and privilege to confer the several Encampment Degrees, having been granted by this Grand Lodge to the several Grand Encampments, in their respective jurisdictions, it is regarded as a solemn compact, that cannot be recalled or revoked by this Body, so long as the said Grand Encampments shall keep inviolate their obligations to this Grand Lodge," is but declaratory of the existing law found in the third Section of Article I of the Constitution of this Grand Lodge ; and this Grand Lodge has the power " to deprive such State, District or Territorial Grand Bodies of their Charters, and annul their authority ; *provided*, that such deprivation or annulment shall only be made for violation of the laws of this Grand Lodge."

The Grand Encampment of Pennsylvania, presented a protest against mergement of the Encampments with Subordinate Lodges.

The Committee on Revision reported that they had completed the work entrusted to them. They collated, revised and corrected the following books, viz: The Subordinate Charge Book, the Subordinate Degree Book, the Rebekah Degree Book, the Subordinate Encampment Book, all of which were accepted and approved.

An amended Form for the Election and Installation of the Officers of the Grand Lodge of the United States was adopted.

The following Grand Officers were elected and installed: M. J. Durham, P. D. G. Sire, of Kentucky, Grand Sire; John W. Stokes, P. G. M., of Pennsylvania, Deputy Grand Sire; James L. Ridgely, P. G. M., of Maryland, Grand Corresponding and Recording Secretary; Joshua Vansant, P. G. M., of Maryland, Grand Treasurer.

The Grand Sire appointed the following: Rev. John W. Venable, P. G. Rep., of Kentucky, Grand Chaplain ; John R. Tompkins, P. G. Rep., of Alabama, Grand Marshal ; John W. Hudson, P. G. Rep., of Wisconsin, Grand Messenger.

The Grand Corresponding and Recording Secretary appointed as his Assistant, Theodore A. Ross, G. Rep., of New Jersey.

1875.

The Grand Lodge met in annnal session, in the City of Indianapolis, on the 20th of September.

A Committee of Arrangements on the part of the Grand Lodge and Grand Encampment of Indiana, met the members

of the Grand Lodge of the United States, as they arrived at
the depot, and conducted them to their hotels. At noon the
officers and members were escorted by the Grand Lodge
and Grand Encampment of Indiana and the Uniformed
Patriarchs of Indianapolis, to the Academy of Music,
where they were welcomed by the Hon. T. A. Hendricks,
Governor of the State, the Hon. John Caven, Mayor of the
City. Bro. O. P. Morton, P. G. M., U. S. Senator, and
Bro, Schuyler Colfax, P. G. Rep. Responses were delivered by the Grand Sire and Grand Secretary. In the
evening, the Governor and Mrs. Hendricks gave a reception to the Grand Lodge of the United States, which
was attended by members of the Order and prominent
citizens of the State. There was a grand parade on the
22nd, in which there were thirteen bands of music, and three
thousand Odd Fellows in line. The festivities of the day
culminated in a grand banquet at the Occidental Hotel,
which three hundred and twenty-five guests attended.

Grand Sire Durham, in his report, said :

One year ago we met in legislative council in the sunny South, in her
Empire State ; to-day we meet in the great Mississippi valley, in one of its
most populous and powerful States. There we were welcomed to that hospitable region, by the authorities of one of her most beautiful cities, by an
honored and respected jurisdiction, and by a devoted and zealous brotherhood. Here the authorities of this great and prosperous State and of this
beautiful city, the representatives of this honored, enlightened jurisdiction, and
of this intelligent fraternity, welcome us to their midst, to their homes and
their hospitalities. These evidences of honor and respect, should impress us
with the high position attained by this Body in public esteem, and stimulate us
to maintain in the future, its past reputation and standing. The future success
of this institution in ameliorating the condition of mankind, in elevating the
character of our members, or in making honorable this Body, depends greatly
upon the care and attention with which your deliberations are marked. Nothing tends so much to retard our progress as hasty and careless legislation ;
and I therefore ask of you great care and study in your deliberations, so that
the laws passed, and decisions made by you, may be in accordance with our
Constitution, and in harmony with the spirit and genius of our Ritual. I am
glad to be able to announce to you the continued increase and prosperity of
our Order, at home and abroad, and to a kind Providence we should render
hearty thanks for all His mercies to us, individually and collectively. Although
our increase is considerable, yet it would have been far greater but for the
general financial condition and distress of the country, which has caused the

dropping of many good and true men, who have been unable to pay their dues.

Reject all doubtful propositions which will introduce new and untried customs and usages into the Ritual and Work of the Order. Mature every law proposed, and consider well its harmony with past legislation, which has worked well, and how it is to tell upon our future prosperity and growth. Let us improve, beautify, and adorn the pathway so well marked out for us, rather than try some unknown route. Let courtesy, kindness, moderation, and brotherly love characterize all your deliberations ; remembering that upon the great Ruler of the Universe we must rely for success, and without whose fostering care all our works are as nothing.

The following decisions of the Grand Sire were approved:

A Subordinate Encampment should not use its funds to procure street Uniforms.

The law authorizing the N. G. of a Lodge to communicate the Semiannual Password to a brother of another Lodge, at the request of the N. G. of the Lodge to which he may belong, under the Seal of the Lodge, applies to the N. G's in the same jurisdiction, and not in different jurisdictions.

A member in good standing in his Lodge, is entitled to pecuniary benefits while sick and unable to attend to his ordinary vocation, although he may have an income sufficient for his support.

It is lawful for a Subordinate Lodge to donate its funds for any purpose within the object and scope of the Order.

A brother in good standing, cannot be kept out of his Grand or Subordinate Lodge while the minutes of the preceding meeting are being read, if he desires to enter, and can work his way into the Lodge.

There is no law compelling Subordinate Lodges to send their members to a Degree Lodge, to receive the Degrees, although the Degree Lodge may be in the same city or town.

The Grand Secretary, in his report, said:

Odd-Fellowship—its promotion, diffusion, and preservation *alone*, assembles this Body of citizens from every State, District and Territory of our confederacy, and from the neighboring nationality of Canada. Like all other institutions devised for the benefit of mankind, it is the fruit of a progressive civilization. By this power, it has been wonderfully advanced and developed in the expansion of its capabilities, and the enlargement of its field of labor. After more than fifty years of unremitting effort in its proper sphere, it has become a fixed institution of society, as a reliable secular aid against the pressure of suffering humanity. It has grown, as many other orders of kindred character, formed in a good degree upon its example, out of the demand for auxiliaries, by the physical, as well as the moral needs of men. Progress and civilization, which are practically correlative terms, are always moving under the light of accumulating experience, constrained by a continuous necessity, as "the mother of invention." All our institutions, whether social, political, religious, or moral, are the creatures of this mystic force, and have been controlled, modified, reformed, and perfected under its processes, so that their present excellence has been graduated from rude and simple originals. Under this law of the social organization, mutual co-operation against the trials of life has been introduced, as alike the instinct of a common humanity and the suggestion of a wise Providence.

Who can calculate the value of such institutions, not only to their immediate membership, but as substantial public supports? Their withdrawal would be seriously felt, not only as the loss of an immense moral power in society, but also from the fact, that their absence would necessarily transfer the burden, which they bear, to the public. Among the many tributaries to the general welfare of this character, which are diffusing blessings upon men, from year to year, noiselessly, yet most effectively, Odd Fellowship by its widely extended resources, has done a colossal work.

Looking from the present standpoint, upon the past of American Odd Fellowship, and from these forming a rational estimate of its future, our hearts may swell with honest pride, in the consciousness that we have not lived in vain. We are here then, not only to legislate for the present needs of this great brotherhood, to promote its unity and thus preserve its healthful life, but to transmit it with increasing power and capability to our descendants. In another half century, it will, in all probability, have girdled the earth with its golden chain, and diffused its blessings upon millions. Can it be a matter of wonder, that in such a cause, we should be here to counsel together for its welfare, to renew our vows of fidelity and devotion to it, and to each other, and to supplicate, with uplifted hearts, for the continued favor of *Him*, who has ever been its firm friend and support, and for the promotion of whose original intendment of fraternity among men, it has unremittingly toiled for so many years? Oh! no, the wonder would be that we could be such unworthy descendants of the noble sires who have bequeathed to us the legacy, as to fail to realize its value and our duty to preserve and perpetuate it.

Warrants were issued, during the recess, for the institution of two Grand Encampments, (Oregon and Nevada), five Subordinate Encampments, six Subordinate Lodges, and one Degree Lodge.

The receipts of the Grand Lodge for the year were, $41,929.86; profit on the sale of supplies, $19,259.48.

The following amounts were expended by the Subordinate Lodges, Encampments and Degree Lodges of the Daughters of Rebekah, respectively:

	LODGES.	ENCAMPMENTS.	REBEKAH.
For relief of members ....,	$933,951,45.	$124,483.01.	$2,662.25.
For relief of widowed families.	160,885.99.	10,002,54.	205.84.
For education of orphans....	16,786.15.	79.68.	11.10.
For burying the dead........	223,545.61.	22,497.82.	691 05.

Forms for Trials and Appeals were adopted. (*See Journal, pages* 6542, 6543, 6544, 6545.)

The following were adopted :

When a Withdrawal Card has been granted to a member, and the recip‚ ient forgets the A. T. P. W., the N. G. of the Lodge, from which the brother withdrew, has authority to again communicate the A. T. P. W. on the pres‚ entation of the Card within one year from the date of its issue.

When any jurisdiction shall suffer under some great calamity, and a relief committee shall be duly authorized to receive and disburse money to the suf‚ ferers, it shall be the duty of the Grand Master of such jurisdiction, to see that the Treasurer of such fund shall execute and deliver to him, a bond to secure the money placed, or to be placed, in his hands for the purposes of relief.

In such an event as is set forth in the above resolution, any committee appointed to administer a relief fund shall be required, within a reasonable time, to make to the Grand Master of the jurisdiction, a full and complete report of their proceedings in the premises, and especially if there should be a surplus of money on hand, to report the amount thereof.

Should any surplus of said moneys be reported, as aforesaid, the Grand Master shall notify the M. W. Grand Sire of the same, who shall forthwith proceed to draw for the same, to the order of the Grand Treasurer.

Any such surplus of moneys, that shall come to the hands of the Grand Treasurer, as aforesaid, shall be invested, and held by him, under the orders of this Grand Lodge, to be kept for such purposes of special relief as may seem best to conserve the purposes for which they were contributed.

If an Odd Fellow shall renounce the Order, he thereby forfeits all bene‚ fits, to which, by law, he may be entitled, from the time of his renunciation.

Hereafter, no appeal will be considered by this Grand Lodge, at any session thereof, unless the papers in such an appeal shall be placed in the hands of the Grand Secretary, at least five days before the commencement of the session.

In granting a Visiting Card, a ballot is not necessary, but the application must be passed upon by the Lodge.

The Grand Lodge and Grand Encampment Degrees, may be conferred upon Past Grands and Past Chief Patriarchs, belonging to Subordinates under the immediate jurisdiction of this Grand Lodge, by a State or Territorial Grand Body, on the presentation of a proper Certificate, signed by the Grand Sire and Grand Secretary, and attested by the Seal of this Grand Lodge.

An Atheist is disqualified for election, and admission to an Encampment.

A member of an Encampment, clothed in street Uniform, presenting himself for admission while the Encampment is transacting its ordinary business, shall be treated the same as if he presented himself without such Uniform.

The Special Committee on Dues and Benefits made another elaborate report, which will be found in the Journal, pages 6601–6606.

1876.

The Grand Lodge met in annual session, in the City of Philadelphia, on September 18th, while the Centennial Exhibition was open.

On the evening of the 18th a meeting was held, entitled, the "Reunion of Past Grand Representatives and Past Grand Officers of the Grand Lodge of the United States." James L. Ridgely was President, and there was a Vice-President from each jurisdiction, and six Secretaries. A programme of interesting exercises elicited the approbation of a large audience. (*See Journal, pages* 7113–7134, 7162.) At a subsequent meeting, on the 21st, a plan of organization was adopted, and officers, for the ensuing year were elected.

The Exhibition Authorities designated September 20th, as "Odd Fellows' Day," when there was a grand parade of the Order through the city, to the Exhibition Grounds. It was conceded to be one of the finest demonstrations ever made in the city. Seventeen thousand five hundred and sixty-eight men were in line, in twenty divisions, with ninety-two brass-bands, and nine flute and drum corps. It was a scene long to be remembered by every Odd Fellow who had the good fortune to witness it. (*See Journal, pages* 7135–7161.)

Grand Sire Durham, in his report, said :

We meet to-day under peculiar circumstances. We are in the last quarter of the nineteenth century, in the centennial year of this great nation, and in the fifty-eighth year of our own existence as an Order. We stand to-day, within sight of the spot where the declaration of a nation's independence was first proclaimed, and within the hearing of that bell which rung out, upon the midnight air, the glad acclaim of a nation's birth. One hundred years ago ! How light the words fall from the careless lips, but how vast and wonderful have been their influence on the destinies of the world and the human race. Dare we gaze upon the wonderful panorama of that period ? Shall we undertake to review, at once, its marvelous developments in the political and moral, the material and scientific, the social, intellectual and religious world ? How the effort mocks our feeble powers. Within this period, which tells the history of our nation, and of our Order, have been wrought the mighty wonders which must forever separate the future from the past. It has been a period of civilization and growth, in which empires have been formed out of the wilderness, grander in proportion, more perfect in organization, and more just in administration, than anything which had ever preceded it. It has been a period at which the coming philosopher, historian and statesman will pause, and seeing nothing beyond, worthy of man, will wander and linger among its monuments, achievements and traditions, as his predecessors have halted, to wander amid the ruins of ancient kingdoms and empires. Within this period, the arts and sciences have opened up new fields of conquest to man, and he has not stopped with the exercise of dominion over the beasts of the field, the fowls of the air and the fish of the sea, but earth, air and sea, have been made his ministers and taught to do his bidding, as if they were things of life and intellect. It has been peculiarly distinguished for the onward growth of associations designed to provide against the wants of impoverished humanity, teaching, also, the sentiment that man's most perfect happiness is in administering to the wants of those around him; and it is the glory of Odd Fellowship to stand pre-eminent, among those organizations most efficient in the inculcation and establishment of these principles, and improved condition of society. This institution could not have been organized and made so prosperous in any other age of the world. But when the mariner's compass had revealed a new world, war and commerce had made man better acquainted with his fellow man ; when the art of printing had stepped in to disseminate truth, when the church, true to her high mission, had proclaimed the idea of one vast brotherhood in the practice of virtue and fraternal love, then it sprang into existence. It was the legitimate offspring of that great moral and social transition, it is the child of progress, it is the work of civilization in the nineteenth century. That such an institution has been founded here, that it has grown in power, influence and greatness, that we are permitted to assemble here, in this grand old city of brotherly love, in this year of rejoicing and general jubilee, to legislate for our common good, we should return thanks to Him who overlooks and shapes the destinies of all things, to whom we must look for our future guidance and prosperity. I am gratified in being able to say that the past year has been one of general growth and prosperity. The social, moral and financial condition of the Order, at home and abroad, is generally good. To you, and to your successors, is committed the future of this great institution. Guard and protect it well. Leading all other charitable institutions in their efforts to better acquaint man with his fellow man, and to make him wiser, better and happier, may we not hope that those who shall come after us to fill these high places, and to participate in the centennial of this Order, shall see it established in every civilized land, practicing the beautiful teachings of Friendship, Love and Truth ? "Then one law shall bind all nations, kindred and tongues, and that law shall be the law of universal love."

The following decisions of the Grand Sire were approved :

The several jurisdictions of the several States, have the right to determine whether the dead can be buried by a committee of the Lodge, or by the whole Lodge.

A Lodge cannot, in a Body as a Lodge, attend the funeral of a deceased

"Ancient Odd Fellow," and conduct the services according to the Ritual of the Order.

It is not illegal that members of the Lodge, by appointment of the N. G., shall, when the Lodge is opened under the head of "The good of the Order," deliver addresses or read essays on Odd Fellowship.

The Seal of a Lodge should only be used in transacting the legitimate business of the Lodge.

The Grand Secretary, in his report, said:

Among the thousands and tens of thousands of acquisitions supplied to the world during the last one hundred years, as the product of genius, skill or industry, no greater blessing has been vouchsafed to the moral nature than the mission of Odd Fellowship. This sentiment is neither idle nor abstract, but like the tree which is known by its fruit, demonstrates its truth by a record visible to the eye of all that may be incredulous. The banding of men in secular and voluntary organization, is modern and eminently instinctive of centenary principles. In the olden times, such offices as Odd Fellowship administers, were chiefly assumed and claimed by the church, not unfrequently exclusively demanded. Now behold the millions and tens of millions applied by it, by kindred Orders, by the municipality and private charities, for which the age is so distinguished, everywhere and among every people. This strong arm of support has been sensibly realized by the public authorities as an extraordinary aid, and is generally conceded.

There are in the historic facts connected with the career of the government, and that of the Order, coincidences and analogies striking in their relation to each other, especially in the creation and assertion of cardinal principles of remarkable sympathy, although they apply to systems, having dissimilar objects, and pursuing opposite paths. Each sets out with a mission for the protection, defence and elevation of the masses ; each had feeble resources, and comparatively inadequate to the end in view ; each encountered powerful and long continued opposition ; each ventured upon an untried experiment, although, on the one hand the general idea of a republic, and on the other, secular benevolence generally, were old, while the special theories entered upon, were new and unprecedented. The two organizations, each in its particular sphere, were, therefore, practically the outgrowth of their time, and each of centenary product instinctively. The one not more the broad truth of popular rights and constitutional liberty, than the other was the divine idea or design of brotherhood, with its inseparable mutual dependence and its correlative obligations. The Fatherhood of God and the brotherhood of man, being indisputable propositions, their application became as a corollary, equally clear and deducible. Thus the coincidence of career is strong, while the logic of cardinal principles and their influence on their subjects and progress under it, present a similar analogy.

We may justly claim that Odd Fellowship is a product of the century, and as such, contributes with becoming patriotic ardor its "offering" to the great American jubilee. It is here, therefore, by its Supreme Grand Lodge, to honor the occasion and itself, by approving the great object, and by offering its homage to the refined civilization, elevated manhood, and broad spirit of brotherhood which it represents. Let us, its votaries, whilst we rejoice in the review of our past work now spread before us in our statistics and their detail, and in the grand promise which the future of our Order presents, drink deeply from the fountain of wisdom, which the extraordinary experience supplies, and let us cherish, with veneration, the political, social and moral truths, which glitter like diamonds upon the chart of human rights, whose proclamation our Fathers boldly ventured one hundred years ago ; the more so, because they are based upon the great idea of Odd Fellowship, that men are brethren, and God, in their creation and original intendment, designed that they should so dwell together.

The work done from 1830 to December 31, 1875, is shown as follows :

Initiations, 980,780; members relieved, 729,189; widowed families relieved, 97,077 ; members deceased, 65,481 ; total relief, $22,273,386,63 ; total receipts, $60,065,926.52 ; present membership, 460,414.

The receipts of the Grand Lodge for the year, were $40,576,71 ; profit on the sale of supplies, $21,433.85.

The following amounts were expended by the Subordinate Lodges, Encampments, and Degree Lodges of the Daughters of Rebekah, respectively :

	LODGES.	ENCAMPMENTS.	REBEKAH.
For relief of members.........	$1,003,749.43	$147,500.62	$4,890.09
For relief of widowed families.	157,923.49	6,927.52	720.29
For education of orphans.....	17,287.23	499.79	129.00
For burying the dead..........	260,430.32	24,734.13	1,023.85

Warrants were issued, during the recess, for one Grand Encampment, (Arkansas), seven Subordinate Encampments, (one in London, England), two Grand Lodges, (Chile and Dakota), and nine Subordinate Lodges, (one in London, England, one in the Sandwich Islands, one in Chile, one in the Netherlands and two in Peru).

The following were adopted :

No Lodge can lawfully permit an Indian to visit it, under any circumstances whatever.

Lodge Libraries are a necessity of the Order, and should, by all means, be encouraged ; and the funds of Lodges may be appropriated for that purpose ; but the manner and measure of such appropriations are proper subjects of local legislation.

When petitioners for the resuscitation of a defunct Lodge are not present at the organization, when the Charter is restored, they are not restored to membership. They must come in by petition.

A Lodge should not "close in regular form" before a public installation, but "the ordinary ceremonies being suspended," the doors are opened and the installation proceeds. After its completion, the Grand Officers retire, and then, all but the members of the Order being excluded, the Lodge closes in form. If the installation takes place in a room other than the Lodge room, there is no objection to declaring a recess, and then proceeding to the hall in which the ceremony is to take place, after which, the Lodge should return to its Lodge room and close in form. If, however, a Lodge should close before installation, and then the G. M. should proceed and install the officers, such installation, though *irregular*, would not be void, and the installed officers would be the legal officers of the Lodge.

Any Grand Lodge, or Grand Encampment, may permit the use of the names and numbers of extinct Subordinate Lodges or Encampments, in their respective jurisdictions, that have been extinct more than twenty years.

In reference to certain resolutions from the Grand Lodge of Colorado, in relation to Life Insurance, the scheme contemplated by the resolutions referred to, is a mere Life Insurance, made compulsory upon every member and every Lodge in the jurisdiction of Colorado. There is no law in our Order which authorizes such legislation, and no authority by which a State Grand Lodge can turn a whole jurisdiction into a Life Insurance Society.

Whenever any Rebekah Degree Lodge, which heretofore has been, or hereafter may be chartered, shall, for thirty days after the time by law required for the making of its annual report, neglect to make and forward such report to the proper officer, it shall be the duty of the Grand Master of the proper jurisdiction, to declare the Charter of such Lodge forfeited, and to reclaim the same.

Lodges have an undoubted right to expel a member who is in contempt of the Lodge, and who refuses to purge himself of such contempt.

A member cannot resign from his Lodge, while charges are pending against him.

The following Grand Officers were elected and installed: John W. Stokes, P. D. G. Sire, of Pennsylvania, Grand Sire; John B. Harmon, P. G. M., of California, Deputy Grand Sire; James L. Ridgely, P. G. M., of Maryland, Grand Corresponding and Recording Secretary; Joshua Vansant, P. G. M., of Maryland, Grand Treasurer.

The following were appointed, the first by the Grand Corresponding and Recording Secretary and the others by the Grand Sire: Theodore A. Ross, P. G. Rep., of New Jersey, Assistant Grand Secretary; Rev. J. W. Venable, P. G. Rep., of Kentucky, Grand Chaplain; John W. Smith, P. G. M., of Connecticut, Grand Marshal; John W. McQuiddy,

P. G. M., of Indiana, Grand Guardian; John W. Hudson, P. G. M., of Wisconsin, Grand Messenger.

Nine P. G. Sires, who were present at this session, were allowed mileage and per diem amounting in the aggregate to $1,224.50.

1877.

The Grand Lodge met in annual session, in the City of Baltimore, on the 17th of September.

Grand Sire Stokes, in his report, said:

In obedience to the commands of the organic law, which brings us together once more in annual council, I have the honor to submit for your consideration, a report of my official acts during the year. The continued depression in the various industries of the people, which seems to be testing and trying every pursuit, interest and enterprise in life, and finally culminating in events that are calculated to bring reproach upon the civilization, manhood and progress of the nineteenth century, has tended to put to the severest test, the faith and confidence of the members in the value and reliability of our organization to fulfill its pecuniary and moral obligations, at all times, towards its members. And the sequel shows a wonderful tenacity of life, and persistent perseverance and courage in the maintenance of their noble and disinterested purpose, to be greatly admired, and presents the most hopeful outlook for the future.

Whilst it is to be regretted that, in some localities, the membership has fallen off, the aggregate returns will exhibit an increased constituency in both branches, over last year, in the United States. We have more than held our own. The ranks that are annually thinned by death, inability and indifference of a large class to pay their dues, have been more than made up with new recruits, presenting to the assembled Representatives a progressive and appreciative constituency, which, under all the adverse circumstances that have so long paralyzed the industries of the country, is cause of congratulation. And we should not fail in making proper acknowledgments to the Supreme Ruler of the Universe for the many favors, which enable us to feel that His love appears to govern in our councils, and that we meet again under the most favorable auspices, with peace, harmony, good will and good order pervading the entire brotherhood.

The following decisions of the Grand Sire were approved:

The Grand Representative should give the A. T. P. W. to the Grand Master or Grand Patriarch of the jurisdiction, who will communicate it to the Grand Secretary or Grand Scribe, and cause it to be communicated to the D. D. Grand Masters, etc.

A member (Daughter of Rebekah), divorced from her husband upon her own complaint, would be entitled to the A. P. W., and the N. G. of her Degree of

Rebekah Lodge would be the proper officer to communicate the same. The husband's standing in his Lodge does not affect her standing in the Rebekah Degree Lodge.

An Indian, with a Withdrawal Card, cannot be a petitioner for, nor become a Charter member of a new Lodge.

The Grand Secretary, in his report, said:

In concluding this review of the work of Odd Fellowship under the Grand Lodge of the United States and the jurisdictions thereunto belonging, our hearts are gladdened and made happy in the contemplation of the scene which rises before us. We behold the Order, which our fathers founded less than sixty years ago, (in that spirit of beneficence, which ennobles the age,) for the elevation of human character, now recognized as one of the potential forces of society. In no age of the world, have greater efforts combined to befriend man. Offices of philanthropy and of general charity, in earlier periods, were administered by the church or its auxiliaries in some form. This vast service no longer confines itself to this narrow sphere. Mankind, irrespective of country, creed or religious sentiment, now reckons such duties to be instinctive, and amongst the highest obligations of life, not less binding upon the secular arm, than upon church and State. To provide for the poor, for the sick, for the ignorant of every class, for the widow, for the orphan, for the really helpless and destitute, is no longer exclusively the command of religion, but is, in all enlightened communities, recognized as a high obligation of the State, which challenges the general approval. On this broad field of benefaction, policy harmonizes with humanity and religion, the abundant fruit of which is seen in all well ordered society. In fact, the common sentiment prevails wherever civilization extends. Nobly have our age and people met this humanity, and illustrated the generous spirit which it has generally awakened. Thousands and tens of thousands emulate each other in works of brotherly love, in every form of charity and by every form of individual or combined instrumentality for the relief of human suffering. The church, the State and the secular arm, however otherwise divided, move in harmony in this cause. Their counsels may differ, but the course pursued leads to the same great end. Each acting from a common heart, strengthens the arm of the other, and adds greatly to the general purpose, by the accord of spirit which prevails and unites the whole. Odd Fellowship is an outgrowth of this spirit and the prevailing sentiment of the times. It has been pursuing its mission, in its own quiet way, for half a century and more, and has enlisted the co-operation of millions of men and of treasure in the great cause, the details of which form its records, which it is our pride to present to you from year to year.

We have not only met all the demands of the sick and the needy, in our seven thousand Lodges and our two thousand Encampments, but have contributed to such other objects of general benevolence as our means would allow. The condition of the Order is a just subject of congratulation to its friends. There is nothing to excite its fears or to create anxiety for its future. On the contrary, its career is auspicious in the highest degree. Ranking among the strongest organizations of the kind in the world, it maintains its prestige triumphantly, and, beyond a satisfactory examination of its system of "Dues and Benefits" and their proper reconstruction, needs no organic legislation. This, although a pressing and vital subject, with a view to its permanent existence, is rather a question of calm and considerate reform than of controversy, addressing itself to the practical sense and wisdom of its rulers, involving, as it does, the life and death of Odd Fellowship, which is inseparably blended with sound finances and a stable system of dues and benefits.

During the year, the Order was introduced into the Netherlands, at Amsterdam, by the institution of Paradise Lodge, No. 1.

The Order in Australasia, at this time, was reported to consist of the Grand Lodges of Australia, Colony of Victoria, 44 Lodges, 2,510 members; New South Wales, 2 Lodges, 160 members; Tasmania, 3 Lodges, 180 members; New Zealand, 17 Lodges, 800 members. Total, 66 Lodges, 3,650 members.

The condition of the Order in Germany, January 1st, 1877, was stated as follows: Grand Lodge of the German Empire, 4 Subordinate Lodges, 133 members; Brandenburg, 12 Lodges, 761 members; Wurttemberg, 13 Lodges, 587 members; Hannover, 8 Lodges, 360 members; Saxony, 5 Lodges, 170 members. Total, 42 Lodges, 2,011 members. Encampments, 5; members, 185.

The condition of the Order in England was represented as not promising, but the good work was stated to be improving in Switzerland. Three new Lodges in the Republic were opened since January 1st.

Warrants were issued, during the recess, for four Subordinate Encampments (one in Peru), and six Subordinate Lodges.

The receipts of the Grand Lodge were $43,881.61; profit on supplies, $14,811.74.

The following table from 1830 to Dec. 31, 1876, is instructive:

Initiations, 1,022,800; members relieved, 773,191; widowed families relieved, 102,754; members deceased, 69,867; total relief, $23,982,887.62; total receipts, $64,633,783.90; present membership, 461,888.

The following amounts were expended by the Subordinate Lodges, Encampments and Degree Lodges of the Daughters of Rebekah, respectively:

	LODGES.	ENCAMPMENTS.	REBEKAH.
For relief of members	$1,030,163.83	$144,795.87	$3,708.01
For relief of widowed families	155,697.97	6,519.90	311.50
For education of orphans	14,947.70	153.73	40.00
For burying the dead	252,316.36	24,440.04	407.90

Article XVII. of the Constitution was amended to the effect that no compensation (except such per diem as the Grand Lodge may think proper) shall be allowed any Grand Representative coming from a jurisdiction beyond the limits of the North American Continent.

It was decided that State Grand Lodges have not the power " to require of the members of their Subordinates the payment of any sum, in the shape of dues, or otherwise, for the establishment or support of Odd Fellows' Libraries."

Eight Forms for Processions were adopted. (*See Journal, pages* 7382-7387.)

The Special Committee on Dues and Benefits, in their report, presented the following, showing the number of days sickness annually, that may be expected among men of a certain age.

At 20 years, 4 days; 25 to 35 years, 5 to 6 days; 45 years, 7 days; 50 years, 9 to 10 days; 55 years, 12 to 13 days; 60 years, 16 days; 65 years, 31 days; 70 years, 74 days.

At this time, with a membership of 453,903, and 230,377 weeks' benefits paid during the year, the Committee showed that, if the sickness was distributed through the brotherhood, each member would have been sick three days and thirteen hours.

The following were adopted :

It is the opinion of this Grand Lodge that a donation of the bound Revised Journals, Digest and Book of Forms, to Grand Representatives who have not received them, as provided for by a standing resolution of this Body, is impolitic and expensive, and should not be continued, and the said resolution is hereby repealed.

Hereafter, the only qualification for office in a Rebekah Degree Lodge shall be : 1st, Such member shall be an actual contributing member in good standing in such Lodge ; 2d, No member shall be eligible to the office of Noble Grand, unless previous service is shown in the office of Vice Grand in a Rebekah Degree Lodge, or in a Subordinate Lodge.

The Term P. W. of the Subordinate Lodge, shall not be applicable to, or used in, a Rebekah Degree Lodge, and the Passwords of the Rebekah Degree Lodge shall alone be used by both sexes, therein, from and after the first day of January next.

It is illegal for a Lodge to extend the time for which a Visiting Card was granted, by endorsement on the back thereof, but in all cases of renewal, or extension, a new Card must be issued.

The printer of the Daily Journal shall be interdicted, by the proper officers of the Grand Lodge, from permitting any person to have access to the manuscripts or matter entrusted to his care ; he is to regard the matter as *private*, and no one shall be allowed to copy therefrom, but every copy printed should be placed in the hands of the officers of the Grand Lodge.

The Grand Secretary and his Assistant, are especially charged with the proper preservation and protection of all property of the Grand Lodge other than supplies, and no additional compensation shall be allowed.

Subordinate Grand Jurisdictions possess the right to establish widows' and orphans, endowments, of any nature whatever, provided they are founded upon a basis of voluntary contributions ; but it is against the organic law of the Order to make forced assessments for the above purpose.

When, from any cause, any separate fund of a Subordinate Lodge shall be found unnecessary, it shall be lawful to otherwise appropriate such fund, or merge it, in whole or in part, in the general fund ; provided, that the object contemplated by such special fund, be otherwise fully protected and secured. And provided further, that provision be fully made to return any donation made to the said special fund, which may be demanded by any donor who may insist upon its being donated to the object for which it was donated ; provided further, that no such appropriation shall be made, unless the same shall first be authorized by the Grand Lodge to which such Subordinate may be attached.

It is competent for a Grand Lodge or Grand Encampment, to permit its Subordinates to make By-Laws requiring payment of dues in advance, provided such requirement shall not work a forfeiture of any rights now guaranteed to members by the laws of this Grand Body.

A Sub-Committee of the Finance Committee, consisting of not less than two of the members residing nearest the City of Baltimore, shall be appointed to examine the books and vouchers of the Grand Treasurer and Grand Corresponding and Recording Secretary; such examination to be made within one week prior to the commencement of each annual session. That to this end, it is suggested that the Grand Sire appoint the Finance Committee, or so many of its members as may be consistent, prior to the close of the annual session, instead of the commencement of the same, as has been the prevailing custom.

A member of a Subordinate Lodge or Encampment, who is in arrears for weekly or funeral dues more than thirteen weeks, is not entitled to the Term Password, or to vote in the Lodge or Encampment, but is a contributing member until suspended, dropped or expelled, in accordance with the requirements of the Constitution, and, as such, is entitled to visit his own Lodge or Encampment. He cannot, however, become entitled to benefits until he shall have paid up in full, all dues and fines, (weekly and funeral) that have accrued against him up to the date of payment, if the By-Laws of the Lodge or Encampment shall so provide; nor then, until the expiration of such time thereafter as may also, by the laws, be provided as a penalty.

A Lodge or Encampment, cannot refuse to receive, in full or in part, the dues of a member prior to his suspension, and no member can be suspended or dropped from membership in the Order, for non-payment of dues, unless at the time of his suspension he shall be indebted to the Lodge or Encampment for one year's dues.

When any member of a Lodge or Encampment, shall neglect or refuse to pay the dues fixed by the laws, for the space of one year, the Secretary or Scribe shall report the same to the Noble Grand or Chief Patriarch, and, unless the Lodge or Encampment otherwise direct, such member shall thereupon be suspended, (he having been first notified of the action that would be taken), a record of which shall be made upon the minutes. The mere fact of a member being over twelve months in arrears, does not constitute him a suspended or dropped member. To render him such, the Lodge or Encampment must formally declare him to be suspended.

1878.

The Grand Lodge met in annual session, in the City of Baltimore, on the 16th of September.

At the last session, the Grand Lodge agreed to meet in Austin, Texas, but owing to the breaking out of the yellow fever in some of the Southern States, the Grand Sire, after having consulted his brother officers and members, exercised extraordinary authority, and by proclamation convened the Grand Lodge in Baltimore.

Seats were drawn for one hundred and forty-six Representatives.

Grand Sire Stokes, in his report, said:

The unparalleled success and popularity of Odd Fellowship in America, it would seem, has given rise to a general desire to emulate its example, by creating, under various names, organizations ostensibly similar in design, until secret beneficial Orders have been multiplied in some localities, far beyond the wants or ability of the people to sustain them, temporarily retarding the progress and success of Odd Fellowship, and rendering the existence of each other precarious and uncertain, thus entailing loss and disappointment upon the people who have been drawn into them by promises of large weekly and funeral benefits, endowment policies, and life insurance, upon the payment of small dues, which a moment's reflection would show, could not, under the most favorable circumstances, (and that whilst their members are young and healthy), be paid but for a few years at most. A glance at the tables of mortality and the laws of our being, will reveal to us the unalterable decrees of Providence, that death will sooner or later come to us all. And the money promised to be paid to the members and their families, on these sad occasions, cannot be realized.

The funds of all beneficial associations must be steadily contributed, in properly adjusted proportion to their promises, so as to make it certain that those with the longest expectations of life can safely and surely rely upon them. Some may and do, of course, die early, and their families may get a much greater amount than they have paid in. This must be expected, it is in fact the capital upon which they expect to do business, and is used as an inducement, indeed I might add as an allurement, to obtain members ; but the heirs of those that die late, will not only get much less than the amount paid, but run the risk of getting nothing at all.

The abundant caution heretofore practised by the G. L. U. S. in this particular, and the rigid enforcement of wholesome and judicious laws in our Order against vice and immorality of all kinds, are the real secrets of our great success, and enable us to point with pride and satisfaction to our past record, as exhibiting to the criticism of a scrutinizing and intelligent people, that our best efforts are put forth in upholding a reliable, exemplary, and useful organization. I therefore feel it to be my duty, with the experience that nearly half a century has afforded, to encourage the members of our Order to an increased interest and zeal in its maintenance, and if possible, to inspire them with a higher and better appreciation of the advantages they enjoy, in holding membership with such a large, reliable, and harmonious body of men, banded together for mutual relief, the preservation of their manhood, and the elevation of the race ; whose boasted pride is in seeing the promises of their brethren everywhere and at all times fulfilled, and their misfortunes alleviated ; and to warn them to beware of all organizations and associations that make large promises on small consideration. If but little is contributed to the funds, and large sums are to be drawn out, some one, in the end, is sure to be disappointed. Rely upon it, it cannot be done, and I beg the members of this great brotherhood to be admonished in time. Again, I would call your special attention to the great objects of our organization ; bear in mind that its earnest and persistent purpose is to assist each other with stipulated and reliable weekly payments, (which we have proclaimed to the world to be the peculiar characteristics of our Order), at such times as members may be unable to help themselves, blended with the further, broader, and grander purposes of *Benevolence* and *Charity*, whenever and wherever misfortune shall lay its heavy hand upon any part or portion of the brotherhood. Any attempt to divert it from the fulfillment of these sacred engagements, or to embrace other features altogether foreign to the original design, must result in weakness, if not in disaster and ruin. Never let it be hampered with seductive schemes of life insurance, which may have nothing to recommend them, but the good name and reputation of the Order they seek to use, that have cost us half a century, in the pursuit of a single purpose, to establish.

The following decision of the Grand Sire was approved:

The Signs, Grips and Passwords of the Order, are designed to speak one universal language to the initiated of every nationality the world over. Therefore the *Annual* and *P. P. W.* of the Degrees are not to be translated into any other language, or spoken other than as they are written, spelled, and pronounced in the English language. The different nations must learn to give them the one universal sound, as nearly as possible, so that the sound of the Word will be as familiar to the ear, as the Signs are to the eye, or the Grip to the touch of the hand ; to the end that an Odd Fellow of any country, may be known and recognized, in any part of the habitable globe, as a brother. The language used in describing and explaining the use, meaning and manner of performing the Signs, Grips, etc., may be in the tongue of the people in which the Lodges are working.

The Grand Secretary, in his report, said:

The business depression in the Order at large, which has prevailed generally for several years, has been growing, and is by common consent referable to its true cause, viz.: the continued paralysis which has pursued commerce and industry. Since the close of our civil war, much of the antecedent capital and wealth of the country has disappeared, as the inevitable effect of that unhappy strife, in the enormous waste of war. It is contended, that the loss of this wealth has not only not been restored, but, to the contrary, the industry of the country, which is the basis of wealth, has been inadequately rewarded, and the products of manufacture and agriculture have been unremunerative. Without venturing to discuss such extraneous subjects in this report, we remark, as germane to the subject, that our Order is not exempt from the influence which business prosperity entails upon all institutions which require the aid of capital. Besides, the foreign world has but recently ceased its bitter strife of war, leaving behind all the evils which follow in its train, including its fearful waste and general business derangement. Hence, we are admonished that the end of financial depression is not yet, and that the blessing of general peace to mankind is still in abeyance, and must await events which ripen as natural fruit, from legitimate and cognate causes. We may reasonably indulge the hope that the future prospect of commerce, agriculture, and general business will soon begin to brighten, and that Odd Fellowship will then revive, and be lifted to its normal vigor, as a potential element and moral force. Meanwhile, it is our duty and privilege to apply the experience acquired, to our proper enlightenment, to deduce wisdom from its pregnant lessons, and to do all that we can to improve and defend the position. To apply ourselves to a judicious and intelligent economy, consistent with our obligations, the just benefactions which arise out of them, and the magnitude of the interests which they involve. There is no cause for alarm.

We may confidently rely upon the Supreme Head of the Order ; we have in past emergencies done so, and He has always proved equal to the crisis, and ever will, beyond all peradventure. The circumstances of our position, we have not improvidently superinduced. The administration has been, as heretofore, wise, economical, and prudent, commensurate with the magnitude and important interests of the million which it represents and sustains, and may be, therefore, confidently relied upon to provide as adequate a finance system in the future as it has done in the long past.

During the recess D. G. Sire Harmon visited the Order in Australasia (*see his report in Journal, pages* 7680–7691), and brought it into harmonious working order, presenting a Charter, similar in its provisions to that granted to the Grand Lodge of the German Empire, to the Grand Lodge of Australasia, having jurisdiction over Australia, Tasmania, New Zealand and other islands. (*See Australasia in a subsequent chapter*).

On June 29th, 1877, the Order was introduced into Denmark. (*See Denmark, in Grand Jurisdictions*).

The following, obtained from the report of the Grand Lodge of the German Empire for the year ending December, 31st. 1877, shows the status of the Order: Grand Lodges, 4 ; Subordinate Lodges, 46 ; members, 1,950 ; brothers relieved, 103 ; widowed families relieved, 19 ; paid for the relief of brothers, $1,869.70 ; widowed families, $335.50 ; education of orphans $212.88 ; burying the dead, $495.45 ; special relief, $145.32 ; total relief, $3,058.85 ; receipts, $18,-615.11. Encampments, 5 ; members, 181.

The Order in the Netherlands was meeting with success. A second Lodge was instituted on the 17th of January, 1878. The membership in the jurisdiction now numbered 80.

In Peru, at this time, the Order consisted of 4 Lodges and 110 members ; 1 Encampment with 19 members.

Warrants were issued, during the recess, for one Independent Grand Lodge, that of Australasia, and eight Subordinate Lodges (one in Denmark and one in the Netherlands).

The following is a condensed history of the Order in reference to the subjects mentioned, from 1830 to

December 31st, 1877: Initiations, 1,059,862; members relieved, 816,155; widowed families relieved, 108,903; members deceased, 74,209; total relief, $25,704,885.68; total receipts, $69,142,260.86; present membership, 454,174.

The revenue of the Grand Lodge was $39,280.54; profit on supplies $15,706.24.

The following amounts were expended by the Subordinate Lodges, Encampments and Degree Lodges of the Daughters of Rebekah, respectively:

	LODGES.	ENCAMPMENTS.	REBEKAH.
For relief of members	$1,029,647.26.	$150,097.07.	$4,279.95.
For relief of widowed families	159,201.99.	5,219.47.	281.50.
For education of orphans	14,985.78.	85.00.	66.18.
For burying the dead	247,022.77.	26,087.55.	641.25.

Section 1, of Article 1, of the Constitution, was amended to read as follows: Section 1. This Lodge shall be known by the name, style and title of *The Grand Lodge of the Independent Order of Odd Fellows.*

The following were adopted:

No Grand Encampment has the power to declare a Past High Priest a Past Chief Patriarch, unless he has also been duly elected a Chief Patriarch by his Subordinate Encampment, and served out his time as such, as provided by the laws of the Order.

When State Grand Officers grant Cards to former members of defunct Lodges, the brother receiving the Card is not entitled to the A. T. P. W. The Card cannot be used for visiting Lodges, but is good for deposit only, by the holder, as an Ancient Odd Fellow.

If a member of an Encampment shall be dropped or suspended for *non-payment of dues* by his Lodge, said act of the Lodge shall not affect the standing of said member in his Encampment, for the term of one year thereafter, provided the Patriarch shall not rest under any disability during the interim, in his Encampment.

The Annual Password of the Degree of Rebekah, made by the Grand Sire, shall only be used when visiting in other jurisdictions than the one to which the visitor belongs, or when the instructions are given in a Subordinate Lodge.

Hereafter, the quorum of a Rebekah Degree Lodge shall consist of seven members, irrespective of sex.

Non-affiliated Odd Fellows, who have been regularly initiated in the Order, and have retained membership therein for at least five consecutive years, and who, at the time of making application for reinstatement or membership, shall be over fifty years of age, and who are not under expulsion for cause, may be admitted to membership, in any Lodge or Encampment, as non-beneficial members, upon such terms as the local law may prescribe.

State Grand Encampments are permitted, if they shall deem it for the best interest of Subordinate Encampments, to make the term of office one year.

A Grand Encampment, cannot amend its Constitution and By-Laws so as to elect its Grand Officers by the Representatives present at its annual session.

The Grand Masters of State, District or Territorial Jurisdictions, are authorized to make a Semi-annual Password for the Degree of Rebekah, which shall be a test of good standing in a Rebekah Degree Lodge, and be used only in the jurisdiction to which it properly belongs, and the instruction in the Ritual, when given in Rebekah Degree Lodges, shall be changed so as to give this Semi-annual Password in the place and stead of the Annual Password.

The unmarried daughters of Odd Fellows of the Fifth Degree, who are above the age of eighteen years, are made suitable candidates for admission into Lodges of the Degree of Rebekah, when proposed by either parent, or by a guardian, and the same rule applies to unmarried sisters of Odd Fellows of the Scarlet Degree, when proposed by their brothers.

As the Rules of Order require that every member is bound to vote unless excused, no member can be deemed present, on a call of the yeas and nays, whose vote, or that of his colleague for him, does not appear upon the roll-call of yeas and nays, or unless he is excused by vote of the Grand Lodge from voting.

The street Uniform for Subordinate Lodges, adopted at last session, was modified. (*See Journal, page 7,790.*)

The following Grand Officers were elected and installed:

John B. Harmon, P. D. Grand Sire., of California, Grand Sire; Luther J. Glenn, P. G. Rep., of Georgia, Deputy Grand Sire; James L. Ridgely, P. G. M., of Maryland, Grand Corresponding and Recording Secretary; Joshua Vansant, P. G. M., of Maryland, Grand Treasurer.

The following were appointed, the first by the Grand Corresponding and Recording Secretary, and the others by the Grand Sire:

Theodore A. Ross, P. G. Rep., of New Jersey, Assistant Grand Secretary; Rev. J. W. Venable, P. G. Rep., of Kentucky, Grand Chaplain; Nathan Taylor, P. G. Rep., of Massachusetts, Grand Marshal; B. H. Woodell, P. G., of North Carolina, Grand Guardian; Charles H. Gatch, P. G. P., of Maryland, Grand Messenger.

1879.

The Grand Lodge met in annual session, in the City of Baltimore, on the 15th of September.

Grand Sire Harmon, in his report, said :

We ought to reduce representation to one from each Grand Body. This would give us a Grand Lodge of eighty-seven members—not counting Chile and Switzerland, and for a long time the membership would be under 100. The truth is, this Lodge should be composed of but one Representative from each State, Territory or Country under our jurisdiction; not one from each Grand Body. This would make a Grand Lodge of forty-eight members at present, with a probable increase to sixty in the next thirty to fifty years, a Body larger than the Senates of most of the States of the Union. Even without consolidation, or segregation of Grand Lodges and Grand Encampments, this result could be reached by a joint election, just as the two Houses of our State Legislatures elect United States Senators in joint convention.

Giving, however, each Grand Lodge and Grand Encampment one Representative, and thus having a Lodge of eighty-seven members, the question is how to raise its revenue. Taxation is generally considered in connection with representation. In the American political mind, the two go together. Hence, whenever it is suggested that we raise our entire revenue by a per capita tax on the whole membership of the Order, the larger jurisdictions object, unless we also give them a representation here, in proportion to the tax paid. This per capita tax is the true plan; it is perfectly just, and could be easily borne by the Subordinates. Examine it. This Body is essential to our system of government. Its expenses must come from the members of the Order, equally or unequally, directly or indirectly. Unless good reason be shown to the contrary, equality should be the rule. To secure it, direct assessment upon each Odd Fellow is the only way. The reason assigned for inequality is, that the State jurisdictions are the units ; that each should have equal power and pay an equal share of the expenses. This was the rule up to 1833, when the present basis of representation and taxation was adopted, except that the tax was $20.00, instead of $75.00. This per capita tax plan was adopted in 1849. Up to that year the mileage and per diem of Representatives was paid by the State Bodies. The Constitution was then amended, so as to pay them out of the treasury of this Lodge ; and to provide funds, an assessment was levied, pro rata, on each State Grand Body, based upon the members under its jurisdiction. Several States protested and the law was repealed. The objection does not seem to have been to the principle of the law, but it was regarded as unnecessary taxation, and as tending to the accumulation of a large surplus fund for idle investment. If such a provision were now to be incorporated into our Constitution, the tax would be light. A tax of seven cents *per capita* on the entire membership, would pay all expenses and enable us to furnish supplies at cost, or a like tax of five and a half cents would pay the expenses of our session, and a small advance on the cost of supplies would pay the other expenses.

The Order in Australasia was represented as flourishing. The Grand Lodge of New Zealand, on November 13th, 1878, reported 1,000 members.

A favorable opportunity offering, a Commission, Charter, books, etc., were forwarded to Barbados, West Indies.

The following decisions of the Grand Sire were approved :

A law of the Grand Lodge of the I. O. O. F. takes effect in each State jurisdiction from the time of its enactment, unless the law, on its face, provides otherwise ; or unless, from the nature of the law, it necessarily requires legislation by the State jurisdiction to carry it into effect.

A brother or sister, not a member of a Rebekah Degree Lodge, is not entitled to the Semi-annual P. W. of Rebekah Degree Lodges, nor can they visit such Lodges within the jurisdiction to which they belong.

The Noble Grand of a Subordinate Lodge, in his capacity as Noble Grand, is not entitled to the Semi-annual P. W. of Rebekah Degree Lodges. That P. W. is to be given only to members of such Lodges.

A Past Grand, member of a Grand Lodge, and in good standing in his Subordinate Lodge, has the right to a seat and vote in his Grand Lodge, on an election of Grand Officers, although he may not have the P. W. of the current term.

The Grand Secretary, in his report, said :

It is the experience of the world, and the teaching of history, supplemented by careful observation, that of all the powers that exert a controlling influence upon society, none exceeds the " moral power." It gives to citizenship the highest incentive to character, which forms the basis and bulwark of society, and supplies the general virtue and intelligence upon which the State most relies ; it is the corner-stone and foundation of all public sentiment, and is so appreciated by all enlightened peoples. Odd Fellowship, thus constituted, is an important organization, not only in controlling the general sentiment, but in educating the popular feeling into a healthful tone. It is difficult, therefore, to estimate its value as a general educator of principles, in directing healthy sentiment in all well-trained communities. It exerts, therefore, its legitimate counsels in erecting, guiding, and enlightening all well-ordered governments, and thus largely contributes to the welfare and happiness of the people. It is in this light especially, that its form of government has had its structure, and to this great end, that it has chiefly been designed as a great public benefactor.

How wisely its principles have been formed, and its practice in conformity thereto applied, the experience of more than half a century, as its records verify, will amply attest.

It is now pursuing the same career which it has occupied since its organization in 1819, and will continue to pursue a like mission for many years yet to come. Who can estimate the good it has accomplished by its persistent and noiseless work of love and mercy, in all its many jurisdictions throughout the world? The inquiry is overwhelming, and the answer to it simply impossible to adequately make ; it fills us with amazement, like an echo from a vast canyon, reverberating in the American solitudes, striking us with awe and veneration by its mighty intonations ; and this course has been going on unremittingly for nearly a hundred years. Such a continued labor of love among men, challenges attention as a great moral power, working the welfare of society in manifold ways, but chiefly by its education in that channel, and by sending out its contributions, of a like character, for the moral and physical wants of the million.   •

In what manner can larger benefit be conferred upon society ? Vice and crime are everywhere rebuked and stamped out of existence by its ministrations, and high-toned influence is imparted ; thus true religion is inspired, and differences of opinion tolerated and respected among men. Society is enlightened and trained under a proper education; the people become happy, industrious, thrifty, and liberty, restrained by law, is supremely triumphant.

We present Odd Fellowship in this garb, before our fellow citizens, after a period of more than a half century of trial, and claim for it the verdict of tolerant sentiment, free from all sect and prejudice.

The condition of the Order in Germany, December 31st, 1878, was represented as follows :

Grand Lodges, 4; Subordinate Lodges, 48; members, 1,967; Encampments, 5; members, 160. Paid for the relief of brothers, $1,678.25; widowed families, $596.75; orphans, $33,00; burying the dead, $187.00; special relief, $20.00; total relief, $2,515.00; total receipts, $17,247.90.

The Order in Great Britain had ceased to exist. In the Netherlands the progress was satisfactory.

An instructive review of the action of the Grand Lodge on the subject of establishing the Order out of the United States, excluding British North America and the Republic of Texas, will be found in the Journal, pp. 7,970–7,973.

Warrants were issued, during the recess, for the Grand Lodge of Quebec, and the Grand Lodge of Washington; also, for one Subordinate Lodge, and Charters were issued for sundry Lodges in Idaho and Washington Territories, to take the place of Charters granted by the Grand Lodge of Oregon.

Degree Lodges of the Daughters of Rebekah, were, as yet, not established in the jurisdictions of Arkansas, British Columbia, Dakota, Florida, Louisiana, Lower Provinces, Maryland, Minnesota, Mississippi, Montana, Quebec, South Carolina, Utah and Washington.

The following is an exhibit of the operations of the entire Order, from 1830 to December 1st, 1878: Initiations, 1,094,965; members relieved, 859,126; widowed families relieved, 115,127; members deceased, 81,648; total relief, $27,468,286.36; total receipts, $73,504,918.00; present membership, 450,238.

The Grand Secretary, in concluding his report, said:

The recapitulation of the several returns, enables me to present Odd Fellowship as highly prosperous. It is no longer experimental as an institution of beneficence in society, but by a long and uninterrupted practice, it has attained the position among men as a great moral power in the community. It has, for many years, been subject to that test, and has been adjudged worthy of public support. Its numerous and varied jurisdictions, at home and abroad, domestic as well as foreign, are reported to be doing well and to be advancing to great success.

The ordinary revenue of the Grand Lodge for the year was $30,222.05; profit on supplies, $15,467.08.

The following amounts were expended by the Subordinate Lodges, Encampments, and Degree Lodges of the Daughters of Rebekah, respectively:

	LODGES.	ENCAMPMENTS.	REBEKAH.
For relief of members.....	$1,043,791.23	$142,652.46	$6,467.01
For relief of widowed families,	145,038.54	6,333.35	480.00
For education of orphans,	14,755.33	120.00	110.00
For burying the dead......	252,980.19	23,888.21	1,726.69

The following were adopted:

Patriarchs who are, or may become, members of a Grand Encampment of one State or jurisdiction, shall be qualified for membership in a Grand Encampment of any other State or jurisdiction.

Grand Lodges be, and are hereby directed, to require Secretaries of Lodges to keep a register of the members of their respective Lodges, who are Patriarchs of Encampments, and also to report to said Encampments, respectively, whenever a member of the same is suspended.

Grand Encampments be, and are hereby directed, to require the Scribes of Encampments to notify each Lodge whose member becomes a Patriarch, on admission to the said Encampment, in order to promptly transmit, one to the other, reciprocal official notifications.

State Grand Lodges are hereby authorized, in their discretion, to make the term of office in their Subordinates one year.

Aged and indigent members of the Order, are not *per se*, as a matter of right, entitled to benefits, the same as those who become disabled from their usual occupation, by sickness or accident.

A revision of the Written and Unwritten Work of the Order, entire, is desirable, and, if properly done, will be promotive of good, regardless of expense.

In the opinion of this Grand Lodge, if a proper revision of the Written and Unwritten Work is made, it will act as an incentive to thousands to take all the Degrees, who heretofore have been disinclined to seek for advancement, and it will bring back into active fellowship, thousands who have drifted out of the Order.

A committee to consist of thirteen members of the Order, learned in the Degrees and their system generally, shall be appointed by the Grand Sire, at this session, who shall be entrusted with the preparation of the said revisions, a majority of whom shall constitute a quorum.

It is not lawful for an Encampment to appropriate money, from its regular funds, for music at the funeral of a Patriarch.

The members of the Order in good standing, in any, or several, or all the Subordinate Grand Jurisdictions, may form themselves into one or more Auxiliary Endowment Benefit Associations, upon the following general conditions. The machinery for working the associations, may be through the Grand Lodges, but no action of said Subordinate Grand Bodies, and Lodges under their jurisdiction, shall in any way bind the moneys or funds of either Grand or Subordinate Lodges, for the purpose of carrying out the provisions which may be adopted by Auxiliary Endowment Benefit Associations, hereinbefore mentioned. The only obligation the several Lodges shall be under, is to secure, without incurring pecuniary liability on the part of said Lodges, from their respective officers, the faithful discharge of such duties as the said Endowment Benefit Associations may impose upon them. Should two or several Subordinate Grand Jurisdictions desire to establish an Auxiliary Benefit Association, on the voluntary plan, arrangements for the same may be agreed upon by the Grand Lodges interested, in keeping with the provisions heretofore stated ; and the Grand Masters and Grand Secretaries of the jurisdictions concerned, shall lend all necessary aid, in the way of correspondence, in their power, Any plan for an Endowment Benefit Association, which may be adopted by one or more Subordinate Grand Jurisdictions, may exist and be controlled by such laws as may be sanctioned by the jurisdictions interested, *all within the terms of the provisions conditioned above.*

The members of the I. O. O. F. may unite with any lawful society, or association, whatsoever, without severing their connection with the Order.

Any Grand Lodge or Grand Encampment, may hold special sessions, as often as may be deemed necessary, in their respective jurisdictions, to give instruction in the Unwritten Work of the Order, and to confer the Past Official, Grand Lodge and Grand Encampment Degrees, respectively.

The special sessions, as above provided for, may be held at such places, within the jurisdiction of such Grand Body, as may be determined by the Grand Master or Grand Patriarch, unless otherwise provided by the laws of the Grand Body. At such sessions, no business shall be transacted other than is provided for in the above resolution.

The Grand Master, the Deputy Grand Master, or the Grand Warden, and **the Grand** Secretary, shall be required to attend such special sessions, but it shall not be obligatory on any other officer, or Lodge Representative to attend. Any Past Grand of said jurisdiction, being in good standing, may attend, and five Past Grands shall constitute a quorum for the transaction of the business of such meetings, or special Degree sessions. The Grand Patriarch, Grand High Priest or Grand Senior Warden, and the Grand Scribe, shall be required to attend all such special sessions of Grand Encampments, and five members of the Grand Encampment of said jurisdiction, being in good standing, shall constitute a quorum. Past officers from any part of the jurisdiction in which such special sessions are held, and entitled to membership in such Grand Body, shall be privileged to attend and receive the Degrees and instruction to be given by the Grand Officers.

Subordinate Lodges be, and they are hereby authorized, to confer the Degree of Rebekah upon all persons that are qualified by the laws of the Order to receive said Degree.

The Grand Masters of State, District or Territorial jurisdictions, in which Rebekah Degree Lodges have been, or may hereafter be instituted, are required to make a Semi-annual Password for the Degree of Rebekah, which shall be a test of good standing in a Rebekah Degree Lodge, and shall be used at the outer door of such Lodge to obtain admission to the ante-room. This Semi-annual Password, shall only be used in the jurisdiction to which it properly belongs, and shall be communicated privately to all persons entitled to receive it.

The Annual Password shall be given, both in Subordinate Lodges and in Rebekah Degree Lodges, and used as a further proof test of membership in the Degree, as well as to enable all members, having the Degree, to visit Subordinate Lodges, when opened for the purpose of conferring the Degree. This Annual Password shall also be used in conjunction with a Card issued by a Rebekah Degree Lodge, when visiting a Rebekah Degree Lodge in jurisdictions other than the one to which the visitor belongs.

Rebekah Degree Lodges shall confer the Degree, on those persons only, who may apply for membership in such Lodge, unless the Rebekah Degree Lodges shall otherwise provide.

A Subordinate Lodge has a right to expend its funds, not otherwise interdicted, to hire watchers to watch its own, or transient members, purchase real estate, build its hall, purchase large and costly frames for Charters and pictures, and many other such articles.

The name, style and title of the Body was now changed to: *The Sovereign Grand Lodge of the Independent Order of Odd Fellows :*

An appropriate Funeral Service, to be held in the Lodge room, was adopted. (*See Journal, pages* 8128–8131.)

The Grand Lodge enacted what was termed the "Dormant Law." Thereafter members suspended for non-payment of dues in Subordinate Lodges and Encampments, were to be classed as *dormant* members. (*See Journal, pages* 8035, 8099, 8100, 8122.) This legislation was repealed the next year.

The Special Committee on the Patriarchal Branch of the Order, reported that the Subordinate Lodges, from 1819 to 1877, inclusive, had lost, by suspension for non-payment of dues, 460,120 members, while the Encampments from 1827 to 1877, inclusive, had lost, from the same cause, 48,429.

1880.

The Grand Lodge met in annual session, in the City of Toronto, Province of Ontario, Dominion of Canada, on the 20th of September. This is memorable, by reason of the fact that this session was the first held by the Grand Lodge out of the limits of the United States.

The members of the Sovereign Grand Lodge assembled at Toronto, on Friday, the 17th of September, in accordance with the wish of the Grand Lodge of Ontario, to receive a city welcome and reception on the Exhibition Grounds of the Agricultural and Industrial Exposition Association. There was a grand parade of the Order on the occasion, fitly described as " an imposing affair, composed of 49 bands, 908 musicians, several thousand Odd Fellows in Regalia, walking; 104 in Regalia, riding, and about 100 carriages." Hon. James Beaty, Jr., Mayor of Toronto, welcomed the Sovereign Grand Lodge to the city, and the President of the Association, Hon. John J. Withrow, to the Grounds, and the Grand Sire responded. In the evening, the Corporation of Toronto gave a banquet to the Sovereign Grand Lodge, in the large dining hall on the Grounds. The next day was occupied by a trip to Penetanguishene, on Georgian Bay, 100 miles from Toronto, where the Body was welcomed by Dr. P. H. Spohn, Reeve, Mayor of the Corporation, and the address, in the absence of the Grand Sire, was responded to by Deputy Grand Sire Glenn.

On Sunday, services were held in St. James' Cathedral by Grand Chaplain Venable, and on Monday, 20th, the officers and members assembled at the Queen's Hotel, and, in full Regalia, were escorted by the Boston and Chicago Uniformed Encampments to their place of meeting, in the Parliament Building.   They were received by the Grand Lodge of Ontario, and cordially welcomed by the Grand Master, W. H. Cole, in a short and felicitous address.

The Sovereign Grand Lodge by invitation, visited Lieutenant-Governor Robinson, and on the invitation of the General Committe on Entertainment, enjoyed a drive through the city, visiting many interesting places.

The Reunion of Past Grand Representatives, Tuesday evening, the 21st, was an interesting and memorable occasion.

Grand Sire Harmon, in his report, said :

Permit me to renew the suggestion, made last year, that this Grand Lodge ought to adopt a system of dues and benefits.   Facts sufficient have been gathered.   The longer the delay the greater the difficulty and the danger.   At all events, a rule could be established for new Lodges.

Further reflection, has confirmed the views on the subjects, (Representation, Taxation etc.,) expressed in my report of last year.   That this Body was then, largely in favor of biennial sessions, and of reducing representation to one from each Grand Lodge and Grand Encampment, I know, because more than three-fourths of the members so said ; and there is little doubt but that the opinion to-day is the same.   What the vote will be on the proposed amendments to the Constitution in these respects, remains to be seen.   Odd Fellows, like politicians, do not always vote their convictions.   Human selfishness and human weakness, often rule in our councils.   It is pleasant for us to come up to this annual feast, and we have not the courage and conscience to say, by our votes, that we come too often, or that there are too many of us for the table spread.   The loaves and fishes will not go round, and we have no power to work a miracle.   Most respectfully, but most earnestly, do I urge every Representative, when these amendments are reached, to speak and vote, not simply as he feels, but as he believes.   I say " speak," because one of the worst evils in this Grand Lodge, is action on important subjects without mature deliberation and without discussion.   Unless some thoughtful, careful and determined member is ever on the alert, the motion " to indefinitely postpone," comes and goes like a whirlwind, and the real voice of the Lodge is not heard.   It will not do to say that, Representatives come here with opinions formed after thorough examination, and, therefore, that discussion is waste of time.   Occasionally this is true, but on many of the most vital issues, the mass of Odd Fellows and the mass of Representatives as well, have not reached conclusions after persistent, digested thought.   On the contrary, after the session closes, nine-tenths of this Grand Lodge go about their business, until a new session summons them to their duties. Many most abstruse and difficult questions, now press us for solution. Intelligent, earnest and honest debate on this floor, would expose ignorance, increase knowledge, and brush away some of the cobwebs which now cover the brain of Odd Fellowship. These questions must be settled by this Lodge. The highest thought and civilization of the Order, should find expression here, in laws and systems fit for the times and for the grand principles we profess ; and yet, Odd Fellowship is to-day, in many respects, cramped and hampered by the action and non-action of its Sovereign Grand Lodge. Sometimes we err in our legislation by keeping ourselves aloof from the masses ; at other times we err by commanding without reason ; and again we err by standing still. What we want is a new, and stronger, and longer pole to our banner, so that it can be lifted high up and be seen of all men, in the very front rank of modern thought and modern humanity.

During the past two years, it has been my privilege to survey and re-survey the field of Odd Fellowship ; and I have become more and more convinced, that its true glory is in its educational and moral power. Its beneficial feature is valuable ; but its value is more in the spirit of industry, of self-help, and of human sympathy engendered by it, than in the money given and received. Hence everything which tends to develop the intellectual and moral features of the Order, should be fostered ; while everything which tends to reduce and degrade it to a merely money institution, should be avoided. We must keep up the sentiment of the Order. It is an idea. Man, humanity, God ! There lies our power. In time, Odd Fellowship will become mainly a beneficial society, or mainly a fraternal society, with just benefits and charity, so commingled, as to make it the embodiment of universal brotherhood.

A handsomely illuminated address, dated Manchester, August 11th, 1879, was received from the Manchester Unity, signed on its behalf by Fred. G. Pownall, D. G. M., M. U., in which the hope is expressed: "That Odd Fellowship may thrive still more and more amongst you, that its principles of Friendship, Love and Truth, may permeate each breast, and that although thousands of miles may separate us, one common *Faith* being ours, one *Hope* uniting us, and one principle of universal *Charity* being our guiding star, we may all work together for the common good of the common weal."

The Order in South America suffered from the war in progress between Chile and Peru.

The following decisions of the Grand Sire were approved:

Prayer is not a part of the Work, at initiations in a Subordinate Lodge, and therefore not admissible.

When special sessions of a Grand Lodge are called, under the law of 1879, either the Grand Master, or the Deputy Grand Master, or the Grand Warden, with the Grand Secretary, can hold the session ; that is, either one of the first three named and the Secretary are sufficient, so far as the officers are concerned ; of course a quorum under the law is requisite.

When a brother visits a Grand or Subordinate Lodge, not his own, he may wear the Encampment Regalia, and Jewel of the highest Degree he has taken ; but he cannot wear such Regalia and Jewel in his own Lodge, Grand or Subordinate.

The Chief Patriarch in office, should continue in that office until the installation of his successor, if the installation of the Chief Patriarch elect is, for any good reason, postponed.

A legally adopted daughter of a Fifth Degree member, is eligible to receive the Degree of Rebekah, where the local civil law provides for adoption, and such adoption creates the legal relation of parent and child, as in no other case, can the applicant be a "daughter," within any definition of that term, and therefore step-daughters are not eligible.

The Grand Secretary, in his report, said :

Twenty years ago the Grand Lodge assembled in the City of Nashville, State of Tennessee. The roll of Representatives, accredited to this session, contains the names of only *two* of the 96 who were members of the Grand Lodge of 1860. Looking over the long list of brothers who have disappeared from this forensic stage, I am constrained to say:

> "I feel like one
> Who treads alone
> Some banquet hall deserted,
> Whose lights are fled,
> Whose garlands dead,
> And all but he departed!"

Year after year, I have had the opportunity of speaking to you words of cheer, even when the heavy clouds of gloom hovered over us and seemed to shut out the faintest gleam of sunlight. During the dark days from 1861 to 1865, when the membership was so depleted that the heart of every true Odd Fellow became sad, and fears for the safety and stability of the Order were felt by many of our best and wisest, I did not despair, but expressed a firm belief that "the undying principle will not perish, but will again, when halcyon peace with healing upon its wing, shall descend in mercy among the children of men, lift its fraternal voice to awaken a kindred and sympathetic pulse in the great heart of the Order."

During the years 1877, 1878 and 1879, we have lost from our fold 15,342 members, reducing the grand aggregate from 456,125 active Odd Fellows in 1876, to 440,783 in 1879, yet there is no cause for despondency, our annual loss from 8106 in 1877 having been reduced to 1508 in 1879.

This Order is not an experiment, but has survived "the pestilence, that walketh in darkness;" the ordeal of fire has not affected it; gaunt famine has fled at its approach, and at its command the sword red with the blood of

fierce conflicts has been sheathed. With its sixty-one years of active minis-
tration in the cause of humanity ; its admirable code of laws ; its systematic
benevolence—attributes that have been widely copied by other organizations—
there is not the slightest room for doubt as to the permanency of the institution. Built upon the immutable corner-stones of Friendship, Love and
Truth, despite the efforts of foes without and enemies within, it will live
to bless mankind in the future as it has in the past. As it has stood, so it
will stand :

> "As some tall cliff that lifts its mighty form,
> Swells from the vale, and midway leaves the storm ;
> Though round its breast the rolling clouds may spread,
> Eternal sunshine settles on its head."

Representatives of a world-wide jurisdiction, standing like watchmen on
the towers of some great castle, you will doubtless take lessons from the past
and so shape your legislation that there may be no step backward ; but that
"progress," shall continue the watchword of the Order.

FAITH with resplendent eyes looks on lovingly, and bids you "fail not,
falter not, weary not in well doing." HOPE bends over you a bow bright
with magnificent promise for the future, inviting you to enter upon and
occupy the uncultivated grounds, and CHARITY, "chief among the
blessed three," with her angelic countenance smiles her approval of your
efforts in the past, encouraging to still greater achievements in the years to
come.

It is my earnest prayer that your deliberations may redound to the good
of the great Order whose destiny is in your hands ; that wide-spread as it has
become, it may be still further extended, encircling the world ; its beautiful
banner float from temples in every habitable portion of the globe ; its anthems
be continually heard, "like the drums of England, from the rising to the setting, and the setting to the rising sun," until it may be truthfully said, "there
are no more worlds to conquer."

The following table exhibits the present condition, and
the entire work of the Order, from 1830 to December 31st,
1879: Sovereign Grand Lodge, 1; Independent Grand
Lodges, (German Empire, Australasia), 2; State, District,
Territorial and Colonial Grand Lodges, 58; Grand Encampments, 40; Subordinate Encampments, 1,851 ; Encampment members, active, 79,813; Subordinate Lodges, 7,276;
Lodge members, active, 449,745 ; Lodge initiations, 1,131,297;
members relieved, 902,845; widowed families relieved, 120,645;
members deceased, 86,351 ; total relief, $29,202,835.56; total
receipts, $77,984,169.72.

The ordinary revenue of the Sovereign Grand Lodge,
for the year, was $31,388.32 ; profit on supplies, $15,778.93.

The following amounts were expended by the Subordinate Lodges, Subordinate Encampments and Degree Lodges of the Daughters of Rebekah, respectively:

	LODGES.	ENCAMPMENTS.	REBEKAH.
For relief of members	$1,062,466.38.	$137,169.07.	$3,181.68.
For relief of widowed families..	140,322.5?.	5,832.04.	498.59.
For education of orphans	13,100.31.	45.30.	26.00.
For burying the dead	257,683.07.	25,250.41.	832.41.

The following is a copy of a commission issued May 6th, 1829, to Thomas Wildey, P. G. Sire ; the original document was presented to the Sovereign Grand Lodge, on the 15th of July, 1880, by Bro. B. F. Zimmerman, P. G. M. and P. G. Rep., of Maryland:

"BUT THE FIRST OF THESE IS CHARITY."

(Emblems—Axe and Sword, Heart and Hand, Three Arrows.)

GRAND LODGE OF UNITED STATES OF THE INDEPENDENT ORDER OF ODD FELLOWS.

To all Loyal Lodges and Worthy Brethren throughout the globe :

THESE PRESENTS, in Friendship, Love and Truth, COME GREETING :

KNOW YE *that* THOMAS WILDEY, being then P. G. S., was on the sixth day of May, 1829, by the vote of all the Lodges and Deputies present, duly elected Grand Sire of the United States of the Independent Order of Odd Fellows, to serve until the first Monday in September, 1833. In traveling he has cognizance of all affairs of the Order, and cherishing that fraternal feeling which our laws and precepts enjoin, we fondly anticipate you will pay due respect to his authority, and that the Lodges of the United States, which are particularly under our jurisdiction, will be guided by his advice and instruction, as being well assured he will act only for the good of the Order, we confidently entrust him with the power.

IN TESTIMONY WHEREOF, we have hereunto set our respective names, in GRAND LODGE OF THE UNITED STATES, at Baltimore, this sixth day of May, in the year of our Lord one thousand eight hundred and twenty-nine, on which day the Grand Seal of said Lodge was annexed.

Seal and Colors (8) of the Order.	THOMAS SCOTCHBURN, D. G. S.	CHARLES BRICE, Rep., Mass.
	ROBERT GOTT, G. G.	JOHN H. CAMPBELL, Rep., Pa.
	AUGUSTUS MATHIOT, G. S.	RICHARD MARLEY, Rep., N.Y.
	JOHN ROACH, Rep., Md.	JOHN BRANNAN, Rep., D. C.

The following were adopted :

When a brother is a member of both a Subordinate Lodge and Encampment, and his Subordinate Lodge shall become extinct, and who, by reason of age or infirmity, cannot successfully apply for membership in another Subordinate Lodge, upon his obtaining a Grand Lodge Card from the Grand Secretary of his jurisdiction, such aged or infirm member, shall be entitled to retain membership in his Encampment, upon said Card.

An unmarried daughter of an Odd Fellow, of the Fifth Degree, who has attained the age of eighteen years, and whose parents are dead, may be admitted to membership in a Lodge of the Degree of Rebekah, when proposed by the N. G. of the Lodge of which her father was a member at the time of his death, or by a member of a Lodge of the Degree of Rebekah, when furnished with a Certificate from the Subordinate Lodge of which the father was a member, that he had attained the Scarlet Degree, and was in good standing at the time of his death.

Any member of this Order, who has been a contributing member twenty-five years, upon change of residence, shall have the privilege of applying for membership in any Lodge at his new place of residence, without first applying for a Withdrawal Card from the Lodge in which he holds membership. Upon election of such brother, by the Lodge to which he shall apply for membership, said Lodge shall notify the Lodge of which he is a member, of such election, when, being free from all charges, and on payment of all dues and fees, upon proper application, he shall be entitled to a Withdrawal Card. Upon deposit of said Card with the Lodge in which he had been elected, he shall be entitled to sign the Constitution and By-Laws, and be received in full membership from such time, upon the payment of the admission fees required by the By-Laws of said Lodge.

Grand Encampments, are hereby authorized, to permit their Subordinates to make suitable rules and regulations for the government of such of their members, in their practice and drill, as choose to uniform : such regulations not to be in conflict with the laws and usages of the Order.

A member of a Subordinate Lodge, can decline to receive sick benefits which are due to him—said act, being in fact, a donation by him to the Lodge. After the reception of such declination by his Lodge, in the absence of local legislation, he is forever debarred from further right to demand said benefits.

No Encampment can adopt any other name than that designated in the Charter, except in the manner provided for changing names, by local Grand Jurisdictions.

In any and every case, notice must be given by the Subordinate Lodge, to the Subordinate Encampment, on the reinstatement of an expelled brother. A Subordinate Lodge is the proper tribunal to try all cases of delinquency, when the charge is cognizable under the laws. It is made the duty of Secretaries to advise Scribes, in a reasonable time, of any member of their Lodges who is also a member of an Encampment, who is suspended, expelled or reinstated.

Grand Encampments and Grand Lodges, that may lawfully change their time of meeting, from annual to biennial sessions, shall be permitted to elect their officers for the term of two years. Grand Bodies having annual sessions, shall, as heretofore, elect their officers for the term of one year.

A wife shall be allowed to testify against her husband, in a case where he is arraigned upon the charge of inflicting *corporal injury* upon her.

The matter of benefits, pecuniary and attentive, is delegated by this Body to Subordinates. But the general rule, presented by uninterrupted usage and custom, and recognized by this Grand Lodge is, that as a Lodge binds itself for benefits to its members, by its By-Laws, so it is bound and no farther, when the same are paid or rendered, as pecuniary or attentive, by another Lodge; and any excess, in money or services, creates no legal obligation ; and the claim therefor, by the Lodge paying the money, or performing the services, on account of a transient or visiting brother, cannot be enforced against his Lodge.

It is a fundamental principle of Odd Fellowship, that a brother in arrears for dues, who is not dropped, is entitled to be visited by the officers of his Lodge, and cared for in sickness, although he may not be entitled to pecuniary benefits. And any provision to the contrary, in the Constitution for Subordinate Lodges, prescibed by any State Grand Lodge, is void.

The Committee on Revision of the Work submitted, in secret session, their report, providing an Initiatory Ceremony, and three Degrees for Subordinate Lodges, and three Degrees for Subordinate Encampments. The committee was continued, to supervise the printing of the books, with authority to make any clerical corrections that might be found necessary to perfect the same.

The following Grand Officers were elected and installed : Luther J. Glenn, P. D. Grand Sire, of Georgia, Grand Sire ; Erie J. Leech, P. G. M., of Iowa, Deputy Grand Sire ; Joshua Vansant, P. G. M., of Maryland, Grand Treasurer ; James L. Ridgely, P. G. M., of Maryland, Grand Corresponding and Recording Secretary.

Brother Ridgely, being unable to attend at the hall, was installed in his room in the Queen's Hotel, on the 22d of September, by the Grand Sire, John B. Harmon, as directed by the Sovereign Grand Lodge.

The following were appointed, the first by the Grand Corresponding and Recording Secretary, and the others by the Grand Sire :

Theodore A. Ross, P. G. Rep., of New Jersey, Assistant Grand Secretary; Rev. J. W. Venable, P. G. Rep., of Kentucky, Grand Chaplain ; Belden Seymour, P. G. Rep., of Ohio, Grand Marshal; J. T. Hornibrook, P. G. M., of Ontario, Grand Guardian ; Charles H. Gatch, P. G. M., of Maryland, Grand Messenger.

1881.

The Sovereign Grand Lodge, met in annual session, in the City of Cincinnati, on the 19th of September, and received a hearty reception from the brethren of Ohio. On Saturday the 17th there was an excursion to Dayton and the National Military Home. Addresses of welcome were delivered by General Patrick, Governor of the Home, and Hon. Samuel Craighead, P. G. Sire, and responded to by Bro. E. J. Leech, Deputy Grand Sire, in the absence of the Grand Sire, who, on account of injury received during his journey to Cincinnati, was unable to visit Dayton. A bountiful collation, in a large pavilion on the grounds, was served to the two hundred and fifty visitors, and the party then enjoyed themselves in examining and admiring the complete arrangements of the well kept "Home." In the evening, Bro. Craighead tendered the Grand Lodge a magnificent reception at his residence in Dayton.

On the morning of the 19th, the Sovereign Grand Lodge was escorted from the Grand Hotel, by the Grand Lodge and Grand Encampment, of Ohio, and Uniformed Patriarchs from Rochester, N. Y., to the place of meeting, where the Body was welcomed by Lieutenant-Governor A. Hickenlooper, for the State of Ohio, Hon. Benjamin Eggleston, in the absence of the Mayor, for the city, and Bro. W. R. Hazlett, Grand Master of the Grand Lodge of Ohio. Grand Sire Glenn responded to the addresses.

The first action of the Body, after organization, was the unanimous adoption, by a rising vote, of the following:

Resolved, That the officers and members of the Sovereign Grand Lodge of the Independent Order of Odd Fellows, speaking for themselves and the half million members of the Order, desire to place upon record, as the first act of their annual session, this expression of their loving sympathy for President James A. Garfield, the suffering victim of a cowardly crime; and, further, to express their admiration for the sublime faith and courage of the patient invalid in his brave fight for life, and their prayerful hope that the dark shadow of death, which now hangs over him, may yet be dissipated, and his valuable life spared to his family, the American people, and the world.

That a copy of the above resolution, certified by our Grand Secretary, and under the Seal of this Grand Body, be forwarded to the family of President James A. Garfield, and the Secretary of State, Hon. James G. Blaine.

That the M. W. Grand Sire transmit, by telegraph, a copy of the resolution just adopted, and a synopsis of the proceedings in reference to the same, to the Honorable Secretary of State, James G. Blaine.

Invitations were received from the Odd Fellows' Monumental Association to join in the procession, and attend the unveiling of the Odd Fellows' Monument in Spring Grove Cemetery, on the 20th; from the General Committee on Entertainment to attend a banquet on the evening of the 22d, and from many Associations of the city, which were accepted, and the Grand Lodge adjourned from Monday until Wednesday, to take part in the parade on Tuesday; but the announcement, on Monday night, of the death of JAMES A. GARFIELD, President of the United States, caused the Grand Sire to issue a proclamation, notifying the officers and members to meet in special session, on Tuesday, the 20th, at 11 o'clock, A. M., "to take such action, as may seem appropriate, in regard to the great affliction to this country, and the world, caused by the sudden termination of the life of the ruler of a great people."

The Body assembled at the hour named, and a committee of eleven reported sympathetic and patriotic resolutions, which were unanimously adopted by a rising vote. (*See Journal, pages* 8686–8687.)

The numerous entertainments projected, were abandoned, but on the afternoon of Tuesday, the 20th, the Grand Lodge attended the unveiling of the Odd Fellows, Monument, in Spring Grove Cemetery. The ceremony was made as simple and unostentatious as possible, on account of the death of President Garfield.

Grand Sire Glenn, in his report, said :

To-day after an absence of thirty-one years, we are assembled in the magnificent Queen City of the West, the far famed Cincinnati, in the State of Ohio, the centre of a population of fifty millions of inhabitants of the United States of America, and your reception here, by your brethren of the Order, by the city authorities, and others, is as cordial as warm hearts and open hands can render.

But you have met here, not merely to participate in the entertainments that have been so lavishly provided for your pleasure and comfort, but to legislate for the best interests of the great brotherhood you represent; to shape the future of this Order, that it may continue to prosper, as the years roll on, and that you may hand it down to posterity, grander and better, (if possible), than you received it from those who have gone before.

To men, who, by long service, have attained the proud positions of Representatives to this Grand Lodge, a word of admonition from me may seem preposterous ; yet, pardon me if I say, I trust your legislation will be marked by a careful discrimination against all projects of doubtful utility ; that you will weigh carefully all matters presented to you, rejecting the bad and holding fast to the meritorious, and thus deserve the respect and confidence of the entire Order, which watches with earnest eyes the deliberations of this Supreme Tribunal of Odd Fellowship.

That you will be faithful to the trust confided to you, I do not doubt, and it is my earnest hope that the record of the fifty-seventh annual session of this Body will be, at least, the equal in wisdom and intelligence of any of the many communications that have preceded it.

It will be the cause of deep regret, pain and sorrow, to every member of this Grand Body, and to the brotherhood generally, to learn that our venerable Grand Secretary, Bro. James L. Ridgely, continues in feeble health. The prayer of every member of the Order, which he has so long and faithfully served, is, that he may yet be restored to vigorous health, and be enabled to resume the position, whose duties, for more than forty years, he has discharged with an ability and fidelity which will never be surpassed, if ever equalled, by those who may follow him.

In consequence of the continued affliction of Bro. Ridgely, the duties of the office of Grand Corresponding and Recording Secretary have fallen upon, and been entirely performed by your most efficient Assistant Grand Secretary, Bro. Theodore A. Ross.

The Grand Sire reported the Order in a healthy and progressive condition, with an increase of 105 Subordinate Lodges, 1 Grand Encampment, 15 Subordinate Encampments, 7,710 Lodge initiations, and 16,159 Lodge members; that the Order in Australasia, Denmark, Germany, Netherlands, Sandwich Islands and Switzerland was prospering; that the new Work adopted by the Sovereign Grand Lodge at Toronto had greatly benefitted the Order.

He called the attention of the Grand Lodge to a circular of the Supreme Temple—Patriarchal Circle, which "seeks to enlist members of the Order in the establishment of 'new Degrees for Uniformed Patriarchs,'" and expressed the opinion that, "the brothers engaged in this 'new Work,' however laudable the motives that prompted them, were treading upon debatable, if not forbidden ground."

The following decisions of the Grand Sire were approved:

A non-affiliated Odd Fellow, who has retained membership in a Lodge of one jurisdiction for ten consecutive years, and has been suspended for non-payment of dues, cannot be admitted as a non-beneficial member in a Lodge of another jurisdiction, on terms prescribed by the latter jurisdiction for the admission of non-beneficial members, without action in the Lodge in which he has been suspended, being first had.

The Odes constitute an integral part of the opening and closing ceremonies of a Subordinate Lodge.

A person permanently so blind as not to be able to distinguish persons and things, although in good financial circumstances, cannot be initiated into the Order. He could not rightly comply with the obligations which Odd Fellows take, upon connecting themselves with the Order.

The laws regulating weekly benefits, apply to both Subordinate Lodges and Encampments. Some benefits, however small, must be paid.

On resolutions relative to the death of a brother, in a Subordinate Lodge, a rising vote may be taken, without giving the voting sign.

Assistant Grand Secretary Ross, in his report, said :

The tables accompanying this report, exhibit a very gratifying gain of 16,159 members in the year 1880, a greater number than we lost in the three years preceding. The Grand and Subordinate Lodges reporting to the Sovereign Grand Lodge, show an aggregate of 456,942 members, the largest number ever returned. From 1865 to 1875, the Order steadily increased from 153,594 members in the former, to 456,125 in the latter, and we now exceed by 817 the highest number heretofore attained, with such assurances, as lead us to believe that the returns for the year 1881, will present a grand array of at least 480,000 members. Add to this, the Order in Germany, and Australasia, which will probably number 15,000, and it will be seen that nearly half a million of men, are to-day, active and earnest workers in the cause of Odd Fellowship.

Within fifty years, nearly eighty-three millions of dollars have been paid into the treasuries of Subordinate Lodges and Encampments, nine hundred and forty-six thousand brothers, and one hundred and twenty-seven thousand widowed families have been relieved, ninety-one thousand brothers buried; orphans have been clothed and educated, and in the fulfilment of the great command of our laws—" Visit the sick, relieve the distressed, bury the dead, and educate the orphan"—we record thirty-one millions of dollars expended, besides the countless thousands of which no just estimate can be made.

The financial condition of this Grand Body is better to-day than ever before ; the receipts of the year, $85,076.33, from ordinary revenue, far exceeding any previous year in its existence. The figures submitted, carefully gleaned, as they have been, from the most reliable sources, may justly excite our pride, and we have a right to exult over the splendid record of the year ; but whilst contemplating the magnificent results that have crowned our efforts in the past, we cannot forget that there is yet more work to do. Our field is boundless, and, comparatively, but a small space has been cultivated. It is your province to extend the sentiment of brotherhood, until our spotless banner shall be unfurled in every city, town and hamlet of the civilized earth, for, let it be remembered : "Wide as the world is our scope, and free as the air is our welcome to the children of men."

That all the labor that has been expended upon this great Order, since the days of 1819, has not been in vain, is manifested by the splendid array of statistics presented to you. As time rolls on, these benefactions to the human race will increase and multiply a thousand fold, and the humble toilers in the vineyard of Odd Fellowship, will feel that they have been abundantly rewarded by the prayers and blessings of thousands of their brethren who have received the benefits of the Order, and the widows and orphans that, without this institution, would have been consigned to the charities of a cold and unfeeling world.

You will doubtless measure up to the full standard of duty required of you ; that there may be no halt in the march of Odd Fellowship ; but that your legislation shall tend to the improvement of the Order where it exists to-day, and extend its operations to every habitable portion of the globe, that its influence may descend

> " As the gentle rain from Heaven
> Upon the place beneath ; twice blessed ;
> Blessing him that gives, and him that takes."

In conclusion, the undersigned deems it his duty to state that, although for several years the Grand Corresponding and Recording Secretary has been unable to give any attention to the details of the annual report from this office, yet the proofs have been submitted to his inspection, and the work has received his approval. I regret to say that, during the last year, it has been impossible, on account of his feeble condition, to consult with that distinguished officer on any matters relating to the business of the office, and this document is the first report of the Grand Secretary, since the organization of " the Grand Lodge of Maryland and of the United States," in 1821, submitted without the sanction and name of James L. Ridgely; a determination arrived at, after consultation with eminent members of the Order, on whose judgment I place the most implicit reliance.*

Therefore, as the entire responsibility for the matter presented in this paper has devolved upon me, I sign it, on behalf of the Grand Corresponding and Recording Secretary.

Warrants were issued, during the recess, for one Grand Encampment, that of Dakota, six Subordinate Lodges, five

---

* Bro. Ridgely was the first Grand Secretary to make a report, so far as the records disclose. At the adjourned session, April 24th, 1840, Bro. Ridgely was elected Grand Corresponding secretary, and a resolution was adopted, directing that officer, "at each annual communication, hereafter, to make a detailed report of the subjects of correspondence," etc. The first report of a Grand Secretary of the Grand Lodge of the United States, was made at the annual session, October 5th, 1840.—(*See Journal, page* 336.)

Subordinate Encampments, and one Degree Lodge of the Daughters of Rebekah.

The following is a statement of the work of the Order from 1830 to December 31, 1880: Sovereign Grand Lodge, 1; Independent Grand Lodges, (German Empire, Australasia), 2; Subordinate Grand Lodges, 58; Subordinate Grand Encampments, 41; Subordinate Encampments, 1,867; Subordinate Lodges, 7,371; Encampment members, 79,950; Lodge members, 466,857; Lodge initiations, 1,175,050; members relieved, 945,895; widowed families relieved, 126,324; members deceased, 90,940; total relief, $30,915,393.96; total receipts, $82,701,157.86.

The following amounts were expended by the Subordinate Lodges, Subordinate Encampments, and Degree Lodges of the Daughters of Rebekah, respectively:

	LODGES.	ENCAMPMENTS.	REBEKAH.
For relief of members	$1,043,695.25	$132,530.48	$3,476.95
For relief of widowed families...	146,001.17	5,502.74	248.00
For education of orphans	13,788.12	20.40	30.00
For burying the dead	268,016.85	27,250.41	862.05

The following were adopted:

Grand Lodges may provide, by law, for conferring the three Degrees of a Subordinate Lodge, upon five or more Initiatory Odd Fellows desiring to form a Lodge of Odd Fellows, to enable them, or any five of them, to petition for a Subordinate Lodge in a locality where no Subordinate Lodge is in operation within a distance of ten miles from the location of said proposed new Lodge.

The Grand Sire, in issuing Warrants to Subordinate Lodges or Encampments, under the jurisdiction of this Grand Lodge, is authorized to use the number of any Lodge or Encampment that has been extinct over twenty years.

On and after July 1st, 1882, all the business of the Subordinate Lodge shall be transacted in the Third Degree, or Degree of Truth. The Lodge shall open in each Degree for the purpose of conferring the Degrees, and each Degree shall be conferred when it is opened in that Degree.

A quorum for Encampments shall be five members, instead of seven, as heretofore.

The unmarried daughters of Odd Fellows, who have attained the age of eighteen years, and whose parents are dead, may be admitted to membership in Lodges of the Degree of Rebekah, when proposed by the Noble Grand of the Lodge to which the father was formerly attached.

A sister member of a Degree Lodge of the Daughters of Rebekah, who was suspended for non-payment of dues, and whose husband died while she was under suspension, and who afterwards married one who was not an Odd Fellow, cannot be reinstated in her Lodge.

The adoption of a report of the Committee on Appeals, is simply an approval, by this Grand Lodge, of the conclusion of the committee in the particular case reported upon, and does not commit this Body to any statements of the laws of the Order, which may be contained in the body of the report. And when the conclusion, arrived at by the Committee on Appeals, is embodied in a resolution, the adoption of the report amounts, in its legal effect, to the adoption of said resolution and nothing more, unless otherwise stipulated in the motion to adopt.

WHEREAS, The Grand Lodge, after mature and deliberate consideration, has decided that the time has now arrived, to make a change in the mode of transacting the business of the working Lodges, and fully recognizing the difficulty that may occur in some localities having a membership, without having the requisite qualifications for participating in the business of the Lodge, desires to give an expression of the deep interest it feels in the entire success of this important movement ; therefore,

It recommends to the different jurisdictions, the exercise of a liberal policy in authorizing the conferring upon all such members, either gratuitously or for a mere nominal charge, the requisite Degrees, to enable the entire Fraternity to participate in the business of the Lodges under the new organization, protecting the Lodges whose laws graduate their benefits according to the Degrees taken, from the payment of such increased benefits to the members accepting the Degrees under all such arrangements.

As to when, and under what circumstances, a Lodge will be bound to pay for a nurse for a member of the same, when he is sick and under the care of another Lodge, in the same or a different jurisdiction, such payment should be made only when, and under no other circumstances, the Lodge of the sick brother, by its By-Laws, provides for the payment of a nurse.

A brother, who has by sickness become blind, is, *prima facie*, entitled to benefits, although in other respects his bodily health may be good.

The Senior Warden can be placed in charge of the door of an Encampment, during regular business, but it must be done by the Chief Patriarch, and not by the Encampment, and when the door is so placed in charge of the Senior Warden, the Inside Sentinel reports to that officer.

The Judiciary Committee construed "unmarried daughters, and unmarried sisters," as entitled to admission to Degree Lodges of the Daughters of Rebekah, to "include daughters and sisters, who once were married, once were under the disability of coverture, but afterward, by death of their husbands, or for other cause, became single women."

Article XXII, of the By-Laws, was amended to read as follows:

The Regalia of the Order shall be as follows, to wit : Collars of Subordinate Lodges shall be white, trimmed with the emblematic color of the Degree intended to be represented, namely : *First Degree*, pink ; *Second Degree*, blue ; *Third Degree*, scarlet ; *Initiatory Degree*, a plain white collar. Rosettes of the appropriate color may be worn upon the collars. The Noble Grand, Secretary, and Treasurer shall each wear a scarlet collar trimmed with white or silver ; the Vice-Grand, a blue collar trimmed in like manner. Supporters of the Noble Grand and Vice Grand, shall wear sashes of the color of the collars of those Officers, respectively ; Warden and Conductor, black sashes ; Scene Supporters, white sashes ; Chaplain, white sash ; Outside Guardian, scarlet sash ; Inside Guardian, scarlet sash.

The position of each Officer shall be indicated by the Jewel of the office.

The above shall apply to all Lodges that may be hereafter instituted, and to all Lodges that shall hereafter procure new Regalia.

A new code of Rules of Order, for the government of the Sovereign Grand Lodge was adopted.

1882.

The Sovereign Grand Lodge met in annual session, in the City of Baltimore, on the 18th of September. Seats were drawn for one hundred and forty-four Representatives.

The Grand Sire announced the death of Grand Secretary James L. Ridgely, which occurred on the 16th of November, 1881. His age was 74 years, 9 months, 20 days.

On being informed, by telegraph, of the sad event, the Grand Sire, at once, went to Baltimore, and issued the following :

SOVEREIGN GRAND LODGE OF THE I. O. O.F.,
OFFICE OF THE GRAND SIRE.
Baltimore, Md., November 19, 1881.

To all whom it may concern :

WHEREAS, Our beloved Brother, James L. Ridgely, Grand Secretary of the Sovereign Grand Lodge, of the Independent Order of Odd Fellows, died on the sixteenth day of November, 1881 ; in accordance with the provisions of Section 9, Article XV., of the By-Laws of the Sovereign Grand Lodge, it devolves upon me to fill the vacancy.

Therefore, I, Luther J. Glenn, Grand Sire, do hereby appoint Theodore A. Ross, of the jurisdiction of New Jersey, now, and for several years past, a resident of Baltimore, Maryland, as Grand Secretary of the Sovereign Grand Lodge of the I. O. O. F., to fill the vacancy caused by the death of Bro. James L. Ridgely.   LUTHER J. GLENN, *Grand Sire.*

The following proclamation was issued, and its requests faithfully and sorrowfully obeyed, throughout the domain of Odd Fellowship.

SOVEREIGN GRAND LODGE OF THE I. O. O. F.

To the officers and members of Grand and Subordinate Lodges and Encampments of the Independent Order of Odd Fellows, throughout the world:

WHEREAS, James L. Ridgely, Grand Secretary of the Sovereign Grand Lodge, who has held that honorable and responsible position since 1840; who came into the Order in 1829, when the Institution was in its infancy, and who devoted his time, his talents, and his influence, in extending this great Institution, until it has expanded the area of its usefulness to all quarters of the globe, and now numbers half a million of members—a wonderful increase from the less than five thousand of 1829, that then constituted the entire strength of the Independent Order of Odd Fellows—has passed away, it seems eminently proper that this great brotherhood should take suitable action to commemorate the death of the foremost Odd Fellow of the world;

Therefore, I, Luther J. Glenn, Grand Sire, do most earnestly request that all Grand and Subordinate Encampments and Lodges throughout the world, drape their rooms in mourning for the space of thirty days from the receipt of this notice, and observe such other ceremonies, as to them may seem proper, to testify the respect, the love, and the unfeigned admiration that every Odd Fellow must feel for the memory of our venerated and departed brother.

Done at the office of the Grand Sire, in the City of Baltimore, this nineteenth day of November, in the year eighteen hundred and eighty-one, and of our Order the sixty-third year. LUTHER J. GLENN, *Grand Sire.*

THEO. A. ROSS, *Grand Secretary.*

Grand Sire Glenn, in his report, said:

It affords me great satisfaction to be able to state, that the progress of the Order, during the year 1881, has been, in every particular, highly gratifying. The roll of membership, notwithstanding the heavy losses by death and suspension, has been largely increased. Lodges have been multiplied; the benefactions have been augmented, and the means of discharging our duty to the sick and afflicted, in the hour of trial and need, have advanced, and kept pace with the growing demands upon the Order.

The country has been generally prosperous; the wheels of industry have moved regularly; bountiful returns have crowned the labors of the husbandman, and with this propitious condition of material affairs, our Order has fully sympathized. It is a proud tribute to the intrinsic excellence of Odd Fellowship, to know, that despite the numerous organizations that have sprung up, within a few years past, our time-honored Institution has not suffered, but that it is stronger and better to-day, than at any former period in its history. For this, as for all other favors and blessings, vouchsafed to our beloved Order, by the Supreme Ruler of the Universe, we should feel and render proper acknowledgments.

The Order was established in Mexico, during the recess, by the institution of Ridgely Lodge, No. 1, City of Mexico. The Grand Encampment of Wyoming, was instituted at Cheyenne.

The following decisions of the Grand Sire were approved :

The Grand Sire has no power to authorize a Lodge, working under the immediate jurisdiction of the Sovereign Grand Lodge, to change the place of meeting from that designated in its Charter.

To suspend or drop a member, for non-payment of dues, the *time* fixed by law, must be regarded, and not the *amount due.* A brother clear on the books on the 1st of January, for instance, cannot be suspended or dropped, until a year thereafter, no matter to what amount his dues may accumulate in the intermediate time, by fines or otherwise.

A Card of Withdrawal having been granted to a member of a Lodge, and before its expiration charges are duly preferred against him, and the Card annulled, and the brother, after trial, was acquitted, his position in the Lodge is the same as if the Card had never been granted.

A petition for a Charter for a Subordinate Lodge, must be signed by five Third Degree members in good standing.

The law in reference to the Lodge in which Withdrawal Cards shall be deposited, has not been repealed or modified.

The law which prevents the name of any person, while living, to be used as the chartered name of a Lodge, cannot be evaded by dropping the given name of the person.

A Grand Lodge has no power to make it obligatory upon the members in its jurisdiction, to subscribe for and take a paper founded by the Grand Lodge, and devoted to the interests of the Order.

Although the By-Laws may be silent on the subject, yet when appointed on a committee, it is the duty of a member of a Lodge to serve, unless excused by the Noble Grand or the Lodge.

After the 1st day of July, 1882, balloting for the Degrees must take place in the Third Degree.

Grand Secretary Ross, in his report, said :

The returns exhibit an addition of 19,006 to the numerical strength of the Order, in the jurisdictions reporting to this Grand Lodge. The temples devoted to Odd Fellowship have been increased, and the three-linked banner has been unfurled upon heretofore forbidden soil. Nearly five millions of dollars were, during the year 1881, paid into the treasuries of the Subordinate Lodges and Encampments, and but little less than two millions of dollars were disbursed for the relief of the unfortunate. The Encampment Branch of the Order, has shared in the prosperity of the Subordinate Lodges, adding more than eleven hundred to the membership, and now numbering nearly eighty-one thousand Patriarchs. And when, to these home returns, we add the statistics of the foreign Bodies of Australasia and Germany, and, counting the grand aggregate of the labors of little more than half a century, we find that eighty-eight millions of dollars have been paid into the Subordinate treasuries, thirty-three millions expended for benefits, one million of brothers relieved, one hundred and thirty-three thousand widowed families assisted, ninety-six thousand brothers buried, the figures are simply astounding. These grand results, cannot fail to gladden the heart of every Odd Fellow, and impress him with the firm belief that, however unstable other institutions of human origin may be, there is something in this Order, some potent influence for good, a power that we fail to fully appreciate, guiding our efforts and directing our energies into the grand channel of success.

If we continue to adhere to the principles of our Ritual, keeping aloof from the disturbing elements that distract and destroy other organizations, we may expect our labors in the future, to be as bountifully blessed, as our efforts in the past.

As the rush-light of a century ago, throwing its faint beams into a wilderness of darkness, has been superseded by the bright electric spark, that illuminates, dazzles, beautifies and adorns the night, penetrating the deepest gloom and transforming dusky shades into the brilliancy of noon-day—so with Odd Fellowship. Its feeble beginnings, in ministering to the sick and distressed, have been multiplied a thousand fold, its humble methods of contributing a few pence to a wandering brother, have, under wise regulations and systematic organization, assumed proportions that, in their magnitude, may well astonish the world.

With these few general remarks on the present condition of the Order, at home and abroad, congratulating you upon the brilliant outcome from the labors of the year that has passed, mingling my tears, with yours, upon the newly-made graves of our departed brothers, and with an earnest prayer that your deliberations may redound to the welfare of the Institution of which you are the head, throughout the world, I respectfully submit this report for the consideration of the Representatives assembled.

Americus Lodge, No. 1, Barbados, ceased to exist.

The revenue of the Sovereign Grand Lodge, for the year, exceeded the expenses in the sum of $17,762.20.

The following amounts were expended by the Subordinate Lodges, Subordinate Encampments, and Degree Lodges of the Daughters of Rebekah, respectively:

	LODGES.	ENCAMPMENTS.	REBEKAH.
For relief of members	$1,130,566.15	$134,218.52	$4,148.22
For relief of widowed families	151,811.99	4,829.83	283.65
For education of orphans	13,981.91	345.00	4.50
For burying the dead	297,411.96	26,616.76	794.64

Warrants were issued, during the recess, for one Grand Encampment, one Subordinate Encampment, and seven Subordinate Lodges.

The ordinary revenue of the Sovereign Grand Lodge, for the fiscal year, was $56,363.31 ; profit on supplies, $36,051.87.

The following were adopted:

The Committee on Printing Supplies, are required to have printed, on the back of all Visiting Cards a proper blank, to be filled by Scribes of Encampments and Secretaries of Lodges, upon the visitation of a Patriarch or brother, embracing date, name and number of Encampment or Lodge.

When a Battalion of Uniformed Patriarchs visits an Encampment in a body, accompanied by either of its first two officers, the members shall be deemed to be in proper Regalia, when clothed in full uniform.

Grand Masters and their duly commissioned and appointed deputies, may, under such rules and regulations as may be prescribed by the Grand Lodges, initiate, for the purpose of instituting a new Lodge, in a locality not less than ten miles from any other Lodge, a sufficient number of applicants to constitute such new Lodge; provided, such persons shall first make regular application for membership, in the Lodge nearest such locality, and upon due reference of such application, examination and report of such committee, according to the By-Laws of such Lodge, and said Lodge shall recommend such persons to membership, by the constitutional vote required for the election of members, which vote shall be certified to the Grand Master, by the Noble Grand and Secretary of such Lodge, under Seal.

The manner of balloting for Degrees, whether by separate ballot for each Degree, or by one ballot for all, is a matter for local legislation.

Persons in the military service of the United States, who have been stationed continuously at one post, for the space of six months or more, may make application for membership in our Order, provided, they apply to the nearest Lodge, or otherwise comply with the laws of the jurisdiction in which the application is made.

It shall not be lawful for any Subordinate Lodge or Encampment, to grant to any member or Patriarch, a Visiting or Traveling Card, who has heretofore applied for and obtained a Visiting or Traveling Card, until such Card shall have been returned to the Secretary of the Lodge, or Scribe of the Encampment, or until such brother or Patriarch shall produce satisfactory proof of the loss or destruction of the same.

When a member of the Order, in possession of a Visiting Card from a Subordinate Lodge or Encampment, obtains money, either from a Lodge, Encampment, or from a Relief Committee, the amount so obtained, shall be endorsed upon such Card, with the date, and by what Lodge, Encampment or Relief Committee furnished, attested by the proper officer.

The several jurisdictions subordinate to the Sovereign Grand Lodge, are recommended to abolish all prefixes to the titles of the State Grand Bodies, and the Officers thereof.

It shall be lawful for a Degree Lodge of the Daughters of Rebekah, to confer the Rebekah Degree upon such members of a Subordinate Lodge, or persons qualified by the laws of the Order to receive the Degree in said Subordinate Lodge, upon the presentation of a Certificate from said Subordinate Lodge, under Seal, setting forth said facts, and coupled with a request to confer the same, without ballot, in the Degree Lodge of the Daughters of Rebekah, and without pecuniary compensation ; provided, that such conferring of the Degree, shall *not* be construed to constitute the recipient thereof, a member of, or entitled to any of the privileges of the said Lodge.

The securities or investments, the property of this Sovereign Grand Lodge, shall be placed, for safe keeping, in the " Safe Deposit and Trust Company," of Baltimore, which shall be designated as the depositary of the Sovereign Grand Lodge, under the direction and supervision of the Grand Treasurer.

The Grand Sire is requested to issue a circular letter, to the Encampment Branch of the Order, calling attention to the adoption of the Degree for Uniformed Patriarchs, and advising of the impropriety of members forming organizations outside of the Order, and the illegality of wearing the Regalia of the Order, under any direction, or regulation, not recognized by the Sovereign Grand Lodge.

The Special Committee, on the death of James L. Ridgely, reported :

An eminently good and great man has gone ; eminent as a citizen of his native City of Baltimore, and State of Maryland, and of the Republic, distinguished during a long and busy career, for probity of character, for purity of private life, and fidelity in public station—more eminent as a member of the Order.

In his young manhood, the cherished friend and valued counselor of the founder of American Odd Fellowship, the associate of Scotchburn, Mathiot, Hall, Rice, Marley, Birkey, Gettys and Boyd, and the trusty and trusted adviser, of each and all of the long line of Grand Sires, from Wildey to and including Harmon, and yet more eminent " in his active service to the Order, in his devotion to its interests, in his entire abnegation of self in his endeavors to place the institution of Odd Fellowship in the uppermost rank of benevolent organizations," and in the unparalleled success which attended his every endeavor.

He lived long, and yet we cannot measure him by years—but by his deeds. They live after him, and shall live in their influence for the good of this great brotherhood, down to the end of time.

His pre-eminent services and exalted character, entitle him to the love of the entire brotherhood, and the esteem and respect of the whole world of civilization.

We should not mourn his departure. Life's work with him was all done, and well done. We do, and should drop the tear of sympathy with his beloved wife and children over his grave, while we rejoice and are glad that RIDGELY ONCE LIVED.

The Special Committee on Dues and Benefits submitted the following :

Grand Lodges and Grand Encampments, are advised to investigate the financial condition of their Subordinates, and to define for them, within certain limits, the rate of dues and benefits.

In the opinion of the Sovereign Grand Lodge, the only classes of benefits advisable are weekly payments to a sick brother, and a funeral benefit on the death of a brother ; all other relief to take the form of special grants, made as circumstances may require, within the limits fixed by the several State jurisdictions.

The Special Funds of a Subordinate should be kept separate and intact·; and when a deficiency occurs in any one of them, it should be replenished by assessments or otherwise, but not by drawing on, or borrowing from, other funds.

Section 3, of Article XIV, of the Constitution, was amended to read as follows:

Dues from Subordinate Lodges or Encampments working under the immediate jurisdiction of this Sovereign Grand Lodge, five per cent. on their receipts.

Article II, of the By-Laws, was amended to provide for the institution of a Subordinate Encampment, on the petition of five, instead of seven qualified members.

Article XXIV, of the By-Laws, was amended to read as follows:

Past Officers of every description, and members in possession of the Encampment Degrees, and all other members of the Order, when visiting Grand or Subordinate Lodges, and when attending the meetings of the Lodges of which they are members, are entitled to wear the Regalia and Jewels pertaining to the highest Degrees they may have taken.

Section 2, of Article XIV, of the Constitution for Subordinate Lodges, was amended to read as follows:

The first Noble Grand and Vice Grand of a new Lodge are entitled to all the Past Official Degrees, provided, such Lodge shall have been instituted at least fourteen meeting nights before the time of the expiration of the regular term, but when less than fourteen meeting nights of a term shall remain at the time of such institution, officers must serve the remainder of the term in which the Lodge was instituted, and to the end of the next ensuing term.

The following Grand Officers were elected and installed:

Erie J. Leech, P. D. Grand Sire, of Iowa, Grand Sire; Henry F. Garey, P. G. M., of Maryland, Deputy Grand Sire; Theodore A. Ross, P. G. Rep., of New Jersey, Grand Secretary; Joshua Vansant, P. G. M., of Maryland, Grand Treasurer.

The following were appointed by the Grand Sire:

Rev. J. W. Venable, P. G. Rep., of Kentucky, Grand Chaplain; John W. McQuiddy, P. G. M., of Indiana, Grand Marshal; Joshua Davis, P. G. Rep., of Maine, Grand Guardian; H. C. Fuhrmann, P. G. Rep., of Minnesota, Grand Messenger.

1883.

The Sovereign Grand Lodge met in annual session, in the City of Providence, Rhode Island, on the 17th of September, and was welcomed by Hon. Augustus O. Bourn, Governor of the State, Hon. Wm. S. Hayward, Mayor of the city, Bro. Hollis M. Coombs, Grand Master of the Grand Lodge of Rhode Island, and Grand Sire Leech responded to the several addresses.

On Sunday, the 16th, by invitation of Bro. Rev. H. W. Rugg, Grand Chaplain of the Grand Lodge of Rhode Island, the officers and members attended service at the Church of the Mediator, and listened to an eloquent sermon by the pastor, Bro. Rugg, on " The Law of Beneficient Association."

A grand parade of the Order took place on Tuesday, September 18th, through the principal streets of the city, which were crowded by thousands of citizens and others eager to see the pageant. It was estimated that the procession contained 5,000 members of the Order, among whom were 1,500 Uniformed Patriarchs. Twenty-six full bands of music and eight drum corps were in line, and made the welkin ring with their enlivening music. On Thursday evening, September 20th, the Mayor tendered a reception to the members of the Sovereign Grand Lodge and their ladies. It was a pleasant and very enjoyable affair, and an unqualified success. The greatest treat offered the visiting brethren was the complimentary excursion to Newport, on Saturday, the 15th. On the way thither, the party landed at Rocky Point and enjoyed a genuine Rhode Island clam-bake. Reaching Newport, carriages were found in waiting to convey the excursionists about the city. The drive along the sea coast was an event long to be remembered by all.

Grand Sire Leech, in his report, said :

Nineteen years ago we met, for the first time in annual session in New England, in the far-famed and classic city of Boston, where first rocked the cradle of liberty in this new world, and held our gathering beneath the shadow of Faneuil Hall. To-day, beholds us again in New England, in the beautiful City of Providence, the adopted home of Roger Williams, the author and founder of that spirit of religious toleration which has made Rhode Island so famous, and aided, more than anything else, in paving the way for the up-building of all such associations as ours, in this our beloved land ; and the hearty welcome with which we have been received here, shows that, in this little State, Odd Fellowship has taken deep root in the hearts of its people, and goes hand in hand with religion, in its offices of benefaction, cheering the widow and orphan, and shielding the needy and distressed from suffering and want.

It is with pleasure, that I am able to state to you, that our progress during the year has been extremely gratifying, and in every particular highly satisfactory. Our *net* gain in membership has been 18,050, which, with the loss of about 2,000 in Kentucky and North Carolina, by the retirement of defunct Lodges they have carried for years, would really make our increase over 20,000—larger, in fact, than that of any previous year. Our finances are in a sound and healthy condition, and we may congratulate ourselves, that at no period in the history of our Order, has the outlook for the future been more bright and promising.

The following decisions of the Grand Sire were approved :

Degree Lodges of the Daughters of Rebekah, and Uniformed Degree Camps, cannot be chartered by the name or title of any living person.

The Revised Rebekah Degree Work adopted at the last session, as soon as distributed, or ready for distribution, is the only legal Rebekah Work extant, and its use in lieu of the old Work is mandatory.

In the absence of the Chief Patriarch, it is not only the right, but the duty, of the Senior Warden to take the place of the superior officer and fulfill all his functions. In the absence of the Chief Patriarch, the Senior Warden is *de facto* Chief Patriarch, and may confer the Degrees. He has the right, however, to invite a Past Chief Patriarch to occupy the chair during initiation, conferring Degrees, or upon occasion of Grand Visitation.

It is legal for the Senior Warden, acting as Chief Patriarch of an Encampment, or the Vice Grand acting as Noble Grand of a Lodge, to give the Term, or the Annual Traveling Password to initiates, or to a brother in good standing, when required.

A By-Law of a Subordinate, granting to a Vice Grand the privilege of calling a special meeting of his Lodge, in the absence from town of the Noble Grand, is legal.

It is legal for a Subordinate to confer a Degree upon a brother from another jurisdiction, holding an authenticated order from his Lodge for such Degree, the said brother being without a Visiting Card and the Annual Traveling Password.

An unmarried half-sister, of a brother of the Order, is entitled, when proposed according to law, to the Degree of Rebekah, and is eligible to membership in a Degree Lodge of the Daughters of Rebekah.

To enable a brother of a Degree Lodge of the Daughters of Rebekah to visit such Lodges, in jurisdictions other than the one to which the brother belongs, he must present a Card from the Degree Lodge of the Daughters of Rebekah, of which he is a member, the same as a sister of such Lodge.

A Subordinate under the immediate jurisdiction of the Sovereign Grand Lodge, cannot issue a Visiting Card for a longer period than one year, but under the general law, (which says a "reasonable time"), Subordinates under State Grand Bodies must be the judges as to what is a "reasonable time;" therefore, a Visiting Card, issued under the general law, for a longer period than one year, is legal.

A brother duly charged with an offense against the laws of the Order, having been tried by the highest tribunal thereof, acquitted and restored to membership, that tribunal having adjourned without day, cannot, at a subsequent session thereof, re-open and re-try the case, its former action being final and conclusive against all parties.

The dues of a member, although suspended, continue to accumulate, and though he does not want to be reinstated, or take a Dismissal Certificate, but desires to pay the dues standing against him at time of suspension, and all that have accrued since, resign his membership and leave the Lodge honorably, the Lodge can refuse to receive the money if he will not allow himself to be reinstated, or receive a Dismissal Certificate. He must be in good standing, or he cannot resign his membership. He should be reinstated, to place him in good standing.

The Grand Sire reported that "Uniformed Degree Camps are being instituted in nearly every jurisdiction, and already number nearly two hundred."

Grand Secretary Ross, in his report, said:

The wildest visions of our fathers, who projected this institution sixty-four years ago did not, could not, contemplate the magnificent results of their enterprise that we chronicle to-day, and not one of the five humble men assembled at the "Seven Stars," in Baltimore, on the 26th of April, 1819, could have foreseen that in less than three score and ten years, more than one and a quarter million of people would be recorded as initiates in this Order, as followers in the footsteps of the originators of Washington Lodge, No, 1.

We may well rejoice and be glad, in reviewing the operations of the year that has passed, and press on to further conquests under our spotless banner, aiding to alleviate the distress that seems universal, by helping the sick, the afflicted and unfortunate, soothing the dreary passage to the tomb, and caring for the destitute widows and orphans. Such is the great work of Odd Fellowship, and its field of labor is everywhere in this wide world, where men are struggling in the great battle of life, where vice and crime prevail, and where sorrow's cry is heard.

A beneficent Providence has smiled upon our efforts, in the years that have passed. The career of the Order has ever been onward and upward, for though clouds have sometimes obscured the bright sun of prosperity, the check in its progress was but momentary, and it has marched on, conquering and to conquer, in the fields of peace and love, scattering the choicest blessings in its pathway.

The following was submitted by Grand Secretary Judge, in letter July 30th, 1883, as the condition of the Order in Australasia :

GRAND LODGES.	LODGES.	MEMBERS.	RELIEF.	LODGE FUNDS.
Victoria.............	55	5,485	$22,547.34	$103,532.02
South Australia.......	22	1,804	7,325.12	18,084.61
New Zealand.........	18	714	2,104.40	20,492.89
New South Wales.....	27	2,028	4,998.69	13,845.00
Totals...........	122	10,031	$36,975.55	$155,954.52

It is evident, from the above, that the Order in this far distant jurisdiction is prospering.

The exhibit of the German Empire, for the year ending June 30th, 1883, is highly satisfactory, as follows :

GRAND LODGES.	LODGES.	ADM'D.	WITHD'N.	DEC'D.	MEMBERS.	RELIEF.	RECEIPTS.
Brandenburg..	9	219	188	15	382	$1,843.62	$5,846.69
Wurttemberg..	12	97	131	8	371	1,637.86	6,436.54
Hannover.....	6	57	117	9	276	1,445.01	6,395.09
Saxony........	5	53	26	4	211	285.38	3,475.12
Germany......	8	96	133	5	316	190.79	5,562.00
Denmark......	4	262	409	3	...	508.40	11,158.74
	44	784	1004	44	1,556	$5,911.06	$38,874.18
Encampments	4	144	155	7	132	....	1,190.62
Total..						$5,911.06	$40,064.80

Germany and Denmark, in the above table, are Subordinates under the Grand Lodge of the German Empire.

The revenue of the Grand Lodge, for the year, amounted to $50,930.48 ; profit on supplies, $26,417.24.

The following exhibits the work of the Order from 1830 to December 31, 1882:

Sovereign Grand Lodge, 1 ; Independent Grand Lodges (German Empire and Australasia,) 2 ; Subordinate Grand Encampments, 42 ; Subordinate Encampments, 1,876 ; Subordinate Grand Lodges, 60 ; Subordinate Lodges, 7,803 ; Encampment members, 85,749 ; Lodge members, 510,414 ; initiations in Subordinate Lodges, 1,273,368 ; members relieved, 1,044,480 ; widowed families relieved, 138,685 ;

members deceased, 101,451 ; total relief, $34,690,988.23 ; total receipts, $92,838,831.83.

The following amounts were expended by the Subordinate Lodges, Subordinate Encampments, and Degree Lodges of the Daughters of Rebekah, respectively :

	LODGES.	ENCAMPMENTS.	REBEKAH.
For relief of members	$1,141,595.49	$129,945.29	$5,163.29
For relief of widowed families.	163,670.72	6,076.96	339.12
For education of orphans.....	12,882.02	....	24.00
For burying the dead.........	311,087.95	27,836.63	1,065.01

Forms for Public Processions were adopted. (*See Journal, pages* 9,315–9,317.)

The following were adopted :

Subordinate Grand Lodges and Grand Encampments, are hereby permitted to exemplify, respectively, the Degrees in the presence of all duly qualified members in good standing, and for that purpose, to admit them to the floor of said Grand Bodies.

It is legal for a Lodge working under the immediate jurisdiction of the Sovereign Grand Lodge, to make a By-Law requiring a candidate, previous to being balloted for, to furnish a physician's Certificate of health, and requiring the candidate to pay the Lodge physician the sum of one dollar therefor.

Any Odd Fellow, who shall hereafter retain membership in, or become a member of, any secret organization not subordinate to this Grand Body, which shall have adopted, or appropriated, to its own use, the Uniform, Regalia, Emblems, Name, Titles, Mottoes, or Initials, of this Order, or any part of them ; or in which qualification for membership is based upon the applicant's standing in this Order ; or in which the applicant is required to obligate himself to prefer said organization, or any member thereof, at the expense of this Order, or any of its members, shall be guilty of conduct unbecoming an Odd Fellow, and a grave offense against Odd Fellowship, and, upon conviction thereof, shall be expelled.

It shall be the duty of the Subordinate Lodge of which such person, so offending, is a member, as well as of every member thereof, to prefer charges against, and bring to speedy trial and sentence, any person so offending. If any such Subordinate Lodge shall unreasonably delay in bringing any member thereof to justice, who shall offend as aforesaid, it shall be the duty of the Grand Lodge of the jurisdiction, within which such Subordinate Lodge is located, and of its officers, to enforce upon such Subordinate Lodge a compliance with the requirements herein imposed, and in case of a refusal or of unreasonable delay, upon the part of such Subordinate Lodge, the same shall be disciplined, if necessary, by such Grand Body to the extent of depriving it of its Charter. Whenever any person shall be put upon trial for such offense as is hereinbefore stated, no person shall serve upon the trial committee who is, at the time, a member of any such organization as the offending brother is charged with being a member.

Whenever it shall come to the knowledge of this Grand Body, that any Subordinate Grand Jurisdiction has failed to require a due compliance with the duties hereinbefore imposed upon Subordinate Grand Bodies, or their officers, such offending jurisdiction shall be deprived of representation upon the floor of this Grand Body, and a surrender of its Charter shall be demanded.

The foregoing resolutions shall not be construed to apply to Odd Fellows' Insurance Associations, or Funeral Benefit Associations, and they shall take effect on the 1st of January, 1884.

The Noble Grand and Recording Secretary of a Lodge, may issue Visiting Cards to members in good standing, when application for the same is made to them in writing.

A Subordinate Lodge may authorize its Noble Grand to cause brothers, visiting by Card, to be examined prior to the opening of the Lodge.

Until otherwise ordered by this Grand Lodge, the Junior Past Grand Sire, if present at the sessions of this Grand Lodge, during the term of his immediate successor, shall receive mileage and per diem.

Subordinate Grand Lodges and Grand Encampments, are hereby fully authorized and empowered, to enact such legislation within their respective Grand Jurisdictions, as shall fully authorize the consolidation of two or more Subordinate Lodges or Encampments, into one Lodge or Encampment.

It shall be the duty of the Recording Secretary of a Subordinate Lodge, when he issues a Visiting Card, to endorse thereon the character of attentive benefits allowed by the By-Laws of such Lodge, and if such By-Laws allow the hiring of nurses during sickness, such fact shall also be stated, together with the compensation allowed per diem for such nurses, which endorsement shall be signed by such Secretary, with the Seal of the Lodge attached.

The Grand Secretary and Grand Treasurer, are hereby authorized to close their books on the 20th of August in each year, and report the financial operations, to and including the day named.

The right to appeal is sacred, and may be made under any, and all circumstances, within the mandates of the law applying to the case.

A member or members of a Subordinate Grand Lodge, may appeal to the Sovereign Grand Body without consent, the only condition being that, the decision of the Subordinate Grand Lodge shall stand as final and conclusive, until reversed by the Sovereign Grand Body.

Unless an officer is present in the Lodge room a majority of the meeting nights of his term, (unless excused from sickness), he is not entitled to the honor of the office.

Past Grand Representative, is not a higher rank or title than Past Grand Master or Past Grand Patriarch.

A Grand Lodge may change its Constitution for Subordinates, making the term of office of Treasurer only one year.

Although a Third Degree member declines to take the Degree of Rebekah, his wife is eligible to membership in a Degree Lodge of the Daughters of

Rebekah, upon a Certificate that her husband is a member of the Third Degree.

It is the duty of any Subordinate Lodge, Encampment, or General Relief Committee of the Order, on application of a brother and the presentation of a properly certified Card, to promptly render the same fraternal sympathy and attention to a traveling or sojourning brother, being sick or disabled, as they would bestow on a sick or disabled brother of their own Lodge or Encampment, and pay such pecuniary benefits as the brother may be entitled to receive from his own Lodge or Encampment, as shown by the endorsement on his Card.

A member suspended or dropped from membership, for non-payment of dues, who makes application for re-instatement and for a Withdrawal Card, may be re-instated, and granted a Final Card, at any time within five years from the date of suspension, upon the payment of one year's dues and the usual price of a Card.

The several Subordinate Grand Bodies, be and they are hereby fully authorized to declare, in the several jurisdictions, what sum of dues or what length of time, a brother shall be in arrears for dues, shall constitute such brother non-beneficial, notwithstanding the decision No. 27, of the Grand Sire, page 8840, Journal of 1882.

Emblems, to be worn as shoulder-straps, to designate the officers of Uniformed Degree Camps, were adopted. (*See Journal, pages* 9367, 9368.)

A suitable Regalia to be worn by the officers of Degree Lodges of the Daughters of Rebekah, was adopted. (*See Journal, page* 9402.)

Article XI, of the By-Laws, was amended, to read as follows:

No Grand Lodge or Grand Encampment, which shall fail or neglect to make its returns to the Grand Secretary on or before the first day of June; which shall be in arrears for money due to this Grand Lodge, shall be allowed to vote by its Representative or Representatives. And no Representative shall be entitled to more than one vote in election for Grand Officers.

1884.

The Sovereign Grand Lodge met in annual session, in the City of Minneapolis, Minnesota, on the 15th of September.

The Grand Lodge was welcomed by the Hon. Eugene Wilson, Mayor Pillsbury, and Grand Master Tefft, to whom the Grand Sire appropriately responded.

The brethren of Minnesota were extremely lavish in their hospitalities. On September 12th, there was a splendid entertainment at Winona; on the 13th, a grand excursion to Lake Minnetonka; on the 15th, a motor ride to Minnehaha

Falls ; on the evening of the same day, the citizens gave an elaborate banquet at the West Hotel to the Grand Lodge and visitors, numbering about four hundred persons; on the 16th, the entertainment was varied by a carriage drive; then a banquet and Reunion of Past Grand Representatives at St. Paul, in the evening, and last, but not least, an excursion to the Dalles of the St. Croix on the 18th, for the ladies accompanying the officers, members and visiting brethren.

Grand Sire Leech, in his report, said :

Representatives—Once more I greet you, as you gather in these seats to enter upon the work of another annual session. Let us reverently thank our Almighty Father for the great privilege granted to so many of us, as we assemble here this morning. I congratulate you, that you are holding the sixtieth annual communication in this great North Star State, in this grand Northwest, and one of eight States in that section of our land which contains nearly one-quarter of the whole membership of the Order. Let us see the roll : Indiana, Illinois, Michigan, Wisconsin, Iowa, Minnesota, Nebraska, Dakota. It is a proud day for the 124,000 Odd Fellows of this vast region of our beloved country, and in their name, and in their behalf, I greet you all.

During the year, there have been instituted four Grand Lodges and two Grand Encampments, besides 189 Subordinate Lodges and 42 Subordinate Encampments. New territory has been invaded and occupied, and our field of labor largely increased. While we have not initiated so large a number of members as in the previous year, yet our growth is healthy, and we now number nearly 506,000, and, taking all things into consideration, the prospects of the Order were never more flattering than at the present time.

He announced the death of Joshua Vansant, Grand Treasurer of the Sovereign Grand Lodge, who died on the 8th day of April, 1884. To fill the vacancy thus occasioned, on the 12th of April, he appointed Alexander L. Spear, P. G. M., and P. G. Rep., of Maryland.

The following decisions of the Grand Sire were approved:

The obligation cannot be used in evidence in court, against a member, in his suit against the Lodge.

The presence of Past Grands at the institution of a Grand Lodge, does not make them Charter members, unless they were petitioners for the Charter.

Although a brother is assaulted by ruffians, and terribly beaten and injured, the Lodge of which he is a member cannot, *lawfully*, appropriate funds from its treasury, for the purpose of offering a reward for the apprehension and conviction of the perpetrators of the outrage.

Grand Secretary Ross, in his report, said:

We cannot point to as grand an array of figures to record the result of the labors of 1883, as was shown in the year immediately preceding, yet there is nothing in the exhibit to discourage us, or to warrant the impression that the Order is not as prosperous now, as it was one year ago. The tables accompanying this report, will fully explain why the net increase in Lodge membership in 1883 was 6,175 less than in 1882, and they will also show that "the command of our law" has been obeyed to the fullest extent, by an increase of $133,388.64 over the year 1882, in the amount expended for relief. It is unnecessary to make any apology for the condition of jurisdictions that exhibit a decrease in membership, and the fact is not, in any sense, a reflection upon them. Local causes conspire to influence results, and we feel sure that, in time, the impediments existing will be removed, and the once flourishing and progressive, but now languishing jurisdictions, will resume their old positions on the roll.

Our hearts must certainly swell with emotion, as we glance at the grand aggregate of the practical work of sixty-five years. We report: 1,318,225 initiated; 1,096,950 brothers aided by weekly benefits, and contributions; 144,805 widowed families assisted; $36,742,136.75 expended for relief, whilst the receipts of Subordinates amounted to $98,227,589.60.

In looking over the entire field of labor, we certainly have occasion to be thankful to "the Giver of all good," that we are enabled to show to the world, that Odd Fellowship is a prospering and ever increasing institution, and that we have the will and the ability, to largely aid in ameliorating the sorrows of the afflicted and the needy.

The fact that the benefactions of the Order are not confined to our own household is widely known, yet it is disputed. It seems only necessary, however, to ask the skeptical to examine the records and learn the extent of the contributions of the Order in times of pestilence and famine, the devastation by fire, and when the surging waters have swept from existence, with scarcely a moment's warning, houses and furniture, the little all, of hundreds and thousands of our fellow citizens. The purse of the genuine Odd Fellow has ever been, and always will be, opened to relieve the distressed, without inquiring their country or their creed.

Under the jurisdiction of the Grand Lodge of the German Empire there were, at the date of the last report, 41 Subordinate Lodges and 4 Encampments. The membership of the Lodges numbered 1,573. The total relief amounted to $2,657.55, and the receipts were $14,595.92.

Warrants were issued, during the recess, for the Grand Lodges of Arizona, Denmark, Idaho, and Manitoba, Canada; Grand Encampments of Montana, and Washington; five Subordinate Lodges and seven Subordinate Encampments.

Uniformed Degree Camps were now distributed, (as far as reports were received,) as follows : Colorado, 3 Camps, 65 members; Delaware, 1 Camp, 34 members; Denmark, 1 Camp, 8 members; Illinois, 27 Camps, 592 members; Michigan, 19 Camps, 378 members; Minnesota, 4 Camps, 100 members; Nebraska, 1 Camp, 26 members; New Hampshire, 9 Camps, 387 members; New York, 18 Camps, 580 members; Pennsylvania, 5 Camps, 151 members; Rhode Island, 2 Camps, 78 members; Vermont, 3 Camps, 83 members; Virginia, 3 Camps, 82 members; Wyoming, 2 Camps, 43 members. Total, 98 Camps, 2,607 members.

The ordinary revenue of the Sovereign Grand Lodge, for the year, was $42,218.57; profit on supplies $2,1754.38.

The following amounts were expended by the Subordinate Lodges, Subordinate Encampments and Degree Lodges of the Daughters of Rebekah, respectively:

	LODGES.	ENCAMPMENTS.	REBEKAH.
For relief of members	$1,239,521.62	$146,910.45	$10,166.90
For relief of widowed families	161,313.18	4,413.25	2,406.11
For education of orphans	12,286.32	285.05	....
For burying the dead	321,637.21	28,771.45	....

The following were adopted :

The several Grand Lodges and Grand Encampments, may, by appropriate legislation, make such provision for benefits for aged, infirm and indigent members as they may deem proper.

Every Subordinate Lodge must open in the Third Degree, and no other form of opening is recognized by our laws. When reduced to the Initiatory, the First or Second Degree, or the Degree of Rebekah, it is the same Lodge, but open for specific purposes only, in a lower Degree. Members can retire from the Lodge room when the Lodge is closed in one Degree, and before it is opened in another. The Subordinate Degree Lodge opened at the beginning, is not closed, in any sense, except to confer Degrees, until formally closed at the end of the session; but when open to confer any lower Degree, any member who has received such Degree is entitled to be admitted.

Brothers of a lower Degree than the Third, are entitled to Visiting Cards, and to visit on the same, as in their own Lodges ; and such Cards shall show whether the holders thereof are beneficial or non-beneficial, and if the former, what benefits are allowed.

A Subordinate Lodge has the legal right to require proficiency in the Unwritten Work of the last Degree taken, as a condition precedent to a candidate advancing to the next higher Degree.

Brothers who have served a term of District Deputy Grand Sire, shall be entitled, at the expiration of such term, to be hailed and addressed as Past District Deputy Grand Sire.

All District Deputy Grand Sires shall be entitled to wear a Jewel, which Jewel shall be, in all respects, similar to the Jewel of the Grand Sire, except that it will be two inches in diameter.

It is the right of a brother to vote a secret ballot, and he has not the right to conceal, or expose, the character of his vote at pleasure, except, in the case of a voluntary motion of all those who cast black balls against an applicant for membership, for a reconsideration of the ballot. In such case, it is lawful for such brothers to expose the character of their votes.

Any Grand Lodge or Grand Encampment may permit the use of the names and numbers of extinct Subordinate Lodges or Encampments, in their respective jurisdictions.

An elective officer of a Grand Lodge can hold, at the same time, the office and discharge the functions of Representative to the Sovereign Grand Lodge.

Under the existing law, past officers cannot be deprived of their rank, simply because they are not members of Grand Lodges or Grand Encampments, but are entitled to their rank by virtue of their having filled said offices, and evidence of such rank should be shown in their Diplomas.

A Dismissal Certificate, when issued, shall show upon its face the highest Degree and rank obtained by the brother to whom the same is issued.

A Past Grand Representative is entitled to rank as such, in every Branch of the Order, of which he is a member.

Unless permitted by local law, a proposed amendment to the By-Laws of a Lodge, after being read at the number of meetings required by the By-Laws of the Lodge, cannot be amended when taken up for action.

The Committee on the subject of the Ridgely Monument are hereby authorized to have erected a monument to Grand Secretary Ridgely, in Harlem Square, in the City of Baltimore, the material to be of granite, with a bronze statute of Bro. Ridgely, the cost of which shall not exceed $20,000.

The trial of a member under charges, who has not attained the Third Degree, must take place when the Lodge is open in the highest Degree to which the member has attained, and the Lodge must be specially opened in such Degree, for that purpose.

A Uniformed Degree Camp, under command of its officers, and in full uniform, can lawfully visit a Subordinate Lodge when in session.

This Grand Lodge does hereby legalize the consolidation of all Lodges or Encampments, made prior to the 22nd day of September, 1883.

The Committee on the State of the Order, in reference to " The Press," reported:

Whilst we should only be too happy to have the support and influence of the secular press, as well as that specially devoted to the interest of our Order, and with the greatest desire to accord to them all honor and credit, for the beneficial results of their labors in the past, we cannot, however, lose sight of the fact, that the controversies in the journals spoken of are, at times, more detrimental than of value, to the Order. The merits of candidates for office in our Order, are frequently discussed by the column, and not in the most enviable terms. Decisions made by Grand Officers, are often published and commented upon, before the Grand Lodges have had an opportunity to approve or reject the same. Opinions of persons, many of whom are not members of the Order, are often promulgated as law, and believed by many, to the detriment of the only authority on the subject, viz., The Sovereign Grand Lodge. Besides these, other indiscretions, of a like character, are constantly committed.

WHEREAS, The periodicals of the Order are not, either directly or indirectly, under the supervision or control of the Sovereign Grand Lodge, or of the Subordinate Grand Lodges ; therefore, be it

Resolved, That all resolutions, heretofore adopted by the Sovereign Grand Lodge, declaring that certain periodicals, or journals, should be regarded as the "Official Organs of the Order," be and they are hereby rescinded.

The Committee on the Patriarchal Branch of the Order, to whom was referred the communication of the Patriarchal Circle, relative to bringing about a union of the Patriarchal Circle and Uniformed Degree Camps, reported :

It is not becoming the dignity of the Sovereign Grand Lodge, to receive the communication, or to treat with the Patriarchal Circle, or any of its Representatives, in relation to the subject matter therein contained.

The legislation reported by the Special Committee on the Supreme Temple, Patriarchal Circle, found on pages 9361, 9362 and 9363, Journal of 1883, was re-enacted and re-affirmed.

It was deemed inexpedient to authorize the establishment of Rebekah Degree Grand Lodges.

A committee of three was appointed, "with instructions to give the Uniformed Degree, and all of the legislation heretofore adopted in relation thereto, careful consideration, ascertain what changes, revisions, alterations, amendments and legislation may be necessary, in order to make the Degree as satisfactory and effective as possible, and to report at the next session."

The Committee on the Degree of Rebekah reported that Subordinate Grand Lodges have authority to form organizations " in which Representatives of Degree Lodges of the Daughters of Rebekah can meet annually for the purpose of promoting the interests of that Branch of the Order, and for social intercourse."

Appropriate resolutions were adopted on the deaths of Isaac M. Veitch, Past Grand Sire, and Joshua Vansant, Grand Treasurer.

The following Grand Officers were elected, and installed : Henry F. Garey, P. D. Grand Sire, of Maryland, Grand Sire; John H. White, P. G. M., of New York, Deputy Grand Sire; Theodore A. Ross, P. G. Rep., of New Jersey, Grand Secretary; Isaac A. Sheppard, P. G. M., of Pennsylvania, Grand Treasurer.

The following were appointed, the first by the Grand Secretary, and the others by the Grand Sire :

Allen Jenckes, P. G. P., of Rhode Island, Assistant Grand Secretary; Rev. J. W. Venable, P. G. Rep., of Kentucky, Grand Chaplain; John T. Jakes, P. G. Rep., of Delaware, Grand Marshal; J. R. Harwell, P. G. Rep., of Tennessee, Grand Guardian; E. H. Whitney, P. G. M., of Michigan, Grand Messenger.

1885.

The Sovereign Grand Lodge met in annual session, in the City of Baltimore, on the 21st of September.

The ceremony of unveiling the Ridgely Monument took place on Tuesday, September 22nd. There was a procession through the streets of the city to Harlem Park, where the monument was erected. Bro. John J. Gallagher, Representative of Delaware, Secretary of the Monument Committee, delivered an address, and presented the structure to the Grand Sire, for the Sovereign Grand Lodge. "Just as his last word was spoken, Bro. M. Muldoon, of Louisville, Ky, architect of the monument, pulled the cords, and the veil parted from the bronze figure of Ridgely, and disclosed his form crowning the top of the granite shaft, his calm face directed towards the east."

The Grand Sire then accepted the monument from the building committee, and made an eloquent and appropriate address. The processional feature of the occasion was somewhat marred by the inclemency of the weather.

The Monument Fund amounted to $19,013.02.
Grand Sire Garey, in his report, said:

Representatives—I congratulate you and the Order that, after a session in
Providence, that land sacred to toleration, and another session at the sources
of the Mississippi, among its wonders of modern civilization, you have returned to this ancient jurisdiction and original birth-place of American Odd
Fellowship. I welcome you to this historic and traditional hall, whose walls
commemorate the line of your illustrious leaders, beneath whose roof your
beautiful rites and fraternal work have been constantly exhibited for fifty-four
years. Around you are the firm foundations of your present prosperity, laid
in the cement of Friendship, Love and Truth ; and, although the workmen are
dust, yet their work remains, as an imperishable memorial of their love for
humanity. Twenty years ago you came to unveil the monument to Wildey ; you
will now receive and approve the monument to the intellectual and moral founder. The one, a tribute to a great soul and a mighty laborer, the other, a tribute to
an intellectual and moral leader, whose varied accomplishments and wonderful
diplomacy, have made those monuments both possible and necessary, as land-
marks of our Order. Other localities may surpass ours in numerical influence,
and material progress in Odd Fellowship, but this is sacred soil. Here is
the first Odd Fellows' hall built and occupied by our Order. Here are the
sites upon which the first American Odd Fellows were initiated, and from which
Wildey went forth to his immortal conquests. Here Wildey and Ridgely met
as types of "Justice and Truth," when "righteouness and peace" may be said
to have "kissed each other" in a solemn covenant which concerned the world.
Here repose the fathers, in great peace, their labors ended—with grateful
tongues, in many languages, inditing their glorious epitaphs. I welcome you,
therefore, to this city, as to the Mecca of our Order.

These are not prosperous days on either side of the Atlantic. We live in
a period of extremes—in which capital and labor have not adjusted their differences ; when money, or its representative, is plentiful, but the channels for
its distribution are not freely open to industry and enterprise. Yet the in-
domitable energy of our countrymen is conspicuously manifest in all directions, and the country, though depressed, is vigorously at work to recu-
perate and prosper. For these reasons, we cannot boast of much material
progress, but it is a source of pride and encouragement that we have kept
our great Body in healthy activity, and find and report it, sound and full of
vitality.

The sixty-sixth anniversary of American Odd Fellowship was celebrated
in this city, and made memorable in our annals, by the laying of the corner-
stone of a monument to the moral architect of the Order. The Grand Lodge
and Grand Encampment of Maryland, with distinguished Odd Fellows from
several jurisdictions, and a large number of our brethren, assembled in this
hall, and, escorted by the Uniformed Patriarchs, proceeded to Harlem Park,
where a large multitude had asssembled. The impressive ceremonies of our
Order were called into requisition, and the corner-stone duly placed, and
cemented at the base of the structure.

RIDGELY MONUMENT, BALTIMORE, MD.

This Grand Lodge is the owner of valuable property in this city, now occupied by its Grand Secretary. A part of the lot upon which this hall is erected was leased from the Grand Lodge of Maryland, subject to an annual rent, upon which valuable improvements have been made, including a fireproof vault for your archives ; the whole costing more than $4,600.00. By the terms of the lease, it was made to terminate at any time that the City of Baltimore might condemn the property for public use, reserving to this Grand Lodge the right to receive from the city the value of its improvements upon the property. The contingency has happened; the city has, by ordinance, condemned the whole of the original lot; plats have been prepared and the assessment of damages is now being made. The ordinance of the city provides for the opening of Lexington street, from Gay to Holliday street, and there seems to be no way of preventing a condemnation of the property and the destruction of all the improvements thereon. This great hall, will, in all probability, soon pass away, and exist only in tradition and history. It, therefore, becomes necessary that provision should be made for protecting the interests of the Sovereign Grand Lodge, as well by securing payment for the loss of its property as by providing proper accommodations for the Grand Secretary and the valuable archives of which he is the custodian. The Grand Lodge of Maryland, has twice succeeded, before the courts, in defeating a similar ordinance, but, taught by that experience, the city officers seem to have prepared a law, which, unless repealed, will appropriate this hallowed soil as a highway, and leave no vestige of this famous temple to succeeding generations. I recommend that a special committee, clothed with all necessary powers to do whatever may be deemed advisable in the premises, be appointed at this session.

The following decisions of the Grand Sire were approved:

When a Lodge is suspended and its Charter taken away, such of its members as belonged to the Encampment Branch, are likewise suspended. In such a case, notice should be given of such suspension, to the respective Encampments to which they belong.

In the installation ceremony, the Seal is put into the hands of the Recording Secretary, and he alone, can officially attest anything for and in behalf of the Lodge.

The Vice Grand, in the absence of the Noble Grand, performs the duties of the Noble Grand, including conferring the Initiatory Degree.

It is not only legal, for a Subordinate Lodge to entertain, permit, or allow charges to be brought against a member who has an application for a Dismissal Certificate before it, after five years from date of suspension, but it is the duty of the Lodge to allow and try such charges.

It is the general law, without exception, that a Charter for a Subordinate Lodge, can only be issued upon the application of five Third Degree members in good standing.

The installation ceremony in a Subordinate Lodge, must always take place when the Lodge is open in the Third Degree.

A D. D. Grand Sire is entitled to "the Honors" when visiting officially.

Grand Secretary Ross, in his report, said :

The results of the year 1884, may be briefly summarized as exhibiting the initiation of more than forty-six thousand, and a net increase exceeding ten thousand, added to our roll, a grand aggregate of 532,467 members enlisted under the banner of Odd Fellowship.

The expenditures for relief amounted to $2,176,269.41, while the Subordinates received into their treasuries $5,530,383.71.

It may be interesting to trace the growth of the Order by decades, and the following is submitted: 1819—Lodges, 1, members, 5; 1829—Lodges, 31, members, 2,000; 1839—Lodges, 130, members, 9,381; 1849—Lodges, 1,727, members, 139,242; 1859,—Lodges, 3,425, members, 177,711; 1869—Lodges, 3,473, members, 268,608; 1879—Lodges, 7,094, members, 450,238, while in 1884, (half a decade,) we have increased to 8,057 Lodges, with a membership of 532,467. If the years to come, in the present decade, present an exhibit equal to the past, we may safely assume that the Order in 1889 will number more than 9,000 Lodges and 620,000 members.

While it is true that we have not, during the last year, planted our banner in any countries not heretofore occupied, we have, at least, added largely to the membership in several foreign jurisdictions, and there are indications that Lodges will be applied for, in localities where Odd Fellowship has been unknown. It seems probable that our temples will soon lift their spires, and our brethren be found earnest laborers in fields that are now shut out from the blessings of this Order. It cannot be doubted, that it is simply a question of time, when Odd Fellowship shall dwell in all the civilized countries of the world, and its benefactions shall descend, "as the gentle rain from Heaven," upon the people of every nation, clime and tongue.

It is my earnest hope that the deliberations of the members of the Sovereign Grand Lodge, at the present session, may be crowned with the success that ought to follow the true and energetic efforts of such an intellectual assembly, and the few disturbing questions that it seems probable will be presented, may be disposed of in a manner that will be entirely satisfactory to all the brethren, and add to the glory and renown of an Order that proclaims : "On earth peace, good will toward men."

The reports showed the existence of 210 Uniformed Degree Camps, with an aggregate membership of 5,943, an increase of 112 Camps and 3,336 members during the year.

The following jurisdictions have no Uniformed Degree Camps : District of Columbia, Maryland, Mississippi, Nevada, South Carolina, Tennessee, Washington, West Virginia.

During the recess, Warrants were issued for the Grand Encampment of Florida, six Subordinate Encampments, and four Subordinate Lodges. Among the latter was Alberta Lodge, No. 1, at Calgary, Canada. Scania Lodge, No. 1, Malmo, Sweden, Europe, was instituted October 29th, 1884.

The Grand Secretary of the Grand Lodge of Australasia, Bro. William Judge, furnished statistics to December 31st, 1884, showing: Subordinate Grand Lodges, 5; Subordinate Lodges, 167; initiated, 4,792; members, 14,664; Grand Lodge Funds, $113,335.00; Subordinate Lodge Funds, $241,480.00; sick allowance paid during 1884, $47,720.00; funeral donations in 1884, $13,965.00; members buried, 96; members' wives buried, 89.

The following statistics are taken from the report of the Grand Lodge of the German Empire:

District Grand Lodges, 5; Subordinate Lodges, 42; members, 1,707; Encampments, 4; members, 146; total relief for the year, $4,795.46; total revenue for the year, $29,547.87.

The ordinary revenue of the Sovereign Grand Lodge for the year, was $34,731.53; profit on supplies, $21,060.38.

The following table shows the work of the Order from 1830 to December 31st, 1884, and its present condition:

Sovereign Grand Lodge, 1; Independent Grand Lodges (German Empire and Australasia), 2; Subordinate Grand Encampments, 45; Subordinate Encampments, 1,943; Subordinate Grand Lodges, 65; Subordinate Lodges, 8,057; Encampment members, 94,589; Lodge members, 532,467; initiations in Subordinate Lodges, 1,364,381; members relieved, 1,151,893; widowed families relieved, 151,222; members deceased, 112,268; total relief, $38,918,406.16; total receipts, $103,757,973.31.

The following amounts were expended by the Subordinate Lodges, Subordinate Encampments and Degree Lodges of the Daughters of Rebekah, respectively:

	LODGES.	ENCAMPMENTS.	REBEKAH.
For relief of members	$1,288,551.46	$158,788.61	$9,934.86
For relief of widowed families	147,645.93	4,709.92	2,985.15
For education of orphans	14,772.47	223.00	....
For burying the dead	339,722.65	30,328.81	....

Bro. C. Kloecker, P. G., was present, as Special Representative from the Grand Lodge of the German Empire.

The Committee on Dues and Benefits reported the following table, as the experience of the Order for the past twelve years:

Rate per member, in decimals, of deaths, of weeks' benefits paid, and of widowed families relieved, under the jurisdiction of the Sovereign Grand Lodge, from 1873 to 1884 :

Year.	Members.	Weeks' Benefits Paid.	Average.	Brothers Buried.	Average.	Widowed Families Relieved.	Average.
1873	414,815	115,289	.2779	4,013	.0096	5,551	.0134
1874	438,701	179,479	.4091	3,889	.0088	5,977	.0136
1875	454,689	211,148	.4667	4,543	.0099	5,931	.0130
1876	456,125	230,398	.5160	4,371	.0094	5,558	.0121
1877	448,019	221,319	.4939	4,284	.0095	5,991	.0133
1878	442,291	237,709	.5368	4,381	.0099	6,162	.0139
1879	440,783	246,768	.5959	4,530	.0102	5,330	.0120
1880	456,942	251,448	.5502	4,504	.0098	5,601	.0100
1881	475,948	285,081	.5989	5,055	.0106	6,287	.0132
1882	496,696	290,750	.5853	5,132	.0103	5,774	.0116
1883	505,871	311,060	.6544	5,211	.0105	5,758	.0113
1884	516,230	323,614	.6268	5,229	.0101	6,076	.0117

The following is the practical outcome of the committee's researches.

Expectation of Life and Sickness, with Dues graded according to Age at Admission—Sick Benefits, $4 per week ; Funeral Benefits, $40 :

Age,	Expectation of Life—Years and Decimals.	Expectation of Sickness for that Year—Weeks and Decimals.	Quarter's Dues.	Age.	Expectation of Life—Years and Decimals.	Expectation of Sickness for that Year—Weeks and Decimals.	Quarter's Dues.
21	41.5	.450	$1.50	41	27.4	.763	$2.28
22	40.8	.455	1.53	42	26.7	.803	2.34
23	40.2	.460	1.56	43	26.	.843	2.40
24	39.5	.465	1.59	44	25.3	.885	2.48
25	38.8	.470	1.61	45	24.5	.930	2.56
26	38.1	.476	1.64	46	23.8	.980	2.63
27	37.4	.483	1.67	47	23.1	1.035	2.71
28	36.7	.491	1.70	48	22.4	1.095	2.80
29	36.	.499	1.74	49	21.6	1.166	2.89
30	35.3	.509	1.77	50	20.9	1.230	2.99
31	34.6	.520	1.81	51	20.2	1.308	3.09
32	33.9	.532	1.85	52	19.5	1.396	3.21
33	33.2	.545	1.89	53	18.8	1.494	3.32
34	32.5	.560	1.93	54	18.1	1.604	3.45
35	31.8	.578	1.97	55	17.4	1.730	3.59
36	31.1	.599	2.01	56	16.7	1.875	3.75
37	30.3	.624	2.06	57	16.	2.040	3.90
38	29.6	.653	2.11	58	15.4	2.230	4.05
39	28.9	.686	2.16	59	14.7	2.450	4.25
40	28.2	.723	2.22	60	14.1	2.700	4.45

The following were adopted :

When members of the Order shall have been suspended or expelled for misconduct, their wives, having received the Degree of Rebekah, shall not be thereby debarred from receiving the Annual Password of the Degree, nor from joining a Degree Lodge of the Daughters of Rebekah.

Grand Lodges and Grand Encampments may elect their officers for a term of one year, or for two years, as their Constitutions may provide.

The time of balloting for Degrees, is a subject for local legislation, and a Subordinate Grand Lodge may, by a general law, provide that one or more weeks shall elapse, from the date of the application, before balloting thereon ; but, in the absence of local legislation, the balloting for Degrees must be upon the same evening on which the application is made therefor.

Appellants must furnish two hundred copies of all appeal papers, as required by the legislation of 1855, page 2,499 of the Journal, and the legislation of 1875, found on page 6,552 of the Journal.

All applications to open, rehear, or review decisions of this Grand Lodge in appeal cases, whether by petition, memorial or otherwise, shall be prepared and forwarded to the Grand Secretary, and under the same rules adopted by this Grand Body for appeals, and be sent to the Committee on Appeals.

When a State, District or Territorial Grand Lodge shall have been duly chartered and instituted, all Subordinate Lodges theretofore existing within said State, District or Territory, and under the immediate jurisdiction of the Sovereign Grand Lodge, by operation of law pass under the jurisdiction of such State, District or Territorial Grand Lodge; and, while such Grand Lodge has not the power to abrogate the Charters or Dispensations, under which such Subordinate Lodges were organized, or to issue Warrants as substitutes therefor, yet such State, District or Territorial Grand Lodge, should issue Charters to such Subordinate Lodges in the usual form, and with the following inscribed upon or across the face thereof : "This Lodge was instituted by —————————, [insert name of officers instituting the Lodge,] on ———————— [insert date of institution,] under and by authority of a Charter [or Dispensation] issued by the Sovereign Grand Lodge, [or the Grand Lodge of the United States,] dated —————————, [insert date of Charter or Dispensation.] [Signatures of present Grand Officers.]" The Subordinate Lodge should be allowed to retain the original Charter or Dispensation.

It is the duty of the Noble Grand, or Chief Patriarch, to *supervise* all ball ballots and declare the result. Grand Jurisdictions, subordinate to the Sovereign Grand Lodge, may authorize their Subordinates to enact By-Laws that the Vice Grand, or Senior Warden, may assist in the examination of the ballot and make known the result of his examination, so far as to state whether the ballot is favorable or unfavorable. The whole matter is left to local legislation, except that the Noble Grand or Chief Patriarch alone, has the prerogative of deciding the result of a ballot.

No member of a Lodge or Encampment, shall vote upon any question relating to the fiscal affairs of his Lodge or Encampment, in the result of which he has a direct *personal* interest ; but may vote upon all questions concerning the leasing or renting of the hall, or other property of his Lodge or Encampment, to any Lodge, Encampment, Rebekah Degree Lodge, Canton, or Uniformed Degree Camp of this Order, and all law in conflict herewith be, and the same is hereby repealed.

No officer of the Sovereign Grand Lodge can serve upon any committee, when the Constitution, By-Laws, or general legislative enactments do not authorize it.

In the absence of the Grand Patriarch, and all Past Grand Patriarchs, a Grand Representative or a Past Grand Representative can install the officers-elect of a Grand Encampment.

In all cases, when a candidate enters a hall to receive a Degree, he should appear without Regalia.

Members of a defunct Subordinate, will be chargeable with dues up to the date when such Subordinate shall legally vote to surrender its Charter, or, in the event of no such action by the Subordinate, then to the date when the Charter shall be sent, by its last officers, to the Grand Lodge or its Executive ; and if no action is taken by the Subordinate or its officers, then to the date when, by local or general authority, the Charter is forfeited.

WHEREAS, The Grand Lodge of the German Empire, by its Special Representative, in attendance at this session, has signified to the Sovereign Grand Lodge, its desire to direct the transaction of ordinary Lodge business, to take place in the Initiatory Degree ; therefore, be it,

Resolved, That if the Grand Lodge of the German Empire shall direct the transaction of ordinary Lodge business to take place in the Initiatory Degree, such direction shall not be held or considered, a violation of the limitation against changes in the Unwritten Work, stipulated in the Charter and compact of the Grand Lodge of the German Empire ; and, further,

Resolved, That these resolutions shall take effect and be communicated immediately, to the Grand Lodge of the German Empire, by the Grand Secretary of the Sovereign Grand Lodge.

Hereafter, every Grand Representative, before entering upon the discharge of his duties in the Sovereign Grand Lodge, shall subscribe to, and file with the Grand Secretary, the following affirmation:

I, upon my honor as an Odd Fellow, declare that I am not now, and was not at the time of my election as Grand Representative to the Sovereign Grand Lodge, a member of the Patriarchal Circle by whatever name known, or of any secret organization, not authorized by this Order, that has ever had as a basis of qualification, membership in this Order of Odd Fellows.

The Committee on the State of the Order, in relation to the property of the Sovereign Grand Lodge, in Baltimore, referred to by the Grand Sire in his report, submitted a resolution (which was adopted), as follows :

That a committee be appointed whose duty it shall be—

1st. To take charge of the interests of this Grand Body in relation to the condemnation of its property, so that full compensation therefor may be recovered, and, if necessary, to employ counsel to represent and protect the interests of the Sovereign Grand Lodge in the premises.

2d. To secure other and temporary quarters for the Grand Secretary, and for the property and archives of this Grand Body, in the event of the condemnation and destruction of the present offices.

3d. To take into consideration the permanent location of the Grand Lodge, whether the same shall be continued at Baltimore, or removed elsewhere ; to make all due inquiry, and to ascertain what inducements may be offered by other cities throughout the land, for the permanent location of this Sovereign Grand Lodge, and to report all facts, propositions and suggestions, with all their acts, to the next session of this Grand Body.

The report of the Special Committee on Revision of the Degree for Uniformed Degree Camps, was considered, amended and adopted. The new Degree was named the "Patriarchs Militant." (*See Journal, pages* 10,111–10,129.)

The Special Committee was continued for another year, to correct and supervise the printing of all books, documents, etc., relating to the Degree, and was directed to copyright the Uniform, Flag, Banner and Jewels, adopted for the Degree of Patriarchs Militant.

A new form of Public Dedication of an Odd Fellows' Hall was adopted. (*See Journal, pages* 10,159–10,167.)

The Grand Lodge of Australasia was, under certain conditions, invested with all the powers and privileges heretofore granted to the Grand Lodge of the German Empire, and permitted to transact the ordinary Lodge business in the Initiatory Degree.

A Special Committee was appointed, to present at next session, "such changes, amendments, alterations, revisions and legislation, as may be necessary to make the Ritual of the Degree Lodges, Daughters of Rebekah, as satisfactory as possible to the several jurisdictions."

A vote of thanks was tendered Canton Excelsior No. 1, of Louisville, Kentucky, for the aid given to the committee, and for the perfect manner in which they exemplified the Degree of Patriarchs Militant.

Bro. J. C. Underwood, G. Rep., of Kentucky, was elected Lieutenant General of the Patriarchs Militant.

The following form of application for membership was recommended :

To the officers and members of ....*No.*....... *working under the jurisdiction of the Grand* .... *of the Independent Order of Odd Fellows
of the*.............. ....

I respectfully request admission into this............,and in consideration of
such admission I promise and agree that, if elected, I will conform to the
Constitution and By-Laws of your ....and those of the Grand
..................of ...., and that I will seek my remedy for all rights on
account of said membership or connection therewith, in the tribunals of the
Order only, without resorting for their enforcement, in any event, or for any
purpose, to the civil courts.

My age is.........years, my occupation is........, my residence...............................
Dated...
Witness........................   Signed........................

1886.

The Sovereign Grand Lodge met in annual session,
in the City of Boston, Massachusetts, on the 20th of September.

By request of the Committee of the Grand Lodge
and Grand Encampment of Massachusetts, the officers and
members of the Sovereign Grand Lodge, assembled in
Boston, on the morning of Saturday, the 18th of September,
to partake of the hospitality of Mayor O'Brien, who invited
the party to an excursion down the harbor, on the steamer
" Nantasket." The boat stopped at Deer Island, where
all lunched and inspected the place, visiting the Chapel of
the prison and listening, with great interest, to the songs of
the children in the institution. On Sunday, the 19th, there
was a special sermon preached by the Rev. George
Landor Perin, in Shawmut Avenue Universalist Church,
before the Sovereign Grand Lodge and the members of
the Order generally.

The Sovereign Grand Lodge was received and welcomed on Monday, the 20th, by Bro. William M. Hill,
Grand Master of the Grand Lodge of Massachusetts, and
Grand Sire Garey made an appropriate reply. On the
evening of the same day there was a splendid banquet held
in Odd Fellows' Hall. On Tuesday evening, the 21st,
there was a Reunion of Past Grand Representatives and
Past Grand Officers of the Sovereign Grand Lodge. The

crowning event of the session was, however, the Grand Parade of Wednesday, the 22d. For splendor and effectiveness it excelled every former one. There were in line about 15,000 brethren, nearly 6,000 being Patriarchs Militant, in their new and showy uniform. It required about two hours for the parade to pass a given point.

Grand Sire Garey, in his report, said :

Twenty-two years have passed since our predecessors met in Massachusetts. The nation was then enveloped in the clouds of civil war, and half the States in the Union were resounding with the clash of arms. The Committee on Seats had drawn the full number required for all the Representatives, but twenty-seven of them were vacant, because ten jurisdictions were struggling with adversity, south of the Potomac. But peace ruled our councils, and Fraternity presided at that meeting. Each vacant chair, as at former sessions, was jealously guarded as the symbol of a living brother, and no action was taken without reference to the known wishes of the distant brotherhood. In that day of intolerance, the Independent Order of Odd Fellows was the only popular Body that led in opening up an era of national toleration. The good work was consummated at the next session, in Baltimore (1865), when the Southern Representatives left their impoverished homes, passed over the still reeking battle-fields, and took their hitherto vacant seats, amidst the tears and shouts of their expectant brethren. This was the first link in a new and more perfect union, a three-fold link which never can be broken— Friendship, Love and Truth.

In 1864 we numbered, in the whole world, so far as reported, but 137,623 members, 39 Grand Lodges, 29 Grand Encampments, 2,118 Lodges, 466 Encampments, and our total revenue was but $1,161,828.65. To-day, we have 517,310 members, 54 Grand Lodges, 44 Grand Encampments, 7,956 Lodges, 1,947 Encampments, and a total revenue, in 1885, of $5,309,688.77. We had then, but one foreign jurisdiction. Twenty-two years ago the Order existed in only one foreign country—the Sandwich Islands—while to-day we find the Odd Fellowship of 1819 flourishing in the Grand Jurisdictions of Australasia and Germany, in the Sandwich Islands, Switzerland, the Netherlands, Denmark, Sweden, Chile, Peru, Mexico and Cuba, and people of other countries evince an ardent desire for the establishment of Lodges of our Order among them.

The following decisions of the Grand Sire were approved :

An appointive officer, who serves for nineteen weeks continually and then resigns, before the end of the term, cannot be elected and installed Vice Grand.

A brother having a Withdrawal Card from his Lodge, is in the same relation with it, as with any other Lodge, except only, that the Lodge issuing the Card has a certain control over him for one year, unless the Card has been elsewhere deposited.

The time fixed by its Constitution, for the meeting of a Grand Lodge, must be observed. A Grand Master has no authority to change the time fixed by law, to an earlier or later period.

The Form of Application for membership, Journal 1885, page 10,188, is not mandatory, but has been left to the discretion of the several Grand Jurisdictions.

No Lodge has a right to refuse admittance to a brother who has a regular Visiting Card, and is correct, etc., for the simple reason that his presence is obnoxious to the Lodge.

A brother cannot hold the two offices of Recording Secretary and Treasurer, at the same time, in any Lodge or Encampment, Grand or Subordinate, in the Order, as the case may be.

It is the duty of a Subordinate Lodge, and its officers, to obey and enforce the laws of the Sovereign Grand Lodge, anything in the Constitution of Grand or Subordinate to the contrary notwithstanding.

No failure to be installed, or to serve, on the part of a Noble Grand elect, or vacation of office after he has assumed his place, can entitle a Vice Grand to the office, unless he has been lawfully elected thereto.

Grand Secretary Ross, in his report, said :

Once more, and for the second time in the history of the supreme head of this Order, the officers and members are assembled in the City of Boston, known as "the Athens of America." Since 1864, many and wonderful changes have taken place throughout the world, but, perhaps, no greater evidence of progress is to be noted than we find in the Institution of Odd Fellowship. Glancing over the records, we ascertain that in the twenty-two years since the session in this historic city, we have added nearly 380,000 to the Lodge and 69,000 to the Encampment membership, in Bodies under the jurisdiction of the Sovereign Grand Lodge, and the roll of Grand and Subordinate Bodies has been increased by 15 Grand Lodges, 15 Grand Encampments, 5,838 Subordinate Lodges and 1,481 Subordinate Encampments. In the same period, the expenditures for the relief of the sick and distressed, the burial of the dead, and the education of orphans, amounted to $31,614,288.29, and the aggregate paid into the treasuries of Subordinates was $86,221,933.08.

In 1864, Degree Lodges of the Daughters of Rebekah were unknown, as it was not until 1868 that authority was given for the establishment of this important and useful Branch of the Order ; and Odd Fellows of a quarter of a century ago, did not dream of a Uniformed Encampment member, or of the existence of more than 300 Cantons of Patriarchs Militant, and a splendid Body of thousands of disciplined Chevaliers, marching under the banner of the Order, to honor the Sovereign Grand Lodge at its annual session. Of the 81 officers and members assembled in Boston in 1864, not one is accredited as a Representative at the session of 1886, and probably not a half dozen of them will be with you in any capacity. The Angel of Death has waved his dark wing over our household, and borne from our midst many of our best beloved and most useful workers ; but the Order prospers. The vacant places are filled with young and enterprising brethren, emulating by their zeal, intelligence, and devotion to Odd Fellowship, the glorious examples left them by Brothers Ridgely, Vansant, Ellison, Kennedy, Williamson, Veitch and their associates, who, twenty-two years ago, met in this beautiful city, in the interest of American Odd Fellowship.

The legislation of the session, now opening, will, no doubt, be transacted in the same careful manner that has marked the previous annual meetings of this Body, and produce good fruit in due season, tending to still further enlarge the sphere of the Order, and plant our banner in countries where the principles of Friendship, Love and Truth, as inculcated and practised by the brethren of our Mystic Union, are now unknown.

> "No pent-up Utica contracts your powers,
> But the whole boundless continent is yours."

The following table shows the statistical history of the Order, on the subjects mentioned, from 1830 to December 31st, 1885:

Initiations in Subordinate Lodges, 1,404,110; widowed families relieved, 157,063; members relieved, 1,208,180; members deceased, 117,904; total relief, $41,154,900.09; total receipts, $109,254,362.08.

The following amounts were expended by the Subordinate Lodges, Subordinate Encampments and Degree Lodges of the Daughters of Rebekah, respectively:

	LODGES.	ENCAMPMENTS.	REBEKAH.
For relief of members	$1,330,547.70	$160,699.01	$11,577.99
For relief of widowed families	145,094.33	4,666.81	3,285.70
For education of orphans	13,918.74	409.04	....
For burying the dead	359,206.10	35,320.37	....

At this session, the Patriarchs Militant Branch of the Order received much consideration from the Grand Lodge. The report of Lieutenant General Underwood, a very voluminous document, will be found on pages 10,533–10,640 of the Journal.

The Special Committee on the location of the office of the Sovereign Grand Lodge, on the 22d of September, made an elaborate report, submitting propositions from Washington, D. C.; St. Louis, Mo.; Indianapolis, Ind.; Philadelphia, Pa.; Chicago, Ill.; and Columbus, O., for the accommodations necessary. The report was adopted after adding:

The Sovereign Grand Lodge should, at this session, take action with a view to determining the question of change of location of its home office, it being expedient that such change be made.

Pursuant to the above action, on the 24th of September the Grand Lodge proceeded to determine, by ballot, the location of the headquarters. The places named above, and the City of Baltimore, Md., were nominated, and on the fifth formal ballot, Chicago received 73 and Columbus 76 votes. Subsequently, a committee was appointed to make all arrangements for the removal of the office, etc.

The following were adopted :

The wife, unmarried daughter, or unmarried sister of an Odd Fellow, of the Degree of Truth, who has attained the age of eighteen years, *if she be a white woman*, may receive the Degree of Rebekah, or be admitted to a Degree Lodge of the Daughters of Rebekah. (This action made an important change in the qualifications for members of the Degree of Rebekah.)

The several Grand Bodies, and Lodges and Encampments subordinate to the Sovereign Grand Lodge, are required to report to this Grand Lodge : 1st. The number of schools and colleges under their control. 2nd. The number of children attending the same. 3rd. The number of children kept at other schools not under the control of the Order. 4th. The amount paid out, per term, on account of the same.

The law regulating the qualifications for membership in the Degree of Rebekah, shall be so amended, as to provide for the admission of the mother (a widow), and unmarried step-daughter of an Odd Fellow.

A Certificate of the Secretary of the Subordinate Lodge, of which the applicant is a member, with the Seal attached, shall accompany all applications for membership made to a Subordinate Encampment, and it is hereby made the duty of every Secretary, to fill out and furnish, to any Scarlet Degree member of his Lodge, who is in good standing, such Certificate, upon application therefor.

The Revised Ritual of the Rebekah Degree, adopted at this session, shall take effect and be the only authorized work for Rebekah Degree Lodges, on and after January 1st, 1887.

In such jurisdictions as authorize the conferring of the Past Official Degrees, only within the Grand Lodges, a member may be eligible to the office of D. D. Grand Master, without being in possession of the Past Official Degrees.

Hereafter, it shall be lawful for the Subordinate Lodges and Encampments of this Order, whenever their regular stated meetings fall upon the National Anniversary, Thanksgiving and other legally established or generally recognized holidays, to omit such sessions.

Grand Lodges may elect their Grand Chaplains.

In all appeals to this Grand Lodge, it shall be required of the appellants to send with their papers, a certified copy of the Constitution and By-Laws of their Grand Body, of the Constitution for Subordinates, and of the By-Laws of the Subordinate Lodge or Encampment involved in the appeal.

Until the Grand Lodge of Australasia shall have had reasonable time to take steps to procure for the same, full power, without further authority from us to itself, it may authorize the transaction of business in the Initiatory Degree in Australasia, as indicated in the report of the Committee on Foreign Relations, adopted at our last annual session, and until our further order in the premises, no further steps be taken to the enforcement, in Australasia, of our rule requiring the transaction of business in the Third Degree.

In addition to the law as found in Section 509, White's Digest, allowing Grand Lodges to open in the Scarlet Degree during the installation of Grand Officers, Grand Lodges and Grand Encampments may also provide for the exemplification of the Degrees of the Order, while open in the Scarlet or Royal Purple Degrees, respectively.

The Grand Lodge accepts the proposition of the Order in Columbus, Ohio, for the second floor of the Temple in that city. (This resolution refers to the removal of the headquarters of the Sovereign Grand Lodge from Baltimore to Columbus. See propositions of the brethren of Columbus, Journal, pages 10,468–10,471.)

A Special Committee of three, and the Grand Sire, Grand Secretary, and Grand Treasurer, shall be raised to carry into effect, as speedily as possible, the determination of this Grand Body; to take control of its property and interests in the City of Baltimore ; to dispose of the same in such manner, and at such time, as shall be to the best interests of this Grand Lodge, or to recover compensation therefor, in the event of its appropriation, and to make and conclude, all contracts and arrangements with the proper authorities, which may be necessary to perfect the transfer and locate its offices in the city of Columbus; also to secure the incorporation of the Sovereign Grand Lodge, under the laws of the State of Ohio.

Article XVIII, of the By-Laws, was amended to read as follows :

Each State, District and Territorial Grand Lodge shall annually be furnished with as many copies of the printed proceedings of this Grand Lodge as it has Subordinate Lodges working under its jurisdiction, to be distributed among its Subordinates, and one-half of such number, but not less than fifteen copies, for its own use.   Each Grand Encampment shall be furnished in the same manner ; and each Lodge or Encampment working under the Warrant of this Grand Lodge shall be furnished with a copy of the proceedings.   The Grand Secretary shall see that this law is carried into effect at as early a date as possible after the close of the annual session of this Grand Lodge.

Appropriate resolutions were adopted on the deaths of Past Grand Sires Glenn and DeSaussure.

The following Grand Officers were elected and installed : John H. White, P. D. Grand Sire, of New York, Grand Sire; John C. Underwood, P. G. M., of Kentucky, Deputy Grand Sire ; Theodore A. Ross, P. G. Rep., of New Jersey, Grand Secretary ; Isaac A. Sheppard, P. G. M., of Pennsylvania, Grand Treasurer.

The following were appointed, the first by the Grand Secretary, and the others by the Grand Sire:

Allen Jenckes, P. G. P., of Rhode Island, Assistant Grand Secretary; Rev. J. W. Venable, P. G. Rep., of Kentucky, Grand Chaplain; Wm. H. Stevenson, P. G. Rep., of Connecticut, Grand Marshal; Walter G. Dye, P. G. Rep., of Minnesota, Grand Guardian; W. H. Frazier, P. G. P., of the District of Columbia, Grand Messenger.

1887.

The Sovereign Grand Lodge met in annual session, in the City of Denver, Colorado, on the 19th of September. The officers and members were cordially welcomed by the brethren of Colorado.

On Saturday morning, the 17th, the visitors were given an excursion to Graymont, over the Union Pacific Road. The party was so large that the train was run in two sections. The scenery was magnificent beyond description; the wonderful "loop," a splendid specimen of railroad engineering, attracted the undivided attention and commanded the admiration of all. The entire day was an occasion of unalloyed pleasure.

On Sunday, the 18th, the Body attended St. John's Cathedral, which was magnificently adorned for the occasion, and listened, with intense interest, to a sermon by Grand Chaplain Venable, and the grand sacred music, rendered by a choir of 150 voices, (accompanied by instrumental music,) described as "magnificent and sublime in the extreme."

On Monday morning, the 19th, the Sovereign Grand Lodge was escorted by the Grand Lodge of Colorado and Patriarchs Militant, to the Grand Opera House, where addresses of welcome were delivered by Hon. Alva Adams, Governor of Colorado; Hon. Wm. Scott Lee, Mayor of Denver, and Bro. J. M. Norman, Grand Secretary, for the Grand Master. Bro. John H. White, Grand Sire, made an appropriate reply.

On Monday evening, September 19th, there was a Reunion of the Past Grand Representatives, and the survivors

JOHN H. WHITE, GRAND SIRE.

of the session of 1865. On Thursday, September 22d, there was a grand parade. The entire number in the procession was estimated at 3,000, of whom about 1,000 were Chevaliers. The streets were thronged, and every available spot was occupied by citizens and strangers, anxious to view the pageant. It is said that the spectators numbered fully 50,000. On this occasion, Denver was in holiday dress, and the day was one to be long remembered.

Grand Sire White, in his report, said:

It is a gratifying fact, that the year which closed with the 31st day of December, 1886, has been a prosperous one for our Order. The increase in membership has been most marked, and, judging from indications, the present year will be much more prosperous than the preceding one. While it is true that some jurisdictions have exhibited a decline in membership, yet the general increase for 1886 was eleven thousand nine hundred and ten (11,910) greater than that of 1885. The causes of decline in certain of the jurisdictions, are apparent to any one at all conversant with the conditions of the particular jurisdictions. It is a marvel to those unacquainted with the organization, the purposes and principles of the Independent Order of Odd Fellows, that, in spite of all the opposition it encounters, amidst the thousand-and-one secret fraternal organizations which have sprung up in the country within the last few years, all appealing to the interests, the passions and prejudices of the public, our grand old Order should continue to march right along, steadily increasing in membership, in wealth, in power and in influence; but to us who know its worth, who have participated in its benefits and shared in its enjoyments, it is no marvel at all. Its principles are rooted deep down in the human heart, its purposes and practices are grateful to the feelings, and in accordance with the impulses of every generous nature. Such an institution must continue to increase and prosper, so long as the nature of man shall remain unchanged, and misery and misfortune encumber the earth.

Much more interest has been manifested in the Degree of Rebekah, for the past year or two, than formerly. In many sections it is doing a vast amount of good. The various conventions that I have attended during the past year have convinced me that more attention should be given to this Branch of the Order, by the law making power. The proceedings of the conventions were characterized by a moderation, courtesy and business tact which would do credit to conventions composed exclusively of the sterner sex. I am satisfied that many Subordinates have been saved by the establishment of Rebekah Lodges in their vicinity. In many jurisdictions there are but few of these Lodges, and they are weak and of no account, but in others they are strong and of great influence upon the members of the Order of both sexes. Those who decry these Lodges, need not join them. They can keep away and allow those who take pleasure in these meetings, and their associations, to go on doing good in their own way. The world of Odd Fellowship is wide enough for all.

The office of the Grand Secretary has been successfully removed from the City of Baltimore, to the City of Columbus, Ohio, of the particulars of which you will be fully advised by the report of the committee.

Complaints have been repeatedly made to me in reference to organizations which are springing up all over the country, denominated Odd Fellows' Benevolent Associations, many of which, it is alleged, are not conducted on a sound basis, and some of which, it is alleged, use fraudulent means to obtain business. A number of these companies have failed to meet their obligations, and it is said are bringing discredit upon the Order. I call your attention to this subject, that measures may be adopted to correct the evils complained of.

The following decisions of the Grand Sire were approved:

The widow of an Odd Fellow, who had received the Degree of Rebekah, during the life of her husband, in his Subordinate Lodge, is eligible to membership in a Rebekah Degree Lodge, upon a Card from the Subordinate of which her husband was a member, although her husband, at the time of his death, was not in good standing in his Subordinate Lodge.

Rebekah Degree Lodges, working under the new Ritual, cannot lawfully give that Work before a Subordinate Lodge open in the Degree of Rebekah. The new Ritual is for the exclusive use of Rebekah Lodges.

The Grand Sire has not the authority to approve the Constitutions of Subordinate Grand Bodies, or amendments thereto, during the recess of the Sovereign Grand Lodge.

When the officers, at installation, retire in charge of the Grand Marshal for examination, they should retire in form—that is, address the Chairs.

A Grand Representative to the Sovereign Grand Lodge, has not the right to introduce to a Subordinate Encampment, visitors whom he knows are not members of the Patriarchal Branch of the Order.

A brother holding a Withdrawal Card out of date, or a Dismissal Certificate, may join in applying for a Charter for a new Lodge of Odd Fellows, but the application must be signed by five Third Degree members, who hold unexpired Withdrawal Cards. The term "brothers of the Order in good standing," as used in Art. I. of the By-Laws, Sovereign Grand Lodge, must be construed to mean, brothers holding unexpired Withdrawal Cards.

Under the law of the Sovereign Grand Lodge, establishing the Degree of the Patriarchs Militant, honorary members cannot be required to wear a cap, belt and sword, in order to sit in a Canton.

Grand Secretary Ross, in his report, said:

In concluding this report, it is indeed gratifying to be able to point to such a splendid record of the labors of our brethren generally, during the last year, as the figures presented unmistakably indicate. The results attained, must astonish the most sanguine of our membership, as, considering the unsettled condition of business affairs throughout the country, the continued clashing of labor and capital, and the lack of employment occasioned thereby, the most ardent and zealous Odd Fellow had grave fears of the effect of the "labor troubles " on the membership, in the year 1886. But, happily, the apprehensions were not realized, and it has been clearly demonstrated, that the brethren have been true to themselves and to the noble Order they connected themselves with, during the serious trials through which they were compelled to pass. The number of members lost by reason of non-payment of dues, in 1886, was 30,085, whilst in 1885 it was 32,555, a difference of 2,470. The net increase of 12,990 in membership, is greater than in any year since 1882, when a gain of 18,050 was reported, and exceeds by 11,910 the increase in 1885. Whether this unexpected result is to be attributed, as some assert, to the Patriarchs Militant organization, is a question upon which members differ. Brethren in positions to know whereof they speak, maintain that in their jurisdictions, the influence of the display element of the Order, has been of great benefit to the Encampments, and if the higher Bodies increase in membership, it is evident that the Subordinate Lodges must also feel the effects ; in fact, be the first to reap the fruits of any new enterprise.

The feeling seems to be growing, that the time has arrived, when suitable provision should be made for the care of aged and indigent members of the Order, in their declining years, and for widows and orphans left destitute, by the removal by death, of their dependence for support. In several States, organizations of this truly benevolent character, are in successful operation, and in other jurisdictions projects for " Homes " have assumed definite shape, promising encouraging results, in the near future, in this important field of labor. Certainly no worthier object than the relief of the helpless, in the hour of need, can enlist the attention and the energies of the members of an institution organized for the aid of the afflicted and distressed, the protection of the widow and orphan, and efforts in this direction demonstrate that the well-known words—

" Failing not when life has perished,
Living still beyond the tomb,"

are not meaningless professions. In view of the movements referred to, it is hoped that future reports from Grand Bodies will show a grand work accomplished in the direction indicated.

The following statements are compiled from reports to the Sovereign Grand Lodge, and give the statistics of the Order from 1830 to December 31st, 1886 :

Initiations in Subordinate Lodges, 1,460,459 ; members relieved, 1,265,268 ; widowed families relieved, 163,573 ; members deceased, 124,060 ; total relief, $43,589,061.87 ; total receipts, $115,014,145.25.

Condition of the Order December 31st, 1886: Sovereign Grand Lodge, 1 ; Independent Grand Lodges, (German Empire and Australasia), 2 ; Subordinate Grand Encampments, 47 ; Subordinate Encampments, 2,016 ; Subordinate Grand

Lodges, 65; Subordinate Lodges, 8,334; Encampment members, 100,223; Lodge members, 547,856.

The following amounts were expended by the Subordinate Lodges, Subordinate Encampments, and Degree Lodges of the Daughters of Rebekah, respectively:

	LODGES.	ENCAMPMENTS.	REBEKAH.
For relief of members..........	$1,381,128.41	$166,454.02	$12,578.01
For relief of widowed families..	137,841.79	5,056.19	3,712.80
For education of orphans..... .	16,060.95	367.53	....
For burying the dead..........	354,169.64	32,943.32	....

During the recess, the Grand Sire issued a proclamation warning members of the Order to have no affiliation with the "Patriarchal Circle." (*See Journal*, 1887, *pages* 10,727, 10,728.)

Charters were issued for four Subordinate Encampments, four Subordinate Lodges, one Degree Lodge of the Daughters of Rebekah, and the Grand Lodge of New Mexico, at Las Vegas. One of the Lodges instituted was Concorde Lodge No. 1, at Havre, France.

A communication was received from James John Stockall, Grand Master of the Manchester Unity, I. O. O. F., expressing a desire to re-open friendly relations, and more particularly that the matter of the old visiting privileges be considered, with a view to their being re-established, under proper circumstances and arrangements. (*See Journal*, *page* 10,731.)

The following were adopted :

That the resolution passed in 1858, (providing that all sessions of the Sovereign Grand Lodge will be held in Baltimore, until further ordered), be rescinded, and that hereafter, when not otherwise ordered, the Sovereign Grand Lodge will hold its sessions in the City of Columbus, Ohio.

State Grand Lodges and Grand Encampments, may provide, by Constitutional enactment, for the erection and maintenance of Homes for aged and indigent Odd Fellows; provided, however, said Bodies shall not make assessments on their Subordinates, for the purpose of erecting and maintaining the same.

A lady member of a Rebekah Degree Lodge, being in good standing, has the right to ask for and receive a Withdrawal Card, and the right to deposit the same, for re-admission to the Order, under the same rules and regulations as govern that subject in Subordinate Lodges.

The permission heretofore given to Australasia to continue the transaction of ordinary Lodge business in the Initiatory Degree, until said amended Grand Charter, (*See page* 10,931, *Journal*), has been made, be and is expressly continued.

If the Grand Lodge of Australasia, having obtained said amended Grand Charter, and said extensive powers and privileges, and having thus been made an Independent Grand Lodge and the true head of the Order in Australasia, shall then direct the transaction of ordinary Lodge business in the Initiatory instead of the Third Degree, this Sovereign Grand Lodge will not regard or hold such direction a violation of the limitation against changes in the Unwritten Work, to be contained in said amended Grand Charter, although a transfer of certain parts of the Unwritten Work to the Initiatory, from a higher Degree, may be made necessary by such direction, as long as the Unwritten Work itself, is not in any manner altered or changed.

The only persons who are the beneficiaries of a funeral benefit are the orphans or dependent relatives of the deceased, or relatives upon whom the deceased was dependent at the time of death. Dependent relatives are relatives who were members of the family of the deceased, and were dependent upon the deceased for support, at the time of death.

The Grand Sire is requested to take such steps as may seem best to him, for bringing about the introduction of our Order into Spain, provided that the same be done without expense to this Grand Lodge.

The Dispensations granted, by authority of the Grand Sire, to Cuban brothers, during the recess of the Sovereign Grand Lodge, to receive the Encampment Degrees in the State of Florida, are hereby ratified.

Active participation in any organization, by whatever name known, purporting to be, or which has purported to be, a part of, or connected with, Odd Fellowship, said organization not being recognized by the Sovereign Grand Lodge, shall be deemed *prima facie* evidence of membership therein, as shall the wearing of any distinctively Odd Fellow's Badge, Emblem, Uniform or Insignia, or any part thereof, in connection with said organization, or the Emblems, Insignia or Uniform thereof.

Any member of any Subordinate Lodge or Encampment of the Order, upon change of residence, shall have the privilege of applying for membership in any Lodge or Encampment, without first applying for a Withdrawal Card from the Subordinate Body in which he holds membership, by first obtaining a Visiting Card from such Body, and depositing the same in the Lodge or Encampment in which he seeks to obtain membership.

Upon election of such brother by the Lodge or Encampment, to which he shall apply for membership, said Body shall notify the Body of which he is a member of such election, when, being free from all charges and the payment of all dues and fees, upon proper application, he shall be entitled to a Withdrawal Card, or a Dismissal Certificate.

Upon deposit of said Card, with said Lodge or Encampment in which he had been elected, he shall be entitled to sign the Constitution and By-Laws, and be received in full membership from such time, upon the payment of the admission fees required by the By-Laws of said Lodge or Encampment.

Grand Masters of the various State jurisdictions, in which Degree Lodges of the Daughters of Rebekah exist, are authorized to appoint Deputies from among the lady Past Grands of such Lodges, to exercise the duties of installation, and such other duties in said Lodges, as their office empowers them to do.

Installing officers for the Rebekah Degree Lodges, are authorized to fill the various positions, in the installation of officers of such Lodges, with lady Past Noble Grands.

The widows' and orphans' fund of the Subordinate Lodges and Encampments, is stamped as a trust fund, for the use and benefit of the widows and orphans whose husbands and fathers, at their death, were members in good standing, in such Lodge or Encampment; and it is illegal and a misapplication of such funds, to donate or appropriate said funds, or any part thereof, to any purpose whatever, except for the direct and individual support and benefit of the widows and orphans who are, under the law, legitimate charges upon such Lodge or Encampment; provided, however, nothing herein shall prevent Subordinates, who may have placed their widows and orphans in an asylum or home, from using their widows' and orphans' fund in defraying the legitimate expenses thereby incurred. And the several Grand Bodies are instructed to see to it, that this law is observed by their Subordinates.

The sum of $500, or so much thereof as the Grand Sire may deem necessary, be, and the same is hereby appropriated, annually, for the purpose of procuring clerical assistance for the Grand Sire, and the Grand Sire is authorized to draw his warrants on the Grand Treasurer, at such times, and in such amounts, as may be required.

It is the duty of every Odd Fellow, when he is away from home and out of his own jurisdiction, to give attention and care to his brethren in distress, and watch with the sick when necessary, as well as when he is within his own jurisdiction.

It is, and shall be the duty of every member of the Order, on taking up his residence away from the vicinity of his own Lodge, to report himself to the Lodge nearest his residence, or when it is equally near, to two or more Lodges, to one thereof, within thirty days after taking up such residence, and in making such report, he shall give the name and number and location of his Lodge, and when requested by the Lodge to which he has reported, shall watch with the sick who, like himself, are away from home and their own jurisdiction; and any such member, so failing to report, shall not be entitled to affiliation with the Order, nor to attention from any Lodge. And this legislation shall not be construed to hinder or prevent any Lodge, or member, from furnishing watchers, or giving attention to any sick or needy brother.

The Grand Sire shall appoint a committee of five, with instructions to investigate this matter, (of Odd Fellows' Benefit Associations), without expense to this Grand Body, and report the facts at the next session of this Sovereign Grand Lodge, and also a system of rules and regulations for inquiring into the condition, business methods, and management of such associations, if the same can be safely done, in the opinion of said committee.

The Grand Lodge of Nevada petitioned the Sovereign Grand Lodge " to organize a National Endowment feature,. under the supervision and control of the Sovereign Grand Lodge," which was referred to a special committee. They reported a resolution designed to obtain the views of the several jurisdictions on the subject. The report was not adopted.

A protest was received by the Grand Sire, from the Grand Lodge of Maryland, against the removal of the headquarters of the Order from Baltimore to Columbus. (*See Journal, pages* 10,719–10,721.)

The Special Committee on Location of the Sovereign Grand Lodge, made a report which contains the agreement between the Lodges and Encampment, owners of the Odd Fellows' Temple, in the City of Columbus, Ohio, and the Sovereign Grand Lodge, and will be found in the Journal, pages 10,873–10,876.

The Committee on the State of the Order, to whom was referred the report of the Special Committee on Location of the Sovereign Grand Lodge, and that portion of the Grand Sire's report relating to the protest of the Grand Lodge of Maryland, reported :

That, in their opinion, the position taken by the Grand Sire is a correct one, and should be approved and adopted by the Sovereign Grand Lodge. That the office of the Grand Secretary has been removed from the City of Baltimore, and located in the City of Columbus, Ohio, and that the said Special Committee, in behalf of the Sovereign Grand Lodge, has received and accepted a sufficient deed of conveyance, securing to the respective parties all of their rights in the premises.

The High Commission submitted the legislation proposed by the Military Council of the Patriarchs Militant, and reported as follows :

After due examination and such alteration as was deemed proper, your commission find nothing in said proposed legislation contrary to the laws of the Order, and therefore report the same to the Sovereign Grand Lodge for its action.

The matter presented, consisted of thirty-one recommendations relating to the organization of the Army into Corps, the rank of officers, etc., as detailed on pages 10,877–10,879,.

Journal; "a decoration to be given to Chevaliers, Patriarchs Militant, and Daughters of Rebekah, who shall be selected because of general worth and service, and looking towards the protection of mothers, wives and daughters of Odd Fellows in their rights, to be worn upon the left breast, by Chevaliers, and at the throat, by the Daughters of Rebekah," and a suitable Ceremony for conferring the same. (*See Journal, pages* 10,881–10,890.)

The several subjects received the approval of the Sovereign Grand Lodge. The Ceremonies referred to, will also be found in the " Book of Forms."

The following report, from the Committee on the Degree of Rebekah, was adopted:

Your Committee on the Degree of Rebekah have read, with great pleasure, the clear and concise statement of the condition of this Degree, as it appears in the report of the Grand Secretary, page 10,795. From this statement, it is plainly shown that this Branch of our Order is meeting with encouragement, and has the endorsement of nearly all the jurisdictions subordinate to this Sovereign Body. We regret to notice, that no reports have been received from seven jurisdictions, for several years past. We suggest that the Grand Secretary again make call on the Grand Secretaries of the delinquent jurisdictions, for an immediate report, and that such reports be incorporated in the tabular statement in the Revised Journal. It is to be hoped that the recognition and introduction of this Degree, will receive the early attention of such jurisdictions as have no Lodges of this Degree within their limits. The condition of this Branch of the Order, is certainly very cheering, there being shown a large increase in the number of Lodges, membership and finances.

A Form of Burial Ceremony for a Daughter of Rebekah was adopted. (*See Journal, pages* 10,983–10,985.)

The By-Laws of the Sovereign Grand Lodge were amended as follows:

Article I., by inserting, after the word "Order," in the first line, the words " of the Degree of Truth." (Qualifications of petitioners for a Subordinate Lodge.)

Article II., by striking out the word " qualified," in the first line, and inserting in lieu thereof " Royal Purple." (Qualifications of petitioners for a Subordinate Encampment.)

The Constitution for Subordinate Lodges, under the immediate jurisdiction of the Sovereign Grand Lodge, was amended as follows:

Article I., Section 1., by striking out of the second line the words, "including one qualified to preside at its sessions," and inserting "of the Degree of Truth." (Number of members required to constitute a Lodge.)

Article VII., Section 4, by striking out "twenty-six nights," in the fourth line, and inserting "a regular term." (Service in an inferior office to be eligible for Vice Grand.)

The Constitution for Subordinate Encampments, under the immediate jurisdiction of the Sovereign Grand Lodge, was amended as follows:

Article VIII., Section 1, by adding after "vacancy," in the fourth line, "except for the two terms after an Encampment has been instituted or revived." (Service in some other elective office to be eligible for Chief Patriarch, or High Priest.)

The Grand Lodge decided that the action of the Grand Sire, in approving By-Laws of Subordinates under the immediate jurisdiction of the Sovereign Grand Lodge, during the recess, is not final, but subject to review by the Grand Lodge.

Appropriate resolutions were adopted relative to the death of Past Grand Sire Moore.

The career of Washington Lodge, No. 1, from its organization, until the surrender of its extraordinary Charter to a Committee of Past Grands, for the purpose of forming a Grand Lodge, and the transactions of the Supreme Body, under its several names, constitute the history of the Order from 1819 to 1887. In the preceding matter, extracts from the eleven thousand pages of the Journals of the Sovereign Grand Lodge are presented, and it can be said, with entire truthfulness, that it has been a very laborious and difficult undertaking to discriminate in the selection of suitable portions of the proceedings. In some instances, a mere reference has been made to important legislation, while in other cases, the full text of the laws was incorporated when it was thought that the entire resolutions would prove more satisfactory than a brief synopsis of them.

The reader of this Chapter must have noticed many changes in the Constitution, By-Laws and general laws of the Order. Such alterations and modifications were to be expected from an institution that, from its incipiency, has been "progressive in its character," and it seems scarcely necessary to say that some of the resolutions presented, will be found at variance with the laws now governing the Order, for the reason that many of the enactments have been repealed and supplanted by later legislation. Repetitions will be found; laws adopted at a session having been affirmed at subsequent meetings, and in some instances, a law previously adopted, has been re-enacted in a modified form. This feature, "progress," has been the great impetus of the Order; its Protean capacity to meet every phase of its growing greatness, is the best proof of the ability and genius of the founders of the institution and their successors. Its untrammeled legislative capacity, wisely preserved, and reserved, is not the least of the evidences of the wisdom displayed by its progenitors. It will be well, therefore, to remember that this Chapter is simply a "History" of the progress of the Order, year after year, in membership, and ministrations in fulfillment of the great command of our laws, and of the transactions of the Supreme Body from the earliest days of Odd Fellowship in America, until the present time. For this reason, some of the legislation, as well as copious extracts from the reports of Grand Officers, are presented under each year. There has been no attempt at *fine writing*, but the action of the Body, as found on the pages of its Journals, is presented in a plain and unpretending form, the effort having been, to "nothing extenuate, nor set down aught in malice." Those who desire to know the laws of the Order, as they are, can have their wishes gratified by perusing the Digest, Book of Forms, and Journals, published by the Sovereign Grand Lodge, and for more detailed information concerning the Order in its infancy, the reader is referred to the "History of American Odd Fellowship, The First Decade, by James L. Ridgely, Historiographer," in which the particulars of the trials, struggles and successes of the pioneers, in the early days of the institution, are elaborately presented.

CHAPTER II.

THE SOVEREIGN GRAND LODGE.

THE legal title of this Body is THE SOVEREIGN GRAND LODGE OF THE INDEPENDENT ORDER OF ODD FELLOWS, and it is at present incorporated under the laws of the State of Maryland. " It is the source of all true and legitimate Odd Fellowship in the United States of America, and possesses such powers and jurisdiction over the whole brotherhood, as are provided in the Constitution and Ritual of the Order. Its authority extends also to such Lodges and Encampments as may be organized under its Charter in foreign countries."

It existed originally, under the name of "*The Grand Lodge of Maryland and of the United States, I. O. O. F.*," and worked under this title until the 15th of January, 1825, when a new Constitution was adopted for the Grand Body, separate and distinct from the Grand Lodge of Maryland, and the name of " *The Grand Lodge of the United States, of the Independent Order of Odd Fellows*," was assumed. September 17th, 1878, the name was changed to "*The Grand Lodge of the Independent Order of Odd Fellows.*" On the 18th day of September, 1879, the present title was adopted. The Act of Incorporation under this new name was approved, and became operative February 26th, 1880.

There are two Independent Grand Lodges: "*The Grand Lodge of the German Empire*," and "*The Grand Lodge of Australasia.*"

On December 31st, 1886, the Sovereign Grand Lodge had enrolled under its banner the following: Independent

Grand Lodges, 2; Subordinate Grand Encampments, 47; Subordinate Encampments, 2,016; Subordinate Grand Lodges, 65; Subordinate Lodges, 8,334; Encampment members, 100,223; Lodge members, 547,856; Degree Lodges of the Daughters of Rebekah, 1,345; members, brothers, 33,333, sisters, 33,958, total Rebekah members, 67,291; Cantons of Patriarchs Militant, 462; Canton members (Chevaliers); 15,259.

The Constitution, By-Laws, and Rules of Order of the Sovereign Grand Lodge, here presented, will give the full and detailed information necessary to understand the system of government practiced by this Supreme authority.

CONSTITUTION
OF THE
SOVEREIGN GRAND LODGE
OF THE
INDEPENDENT ORDER OF ODD FELLOWS,

Adopted at the Annual Session of that Grand Body, Held at the City of Baltimore, on the 4th Day of September, A. D. 1854, and Year of the Order in North America the 36th, with all Amendments which have been made Thereto up to the Session of 1887, Inclusive. •

ARTICLE I.

SECTION 1. This Lodge shall be known by the name, style and title of the SOVEREIGN GRAND LODGE OF THE INDEPENDENT ORDER OF ODD FELLOWS.

§ 2. It is the source of all true and legitimate Odd Fellowship in the United States of America, and possesses such powers and jurisdiction over the whole brotherhood, as are provided in the Constitution and Ritual of the Order. Its authority extends also to such Lodges and Encampments as may be organized under its Charter in foreign countries.

§ 3. By virtue of Charters granted by it, all State, District and Territorial Grand Lodges and Grand Encampments exist, and with it rests the power, by a majority of two-thirds of the votes cast, to deprive such State, District or Territorial Grand Bodies of their Charters, and to annul their authority; *provided*, that such deprivation or annulment shall only be made for violation of the laws of this Grand Lodge. No more than one Grand Lodge and Grand Encampment shall be chartered in any State, District or Territory. All Grand Bodies working under Charters granted by this Grand Lodge are supreme for all local legislation and appellate jurisdiction within their respective limits, except as is hereinafter provided.

HALL OF THE SOVEREIGN GRAND LODGE, COLUMBUS, O.

§ 4. With the consent of the Grand Lodge or Grand Encampment of a State, District or Territory, an appeal may be had by any Subordinate Lodge or Encampment to the Sovereign Grand Lodge; such consent, however, not being necessary when an expelled Lodge or Encampment, after having surrendered to its Grand Lodge or Grand Encampment all its effects, appeals from such decision. Appeals may also be heard from a member or members of a State, District or Territorial Grand Lodge or Grand Encampment from the decision thereof; but in all cases the decision of the State, District or Territorial Grand Lodge or Grand Encampment shall be final and conclusive until reversed by this Grand Lodge on a direct appeal therefrom.

§ 5. To this Grand Lodge belongs the power to regulate and control the Unwritten Work of the Order, and to fix and determine the customs and usages in regard to all things which appertain thereto. And to it alone belongs the power to provide and establish suitable Lectures and other Written Work therefor. But the Unwritten Work of the Order shall in no wise be altered or amended, except by a four-fifths vote of the members of this Grand Lodge ; nor shall the Written Work of the Order be in any wise altered or amended, except with the concurrence of two-thirds of the members of this Grand Lodge.

§ 6. To this Grand Lodge is reserved the power to establish the Independent Order of Odd Fellows in such countries, domestic or foreign, wherein the same has not yet been established.

§ 7. To this Grand Lodge belongs the immediate jurisdiction over all Subordinate Lodges and Encampments in such countries, domestic or foreign, as are without Grand Lodges or Grand Encampments.

§ 8. To it belongs the power to enact all laws of general application to the Order.

§ 9. All power and authority in the Order not reserved to this Grand Lodge by this Constitution is hereby vested in the various State, District and Territorial Grand Bodies.

ARTICLE II.

This Grand Lodge shall be composed of the following members, to wit: A Grand Sire, Deputy Grand Sire, Grand Secretary, Grand Treasurer, Grand Chaplain, Grand Marshal, Grand Guardian, Grand Messenger, and Grand Representatives from the several State, District or Territorial Grand Lodges and Grand Encampments working under legal unreclaimed Charters granted by this Sovereign Grand Lodge.

ARTICLE III.

Section 1. The officers of this Grand Lodge shall be the Grand Sire, Deputy Grand Sire, Grand Secretary and Grand Treasurer, who shall be elected by ballot, by a majority of all the votes cast, biennially, at the stated communication of this Grand Lodge in September; and shall be installed into their respective offices at the conclusion of said stated communication.

§ 2. The Grand Chaplain, Grand Marshal, Grand Guardian and Grand Messenger shall be nominated by the Grand Sire, and, if approved by the Grand Lodge, shall be installed into their respective offices immediately after the installation of the elective officers.

§ 3. Should any of the elective officers fail to appear to be installed at the time provided, the particular office or offices shall be declared vacant, and the Sovereign Grand Lodge shall in that event proceed to a new election to fill such vacancy or vacancies, and the officer or officers so elected shall be accordingly installed.

§ 4. All the officers, both elective and appointed, shall attend each meeting of the Sovereign Grand Lodge, and perform such duties as are enjoined by the laws and regulations of the Order, and such as may be required by the presiding officer ; and shall receive such compensation as is hereinafter provided.

§ 5. No officer, who is not a Representative, shall be permitted to vote, except the Grand Sire in case of an equal division ; the elective officers shall have the power of debating and making motions, but shall not have the privilege of voting unless they be Grand Representatives. The appointed officers, unless they be Representatives, shall not be allowed to take part in the proceedings and debates of the Sovereign Grand Lodge, except by a vote of the majority thereof.

ARTICLE IV.

SECTION 1. The Grand Sire shall preside at all meetings of the Sovereign Grand Lodge, preserve order, and enforce the laws thereof. He shall have the casting vote whenever the Lodge shall be equally divided, other than upon a ballot for officers, but shall not vote upon any other occasion. He shall appoint all committees not required to be raised by ballot, and appoint all District Deputy Grand Sires. During the recess of this Grand Lodge he shall have a general superintendence of the interests of the Order. He may hear and decide such appeals as may be submitted to him by the several State Grand Lodges and Grand Encampments, or by the Subordinate Lodges or Encampments under the immediate jurisdiction of this Grand Lodge. He may hear and decide such questions, other than questions arising out of the Constitutions of the several State, District or Territorial Grand Lodges or Grand Encampments, as may be submitted to him by the several State Grand Lodges and Grand Encampments, or by the Grand Masters or Grand Patriarchs thereof, or by the Grand Representatives, or by the Subordinate Lodges or Encampments under the immediate jurisdiction of this Sovereign Grand Lodge. And his decision upon all appeals and questions so submitted to him shall be binding upon the Bodies or persons submitting the same until reversed by this Grand Lodge. He is empowered to receive petitions and grant Warrants for the opening of new Lodges and Encampments, Grand or Subordinate, in places where Grand Bodies established by this Grand Lodge may not exist; and all Warrants so granted by him shall be of force until recalled by this Grand Lodge. At every communication of this Sovereign Grand Lodge he shall make a report in writing of all his official acts and decisions during the recess.

§ 2. During his term of service he shall not hold any office in any State, District or Territorial Grand or Subordinate Lodge or Encampment.

§ 3. In case of the death, resignation or removal from office of the Grand Sire, or in case he should absent himself for six months or upward beyond the limits of the United States and the British North American possessions, or in case of his inability, from physical causes, to discharge the duties of his office, the Deputy Grand Sire shall act in his place, and shall have and enjoy all the powers and privileges, and exercise the duties of said office until the next communication of this Sovereign Grand Lodge. In case of the death, resignation, removal, absence, or inability of both the Grand Sire and Deputy Grand Sire, all said duties and powers shall be exercised by the Junior Past Grand Sire competent to fill said office, and at the first communication thereafter, the Sovereign Grand Lodge shall proceed to elect and install a Grand Sire for the unexpired term, and to fill any vacancy that may be occasioned thereby; *provided, however*, that a mere temporary or transient visit beyond said limits, not exceeding the aforesaid period of time, shall not be so construed as to work a forfeiture of the office.

ARTICLE V.

The Deputy Grand Sire shall open and close the meetings of the Sovereign Grand Lodge, support the Grand Sire by his advice and assistance, and preside in his absence. In case of the removal, death, resignation or inability of the Grand Sire, the powers and duties of the said office shall devolve on the Deputy Grand Sire for the unexpired term as provided in section three of article four.

ARTICLE VI.

The Grand Secretary shall make a just and true record of all the proceedings of the Sovereign Grand Lodge, in a book provided for that purpose; keep the Journal of all secret sessions, and preserve and keep the evidences of the Unwritten Work, and such alterations as may, from time to time, be made therein, and all other records appertaining to the Work of the Order, and the explanations and lectures relative thereto; summon the members to attend all special meetings; keep accounts between the Sovereign Grand Lodge and the Grand and Subordinate Lodges and Encampments under its jurisdiction; read all petitions, reports and communications; write all letters and communications; carry on, under the direction of the Sovereign Grand Lodge or Grand Sire, its correspondence; and transact such business of the Sovereign Grand Lodge appertaining to his office as may be required of him by the Sovereign Grand Lodge. All communications transmitted or received by him, officially, shall be laid before the Sovereign Grand Lodge. He shall receive for his services such compensation as the Sovereign Grand Lodge shall from time to time determine.

ARTICLE VII.

SECTION I. The Grand Treasurer shall keep the moneys, and all the evidences of debt, cases in action, deeds, etc., of the Sovereign Grand Lodge, and pay all orders drawn on him by the Grand Secretary. He shall lay before the Sovereign Grand Lodge at its stated communication in September, annually, a full and correct statement of his accounts. Before his installation he shall give a bond, with at least two sureties, to the Sovereign Grand Lodge, in such sum as may from time to time be fixed; and shall receive such compensation as the Sovereign Grand Lodge shall determine.

§ 2. No money shall be drawn from the treasury but in consequence of appropriations made by the Sovereign Grand Lodge.

ARTICLE VIII.

SECTION 1. The Grand Chaplain shall perform such duties as appertain to his office, and as may, from time to time, be required by the Sovereign Grand Lodge relative thereto.

§ 2. The Grand Marshal shall assist the Grand Sire in performing his duties in such a manner as may, from time to time, be required, and perform all the duties generally, appertaining to such office.

§ 3. The Grand Guardian shall prove every brother before admitting him, and allow none to depart without the usual formality.

§ 4. The Grand Messenger shall perform such duties as the Sovereign Grand Lodge may, from time to time, require for the convenience and comfort of the members; and for his services he shall receive such compensation as the Sovereign Grand Lodge shall determine.

ARTICLE IX.

SECTION 1. Grand Representatives shall be chosen by the several State, District and Territorial Grand Lodges and Grand Encampments for the term of two years, and shall be divided into two classes, whose seats shall be vacated annually by rotation. And if vacancies occur by death, resignation or otherwise, during the recess of the Grand Lodge or Grand Encampment of any State, District or Territory, such vacancies shall be filled in the manner pointed out by the Constitution of such State, District or Territorial Grand Lodge or Grand Encampment.

§ 2. Grand Representatives shall be apportioned as follows, viz.: To every State, District or Territorial Grand Lodge or Grand Encampment, having under its jurisdiction one thousand or less members in good standing, one Grand Representative; to every State, District or Territorial Grand Lodge or Grand Encampment, having under its jurisdiction over one thousand members in good standing, two Grand Representatives; and no State, District or Territorial Grand Lodge or Grand Encampment shall have over two Grand Representatives.

§ 3. A Grand Representative must be a Past Grand in good standing, and a member of a Lodge in good standing. He must have received the Royal Purple Degree, be a member in good standing of an Encampment in good standing; and he must reside in the State, District or Territory in which the Grand Lodge or Grand Encampment which he represents is located. No Representative shall represent more than one Grand Body at the same time.

§ 4. Grand Representatives shall be furnished by the Grand Bodies which they represent with such Certificates as shall be required by law.

§ 5. In case of contested elections, this Sovereign Grand Lodge shall determine to whom the contested seat belongs.

ARTICLE X.

Past Grand Sires shall be admitted to seats in this Grand Lodge, with the power of debating and making motions, but shall not have the privilege of voting unless they be Grand Representatives.

ARTICLE XI

SECTION 1. This Grand Lodge shall have the power, a majority consenting thereto, to impeach and try any of its officers or members, and, with the concurrence of two-thirds of the votes cast, to expel from office or membership therein any officer or member so impeached and convicted; *provided*, that a copy of the charges preferred shall have been furnished to the accused at least three days before trial.

§ 2. During the trial of any impeachment, the officer or member under impeachment shall be debarred the exercise of his office or the privilege of his membership, but may be heard in his own defense.

§ 3. Suspension or expulsion from the Subordinate Lodge or Encampment to which an officer or member of this Grand Lodge belongs shall operate as a suspension or expulsion from office or membership in this Sovereign Grand Lodge, and the vacancy thereby created shall be filled in the manner hereinbefore prescribed.

ARTICLE XII.

This Grand Lodge shall meet annually on the third Monday of September, at 9 o'clock, A. M., at such place as the Sovereign Grand Lodge shall, from time to time, determine. It may also meet on its own adjournments. It may also meet specially on the call of the Grand Sire, of which the Grand Sire shall cause three months' notice to be given to the Representatives of the several State, District or Territorial Grand Lodges and Grand Encampments, communicating to them the purpose for which the special meeting is called ; and in no case shall any business be transacted at a special meeting, unless notice thereof has been given as above stated; *provided*, that if it shall be impracticable, from the prevalence of contagious disease, or any other cause, for the annual session to be held at the place designated therefor, the Sovereign Grand Lodge shall have the power to determine at what date or place said session shall be held; or if the Sovereign Grand Lodge be not in session when such emergency occurs, such power may be exercised by the Grand Sire.

ARTICLE XIII.

SECTION 1. Representatives from a majority of the whole number of State, District and Territorial Grand Bodies shall be necessary to form a quorum for the transaction of business; but a smaller number may adjourn from day to day, and may receive and act upon the credentials of new members, except in contested elections.

§ 2. This Grand Lodge shall be the judge of the Certificates or returns and qualifications of its members.

§ 3. It may determine the rules of its proceedings, and from time to time adopt such Rules of Order as it may see fit.

§ 4. A Journal of its Proceedings shall be kept and published annually, except such proceedings as are had in secret session.

§ 5. Voting for officers shall be by ballot. All other voting shall be *viva voce*, or by yeas and nays, as the Sovereign Grand Lodge may determine.

The yeas and nays may be demanded by one-fifth of the Representatives present, and shall be entered upon the Journal.

§ 6. All questions shall be decided by a majority vote, except in such cases as a specific majority is required.

ARTICLE XIV.

The revenue of the Sovereign Grand Lodge shall be as follows, viz.:

1. Fees for Charters of Grand Lodges or Encampments, or Subordinate Lodges or Encampments working under its immediate jurisdiction, thirty dollars.

2. Dues from State, District or Territorial Grand Lodges and Encampments, seventy-five dollars per annum for each vote they shall be entitled to in this Grand Lodge.

3. Dues from Subordinate Lodges or Encampments, working under the immediate jurisdiction of this Sovereign Grand Lodge, five per cent. on their receipts.

4. Proceeds of the sales of Books, Cards, Diplomas, Odes and Certificates.

ARTICLE XV.

SECTION 1. To be an officer of this Sovereign Grand Lodge, one nominated must have received the Grand Lodge and Grand Encampment Degrees and be a member in good standing of a Subordinate Lodge and Encampment in good standing.

§ 2. The nomination and election of officers shall take place on the same day, to wit, the second day of the communication at which officers are to be elected. The nominations for each office shall be immediately succeeded by the election for the same, and before the nominations and election for the next office.

ARTICLE XVI.

SECTION 1. The members of the Order from each State, District or Territory under the jurisdiction of this Sovereign Grand Lodge shall be entitled to admission into the Lodges or Encampments of every other State, District, or Territory, upon proving themselves according to the established Work of the Order and the production of a proper Card.

§ 2. No person shall be entitled to admission to the Order except free white males of good moral character, who have arrived at the age of twenty-one years, and who believe in a Supreme Being, the Creator and Preserver of the Universe; *provided, however,* that in Australia, New Zealand, and other countries not on the continent of North America, in which the Order has been or may hereafter be established, and a Grand Lodge or Grand Lodges formed, the qualification as to age shall be left to local legislation.

§ 3. No citizen of one State, District or Territory wherein Lodges or Encampments are established, shall be admitted to membership in a Lodge or Encampment of another State, District or Territory, without the previous consent of the Grand Lodge or Grand Encampment, or Grand Master or Grand Patriarch of the State, District or Territory whereof such citizen is a resident.

§ 4. A member of the Order suspended or expelled from a Lodge or Encampment in any jurisdiction or sovereignty shall not be admitted to membership in a Lodge or Encampment in another jurisdiction or sovereignty, without the previously obtained consent of the Lodge or Encampment from which he is suspended or expelled; *provided, however*, that members suspended or dropped for the non-payment of dues only may be admitted to membership in another jurisdiction or sovereignty upon such conditions and under such rules and regulations as this Grand Lodge may have prescribed, or may at any time adopt.

ARTICLE XVII.

The Officers and Grand Representatives (except such officers as receive stated salaries) shall receive a compensation for their services, to be fixed by law, and paid out of the treasury of the Sovereign Grand Lodge, provided that this Grand Lodge shall not allow a compensation (except such per diem as it may think proper) to any Grand Representative coming from a jurisdiction beyond the limits of the North American Continent.

ARTICLE XVIII.

With the previous consent and approval, from time to time expressed, of this Grand Lodge, the Grand Sire may accredit any officer or member of this Sovereign Grand Lodge as a special Grand Representative near the Grand Lodge of any sovereign jurisdiction in Odd Fellowship recognized by this Grand Lodge; and in such case the necessary expenses of such special Grand Representative's visit shall be defrayed from the treasury of this Grand Lodge. And any officer or member of any such foreign Grand Lodge, who may be duly accredited from the same as a special Grand Representative near this Grand Lodge, shall be admitted to a seat on the floor of this Grand Lodge, and shall have a deliberate voice, but not a vote, in the proceedings thereof.

ARTICLE XIX.

By-Laws in conformity with this Constitution may be made, which shall not be altered or amended unless such amendment be proposed at a stated annual communication, and acted upon at the same session, but not on the day on which it is offered, and adopted by two-thirds of the votes given.

ARTICLE XX.

This Constitution, and the By-Laws which shall be made in pursuance thereof, shall be the supreme law of the Order, and be binding upon the State, District and Territorial Grand Lodges and Grand Encampments under the jurisdiction of this Grand Lodge.

ARTICLE XXI.

This Constitution shall not be altered or amended except by a proposition therefor, made in writing, at a regular annual communication, by one or more Representatives from three different States, which shall be entered on the Journal and lie over until the next regular annual communication. At the next regular annual communication after being offered, such proposed alteration or amendment may be considered, and if agreed to by a vote of three-fourths of the members present, on a call of the yeas and nays, such proposed alteration or amendment shall become a part of this Constitution.

BY-LAWS.

ARTICLE I.

Upon the petition of five brothers of the Order, of the Degree of Truth, in good standing, praying for a Charter to institute a Subordinate Lodge in a State, District or Territory where a Grand Lodge has not been established, this Lodge may grant the same. Each Subordinate Lodge receiving a Warrant from the Sovereign Grand Lodge of the Independent Order of Odd Fellows shall be instituted by a Past Grand of the Order, regularly deputed therefor by the Grand Sire, who shall deliver to such Lodge the Warrant and Charge Books, and shall, at the institution thereof, give all necessary instruction. Such Lodge shall be visited at least once a year by the Grand Sire, or some Past Grand deputized by him for that purpose, or by a District Deputy Grand Sire.

ARTICLE II.

Upon the petition of five Royal Purple members of the Order, in good standing, praying for a Warrant to institute an Encampment in a State, District or Territory where a Grand Encampment has not been established, this Grand Lodge may grant the same. Every Encampment receiving a Warrant from this Grand Lodge shall be instituted by the Grand Sire, or a qualified Patriarch, who shall deliver to such Encampment the Warrant and Charge Books, and such instructions as may be necessary. Such Encampment shall be visited at least once a year by the Grand Sire, or by some Patriarch deputized by him for that purpose, or by the District Deputy Grand Sire.

ARTICLE III.

Subordinate Lodges and Encampments working under the immediate jurisdiction of this Grand Lodge shall transmit to the Grand Secretary, *annually*, reports containing the same information as is required from Grand Lodges and Grand Encampments by article ten of these laws. The report shall be accompanied by the dues in current money.

ARTICLE IV.

Ten or more Subordinate Lodges or five or more Encampments, located in any State, District or Territory where a Grand Lodge or Grand Encampment has not been established, having seven Past Grands or Past Chief Patriarchs, in good standing, may petition the Sovereign Grand Lodge of the Independent Order of Odd Fellows, in writing, praying for the Charter of a Grand Lodge or Grand Encampment in such State, District or Territory; which, if approved of by a majority of the votes given, shall be granted; and such Grand Lodge or Grand Encampment shall be instituted by the Grand Sire, or some qualified brother or Patriarch whom he shall deputize for that purpose; *provided*, that nothing contained in this article shall operate to prevent the Grand Lodge from entertaining and granting, or instructing the Grand Sire to grant in the recess, the application for a Grand Charter to any less number of Lodges or Encampments who may regularly petition therefor, and accompany the petition with reasons which shall be deemed satisfactory for such grant, by two-thirds of the members of the Grand Lodge at any regular session.

ARTICLE V.

All applications for Charters of Grand Lodges or Grand Encampments must be by a vote of a majority of the Lodges or Encampments within the State, District or Territory, as follows: When ten or more Lodges or five or more Encampments shall agree in the opinion that a Grand Lodge or Grand Encampment will contribute to the general interest, notice thereof shall be given to all the Lodges or Encampments in the State, District or Territory, inviting them to meet for consultation at some convenient time and place. Each Lodge or Encampment shall appoint one or more of its Past Grands or Past Chief Patriarchs or Past High Priests, as Representatives, to meet in convention to consider the propriety of applying for a Grand Charter as well as to determine upon the place for the location of the Grand Lodge or Grand Encampment (both of which questions shall be decided by a majority vote, which majority vote must represent at least ten Lodges or five Encampments). Should any Lodge or Encampment neglect or refuse to send a Representative, or should the Representative, from accident or other cause, fail to attend, it shall not operate to defeat the proceedings of such as may assemble, provided a sufficient number be present to comply with the preceding requirements. Each Subordinate Lodge or Encampment shall furnish to its Representative a statement, under the Seal of the Lodge or Encampment, of the number of Past Grands or Past Chief Patriarchs, in good standing, belonging to it. At the meeting of these Representatives the votes shall be by Lodges or Encampments, and the application shall be in the following form, to wit:

To the Sovereign Grand Lodge of the INDEPENDENT ORDER OF ODD FELLOWS:

The petition of ....Lodge (or Encampment) No. 1, ... No 2, ... No. 3, of...............respectfully represents that at present they work under Warrants granted by your Body; that at present they have...............Past Grands (or Past Chief Patriarchs) in good standing. They are of opinion that it would be of advantage to the Order to establish a Grand Lodge (or Grand Encampment) in the............... They therefore pray your Body to grant a Charter for a Grand Lodge (or Grand Encampment) in the...............to be located at...............

Witness our hands and Seals this...............day of...............18. .

A. B., Representative of No. 1.
C. D., Representative of No. 2.
E. F., Representative of No. 3.

ARTICLE VI.

All traveling and other expenses of the Grand Sire, or of the Past Grand or Patriarch deputed by him to institute a Grand or Subordinate Lodge or Encampment, shall be paid by such Lodge or Encampment.

Article VII.

Applications for Grand or Subordinate Lodges or Encampments must be accompanied by the fee for the same, which shall be returned if the Charter is not granted.

Article VIII.

Each Grand Lodge and Grand Encampment shall have a Grand Seal, an impression whereof in wax shall be sent to the Grand Secretary, and be deposited in the archives of the Sovereign Grand Lodge of the Independent Order of Odd Fellows.

Article IX.

The Constitution of each Grand Lodge or Encampment chartered by this Grand Lodge, immediately on its adoption, shall be forwarded to this Grand Lodge for its approval.

Article X.

Annual returns shall be made by each State, District or Territorial Grand Body, in which shall be embraced the names of the Grand Master and Grand Secretary, or Grand Patriarch and Grand Scribe, the time and place of the next annual session, the number of Subordinates under its jurisdiction, and the aggregate membership in good standing in the same; as well as the aggregate number of initiations, reinstatements, admissions by Cards, withdrawals by Cards, expulsions and deaths, and the number suspended or dropped; the number of brothers relieved, and the amount of such relief; the number of widowed families relieved, and the amount of relief; the amount paid for burying the dead; the amount paid for the education of orphans, and the whole amount of receipts. Forms for these reports shall be furnished by this Grand Lodge. Said returns shall be made to the Grand Secretary on or before the first day of April, and shall be accompanied with the dues thereon, in current money at par in the City of Baltimore, Maryland.

Article XI.

No Grand Lodge or Grand Encampment which shall fail or neglect to make its returns to the Grand Secretary on or before the first day of June ; which shall be in arrears for money due to this Grand Lodge shall be allowed to vote by its Representative or Representatives. And no Representative shall be entitled to more than one vote in elections for Grand Officers.

Article XII.

No person shall at the same time hold membership in more than one Grand and Subordinate Lodge and one Grand and Subordinate Encampment ; nor shall any Lodge or Encampment confer Degrees upon any member of another Lodge or Encampment without the consent of the Lodge or Encampment to which the member belongs, given under its Seal.

Article XIII.

When a Grand Lodge or Grand Encampment shall have been duly chartered in any State, District or Territory, all the Lodges and Encampments in said State, District or Territory working under the jurisdiction of the Sovereign Grand Lodge of the Independent Order of Odd Fellows, shall thereafter be declared subordinate to, and under the jurisdiction of, the Grand Lodge or Grand Encampment of the State, District or Territory in which they are located ; and no Lodge or Encampment situated in one State, District or Territory can be made subordinate to the Grand Lodge or Grand Encampment of another State, District or Territory; *provided, however*, that any Subordinate Lodge or Encampment, working under the immediate jurisdiction of the Sovereign Grand Lodge of the Independent Order of Odd Fellows in any State, District, or Territory, may, at its own request, be made subordinate to any contiguous State Grand Lodge or Grand Encampment.

ARTICLE XIV.

No brother can be admitted to visit or deposit his Card in a Lodge or Encampment out of the State, District or Territory where he resides, unless he presents a Card as furnished under the signatures of the proper officers and Seal of the Lodge or Encampment of which he is a member, and signed on the margin in his own proper handwriting, and prove himself in the A. T. P. W., and in the Degree in which the Lodge is open; *provided*, nevertheless, a brother may always visit, if introduced by a Grand Representative, or any elective officer of the Grand Lodge or Grand Encampment within whose jurisdiction he wishes to visit, or by a District Deputy Grand Sire in a jurisdiction where no Grand Body exists, Grand Representatives of either branch being hereby authorized to introduce visiting brothers into both Subordinate Lodges and Encampments in their several jurisdictions; but in all such cases the presiding officer of the same shall be satisfied that the brother introducing such a visitor is a Grand Representative of the jurisdiction to which said Lodge or Encampment belongs. *And provided further*, that the holder of a Dismissal Certificate regularly issued by a Lodge or Encampment may deposit the same in any other Lodge or Encampment, as the case may be, under such rules and upon such conditions as the jurisdiction in which it is offered for deposit, may prescribe; but he shall not be required to be in possession of the A. T. P. W., nor can he visit a Lodge or Encampment by virtue of such Certificate.

ARTICLE XV.

At each annual session the Grand Sire shall appoint in each State, District and Territory in which there is not a Grand Lodge and a Grand Encampment, an officer to be styled " District Deputy Grand Sire," whose duty it shall be to act as the special agent of this Grand Lodge in relation to the matters herein specified, namely:

1. To act for the Grand Sire, and by his direction to perform whatever may have been ordered to be done by the Sovereign Grand Lodge of the Independent Order of Odd Fellows in the particular district for which the D. D. Grand Sire may be appointed.

2. To act as the Representative of this Grand Lodge, and perform all such matters relating to the Order in his district as the Grand Sire shall direct.

3. To obey all special instructions of the Grand Sire in relation to anything which that officer is required to do for the good of the Order.

4. To act as the agent of the Grand Secretary, and to obey the special directions of that officer.

5. To have a general supervision over all Subordinate Lodges and Encampments in his district, which work under Charters granted by the Sovereign Grand Lodge of the Independent Order of Odd Fellows.

6. To make semi-annual reports of his acts and doings to the Grand Sire.

7. District Deputy Grand Sires shall in no case interfere, as officers of this Grand Lodge, with the State Grand Lodges or Grand Encampments.

8. To qualify a brother for the appointment of District Deputy Grand Sire, he must be a regular contributing member of a Subordinate Lodge and Encampment, and must have attained the rank of Past Grand and of the Royal Purple Degree; and in States where Grand Encampments may be established, he must also be a member of such Grand Encampment. The appointment of District Deputy Grand Sires shall be made at each annual session, to continue for one year, but they may be removed for cause by the Grand Sire during recess.

9. The Grand Sire shall have power to fill, by appointment, all vacancies that may occur during the recess of the Grand Lodge from resignation, sickness or disability, or other causes, which are not provided for by the Constitution; such appointments to last until filled by election or otherwise, as provided by law for the election or appointment of such officers.

Article XVI.

The Representative or Representatives of each Grand Lodge and Grand Encampment shall be examined by the Deputy Grand Sire as to their qualifications for the office, previous to taking seats in the Sovereign Grand Lodge of the Independent Order of Odd Fellows; and on taking their seats each shall be furnished by the Grand Secretary with a copy of the Constitution, Rules of Order and Laws of this Grand Lodge.

Article XVII.

Each State, District and Territorial Grand Lodge or Grand Encampment shall furnish its Representative or Representatives with all documents and papers necessary in the discharge of the duties of their office.

Article XVIII.

Each State, District and Territorial Grand Lodge shall annually be furnished with as many copies of the printed proceedings of this Grand Lodge as it has Subordinate Lodges working under its jurisdiction, to be distributed among its Subordinates, and one-half of such number, but not less than fifteen copies, for its own use. Each Grand Encampment shall be furnished in the same manner. And each Lodge or Encampment working under the Warrant of this Grand Lodge shall be furnished with a copy of the proceedings. The Grand Secretary shall see that this law is carried into effect at as early a date as possible after the close of the annual session of this Grand Lodge.

Article XIX.

All dues and moneys for this Grand Lodge shall be paid to the Grand Secretary, and by him be immediately paid over to the Grand Treasurer, who shall give his receipt for the same.

Article XX.

All State, District and Territorial Grand Lodges and Grand Encampments shall enforce upon their Subordinates a strict adherence to the Work of the Order, according to the Forms furnished by the Sovereign Grand Lodge of the Independent Order of Odd Fellows, and shall be held responsible for any irregularities that they may allow under their jurisdictions. They shall neither adopt nor use, or suffer to be adopted or used, in their jurisdiction, any other Charges, Lectures, Degrees, Ceremonies, Forms of Installation or Regalia than those prescribed by the Sovereign Grand Lodge of the Independent Order of Odd Fellows.

Article XXI.

All Grand and Subordinate Lodges and Encampments under this jurisdiction may at all times open and close their meetings with prayer.

Article XXII.

The Regalia of the Order shall be as follows, to wit: Collars of Subordinate Lodges shall be white, trimmed with the emblematic color of the Degree intended to be represented, namely, *First Degree*, pink; *Second Degree*, blue; *Third Degree*, scarlet; *Initiatory Degree*, a plain white collar. Rosettes of the appropriate color may be worn upon the collar.

Among those who may have attained the Royal Purple Degree, rosettes composed of black, yellow and purple may be worn on the collars, either in connection with the other colors or as a separate rosette.

The Noble Grand, Secretary and Treasurer shall each wear a scarlet collar trimmed with white or silver; the Vice Grand, a blue collar trimmed in like manner. Supporters of the Noble Grand and Vice Grand shall wear sashes of the color of those officers respectively; Warden and Conductor, black sashes; Scene Supporters, white sashes; Chaplain, white sash; Outside Guardian, scarlet sash; Inside Guardian, scarlet sash.

The position of each officer shall be indicated by the Jewel of the office.

Past Grands shall wear scarlet collars or sashes, trimmed with white. The collars or sashes may be trimmed with silver lace or fringe, and those having attained the Royal Purple Degree may have trimmings of yellow metal.

The Grand Officers and Past Grand Officers of Grand Lodges shall wear the Regalia of Past Grands, as above defined.

The Encampment Regalia shall be black aprons and gloves; Patriarchs who have attained the Royal Purple Degree, purple collars or baldrics, trimmed with yellow lace or fringe. Past Chief Patriarchs shall wear purple collars or sashes, trimmed as above defined.

The Regalia for Grand Representatives shall be a collar of purple velvet, not more than four inches in width, with a roll of scarlet velvet, the trimmings to be of white and yellow metal, and the collar to be united in front with three links, to which may be suspended such medal or medals as the member may be entitled to wear.

Past Grand Representatives and the officers and past officers of the Sovereign Grand Lodge of the Independent Order of Odd Fellows shall wear the Regalia above described for Grand Representatives.

The Jewel of the Grand Sire and Past Grand Sires shall be a medal three inches in diameter, of yellow metal, on one side of which shall be the coat of arms of the United States, surrounded by an ornamental edging of silver.

Grand Representatives and Past Grand Representatives shall be entitled to wear medals of the size and style above, with the coat of arms of the State represented.

The Regalia for a Past Grand, who is also a Past Chief Patriarch, may, in lieu of any other Regalia to which he may be entitled, be a scarlet collar trimmed with white, the collar not to be more than five and a half inches wide; with a roll of purple two inches wide, trimmed with yellow, the collar to be united in front with three links. The above described Regalia may be worn by a brother who has passed the chairs in a Lodge and in an Encampment, in any Grand or Subordinate Lodge or any Grand or Subordinate Encampment. The collar may be of scarlet velvet, with white metal trimmings, and the roll of purple velvet, with yellow metal trimmings.

ARTICLE XXIII.

State Grand Lodges are prohibited from conferring the Grand Lodge Degree for a pecuniary consideration, with a view of increasing their revenue, or for any other consideration except the regular performance of the duties of the Noble Grand's chair—the said Degree having been designed as a reward for faithful service in the Subordinate Lodges.

ARTICLE XXIV.

Past Officers of every description, and members in possession of the Encampment Degrees, and all other members of the Order, when visiting Grand or Subordinate Lodges, and when attending the meetings of the Lodges of which they are members, are entitled to wear the Regalia and Jewels pertaining to the highest Degrees which they may have taken.

ARTICLE XXV.

The A. T. P. W. is primarily designed for the use of brethren who are traveling beyond the limits of the jurisdiction to which they belong, but may also be used in the jurisdiction to which brothers belong who have received it in good faith for said primary purpose; and in order that each brother may be properly instructed in it, and visiting brethren from other jurisdictions be properly examined, the two highest elective officers of a Lodge, and the Chief Patriarch and Senior Warden of an Encampment, are to be privately put in possession of the Word, at the time of their installation, that they may be qualified either to give or receive it. The Grand Master and Grand Patriarch of a State, and their regular deputies, should also be in possession of it.

ARTICLE XXVI.

The fiscal year of this Grand Lodge shall commence on the first day of January and terminate on the thirty-first day of December, and all Grand and Subordinate Lodges and Encampments shall make their annual reports as required by Article X, to correspond with the fiscal year.

ARTICLE XXVII.

The Subordinate Lodges and Encampments working under the immediate jurisdiction of this Grand Lodge, which fail to make their returns for one year, shall forfeit their Charters, and whenever such remissness occurs the Grand Sire shall take proper measures to enforce the law.

ARTICLE XXVIII.

SECTION 1. There shall be appointed at each annual session, immediately before the final adjournment, a Committee on Printing Supplies, to consist of five members, including the Grand Secretary and the Grand Treasurer.

§ 2. The members of the committee shall hold their respective positions until the following annual session. The committee shall have power to sit during the recess, and shall report in detail at each annual session of the Grand Lodge. Vacancies that may occur in the committee shall be filled by the Grand Sire.

§ 3. The committee shall organize by the election of a chairman and a secretary, and shall hold a session immediately after the final adjournment of the Grand Lodge, and afterward upon the call of the chairman, but not oftener than four times within twelve months. They shall be entitled to such mileage and per diem as this Grand Lodge may from time to time determine.

§ 4. The Committee on Printing Supplies shall have power and authority to contract for all the necessary printing of the Grand Lodge, and for the furnishing of all needed supplies for the office of Grand Secretary, and for all materials and work which may be required in said office, in such manner and upon such terms as the committee shall deem for the best interests of the Grand Lodge.

§ 5. The committee shall keep a journal of its proceedings, and open such books of accounts and of printing supplies as shall show at any time the quantity of supplies on hand, and the amount ordered by the committee, and adopt such regulations in relation to the supply stock as they shall deem necessary.

§ 6. All bills for printing supplies, materials furnished, or for work done by authority of the committee, shall be audited and passed upon by the Committee on Printing Supplies, and, unless thus approved, shall not be paid unless the Grand Lodge shall order otherwise.

§ 7. All provisions of law heretofore adopted that are in conflict with the foregoing are hereby declared to be repealed.

ARTICLE XXIX.

The Sovereign Grand Lodge of the Independent Order of Odd Fellows will neither entertain nor consider any inquiry as to what are the laws or usages of the Order, unless the same be brought before the Body by an appeal from the decision of a Lodge or Encampment, or unless the same be presented by a Grand Lodge or Grand Encampment.

ARTICLE XXX.

No resolution, order, or other action of the Sovereign Grand Lodge of the Independent Order of Odd Fellows shall operate to change, alter or amend any of these By-Laws, unless said resolution, order or other action shall, upon its face and by its terms, assume to make such change, alteration or amendment, and shall state distinctly the particular By-Law to be affected.

ARTICLE XXXI.

All former laws and regulations inconsistent with the provisions of these general laws are hereby repealed.

RULES OF ORDER.

Adopted 1881.   *Journal,* 8675, *and as since amended.*

GRAND SIRE.

1. The Grand Sire shall take the chair at the hour of meeting of the Sovereign Grand Lodge, immediately call the members to order, and on the appearance of a quorum, cause the Journal of the Proceedings of the last day's sitting to be read.

2. He shall organize the Sovereign Grand Lodge on the first day of its communication, by directing the Grand Secretary to call the names of the Officers and Representatives. He shall then direct the Deputy Grand Sire and Grand Marshal to examine the Representatives present and report to him the result; and if all are correct and a quorum be present, he shall call on the Grand Chaplain to offer a prayer. He shall then direct the Deputy Grand Sire to proclaim the Sovereign Grand Lodge duly opened.

3. He shall, after the organization of the Sovereign Grand Lodge, present a report of his acts and doings during the recess.

4. He shall, at the commencement of each communication, appoint the following Standing Committees, viz.:

On the State of the Order, to consist of nine members.
On the Judiciary, to consist of nine members.
On Legislation, to consist of nine members.
On Finance, to consist of nine members.
On Constitutions, to consist of nine members.
On Foreign Relations, to consist of nine members.
On the Patriarchal Branch of the Order, to consist of nine members.
On the Degree of Rebekah, to consist of nine members.
On Correspondence, to consist of nine members.
On Petitions, to consist of nine members.
On Returns, to consist of nine members.
On Unfinished Business, to consist of nine members.

On Miscellaneous Business, to consist of nine members.
On Grand Bodies not Represented, to consist of nine members.
On Credentials, to consist of five members.
On Printing Supplies, to consist of five members.
On Mileage and Per Diem, to consist of seven members.
On Drawing for Seats, to consist of three members.

5. He shall appoint a Committee on Appeals, two months prior to each communication, to consist of nine members, which committee shall meet on the Wednesday preceding the meeting of the Sovereign Grand Lodge, and consider such appeals as may be presented to them; and no appeal shall be considered by the committee except by direction of the Sovereign Grand Lodge, unless filed with the Grand Secretary by the first day of the meeting of the committee; and the Grand Secretary shall, upon receipt thereof, forward the same to the chairman of the committee.

6. He shall, unless otherwise ordered, appoint all Special Committees ordered by the Sovereign Grand Lodge from time to time.

DUTIES OF THE CHAIR.

7. The Grand Sire shall preserve order and decorum during the sessions and shall have general control of the hall in which the Sovereign Grand Lodge holds its sessions.

8. He shall sign all papers and documents requiring his signature, and decide all questions of order, subject to an appeal to the Sovereign Grand Lodge, by any member; on which appeal no member shall speak more than once, unless by permission of the Sovereign Grand Lodge.

9. He shall rise to put a question, but may state it sitting, and shall put the question in this form, to wit.: "As many as are in favor (as the question may be), say Aye;" and after the affirmative voice is expressed, "As many as are opposed, say No;" if he doubts, or a division is called for, the Lodge shall divide; those in the affirmative of the question shall first rise from their seats, and then those in the negative, and shall remain standing until counted by the Grand Officers, which being reported, he shall rise and state the decision.

10. He shall not be permitted to vote unless the Sovereign Grand Lodge be equally divided, when he may give the casting vote, except on roll call.

11. When two or more members rise to speak, the Grand Sire shall name the member who is entitled to the floor.

DECORUM AND DEBATE.

12. When any member desires to speak or deliver any matter to the Sovereign Grand Lodge, he shall rise and respectfully address himself to the Grand Sire, and on being recognized, may address the Sovereign Grand Lodge from his seat, or from the Grand Secretary's desk, and shall confine himself to the question under debate, avoiding personality.

13. A member shall not speak more than once to the same question without leave, until every member who chooses to speak shall have spoken.

14. While the Grand Sire is putting a question or addressing the Sovereign Grand Lodge, a member shall not walk out of, or across the room, nor when

a member is speaking, pass between him and the chair; and during the session of the Sovereign Grand Lodge no member shall wear his hat, or remain by the Grand Secretary's desk during the call of the roll or the counting of ballots, or smoke upon the floor of the Sovereign Grand Lodge; and the Grand Marshal is charged with the strict enforcement of this rule.

15. Upon every roll call the names of the members shall be called alphabetically by surname; when two or more members have the same surname, the name shall be followed by the jurisdiction represented; and after the roll has been once called the Grand Secretary shall call, in alphabetical order, the names of those not voting; and thereafter the Grand Sire shall not entertain a request to record a vote.

16. Every motion made to the Sovereign Grand Lodge, and entertained by the Grand Sire, shall be reduced to writing on the demand of any member, and shall be entered on the Journal with the name of the member making it, unless it is withdrawn the same day.

17. When a question is under debate, no motion shall be received but to adjourn, to take a recess, to lay on the table, for the previous question (which motions shall be decided without debate), to postpone to a time certain, to refer, to amend, to commit or to postpone indefinitely, which several motions shall have precedence in the foregoing order; and no motion to postpone to a time certain, to refer, or to postpone indefinitely, being decided, shall be again allowed on the same day at the same stage of the question. A motion to adjourn and to take a recess shall always be in order.

18. On the demand of any member, before the question is put, a question shall be divided, if it includes propositions so distinct in substance that one being taken away a substantive proposition shall remain.

19. A motion to strike out and insert is indivisible, but a motion to strike out being lost, shall neither preclude amendment nor motion to strike out and insert; and a motion or proposition on a subject different from that under consideration shall not be admitted under color of amendment.

20. The previous question being ordered by a majority vote, shall have the effect to cut off all debate, and bring the Sovereign Grand Lodge to a direct vote upon the immediate question or questions upon which it has been asked and ordered. The previous question may be asked and ordered upon a single motion, a series of motions allowable under the rules, or an amendment or amendments, or may be made to embrace all motions and amendments. It shall be in order pending the motion for the previous question, and before it has been ordered, for the Grand Sire to entertain and submit a motion to commit, with or without instructions to a Standing or Select Committee, which motion to commit shall be decided without debate.

21. All incidental questions of order arising after a motion is made for the previous question, and pending such motion, shall be decided, whether on appeal or otherwise, without debate.

22. Any member who has voted in favor of the decision may move for the reconsideration thereof, and such motion shall take precedence of all other questions, except a motion to adjourn, or to take a recess, or orders of the day.

23. When a motion or proposition is under consideration, a motion to amend and a motion to amend the amendment shall be in order, and it shall also be in order to offer a further amendment by way of substitute, to which one amendment may be offered, but which shall not be voted on until the original matter is perfected.

24. All questions relating to priority of business shall be decided without debate.

25. A rule shall not be suspended except by a two-thirds vote. When a motion to suspend the rules has been seconded, it shall be in order, before the final vote is taken thereon, to debate the proposition to be voted upon, and the same right of debate shall be allowed whenever the previous question has been ordered on any proposition on which there has been no debate.

26. When the reading of a paper, other than the one upon which the Grand Lodge is called to give a final vote, is demanded, and the same is objected to by any member, it shall be determined without debate by vote of the Sovereign Grand Lodge.

27. A member shall not be permitted to speak or vote unless clothed in proper Regalia.

28. During the progress of a ballot for an officer, a motion cannot be entertained, or debate or explanation permitted.

29. Every officer and member shall be designated by his proper title or office, according to his standing in the Order.

30. A member shall not interrupt another while speaking, unless to explain, or to call him to order for words spoken.

31. If a member while speaking shall be called to order, he shall, at the request of the chair, take his seat until the question of order is determined when, if permitted, he may proceed again.

32. When a blank is to be filled the question shall be taken first upon the highest sum or number, and the longest or latest time proposed.

33. No matter shall be considered at any morning session of the Sovereign Grand Lodge until all the committees shall have had an opportunity of presenting reports; and the Grand Sire shall call for reports of committees in the order of their appointment.

34. It is the duty of a committee appointed at one communication to perform a duty, to report at the next, although some of the members of the committee have ceased to be members of the Sovereign Grand Lodge.

35. Any member has the right to protest, and to have his protest spread upon the Journal.

36. Every member must, unless excused by the Sovereign Grand Lodge, serve on committees and accept nominations.

AMENDMENTS TO THE CONSTITUTION AND BY-LAWS.

37. Propositions for the amendment of the Constitution, made in conformity with Article XXI. of the Constitution, may be made and entered on the Journal as a matter of course, without any action of the Sovereign Grand Lodge. This rule shall also apply to all such reports of Standing Committees as are required to lie on the table one day under Rule 42.

COMMITTEES.

38. The first named member of each committee shall be the chairman, and, in his absence, or being excused by the Sovereign Grand Lodge, the next named member, and so on, as often as the case shall happen, unless the committee, by a majority of its members, elect a chairman.

39. Business presented to the Sovereign Grand Lodge shall be referred as follows:

To the Committee on the State of the Order, all questions in relation to the Work of the Order.

To the Committee on the Judiciary, all questions in relation to the construction of the laws of the Order, and the decisions of the Grand Sire upon questions of law.

To the Committee on Legislation, all proposed new legislation, and repeal of existing laws.

To the Committee on Finance, all matters in relation to the finances of the Sovereign Grand Lodge, and all propositions involving an appropriation of money or supplies.

To the Committee on Appeals, all appeals from the action of Grand Jurisdictions, and from Subordinate Lodges and Encampments under the exclusive jurisdiction of this Sovereign Grand Lodge.

To the Committee on Constitutions, all amendments to the Constitutions of Subordinate Grand Bodies, or of Subordinate Lodges and Encampments under the exclusive jurisdiction of this Sovereign Grand Lodge.

To the Committee on Foreign Relations, all matters in relation to the Order in foreign countries as shall be referred to it.

To the Committee on the Patriarchal Branch of the Order, such matters relating to Patriarchal affairs as shall be referred to it.

To the Committee on the Degree of Rebekah, all matters relating to that Degree and to such Degree Lodges as shall be referred to it.

To the Committee on Correspondence, all correspondence in relation to the business of the Sovereign Grand Lodge, or the Order, requiring action by this Sovereign Grand Lodge.

To the Committee on Petitions, all petitions and memorials requiring action by this Sovereign Grand Lodge.

To the Committee on Returns, all returns from Grand Jurisdictions, and from Subordinate Lodges and Encampments under the exclusive jurisdiction of this Sovereign Grand Lodge.

To the Committee on Unfinished Business, the duty of examining the Journal of prior sessions, and to report such matters as remain undetermined.

To the Committee on Miscellaneous Business, all matters not herein specified for reference to any other committee.

To the Committee on Grand Bodies not Represented, all matters relating to such Grand Bodies requiring action by this Sovereign Grand Lodge.

To the Committee on Credentials, the Credentials of the Representatives.

To the Committee on Printing Supplies, such matters as are prescribed in the twenty-eighth By-Law of the Sovereign Grand Lodge.

To the Committee on Mileage and Per Diem, all matters in relation to the mileage and per diem of the officers and Representatives.

To the Committee on Drawing for Seats, the duty of drawing the seats to be occupied by the Representatives during the session of the Sovereign Grand Lodge.

40. The Committee on Credentials shall have leave to report at any time.

41. The question of reference of any proposition shall be decided without debate, in the following order, viz.: A Standing Committee, A Select Committee.

42. The report of a committee shall not be acted upon on the day of its presentation, except reports from the Committee on Credentials and the Committee on Drawing for Seats; *provided*, that subjects reported back as being improperly referred may, without a suspension of this rule, be referred to the proper committee.

43. When a report of the Committee on Appeals, or a resolution accompanying the same, is regularly before the Sovereign Grand Lodge, and action is being had thereon, the statement of facts contained in the report of the committee and in the record of appeal, shall be deemed conclusive; provided both parties to the appeal have been heard or have had an opportunity to be heard, and the report shall so state, and it shall not be in order to make any statement in debate thereon, inconsistent with the facts so stated in such report or record. This rule shall not apply when action is had upon a motion to recommit such report with instructions.

44. Any proposition offered for reference to any Standing Committee, which shall require an entry in full upon the Journal, shall be submitted in duplicate, either in print or in manuscript; and, if in writing, it shall be on paper not less in size than half a page of foolscap.

45. When the Sovereign Grand Lodge has, by vote, determined to adjourn for the day, or the hour of adjournment has arrived, before declaring the Body adjourned, the Grand Sire shall call upon the chairmen of the several Standing Committees to give any notice they may desire with regard to the time and place of meeting of the several committees.

ORDER OF BUSINESS.

46. The business of the Sovereign Grand Lodge shall be transacted in the following order:

1. The Sovereign Grand Lodge shall be opened in due form.
2. The roll of Officers and Representatives shall be called.
3. Appointment and Report of Committee on Credentials.
4. Appointment and Report of Committee on Drawing for Seats.
5. Appointment of other Standing Committees.
6. The Journal of the previous day's session shall be read and passed upon.
7. Reports of the Grand Sire, Grand Secretary and Grand Treasurer shall be presented.
8. Petitions and Memorials may be received.
9. Communications presented and read.

10. Reports of Standing and Select Committees received.

11. Calling the jurisdictions for the presentation of resolutions, etc.

12. Consideration of reports of committees.

13. Deferred and new business may be considered.

14. This order of business may be transposed, or dispensed with, by the Sovereign Grand Lodge.

15. When the business is concluded the Grand Chaplain shall offer a prayer, and the Deputy Grand Sire shall proclaim the Sovereign Grand Lodge duly closed.

The Sovereign Grand Lodge has prescribed Uniform Constitutions for the Subordinate Lodges and Encampments under its immediate jurisdiction, which will be found in the Digest.

The following is a list of all the officers of the Grand Lodge of Maryland and of the United States, I. O. O. F.; the Grand Lodge of the United States, I. O. O. F.; the Grand Lodge of the Independent Order of Odd Fellows, and the Sovereign Grand Lodge of the I. O. O. F., the several names of the Supreme Authority of the Order, from 1821 to the present time:

GRAND MASTER.

1. Thomas Wildey, February 22d, 1821—February 22d, 1825; Baltimore, Maryland.

DEPUTY GRAND MASTER.

1. John P. Entwisle, February 22d, 1821—February 22d, 1823; Baltimore, Maryland.

2. John Welch, February 22d, 1823—February 22d, 1825; Baltimore, Maryland.

GRAND WARDEN.

1. William S. Couth, February 22d, 1821—August 22d, 1822; Baltimore, Maryland.

2. Thomas Mitchell, August 22d, 1822—February 22d, 1825; Baltimore, Maryland.

GRAND CONDUCTOR.

1. William Larkam, August 22d, 1821—August 22d, 1823; Baltimore, Maryland.

2. P. G. Anstice, August 22d, 1823—November 22d, 1823; Baltimore, Maryland.

3. Charles Common, November 22d, 1823—February 22d, 1823; Baltimore, Maryland.

GRAND SIRE.

1. Thomas Wildey, 1825-1833; Baltimore, Maryland. Died, October 19th, 1861.

2. James Gettys, 1833–1835; Georgetown, District of Columbia. Died, August 15th, 1844.
3. George Keyser, 1835–1837, Baltimore, Maryland. Died, September 19th, 1837.
4. Samuel H. Perkins, 1837–1840; Philadelphia, Pennsylvania. Died, May 22d, 1874.
5. Zenas B. Glazier, 1840–1841; Wilmington, Delaware. Died, November 11th, 1858.
6. John A. Kennedy, 1841–1843; New York City, New York. Died, June 20th, 1873.
7. Howell Hopkins, 1843–1845; Philadelphia, Pennsylvania. Died, June 5th, 1858.
8. Thomas Sherlock, 1845–1847; Cincinnati, Ohio.
9. Horn R. Kneass, 1847–1849; Philadelphia, Pennsylvania. Died, December 12th, 1861.
10. Robert H. Griffin, 1849–1851; Savannah, Georgia. Died, December 14th, 1855.
11. William W. Moore, 1851–1853; Washington, District of Columbia. Died, December 23d, 1886.
12. Wilmot G. DeSaussure, 1853–1855; Charleston, South Carolina. Died, February 1st, 1886.
13. Wm. Ellison, 1855–1857; Boston, Massachusetts. Died, August 23d, 1877.
14. George W. Race, 1857–1858; New Orleans, Louisiana. Died, June 17th, 1881.
15. Samuel Craighead, 1858–1860; Dayton, Ohio.
16. Robert B. Boylston, 1860–1862; Winnsborough, South Carolina. Died, September 5th, 1865.
17. James B. Nicholson, 1862–1864; Philadelphia, Pennsylvania.
18. Isaac M. Veitch, 1864–1866; St. Louis, Missouri. Died, May 22d, 1884.
19. James P. Sanders, 1866–1868; Yonkers, New York.
20. E. D. Farnsworth, 1868–1870; Nashville, Tennessee.
21. Frederick D. Stuart, 1870–1872, Washington, District of Columbia. Died, January 25th, 1878.
22. Cornelius A. Logan, 1872–1874; Leavenworth, Kansas.
23. Milton J. Durham, 1874–1876; Danville, Kentucky.
24. John W. Stokes, 1876–1878; Philadelphia, Pennsylvania. Died, February, 7th, 1888.
25. John B. Harmon, 1878–1880; San Francisco, California.
26. Luther J. Glenn, 1880–1882; Atlanta, Georgia. Died, June 9th, 1886.
27. Erie J. Leech. 1882–1884; Keokuk, Iowa.
28. Henry F. Garey, 1884–1886; Baltimore, Maryland.
29. John H. White, 1886–1888; Albion, New York.

DEPUTY GRAND SIRE.

1. John Welch, 1825–1829......................................Maryland.
2. Thomas Scotchburn, 1829–1833............................Maryland.
3. Robert Neilson, 1833–1835................................Maryland.

4, John Pearce, 1835–1837..............................Pennsylvania
5. Frederick Leise, 1837–1840 ....New York.
6. William W. Moore, 1840–1841.................District of Columbia.
7. Horn R. Kneass, 1841–1843............................Pennsylvania.
8. William S. Stewart, 1843–1845.............................Missouri.
9. Albert Case, 1845–1847..............................South Carolina.
10. Newell A. Thompson, 1847–1849......... ....Massachusetts.
11. Asher B. Kellogg, 1849–1851..................... ....Michigan.
12. Herman L. Page, 1851–1853..... ....Wisconsin.
13. Horace A. Manchester, 1853–1855......................Rhode Island.
14, George W. Race, 1855–1857............................. Louisiana.
15. Timothy G. Senter, 1857–1858................... ....New Hampshire.
16. Edward H. Fitzhugh, 1858–1860......................... ....Virginia.
17. Milton Herndon, 1860–1862............. ....Indiana.
18. William H. Young, 1862–1864................ .... Maryland.
19. James P. Sanders, 1864–1866............................New York.
20. E. D. Farnsworth, 1866–1868..............................Tennessee.
21. Frederick D. Stuart, 1868–1870..................District of Columbia.
22. Cornelius A. Logan, 1870–1872...............................Kansas.
23. Milton J. Durham, 1872–1874.................................Kentucky.
24. John W. Stokes, 1874–1876............................Pennsylvania.
25. John B. Harmon, 1876–1878................................California.
26. Luther J. Glenn, 1878–1880.................................Georgia.
27. Erie J. Leech, 1880–1882......... ....Iowa.
28. Henry F. Garey, 1882–1884............................. ...Maryland.
29. John H. White, 1884–1886................................New York.
30. John C. Underwood, 1886–1888.............................Kentucky.

GRAND SECRETARY.

1. John Welch, of Maryland... ....Installed, February 22d, 1821.
2. John P. Entwisle, of Maryland...........Installed, February 22d, 1823.
3. William Williams, of Maryland ....Installed, March 30th, 1825.
4. John J. Roach, of Maryland...................Installed, May 1st, 1828.
5. Augustus Mathiot, of Maryland..............Installed, May 4th, 1829.
6. Samuel Prior, of Pennsylvania...........Installed, September 3d, 1833.
7. Robert Neilson, of Maryland ....Installed, October 9th, 1835.
8. William G. Cook, of Maryland............. Installed, April 23d, 1840.
9. James L. Ridgely, of Maryland..........Installed, September 22d, 1841.
10. Theodore A. Ross, of New Jersey ....Installed, September 23d, 1882.
    Bro. Ross was appointed Grand Secretary, on the 19th of November, 1881,
    by the Grand Sire, to fill the vacancy occasioned by the death of Bro.
    Ridgely.

ASSSISTANT GRAND SECRETARY.

1. Maurice Fennell, of Maryland............Appointed, August 22d, 1823.
2. Theodore A. Ross, of New Jersey......Appointed, December 1st, 1873.
3. Charles R. Ross, of New Jersey..........Appointed, October 9th, 1882.
4. Allen Jenckes, of Rhode Island............Appointed, October 1st, 1883.

GRAND TREASURER.

1. John Boyd, of Maryland.................Installed, February 22d, 1821.
2. Augustus Mathiot, of Maryland..........Installed, September 3d, 1833.
3. Charles Mowatt, of New York.............Installed, October 9th, 1835.
4. Andrew E. Warner, of Maryland...........Installed, October 5th, 1836.
5. Joshua Vansant, of Maryland.............Installed, September 5th, 1853.
6. Alexander L. Spear, of Maryland, was appointed, April 12th, 1884, by the Grand Sire, to fill the vacancy occasioned by the death of Bro. Vansant.
7. Isaac A. Sheppard, of Pennsylvania......Installed, September 20th, 1884.

GRAND CHAPLAIN.

1. Rev. Sater T. Walker, of Maryland..........Installed, October 9th, 1835.
2. Rev. Geo. M. Bain, of Virginia...............Installed, April 25th, 1840.
3. Rev. Isaac D. Williamson, of New York..Installed, September 24th, 1841.
4. Rev. Albert Case, of South Carolina......Installed, September 19th, 1843.
5. Rev. James D. McCabe, of Virginia.....Installed, September 16th, 1845.
6. Rev. E. M. P. Wells, of Massachusetts..Installed, September 18th, 1849.
7. Rev. Junius M. Willey, of Connecticut..Installed, September 15th, 1851.
8. Rev. Reuben Jones, of Arkansas........Installed, September 15th, 1856.
9. Rev. James D. McCabe, of Virginia.....Installed, September 21st, 1857.
10. Rev. A. Paul Repiton, of North Carolina, Installed, September 19th, 1859.
11. Rev. E. M. P. Wells, of Massachusetts..Installed, September 21st, 1860.
12. Rev. Isaac D. Williamson, of Ohio.....Installed, September 18th, 1862.
13. Rev. J. W. Venable, of Kentucky.......Installed, September 26th, 1868.

GRAND MARSHAL.

1. Samuel Lucas, of Maryland...............Installed, October 9th, 1835.
2. William Curtis, of Pennsylvania.... .....Installed, September 19th, 1843.
3. John G. Treadwell, of New York.......Installed, September 16th, 1845.
4. Smith Skinner, of Pennsylvania........Installed, September 20th, 1847.
5. John R. Johnson, of Georgia...........Installed, September 18th, 1849.
6. H. A. Crane, of Georgia.............. .Installed, September 9th, 1850.
7. John Sessford, Jr., of the District of Columbia, Installed, Sept. 15th, 1851.
8. James M. Cassady, of New Jersey.......Installed, September 5th, 1853.
9. James W. Hale, of New York..........Installed, September 17th, 1855.
10. Augustus M. Foute, of Mississippi......Installed, September 21st, 1857.
11. Isaac M. Tucker, of New Jersey.......Installed, September 24th, 1858.
12. E. D. Farnsworth, of Tennessee........Installed, September 21st, 1860.
13. B. W. Dennis, of Michigan............Installed, September 18th, 1862.
14. Joseph Kidder, of New Hampshire.......Installed, September 23d, 1864.
15. John S. Heiss, of Pennsylvania.........Installed, September 21st, 1866.
16. John W. Orr, of New Jersey............Installed, September 26th, 1868.
17. J. Griswold, of New Jersey.........................Appointed in 1869.
18. Stuart W. Cayce, of Alabama..........Installed, September 24th, 1870.
19. Caleb Rand, of Massachusetts.........Installed, September 21st, 1872.
20. John R. Tompkins, of Alabama........Installed, September 26th, 1874.

21. John W. Smith, of Connecticut..........Installed, September 23d, 1876.
22. Nathan Taylor, of Massachusetts........Installed, September 21st, 1878.
23. Belden Seymour, of Ohio...............Installed, September 27th, 1880.
24. John W. McQuiddy, of Indiana..........Installed, September 23d, 1882.
25. John T. Jakes, of Delaware............. Installed, September 20th, 1884.
26. William H. Stevenson, of Connecticut ...Installed, September 25th, 1886.

GRAND GUARDIAN.

1. John Boyd, of Maryland.................Installed, February 22d, 1821.
2. Thomas Mitchell, of Maryland ....Installed, March 30th, 1825.
3. Robert Gott, of Maryland.....................Installed, May 4th, 1829.
4. Thomas Moore, of Maryland..............Installed, September 3d, 1833.
5. William Crouch, of Maryland...............Installed, October 9th, 1835.
6. Gotlieb F. Buhre, of Maryland..............Installed, October 3d, 1837.
7. William Warren, of Maryland...........Installed, September 24th, 1841.
8. Richard Brandt, of New Jersey..........Installed, September 19th, 1843.
9. Levin Jones, of the District of Columbia.Installed, September 16th, 1845.
10. Samuel L. Harris, of the District of Columbia.Installed, Sept. 20th, 1847.
11. Solomon H. Lewyt, of Maryland........Installed, September 15th, 1851.
12. Augustus Pfaff, of Pennsylvania.... ....Installed, September 18th, 1862.
13. John W. Foss, of Illinois...............Installed, September 21st, 1866.
14. J. W. Smith, of Connecticut............Installed, September 26th, 1868.
15. James Smith, of Ontario................Installed, September 24th, 1870.
16. Albert Cohen, of Arkansas............Installed, September 21st, 1872.
17. William H. Foulk, of Delaware.........Installed, September 20th, 1875.
18. John W. McQuiddy, of Indiana.........Installed, September 23d, 1876.
19. B. H. Woodell, of North Carolian....,..Installed, September 21st, 1878.
20. J. T. Hornibrook, of Ontario, Canada...Installed, September 27th, 1880.
21. Joshua Davis, of Maine.................Installed, September 23d, 1882.
22. J. R. Harwell, of Tennessee............Installed, September 20th, 1884.
23. Walter G. Dye, of Minnesota...........Installed, September 25th, 1886.

GRAND MESSENGER.

1. John E. Chamberlain, of Maryland..........Installed, October 3d, 1837.
2. John W. Hudson, of Wisconsin..........Installed, September 21st, 1872.
3. Charles H. Gatch, of Maryland...........Installed, September 21st, 1878.
4. Henry C. Fuhrmann, of Minnesota.......Installed, September 23d, 1882.
5. E. H. Whitney, of Michigan............Installed, September 20th, 1884.
6. W. H. Frazier, of the District of Columbia, Installed, September 25th,1886.

SESSIONS OF THE SOVEREIGN GRAND LODGE, OUT OF THE CITY OF BALTIMORE, HAVE BEEN HELD AT THE FOLLOWING TIMES AND PLACES.

In 1833, June 7th, Adjourned Session, in Philadelphia, Penn.
In 1834, January 8th, Adjourned Session, in Washington, D. C.
In 1834, August 16th, Adjourned Session, in New York, N. Y.
In 1839, October 7th, Regular Session (no quorum), in Philadelphia, Penn.
In 1850, September 9th, Adjourned Session, in Cincinnati, O.

In 1850, September 16th, Regular Session, in Cincinnati, O.
In 1853, September 5th, Regular Session, in Philadelphia, Penn.
In 1860, September 17th, Regular Session, in Nashville, Tenn.
In 1864, September 19th, Regular Session, in Boston, Mass.
In 1867, September 16th, Regular Session, in New York, N. Y,
In 1869, September 20th, Regular Session, in San Francisco, Cal.
In 1871, September 18th, Regular Session, in Chicago, Ill.
In 1874, September 21st, Regular Session, in Atlanta, Ga.
In 1875, September 20th, Regular Session, in Indianapolis, Ind.
In 1876, September 18th, Regular Session, in Philadelphia, Penn.
In 1880, September 20th, Regular Session, in Toronto, Ontario, Canada.
In 1881, September 19th, Regular Session, in Cincinnati, O.
In 1883, September 17th, Regular Session, in Providence, R. I.
In 1884, September 15th, Regular Session, in Minneapolis, Minn.
In 1886, September 20th, Regular Session, in Boston, Mass.
In 1887, September 19th, Regular Session, in Denver, Col.

The mileage and per diem paid to the Representatives and Officers of the Sovereign Grand Lodge, for attendance at its annual sessions, from 1850 to 1887, inclusive, was as follows:

1850, $7,929.20; 1851, $8,079.30; 1852, $7,856.50; 1853, $9,142.50; 1854, $10,614.50; 1855, $10,948.20; 1856, $10,995.30; 1857, $10,996.83; 1858, $10,575.80; 1859, $10,452.00; 1860, $11,668.90; 1861, $4,760.16; 1862, $4,705.48; 1863, $7,403.50; 1864, $8,121.90; 1865, $10,316.10; 1866, $11,849.50; 1867, $14,776.20; 1868, $15,144.70; 1869, $17,582.60; 1870, $14,168.40; 1871, $16.969.80; 1872, $16,600.20; 1873, $16,950.00; 1874, $20,030.70; 1875, $18,323.00; 1876, $20,553.10; 1877, $18,853,00; 1878, $13,942.95; 1879, $16,081.75; 1880, $16,331.40; 1881, $15,149.25; 1882, $19,228.98; 1883, $21,773.00; 1884, $22,505.19; 1885, $20,890.74; 1886, $24,238.84; 1887, $28,130.80. Total, $544,640.27. The average amount per year is $14,332.64.

From the formation of the Grand Lodge of Maryland and of the United States in 1821, to the close of the session of 1887, the deaths of the following number of officers, past officers and members of the Supreme Body will be found on the pages of the journals: 1 Grand Sire and Past Grand Representative; 1 Deputy Grand Sire and Past Grand Representative; 15 Past Grand Sires and Past Grand Representatives; 1 Past Grand Sire, Past Grand Master and

Past Grand Patriarch; 3 District Deputy Grand Sires and Past Grand Masters; 7 Past Deputy Grand Sires and Past Grand Representatives; 1 Past Deputy Grand Sire, Past Grand Secretary and Past Grand Representative; 1 Past Grand Secretary, Past Grand Treasurer and Past Grand Representative; 1 Grand Treasurer, and Past Grand Representative; 1 Past Grand Treasurer and Past Grand Representative; 4 Past Grand Chaplains and Past Grand Representatives; 1 Grand Secretary and Past Grand Representative ; 3 Past Grand Marshals and Past Grand Representatives; 1 Past Special Deputy Grand Sire for Germany and Switzerland and Past Grand Representative; 1 Past Assistant Grand Secretary and Past Grand Representative; 18 Grand Representatives; 301 Past Grand Representatives other than those above mentioned; 1 Past Grand; 1 Grand Secretary and Grand Representative elect. All the officers referred to above, were those of the Supreme Body under its several names.

THE GRAND LODGE OF THE GERMAN EMPIRE.

For a complete history of the introduction of the Order into Germany the reader is referred to pages 4706–4711, 4725–4740, 5005–5039 of the Journal of the Sovereign Grand Lodge. This Grand Body was instituted at Frankfort, December 28th, 1872. Hugo Wollheim was elected and installed Grand Sire.

The following additional officers were installed: M. Bernheim, Deputy Grand Sire; Otto Schaettle, Grand Secretary; William Altvater, Grand Marshal; E. Wenzel, Grand Chaplain; S. Spiro, Grand Guardian; G. Berlin, Grand Messenger.

The following is the Charter granted it by the Sovereign Grand Lodge:

CHARTER OF THE GRAND LODGE OF THE GERMAN EMPIRE.
I. O. O. F.
FRIENDSHIP, LOVE, AND TRUTH.

To all whom it may concern :

Know Ye, That the Grand Lodge of the United States of the Independent Order of Odd Fellows, the source of all true and legitimate Odd Fellowship in the United States of America, and by virtue of its constitutional power authorized to organize Lodges and Encampments, Grand and Subordinate, in foreign countries, doth hereby, upon application of Germania Lodge, No. 1; Borussia Lodge, No. 2; Teutonia Lodge, No. 3; Templar Lodge, No. 4; Concordia Lodge, No. 5; Humboldt Lodge, No. 6, of Prussia; Wurttemberg Lodge, No. 1; Donau Lodge, No. 2; Schiller Lodge, No 3, of Wurttemberg; and Saxonia Lodge, No. 1, of Saxony, create and erect into a distinct sovereignty in Odd Fellowship the said Lodges, under the name and title of " The Grand Lodge of the German Empire," with independent power in all matters relating to Odd Fellowship within the said jurisdiction, except as follows:

FIRST—The said Grand Lodge shall not at any time hereafter, in anywise alter or repudiate any of the Signs, Tokens, Passwords, Lectures, or Charges, or any other portion or part of either the Written or Unwritten Work of the Order, as known and practiced within the jurisdiction of this Grand Lodge.

SECOND—This Grand Lodge reserves to itself the right to give said Grand Lodge of the German Empire the Annual Traveling Password to be used within the jurisdiction thereof, and to prescribe the Form of Card; and both jurisdictions shall use the same Traveling Password.

THIRD—That said, "The Grand Lodge of the German Empire," shall have power, subject to the exceptions hereinabove provided, to establish and grant Charters to other Subordinate Lodges and Encampments, and to other Grand Lodges and Grand Encampments within the German Empire, and within such other Germanic European countries as may hereafter be attached to said jurisdiction by consent of this Grand Lodge; and when such other Lodges or Encampments, Subordinate or Grand, shall be so established, they shall sustain the same relations to said "The Grand Lodge of the German Empire" as like Lodges and Encampments sustain to this Grand Lodge; and Farnsworth Encampment, No. 1, at Berlin, Prussia, is hereby placed under the jurisdiction of said "The Grand Lodge of the German Empire," if and when established.

Given under my hand and the Seal of the Grand Lodge of the United States, at the City of Baltimore, in the State of Maryland, this nineteenth day of September, 1872, and of our Order the fifty-fourth.

FRED D. STUART, *Grand Sire.*

JAMES L. RIDGELY, *G. Cor. and Rec. Secretary.*

The report of the Special Committee of officers designated to conclude an agreement with the Grand Lodge of the German Empire, allowing that Body certain privileges under certain restrictions, as well as the report of the Sub-Committee on Revision, which presents in detail the reservations to be made in said agreement, will be found in the Journal of 1884, pages 9653–9658.

SUPPLEMENTAL CHARTER ISSUED TO THE GRAND LODGE OF THE GERMAN EMPIRE.

By Authority of the Sovereign Grand Lodge of the Independent Order of Odd Fellows.

The Grand Sire, Deputy Grand Sire, and Grand Secretary, issue this as a Supplement to the Charter granted by the Grand Lodge of the United States, September 19th, 1872, to the Grand Lodge of the German Empire, as printed in Journal of 1878, pages 7604–7605:

WHEREAS, So much of provision "First" of the said document as prohibits the Grand Lodge of the German Empire from altering the Written Work of the Order, was repealed by the action of the Sovereign Grand Lodge at the session, September, 1883, as stated in the "Agreement" transmitted to the Grand Lodge of the German Empire, April 30th, 1884, it is hereby declared:

First—That the said Grand Lodge of the German Empire shall not at any time, hereafter, in anywise alter or repudiate any of the Signs, Tokens, Passwords, Grips, or any part or portion of the Unwritten Work of the Order, as now known and practiced, or as may hereafter be prescribed by the Sovereign Grand Lodge of the Independent Order of Odd Fellows.

Second—That as to the Ritual, or Written Work, contained in the printed Books of Lectures and Charges, the Grand Lodge of the German Empire shall retain the substance, (that is to say, the legends, sentiments and principles therein contained shall forever remain the same as prescribed and authorized by the Sovereign Grand Lodge,) but may change the form of any and all of these in language and matter, (always preserving the substance) so as to conform the same to the language and genius of their own people.

Third—The said Grand Lodge of the German Empire, I. O. O. F., hereby agrees and covenants that the Sovereign Grand Lodge shall reserve to itself the right and power to give to the Grand Lodge of the German Empire the Annual Traveling Password and Explanation, and the Annual Password of the Degree of Rebekah, to be used within the jurisdiction of the Grand Lodge of the German Empire, and both the Sovereign Grand Lodge of the Independent Order of Odd Fellows, and the Grand Lodge of the German Empire, of the Independent Order of Odd Fellows, shall use the same A. T. P. W. and Explanation, and A. P. W. of the Degree of Rebekah.

All the covenants of the original Charter that do not conflict with the above are to be and remain in full force and virtue, and the special stipulations named in the "Agreement" referred to, are to be strictly adhered to.

Given under our hands and the Seal of the Sovereign Grand Lodge of the Independent Order of Odd Fellows, at the City of Baltimore, in the State of Maryland, United States of America; this first day of August, one thousand eight hundred and eighty-four, and of our Order the sixty-sixth year.

ERIE J. LEECH, *Grand Sire.*
HENRY F. GAREY, *Deputy Grand Sire.*
THEO. A. ROSS, *Grand Secretary.*

At the session of the Sovereign Grand Lodge in 1885, the following was presented:

To the Sovereign Grand Lodge of the Independent Order of Odd Fellows:

In behalf of the Grand Lodge of the German Empire, as the Special Representative of which, I attend this session of your Body, I respectfully state that the Grand Lodge of the German Empire desires to empower and direct its Subordinates to transact ordinary Lodge business in the Initiatory Degree, deeming such a course for the great and manifest good of the Order in Germany, and tending to increase largely the membership of such Subordinate Lodges.

But, since doubts exist whether, under the terms and limitations of our Charter, and our agreement with the Sovereign Grand Lodge, the Grand Lodge of the German Empire can lawfully give such direction, in behalf and in the name of the Grand Lodge of the German Empire, I present this subject to you, asking you either to declare that we may take the proposed action, or to take order with a view to a new grant in the way of an amendment to our Charter and compact to the extent indicated in the above, which amendment the Grand Lodge of the German Empire hereby signifies its readiness to accept in due legal form.

Respectfully submitted,

K. KLOECKER,

Special Representative of the Grand Lodge of the German Empire.

The Committee on Foreign Relations made a report on the subject, (which was adopted), as follows:

WHEREAS, The Grand Lodge of the German Empire, by its Special Representative, in attendance at this session, has signified to the Sovereign Grand Lodge its desire to direct the transaction of ordinary Lodge business to take place in the Initiatory Degree; therefore, be it

Resolved, That if the Grand Lodge of the German Empire shall direct the transaction of ordinary Lodge business to take place in the Initiatory Degree, such direction shall not be held or considered a violation of the limitation against changes in the Unwritten Work, stipulated in the Charter and compact of the Grand Lodge of the German Empire; and, further,

Resolved, That these resolutions shall take effect and be communicated immediately to the Grand Lodge of the German Empire by the Grand Secretary of the Sovereign Grand Lodge.

DISTRICT OF BRANDENBURG.

Germania Lodge, No. 1, was instituted at Berlin, April 2d, 1871.

The Grand Lodge was instituted at Berlin, July 16th, 1873.

Farnsworth Encampment, No. 1, was instituted at Berlin, April 22d, 1871.

Minerva Degree Lodge, No. 1, was instituted at Berlin, April 27th, 1872.

Einigkeit (Harmony) Rebekah, No. 1 (a Degree Lodge of the Daughters of Rebekah), was instituted at Berlin, April 28th, 1872.

DISTRICT OF WURTTEMBERG.

Wurttemberg Lodge, No. 1, was instituted at Stuttgart, December 1st, 1870, by Special Deputy Grand Sire, John F. Morse.

The Grand Lodge was instituted at Stuttgart, April 30th, 1874, by Grand Sire, F. S. Ostheim.

DISTRICT OF HANNOVER.

Lessing Lodge, No. 1, was instituted at Braunschweig, November 30th, 1873.

The Grand Lodge was instituted at Hannover, November 15th, 1874.

DISTRICT OF SAXONY.

Saxonia Lodge, No. 1, was instituted at Dresden, June 6th, 1871.

The Grand Lodge was instituted at Dresden, December 30th, 1876.

Lessing Encampment, No. 1, was instituted at Dresden, December 26th, 1872, by O. Arnoux, District Deputy Grand Sire for Saxony.

DISTRICT OF SILESIA AND POSEN.

The Grand Lodge was instituted at Breslau, May 3d, 1885, by the Deputy Grand Sire, Dr. Ascherson and Bro. F. Meyendorf, Grand Secretary.

Statistics of the Order in Germany, June 30th, 1887:

GRAND LODGES.	SUBORDINATE. LODGES.	MEMBERS.	TOTAL RELIEF.	TOTAL RECEIPTS.
Brandenburg..............12		568	$1,214.74	$5,947.00
Hannover................. 6		243	243.25	2,960.08
Saxony................... 4		253	272.50	2,458.27
Silesia-Posen.............. 4		222	410.48	2,579.11
Wurttemberg..............10		396	701.12	4,017.35
Under G. L. of G. E....... 8		. 250	146.88	3,250.88
	44	1,932	$2,988.97	$21,212.69
Encampments............. 4		163	50.30	329.82
			$3,039.27	$21,542.51

The subjoined list of Lodges and Encampments, in Europe, with time and place of meeting, has been compiled for the use of brethren visiting Europe. It is believed to be the only correct list ever published in the United States.

MONDAY.

Aarhuus, Denmark, Skjalm Hvide Encampment, No. 4.

Berlin, Germany, Germania Lodge, No. 1, Alte Jacob Str. 128, II.

Bern, Switzerland, Fellenberg Lodge, No. 3, Zwiebelngaesschen, 20.

Bremen, Germany, Hansa Lodge, No. 1, Schuesselkorb, No. 2.

Chemnitz, Germany, Becker Lodge, No. 6, Spitzgasse, Logenhaus.

Copenhagen, Denmark, Progress Lodge, No. 4.

Copenhagen, Denmark, Union Lodge, No. 7.

Dresden, Germany, Alemannia Lodge, No. 2, Zahnsgasse 23, I.

Frankenthal, Germany, Palatina Lodge, No. 4., Kaufmaennisches Haus.

Hannover, Germany, Copernicus Encampment, No. 3, Escher Str. 2.

Hannover, Germany, Degree Lodge, 'Zu den drei Ringen," Schiller Str. 7.

Hannover, Germany, Koenigin Louise, Rebekah Degree Lodge, No. 2, Schiller Str. 7.

Magdeburg, Germany, Magada Lodge, No. 3, Breite Weg. 140.

Muenchen, Germany, Liebig Lodge, No. 3, Mitterer Str. 3.

Nestved, Denmark, Nestved Lodge, No. 12.

Posen, Germany, Kosmos Lodge, No. 1, Wilhelm Str. 26.

Stuttgart, Germany, Schiller Lodge, No. 3, Kanzlei Str. 22.

TUESDAY.

Aarhuus, Denmark, St. Olaf Lodge, No. 14.

Altona, Germany, Stormaria Lodge, No. — Holsteinsches Haus, II.

Amsterdam, Netherlands, Mount Sinai Lodge, No. 2, Korte spinhuis steeg 1.

Basel, Switzerland, St. Jacob Lodge, No. 6, Blumenrain 12.

Berlin, Germany, Concordia Lodge, No. 5, Alte Jacob Str. 128, II.

Biel, Switzerland, Rousseau Lodge, No. 4, Schuetzenhaus Str.

Braunschweig, Germany, Lessing Lodge, No. 1, Ocker Str. (Logenhaus.)

Copenhagen, Denmark, Scandinavia Lodge, No. 2.

Copenhagen, Denmark, Columbus Lodge, No. 11.

Dresden, Germany, Lessing Encampment, No. 1, Zahnsgasse 23.

Frederiksberg, Denmark, Valdemar Lodge, No. 21.

Freiburg, Germany, Rotteck Lodge, No. 2, Lehener Str. 22.

Goerlitz, Germany, Silesia Lodge. No. 10, Peters Str. 4.

Iserlohn, Germany, Westfalia Lodge, No. 1, Bohnen Str. 4, I.

Leipzig, Germany, Lipsia Lodge, No. 3, Packhof Str. 3.

Mannheim, Germany, Spinoza Lodge, No. 5, Badener Hof; Lit. G. 6, No. 3.

Muelheim, Germany, Rheinland Lodge, No. 1, Rest. Broichhausen.

Nuernberg, Germany, Noris Lodge, No. 2, Vembo-Haus.

Odense, Denmark, Fyen Lodge, No. 5.

Randers, Denmark, Absalon Lodge, No. 18.

Ringkberg, Denmark, St. Blicher Lodge, No. 17,

Ulm, Germany, Donau Lodge, No. 2, Rebengasse C. 130.

Zuerich, Switzerland, Helvetia Lodge, No. 1, Trittligasse.

WEDNESDAY.

Augsburg, Germany, Holbein Lodge, No. 6, Blaues Kruegel am hintern Lech.

Berlin, Germany, Socrates Lodge, No. 8, Alte Jacob Str. 128.

Berlin, Germany, Humbolt Lodge, No. 6, Brueder Str. 2.

Breslau, Germany, Morse Lodge, No. 2, Ohlauer Str. 79, II.

Copenhagen, Denmark, Denmark Lodge, No. 1.

Copenhagen, Denmark, Venskabs Lodge, No. 13.

Dresden, Germany, Saxonia Lodge, No. 1, Zahnsgasse 23.

Frankfurt, Germany, Goethe Lodge, No. 2, Str. Nuernbergerhof 7.
Hannover, Germany, Hoelty Lodge, No. 11, Escher Str. 11.
Havre, France, Concorde Lodge, No. 1, 60 Rue Victor Hugo.
Inowrazlaw, Germany, Astraea Lodge, No, 2, Siegesmund Str.
Kallundborg, Denmark, Andreas Lodge, No. 9.
Karlsruhe, Germany, Hebel Lodge, No. 6, Karl Str. 17 A. II.
Kiel, Germany, Holsatia Lodge, No. 1, Schuhmacher Str. 4, I.
Kjoge, Denmark, Niels Juel Lodge, No. 22.
Kolding, Denmark, Odin Lodge, No. 15.
Magdeburg, Germany, Wilhelm zur Gerechtigkeit Lodge, No. 24, Breite
    Weg. 3a.
Metz, Germany, Abendstern Lodge, No. 1, Marcellen Str. 25.
Stuttgart, Germany, Uhland Encampment, No. 1, Kanzlei Str.
Stuttgart, Germany, Staufen Lodge, No. 4, Thor Str. 29.

THURSDAY.

Amager, Denmark, Chr. IV. Lodge, No. 23.
Amsterdam, Netherlands, Paradise Lodge, No. 1, Korte spinhuis steeg 1.
Assens, Denmark, Villemoes Lodge, No. 16.
Baden, Switzerland, Pestalozzi Lodge, No. 2, Zur Krone.
Berlin, Germany, Templar Lodge, No. 4, Alte Jacob Str. 128, II.
Copenhagen, Denmark, Nordstjernen Lodge, No. 3.
Copenhagen, Denmark, Wildey Lodge, No. 10.
Dresden, Germany, Humanitas Lodge, No. 4, Zahnsgasse 23.
Duerkheim, Germany, Haardt Lodge, No. 7, Wormser Str. 55.
Erfurt, Germany, Thuringia Lodge, No. 4, Loewengasse.
Hannover, Germany, Leibniz Lodge, No. 7, Escher Str. 11.
Malmo, Sweden, Scania Lodge, No. 1.
Mannheim, Germany, Badenia Lodge, No. 1, Lit. C. 2. No. 22, I.
Muenchen, Germany, Bavaria Lodge, No. 1, Mitterer Str. 3.
Stuttgart, Germany, Wuerttemberg Lodge, No. 1, Kanzlei Str. 22.
Varde, Denmark, Holger Danske Lodge, No. 20.
Waldenburg, Germany, Hochwald Lodge, No. 3 Backergasse 2a, H.

FRIDAY.

Berlin, Germany, Borussia Lodge, No. 2, Alte Jacob Str. 128, II.
Cassel, Germany, Hassia Lodge, No. 12, Gruener Weg. 18.
Copenhagen, Denmark, Eureka Lodge, No. 6.
Copenhagen, Denmark, Ridgely Lodge, No. 19.
Duesseldorf, Germany, Hohenzollern Lodge, No. 2, Herzog Str. 37, I.
Egeln, Germany, Helmuth Lodge, No. 2, Hotel zum Weissen Schwan.
Hildesheim, Germany, Roland Lodge, No. 9, Golarsche Str. 4a.
Lemvig, Denmark, Marcellus Lodge, No. 8.
Neumuenster, Germany, Nordalbingia Lodge, No. 2, Luetzen Str. 8, II.
Schaffhausen, Switzerland, Rheinfall Lodge, No. 9, Frohnwaagplatz.

SATURDAY.

Copenhagen, Denmark, Knud Lavard Encampment, No. 2.

Copenhagen, Denmark, Niels Ebbesen Encampment, No. 3.
Copenhagen, Denmark, Valdemar Encampment, No. 1.
Trelleborg, Sweden, Veritas Lodge, No. 2.

SUNDAY.

Berlin, Germany, Beethoven Lodge, No. 18, Alte Jacob Str. 128.
Berlin, Germany, Farnsworth Encampment, No. 1, Alte Jacob Str. 128, II.
Berlin, Germany, Victoria Encampment, No. 2, Breite Str. 5.
Berlin, Germany, Degree Lodge, Alte Jacob Str. 128, II.
Berlin, Germany, Einigkeit Rebekah Degree Lodge, No. 1.
Lychen, Germany, Teutonia Lodge, No. 3, Logengebauede.
Muehlhausen, Germany, Molhusia Lodge, No. 5, Schwarzer Adler.
St. Gallen, Switzerland, Saentis Lodge, No. 7, Dep. z. St. G. Kant. Bankgeb.

THE GRAND LODGE OF AUSTRALASIA.

From the time (1858,) the first communication from Odd Fellows in Australia was received, the subject of bringing the Order in this distant land under the jurisdiction of the Grand Lodge of the United States, received more or less attention; but nearly ten years passed before the desired union was consummated.

The institution seeking affiliation with the American Order was known as "*The Ancient Independent Order of Odd Fellows,*" to distinguish it from other organizations in the Colony. When the Order in Australia was received by the Grand Lodge of the United States, it consisted of the Grand Lodge of Victoria, 40 Lodges, and 1976 members; the Grand Lodge of Tasmania, 7 Lodges, and 592 members; the Grand Lodge of South Australia, 22 Lodges, and 1,640 members. The Grand Lodge of Victoria was the only one of these which applied for a Charter from the Grand Lodge of the United States. Pursuant to this application, A. D. Meacham, Special Deputy Grand Sire visited Australia and instituted the Grand Lodge of Australia, at Geelong, February 22d, 1868. The following Officers were installed: William Stirling, Grand Master; John W. Dickinson, Deputy Grand Master; James Brewster, Grand Warden; A. I. Cohen, Grand Secretary; John Hedrick, Grand Treasurer.

CHARTER GRANTED TO THE GRAND LODGE OF AUSTRALIA,
I. O. O. F.

FRIENDSHIP, LOVE AND TRUTH.

To all whom it may concern:

Know ye, That the Grand Lodge of the United States of the Independent Order of Odd Fellows, as the source of all true and legitimate Odd Fellowship in the United States of America, and by virtue of its constitutional authority to organize Lodges and Encampments, Grand and Subordinate, in foreign countries, doth hereby create and erect into a distinct sovereignty the various Lodges of Odd Fellows heretofore existing in Australia by the name and title of "*The Grand Lodge of I. O. O. F. of Australia*," with power in all matters relating to Odd Fellowship within the said province, except in the following respects, viz.:

That the said "The Grand Lodge of Australia" shall not at any time hereafter in anywise *alter* or *repudiate* any of the Signs, Tokens, Passwords, Lectures or Charges, or any part or portion of either the Written or Unwritten Work of the Order, as known and practiced within the jurisdiction of the Grand Lodge of the United States.

That this Grand Lodge reserves to itself the right to give to the said "The Grand Lodge of Australia" the Annual Traveling Password, to be used within the jurisdiction of the said "The Grand Lodge of Australia," and both jurisdictions *shall* use the same Traveling Password.

That the qualifications for membership in the Subordinate Lodges within the jurisdiction of the said "The Grand Lodge of Australia" shall be identical with those established for membership in Subordinate Lodges within the jurisdiction of the Grand Lodge of the United States.

Otherwise, this Dispensation to be of no force or effect.

Given under my hand and the Seal of the Grand Lodge of the United States, at the City of Baltimore, in the State of Maryland, this twenty-second day of February, in the year of our Lord one thousand eight hundred and sixty-eight, and of our Order the forty-ninth year.

[SEAL]   JAMES P. SANDERS,
                                                              Grand Sire.

JAMES L. RIDGELY,
   Corresponding and Recording Secretary.

(*Journal of* 1868, *page* 4,295.)

In 1877, a copy of the report of the Committee on Foreign Relations, Journal page 7463, declaring the Clearance Card printed by the Grand Lodge of Australia "is illegal, and is issued in contravention of the terms of the Charter," etc., was transmitted to that Body, and Bro. J. H. B. Curtis, Grand Secretary, in letter dated November 28th, 1877, forwarded a copy of the Charter held by the Grand Lodge of Australasia, which contains instead of the third paragraph above, the following: "The Grand Lodge of the United States and both jurisdictions shall use the same Traveling Password." A resolution of the Standing Committee, protested "against the groundless accusation of having violated its Charter, which does not contain one single word in reference to Clearance or Visiting Cards, but merely states that we are to use the same Traveling Password." The interesting correspondence on this subject can be seen on page 7577, Journal of 1878.

The Grand Lodge of New Zealand was instituted at Dunedin, March, 11th, 1869, by A. D. Meacham, Special Deputy Grand Sire. The Charter was granted by the Grand Lodge of Australia, and a copy of it will be found on page 7688, Journal of 1878. New Zealand claimed to be independent, although the creature of the Grand Lodge of Australia. These conflicting claims were of course not productive of that harmony that should prevail to insure success to the Order.

In 1878, John B. Harmon, Deputy Grand Sire, was sent as Special Commissioner to Australia and New Zealand, to work out a solution of the difficulty. The following mode of procedure was agreed upon:

First—To erect into a Sovereignty, similar to the Grand Lodge of the German Empire, the Lodges and Encampments, Grand and Subordinate, in Australia, New Zealand, and Tasmania, under the name of "*The R. W. Grand Lodge of Australasia, I. O. O. F.*," with jurisdiction over the whole of that country, and with a Charter from the G. L. U. S.

Second—To have the Grand Lodges of Australia and New Zealand surrender their existing Charters, and each to accept a new one from said Grand Lodge of Australasia, except that in the case of Australia the Charter should be to the Grand Lodge of Victoria, with jurisdiction over the Subordinates in that colony, leaving the Subordinates in the other Colonies of Australia, and Tasmania, under the direct jurisdiction of the Grand Lodge of Australasia, until Grand Lodges were established; or attaching such Subordinates to the Grand Lodge of Victoria, as should be deemed best; thus inaugurating in Australasia a governmental system precisely like our own.

The Grand Lodges of Australia and New Zealand consented to the plan, and Bro. Harmon instituted, at Melbourne, on the 1st day of July, 1878, the Grand Lodge of Australasia and installed the following officers:

Wm. Stirling, Grand Sire; Michael Kidston, Deputy Grand Sire; J. H. B. Curtis, Grand Secretary; Jno. Moir, Grand Treasurer; Fred. Batcheldor, Grand Marshal; T. W. Wright, Grand Guardian; Wm. Judge, Grand Messenger.

CHARTER FOR THE GRAND LODGE OF AUSTRALASIA.

INDEPENDENT ORDER OF ODD FELLOWS.

To all whom it may concern:

Know ye, That the Grand Lodge of the United States of the Independent Order of Odd Fellows, as the source of all true and legitimate Odd Fellowship in the United States of America, and by virtue of its constitutional authority to organize Lodges and Encampments, Grand and Subordinate, in foreign countries, doth hereby create and erect into a distinct sovereignty the various Grand and Subordinate Lodges and Encampments now existing in the country known as Australasia, including Australia, Tasmania, New Zealand, and other islands, by the name and title of

THE RIGHT WORTHY GRAND LODGE OF AUSTRALASIA, I. O. O. F.,

to be independent of the Grand Lodge of the United States in all respects, excepting as follows:

First. The said Grand Lodge of Australasia shall not at any time hereafter in anywise alter or repudiate any of the Signs, Tokens, Passwords, Lectures or Charges, or any other portion or part of either the Written or Unwritten Work of the Order as known and practiced within the jurisdiction of the Grand Lodge of the United States.

Second. This Grand Lodge reserves to itself the right to give said Grand Lodge of Australasia the Annual Traveling Password to be used within the jurisdiction thereof, and to prescribe the form of Card; and both jurisdictions shall use the same Traveling Password; and also, the right to furnish all books containing the Lectures and Charges, and such Cards and Certificates as are now or may hereafter be prescribed by it.

Third. The qualifications for membership in the Subordinates within the jurisdiction of the said Grand Lodge of Australasia shall be as provided in Section 2, Article XVI. of the Constitution of the Grand Lodge of the United States.

The said Grand Lodge of Australasia shall have power to establish and grant Charters to other Subordinate Lodges and Encampments, and to other Grand Lodges and Grand Encampments within its jurisdiction; and when such other Lodges or Encampments, Subordinate or Grand, shall be so established, they shall sustain the same relations to the said Grand Lodge of Australasia as like Lodges and Encampments sustain to this Grand Lodge.

The said Grand Lodge of Australasia shall pay due respect to the Grand Lodge of the United States, and conform to the provisions of this instrument, otherwise this Dispensation to be of no force or effect.

Given under our hands and the Seal of the Grand Lodge of the United States, at the City of Baltimore, in the State of Maryland, this the fourth day of March in the year of our Lord one thousand eight hundred and seventy-eight, and of our Order the fifty-ninth.

[SEAL.]   JOHN W. STOKES, *Grand Sire.*

JAS. L. RIDGELY, *Grand Cor. and Rec. Secretary.*

  (*See Journal of* 1878, *pages* 7533, 7564–7592, 7680–7690.)

After the adoption, by the Sovereign Grand Lodge, in 1881, of the resolution requiring Subordinate Lodges to transact all business while open in the Third Degree, the authorities in Australasia objected to the provision and sought permission for the Lodges in that country to transact the ordinary Lodge business while open in the Initiatory Degree. At the sessions of 1885 and 1886 the Sovereign Grand Lodge acceded to the request, on certain conditions, and in 1887 the following were adopted:

Resolved, That as soon as the Grand Lodge of Australasia having become a legally existing incorporated Body, with full legal power to enforce its mandates upon its Subordinates, or with the written proper consent of all its Subordinate Provincial Grand Lodges, or having been, by the solemnly attested written declaration of all of said Provincial Grand Lodges, acknowledged as the supreme head of the Order in Australasia in all things that it may, under its Charter from this Grand Lodge, legislate upon, and with power to enforce its action and mandates, shall, in proper form, ask to receive and be invested with all the powers and privileges heretofore by us given and granted to the Grand Lodge of the German Empire, as defined in the amended Charter to that Grand Lodge, and our agreements and stipulations with the same, it shall be granted, have and receive all and singular the said powers and privileges, subject only to like limitations as are contained in the Grand Charter to, and agreements with, the Grand Lodge of the German Empire, and in the same manner, and under the same formalities in which the latter received the same; and an amended Grand Charter shall be made and tested acccordingly, to take the place of the Grand Charter now held by said Grand Jurisdiction of Australasia.

Resolved, That the permission heretofore given to Australasia to continue the transaction of ordinary Lodge business in the Initiatory Degree, until said amended Grand Charter has been made, be, and is expressly continued.

Resolved, That if the Grand Lodge of Australasia, having obtained said amended Grand Charter, and said extensive powers and privileges, and having thus been made an Independent Grand Lodge, and the true head of the Order in Australasia, shall then direct the transaction of ordinary Lodge business in the Initiatory instead of the Third Degree, this Sovereign Grand Lodge will not regard or hold such direction a violation of the limitation against changes in the Unwritten Work to be contained in said amended Grand Charter, although a transfer of certain parts of the Unwritten Work to the Initiatory from a higher Degree may be made necessary by such direction, as long as the Unwritten Work itself is not in any manner altered or changed.

Victoria Encampment, No. 1, was instituted at Melbourne, October 29th 1868.

The Grand Encampment of Victoria, was instituted at Melbourne, June 18th, 1869.

Condition of the Order, December 31st, 1886:

Grand Lodges.	Number of Lodges.	Number of Members.	Funds of Grand Lodges.	Funds of Subordinate Lodges.	Sick Pay for the Year.	Funeral Donations for the Year.
Victoria*..........	57	5,981	$112,509	$151,652	$68,288	$21,321
New South Wales.	59	5,055	29,037	50,128	41,563	9,150
South Australia....	33	2,676	21,802	40,767	41,562	5,667
New Zealand......	25	1,378	21,136	39,999	5,940	2,750
Tasmania.........	7	633	4,860	8,071	6,905	850
Totals	181	15,723	$189,344	$290,617	$164,258	$39,738

*Including Queensland, (4 Lodges, 228 members) which is attached, at present, to the Grand Lodge of Victoria.

There are three Grand Encampments, viz: Victoria; New South Wales; South Australia, with, probably, ten Subordinates, and two hundred and fifty members. Accurate statistics concerning this Branch of the Order in Australasia cannot be obtained.

(*See New South Wales, New Zealand, South Australia, Tasmania and Victoria, in the Chapter on Grand Jurisdictions.*)

CHAPTER III.

THE GRAND JURISDICTIONS OF ODD FELLOWSHIP AND THEIR BEGINNINGS.

MARYLAND.

WASHINGTON LODGE, No. 1, was organized at the house of Wm. Lupton, Sign of the Seven Stars, Second Street, in the City of Baltimore, on the 26th of April, 1819, by Thomas Wildey, N. G.; John Welch, V. G.; John Duncan, John Cheathem and Richard Rushworth. These brethren met at the invitation of Thomas Wildey, and intended to work according to the usages of the Union or London Order. February 1st, 1820, the Duke of York's Lodge, Preston, England, granted to Washington Lodge a Dispensation, which was received October 23d, 1820, and accepted.

February 22d, 1821, Washington Lodge surrendered its Charter to the Grand Lodge of Maryland and of the United States, which was instituted that day and the following Officers were installed: Thomas Wildey, G. M.; John P. Entwisle, D. G. M.; William S. Couth, G. W.; John Welch, G. Sec.; John Boyd, G. T.; John Boyd, G. Guar.

At a meeting of the Grand Committee, April 15th, 1824, it was resolved, " That the Grand Charter of Maryland and of the United States be vested in the Past Grands of the Grand Lodge of the United States, and that Maryland shall receive a Grand Charter from the same, and thereupon resign all claim or title to or from it other than in common with the other Grand Lodges ; which said Grand Charter shall have and contain, in the engrossing thereof, a clause representing the said investment and condition ;

and further, that the Grand Lodge of Maryland and of the United States doth give the said Charter on condition that they keep the Grand Lodge of the United States in Maryland."

January 15th, 1825, the separation of the Grand Lodge of Maryland and of the United States was effected, and a Constitution for the G. L. U. S. adopted. The proceedings of the Grand Lodge of Maryland after this session were in the capacity of a State Grand Lodge.

On the 6th of May, 1827, a number of members of the Grand Lodge of Maryland applied to that Body for a Charter to institute an Encampment of Patriarchs, with power to confer the Patriarchal, Golden Rule and Royal Purple Degrees, on Scarlet members in good standing. On the 15th of the same month, the Grand Lodge granted the Charter, and June 14th, 1827, the following Officers were installed: John Boyd, C. P.; Thomas Wildey, H. P.; Thomas Scotchburn, S. W.; Richard Marley, Scr.; J. J. Roach, J. W.; E. Wilson, Guar. It was first called the Encampment Lodge, then Encampment, No. 1, and finally, on August 24th, 1832, it adopted the title of Jerusalem Encampment, No. 1, I. O. O. F., which it bears to this day.

When two Encampments had been organized under the jurisdiction of the Grand Lodge of Maryland, that Body signified its willingness to transfer to a Grand Encampment all its rights in the premises; whereupon, on September 5th, 1831, a petition was presented from Patriarchs James L. Ridgely, Joseph Bannister, John Boyd, P. C. P., Augustus Mathiot, C. P., of No. 2, Samuel Lucas, C. P., of No. 1, and Thomas Scotchburn, P. C. P., praying for a Charter for a Grand Encampment in Baltimore. The Charter was at once granted, and the Grand Encampment instituted on the 31st of December, 1831, when the following Officers were installed: Thomas Wildey, G. P.; Samuel Lucas, G. H. P.; John H. O'Donovan, G. W.; McClintock Young, G. Scr.; John Boyd, G. T.; John N. Murphy, G. Janitor; William Hall, Asst. G. Janitor. This was the first grant by the G. L. U. S., of a Grand Encampment Charter.

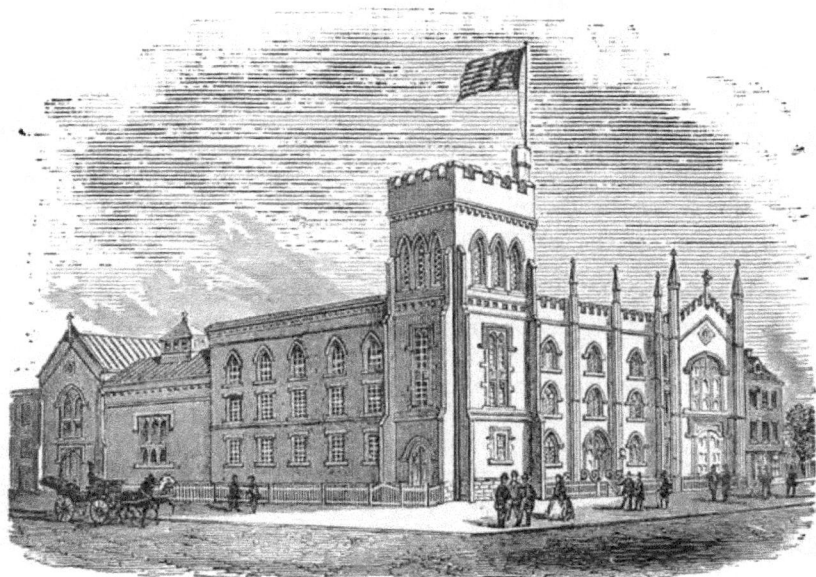

ODD FELLOW'S HALL, BALTIMORE, MD.
(*The First Erected in America.*)

December 31st, 1886, there were 107 Subordinate Lodges and 9,052 members; 26 Encampments and 1,278 members.

MASSACHUSETTS.

Massachusetts Lodge, No. 1, was organized on the self-institution principle, at Boston, on the 26th of March, 1820, and was composed of the following: James B. Barnes, N. G.; H. D. Fregere, V. G.; Thomas Kennedy, Sec.; James B. Eaton, T.; Jacob Myers, W. It worked, until some time in 1822, under the impression that it was the only Lodge in the country. A correspondence took place between the brethren of Baltimore and Boston, in which the latter were persuaded that the former possessed the legal and sole Grand Lodge of the United States. Thereupon it resulted that Massachusetts Lodge, No. 1, was chartered, and instituted June 9th, 1823.

When the Grand Sire visited Boston in 1833, he was informed that no Grand nor Subordinate Lodge existed. The Charter was reclaimed, but was restored, and the Lodge reorganized June 22d, 1841.

The Grand Lodge was instituted at Boston, June 11th, 1823, and the following Officers were installed: Daniel Hersey, G. M.; Henry Solomon, D. G. M.; James B. Barnes, G. W.; William Bishop, G. Sec.; John Snowden, G. Guar.; James B. Eaton, G. C.

The Order was practically dead in this State from 1832 to 1841. This resulted from contentions, discord, jealousy and adverse legislation on the part of the State. The Legislature of Massachusetts in 1834 passed a law making it highly penal in any person to " administer or take an oath, affirmation, or obligation in the nature of an oath." The Grand Lodge of the United States, in order to assist the brethren out of these legal difficulties, adopted the following resolution: " That so long as the law of Massachusetts, relating to illegal oaths, remains in force, the Lodges in Massachusetts be authorized to admit members, confer degrees and install

Officers, etc., on the pledge of honor, and that the oath be dispensed with."

In 1833, the Charter was reclaimed by the Grand Sire, and the Subordinate Lodges required to report directly to the Grand Lodge of the United States. The Charter was restored and the Grand Lodge re-established December 23d, 1841, and the following Officers were installed: Daniel Hersey, G. M.; Thomas Barr, D. G. M.; Aaron Andrews, G. W.; Albert Guild, G. Sec. and T.

A Dispensation was issued January 20th, 1843, for an Encampment, at Boston, to be known as Massasoit Encampment, No. 1. It was instituted February 11th, 1843.

The Grand Encampment was instituted at Boston, March 22d, 1844, and the following Officers were installed: Daniel Hersey, G. P.; Edward Tyler, G. H. P.; Thomas Barr, G. S. W.; Samuel R. Slack, G. Scr.; Hezekiah Prime, G. T.; John S. Ladd, G. J. W.

December 31st, 1886, there were 179 Subordinate Lodges and 32,759 members; 56 Encampments and 7,809 members; 50 Rebekah Degree Lodges and 6,685 members.

NEW YORK.

Columbia Lodge, No. 1, at Brooklyn, was organized on the self-institution plan in 1822. Other and similarly instituted Lodges existed in New York.

On the 14th of November, 1822, the "Loyal Beneficent Duke of Sussex Lodge, No. 2," of Liverpool, England, granted Columbia Lodge the following Charter:

This Dispensation and these Presents, granted from the Loyal Beneficient Duke of Sussex Lodge of Independent Odd Fellows, No. 2, of the Liverpool District, held at the house of Brother James Whittaker, Regent Tavern, Scotland Place, in the town of Liverpool, in the County Palatine of Lancaster, in the United Kingdom of Great Britain and Ireland, to Five brothers of the said Independent Order of Odd Fellows, to enable them to open and establish a Lodge under the title of the Columbia Lodge, No. 1, to be held at the house of Brother James Claridge, No. 49 Main Street, Brooklyn, Long Island, New York, United States. This Dispensation, and these Presents, are not to be altered or amended without the consent of the Officers and brothers of the Loyal Philanthropic Liverpool District Grand Lodge, No. 1, of Independent Odd

Fellows, as well as of the Officers and brothers of the above mentioned Loyal Beneficent Duke of Sussex Lodge, No. 2, of the Liverpool District (the Mother Lodge of the Columbia). It is hereby enjoined that the brothers of the Columbia Lodge meet at such times and on such conditions as are expressed in the By-Laws of the Independent Order of Odd Fellows; and that they do upon oath see that this Dispensation and these Presents be not altered or destroyed; that they do not initiate a person into this our Order for a less sum than the laws (presented to them with this Dispensation by the said Beneficent Duke of Sussex Lodge) express, so that the Lodge and Order may be kept truly respectable; that they do not open any other Lodge of the Order without the consent of the aforesaid Grand Lodge; and that they do appoint Officers in the said Lodge to execute these Presents. In consideration of the sum of two pounds and two shillings, to be remitted to the said Beneficent Duke of Sussex Lodge for this Dispensation. It is agreed that the Officers and brothers of the Columbia Lodge shall not deviate from the principles of the Grand Lodge; and that should any dispute arise so as to cause a matter in question in the said Columbia Lodge, which they cannot conveniently settle, they shall refer the same to a Committee of Past Grands to settle and do justice to the parties concerned in the said matter in question; and that the Officers and brothers of the said Columbia Lodge shall comply with the Dispensation and these Presents, and observe and conform themselves strictly to the laws of the Independent Order of Odd Fellows, according to the purport, principle, true intent and meaning thereof. It is also agreed that the brothers of the said Columbia Lodge, by and with the consent of the Liverpool District Grand Lodge (hereby given), shall elect, appoint and authorize (from time to time), fit and proper persons as Officers, to put in execution, and to enforce a due observance (as aforesaid), of the laws and regulations of the Independent Order; and should they (the brothers of the said Columbia Lodge), hereafter wish to remove the Lodge, they shall show sufficient cause for such removal. Lastly, it is agreed that if at any time hereafter it should happen that the said Columbia Lodge should be destroyed by fire or otherwise, the said Beneficent Duke of Sussex Lodge, or any other Lodge of the Independent Order, shall relieve their distress, in case of necessity.

Granted the 14th day of November, one thousand eight hundred and twenty-two, by the parties concerned in these Presents, who have hereunto subscribed their names and affixed the Seal of the Liverpool District as witnesses.

P. G. M. JOHN WILLIAMSON,	N. G. JOHN DODGSON,
P. G. M. T. C. STANISTREET,	V. G. ROBERT BULMER,
G. M. JAMES CLARKE,	S. JOHN ACKERS,
P. G. M. WILL. RENSHAW,	[L. S.] P. V. G. JOSEPH WILKINSON,
[L.S.] P. D. G. M. JOHN EVANS,	P. S. JOSEPH CONOLLEY,
P. G. M. WILLIAM SPENCER,	C. S. GEO. BRADGATE.
P. G. WILLIAM SMITH,	
[L.S.] P. G. ISAAC WARBECK, pr. procuration of G. B.	
P. G. WILL. SPENCER,	
P. G. GEO. BRADGATE,	
P. G. WILL. RENSHAW,	
P. G. JOHN DAVIES.	

On the receipt of this Charter, Columbia claimed a superior authority over the other Lodges, which, of course, was
vigorously contested. At this stage of affairs Grand Master
Wildey visited the Lodge, and the result of his efforts was
the formal application for a Charter for a Grand Lodge,
which was granted, and was dated June 4th, 1823.

On the 24th of June, 1823, the Grand Lodge was insti-
tuted, and the following Officers were installed: John B.
Robinson, G. M.; James Simister, D. G. M.; John Grant,
G. W.; James Claridge, G. Sec.; Russell Watts, G. Guar.

Columbia Lodge surrendered to the Grand Lodge of
Maryland and of the United States, the Charter received
from England, and received in lieu thereof, the Charter
dated June 4th, 1823.

The seat of the Grand Lodge was moved to Albany in
1828, but by what authority does not appear. October 9th,
1835, the Grand Lodge was permitted to hold its sessions
either in New York or in Albany. The Charter was forfeited May 17th, 1837. A Charter for a Grand Lodge, at
New York, was granted to six petitioning Lodges, and the
Grand Lodge was instituted November 21st, 1838, and the
following Officers were installed: James Alcock, G. M.;
Willct Charlock, D. G. M.; Chas. McGowan, G. Sec.; Geo.
Chatillon, G. T.

New York Encampment, No. 1, existed at Albany. It
does not appear how or when this Encampment was instituted. It is mentioned in the Grand Lodge Journal of 1834.
Mount Horeb Encampment, No. 2, received its Warrant
from No. 1, but in 1838 the G. L. U. S. granted it a Charter,
the powers relative to Encampments in New York having
reverted to the G. L. U. S. in 1837.

The Grand Encampment was instituted at New York
City, August 18th, 1839, and the following Officers were
installed: Charles McGowan, G. P.; Theodore Frost,
G. H. P.; Wilson Small, G. S. W.; James Alcock, G. Scr.;
John A. Kennedy, G. T.

At the session of 1849 two Grand Lodges and two
Grand Encampments were permitted in this jurisdiction, in
order to restore harmony. The Grand Lodge and Grand

Encampment of Southern New York were the original Grand Bodies, and occupied the territory corresponding to the Southern Judicial District of the State, as defined by Act of Congress. The Grand Lodge and Grand Encampment of Northern New York occupied the territory included in the Northern Judicial District. The Charter of the Grand Lodge of Northern New York was presented by Grand Sire Griffin, October 12th, 1849.

The Charter of the Grand Encampment of Northern New York was presented by W. W. Dibblee, Special Deputy, February 5th, 1850.

The two Grand Lodges and the two Grand Encampments, respectively, were consolidated in 1866.

December 31st, 1886, there were 514 Subordinate Lodges and 44,191 members; 95 Encampments and 5,839 members; 76 Rebekah Degree Lodges and 5,984 members.

PENNSYLVANIA.

Pennsylvania Lodge, No. 1, was self-instituted at Philadelphia, December 26th, 1821. John B. Robinson, P. G., of Franklin Lodge, New York, while in Philadelphia on a business trip, invited, through the public papers, the brethren of the city to organize a Lodge. The following brothers met at the house of John Upton, at No. 66 Dock Street, and instituted the Lodge: John Pearce, N. G.; James Day, V. G.; John B. Robinson, Sec.; John Upton, T.; Samuel Croucher, Guar.

The first member admitted was Thomas Hepworth, who immediately took the place of Bro. Robinson as Secretary.

The Lodge was prosperous from the first, and nothing was wanting to render it stable, except the vitality that comes from a Warrant granted by the proper authority. The Lodge soon felt that a Charter was necessary, and applied to Columbia Lodge, New York, for a Dispensation. Pending this application, Grand Master Wildey, on his way to New York and Boston, stopped in the city, and visited the Lodge. He persuaded the brethren to petition the Grand Lodge of Maryland and of the United States for a Charter.

Grand Secretary Entwisle received the following letter:

PHILADELPHIA, June 6th, 1823.

RESPECTED BROTHER :—We have the pleasure to inform you that G. M. Wildey arrived in Philadelphia on Sunday, in good health. We assembled a few brothers by two o'clock; the information we received from our worthy brother was pleasing and instructive. This Lodge had come to the determination to take a Dispensation, Charter, and Degrees; and hearing that a Lodge in New York received a Dispensation from England, we had applied for one from them before the arrival of Brother Wildey.

Brother Wildey wrote us a letter from New York, which we received this morning. His letter gives us such information as to enable us to apply to the Grand Lodge of Maryland and the United States for a Charter, etc.; and he says he will, on his return, prepare us with other documents.

Wishing you every blessing this world can afford, we remain in the bonds of F., L. and T.,

WM. MATHEWS, N. G.   AARON NICHOLS, P. G.
JNO. STURGIS, V. G.   NATH'L LONGMIRE, Secretary.
THOS. HEPWORTH, P. G.

The Charter was at once granted, and Grand Master Wildey, on his return, instituted Pennsylvania Lodge, No. 1, June 27th, 1823.

At the same time that the Charter for Pennsylvania Lodge was given, a Charter was granted for a Grand Lodge to be located in Philadelphia. Grand Master Wildey, on the above date, instituted the Grand Lodge, and installed the following Officers: Aaron Nichols, G. M.; Thomas Small, D. G. M.; Benjamin Richardson, G. W.; Benjamin Daffin, G. Sec.; Joseph Richardson, G. T.

A new Charter was granted May 1st, 1827.

The Grand Encampment was instituted at Philadelphia, by Charter from the Grand Lodge of Pennsylvania, June 19th, 1829, when the following Officers were installed : Isaac Brown, G. P.; James M. Mullen, G. H. P.; Andrew Anderson, G. S. W.; Thomas Small, G. Scr.; John Postill, G. T.; Lawrence O'Connor, G. J. W.; Adam Hamerick, G. Guar.

An Encampment of Patriarchs was chartered by the Grand Lodge of Pennsylvania, August 16th, 1829. It was subsequently known as Philadelphia Encampment, No. 1.

In 1840 the Grand Lodge of Pennsylvania adopted the following:

Resolved, That the Grand Lodge of Pennsylvania will relinquish all jurisdiction over Encampments in this State, to the Grand Lodge of the United States.

This was done in order to do away with the anomalous condition of independence of the Encampments. The Grand Encampment surrendered its Charter, received from the Grand Lodge of Pennsylvania, to the Grand Lodge of the United States, which then granted a new Charter, with a note appended thereto, reciting the date of the Charter from the Grand Lodge of Pennsylvania, in order that the former rank of seniority might be preserved. The Grand Encampment was also directed to recall the Charters heretofore granted to Subordinates, and issue new ones of the same tenor, so far as the same was not inconsistent with the new jurisdiction, noting on each the date of the old Charter.

The Charter granted by the Grand Lodge of the United States, was presented on the 26th of October, 1841.

December 31st, 1886, there were 932 Subordinate Lodges and 81,480 members; 204 Encampments and 12,674 members; 78 Rebekah Degree Lodges and 2,138 members.

DISTRICT OF COLUMBIA.

November 12th, 1827, a petition was presented from Thomas M. Abbett, Robert Boyd, John Cragg, Thomas Smith, and Samuel Knapp, praying for a Charter for a Lodge at Washington, to be known as Central Lodge No. 1. The Charter was granted, and the Lodge instituted November 26th, 1827.

September 28th, 1828, a petition was presented from Thomas M. Abbett, John Wells, Robert Boyd, James Gettys, and James Ashton, Past Grands, praying for a Charter for a Grand Lodge at Washington, which was at once granted, and the Grand Lodge was instituted November 24th, 1828, when the following Officers were installed: Thomas M. Abbett, G. M.; James Gettys, D. G. M.; John Wells, Jr., G. Sec.; Robert Boyd, G. W.; James Ashton, G. Guar.; Francis King, G. C.

June 7th, 1833, a petition was presented from Wm. W. Moore, James Gettys, George M. Davis, Robert Boyd, Wm. H. Mauro, Thomas Stelle, Joseph Burrows, and Wm.

L. Bailey, praying for a Charter for an Encampment of Patriarchs at Washington, to be known as Columbia Encampment, No. 1. The Charter was granted, and when the G. L. U. S. met in Washington, January 8th, 1834, the Encampment was instituted.

The Grand Encampment was instituted by D. D. G. Sire Moore, at Alexandria, April 25th, 1846, when the following Officers were installed: Wm. Towers, G. P.; L. A. Gobright, G. H. P.; J. T. Clements, G. S. W.; J. W. Hodgson, G. J. W.; Chas. Calvert, G. Scr.; Wm. G. Deale, G. T.; James H. DeVaughn, G. Sent. Its location was changed to Washington, September 23d, 1846, Alexandria having been retroceded by Congress to Virginia.

This was the first jurisdiction in the United States under the immediate control of the Grand Lodge of the United States.

December 31st, 1886, there were 15 Subordinate Lodges and 1,620 members; 4 Encampments and 460 members; 2 Rebekah Degree Lodges and 114 members.

DELAWARE.

May 27th, 1830, a petition was received from George McFarlane, James McNeale, Thomas Hill, Simon Robinson, John Scott, Joseph Smith, James Platt, Nelson Ball, and L. Manchester, praying for a Charter for a Lodge at Wilmington, to be known as Delaware Lodge, No. 1. The Charter was granted, and the Lodge was instituted in June, 1830.

February 22d, 1831, a petition was presented from Brothers McAnnal, Scott, McNeale, Robinson, and McFarlane, Past Grands, praying for a Charter for a Grand Lodge at Wilmington, and it was granted. The Grand Lodge was organized June 27th, 1831, when John Scott was installed Grand Master. In September of the same year, the Charter was forfeited, but returned March 5th, 1833, and the Grand Lodge was reinstituted June 12th, 1833, with the following Officers: James S. White, G. M.; Joseph S. Hedges, D. G. M.; Jacob M. Garretson, G. W.; Jacob K. Higgins, G. Sec.; Thomas Hill, G. T.; Simon Robinson, G. Rep.

Delaware Encampment, No. 1, at first worked under a Charter received from Jerusalem Encampment, No. 1, of Maryland, but September 5th, 1834, application was made to the G. L. U. S. for a Charter, which was granted on the same day.

The Grand Encampment was instituted at Wilmington, August 2d, 1848, when the following Officers were installed: Henry F. Askew, G. P.; Robert B. McDonnell, G. H. P.; F. H. Reynolds, G. S. W.; William M. Sink, G. J. W.; John A. Willard, G. Scr.; Joseph String, G. T.; Edward McIntire, G. I. Sent.; George Gill, G. O. Sent.

December 31st, 1886, there were 32 Subordinate Lodges and 2,431 members; 9 Encampments and 358 members; 1 Rebekah Degree Lodge and 75 members.

OHIO.

Brothers Nathaniel Estling, C. Harkin, James W. Brice, Jacob W. Holt, Thomas L. Bedford, and John Gill petitioned, September 26th, 1830, for a Charter for a Lodge at Cincinnati, which was granted October 31st, 1830, and the Lodge named Ohio, No. 1. Brother James Paul, Representative of Pennsylvania to the G. L. U. S., was appointed to institute the Lodge, which he did December 23d, 1830. The following Officers were then installed: Jacob W. Holt, N. G.; James Brice, V. G.; Samuel Cobb, Sec.; Nathaniel Estling, T.

September 5th, 1831, a petition for a Grand Lodge was received from sundry Past Grands of Cincinnati, viz.: Nathaniel Estling, J. Joseph, Richard G. Cheavens, Jacob Holt, and James W. Brice, and referred to a Special Committee of three, who reported:

"That having no evidence that the petitioners had regularly passed the chair of the N. G., and thus rendered themselves legally competent, would therefore earnestly recommend that the Grand Secretary transmit a copy of this report to the applicants, and upon satisfactory information being obtained on that point, the Grand Lodge grant the Charter." A foot-note on page 116 of the Journal of the

Grand Lodge of the United States reads as follows: "It subsequently appearing that there were a sufficient number of Past Grands in membership in Ohio, the Grand Charter was accordingly issued, and the Grand Lodge was instituted January 28th, 1832. The following Officers were installed: David Stuart, G. M.; Samuel Pell, D. G. M.; Hiram Marks, G. W.; Samuel Cobb, G. Sec.; William W. West, G. T."

There is a dispute as to the time of the institution of the Grand Lodge of Ohio. The old Seal of the Body bore the date of January 28th, 1832, but that Grand Lodge now claims that the Lodge should date from January 2d, 1832, as they have printed proceedings of the Grand Lodge of Ohio dated Monday evening, January 2d, 1832. Neither this account, nor the foot-note above mentioned, agrees with that furnished by the report of Grand Sire Wildey, which will be found on pages 122–125 of the Journal of the Grand Lodge of the United States. On page 124 we read:

"After having remained with the brothers of Louisville some six days, I resumed my journey, and landed among the brothers of Cincinnati on the 4th of February (1833), where again I was most cordially received and welcomed by them. All preparations having been made for the organization of the Grand Lodge, in accordance with public notice, the members assembled on Thursday morning, February 7th, at their hall," etc. The Grand Sire on this tour instituted the Grand Lodge of Louisiana before he returned to Cincinnati. On page 132 of the Journal of the Grand Lodge of the United States, there will be found an account of the Grand Sire, adjusted to March 4th, 1833, (he reached home on the 21st of February,) wherein he acknowledges the receipt of $50 for the Louisiana Charter and $50 for the Ohio Charter.

On pages 1960, 1961, Journal of the Grand Lodge of Ohio for 1878, there appears the following:

"The Secretary (of the Grand Lodge of Ohio) was ordered January 25th, 1832, to write to the Grand Lodge of the United States to give them the necessary information relative to the Grand Lodge of Ohio, as well as to inform them that we received a letter from them directing us to commence the said Grand Lodge; but as yet have not received any other authority; and to request them to send us any books, papers, or any other matters that may be useful to us in their opinion. Although the regular 'formation' of the Grand Lodge did not take place until 1833, the one organized under dispensation on January 2d, 1832, was to all intents and purposes a Grand Lodge, and exercised all the powers of such a Body."

The following is the list of the first Officers of the Grand Lodge of Ohio, as taken from its Journal of 1878, page 1962: Richard G. Cheavens, G. M.; Samuel Peel, D. G. M.; J. G. Joseph, G. W.; Jacob W. Holt, G. C.; William West, G. T.; Samuel Cobb, G. Sec.

After a review of the case the conclusion arrived at is, that the Grand Lodge was not "regularly" instituted until February 7th, 1833, when it was done by the Grand Sire.

The removal of the Grand Lodge to Columbus was approved September 20th, 1851.

Wildey Encampment, No. 1, was instituted at Cincinnati, December 7th, 1832, by Grand Sire Wildey.

The Grand Encampment was instituted at Cincinnati, September 24th, 1839. The following Officers were installed: R. R. Andrews, G. P.; William S. Kelley, G. H. P.; Samuel B. Neill, G. S. W.; Jacob Keller, G. Scr.; William Runnells, G. T.; James Read, G. J. W.; Jacob Ernst, G. Sent.

December 31st, 1886, there were 676 Subordinate Lodges and 49,267 members; 187 Encampments and 10,926 members; 120 Rebekah Degree Lodges and 7,219 members.

LOUISIANA.

February 20th, 1831, a petition was presented from Joel C. Davis, Francis C. Davis, Wm. J. Orr, Joseph Price, William Willis, Jno. F. Barnes, Wm. Brown, Joseph F. Irish, John Malone, and Daniel Buckley, praying for a Charter for a Lodge at New Orleans, to be known as Louisiana Lodge, No. 1. The Lodge was instituted in 1831.

A Charter was granted for the Grand Lodge March 5th, 1832, and the Body was instituted, and the following Officers were installed January 6th, 1833: Joel C. Davis, G. M.; Mellville Crossman, D. G. M.; Wm. Collerton, G. W.; A. W. Scates, G. Sec.; David Sidle, G. T.

March 5th, 1832, a petition was presented from Brothers Joel C. Davis, Francis C. Davis, T. Lossing, Wm. Colliston, Thomas Vernon, Mellville Crossman, A. W. Scates, and David Sidle, for an Encampment of Patriarchs, at New Orleans, to be known as Wildey Encampment, No. 1. The Encampment was instituted January 6th, 1833.

The Grand Encampment was instituted at New Orleans February 10th, 1848, and the following Officers were installed: Rev. Chas. W. Whitall, G. P.; Henry Thomas, Jr., G. H. P.; Geo. Hooper, G. S. W.; H. W. Olmstead, G. Scr.; S. W. Kirkland, G. T.; H. P. Andrews, G. J. W.

December 31st, 1886, there were 20 Subordinate Lodges and 751 members; 5 Encampments and 135 members.

NEW JERSEY.

New Jersey Lodge, No. 1, at Camden, was chartered March 30th, 1829.

The Grand Lodge was instituted at Trenton, August 3d, 1833, when the following Officers were installed: John Pearce, G. M.; Crispin Taylor, D. G. M.; William Thompson, G. W.; S. Sutton, G. Sec.; John R. Graham, G. T.; John Pearce, G. Rep.

Industry Encampment, No. 1, was instituted at Paterson, by Grand Sire Wildey, July 4th, 1833. This Encampment became extinct in 1840, but was revived in 1845.

The Grand Encampment was instituted at Trenton, and its permanent location fixed at Newark, May 11th, 1843, when the following Officers were installed: Wm. C. Brannin, G. P.; Samuel B. Scattergood, G. H. P.; Staats S. Morris, G. S. W.; Edward D. Weld, G. Scr.; Wm. Closson, G. T.; Henry C. Boswell, G. J. W.

December 31st, 1886, there were 206 Subordinate Lodges and 18,775 members; 51 Encampments and 2,686 members; 17 Rebekah Degree Lodges and 1,267 members.

KENTUCKY.

March 5th, 1833, a petition was presented from N. Estling, S. S. Lyon, S. Waters, T. H. Breece, G. G. Wright, J. Barclay, J. J. Roach, and T. Mayberry, (working under a Dispensation from the Grand Sire,) for a Charter for Boone Lodge, No. 1, at Louisville, and it was granted. The Lodge was instituted January 24th, 1833.

September 1st, 1835, a petition was presented from J. J. Roach, John Hawkins, Stephen Barclay, Joseph Metcalf, S. S. Lyon, Joseph Barclay, Henry Wolford, Thomas Devan, and Benjamin Moses, Past Grands, praying for a Charter for a Grand Lodge at Louisville. It was granted the same day and the Grand Lodge was instituted September 14th, 1836, when the following Officers were installed: Wm. S. Wolford, G. M.; A. W. R. Harris, D. G. M.; Charles Q. Black, G. Sec.; Henry Wolford, G. T.

August 18th, 1834, a petition was presented from Joseph Barclay, Stephen Barclay, Thos. H. Brice, H. Wolford, George Scott, John Hawkins, Joseph Metcalf, F. Samiento, Wm. Hunt, W. P. Canby, H. H. Moray, and Patriarch J. J. Roach, for an Encampment of Patriarchs at Louisville, to be known as Mt. Horeb Encampment, No. 1. The Encampment was instituted in 1834.

The Grand Encampment was instituted at Louisville, November 21st, 1839, when the following Officers were installed: Henry Wolford, G. P.; Peleg Kidd, G. H. P.; Levi White, G. S. W.; Jesse Vansickle, G. J. W.; S. S. Barnes, G. Scr.; John Thomas, G. T.

December 31st, 1886, there were 168 Subordinate Lodges and 6,948 members; 36 Encampments and 1,561 members; 22 Rebekah Degree Lodges and 806 members.

INDIANA.

October 6th, 1835, a petition was presented from Joseph Barclay and others, praying for a Charter for a Lodge at New Albany, to be known as New Albany Lodge, No. 1. The Lodge was chartered October 14th, 1835, and instituted February 4th, 1836.

The Grand Lodge was instituted at New Albany, August 14th, 1837, when the following Officers were installed: Joseph Barclay, G. M.; Richard D. Evans, D. G. M.; Henry H. West, G. W.; Jared C. Jocelyn, G. Sec.; John Evans, G. T. In 1841 its removal to Madison was authorized, and in 1845 its removal to Indianapolis was authorized and effected.

During the recess of the G. L. U. S., the Grand Sire issued a Dispensation for an Encampment at New Albany, to be known as Jerusalem Encampment, No. 1. October 5th, 1836, the Dispensation was ratified. This Encampment became extinct, but its Charter was restored in 1848 by the Grand Sire, whose action was confirmed September 19th, 1849.

The Grand Encampment was instituted at Indianapolis, January 10th, 1848, and the following Officers were installed: Christian Bucher, G. P.; P. B. Brown, G. H. P.; J. P. Chapman, G. S. W.; A. W. Gordon, G. J. W.; Willis W. Wright, G. Scr.; E. Hidderly, G. T.; D. Craighead, G. Sent.

December 31st, 1886, there were 552 Subordinate Lodges and 26,270 members; 131 Encampments and 5,958 members; 234 Rebekah Degree Lodges and 5,464 members.

VIRGINIA.

Brothers James Crawford, L. W. Bowman, Wm. Compton, Seth Pollard, and Wm. Bailey presented a petition May 4th, 1833, praying for a Charter for Virginia Lodge,,

No. 1, to be located at Harper's Ferry. It was at once granted.

The Grand Lodge was instituted at Richmond, August 19th, 1837, when the following Officers were installed: George J. Roche, G. M.; Henry T. Cook, G. W,; James Nesbitt, G. Sec.; Geo. M. Bain, G. Chap.

Abram's Encampment, No. 1, was instituted at Wheeling, January 11th, 1836. When Virginia was divided, this Encampment belonged to West Virginia.

The Grand Encampment was instituted at Portsmouth, November 15th, 1842, and the following Officers were installed: Jacob Hull, Jr., G. P.; Mallory Dickson, G. H. P; Isaac R. Bagley, G. S. W.; Wm. G. Webb, G. Scr.; Samuel Hartshorn, G. T.; Wm. Ashley, G. J. W.

By authority of the Grand Sire, Greble Lodge, No. 1, was instituted at Fortress Monroe, February 2d, 1865, and September, 1865, it was transferred to the jurisdiction of Virginia.

December 31st, 1886, there were 55 Subordinate Lodges and 3,416 members; 14 Encampments and 469 members.

MISSISSIPPI.

Mississippi Lodge, No. 1, was instituted at Natchez, February 6th, 1837, when the following Officers were installed: Marine Ruffner, N. G.; William Dale, V. G.; Wm. F. Stanton, Sec.

The Grand Lodge was instituted at Natchez, May 4th, 1838, when the following Officers were installed: M. Ruffner, G. M.; Wm. Dale, D. G. M.; E. P. Pollard, G. W.; J. S. Goddard, G. Sec.; Joseph Robinson, G. T.

Wildey Encampment, No. 1, was instituted at Natchez, in 1838, by the Traveling Agent.

The Grand Encampment was instituted at Natchez, January 17th, 1848, and the following Officers were installed: Jno. R. Stockman, G. P.; Cyrus S. Megoun, G. H. P.; Thos. Hackett, G. S. W.; C. Theodore Vennigerholz, G. Scr.;

Samuel Barnes, G. T.; L. K. Barber, G. J. W.; Chas. Stietenroth, G. Sent.

December 31st, 1886, there were 28 Subordinate Lodges and 956 members; 12 Encampments and 245 members.

MISSOURI.

August 18th, 1834, a Charter was granted for Traveler's Rest Lodge, No. 1, at St. Louis, and the Lodge was instituted June 3d, 1835. (The date on its Cards is June 12th.)

The Grand Lodge was instituted at St. Louis, June 13th, 1838, when the following Officers were installed: John Dawson, G. M.; William Blackburn, D. G. M.; Henry M. Brown, G. W.; William S. Stewart, G. Sec.; G. D. Darlington, G. T.; Robert Cathcart, G. C.; William Metcalf, Jr., G. Guar.

Wildey Encampment, No. 1, was instituted at St. Louis, by the Traveling Agent, Thomas Wildey, in June, 1838.

The Grand Encampment was instituted at St. Louis, February 25th, 1846, and the following Officers were installed: Girard B. Allen, G. P.; E. F. Macdonough, G. H. P.; W. C. Corley, G. S. W.; James Robinson, G. Scr.; E. H. Shephard, G. T.; Theodore Betts, G. J. W.

December 31st, 1886, there were 376 Subordinate Lodges and 15,154 members; 78 Encampments and 2,217 members; 31 Rebekah Degree Lodges and 1,089 members.

ILLINOIS.

During the recess of the G. L. U. S., a Dispensation was issued to form Western Star Lodge, No. 1, at Alton. The Lodge was instituted June 11th, 1836.

The Grand Lodge was instituted at Alton, August 22d, 1838, when the following Officers were installed: S. C. Peirce, G. M.; A. Botkin, D. G. M.; D. P. Berry, G. W.; S. L. Miller, G. Sec.; J. R. Woods, G. C.

September 24th, 1841, the Grand Lodge was authorized

ODD FELLOW'S HALL, ST. LOUIS, MO.

to remove its location to Springfield, which was consummated April 25th, 1842.

Wildey Encampment, No. 1, was instituted at Alton, July 11th, 1838. The Charter was reclaimed in 1844, but was restored September 19th, 1849.

The Grand Encampment was instituted at Peoria, July 24th, 1850, by D. D. G. Sire Charles H. Constable. The following Officers were installed: Charles H. Constable, G. P.; George W. Woodward, G. H. P.; F. Scammon, G. S. W.; John Tillson, Jr., G. J. W.; S. A. Corneau, G. Scr.; Isaac S. Hicks, G. T.

December 31st, 1886, there were 669 Subordinate Lodges and 31,806 members; 174 Encampments and 5,733 members; 91 Rebekah Degree Lodges and 4,629 members.

CONNECTICUT.

Quinnipiac Lodge, No. 1, was instituted at New Haven, September 3d, 1839.

The Grand Lodge was instituted at New Haven, November 15th, 1840, and the following Officers were installed: Frederick Crosswell, G. M.; J. B. Gilman, D. G. M.; J. C. Palmer, G. W.; Wm. E. Vibbert, G. Sec.; Samuel Bishop, G. T.

Sassacus Encampment, No. 1, was instituted at New Haven, August 19th, 1841.

The Grand Encampment was instituted at New Haven, by Wilson Small, P. G. P., April 20th, 1843, when the following Officers were installed: Robinson S. Hinman, G. P.; C. W. Bradley, G. H. P.; Richard S. Pratt, G. S. W.; Wm. E. Sanford, G. Scr.; Samuel Bishop, G. T.; T. C. Bordman, G. J. W.

December 31st, 1886, there were 59 Subordinate Lodges and 10,107 members; 22 Encampments and 2,614 members; 16 Rebekah Degree Lodges and 1,439 members.

TEXAS.

Lone Star Lodge, No. 1, was instituted at Houston, July 25th, 1838. This was the first Lodge opened in a foreign land by authority of the Grand Lodge of the United States.

The Grand Lodge was instituted at Houston, April 29th, 1841, and the following Officers were installed: J. A. Young, G. M.; C. W. Buckley, D. G. M.; W. M. Carper, G. W.; J. W. White, G. Chap.; J. N. O. Smith, G. Sec.; A. Ewing, G. T.; Joseph Waterman, G. C. It was subsequently removed to Galveston.

Lone Star Encampment, No. 1, was instituted at Galveston, November 23d, 1847.

The Grand Encampment was instituted at Galveston, December 3d, 1853, by D. D. G. Sire Anson Jones, and the following Officers were installed: C. R. Hughes, G. P.; J. M. Gibson, G. H. P.; S. J. Durnett, G. S. W.; E. P. Hunt, G. Scr.; J. S. Vedder, G. T.; Oscar Farish, G. J. W.; Wm. M. Carper, G. Sent.

December 31st, 1886, there were 170 Subordinate Lodges and 4,450 members; 40 Encampments and 790 members; 3 Rebekah Degree Lodges and 71 members.

TENNESSEE.

Nashville Lodge, No. 1, at Nashville, was authorized by the Traveling Agent in 1839. (In Journal of the Grand Lodge of Tennessee, September 8th, 1841, No. 1 is styled "Nashville;" October 5th and December 18th, 1841, it is called "Tennessee.")

The Grand Lodge, was instituted at Nashville, August 10th, 1841, when the following Officers were installed: Timothy Kezer, G. M.; Robert A. Barnes, D. G. M.; W. H. Calhoun, G. W.; W. P. Hume, G. Sec.; Geo. H. Forsyth, G. T.

Ridgely Encampment, No. 1, was instituted at Nashville, December 20th, 1842.

The Grand Encampment was instituted at Nashville, July 21st, 1847, and the following Officers were installed: Geo. W. Wilson, G. P.; Donald Cameron, G. H. P.; N. E. Perkins, G. S. W.; C. K. Clark, G. J. W.; G. P. Smith, G. Scr.; John Cattart, G. T.

December 31st, 1886, there were 125 Subordinate Lodges and 3,420 members; 18 Encampments and 352 members; 5 Rebekah Degree Lodges and 141 members.

SOUTH CAROLINA.

South Carolina Lodge, No. 1, was instituted at Charleston, by the Traveling Agent, Thomas Wildey, in 1840.

In 1822 an effort was made to establish a Lodge in Charleston. Bros. Dyott, Robinson, and Parkerson, from Pennsylvania, united with two brothers from England to form a Lodge the name of which is now unknown. It is claimed that a Charter was obtained from Philadelphia; but as the Lodge there was at that time without a Charter itself, it is far from likely that it gave what it did not itself possess. The first session of this unknown and name-lost Lodge was held at S. Scyle's hall, in Meeting Street, and afterwards at Roach's hall, Chalmers Street. It continued operations for about two years. John Dyott was the first N. G.; the other Officers are unknown. (*See Journal, page* 306.)

The Grand Lodge was instituted at Charleston, November 29th, 1841, and the following Officers were installed: Jno. H. Honour, G. M.; Peter Della Torre, D. G. M.; Rev. Albert Case, G. W.; S. Thomas, Jr., G. Sec.; J. E. Walker, G. T.

Palmetto Encampment, No. 1, was instituted at Charleston, February 21st, 1842.

The Grand Encampment was instituted at Charleston, August 11th, 1843, and the following Officers were installed: Peter Della Torre, G. P.; James H. Taylor, G. H. P., James H. Adams, G. S. W.; S. A. Hurlbut, G. Scr.; W. H. Gibbes, G. T.; Jno. Schnierle, G. J. W.

December 31st, 1886, there were 16 Subordinate Lodges and 611 members; 4 Encampments and 52 members.

ALABAMA.

Alabama Lodge, No. 1, was instituted at Mobile, April 23d, 1837.

The Grand Lodge of Alabama was instituted at Mobile, December 13th, 1841, when the following Officers were installed : Charles J. B. Fisher, G. M.; C. A. Kelley, D. G. M.; Ezekiel Salomon, G. W.; Thomas C. Rawlins, G. Sec.; James Martin, G. T.

In May, 1838, Thomas Wildey, Traveling Agent, while in Mobile, granted a Charter for Ararat Encampment, No. 1, at Mobile, and instituted the Encampment and installed the Officers.

The Grand Encampment was instituted at Mobile, June 13th, 1848, and the following Officers were installed : Robt. O. Shaw, G. P.; Wm. E. Jennings, G. H. P.; Chas. M. Hansford, S. W.; Samuel Penny, G. Scr.; Sol. J. Jones, G. T.; Robt. Cowan, G. J. W.

December 31st, 1886, there were 33 Subordinate Lodges and 1,507 members; 7 Encampments and 186 members; 6 Rebekah Degree Lodges and 554 members.

NORTH CAROLINA.

Weldon Lodge, No. 1, at Weldon, was chartered March 22d, 1841, and instituted April 26th, 1841.

The Grand Lodge was instituted at Wilmington, January 6th, 1843, when the following Officers were installed : John Campbell, G. M.; R. H. Worthington, D. G. M.; John MacRae, G. W.; W. S. G. Andrews, G. Sec.; Alexander MacRae, G. T.; Rev. A. Paul Repiton, G. Chap. In 1848 the place of meeting was changed to Raleigh, and in 1851 Wilmington was again selected.

Campbell Encampment, No. 1, was instituted at Wilmington, January 5th, 1843.

The Grand Encampment was instituted at Wilmington, July 16th, 1847, and the following Officers were installed: Israel Disosway, G. P.; William D. Cook, G. H. P.; John C. Wood, G. S. W.; Duncan G. McRea, G. J. W.; Alfred Bryant, G. Scr.; Junius D. Gardner, G. T.; W. C. Howard, G. Sent.; T. L. Guess, D. G. Sent. In 1861 the Body ceased working, but was revived at Goldsboro', November 23d, 1871.

December 31st, 1886, there were 36 Subordinate Lodges and 1,169 members; 10 Encampments and 210 members.

GEORGIA.

Oglethorpe Lodge, No. 1, was instituted at Savannah, March 3d, 1842.

The Grand Lodge was instituted at Savannah, November 13th, 1843, when the following Officers were installed: Alvan N. Miller, G. M.; Guy L. Warren, D. G. M.; Elisha Parsons, G. W.; George W. Miller, G. Sec.; Elisha H. Rogers, G. T. In 1850 the Grand Lodge was authorized to remove to Macon.

Magnolia Encampment, No. 1, was instituted at Savannah, August 16th, 1843.

The Grand Encampment was instituted at Macon, July 12th, 1847, by Wiley Williams, D. D. G. Sire. The following Officers were installed: Wiley Williams, G. P.; Jackson Barnes, G. H. P.; John C. Snead, G. S. W.; Jackson DeLoache, G. J. W.; George Patten, G. Scr.; Midas L. Graybill, G. T.; James M. Bivins, G. Sent.; Robert H. Griffin, G. Rep.

December 31st, 1886, there were 49 Subordinate Lodges and 2,038 members; 10 Encampments and 422 members; 2 Rebekah Degree Lodges and 108 members.

MAINE.

Maine Lodge, No. 1, was instituted at Portland, August 25th, 1843.

The Grand Lodge was instituted at Portland, March

18th, 1844, and the following Officers were installed : George W. Churchill, G. M.; Lucius H. Chandler, D. G. M.; James Smith, G. W.; David Robinson, Jr., G. Sec.; J. N. Winslow, G. T.

Machigonne Encampment, No. 1, was instituted at Portland in 1843.

The Grand Encampment was instituted at Portland, October 23d, 1845, when the following Officers were installed: Theophilus C. Hersey, G. P.; Rev. James Pratt, G. H. P.; Allen Haines, G. S. W.; David B. Cleaves, G. J. W.; Nathaniel F. Deering, G. Scr.; Edward Wheeler, Jr., G. T.; Geo. H. Gardiner, G. Sent.

December 31st, 1886, there were 112 Subordinate Lodges and 16,041 members; 45 Encampments and 4,292 members; 23 Rebekah Degree Lodges and 2,434 members.

RHODE ISLAND.

Friendly Union Lodge, No. 1, was instituted at Providence in June, 1829. It became extinct in 1835, but was reopened August 19th, 1843, when the following Officers were installed: William E. Rutter, N. G.; Thomas Charnley, V. G.; James Wood, Sec.; Joseph G. Charnley, T.

The Grand Lodge was instituted at Providence, June 15th, 1844, and the following Officers were installed: James Wood, G. M.; Joseph G. Charnley, D. G. M.; John Hully, G. W.; John Harper, G. Sec.; Mathew Taylor, G. T.

Narragansett Encampment, No. 1, was instituted at Providence, April 9th, 1844.

The Grand Encampment was instituted at Providence, June 11th, 1849, and the following Officers were installed: James Wood, G. P.; Wm. B. Hubbard, G. H. P.; I. B. Purington, G. S. W.; H. A. Manchester, G. Scr.; George W. Ham, G. T.; Hiram Thayer, G. J. W.; John W. Watson, G. Sent.; H. L. Webster, G. Rep.

December 31st, 1886, there were 45 Subordinate Lodges and 5,539 members; 18 Encampments and 1,735 members; 18 Rebekah Degree Lodges and 1,524 members.

NEW HAMPSHIRE.

Granite Lodge, No. 1, was instituted at Nashua, September 11th, 1843.

The Grand Lodge was instituted at Concord, July 9th, 1844, and the following Officers were installed: David Philbrick, G. M.; Eben Francis, D. G. M.; Walter French, G. W.; George H. H. Silsby, G. Sec.; Chas. T. Gill, G. T. ; G. W. Montgomery, G. Chap.

Nashoonon Encampment, No. 1, was instituted at Nashua, May 9th, 1844.

The Grand Encampment was instituted at Concord, October 28th, 1845, and the following Officers were installed: Nathan B. Baker, G. P.; E. P. Emerson, G. H. P.; Geo. W. Towle, G. S. W.; Samuel H. Parker, G. Scr.; E. O. Laughton, G. T. ; Walter French, G. J. W.; David Philbrick, G. Sent.

December 31st, 1886, there were 73 Subordinate Lodges and 9,483 members; 29 Encampments and 2,689 members; 30 Rebekah Degree Lodges and 3,876 members.

MICHIGAN.

Michigan Lodge, No. 1, was instituted at Detroit, December 4th, 1843.

The Grand Lodge was instituted at Detroit, November 5th, 1844, and the following Officers were installed: Wm. Duane Wilson, G. M.; Wm. N. Choate, D. G. M.; Benjamin F. Hall, G. W.; Adrian R. Terry, G. Sec.; John Robinson, G. T. ; Joshua R. Smith, G. C.

Michigan Encampment, No. 1, was instituted at Detroit, April 11th, 1844.

The Grand Encampment was instituted at Kalamazoo, February 4th, 1847, and the following Officers were installed: Jno. Winder, G. P.; J. C. Larrimore, G. H. P.; Wm. N. Choate, G. S. W.; D. S. Walbridge, G. Scr.; Geo. W. Hoofman, G. J. W.; Wm. J. Baxter, G. T.; D. D. Sinclair. G. Sent.

December 31st, 1886, there were 367 Subordinate Lodges and 17,302 members; 97 Encampments and 2,954 members; 98 Rebekah Degree Lodges and 3,398 members.

CANADA.

Prince of Wales Lodge, No. 1, was instituted at Montreal, August 10th, 1843, by Alfred Moore, Special D. G. Sire, and the following Officers were installed: Weatherill Taylor, N. G.; John H. Hardie, V. G.; William Rodden, Sec.; Joseph Kirkup, T.

The Grand Lodge was instituted at Montreal, November 16th, 1844, and the following Officers were installed: W. M. B. Hartley, G. M.; George Matthews, D. G. M.; Thos. Hardie, G. W.; Wm. A. Selden, G. Sec.; Stephen Charles Sewell, G. T.

Hochelaga Encampment, No. 1, was instituted at Montreal, April 2d, 1844, and the following Officers were installed: George Matthews, C. P.; William Rodden, H. P.; John H. Hardie, S. W.; John M. Gilbert, Scr.; John O. Brown, S. W.; S. C. Sewell, T.; Joseph Kirkup, Sent.

The Grand Encampment was instituted at Montreal, September 3d, 1846, and the following Officers were installed: George Matthews, G. P.; J. R. Healey, G. H. P.; G. H. Hamilton, G. S. W.; Wm. Hilton, G. Scr.; H. H. Whitney, G. T.; J. Gilbert, G. J. W.

In 1846 the Grand Lodge and Grand Encampment of Canada requested to be erected into a distinct sovereignty, under the title of " The Grand Lodge of British North America," which request was granted, and this jurisdiction was so named until 1853. The Charter of this Grand Lodge was dated September 24th, 1846, and it was surrendered October 14th, 1853, and its territory divided into three Districts, viz.: Canada East, Canada West, and the Lower Provinces.

The Dominion of Canada was founded in 1867 by the union of Canada East, Canada West, New Brunswick, and Nova Scotia. Canada West then became the Province of

Ontario. September 21st, 1867, the Grand Lodge of Canada West became the Grand Lodge of Ontario. Canada East became the Province of Quebec, and the Grand Lodge of Canada East became, by the revival of the Order in this Province in 1874, and the institution of the Grand Lodge on October 30th, 1878, the Grand Lodge of Quebec.

In 1870 the Dominion of Canada purchased from the Hudson's Bay Company all its vast territory, and, of portions of it, formed the Provinces of Manitoba and British Columbia. The rest of the Hudson's Bay Company's domain is called the North Western Territories, in which there are three "Districts," wherein the Order is planted, viz.: Assiniboia, Alberta, and Saskatchewan.

WISCONSIN.

In the Journal of 1835, page 183, the following is found : "A petition was presented from Edward Cooke, William Ball, Andrew Romfry, William Palkinghorn, John Cole, Richard Johns, George Mitchell, John Cassely, John Rich, Ralph Goldsworthy, John Cock, Joseph R. James, and Edmund Paul, praying for a Charter for a Lodge to be located at Mineral Point, Iowa Territory, to be styled Iowa Lodge, No. 1." The Charter was dated August, 1835, and it was surrendered in May, 1844. This Lodge was created in 1835, before the Territory comprising the present State of Iowa was separated from Wisconsin. That separation took place in 1838, being the same year in which the Encampment mentioned below, and Lafayette Lodge, No. 2, were instituted at Mineral Point.

Grand Sire Sherlock, in his report of 1846, said: "An application was received from four Lodges in Wisconsin for a Grand Lodge Charter, and a remonstrance against the same from three other Lodges. There was so slight an approach to unanimity in this instance that no action was had in the matter." The By-Law, however, which then regulated the subject, was changed, and a Grand Lodge authorized as soon as the conditions of the new law were complied with.

The Grand Lodge was instituted at Milwaukee, June 9th, 1847, and the following Officers were installed: John D. Kinsman, G. M.; A. Kent, D. G. M.; Wm. M. Cunningham, G. W.; Rufus King, G. Sec.; Eli Bates, G. T.; D. McDonald, G. C. Wm. Duane Wilson, D. D. G. Sire, was elected its first Grand Representative to the Grand Lodge of the United States.

The Traveling Agent, P. G. Sire Wildey, in his report, Journal of 1838, page 271, said : " Your Agent here (Mineral Point) opened an Encampment and an additional Lodge upon proper application, and I have no doubt that the Order will steadily advance in Iowa. I had the pleasure during my sojournment among them, to participate in the ceremony of laying the corner-stone of a spacious hall, which they are now erecting."

October 5th, 1838, the Charter given by P. Grand Sire Wildey to the above-mentioned Encampment instituted by him August 3d, 1838, was confirmed. Its title was Wildey Encampment, No. 1. (*See Journal, pages* 287, 288.) It appears that there were three Encampments in Wisconsin, each numbered 1, viz.: Wildey, Milwaukee, and Wisconsin. On page 887 of the Journal of 1846, it appears that a Charter had been issued for Milwaukee Encampment, No. 1. The grant of this Charter was confirmed September 26th, 1846. A mistake was made in the name, as Wisconsin Encampment, No. 1, was the name designated in the petition. The name of the place and the name of the Encampment were interchanged. The semi-annual report of Wisconsin Encampment, No. 1, for the six months ending December 31st, 1847, is signed by M. E. Lyman, C. P.; Francis G. Tibbits, H. P.; Wm. Brown, Scr.

The Grand Encampment was instituted at Kenosha, March 8th, 1849, by Wm. Duane Wilson, D. D. G. Sire.

December 31st, 1886, there were 300 Subordinate Lodges and 14,983 members; 71 Encampments and 1,858 members; 75 Rebekah Degree Lodges and 2,093 members.

VERMONT.

Green Mountain Lodge, No. 1, was instituted at Burlington, January 14th, 1845.

The Grand Lodge was instituted at Montpelier, December 29th, 1847, by Newell A. Thompson, D. Grand Sire. The following Officers were installed: Samuel H. Price, G. M.; James Michell, D. G. M.; Charles W. Bradbury, G. W.; Charles S. Dana, G. Sec.; Ira S. Town, G. T.; J. H. Willis, G. Chap.; Eli Ballou, G. Rep.; Thomas Chubbuck, G. Mar.; William T. Burnham, G. C.; A. B. Childs, G. Guar.

Winooski Encampment, No. 1, was instituted at Montpelier, July 14th, 1846.

The Grand Encampment was instituted at Rutland, June 21st, 1871, by Fred. D. Stuart, Grand Sire. The following Officers were installed: Sewall Morse, G. P.; J. H. Simmons, G. H. P.; J. Baker, G. S. W.; C. G. Peterson, G. Scr.; J. E. McNaughton, G. T.; Timothy Vinton, G. J. W.; Wm. H. Beebe, G. Sent.

December 31st, 1886, there were 31 Subordinate Lodges and 2,101 members; 12 Encampments and 605 members; 8 Rebekah Degree Lodges and 791 members.

IOWA.

Washington Lodge, No. 1, was instituted at Burlington, April 4th, 1844.

The Grand Lodge was instituted at Bloomington, May 1st, 1848, by John G. Potts, D. D. G. Sire. The following Officers were installed: J. Whitfield Garner, G. M.; Amos Mathews, D. G. M.; Samuel McCormick, G. W.; Richard Cadle, G. Sec.; Joseph Bridgeman, G. T.; Wm. Patterson, G. Chap.; J. T. B. Martin, G. Mar.; Benj. Rupert, G. Guar.; Wm. Longley, G. C.

Halcyon Encampment, No. 1, was instituted at Dubuque, February 25th, 1847.

The Grand Encampment was instituted at Muscatine, June 17th, 1852, by Amos Mathews, D. D. G. Sire. The following Officers were installed: B. F. Davis, G. P.; William G. Anderson, G. H. P.; Joseph Bridgeman, G. S. W.; Richard Cadle, G. Scr.; D. G. McCloud, G. T.; William Garrett, G. J. W.

December 31st, 1886, there were 465 Subordinate Lodges and 21,461 members; 120 Encampments and 4,039 members; 80 Degree Lodges of the Daughters of Rebekah and 3,845 members.

ARKANSAS.

April 22d, 1840, the Traveling Agent reported that in the recess of the Grand Lodge he had granted a Charter for Far West Lodge, No. 1, at Little Rock. It was instituted August 12th, 1839.

The Grand Lodge was instituted at Little Rock, June 11th, 1849, when the following Officers were installed: James M. Danley, G. M.; R. W. Johnson, D. G. M.; J. F. Wheeler, G. W.; F. G. Garrit, G. Sec.; A. J. Hutt, G. T.

Eagle Encampment, No. 1, was instituted at Helena, August 31st, 1847. The Charter was at one time recalled, but was restored April 23d, 1869.

The Grand Encampment was instituted at Little Rock, October 14th, 1875, and the following Officers were installed: P. O. Hooper, G. P.; Thomas R. Welch, G. H. P.; S. R. Reid, G. S. W.; W. R. Cox, G. Scr.; George Heckler, G. T.; R. M. Johnson, G. J. W.

December 31st, 1886, there were 65 Subordinate Lodges and 1,592 members; 4 Encampments and 91 members; 11 Rebekah Degree Lodges and 201 members.

FLORIDA.

Florida Lodge, No. 1, was instituted at Black Creek, East Florida, August 11th, 1841, and was soon after permitted to remove to Jacksonville.

The Grand Lodge was instituted at Tallahassee, March 4th, 1851. The following Officers were installed: B. W.

Taylor, G. M.; J. H. Verdier, D. G. M.; J. R. Meginniss, G. W.; M. D. Papy, G. Sec.; S. S. Knight, G. T.

Florida Encampment, No. 1, was instituted at•Jacksonville, in 1846. It ceased work in 1861, but was reinstated June 29th, 1876.

The Grand Encampment was instituted at Waldo, April 15th, 1885. The following Officers were installed: George S. Hallmark, G. P.; Jacob Huff, G. H. P.; J. A. Hooton, G. S. W.; A. A. Thompson, G. Scr.; N. C. Pettit, G. T.; J. C. Thomas, G. J. W.

December 31st, 1886, there were 20 Subordinate Lodges and 555 members; 7 Encampments and 122 members.

MINNESOTA.

Minnesota Lodge, No. 1, was instituted at Stillwater, August 1st, 1849.

The Grand Lodge was instituted at St. Paul, May 5th, 1853, by John G. Potts, D. D. G. Sire, who installed the following Officers: N. Greene Wilcox, G. M.; B. W. Brunson, D. G. M.; G. B. Dutton, G. W.; A. Bryant, G. Sec.; S. W. Walker, G. T.

Minnesota Encampment, No. 1, was instituted at St. Paul, September 1st, 1851, by D. D. G. Sire Potts. None of the Charter members or applicants had the Encampment Degrees; they were conferred on the petitioners prior to the institution of the Encampment by the D. D. G. Sire, assisted by Bros. Stahl and Davis.

The Grand Encampment was instituted at St. Peter, June 7th, 1871, by Charles D. Strong, D. D. G. Sire. The following Officers were installed: C. D. Strong, G. P.; E. K. Smith, G. H. P.; H. M. Rice, G. S. W.; Joseph Lewis, G. Scr.; Joseph Lewis, G. T.; J. W. Everstine, G. J. W.; J. F. Williams, G. Rep.; Rudolph Sieber, G. Sent.; M. Markham, G. Mess.

December 31st, 1886, there were 107 Subordinate Lodges and 6,471 members; 28 Encampments and 1,208 members.

CALIFORNIA.

The first legitimate step to establish Odd Fellowship in California, was taken in the City of Philadelphia. January 16th, 1849, a Charter was issued by Grand Sire Horn R. Kneass to Brothers Samuel J. Torbert, Charles Justis, Jr., Frank M. Caldwell, George H. Weaver, John Willits, and James Smiley, petitioners, for California Lodge, No. 1, to be located at San Francisco. Three of these brothers left Philadelphia with the books and papers, and arrived in San Francisco on the 20th day of May, 1849. The books and documents authorizing the Lodge were confided to Bro. James Smiley, who, with others zealous in the cause, persevered in the work until they had secured a sufficient number of brothers in possession of Final Cards to assist in making up the complement of Charter members required by the laws under which they had secured the Warrant. On the 21st of September, 1849, California Lodge, No. 1, was instituted by Bro. James Smiley, P. G., of Pennsylvania. The early records of this Body having been destroyed in one of the many fires that visited the city, the recollections of the brethren who participated in the establishment of the Lodge, were drawn upon for the data. By them, assisted by such books as are now in existence, it appears that Bro. R. H. Taylor, the first Noble Grand; H. W. Henley, Vice-Grand; E. C. Franklin, Secretary; John M. Coughlin, Treasurer, and Bros. Julius Rose, William Burling, J. N. Dall, David Jobson, and Lewis Tramble comprised, and are entitled to the honor of organizing, the first Lodge and planting the standard of charity and mutual relief on the shores of the Pacific.

As early as 1847 there was an association formed and working as a regularly organized Lodge, having all the paraphernalia, books, etc., to successfully carry on the Work. Bro. E. P. Jones, a prominent citizen of the town, was at its head. This organization was in successful operation until the discovery of gold in May, 1848, when the members were

ODD FELLOW'S HALL, SAN FRANCISCO, CAL.

seized with the excitement common to all citizens of the State, and concluded to suspend the meetings of the Lodge, and all went to the mines. Previous to doing so, they destroyed the books, etc., to prevent them falling into improper hands, and packed the Regalia carefully away. Thus ended the first organization of the Order in California.

An unsuccessful attempt to organize a Lodge was made in August, 1849. The brothers of the Order were called together by a novel, as well as in an odd, manner; which was, the ringing of a bell through the streets, and the crier announcing the fact that a meeting of all Odd Fellows was called at the school-house, to consider the subject of organizing a Lodge of the Independent Order of Odd Fellows. The call was responded to by a large number of brothers, representatives being present from each State of the Union; yet, among the Odd Fellows present, it was found impossible to collect the requisite number of brothers who were qualified to be Charter members; consequently, this effort failed.

It is stated that April 11th, 1853, a committee reported to a convention of Past Grands the "estimate of charitable donations throughout the State, at one hundred thousand dollars, and of which, not over fifteen hundred of that amount has been donated to members of our own Lodges. Of this enormous sum, not more than six hundred dollars have been returned by Lodges on the Atlantic side."

All the above information was obtained from Vol. I. of the Journal of Proceedings of the Grand Lodge of California.

The Grand Lodge was instituted at San Francisco, May 17th, 1853. The following Officers were installed: Samuel H. Parker, G. M.; John F. Morse, D. G. M.; E. W. Colt, G. W.; T. Rodgers Johnson, G. Sec.; John M. Coughlin, G. T.; I. Zachariah, G. Mar.; L. F. Zantzinger, G. C.; A. J. Lucas, G. Guar.

Golden Gate Encampment, No. 1, was instituted at San Francisco, February 1st, 1853. The following Officers were installed: James W. Young, C. P.; John M. Coughlin,· H. P.; L. Ryan, S. W.; T. Rodgers Johnson, Scr.; D. Norcross, T.; John S. Eagan, J. W.

The Grand Encampment was instituted at San Francisco, January 8th, 1855. The following Officers were installed by Matthew Purdin, D. D. G. Sire: S. H. Parker, G. P.; Prescott Robinson, G. H. P.; E. W. Colt, G. S. W.; T. Rodgers Johnson, G. Scr.; W. H. Watson, G. T.; Geo. Borradaile, G. J. W.

December 31st, 1886, there were 303 Subordinate Lodges and 24,375 members; 74 Encampments and 4,641 members; 89 Rebekah Degree Lodges and 5,669 members.

LOWER PROVINCES.

After the Grand Lodge of British North America had surrendered its authority to Grand Sire DeSaussure (October 14th, 1853), the Grand Sire appointed separate District Deputy Grand Sires for Canada East, Canada West, and the Lower Provinces. Past Grand E. G. Fuller had charge of the Lower Provinces.

Past Grand Sire Ellison, assisted by Alfred Mudge, Grand Secretary of the Grand Lodge of Massachusetts, instituted the Grand Lodge of the Lower Provinces, at Halifax, July 26th, 1855, and installed the following Officers: Charles H. Hamilton, G. M.; Thomas Abbott, D. G. M.; Daniel Dickson, G. W.; Samuel C. West, G. Sec.; William J. Williams, G. T.; Charles Bent, G. Chap.; Elbridge G. Fuller, G. Rep.; William Grant, G. Mar.; David W. Ross, G. C.; William Knight, G. Guar. In his report to Grand Sire DeSaussure, he mentioned Acadia, Cobequid, and Eastern Star Lodges and Mamberton Encampment. At the annual session of the Grand Lodge held in 1869, three Lodges and one Encampment were reported: Eastern Star Lodge, No. 2; Fuller Lodge, No. 5; Norton Lodge, No. 6; Stuart Encampment, No. 10.

When Eastern Star Lodge was first instituted, its number was 34. (*See Canada.*)

December 31st, 1886, there were 40 Subordinate Lodges and 2,303 members; 5 Encampments and 148 members; 2 Rebekah Degree Lodges and 133 members.

ONTARIO.

This jurisdiction was formerly called Canada West. (*See Canada.*)

The Grand Lodge was instituted at Brockville, August 23d, 1855, by Thomas Reynolds, D. D. G. Sire. The following Officers were installed: Thomas Reynolds, G. M.; Chauncey Yale, D. G. M.; Anthony Dixon, G. Sec.; John Cameron, G. W.; G. T. Claris, G. T.; Geo. Sherwood, G. Mar.; Charles E. Ewing, G. C.; William Fitzsimmons, G. Guar.

The Grand Encampment was instituted at Hamilton, August 6th, 1869, by James Woodyatt, D. D. G. Sire. The following Officers were installed: James Woodyatt, G. P.; Samuel G. Dobson, G. H. P.; Edmund Beltz, G. W.; M. D. Dawson, G. Scr.; Geo. Irwin, G. T.; A. D. Clement, G. J. W.; James Smith, G. Rep.

December 31st, 1886, there were 210 Subordinate Lodges and 14,856 members; 64 Encampments and 3,032 members.

OREGON.

February 15th, 1846, Albert Guild, D. D. G. Sire, of Massachusetts, under a misapprehension of his authority, granted a Dispensation to Gilbert Watson, P. G. (who with a large company left Boston for Oregon), for Oregon City Lodge, No. 1, to be located at Oregon City. At the session of the G. L. U. S. in September, "a charter in due form" was "granted to Bro. Gilbert Watson and his co-petitioners as a substitute for the illegal charter." In 1847, Grand Secretary Ridgely reported that the Charter was sent as directed, and it appears that the document was used for Excelsior Lodge, Honolulu, S. I.

Chemeketa Lodge, No. 1, was instituted at Salem, December 6th, 1852.

The Grand Lodge was instituted at Oregon City, May

23d, 1856, by E. M. Barnum, D. D. G. Sire. The following Officers were installed : E. M. Barnum, G. M.; H. W. Davis, D. G. M.; H. F. Stryker, G. W.; Wm. P. Burns, G. Sec.; Charles Pope, G. T.; Amory Holbrook, G. Rep.

Ellison Encampment, No. 1, was instituted at Portland, September 25th, 1857.

The Grand Encampment was instituted at Portland, March 29th, 1875, by A. Noltner, Special D. G. Sire, and the following Officers were installed: A. J. Marshall, G. P. F. G. Schwatka, G. H. P.; J. F. Backensto, G. S. W.; J. M. Bacon, G. Scr.; I. R. Moores, G. T.; J. J. Walton, Jr., G. J. W.; A. J. Apperson, G. Mar.; E. H. Stolte, G. Sent.; Wm. Braden, D. G. Sent.

December 31st, 1886, there were 82 Subordinate Lodges and 3,560 members; 20 Encampments and 671 members; 13 Rebekah Degree Lodges and 378 members.

NEBRASKA.

Nebraska Lodge, No. 1, was instituted at Nebraska City, May 28th, 1855.

The Grand Lodge was instituted at Nebraska City, April 27th, 1858, by C. F. Holley, D. D. G. Sire. The following Officers were installed: C. F. Holley, G. M.; J. W. Stull, D. G. M.; H. W. Cook, G. W.; R. W. Furnas, G. Sec.; J. Hamlin, G. T.; M. W. Brown, G. Mar.; H. R. Newcomb, G. C.; Geo. Allen, G. Guar.; W. L. Boydston, G. Mess.

Ridgely Encampment, No. 1, was instituted at Nebraska City, May 3d, 1862.

The Grand Encampment was instituted at Lincoln, July 1st, 1872, and the following Officers were installed: D. A. Cline, G. P.; John Hamlin, G. H. P.; W. L. Wells, G. S. W.; John Evans, G. Scr.; D. H. Wheeler, G. T.; H. A. Wakefield, G. J. W.; St. John Goodrich, G. Rep.

December 31st, 1886, there were 136 Subordinate Lodges and 5,610 members; 22 Encampments and 639 members; 27 Rebekah Degree Lodges and 487 members.

KANSAS.

Shawnee Lodge, No. 1, was instituted at Tecumseh, June 12th, 1857.

The Grand Lodge was instituted at Tecumseh, June 2d, 1858, by J. C. Hemingray, Special D. G. Sire, and the following Officers were installed: John Collins, G. M.; Thomas Plowman, D. G. M.; C. A. Logan, G. W.; G. W. Brown, G. Sec.; H. W. Martin, G. T.; V. W. Kimball, G. Chap.; W. A. Shannon, G. Mar.; Wm. McKay, G. C.; B. D. Castleman, G. Guar.; John A. Fligor, G. Mess.

Far West Encampment, No. 1, was instituted at Leavenworth, March 14th, 1849.

The Grand Encampment was instituted at Leavenworth, October 9th, 1866, and the following Officers were installed: R. A. Randlett, G. P.; Z. E. Britton, G. H. P.; E. S. Scudder, G. S. W.; Wm. Farren, G. J. W.; Samuel F. Burdett, G. Scr.; James S. Crow, G. T.; W. C. Zentmyer, G. Guar.

December 31st, 1886, there were 305 Subordinate Lodges and 12,885 members; 67 Encampments and 2,121 members; 82 Rebekah Degree Lodges and 3,346 members.

WEST VIRGINIA.

The Grand Lodge was instituted at Wheeling, December 5th, 1865, and the following Officers were installed: J. M. Bickel, G. M.; J. H. Duval, D. G. M.; Wm. Taylor, G. W.; Thomas G. Steele, G. Sec.; R. T. Roberts, G. T.; C. Koonce, G. Mar.; W. R. Kelley, G. C. (*See Virginia.*)

The Grand Encampment was instituted at the same time and ·place, and the following Officers were installed: Thomas G. Steele, G. P.; Joseph Tollivar, G. H. P.; L. F. Beeler, G. S. W.; Wm. Taylor, G. J. W.; Wm. W. Blanchard, G. Scr.; R. T. Roberts, G. T.

· The Order in this State was taken under the control of the Grand Lodge of the United States in 1863. The Representatives of eleven Lodges petitioned for a Grand Lodge Charter in 1863. It was refused, although it represented 173 Past Grands. (*See Journal, pages* 3,511, 3,526, 3,583.)

Five Subordinate Encampments at the same time petitioned for a Grand Encampment Charter. This, too, was refused for reasons stated at length in the report of the Committee on Petitions, Journal of 1863, page 3,583.

In 1862 and 1863 the Grand Sire communicated the A. T. P. W. and the A. P. W. of the Degree of Rebekah to Thomas G. Steele, P. G. M., for the benefit of the brethren, as there was no mail communication with the Grand Master of Virginia, who resided at Norfolk.

December 31st, 1886, there were 80 Subordinate Lodges and 3,629 members; 21 Encampments and 607 members; 7 Rebekah Degree Lodges and 274 members.

NEVADA.

Wildey Lodge, No. 1, was instituted at Gold Hill, April 1st, 1862, by Levi Hite, Grand Warden of the Grand Lodge of California, under a commission issued by T. R. Kibbe, Grand Master, of California.

Until the year 1867, the Lodges in Nevada were under the jurisdiction of the Grand Lodge of California.

The Grand Lodge was instituted at Virginia City, January 21st, 1867, by Daniel Norcross, D. D. G. Sire, and the following Officers were installed: John S. Van Dyke, G. M.; J. W. Tyler, D. G. M.; P. J. H. Smith, G. W.; R. H. Taylor, G. Sec.; R. M. Black, G. T.; J. E. Sabine, G. Rep.; John A. Collins, G. Chap.; J. B. Brazelton, G. Mar.; C. Finley, G. C.; J. L. Beam, G. Guar.; C. C. Wright, G. H.

Pioneer Encampment, No. 1, was instituted at Virginia City, July 17th, 1864, by T. Rodgers Johnson, G. Scr., of California.

The Grand Encampment was instituted at Carson City, March 2d, 1875, by D. O. Adkison, Special D. G. Sire, and the following Officers were installed: J. C. Smith, G. P.;

W. H. Hill, G. H. P.; G. W. Chedic, G. S. W.; F. V. Drake, G. Scr.; Geo. Tufly, G. T.; C. W. Jones, G. J. W.; C. H. Maish, G. I. Sent.; J. V. Peers, G. O. Sent.; H. O. Douchy, G. Mar.; E. L. Stern, G. Rep.

December 31st, 1886, there were 26 Subordinate Lodges and 1,433 members; 9 Encampments and 364 members; 3 Rebekah Degree Lodges and 135 members.

COLORADO.

Union Lodge, No. 1, was instituted at Denver, August 18th, 1864.

The Grand Lodge was instituted at Denver, November 30th, 1867, by J. H. Jay, Special D. G. Sire. The following Officers were installed: R. G. Buckingham, G. M.; H. E. Hyatt, D. G. M.; John Chamard, G. W.; J. W. Ratliff, G. Sec.; Hermann H. Heiser, G. T.

Colorado Encampment, No. 1, was instituted at Central City, May 23d, 1867.

The Grand Encampment was instituted at Denver, March 13th, 1873, by Clarence P. Elder, Special D. G. Sire. The following Officers were installed: Clarence P. Elder, G. P.; James M. Fowler, G. H. P.; Fred. J. Stanton, G. S. W.; J. W. Ratliff, G. Scr.; R. G. Buckingham, G. T.; Alonzo Furnald, G. J. W.

December 31st, 1886, there were 60 Subordinate Lodges and 3,448 members; 25 Encampments and 850 members; 4 Rebekah Degree Lodges and 141 members.

VICTORIA, AUSTRALASIA.

The Grand Lodge was instituted at Geelong, February 22d, 1868, by A. D. Meacham, Special D. G. Sire. The following Officers were installed: William Stirling, G. M.; John W. Dickinson, D. G. M.; James Brewster, G. W.; A. I. Cohen, G. Sec.; John Hendrick, G. T.

Victoria Encampment, No. 1, was instituted at Melbourne, October 29th, 1868.

The Grand Encampment of Victoria was instituted at Melbourne, June 18th, 1869. (*See Grand Lodge of Australasia, Chapter II.*)

December 31st, 1886, there were 57 Subordinate Lodges and 5,981 members.

NEW ZEALAND, AUSTRALASIA.

The Grand Lodge was instituted at Dunedin, March 11th, 1869, under a Charter from the Grand Lodge of Victoria. At the session of the Grand Lodge of Victoria, held in Ballarat, September 3d, 1868, the Subordinate Lodges of New Zealand asked for and obtained permission to organize themselves into a separate Grand Body, and receive a Charter either from the Grand Lodge of Victoria or from the Grand Lodge of the United States. The Lodge was instituted by A. D. Meacham, Special D. G. Sire, and the following Officers were installed: B. C. Haggitt, G. M.; Hugh Gourley, D. G. M.; John Lenton, G. W.; James Michie, G. Sec.; Morris Joel, G. T.; Henry Logan, G. Mar.; S. Loudon, G. C.; J. J. Martin, G. Chap.; D. McPherson, G. Guar. (*See Grand Lodge of Australasia, Chapter II.*)

December 31st, 1886, there were 25 Subordinate Lodges and 1,378 members.

SWITZERLAND, EUROPE.

Helvetia Lodge, No. 1, was instituted at Zurich, June 19th, 1871, by Jno. F. Morse, Special D. G. Sire for the Germanic States and Switzerland. The following Officers were installed: C. Heinrich, N. G.; Ed. Altenhofer, V. G.; Adolph Zundel, R. Sec.; G. Rau, P. Sec.; C. Sequin, T.

The Grand Lodge was instituted at Zurich, April 22d, 1874, by F. S. Ostheim, Grand Sire of the Grand Lodge of the German Empire. The following Officers were installed: John Emanuel Grob, G. M.; J. C. Brand, D. G. M.; M. Amman, G. W.; G. Anner, G. Sec.; C. Siegfried, G. T.; E. Altenhofer, G. Rep.

December 31st, 1886, there were 5 Subordinate Lodges and 179 members.

BRITISH COLUMBIA.

Victoria Lodge, No. 1, was instituted at Victoria, March 10th, 1864. A new Charter was given March 18th, 1874, in place of the Charter issued by the Grand Lodge of California. (*See Canada.*)

The Grand Lodge was instituted at Victoria, April 25th, 1874, by A. Noltner, Special D. G. Sire. The following Officers were installed : J. S. Drummond, G. M.; H. V. Edmonds, D. G. M.; John Weiler, G. W.; J. D. Robinson, G. Sec.; E. B. Marvin, G. T.; C. Gowan, G. Mar.; C. Haywood, G. C.; Joseph York, G. Guar.; J. A. Meldram, G. H.

Vancouver Encampment, No. 1, was instituted at Victoria, January 24th, 1871. A new Charter was given March 18th, 1874, in place of the Charter issued by the Grand Encampment of California.

December 31st, 1886, there were 7 Subordinate Lodges and 700 members ; 4 Encampments; the membership in two was 47. The other Encampments reported to the Grand Encampment of Washington.

WYOMING.

Cheyenne Lodge, No. 1, was instituted at Cheyenne, April 15th, 1868. At this time Wyoming formed a part of Dakota, and it was stated in the Warrant that the Lodge was to be located in Dakota.

The Grand Lodge was instituted at Laramie City, April 27th, 1874, by C. P. Elder, Special D. G. Sire. The following Officers were installed : W. L. Kuykendall, G. M.; Louis Miller, D. G. M.; P. Hamma, G. W.; L. Kabis, G. Sec.; H. Haas, G. T. ; H. Garbinatti, G. Rep.; Geo. Little, G. Mar.; L. O. Benedict, G. C. ; H. Tuttle, G. Guar.; J. H. Bramer, G. Mess. ; T. J. Webster, G. H.

Wyoming Encampment, No. 1, was instituted at Laramie City, September, 1870.

The Grand Encampment was instituted at Cheyenne, November 29th, 1881, by H. Altman, Special D. G. Sire.

The following Officers were installed : W. L. Kuykendall, G. P.; Fred. Ruprecht, G. H. P.; L. Kabis, G. S. W.; J. O. Fischer, G. J. W.; Louis Miller, G. Scr.; Mark Jennings, G. T.; H. Altman, G. Rep.

December 31st, 1886, there were 12 Subordinate Lodges and 504 members; 6 Encampments and 146 members; 3 Rebekah Degree Lodges and 122 members.

UTAH.

Utah Lodge, No. 1, was instituted at Salt Lake City, July 29th, 1865.

The Grand Lodge was instituted at Salt Lake City, June 29th, 1874, by J. C. Hemingray, Special D. G. Sire. The following Officers were installed : F. Auerbach, G. M.; Sol. Levy, D. G. M.; M. B. Edinger, G. W.; A. T. Riley, G. Sec.; D. Cram, G. T.

Oquirrh Encampment, No. 1, was instituted at Salt Lake City, July 15th, 1873.

The Grand Encampment was instituted at Salt Lake City, February 22d, 1888, and the following Officers were installed : Alexander Rogers, G. P.; Louis Hyams, G. H. P.; Theo. W. Whiteley, G. S. W.; George Arbogast, G. J. W.; J. J. Thomas, G. Scr.; John T. Buckle, G. T.

December 31st, 1886, there were 8 Subordinate Lodges and 498 members; 2 Encampments and 96 members.

MONTANA.

Montana Lodge, No. 1, was instituted at Helena, July 2d, 1867, by H. S. Norcom, D. D. G. Sire.

The Grand Lodge was instituted at Helena, July 16th, 1874, by D. H. Cuthbert, Special D. G. Sire. The following Officers were installed : D. H. Cuthbert, G. M.; L. E. Holmes, D. G. M.; J. A. Hyde, G. W.; Arch. Graham, G. Sec.; E. Frank, G. T.; J. A. Bradley, G. Mar.; C. Hale, G. C.; D. Vincent, G. Guar.; P. Lansing, G. H.

Rocky Mountain Encampment, No. 1, was instituted at Helena, July 17th, 1872.

The Grand Encampment was instituted at Helena, November 16th, 1883, and the following Officers were installed: J. W. Johnson, G. P.; Wm. Hamilton, G. H. P.; Charles Hoepfner, G. S. W.; George Pascoe, G. J. W.; Wm. Bachr, G. Scr.; Isaac Marks, G. T.; Jacob Loeb, G. Rep.

December 31st, 1886, there were 22 Subordinate Lodges and 1,060 members; 7 Encampments and 234 members; 1 Rebekah Degree Lodge and 101 members.

DAKOTA.

Dakota Lodge, No. 1, was instituted at Yankton, May 25th, 1870.

The Grand Lodge was instituted at Yankton, October 13th, 1875, by William Blatt, Special D. G. Sire. The following Officers were installed: Ezra W. Miller, G. M.; Norman Learned, D. G. M.; J. P. Knight, G. W.; Ralph R. Briggs, G. Sec.; August Siebrecht, G. T.

Royal Purple Encampment, No. 1, was instituted at Vermillion, May 22d, 1874,

The Grand Encampment was instituted at Yankton, August 10th, 1881, by Wm. Blatt, Special D. G. Sire. The following Officers were installed: F. S. Emerson, G. P.; D. S. Dodds, G. H. P.; C. F. Mallahan, G. S. W.; A. E. Ronne, G. Scr.; Fred. Schnauber, G. T.; Chas. Eiseman, G. J. W.; R. R. Briggs, G. Rep.

December 31st, 1886, there were 87 Subordinate Lodges and 3,462 members; 21 Encampments and 598 members; 3 Rebekah Degree Lodges and 129 members.

CHILE.

Valparaiso Lodge, No. 1, was instituted at Valparaiso, April 15th, 1874, by C. A. Logan, Grand Sire, who, on the evening of April 14th, made the following persons Odd Fellows of the Scarlet Degree: Henry von Dessauer, August Moller, Jas. Dimalow, and Wm. H. Nugent. With these newly-made brethren and the following with Cards, he instituted the Lodge: Wm. J. De Gress, J. I. Plunkett, and Alex. Boulet. After the institution, two members were initiated; and three weeks thereafter the membership numbered thirty-two.

The Grand Lodge was instituted at Valparaiso, November 18th, 1875, by C. A. Logan. Past Grand Sire, Special D. G. Sire, and the following officers were installed: George S. Brown, G. M.; Henry von Dessauer, D. G. M.; Charles L. Rowsell, G. W.; Wm. J. De Gress, G. Sec.; Charles Hubner, G. T.

Southern Watch Encampment, No. 1, was instituted at Valparaiso, November 18th, 1875.

December 31st, 1886, there were 5 Subordinate Lodges and 263 members.

SOUTH AUSTRALIA.

The Grand Lodge was instituted at Adelaide, September 30th, 1878, by William Stirling, Grand Sire of Australasia, assisted by Frederick Batcheldor, P. G. Master.

(*See Grand Lodge of Australasia, Chapter II.*)

December 31st, 1886, there were 33 Subordinate Lodges. and 2,676 members.

QUEBEC.

Mount Royal Lodge, No. 1, was instituted at Montreal, December 13th, 1870.

The Grand Lodge was instituted at Montreal, October 30th, 1878, by C. T. Campbell, Special D. G. Sire. The following Officers were installed: Wales L. Lee, G. M.; Wm. Boutelle, D. G. M.; Lyon Silverman, G. W.; A. A. Murphy, G. Sec.; J. H. Field, G. T.; A. A. Murphy, G. Rep. J. C. Becket, G. Chap.; A. A. Maver, G. Mar.; T. H. Christmas, G. C.; H. A. Jackson, G. Guar.

Montreal Encampment, No. 1, was instituted at Montreal, November 6th, 1874.

December 31st, 1886, there were 13 Subordinate Lodges and 773 members. (*See Canada.*)

WASHINGTON.

Olympia Lodge, No. 1, was instituted at Olympia, July 13th, 1855.

The Grand Lodge was instituted at Olympia, November 26th, 1878, by H. G. Struve, D. D. G. Sire. The following Officers were installed: John M. Swan, G. M.; G. T. McConnell, D. G. M.; Abe Reiss, G. W.; N. W. Lane, G. Sec.; J. P. Chilberg, G. T.; W. W. Evans, G. Rep.; H. C. Bostwick, G. Mar.; Frank Hanford, G. C.; James Weir, G. Guar.; Charles Niemeyer, G. H.

Alpha Encampment, No. 1, was instituted at Olympia, April 14th, 1875.

The Grand Encampment was instituted at Walla Walla, May 14th, 1884, by J. V. Meeker, D. D. G. Sire, and the following Officers were installed: N. S. Porter, G. P.; H. E. Holmes, G. H. P.; J. V. Meeker, G. S. W.; J. M. Stout, G. J. W.; Le F. A. Shaw, G. Scr.; G. W. Hall, G. T.; E. Baumeister, G. Rep.; T. N. Ford, G. Mar.; W. D. Scott, G. I. Sent.; B. F. Young, G. O. Sent.

December 31st, 1886, there were 44 Subordinate Lodges and 1,808 members; 11 Encampments and 326 members; 7 Rebekah Degree Lodges and 327 members.

NEW SOUTH WALES.

The Grand Lodge was instituted at Sydney, October 26th, 1880, by Grand Sire Stirling, of the Grand Lodge of Australasia, assisted by the Grand Secretary, William Judge, and J. Munday, Grand Master of the Grand Lodge of Victoria. There were present Representatives from fifteen Subordinate Lodges. The following Officers were installed: W. E. Langley, G. M.; H. H. Greene, D. G. M.; R. S. Cannon, G. Sec.; A. F. Abreu, G. T.; M. L. Kilborne, G. W.; J. Jay, G. Mar.; W. H. Burne, G. C.; J. B. Stow, G. Guar., J. Ross, G. H.

December 31st, 1886, there were 59 Subordinate Lodges and 5,055 members.

(*See Grand Lodge of Australasia, Chapter II.*)

TASMANIA.

The Grand Lodge was instituted at Launceston, December 4th, 1882, by P. G. Sire Stirling and Grand Secretary Judge. The following Officers were installed : James Wallace, G. M.; Alexander Rankin, D. G. M.; James Allen, G. W.; William Edmond, G. T.; George Good, G. Sec.; W. W. Wilks, G. Chap.; D. Sweeney, G. Guar.; G. A. Good, G. Mar.; Lionel Levy, G. C.; T. U. Dunian, G. H.

(*See Grand Lodge of Australasia, Chapter II.*)

December 31st, 1886, there were 7 Subordinate Lodges and 633 members.

MANITOBA.

Manitoba Lodge, No. 1, was instituted at Winnipeg, August 18th, 1873.

The Grand Lodge was instituted at Winnipeg, October 24th, 1883, by John P. Young, D. D. G. Sire. The following Officers were installed: C. D. Anderson, G. M.; J. P. Young, D. G. M.; L. T. Owen, G. W.; James D. Conklin, G. Sec.; W. J. Watson, G. T.; John Dodimead, G. Mar.; J. D. Bowley, G. C.; W. L. Hutton, G. Chap.; Harry Jamison, G. Guar.

Harmony Encampment, No. 1, was instituted at Winnipeg, May 25th, 1874.

December 31st, 1886, there were 13 Subordinate Lodges and 1,005 members ; 3 Encampments and 127 members.

IDAHO.

Pioneer Lodge, No. 1, was instituted at Idaho City, February 16th, 1864, by the Grand Lodge of Oregon. The Sovereign Grand Lodge gave it a new Charter, dated April 25th, 1879.

The Grand Lodge was instituted at Boise City, November 13th, 1883, by William C. Beachey, D. D. G. Sire. The following Officers were installed : G. W. Brumm, G. M. ;

John Upham, D. G. M.; D. B. Kimmel, G. W.; Wm. C. Beachey, G. Sec.; John Lemp, G. T.; M. B. Gwinn, G. Rep.; Daniel Jones, G. Mar.; Wm. H. Davison, G. C.; Nels. Mathison, G. Guar.; A. L. Simondi, G. H.

Idaho Encampment, No. 1, was instituted at Boise City, July 10th, 1876.

December 31st, 1886, there were 17 Subordinate Lodges and 547 members; 1 Encampment and 37 members; 3 Rebekah Degree Lodges and 113 members.

DENMARK.

Denmark Lodge, No. 1, was instituted at Copenhagen, June 29th, 1878, by J. C. Praetorius, Grand Sire of the Grand Lodge of the German Empire.

The Grand Lodge was instituted at Copenhagen, April 21st, 1884, by Andreas Holck, D. D. G. Sire, and the following Officers were installed: Andreas Holck, G. M.; J. Rath, D. G. M.; L. Simmonsen, G. W.; John Hansen, G. Sec.; L. P. Olsen, G. T.; Jeppe Hansen, G. Chap.; C. Borup, G. Mar.; M. Rand, G. C.; A. Petersen, G. Guar.; J. C. Thorndal, G. H.

Valdemar Encampment, No. 1, was instituted at Copenhagen, July 1st, 1881.

December 31st, 1886, there were 21 Subordinate Lodges and 1,923 members; 4 Encampments and 401 members; 1 Rebekah Degree Lodge and 102 members.

ARIZONA.

Arizona Lodge, No. 1, was instituted at Prescott, July 13th, 1868.

The Grand Lodge was instituted at Phœnix, April 26th, 1884, by Clark Churchill, D. D. G. Sire. The following Officers were installed: Wm. Wilkerson, G. M.; W. A. Hancock, D. G. M.; W. L. Whepley, G. W.; N. A. Morford, G. Sec.; Perry Wildman, G. T.; J. E. Wharton, G. Mar.; J. M. Gregory, G. C.; Patrick Hamilton, G. Guar.; O. J. Thibodo, G. H.

Granite Encampment, No. 1, was instituted at Prescott, July 22d, 1884.

December 31st, 1886, there were 6 Subordinate Lodges and 326 members; 1 Encampment and 26 members; 2 Rebekah Degree Lodges and 48 members.

NEW MEXICO.

Montezuma Lodge, No. 1, was instituted at Santa Fe, July 19th, 1851. The Charter was reclaimed in 1858.

Paradise Lodge, No. 2, was instituted at Santa Fe, March 8th, 1852.

The Grand Lodge was instituted at Santa Fe, September 8th, 1887, and the following Officers were installed: A. C. Sloan, G. M.; C. L. Hubbs, D. G. M.; C. T. Russell, G. W.; P. H. Kuhn, G. Sec.; J. T. Newhall, G. T.

Ridgely Encampment, No. 1, was instituted at Santa Fe, in 1853. The Charter was reclaimed in 1858.

James L. Ridgely Encampment, No. 1, was instituted at Silver City, March 11th, 1882.

December 31st, 1886, there were 8 Subordinate Lodges and 307 members; 4 Encampments and 78 members.

WALES.

The Friendly Ivorians Lodge, No. 1, at Tredegar, was instituted June 27th, 1844, at Liverpool, England.

The New Covenant Lodge, No. 2, at Monmouth, was also chartered, and instituted at Liverpool, England, June 27th, 1844.

The Grand Lodge of the Principality of Wales was instituted at Liverpool, England, June 27th, 1844.

Thomas Wainwright Colburn, P. G., of Suffolk Lodge, No. 8, of Massachusetts, and George Bolsover, P. G. M., of Stockport, England, instituted the above named Lodges, but they soon ceased to exist, and all intercourse with both England and Wales terminated in 1846.

ENGLAND.

Pioneer Lodge, No. 1, was instituted at Stockport, in 1845. It soon after ceased to work.

Thomas Wildey Lodge, No. 1, was instituted at London, November 17th, 1875, by R. H. Morrison, Past Grand Rep. of Michigan, Special D. G. Sire.

Anglo American Encampment, No. 1, was instituted at London, November 17th, 1875, by R. H. Morrison, Special D. G. Sire.

The existence of the Lodge and Encampment terminated in 1878.

SANDWICH ISLANDS.

Excelsior Lodge, No. 1, was irregularly instituted at Honolulu, December 10th, 1846, by Gilbert Watson, D. D. G. Sire for Oregon, in the exercise of powers supposed to belong to him as such District Deputy, under a commission erroneously granted by D. D. G. Sire Guild, of Massachusetts, in 1844. The Charter granted by the G. L. U. S. in 1846 (Journal, 959), for a Lodge at Oregon City, Oregon, Grand Secretary Ridgely stated in his report at session of 1847 (Journal, page 1044), was sent to Bro. Watson by a brother who sailed for Honolulu in June, 1847. This document was delivered to Excelsior Lodge as its Charter; but September 11th, 1849, Alexander V. Fraser, Special Deputy for the Pacific Coast, reclaimed it and returned it to Baltimore, presenting to the Lodge a valid Charter, granted in 1847, on the recommendation of the Grand Sire.

At the session of 1847, Pacific Lodge, No. 1, a self-instituted Lodge, and a rival to Excelsior, asked for a Charter, which was refused.

Polynesia Encampment, No. 1, was instituted at Honolulu, February 10th, 1854.

December 31st, 1886, there were 2 Subordinate Lodges and 172 members; 1 Encampment and 42 members.

PERU.

Lima Lodge, No. 1, was instituted at Lima, January 3d, 1872, by James Pascoe, who was authorized to act in the premises by Lewis Soher, of California, P. G. P., Special D. G. Sire. There are two other Lodges: Fortschritt, No. 3, in Lima, and Chalaco, No. 4, in Callao.

Atahualpa Encampment, No. 1, was instituted at Lima, September 22d, 1876.

December 31st, 1886, there were 3 Subordinate Lodges and 138 members; 1 Encampment and 43 members.

INDIAN TERRITORY.

Caddo Lodge, No. 1, was instituted at Caddo, Choctaw Nation, May 8th, 1875, by B. F. Christian, P. G. M., Special D. G. Sire.

Ridgely Encampment, No. 1, was instituted at McAllister, March 27th, 1884.

December 31st, 1886, there were 5 Subordinate Lodges and 257 members; 2 Encampments and 75 members.

NETHERLANDS.

Paradise Lodge, No. 1, was instituted at Amsterdam, Holland, March 19th, 1877, by F. S. Ostheim, Special D. G. Sire and P. G. Sire of the Grand Lodge of the German Empire.

Prior to the institution, and at a preliminary meeting, seventeen candidates were elected, all of whom were initiated. June 30th, 1877, the report of the Lodge furnished the following information: Charter members, 6; initiated, 26; Fifth Degree, 11; Initiatory, 21; Degrees conferred, 62; receipts, $467.

There is another Lodge, Mt. Sinai, No. 2, located in Amsterdam.

December 31st, 1886, there were 2 Subordinate Lodges and 102 members.

WEST INDIES.

In November, 1869, a Mr. J. A. Bibby, of Barbados, opened a correspondence in reference to obtaining a Charter for a Lodge. The correspondence on the subject continued, and at the session of 1877, the Grand Lodge not having sufficient information to enable them to act intelligently in the premises, recommended the Grand Officers to continue the correspondence.

A Charter was intrusted to Archibald Bayne, Special D. G. Sire, who instituted Americus Lodge, No. 1, at Bridgetown, Barbados, November 4th, 1879. The Lodge ceased to work early in 1882.

MEXICO.

Ridgely Lodge, No. 1, was instituted at the City of Mexico, August 5th, 1882, by W. J. De Gress, Special D. G. Sire, formerly Grand Secretary of, and, in 1876–7, Grand Representative from, the Grand Lodge of Chile.

In 1848 an application was made for a Lodge (Hope, No. 1,) at Vera Cruz, which was declined, and no further efforts were made to plant the Order in this Republic until 1882.

Juarez Lodge, No. 2, was instituted March 16th, 1885, at the same place.

December 31st, 1886, there were 2 Subordinate Lodges and 91 members.

CUBA.

Porvenir Lodge, No. 1, was instituted at Havana, August 26th, 1883, by Evaristo Valdes Galindo, Special D. G. Sire. The report of the Lodge for the year ending December 31st, 1883, showed a membership of twenty-five, good work for the four months of its existence. There are at present six other Lodges, as follows: Fraternidad Universal, No. 2; Cuba, No. 3; Havana, No. 4; America, No. 5; Regla, No. 6; Hijos del Trabajo, No. 7.

December 31st, 1886, there were 7 Subordinate Lodges and 329 members.

NORTH-WEST TERRITORIES OF CANADA.

ASSINIBOIA.—Valley Lodge, No. 1, was instituted at Moose Jaw, December 28th, 1883, and was placed under the jurisdiction of the Grand Lodge of Manitoba.

December 31st, 1886, there were 2 Subordinate Lodges and 55 members. (*See Canada.*)

ALBERTA.—Alberta Lodge, No. 1, was instituted at Calgary, December 26th, 1884.

Alberta Encampment, No. 1, was instituted at Calgary, January 11th, 1887.

December 31st, 1886, there was 1 Subordinate Lodge and 51 members; 1 Encampment. (*See Canada.*)

SASKATCHEWAN.—Saskatchewan Lodge, No. 1, was instituted at Battleford, May 2d, 1888. The village is 200 miles from the C. P. Railroad; the nearest town is 160 miles distant, and the nearest Lodge is 312 miles from Saskatchewan, No. 1.

SWEDEN.

Scania Lodge, No. 1, was instituted at Malmo, October 29th, 1884, by Andreas Holck, D. D. G. Sire. It is now under the jurisdiction of Denmark.

FRANCE.

Concorde Lodge, No. 1, was instituted at Havre, March 2d, 1887, by L. Bourdonnay, Special D. G. Sire, P. G. of Concorde Lodge, No. 43, New York. The following Officers were installed: Laurent Vincent Lefebvre, N. G.; Marcel Hibert, V. G.; Eugene Omnes, R. Sec.; Honorè Dautreleau, P. Sec.; Henry Rousselet, T. July 14th, 1887, the Lodge numbered 94 members, with twelve applications pending. It was intended, as soon as the membership reached one hundred members, to open Lodge No. 2.

—THE utmost care has been taken to obtain correct dates of the institution of the Bodies mentioned in this chapter. The Journals of the Grand Lodge of the United States, of Subordinate Grand Lodges and Grand Encampments, returns of institution, letters, reports, and, indeed, all sources of information accessible, embracing many thousand pages of printed and written documents, have been carefully examined to procure the desired knowledge. In many instances very conflicting statements have been encountered, and from the many almost similar cases, the following are cited as examples of the difficulties that were presented at almost every step: The date of institution of a Grand Lodge is given in the Journal of the Grand Lodge of the United States; in the printed proceedings of the State Grand Lodge a different date was found; in a report of one of its Grand Master's another, and in an address by the Grand Secretary of the State Grand Lodge still another day of institution is stated. Thus we have four different times, all, presumably, by the best authority, from which to select. In another case the Instituting Officer reported January as the time, while on the Seal of the Body the date of institution is named as in September of the previous year. Another instance may be mentioned: A Grand Body, having had three Seals made (at different times), three different dates are given for the institution of the Body. The earlier the organization, the greater, generally, has been the difficulty in obtaining correct information. In the printed reports of the Traveling Agent, Bro. Wildey, it will be found that, with few exceptions, he stated the facts of the institutions, but did not mention the days on which he organized the Bodies, and it may be well to remark that manuscript copies of his reports cannot be found in the archives of the Sovereign Grand Lodge. In all instances, when the reports of Instituting Officers could be found, they have been accepted as authority. One great error in this connection appears to have occurred by well-meaning brethren substituting the day of the meeting usually held preliminary to the organization, for the time of the actual institution of the Body.

The orthography of proper names has also been a perplexing impediment in the researches deemed necessary. In the Journals of the Order, in its infancy, very little attention appears to have been given to printing names correctly. Reports, petitions, cards, and letters, have been carefully scrutinized to obtain correct information on this subject, and thus material changes in names, as they appear in the printed Journals, will be found in this chapter, it having been assumed that the autographs were right.

It seems scarcely necessary to say that the determination to present the foregoing sketch of Grand Jurisdictions in as correct a shape as possible, has been accomplished by a great amount of research and labor, hour after hour having been devoted to the pursuit of facts that, when acquired, a few minutes were sufficient to place on paper.

CHAPTER IV.

THE ENCAMPMENT BRANCH OF THE ORDER.

By J. Fletcher Williams, P. G. M., of Minnesota.

THE Encampment Branch of our Order, as the newly made Patriarch finds it at the present day, with its well-matured and strong organization, its fascinating and impressive Ritual, and its perfectly organized system of laws and usages, is vastly different from the crude and fragmentary institution which the founders of our Order in America were experimenting with some sixty, or more, years ago. In fact, from that embryotic state, it has, by a slow, but steady system of evolution, developed into its present proud maturity, perfection and strength.

The Encampment, as such, or even the Patriarchal Degrees, were quite unknown and unthought of, at the period when our Order was struggling into existence in Baltimore, in 1819. Wildey and his coadjutors, in their little meetings, knew nothing but the three original Degrees received from England: 1. The White. 2. The Blue. 3. The Scarlet. And there appears to have been no others in the printed Ritual of the Manchester Unity, as late as 1824. In 1820 the "Covenant" and "Remembrance" Degrees were added to the structure in America, and were taken by Bro. Wildey to England in 1826.

The first mention we find of what is now known as an Encampment Degree is in the Journal of the Grand Lodge of Maryland and of the United States, February 22d, 1821, where it is recorded: "Past Grand Larkam having been duly admitted to membership, the Golden Rule Degree was conferred on five Past Grands." This Degree had recently been constructed, and communicated to the head of the

American Order, and it became, thereafter, a part of the
Ritual of the American Lodges. The Degree is also men-
tioned in the records of 1822, 1823 and 1824, as the Fourth
Degree.

At the session of the Grand Lodge, March 30th, 1825, it
was

Ordered, That the Grand Lodge be informed that there is a color on their
Charter for a Degree, which they have not received, and that it will be forwarded as soon as possible.

A foot note, on page 76 Journal, states:

The Degree here alluded to was the Royal Purple. It had been but
recently received, and owing to the want of the appropriate Lectures, was at
the time known only to G. M. Wildey and D. G. M. Scotchburn, of Maryland.

The two foregoing Degrees seem to have become at once,
a secure part of the Ritual in America, as, April 25th, 1826,
an amendment was adopted to the Constitution of the Grand
Lodge of the United States, providing that the fee for "a
State Grand Charter, together with the G. R. and R. P., or
Fifth, Degrees, be charged at $20." At the same session it is
recorded, "the Patriarchal Degree having been received
from England," etc. This Degree was acquired in England
by Past Grand McCormick, of Maryland, and by him communicated to the American Lodges. "This Degree, (says
Ridgely), completed the Superior Degrees of the Order, and
though last in order of time, was put first in the Encampment Work."

The above Degree, and in fact all the Degrees of the
Order were then very crude and imperfect. The Subordinate Lodge Degrees had printed Lectures at that time,
but we infer, from some facts on record, that the Patriarchal
Degrees did not have this advantage for some time after
they were worked in this country, for it was not until 1826
that the Grand Lodge of Maryland ordered the Patriarchal
Degree to be printed. Meantime the Lectures may have
been delivered in a sort of extempore manner, or possibly
read from manuscript. But the Work was undoubtedly very
crude, and perhaps rude. The Ceremonies of the Degrees,
as conferred at that time, were very different from those in
the present Ritual and not much exists of the originals,

except the names. Three revisions, since, in 1835, 1845 and 1880, have clothed what was then a mere fragment, or skeleton, with beauty and solemnity.

Having thus given the genealogy of the Patriarchal Branch, let us now briefly glance at the separate history of each Degree, in the order we find them.

THE GOLDEN RULE DEGREE.

The records show that on the organization of the Grand Lodge of Maryland and of the United States, February 22d, 1821, this Degree was conferred on five Past Grands, who, with Grand Master Wildey, composed the Body at this session, and a resolution was adopted: "That each member pay to the Grand Lodge *seventy-five cents* for the Golden Rule Degree." The Degree was also conferred February 22d, May 22d, August 22d, November 22d, 1822; February 22d, May 18th, August 22d, November 22d, 1823; February 22d, August 23d, November 22d, 1824, on members on their admission to the Grand Lodge, after being elected to receive the Degree. August 22d, 1822, it was "*Resolved*, That the sum of *one dollar* be charged for the Golden Rule Degree," and November 22d, 1823, "that the election to the Fourth (G. R.) Degree shall be by ballot."

Ridgely records that at the time of its introduction (1821) the Degree was "a barren sketch, without drapery." It was supposed to have taught the Golden Rule enunciated by the founder of the Christian Church, with little but a Sign and Password. It had no Lecture, but whatever its tangible substance was, its teachings must have been regarded as valuable, since Article 7 of the Constitution of the Grand Lodge of Maryland and of the United States adopted in 1821, required that it be "read every quarter," in the Grand Lodge; and in 1826, the Grand Lodge of Maryland "ordered, that the Fourth (G. R.) Degree be read." (It had probably by this time been printed—or the printing ordered, at least.) It is safe to say, that this Degree was, from the start, a grand success. The lessons which it teaches are of the sublimest nature, and the ceremonies by which they are impressed are so pertinent and attractive that in all the years following its adoption, the Golden Rule has generally been spoken of, by intelligent Odd Fellows, as the finest Degree of the Order.

THE ROYAL PURPLE DEGREE.

The Royal Purple Degree was designated, on its introduction, to the Grand Lodge of the United States in 1825, as the " Fifth Degree," and very properly, too, as it followed chronologically after the Golden Rule Degree, which appears on the records as the " Fourth." It was subsequently known as the " Past Grand's Degree," then the " Mazarine Blue Degree," afterwards "the Purple," and finally the " Royal Purple.", Bro. Ridgely, who became an active member soon after this date, and knew intimately all, or nearly all, the founders of the Order in Maryland, says it is undoubtedly an American production. By whom it was written, has not been ascertained. It was, at the time, attributed by some to Wildey, perhaps because he was the first to introduce and confer it. But Wildey certainly could not have written its Lecture, because he did not possess the education and literary skill to produce it. The Degree was well received, and soon became firmly established.

THE PATRIARCHAL DEGREE.

About the same time that our American brethren were clothing the Royal Purple Degree with some drapery worthy of it, (1825) a new Degree was being prepared by a Bro. Smith, at Wigan, England. He submitted this work to a committee of the Manchester Unity there, and it was approved and adopted. The summer of the same year, Past Grand McCormick, of Maryland, visited England, and received the Degree. Returning to America, he imparted it to the Grand Lodge of the United States, September 25th, 1825, and on the 18th of October it was communicated to the Grand Lodge of Maryland. In 1826 the Grand Lodges of Pennsylvania, New York, and Massachusetts, were invested with it.

Thus, we find the Order in America, in 1825, in posses-sion of these three Degrees, as yet, imperfect, fragmen-tary, and having no place in a standard Ritual. But their field, at best, was a limited one. They could only be conferred on the few Past Grands who might secure admit-tance into the Grand Lodges, at their sessions. What then, were the prospects for the new Degrees? In 1825, there were only four Grand Lodges under the jurisdiction of the Grand Lodge of the United States, with a total of *nine* Sub-ordinate Lodges, and an aggregate membership of less than 500. Into such a narrow and unpromising field as this, the Patriarchal Degrees were launched; but brighter prospects appeared in the near future and they soon became a separate and, in some respects, an independent Branch of the Order.

Prior to this period, the word "Encampment" was prob-ably unknown in our Order. The first mention of the Encampment, as a special organization, is found in the rec-ords of the Grand Lodge of the United States, May 1st, 1828, being a report from the Grand Lodge of Maryland, which stated "that an Encampment of Patriarchs had been formed during the year, the establishment of which is considered a great improvement in the Order, as it will be the means of extending useful knowledge to brothers who have not become members of a Grand Lodge." This was a thing utterly without precedent in the usages of the Order. It had cer-tainly not been known in England, where, to this day, only the Subordinate Lodge confers all the Degrees known to the Order there.

Ridgely, the historian, speaking of this departure, in the Grand Lodge of Maryland, May 15th, 1827, said: "A novel and startling feature was proposed. This was, that a Lodge should be chartered for the sole purpose of conferring the Partriarchal, Golden Rule, and Royal Purple Degrees, and that the Grand Lodge should resign the right to confer them into the hands of the members of the proposed Body. These Degrees had heretofore been conferred only upon Past Grands, and that in the Body of the Grand Lodge itself.

The new Lodge was to confer them on members of the Fifth Degree."

The records of the Grand Lodge of Maryland show that, in accordance with the above views a petition was drawn up and presented to it, signed by a number of influential members, praying for such a Charter, and it was duly granted, May 15th, 1827. The new Body was known as "Encampment Lodge No 1." In 1830 it reported only 30 members. It is probable that it was first started simply as an experiment, but it was the beginning of a most important movement. After working for some months, the old Charter was recalled on account of its "being defective in orthography," and a new one was granted, dated January 16th, 1829, in which it is called an "Encampment of Patriarchs." It had also the power bestowed upon it "to grant Dispensations for opening an Encampment to all faithful Odd Fellows throughout the globe." It subsequently adopted as its name "Jerusalem Encampment No. 1."

Pennsylvania appears to have been the first jurisdiction to follow the lead of the Baltimore Patriarchs. September 29th, 1828, a petition from ten members of the Patriarchal Degree was presented to the Grand Lodge of that State for a Warrant "to form an Encampment of Patriarchs," which request was granted December 20th, and the Warrant issued, but no further steps seem to have been then taken. June 16th, 1829, however, the Grand Lodge of Pennsylvania resolved that it would "grant a Warrant for the opening of a Grand Encampment, and that the recommendation of said Grand Encampment shall be necessary, at all times, to all petitions that shall be offered to this Grand Lodge, for Warrants for Subordinate Encampments that may hereafter be applied for."

It is not improbable that the new institution was looked on with some doubt at first. Heretofore, the power to organize Encampments, had resided in the Grand Lodges; but these Degrees were "a new departure"—higher than the other Degrees of the Order, and those who were to receive them would, in a measure, be separated by a grander

rank in the brotherhood, from the very ones who had empowered them to exist. So new, and immature, was still
everything connected with the Encampment Branch, that
regulations to harmonize all conflicting authority and
interests, were necessary, if the new Branch was to succeed,
and these were slowly developed, as we shall see.

The Pennsylvania Grand Encampment, before mentioned, was organized June 19th, 1829, and conferred the
Degrees until a Subordinate was organized. August 13th,
1829, a petition for this purpose was received, and on the
16th the first Subordinate Encampment was opened in Philadelphia. This ultimately became Philadelphia No. 1, and
soon four others followed. In the Grand Lodge of the
United States in 1830, the Representative of Pennsylvania
reported that there was *working under the Grand Lodge*, a
Grand Encampment containing 10 members, and an Encampment subordinate to it, containing 80 contributing members."
In 1840, the Grand Lodge of Pennsylvania relinquished to
the Grand Lodge of the United States all jurisdiction over
the Encampment Branch, following the example of the
Grand Lodge of Maryland.

At the session of the Grand Lodge of the United States
in 1831, a Charter was granted for a Grand Encampment in
Maryland, the first Charter of this nature which that Body
had issued. It was instituted December 31st, 1831, but the
Grand Lodge of Maryland was still exercising its jurisdiction over the Encampment Branch in that State. However,
on January 17th, 1832, it "relinquished all the rights, if any,
the said Grand Lodge now possesses over Encampments in
this State." There were then two Subordinates in Maryland.

It soon became apparent that some supreme or central
head was necessary to control and manage the new Branch
of the Order, to ensure uniformity of Work, and decide all
questions arising. In 1833 the Grand Lodge of the United
States adopted an amended Constitution and By-Laws and
the second section of the latter provided for issuing Warrants to open Encampments in States, Districts or Territories
where a Grand Encampment had not been established. It had

further added to the importance and value of the Patriarchal
Degrees by declaring, in 1831, the Royal Purple Degree a
necessary qualification for Grand Representative.

In New York the Encampment Branch did not have
such smooth sailing as in the States above named. The
Grand Lodge of the United States had, in 1829, conferred on
the Grand Lodge of New York power to charter Subordinate Encampments, and it had so chartered one in Albany,
giving it the power, usual at that time, of chartering other
Encampments in that State. In 1834, certain brothers in New
York City petitioned the Grand Lodge of the United States
for a Charter for an Encampment. Notwithstanding the
By-Law adopted in 1833 this was declined on the ground
that the power to grant such a Charter, resided in the
Encampment in Albany, and application must be made to it.
The petitioners were not very willing to accept a Charter
from such a source, but seeing no other way, applied for,
and obtained a Dispensation. Not long after, the members of
the parent Encampment, having seceded from the authority
of the Grand Lodge of the United States, the power of chartering Encampments reverted to the latter Body, by recall
of the Charter of the Grand Lodge of New York, in 1837.
Then a new Charter was granted to Hebron Encampment,
No. 2, New York City. On the 18th day of August, 1839,
the Grand Encampment of New York was instituted and
became the supreme authority for the Encampment Branch
in said State.

An Encampment was opened in Massachusetts in 1829,
as reported by the Movable Committee, page 109, Journal,
which shared the reverses of the Order in that State, and it
was not until March 22d, 1844, that a Grand Encampment
was instituted.

While the foregoing details may not be interesting to
all readers, they are, in some sense, necessary to the com-
pleteness of this history, to show the difficulties and hindrances through which the Encampment Branch passed,
before becoming firmly established. Its growth, as may
well be supposed, was quite slow in the first two decades of

its existence. In 1834, the Grand Encampments of Maryland and Pennsylvania reported to the Grand Lodge of the United States, 2 Subordinates each. Other Subordinates, in care of that Body, were located in New York, New Jersey, Delaware, Ohio, and Louisiana, in all, 5. But from this period, largely due, probably, to the energetic and enthusiastic labors of Past Grand Sire Wildey, who traveled throughout most of the settled States, instituting Lodges and Encampments, it grew gratifyingly, and Grand Encampments were soon instituted in the following States: Kentucky and New York in 1839; Ohio in 1840; New Hampshire and Maine in 1845; District of Columbia and Canada. in 1846; Indiana, Georgia, Tennessee, North Carolina and Michigan, in 1847.

The first formal reports were for the year ending October, 1838, from the 13 Subordinates under the immediate jurisdiction of the Grand Lodge of the United States representing 414 members, but no reports were received from Grand Encampments until the session of 1840, when reports for the year ending September, 1839, were received from the Grand Encampments of Maryland and New York, the former having 5, the latter 2 Subordinates. Of the 22 Subordinates the reports from 16 exhibited 565 members.

The Revision of 1835, was an important step forward, for the Encampment Branch. That action did not materially change the construction of the Patriarchal Degrees, but added substance to them. The Order, and its personnel, had radically changed, since the days when Father Wildey and a small group of his countrymen, mostly mechanics in humble life, used to meet convivially in the upper room of a tavern, and there initiate and confer Degrees on the few applicants. Its capabilities as a great fraternal association had become patent to many thinking persons, and men of culture, education, and honorable position in society, were seeking membership, and demanding that its Ritual should be made a system of teaching the grand truths of human brotherhood more consonant with the intellectual wants of its membership.

Another move which also aided the growth of the Order, was the translation, in 1840, of the Encampment Ritual, into German, and at the same session a still further advance was made towards strengthening the Patriarchal Branch, by a proposition to give to Grand Encampments the same representation in the Grand Lodge of the United States, that Grand Lodges had at that time. The movement did not succeed at that session, but was renewed at the session of 1841, and adopted. Representatives from Grand Encampments took their seats for the first time at the session of 1842, when Maryland and New York delegates appeared, and it was an important era for the Patriarchal members, giving them, for the first time, a full representation, and an equal voice in the legislation for the Order.

In 1842, a still farther progress was made, by the adoption of the Grand Encampment Degree, a matter that had been agitated as early as the session of 1835. The Past Official Degrees of P. H. P. and P. C. P. were also adopted and promulgated, and were in force until September 20th, 1844, when they were withdrawn.

At the session of 1843, seven Grand Encampments were represented. Other important occurrences now claimed the attention of the brethren in this country. The disaffection between the Order in America, and that in England, had been gradually growing greater, for several years, and it now culminated in a complete and final separation and alienation by the adoption of the resolution on page 577 Journal.

THE REVISION OF 1845.—In 1846, the Revised Work which had been adopted at the session of the year previous, went into effect, thus giving the Order the beautiful Ritual which our older members recollect was in force from 1846 to 1881. But few now remain in active membership, who worked under the Patriarchal Ritual that was in use prior to the revision referred to, but these declare that the one adopted in 1845 was vastly superior to its predecessor, and the system of Patriarchal Degrees had now reached a consistency of beauty, solidity and interest, which was a great improvement on any previous attainment.

As was to be expected, the Encampment Branch at once took a rapid forward movement. In 1845 there were 146 Subordinate Encampments and 6,847 members. Five years later, (1850) there were 499 Subordinates and 19,722 members. And in 1855 there were reported 30 Grand Encampments, 630 Subordinates, and 23,081 members. But even in the midst of this prosperity the reefs were not far off.

Very many of the readers of this sketch can remember that, under the Ritual used from 1845 to 1881, the complaint was made by the membership, that the Subordinate Degrees lacked a certain element of dramatic interest, which the Encampment Degrees possessed. Members going through the five Lodge Degrees often felt surprised, and even disappointed, at their bareness. But on entering the Encampment (if they did not become discouraged before going thus far) they found their desire fully gratified. In time, this led many of the members to become somewhat dissatisfied with, and tired of the Lodge Work, where there was so little opportunity to display dramatic skill, and this feeling, perhaps, reacted eventually on the Order at large, retarding its zeal and activity. In seeking a cause for this, very many good and loyal Odd Fellows arrived at the conclusion that since the Encampment Degrees were said to be so interesting and beautiful, while the Subordinate Degrees were not, it would be a good move to dispense with the Patriarchal Branch, and attach its Degrees to the Subordinate Lodge.

The Mergement agitation then commenced in Grand Bodies, and in the periodicals of the Order, and for some years caused heated debates in the Grand Lodge of the United States, to some extent injuring and retarding the growth of the Encampment Branch, during that period, by filling the minds of the membership at large, with distrust of its permanency. The Mergement movement first makes its appearance on the records of that Body, by a petition from the Grand Encampment of Wisconsin, presented at the session of 1851, "to abolish Encampments." It promptly received a quietus, but a similar proposition made its appearance in 1853,

and this time with more support, but it was indefinitely postponed. In 1854, however, similar requests were received
from several Grand Bodies, and referred to the Legislative
Committee, who reported in favor of the measure, and
appended a resolution providing that a Special Committee
of five be appointed to prepare a plan of mergement, and
report at the next session. The report was tabled, but the
resolution was adopted, and the committee was appointed.
At the session of 1855, the committee reported, at length, a
plan to merge the two Branches, but for some reason the
Grand Lodge refused to consider it. (*See Journal, pages
2455–2458.*) Thus the movement went over to the session of
1856, when its friends opened the campaign early in the session, by a resolution authorizing the appointment of a committee of five "to report a revision of the Work and Lectures of
the Patriarchal and Subordinate Lodge Degrees,—abolishing
the Patriarchal as a separate and distinct Branch, and
merging the same in the Subordinate Lodges ; retaining the
same number of Degrees that now exist, but reducing them
as to length, and otherwise improving them, etc., and report
at the next session." After much earnest debate, the first
portion of the resolution, down to and including the word
"Degrees," where it first occurs, was adopted, and the rest
of it rejected. But the next day, when the Grand Lodge
was about to proceed to ballot for the Committee on
Revision, so provided for, the resolution was reconsidered,
and laid on the table.

The irrepressible conflict, however, was renewed in
1857, in the shape of resolutions from the Grand Lodge of
New York in favor of the proposal rejected at the previous
session, and they were referred to the Committee on the State
of the Order, who reported in favor of the general proposition,
and added a resolution that a Special Committee of five be
appointed, " with instructions to revise the entire Secret
Work, and report at the next session a plan for merging the
Degrees; and also report suitable Charges and Lectures
which would be appropriate after such merging." Much
debate ensued when this report was considered, and it was
finally indefinitely postponed.

This was almost the end of the mergement agitation—certainly in any definite form in the Grand Lodge of the United States. Some feeble references to it were made, now and then, and in 1874 a protest of the Grand Encampment of Pennsylvania against "Mergement," was presented, and will be found on pages 6223, 6224, Journal; and to dispose of this vexatious question for all time, the Grand Lodge of the United States declared:

"That the sole right and privilege to confer the several Encampment Degrees having been granted by this R. W. Grand Lodge to the several Grand Encampments in their respective jurisdictions, it is regarded as a solemn compact, that cannot be recalled or revoked by this Body, so long as the said Grand Encampments shall keep inviolate their obligations to this R. W. Grand Lodge," is but declaratory of the existing law found in the third Section of Article I. of the Constitution of this Grand Lodge; that this Grand Lodge has the power "to deprive such State, District, or Territorial Grand Bodies of their Charters, and annul their authority; *provided*, that such deprivation or annulment shall only be made for violation of the laws of this Grand Lodge."

Thus the advocates of "Mergement" learned that their plans could not be accomplished except by the voluntary surrender of all Encampment Charters.

Just when the benefit system was engrafted on the Encampment Branch, it is impossible to say. The first reports on the subject are found in the Journal of 1845, page 823. There are many members who believe that its adoption was unwise; that it was not necessary or in accordance with the original intention of the Patriarchal Branch; that the benefit system of the Lodge is sufficient for the wants of the membership in that direction, or should be made so, if not, and that attaching it to the Encampment Degrees, which were originally designed for more elevated enunciation and better promulgation of the principles of the Order, really injured the Encampments, rather than added to their strength.

THE UNIFORMED MOVEMENT is an interesting chapter in the history of the Patriarchal Branch, and the rise and development of the enterprise deserves consideration. For two or three years prior to 1870, there was a growing agitation in Encampments for the adoption of a Uniform, to be worn by Royal Purple members in street parades. It was urged, by its advocates, that other societies had such marching Regalia, and that, if the Odd Fellows did not also adopt one, our Order would lose ground in the competition, as men, who otherwise would join us, would be attracted elsewhere. Many conservative Odd Fellows warmly opposed the project, fearing that its adoption would appear as if we were simply aping other associations, the Knights Templar, for instance; and besides, the Odd Fellows were usually men of limited means, who could not afford the expense of such displays. It is known that some Encampments did adopt and wear the proposed Uniform, in advance of any specific authority, as we find that Grand Sire Farnsworth, under date of March 15th, 1870, issued a proclamation forbidding the wearing of "swords, chapeaux, gauntlets and so forth," and terming it "an innovation upon our system." At the session of 1870, the above fact was embodied by the Grand Sire, in a decision, that "chapeaux, crooks, swords and belts, and all military paraphernalia" not prescribed by law, "are accordingly inadmissible." This decision, being referred to the Committee, on the State of the Order, was approved by them, and the words "as Regalia" added to the words above quoted; but when the report came up for consideration, these words were stricken out, and the decision as presented was adopted. But the advocates of the Uniformed movement, were not to be baffled thus. At the same session, Representative Perkins, of Massachusetts, moved the following, which was referred to the Legislative Committee:

That Subordinate Encampments, when they appear in public, may wear such uniform style of head dress, as may be approved by the Grand Patriarch of the jurisdiction.

The committee recommended the adoption of the resolution, as it "would not be a violation of any law of the Order," and their report was adopted. This legislation was, in fact, the entering of the wedge, and was the first step towards the complete legalization of the Uniform. At the session of 1871, Grand Sire Stuart reported:

Under this legislation, authority has been claimed, and exercised, to wear in procession, the very specific costume, to wit: chapeaux, crooks, swords, and belts, and military paraphernalia, which the Grand Lodge had already declared to be *Regalia*, and as such, inadmissible." He further stated, that having been called on for an opinion, he had "replied that such a claim was wholly unwarranted." Finding that it was intended to wear the forbidden Uniform, despite his prohibition, the Grand Sire issued a proclamation officially declaring "such practice to be wholly illegal and improper," etc. That portion of the Grand Sire's report was referred to a Special Committee, who reported, concurring in the views of the Grand Sire, and recommending their approval. The committee further gave it as their opinion "that the wearing of chapeaux, swords, belts, and gauntlets, by Odd Fellows in public processions * * *. was a flagrant violation of law," etc., and hoped the opinions of the Grand Lodge, as indicated, would be sufficient "to put down, at once, everything like insubordination and disobedience to our laws," etc.. This report was considered by the Grand Lodge on a subsequent day, and the word "chapeaux" sticken out, and the report was then adopted. Nothing further seems to have been done, until the session of 1872, when Representative Rand, of Massachusetts, moved the following:

Whereas; The wearing of a uniform style of dress, on occasions of street parades, by the Encampments of several jurisdictions, has proved a great success in securing membership, inspiring interest, and adding largely to the financial operations of this Branch of our Order; therefore, *Resolved*, That Encampments be permitted to wear such style of street Uniforms, on parade, as may be sanctioned by the Grand Encampments of their respective jurisdictions.

The resolution was referred to a Special Committee, which reported, recommending the adoption of a resolution "that Encampments be permitted to wear such style of street Uniform, on parade, as may be sanctioned by the Grand Encampments of their respective jurisdictions," etc. The report was adopted, and thus the Uniformed movement was an assured fact.

At the session of 1873, the proceeding of the Grand Encampment of Missouri in favor of the adoption of "a uniform parade dress for the entire Body of Patriarchs," was presented. The committee to whom it was referred, reported that "the matter is properly committed to the State jurisdictions"; and regarded the proposed legislation as inexpedient; in which views the Grand Lodge concurred. During the same session, however, a resolution was adopted, ordering the appointment of a Special Committee of five, "whose duty it shall be to report to this Grand Body, at its next session, a suitable street Uniform, which may be used by Subordinate Lodges and Encampments on parade, in order that street Uniforms be the same in all jurisdictions." The committee was accordingly appointed, and reported, at the session of 1874, "the Uniform of the Patriarchal Branch of the Order to be worn on public occasions," and the report was adopted.

The subject of a Degree for Uniformed Patriarchs, began to be agitated soon after the foregoing action. It was not, however, until 1879 that it assumed a tangible form. At the session that year, a Special Committee on the Patriarchal Branch, reported against the creation of such a Degree, on the ground that it would be impracticable; which report was adopted. It was enacted, however, that Uniformed Patriarchs may make rules for their own government. At the session of 1881, the demand for a special Degree became stronger. Several jurisdictions had directly asked for it, by resolution, and the subject was referred to the Committee on the Patriarchal Branch, which recommended that a Special Committee of five be appointed to prepare and report, at the next session, "a Degree suitable and appropriate for the purposes desired," etc. This report was adopted, and the committee was appointed, with the proviso that the adoption of the resolutions "shall in no way commit the Grand Lodge to the adoption of a Degree for Uniformed Patriarchs, nor shall any expense be incurred for the production of the said Degree, by this Grand Lodge." At the session of 1882, the Degree for Uniformed

Patriarchs was reported by the above committee, and adopted by the Sovereign Grand Lodge, by the decisive vote of 119 yeas, 22 nays; together with other provisions necessary, and the entire Uniformed portion of the Encampments was thus got into complete working order. It had a very good measure of success, and at the session of 1884 the Grand Secretary reported that the returns to July 1st, 1884, exhibited 98 Uniformed Degree Camps as chartered and in working order, with 2,607 members, and that reports had not been received from seventeen jurisdictions, in which Camps had been organized.

About this period, a very anomalous state of things occurred, which, for several years, was the occasion of much controversy in the Order. Some time in 1881, certain Odd Fellows in Wisconsin, who had been ardent advocates of a Degree for Uniformed Patriarchs, addressed circulars to members in other localities, asking them to become members of an organization, or secret society, called " *The Patriarchal Circle.*" At the session of the Sovereign Grand Lodge, September, 1881, Grand Sire Glenn, in his report, thus referred to the matter:

A short time since a circular, under the caption "Supreme Temple—Patriarchal Circle, Milwaukee, Wisconsin," and signed by Lawrence Demmer, Secretary, etc., was forwarded to me from a western jurisdiction. This circular, as you will perceive by the copy herewith submitted, seeks to enlist members of the Order in the establishment and propagation of "new Degrees for Uniformed Patriarchs." Believing that the brothers engaged in this "new Work," however laudable the motives that prompted them, were treading upon debatable, if not forbidden, ground, I deem it my duty to bring the matter to the attention of the Sovereign Grand Lodge, in order that you may, if in your judgment it be necessary, take proper action on the subject.

The Committee on the Patriarchal Branch, to whom the subject was referred, reported that they had considered the matter and made it the substance of another report, meaning the one providing for the appointment of a committee to prepare a Degree, as heretofore stated. No further mention of the matter was made at this session.

In 1882, Grand Sire Glenn again called attention to the Patriarchal Circle, and the subject was referred to a Special

Committee, which reported that the organization referred to, was unlawful, and "that the Grand Sire be requested to issue a circular letter to the Encampment Branch of the Order, calling attention to the adoption of the Degree for Uniformed Patriarchs, and advising of the impropriety of members forming organizations outside of the Order," etc. Accordingly, on the 13th day of October, 1882, Grand Sire Leech issued his proclamation reciting the action of the Sovereign Grand Lodge, and expressing the opinion that the brotherhood would at once comply with the supreme law. In this he was disappointed, and on the 10th day of April, 1883, felt compelled to issue another proclamation, warning the members to desist from their contempt and defiance of the legislation of the Grand Lodge, "under the penalty presented for a violation of the laws and regulations of the Order in that behalf."

At the session of 1883, the Grand Sire reported that his proclamation had produced little, or no effect, on those violating the law, etc. The subject was referred to a Special Committee, which presented a lengthy report, (to be found on pages 9361, 9362, 9363, Journal) submitting resolutions, approving the action of the Grand Sire; requiring Subordinate Lodges to bring to trial, and, if convicted, expel any of its members "who shall hereafter retain membership in, or become a member of, any secret organization not subordinate to this Grand Body, which shall have adopted or appropriated to its own use the Uniform, Regalia, Emblems, Name, Titles, Mottoes or Initials of this Order, or any part of them ; or in which qualification for membership is based upon the applicant's standing in this Order; or in which the applicant is required to obligate himself to prefer said organization, or any member thereof, at the expense of this Order or any of its members." The report was adopted, with the provision that the resolutions should take effect on the 1st of January, 1884.

When the Sovereign Grand Lodge assembled in 1884, Grand Sire Leech reported that the enactment of the year previous had not been obeyed, and that the members of the

Patriarchal Circle were still continuing their unlawful work. Believing in a trial of some "heroic remedy," Representative Lawrence, of Massachusetts introduced resolutions providing "that no person shall hereafter be initiated into this Order, or installed into any official position whatever," unless he made an affirmation that he was not at the time a member of the Circle, and would not become such, during his membership in the I. O. O. F. This resolution was referred to the Committee on the Patriarchal Branch of the Order, who made thereon a lengthy report recommending the adoption of Representative Lawrence's resolution, or one similar, and re-enacting and re-affirming the legislation of 1883. The report was adopted. Thus the action had at the session of 1883 was reasserted and strengthened at the session of 1884, and again, in 1885. Grand Sire Garey, at the latter session, reported that the legislation hitherto had, "has been utterly inoperative and of no effect." The correspondence on this subject will be found on pages 9870 to 9876 Journal. The Committee on the Judiciary reported, recommending prompt and energetic measures to terminate the membership of every Odd Fellow who might also be a member of the Patriarchal Circle. The resolutions proposed by them, required that after January 1, 1886, any Odd Fellow who should retain his membership in the Patriarchal Circle, should be expelled from his Lodge, and the Grand Sire was clothed, during the recess, with all the power and authority of the Sovereign Grand Lodge to prevent the members of this Order remaining in, or becoming members of the Patriarchal Circle, and to see that this demand was observed, under forfeiture of the Charters of Grand Bodies neglecting or refusing, to compel their Subordinates to obey the law. Also, that every Grand Representative, before entering on his duties should subscribe an affirmation that he is not now, and was not at the time of his election a member of the Patriarchal Circle. This report was adopted by the Grand Lodge. November 10th, 1885, Grand Sire Garey issued a proclamation to Grand Masters, directing them to enforce the order of the Sovereign Grand Lodge, and giving notice of his determination "to execute the law whenever the facts shall justify me in so doing." The order was complied with in most jurisdictions; many trials of individual members took place, with varying results, and a few Charters were taken away. At the session of 1886, Grand Sire Garey, in his report, stated that he "was confident that the moral effect of last year's action would alone go far towards settling the whole difficulty," and expressed the opinion "that the Patriarchal Circle will no longer be a factor to be used to embarrass any part of our work."

THE PATRIARCHS MILITANT.

At the session of 1883, a resolution was adopted, referring to the Committee on the Patriarchal Branch, the duty of reporting at the next session a more suitable name for the Uniformed Degree. The Committee reported at the session of 1884, recommending that the entire subject of the Uniformed Degree, and all the legislation heretofore adopted in relation thereto, be confided to a Select Committee of three, who should carefully consider the matter, "ascertain what changes, revisions, alterations, amendments and legislation may be necessary in order to make the Degree as satisfactory and effective as possible, and report the same at the next session." This report was adopted, and the Grand Sire appointed as the committee: Reps. Albin, of New Hampshire; Underwood, of Kentucky; Stevens, of Minnesota. At the session of 1885, the committee reported, at length, a revised Degree, to be called "The Patriarchs Militant," the members of which were to be termed "Chevaliers." The Degree was adopted, and virtually superseded the previous "Uniformed Camp Degree," attaining a popularity that assures its success and proves its inherent merits.

PRESENT CONDITION OF THE PATRIARCHAL BRANCH.

After reading the history of the Patriarchal Branch, as detailed in the preceding pages, and of its early struggles and slow development, from the rude germ of its being, through years of growth and expansion, to its present condition, the report of Theo. A. Ross, Grand Secretary of the S. G. Lodge, exhibiting the Encampment statistics for the year 1886, forms a fitting finale to the record:

December 31st, 1886, number of members, 96,796; number of Subordinate Encampments, 1,996; paid for relief of Patriarchs, $166,454.02; paid for relief of widowed families, $5,056.19; paid for burying the dead, $32,943.32; paid for special cases of relief, $4,161.39; total relief granted in 1886, $208,614.92; total receipts, $496,268.05. September 1st, 1887, there were 462 Cantons, and 15,259 members, (Chevaliers) in the Patriarchs Militant Branch.

SYNOPSIS OF THE PATRIARCHAL DEGREES.

Patriarchal Degree: In the midst of life, such as we find it around us in modern days, with much that is fictitious and misleading, it is profitable to study the simple and quiet lives of the Patriarchs of old. They dwelt mostly in tents, and subsisted by raising flocks and herds. They had many virtues, that have almost disappeared from society, as it is constituted at the present day. They cultivated, to an eminent degree, the duty of hospitality, giving bread and salt to the wayfarer and stranger, after being satisfied, however, that he was not an enemy in disguise, but a true and honest man. They had also a simple but thorough trust in God. Their virtues, and pure, peaceable, honest lives are well narrated in the sacred Scriptures. In entering their country, you are like a pilgrim crossing the plain, or wilderness of Paran, in which you may meet trials that will test your faith and sincerity. A guide is needed, to vouch for your character and good intentions. If challenged, by those you meet, and who are suspicious of you, it is always the best policy to tell the truth; that you are simple herdsmen, desiring to find employment, and ultimately to become Patriarchs. Let us approach the tents of these pastoral chieftains at Beersheba, and see them. Perhaps Abraham, their Sheik, is here. Abraham was one of the most noted of the Patriarchs of old, whose faith was severely tried by God, being commanded by Him to sacrifice his son, Isaac. But the sacrifice was not completed, because Abraham had shown his faith and trust in God, by his willingness to obey him implicitly. In becoming a herdsman, you must use the Crook, the implement of that vocation. It was used by the Patriarchs of old, and we now seek to revive their simplicity and purity, and thus prepare the way for the universal brotherhood.

Golden Rule Degree: This Degree is devoted to the principal of toleration. It teaches that we must permit others to think and act according to their convictions of duty. Mankind is so constituted that it is impossible that all should think alike. Look around you. You will see that the great human family is composed of numerous races, each differing from the others, in language, religion, complexion, and customs. Many of them are so degraded and ignorant, that they are ever ready to sacrifice those who differ with them. But no brave, true man should shrink from avowing his sentiments and principles, through fear of others, even though the sword, or rack, or dungeon should await him. The teachings of Odd Fellowship, however, if extended over the world, would do away with such intolerance, and all men would become brothers, and all the races of earth would bow before the common altar of our Order. The Golden Rule would then be practiced by all men, and many, if not all, the wrongs of society would cease. As Odd Fellows, therefore, it is our duty to labor for the coming of that era, when the weapons of war shall be changed into the implements of peace, and Love shall sway all hearts.

Royal Purple Degree: All mankind appear to have a common feeling, that ultimate rest is the natural sequel of the turmoil of life, and are certain that repose cannot be had in this world. Life is a course of temptations, and difficulties and struggles. Happy is he, who once entered on its turmoil, shall find a guide who can warn him to shun the dangers and pitfalls that have caused moral ruin to so many. It is like one journeying through a wilderness by night, amidst tangled thickets, rough rocks, over roaring streams or frail bridges, down dizzy steeps, groping his slow way though the blinding storm, lighted only by the lightning's flash. The siren voice of temptation is heard on one hand, and the horrid sounds of war on the other. But the poor pilgrim will, by courage and patience, at last reach the haven so longed for, where he will find light, and safety and repose. Here, we see around us, many Emblems, that teach lessons of the highest wisdom. May we all profit by their silent lectures.

CHAPTER V.

THE PATRIARCHS MILITANT.

Examined and approved by John C. Underwood, Commander of the Patriarchs Militant.

AT the session of 1870, the following resolution was adopted: "That Subordinate Encampments, when they appear in public, may wear such uniform style of head-dresses as may be approved by the Grand Patriarch of the jurisdiction." The Legislative Committee, in reporting the resolution for adoption, said that although "this Grand Lodge has decided that chapeaux, crooks, swords and belts, etc., are inadmissible as Regalia, we do not understand that it is proposed to adopt any head-dress as a Regalia of the Order, but simply to secure, in a given locality, a uniformity in that portion of the dress of persons appearing in public procession."

February 14th, 1871, Grand Sire Stuart issued the following proclamation:

To All Whom It May Concern:

WHEREAS, At the September session, 1870, of the R. W. Grand Lodge of the United States, held at the City of Baltimore, State of Maryland, it was formally resolved, "That no Regalia is legitimate, except that prescribed by law; chapeaux, crooks, swords and belts, and all military paraphernalia, not so prescribed, are accordingly inadmissible." And whereas, *nevertheless*, it has been known to me that in some jurisdictions, under color of a resolution which authorizes uniformity in head-dress, passed at the last session, chapeaux, swords and belts are being worn:

Now, therefore, I, Fred. D. Stuart, M. W. Grand Sire, by authority of law, do hereby officially declare such practice to be wholly illegal and improper, and do direct all Grand Patriarchs to take order in the premises accordingly.

The Grand Sire, in his report, expressed himself in favor of an improved Regalia for the Patriarchal Branch. He believed "that there was talent and genius enough in our Order to conceive and elaborate, with skill and taste, this idea, without borrowing from or poaching upon the Regalia of other societies." On his recommendation, the subject was referred to a Special Committee, whose report that the wearing of chapeaux, etc., "was a flagrant violation of law," etc., was amended by striking out the word "Chapeaux." The real need of a suitable street Uniform and the increasing demand from jurisdictions for it, induced the Grand Lodge, at the session of 1872, to adopt the following :

That Encampments be permitted to wear such style of street Uniform, on parade, as may be sanctioned by the Grand Encampments of their respective jurisdictions; but under no circumstances shall the funds of an Encampment be appropriated to meet any expense incurred thereby.

On Friday, September 22d, 1882, the Sovereign Grand Lodge adopted the Degree for Uniformed Patriarchs by a vote of 119 yeas to 22 nays. Grand Encampments were authorized to institute " Uniformed Degree Camps for Uniformed Patriarchs," at such places as they might deem proper, within their territorial limits. (*See Journal, page* 9,111.)

The Special Committee on the Degree was continued, to "report, at the next annual session, such changes, if any, that they may deem necessary to perfect the work of said Degree." At the session of 1883, the committee reported two resolutions relating to the Uniform and distinguishing Emblems to be worn as shoulder-straps. (*See Journal, pages* 9,367, 9,455.)

The following preamble and resolution were adopted :

WHEREAS, It is desirable to perpetuate and popularize the Uniformed Degree of the Patriarchal Branch of the Order, and inasmuch as the present name of Comrades of the Uniformed Degree Camp is not considered to be as distinctive or desirable as might be ; therefore,

Resolved, That the matter of selecting a more appropriate name for said Degree be referred to the Committee on the Patriarchal Branch of the Order, with instructions to report a suitable name for the same, at the next session of the Sovereign Grand Lodge.

That committee reported, at the session of 1884, the following resolution, which was adopted :

That a committee of three be appointed by the Grand Sire, with instructions to give the Uniformed Degree and all the legislation heretofore adopted in relation thereto, careful consideration, ascertain what changes, revisions, alterations, amendments, and legislation may be necessary in order to make the Degree as satisfactory and effective as possible, and report the same at the next session of this Grand Body for its consideration.

The Chair named as the committee :

Reps. Albin, of New Hampshire ; Underwood, of Kentucky ; Stevens, of Minnesota.

This Special Committee on Revision, etc., of the Uniformed Degree submitted a report which was amended and adopted. (*See Journal, pages* 10,108-10,129.)

This action was the introduction of what is now well-known as THE DEGREE OF PATRIARCHS MILITANT.

It was exemplified before the Grand Lodge by the Royal Purple Degree Odd Fellows, now known as Canton Underwood, No. 7, of Louisville, Kentucky. The Grand Lodge tendered them a vote of thanks "for the great aid which they gave to the committee, and for the soldierly, chivalrous and perfect manner in which they exemplified the Degree of Patriarchs Militant." The new Degree's fitness and adaptability for the purposes intended were at once apparent. It was seized with such eagerness and avidity that at the next session there was reported a membership of 12,073, distributed among 356 Cantons. Its success was assured from the first, and thereafter needed only such appropriate legislation as experience and the growing wants of the organization might require. At each session thereafter additional legislation has been enacted.

The report of the Commander of the Patriarchs Militant, Lieutenant-General Underwood, submitted to the Sovereign Grand Lodge, at the session of 1886, will be found in the Journal, pages 10,533-10,640, and the report of the Supervisory Committee on page 10,522.

At the session of 1887, the High Commission, consisting of the Grand Sire, Deputy Grand Sire, and the Chairman of the Committee on the Judiciary, submitted, with certain amendments, the action of the Military Council adopting thirty-one articles relating to the Patriarchs Militant organ-

JNO. 'C. UNDERWOOD,
Deputy Grant Sire and Commander of the Patriarchs Militant.

ization ; three Degrees, entitled, " The Grand Decoration of Chivalry, to be conferred by the Commander of Patriarchs Militant upon Chevaliers whom he shall select;" " The Decoration of Chivalry by the Commanders of Departments upon Chevaliers whom they may select and those recommended by Cantons," subject to conditions named in the organization, and " The Decoration of Chivalry for a Lady, to be conferred by the Commander of Patriarchs Militant upon Daughters of Rebekah selected by himself, and by Commanders of Departments upon such Daughters of Rebekah and other Ladies, who are the wives of Chevaliers, as may be recommended by Lodges of the Degree of Rebekah." (*See Journal, pages* 10,876–10,890.)

Representative John C. Underwood, of Kentucky, on the 26th day of September, 1885, was elected the first Lieutenant-General of the Patriarchs Militant.

The adoption of this Degree filled, at once, a void in the wants of the Order, and this was fully attested by its rapid and unexampled growth. In one short year it attained a condition of development not easily reached, except by *years* of active and unceasing effort. The display made by the Patriarchs Militant, in Boston, in 1886, exceeded the wildest dreams or hopes of the Order. It was a revelation as gratifying, as instructive, and was strikingly indicative of the latent powers and possibilities for good inherent in the Order, awaiting but the man and the hour to evolve them from darkness to light. Its influence upon the Order at large has been of marked benefit. The Commander, in his report, said in this connection:

> The great desideratum is growth and advancement, which I consider has been aided in an eminent degree by the Militant Branch, and therefore I unhesitatingly denominate the P. M. Degree an *adjunct* to the I. O. O. F., well calculated to materially aid its progress numerically, in wealth of finances, in the disciplining of its members, and in its benevolent, moral, chivalrous and honorable teachings, and as such it should be recognized.

The name " Patriarch Militant " is interpreted to mean " a peaceful ruler serving as a soldier," or " a just soldier." The motto of the just soldier is " universal justice " (*justitia universalis*), and his battle-cry, "peace or war" (*pax aut bellum*); peace if possible, war if necessary.

ORGANIZATION.

THE CANTON.—The unit of organization of this Military Degree is termed a "Canton," the familiar name of one of the political divisions of Switzerland.

To be eligible to membership in a Canton a brother must be a Patriarch, of the Royal Purple Degree, in good standing in his Lodge and Encampment.

A Canton consists of at least fifteen (15) members, who are called "Chevaliers," when addressed.

Fifteen Patriarchs, of the Royal Purple Degree, desiring to form a Canton, shall make application to the Lieutenant-General for a Warrant therefor, through the Department Commander, if there be one, and shall be recommended by the Grand Encampment of the jurisdiction in question, if in session at the time of application ; but if not, then to be certified to by the Board of Grand Officers, if there be such a Board, and if not, by the Grand Patriarch ; the certification in both the latter cases to be subject to the approval of the Grand Encampment when convened. All Warrants are issued in the name of the Sovereign Grand Lodge, signed by the Lieutenant-General, and approved, as above stated, by the Grand Encampment of the jurisdiction in which the Canton is located. Commanders of Departments must approve and cause all applications for Warrants to establish Cantons to be properly certified to, as to the rank and standing of the applicants, by the Board of Grand Officers, or by the Grand Patriarch, as the case may be. Should the Commanders of Departments disapprove applications, they must set forth fully, in writing, their reasons therefor.

They will mail applications for Warrants to establish Cantons, direct to the Commander P. M., without forwarding the same through military channels.

If the application be favorably received by the Lieutenant-General, he shall select a competent officer through the Department Commander, or the Grand Patriarch, to muster the applicants into the service and enroll their names upon the roster of the proposed Canton. As soon as this is done, the mustering officer shall hold an election for officers of the new Canton. Nominations shall be made and the several positions filled by ballot-vote, a majority vote of the number shall, in all cases, decide the election.

Applications for Warrants for Cantons, must be accompanied by a type-written or a printed roster of the Charter names, to avoid the difficulty of deciphering strange names.

The commissioned Officers of a Canton shall consist of a Captain, who shall be Commandant, a Lieutenant, and Ensign ; and the non-commissioned Officers shall be, a Clerk, an Accountant, a Standard-Bearer, a Guard, a Sentinel, and a Picket, who shall rank in the order named.

The first five shall be elected annually by the members of the Canton, and the remaining four shall be appointed by the Captain, and hold office at his will, for the period he serves as Commandant.

All Chevaliers in good standing, shall be eligible to office in their respective Cantons.

Cantons may, at their option, select suitable names, and shall be numbered in Departments according to the date of their organization.

An applicant for membership in a Canton need not belong to the jurisdiction in which the Canton is located, but shall furnish with application, a Certificate of membership and good standing in his Encampment, and it will require a three-fourths ball-vote of the members present, at the time the ballot is taken, to elect.

Cantons shall hold regular monthly meetings, or "cantonments," at which nine (9) members shall constitute a quorum. The law requires that Cantons shall have at least one regular monthly cantonment, but there is nothing to prevent them from having semi-monthly cantonments, or even regular cantonments every week.

On the night of the regular cantonment, next before the 26th of April of each year, an election shall be held in every Canton of Patriarchs Militant for Commandant and subordinate elective officers. The Clerks of the various Cantons shall hold said elections, and make report thereof to the Adjutant of the Battalion or Regiment, which report shall be attested by the retiring Commandant. The Clerks will make returns of said elections on seven sheets, blanks furnished for the purpose, and will also fill out seven blanks for the Report, showing the result of the muster and inspection of their Cantons, respectively, on the 26th of April of each year, and transmit as follows : One copy, marked " unofficial," direct to the Lieutenant-General; one copy direct to the Commander of the Department; five copies to the Adjutant of the Regiment to which the Canton is attached—one copy for regimental file, and four to be forwarded by the Adjutant through military channels: One, to the Assistant Adjutant-General of the Brigade; one, to the Assistant Adjutant-General of the Division ; one, to the Assistant Adjutant-General of the Army Corps ; and one to the Deputy Adjutant-General at Army Headquarters. For such clerical services, the Clerks should be paid a reasonable remuneration by the Cantons.

All returns of elections and appointments to office must be accompanied by the written acceptances of the Chevaliers so elected and appointed, together with check, or money order, in payment for commissions. On and after April the 26th, 1888, instead of the present fees charged for the Commissions and non-commissioned Warrants of Canton Officers, an annual Canton Tax shall be collected, of twelve dollars for each Canton, and for Grand Cantons at the rate of ten dollars for each Component.

It is necessary for a Canton to have a Patriarchs Militant Seal. Seals are among the list of " Supplies " and must be obtained as other supplies. Seals not approved will carry no force with them, and papers to which they are attached will not be regarded as official. It is a direct requirement of law, that all official documents emanating from Cantons, shall have an impression of the regulation Seal of the Patriarchs Militant stamped upon the paper, to make the communication official.

The Clerk is the Secretary and has charge of the Seal, the roster, minute book, order book, etc. It is his duty to make out all necessary reports, and, when attested by the Commandant, forward them to the Adjutant of the Battalion or Regiment to which the Canton may be attached.

The Accountant is the Treasurer of the Canton and should give satisfactory bond, approved by the Commandant of the Canton.

The Organic Regulations for Cantons are obligatory to the letter. The general By-Laws for Cantons may be modified to suit particular cases and localities, and in such instances, they must be forwarded to the Lieutenant-General for approval and will not go into effect until they are approved by such Commander.

The Organic Regulations and By-Laws for Cantons, must be ordered of the Chief of Supplies at Army Headquarters, by the Commandants of Cantons.

The annual parade shall be on the 26th day of April, but if this day should be Sunday, then on the preceding or following day.

Cantons shall not turn out for public display with less than twenty-seven (27) rank and file, but may parade upon occasions of the burial of a Chevalier, with less than the above minimum number ; and at other times by permission of the Commander of the Department. Each Canton, when on parade, shall carry the Patriarchs Militant Banner. For description of Banner, see Journal of 1885, pages 10,122, 10,123, and pages 239, 240 of the Report of the Lieutenant-General to the S.G.L., at Session of 1887. A Canton may be allowed to parade: Anywhere under Dispensation from the Lieutenant-General ; at any place within the bounds of the Army Corps to which it is attached, under Dispensation from the Corps Commander ; at any place within the bounds of the Grand Department or Division, in which it is located, under Dispensation of the Officer in command of the Grand Department, or the Major-General of the Division ; at any place within the bounds of the Department, in which it is located, under Dispensation from the Commander of the Department. A Canton cannot be compelled to turn out for parade or drill, except on the 26th of April. When ordered out at any other time, the Canton may determine, by vote, whether it will or will not turn out, and inform the Officer of its decision, without incurring the penalty of court-martial. When a Canton parades, it may also display the P. M. Colors in conjunction with the P. M. Banner. All bands of music with Cantons, for the time of inspection, review, and parade, will be under the control of the regimental Officer in command.

Chevaliers holding active membership in Cantons, will not be allowed to turn out in Uniform and parade with their Encampments in an Odd Fellows' procession where the Patriarchs Militant form a part. If they appear in Uniform, under the above circumstances, they must parade with their respective Cantons, unless excused by the Lieutenant-General.

Permission will be granted to Chevaliers, allowing them to parade with their Lodges and Encampments in processions embracing their Cantons, whenever sufficient reason for so doing shall be presented to the Lieutenant-General; but, in all cases where such permission shall be granted, the Chevaliers acting under said permits, must parade in ordinary Lodge or Encampment Regalia.

Cantons take rank in Battalions according to the age of organization, and are thrown into particular Battalions for local reasons.

The fiscal year ends on the 26th of April, and at the first meeting of the Canton thereafter, the annual report of the Officers shall be considered and audited, and after adoption and attestation as correct, by the Captain or Commandant, the Clerk shall make out duplicates and forward immediately to the Adjutant of the Regiment, so as to reach the Adjutant-General's office not later than July 1st at furthest, so that he may prepare his report to the Sovereign Grand Lodge.

Each Canton shall furnish its armory, necessary equipment, and defray all its requisite expenses.

The outfit for a newly opened Canton consists of Warrant, three Degree Books, proclamation, military blanks, etc., which are furnished at a cost of $20.00. The same outfits shall be furnished Cantons created from Bodies already organized, composed of Odd Fellows, who have attained the Royal Purple Degree, and who desire to be merged into the Patriarchs Militant, at actual cost, $10.00.

Each Canton operating under a Warrant, will be allowed to purchase three additional Rituals.

Cantons may elect honorary members, from Odd Fellows possessing the Royal Purple Degree, who shall not be required to purchase a dress Uniform, or turn out in parades or funerals. Honorary members are required to have fatigue caps, belts, and swords, in order that they may work their way into, and out of, cantonments, but they are not required to wear the above articles in order to sit in a Canton. Cantons are recommended to procure, and have accessible at the Out-posts, a limited supply of fatigue caps, belts, and swords for the use of honorary members and visiting Chevaliers generally, who may be without the necessary equipment to work the Degree.

Honorary members are required to pay their proportionate part toward defraying the expenses of the Canton; they may discuss, but will not be allowed to vote upon questions brought before the Canton.

A system of dues, but not of benefits, may be adopted by each Canton for military purposes.

The countersign, to be given at the outer door, shall be universal, and necessary to gain admission into a Canton. It shall be selected annually by the Grand Sire, and by him communicated to the Lieutenant-General, who shall promulgate it through the army. The Commandant of the Canton shall promulgate it at the muster and inspection of his command on the anniversary of the Order, the 26th of April, and the 25th or 27th, when the 26th falls on Sunday.

The right of appeal through proper military channels to the Sovereign Grand Lodge, by any Chevalier, from the action of his Canton, and by any Canton, from the action of any Officer, provided for by law, is expressly granted.

All Bodies desiring to join the Degree by merging into a Canton, must apply for the necessary military Warrant, Officers' Commissions, etc.

All applicants for Warrants to establish Cantons shall possess regulation Uniforms, and appear in the same upon the mustering of the Canton.

The Commander of Patriarchs Militant shall issue to Chevaliers of defunct Cantons, Certificates of honorable discharge upon application therefor, and the payment of the fee of one dollar ($1), which, together with certified evidence of good standing in a Subordinate Encampment, may be deposited with other Cantons, and, by means thereof, membership therein obtained.

The Cantons in a Department to which there has not been assigned a Commander, will report to the special Aid-de-Camp of the Lieutenant-General in such Department

The Lieutenant-General is clothed with the power to convene courts-martial for the purpose of investigating any and all acts perpetrated by a Chevalier, Canton, or other Organization of the P. M., and approve or reject the finding of the court-martial as he may deem proper.

Officers and members of the Sovereign Grand Lodge are entitled to visit Cantons, during the terms of their active membership in that Grand Body, regardless of membership in a Canton. They will be required to work their way into a cantonment, as any Chevalier.

Commandants of Cantons are to see that the history of the original organization of the Bodies from which the Cantons sprang, respectively, properly authenticated, is prepared and forwarded to the Lieutenant-General.

Hereafter in estimating the strength of Cantons in the roster of Battalions and Regiments, the active Chevaliers only, shall be reported as bearing swords, and the mention of honorary members shall be made as such.

Orders issued by superior Officers in plain violation of the law creating the Degree, are of no binding force upon Cantons or Chevaliers, and may be disregarded.

A Chevalier cannot be expelled from membership in a Canton without trial.

Chevaliers in Uniform will refrain from frequenting bar-rooms and places where intoxicating drinks are sold, and from any and all objectionable places, under penalty of a court martial, if reported.

All Officers' Commissions shall be made out in the Adjutant-General's Department, and fees charged and collected for the same, as follows: For Non-commissioned Warrants, $1.00; Ensign's Commission, $1.50; Lieutenant's Commission, $2.00; Captain's Commission, $3.00.

The Lieutenant-General may, at his discretion, cause the retiring Commandant of a Canton to muster his successor and other Officers-elect, and shall, at will, issue muster Commissions to that effect. The retiring Commandant of a Canton will be commissioned to install and muster his successor when practicable.

The installation and muster of the Officers of a Canton in public is admissible, where the Canton is properly uniformed and can make a creditable display. Permission to do so, must be obtained from the Commander of the Department, who is authorized to grant Dispensations for the purpose, when, in his judgment, the membership of the Canton, the condition of Uniforms, etc., will enable it to make such a display as will be creditable to the Degree. The public installing ceremony must be performed without the use of books.

Chevaliers of all grades, composing the rank and file of the Army, will appear in dress Uniform, as prescribed by law, when on inspection, parade, and review, without local Badge or Jewel, and with handkerchief and watch chain concealed.

Chevaliers will not be allowed to drop out of line, unless for unavoidable cause, and then only by permission of the Officers in command of their respective Cantons.

Chevaliers should not use their Uniforms, or loan them to others to be used for purposes other than those pertaining to the I. O. O. F., wherein the Military Branch is represented.

THE GRAND CANTON.—It is intended that the maximum number of members of a Canton shall be sixty-three (63), and if the overplus beyond this number amounts to twenty-seven (27), making ninety (90) members in all, then these twenty-seven members shall elect a second set of Officers—Captain, Lieutenant, Ensign, etc.,—thus making two Cantons, which shall have two separate organizations, but united together in one Body called a "Grand Canton." The senior Captain shall be Commandant of the Grand Canton. His Canton shall take precedence in parades, and he shall command when the Body is turned out as a Grand Canton.

Should the Grand Canton increase in membership in multiples of 63 and a fraction of 27, then each 63, and the overplus of 27 shall form a new Canton, as above, and this may continue until the Grand Canton comprises twelve (12) Cantons, which are to be organized into a Regiment, with a Colonel as Commandant, and the several Captains as Commandants of their respective Cantons.

No Grand Canton shall parade with less than twenty-seven Chevaliers, rank and file, in each Component Canton.

There shall be issued a special Warrant authorizing a Grand Canton, and, when desired, regular Warrants for each Canton comprising such Grand Canton.

In the election of a Commandant for a Grand Canton, when the Body comprises two or three Components, it is not obligatory for the Canton to promote Officers of any grade; it is within the power of the Body to elect Officers from the Chevaliers in the ranks, under the general elective franchise of the organization. Where two or more Captains are retained in office, the senior by virtue of past service, if acceptable to the Grand Canton, should be designated as the Commandant. Where there is no perceptible seniority between such Officers, the Canton, as a Body, must select and designate the Commandant from among the Captains; in fact, the Grand Canton possesses the inherent right to select its Commandant from among the Captains of its Components; and it is suggested that other Officers of the Grand Canton should be designated to act as Lieutenant and Ensign for Degree work, being selected according to their fitness for such floor positions.

Where the Commandant of a Grand Canton ranks as a Field Officer, he must be elected by the commissioned Officers of the various Components of the Grand Canton.

Components of Grand Cantons, holding and operating under separate Warrants, will be allowed to procure three additional Rituals.

THE BATTALION.—Four Cantons shall constitute a Battalion. When four Cantons shall have mustered into the Patriarchs Militant, the Adjutant-General shall, in the name of the Lieutenant-General, issue orders for the election of the Battalion Major, who shall command the Battalion, and be elected every two years by the commissioned Officers of the Cantons composing the command. There are therefore three Majors to a Regiment.

The Major of a separate Battalion shall appoint the Battalion Staff, after the manner of appointment of a Regimental Staff. Battalions, generally, are allowed regular Staffs, at the option of the Majors commanding.

STAFF OF A MAJOR COMMANDING A SEPARATE BATTALION.—An Adjutant, with rank of Lieutenant; Quartermaster, with rank of Lieutenant; Commissary, with rank of Lieutenant; Assistant Surgeon, with rank of Captain; Chaplain, with rank of Lieutenant.

NON-COMMISSIONED.—An Acting Quartermaster Sergeant; Acting Commissary Sergeant; Acting Color Sergeant; Acting Equipment Sergeant; Acting Hospital Sergeant.

The fee for a Major's Commission shall be $4.00.

When two Battalions shall have been mustered into service, the Adjutant-General shall, in the name of the Lieutenant-General, issue orders for the election of a Lieutenant-Colonel to command them.

The fee for a Lieutenant-Colonel's Commission shall be $4.50. A Lieutenant-Colonel may command from six to ten Cantons.

Battalions take rank in regimental line according to date of separate formation. Battalions form in regimental organization as follows: The first Battalion on the right of the line, the second Battalion next to the first, and the third next to the second; and when there is a fourth Battalion temporarily assigned to the Regiment, it will form next to the third, at left of the line. When the Battalions are formed for regimental drill and parade, the Staffs of the several Battalions will form as the right Canton of the Regiment; the commissioned Officers forming the first Platoon, and the non-commissioned Officers forming the second Platoon; the senior Adjutant will act as Captain and take command of the Canton; the 2nd Adjutant will act as Lieutenant, and the junior Adjutant as Ensign. All are to be attached to the 1st Battalion, and under command of the Major thereof.

Staffs of regular Battalions forming Regiments, are not mounted Officers, except by courtesy on special occasions, and are required at regimental drills and parades to form as the right Canton of the Regiment.

That the Officers, forming the file of the first Platoon of the right Canton, may be dressed uniformly, the Captains, Assistant Surgeons on the Staffs of regular Battalions, should, in uniforming, procure single-breasted coats. The Officers constituting the Staffs of regular Battalions, should equip with Line Officers' swords. The Uniforms and Equipments for Officers forming the Staffs of regular Battalions are similar to those for Officers forming the Staffs of separate Battalions and Regiments, except in the details mentioned in preceding regulations.

The Officers comprising the Staffs of regular Battalions should drill as Chevaliers, that they may be able to form a well-drilled Canton at regimental drills and parades.

Majors of separate Battalions shall audit the accounts of their Staff Officers, holding fiduciary trusts, and shall attest all reports of a financial nature, after they have been audited and found correct.

Full Battalions will be allowed to have bands of music at the option of the Colonels of their respective Regiments.

Battalion Colors must be massed with those of the Regiment.

THE REGIMENT.—A Regiment shall consist of twelve Cantons organized into three Battalions. When three Battalions or twelve Cantons shall have been mustered into service, the Adjutant-General shall, in the name of the Lieutenant-General, issue orders for the election of the Officers of the Regiment. The Colonel and Lieutenant-Colonel shall be elected every two years by the three Majors and other commissioned Officers of the Cantons composing the Regiment. The Colonel shall appoint the commissioned and non-commissioned Staff of the Regiment from the command, and any vacancies caused by such appointments, shall be regularly filled by election, or appointment, as may be necessary.

A Colonel may command from ten to sixteen Cantons.

The fee for a Colonel's Commission shall be $5.00; for a Regimental Staff Officer's Commission, $3.50.

STAFF OF A COLONEL COMMANDING A REGIMENT.—An Adjutant, with rank of Captain; Quartermaster, with rank of Captain; Commissary, with rank of Captain; Surgeon, with rank of Major; Assistant Surgeon, with rank of Captain; Chaplain, with rank of Captain; Banneret, with rank of Lieutenant.

NON-COMMISSIONED.—A Sergeant-Major; Quartermaster-Sergeant; Commissary-Sergeant; Color-Sergeant; Equipment-Sergeant; Hospital-Sergeant; Trumpeter.

Colonels of Regiments shall audit the accounts of their Staff Officers, holding fiduciary trusts, and shall attest all reports of a financial nature, after they have been audited and found to be correct.

Regiments take precedence in Brigade formations, according to dates of their Colonels' Commissions.

For description of Regimental Flag, see Journal of 1885, pages 10,536, 10,537, and page 241 of the Report of the Lieutenant-General to the S. G. L., at session of 1887.

THE BRIGADE.—Three Regiments shall form a Brigade. When three Regiments shall have been mustered into service, the Adjutant-General shall, in the name of the Lieutenant-General, issue orders for the election of the Officers of the Brigade.

A Brigadier shall be elected every three years by the Field Officers of the Brigade, and shall appoint the Brigade Staff from the command.

A Brigadier may command from two to four Regiments.

The fee for a Brigadier's Commission shall be $6.00; for Brigade Staff Officer's Commission, $4.00; for Aids' to Staff Brigadiers Commissions, $4.00.

STAFF OF A BRIGADIER, COMMANDING A BRIGADE.—Chief of Staff, a Lieutenant Colonel; Assistant Adjutant-General, with rank of Major; Assistant Inspector-General, with rank of Major; Assistant Quartermaster-General, with rank of Major; Assistant Commissary-General, with rank of Major; Assistant Chief of Equipment, with rank of Major; Assistant Surgeon-General, with rank of Major; Assistant Judge-Advocate-General, with rank of Major; Brigade Chaplain, with rank of Major; Banneret, with rank of Captain; Two Aids-de-Camp, each with rank of Captain.

Staff Brigadiers shall have one Aid-de-Camp each, with rank of Captain.

Staff Assistant Adjutant-General of a Brigade shall have an Assistant Adjutant-General, as Clerk, with rank of Captain.

Brigades shall take rank in line, in Division formation, by assignment of the Division Commander.

The Assistant Adjutant-General of a Brigade shall, when necessary, and when specially authorized so to do, hold an election for the Field Officers thereof, upon the following basis, and make return on seven sheets: The Line Officers of each Battalion voting for the Major of the Battalion; the Majors-elect and Line Officers voting for the Lieutenant-Colonel of the Regiment; or if the Regiment comprises four Battalions, the Majors-elect and Line Officers of each double Battalion voting for the Lieutenant-Colonel thereof; and the Lieutenant-Colonel (or Lieutenant-Colonels), Majors-elect, and Line Officers voting for the Colonel of the Regiment. He will make return upon blanks, file one copy, and forward: One copy, marked "unofficial," inclosing fees for Commissions, direct to the Lieutenant-General; one copy direct to the Commander of the Department; and, obtaining the approval of the Brigadier upon the four remaining copies, forward one to the Adjutant of the Regiment for file; three to the Assistant Adjutant-General of Division, who will obtain the approval of the Major-General, file one, and forward two to the Assistant Adjutant-General of the Corps, who will obtain the approval of the Corps Commander, file one, and forward the remaining copy to the Deputy Adjutant-General at Army Headquarters.

A Brigadier commanding a Brigade shall audit the accounts of his Staff Officers holding fiduciary trusts, and shall attest all reports of a financial nature, after they have been audited and found to be correct.

For a description of the Brigade Flag, see Journal of 1886, page 10,536, and page 241 of the Report of the Lieutenant-General to the S. G. L., at session of 1887.

THE DIVISION.—Three Brigades shall form a Division. When three Brigades shall have been mustered into service the Adjutant-General shall, in the name of the Lieutenant-General, issue orders for the election of a Major-General to command the Division.

A Major-General of Division shall be elected every four years by the Brigadiers and Colonels having commands within the Division, and shall appoint the Division Staff from the command.

A Major-General may command from two to four Brigades.

The fee for a Major-General's Commission shall be $10.00; for Major-General's, Heads' of Staff Departments Commissions, $10.00; for Division Staff Officer's Commission, $5.00.

The Major-General-elect, upon the reception of his Commission, will assume command of the Division to which he is assigned, appoint his Staff, and forward the names of Chevaliers nominated, inclosing their acceptances and fees for Commissions, that the nominations may be approved and the Commissions issue.

STAFF OF A MAJOR-GENERAL COMMANDING A DIVISION.—Chief of Staff, a Colonel; Assistant Adjutant-General, with rank of Lieutenant-Colonel; Assistant Inspector-General, with rank of Lieutenant-Colonel; Assistant Quartermaster-General, with rank of Lieutenant-Colonel; Assistant Commissary-General, with rank of Lieutenant-Colonel; Assistant Chief of Equipment, with rank of Lieutenant-Colonel; Assistant Surgeon-General, with rank of Lieutenant-Colonel; Assistant Judge-Advocate-General, with rank of Lieutenant-Colonel; Division Chaplain, with rank of Lieutenant-Colonel; Banneret, with rank of Major; Three Aids-de-Camp, each with rank of Major.

Staff Major-Generals have two Aids-de-Camp, each with rank of Major.

Staff Assistant Adjutant-General of a Division shall have an Assistant Adjutant-General, as Clerk, with rank of Major.

Divisions take rank per order of the Lieutenant-General.

The Assistant Adjutant-General of a Division will hold and make return of the election held for a Brigadier, either at an "Assembly" of the Field Officers of the Battalions and Regiments constituting the Brigade, or from written proxy votes forwarded by the Officers of such grade from a distance, on blanks. He will fill out five sheets of official returns on blanks, file one copy, and forward: One copy, marked "unofficial," inclosing fees for Commissions, direct to the Lieutenant-General; one copy to the Assistant Adjutant-General of the Brigade, for file; two copies, approved by the Major-General of Division, to the Assistant Adjutant-General of the Army Corps, who will obtain the approval of the Corps Commander, file one, and forward the remaining copy to the Deputy Adjutant-General at Army Headquarters.

Officers in command of Battalions, Regiments, Brigades, and Divisions will be allowed to procure one copy of the Ritual each, for individual use.

Generals of Divisions shall audit the accounts of their Staff Officers holding fiduciary trusts, and shall attest all reports of a financial nature, after they have been audited and found to be correct.

For description of Division Flag, see Journal of 1886, page 10,536, and pages 241, 242 of the Report of the Lieutenant-General to the S. G. L., at session of 1887.

THE ARMY CORPS.—Two or more Divisions shall form an Army Corps.

The number of Army Corps, in the United States and Canada, is limited to four.

The Officer to be placed in command of an Army Corps shall be selected by the Commander of the Patriarchs Militant from the Generals in command of troops, and be commissioned Corps Commander with rank of Major-General. He shall appoint his Staff from the command.

STAFF OF A MAJOR-GENERAL COMMANDING AN ARMY CORPS.—Chief of Staff, a Brigadier; Assistant Adjutant-General, with rank of Colonel; Assistant Inspector-General, with rank of Colonel; Assistant Quartermaster-General, with rank of Colonel; Assistant Commissary-General, with rank of Colonel; Assistant Chief of Equipment, with rank of Colonel; Assistant Surgeon-Gencral, with rank of Colonel; Assistant Judge-Advocate-General, with rank of Colonel; Assistant Chaplain-General, with rank of Colonel; Banneret, with rank of Lieutenant-Colonel; Four Aids-de-Camp, each with rank of Lieutenant-Colonel.

Staff Assistant Adjutant-General of an Army Corps shall have an Assistant Adjutant-General, as Clerk, with rank of Lieutenant-Colonel.

An Army Corps takes rank per order of the Lieutenant-General.

The Assistant Adjutant-General of an Army Corps will hold and make return of the election held for a Major-General, either at an "Assembly" of the Generals of Brigades and Colonels of Regiments, constituting the Division, or by written proxy votes, forwarded by Officers of such grades from a distance, on blanks. He will fill out four sheets of official returns on blanks, file one copy, and forward: One copy, marked "unofficial," inclosing fees for Commissions, direct to the Lieutenant-General; one copy to the Assistant Adjutant-General of the Division, for file; and, obtaining the approval of the Corps Commander, forward the remaining copy to the Deputy Adjutant-General at Army Headquarters.

Generals of Army Corps shall audit the accounts of their Staff Officers holding fiduciary trusts, and shall attest all reports of a financial nature, after they have been audited and found to be correct. Commanders of Army Corps will be allowed to procure a set of three Rituals for Headquarters' purposes.

For a description of the Army Corps Flag, see page 242, of the Report of the Lieutenant-General to the S. G. L., at session of 1887.

The Commanders of Battalions, Regiments, Brigades, Divisions, and Army Corps shall hold active membership in a Canton forming part of the command, except where for good and satisfactory reasons the Commander of P. M. shall deem proper to grant and issue a Dispensation to the contrary.

THE ARMY.—The Army shall embrace the entire rank and file of the Patriarchs Militant. The Grand Sire shall be *ex-officio* the Commander-in-Chief, and shall issue his instructions through the Lieutenant-General, who shall be the active Commander of the Army. He shall attain the office by regular promotion from Captain-General. His Commission shall be issued by the Grand Sire and attested by the Grand Secretary of the Sovereign Grand Lodge. All other Commissions shall be issued by authority of the Grand Sire, as the head of the Order, but shall be signed by the Lieutenant-General, as his active representative, and be attested by the Adjutant-General, Deputy Adjutant-General, or an Assistant Adjutant-General. He shall appoint the general Staff of the Army, and his Aids-de-Camp, and be the active Commander for three years. The Captain-General shall be elected every three years by the general Officers of the Army, and shall appoint his Aids-de-Camp. He shall succeed to the active command of the forces, with rank of Lieutenant-General, at the expiration of such three years term. He is entitled to three Aids-de-Camp, each with rank of Lieutenant-Colonel. The Grand Treasurer of the Sovereign Grand Lodge shall be *ex-officio* Quartermaster-General. All commissioned Staff appointments shall be for the period of office held by the appointing Officer.

STAFF OF THE LIEUTENANT-GENERAL, COMMANDER P. M.—A Captain-General, who shall be Chief of Staff of the Army; Adjutant-General, with rank of Major-General; Assistant Adjutant-General, with rank of Brigadier; Deputy Adjutant-General, with rank of Colonel; Inspector-General, with rank of Major-General; Quartermaster-General, who must be the Grand Treasurer of the Sovereign Grand Lodge, with rank of Major-General; Commissary-General, with rank of Major-General; Chief of Equipment, with rank of Major-General; Surgeon-General, with rank of Major-General; Judge-Advocate-General, with rank of Major-General; Chaplain-General, with rank of Major-General; Six Brigadiers, general Staff Corps; Such general Officers, whose terms of service have expired, as may be attached to the Staff of the Army by the Commander; Four Aids-de-Camp, each with rank of Colonel; A Banneret, with rank of Colonel; A Special Aid-de-Camp, with rank of Lieutenant-Colonel, for each Department, and by sanction of the acts of the Commander, additional Staff Officers of various Grades and Corps, during the introduction of the P. M. movement, etc.

The fee for the Lieutenant-General's Commission shall be $25; for the Captain-General's Commission, $15; for Aid's, on Staff of Lieutenant-General, Commission, $7; for Aid's, on Staff of Captain-General, Commission, $6.

For description of Commander's Flag, see Journal of 1886, page 10,535, and pages 242, 243 of the Report of the Lieutenant-General to the S. G. L., at session of 1887.

RANK AND PRECEDENCE—GRADE.—The Grand Sire *ex-officio* the Commander-in-Chief.

COMMISSIONED OFFICERS.—1. A Lieutenant-General, shall be in active command of the forces; 2. A Captain-General, shall be second in command and Chief of Staff; 3. A Major-General, shall command an Army Corps; 4. A Major-General, shall command a Division; 5. A Brigadier, shall command a Brigade; 6. A Colonel, shall command a Regiment; 7. A Lieutenant-Colonel, shall be second in command of a Regiment; 8. A Major, shall command a Battalion; 9. A Captain, shall be the Commandant of a Canton; 10. A Lieutenant, shall be second in command of a Canton; 11. An Ensign, shall be third in command of a Canton.

NON-COMMISSIONED OFFICERS.—1.A Sergeant-Major; 2. A Quartermaster-Sergeant; 3. A Commissary-Sergeant; 4. A Color-Sergeant; 5. An Equipment-Sergeant; 6. A Hospital-Sergeant; 7. A Trumpeter; 8. A Clerk; 9. An Accountant; 10. A Standard Bearer.

TURM OF HORSE.—The organization of a mounted command of *retired* officers, to be mainly used for escort duty, and the unit of which shall be designated a "Turm of Horse," shall be divided into two Troops and four Platoons, and consist, in maximum strength, of ninety-six Cavaliers and seven Officers. The Officers of such command shall consist of a Colonel, the Commandant; two Lieutenant-Colonels, in command of the first and second Troops; four Majors, in command of the first, second, third, and fourth Platoons; and the seven Officers shall have issued to them live Commissions designating their rank and command. The Turm of Horse shall be drilled in the simpler movements of the Patriarchs Militant Tactics, suitably changed and adapted for Cavaliers. Past Officers organized as a Turm of Horse, may hold membership in Cantons, regardless of location, and will not be required to turn out and drill, as Chevaliers in the line, with their Cantons; but will be required to attend practice and mounted drills of their Platoons, Troops, and the Turm of Horse to which they belong. Officers of a Turm of Horse, when mounted, shall carry lances resting in the stirrup-sockets and extending upwards, back of their right shoulders, and use swords only as arms; file Cavaliers, when mounted, will use swords or lances in obedience to orders.

DEPARTMENTS AND GRAND DEPARTMENTS.—The district organization of the forces constituting the military branch of the Order shall be by States, Territories, Provinces, etc., wherein there are, at the time, Grand Encampment jurisdictions of the I. O. O. F. All the Cantons within the limits of any such Grand Jurisdiction, shall be formed into a military command and be termed a Department. For perfecting the mobilization of the Army, the Lieutenant-General shall so combine the troops of the different Departments as to band together the Chevaliers of near and congenial jurisdictions in the organization of Regiments, Brigades, and Divisions. Where the troops of Departments are combined with those of other Departments in the formation of Brigades and Divisions, the combined Departments shall be designated as Grand Departments. Several Departments or Grand Departments, forming a general section of the country, will be denominated a Division.

There are, at present, five Divisions, two Grand Departments, and forty-five Departments: The Division of the North, composed of the following Departments: Maine, New Brunswick, New Hampshire, Quebec, and Vermont; The Division of the East, composed of Connecticut, Massachusetts, and Rhode Island; The Division of the Atlantic, composed of Columbia, Delaware, Manitoba, Maryland, New Jersey, New York, North Carolina, Ontario, Pennsylvania, and Virginia; The Division of the Ohio, composed of Alabama, Georgia, Indiana, Kentucky, Ohio, Tennessee, and West Virginia; The Division of the Lakes, composed of Dakota, Illinois, Iowa, Michigan, Minnesota, Montana, Nebraska, Wisconsin, and Wyoming; The Grand Department of the Mississippi, composed of Colorado, Kansas, Louisiana, Missouri, and Texas; The Grand Department of the Pacific, composed of Arizona, California, Nevada, Oregon, Utah, and Washington.

The following table exhibits the Departments, the number of Cantons and members in each Canton, at the end of the Patriarchs Militant Year, April 26th, 1887:

NAME OF DEPARTMENT.	Number of Cantons.	Number of Members.
Alabama	1	28
Arizona	1	27
California	21	761
Columbia	4	89
Connecticut	20	794
Colorado	8	240
Dakota	9	206
Delaware	1	36
Georgia	3	80
Illinois	34	1,042
Indiana	25	769
Iowa	17	456
Kansas	10	216
Kentucky	12	435
Louisiana	1	35
Maine	21	961
Manitoba	1	31
Maryland	2	67
Massachusetts	52	2,280
Michigan	26	646
Missouri	16	440
Minnesota	8	251
Montana	4	68
Nebraska	3	88
New Brunswick	1	19
New Hampshire	12	503
New Jersey	8	233
New York	26	878
Nevada	2	45
North Carolina	1	25
Ohio	54	1,661
Ontario	10	329
Oregon	1	26
Pennsylvania	19	575
Quebec	1	45
Rhode Island	9	366
Tennessee	1	27
Texas	3	79
Utah	1	29
Vermont	4	153
Virginia	2	63
Washington	1	25
West Virginia	1	23
Wisconsin	2	58
Wyoming	3	51
Totals	462	15,259

The Lieutenant-General estimated that the membership had increased from the above date to September 19th, 1887, when the Sovereign Grand Lodge met in annual session, and at that time approximated 18,000 or more Chevaliers.

The Army, at the present time, is composed of three Corps. The first Army Corps comprises the Divisions of the North and East; the second Army

Corps, the Divisions of the Atlantic and Ohio; the third Army Corps, the Division of the Lakes and Grand Department of the Mississippi.

MILITARY COUNCIL.—A Military Council, consisting of the Field and General Officers of the Army, shall be held annually, at least one week prior to the meeting of the Sovereign Grand Lodge. Such Body shall have the right to determine upon and proffer such legislation, relating to the Patriarchs Militant, as it may deem proper and expedient, and shall present the same to a High Commission consisting of the Grand Sire, Deputy Grand Sire, and Chairman of the Committee on the Judiciary of the Sovereign Grand Lodge. Such Commission shall report the legislation proposed, to the Sovereign Grand Lodge for its action; but this shall not preclude the Sovereign Grand Lodge from originating legislation for this Degree. The Lieutenant-General shall preside over the Military Council, and shall vote as a member, and in case of a tie, shall give another and a casting vote. When the Military Council is in session, the Lieutenant-General will occupy the principal chair, with an Aid on each side. The Captain-General will sit further to his left, and be accompanied by an Aid, and shall preside during a temporary absence of the Lieutenant-General. The Adjutant and Quartermaster-General shall both sit to the right of the presiding Officer, the Adjutant-General being nearest his station. An Officer of the Day, with Sentinel, shall have charge of the door. The members of the Military Council comprise all General Officers of the Army in active commission, regardless of Corps or Command, and the Field Officers of Battalions and Regiments. It is to the best interest of the Patriarchs Militant that the Military Council shall be convened during the summer months, and that the annual parade of the Army shall occur at the time and place selected by the Commander P. M. for holding the Council. As a general rule, to be followed in determining the points at which to convene the Military Council, the Commander P. M. should consider the accessibility of the location, its fitness for a parade and display occasion, and the possibility of making cheap excursion rates for the round trip, from the greatest number of points where P. M. troops are located. A Board of thirteen Officers shall be appointed by the Commander P. M. to draft rules for the government of the Military Council when in session, and present such general suggestions as they may deem important, and to the interest of the Degree and Army, and make report thereof, at the next annual session of the Military Council.

MISCELLANEOUS.—In the election for Field and General Officers, the Officers in command of troops, only, shall vote; the votes shall be of two classes, viz: *Oral*, upon a call of the roster, at an "Assembly" of Officers for any election, or by *sealed written proxy* forwarded to the Officer holding the election; an *oral* vote may be changed by the Officer casting it at any time prior to the announcement of the vote; a *written proxy* vote may be withdrawn, changed, and re-delivered at any time prior to the hour fixed for opening proxies; all elections shall be held under written orders, and a copy thereof shall be filed with the returns, and the *written proxies*, if any, shall be filed and forwarded to Army

Headquarters with the election returns; *personal* representatives or *telegraph* proxies shall not be legal.

Officers holding the following positions shall, when necessary, and when specially authorized so to do, hold elections as follows: The Assistant Adjutant-General of a Brigade, for the Field Officers thereof; the Assistant Adjutant-General of a Division, for the Brigadiers commanding Brigades therein; the Assistant Adjutant-General of a Corps, for the Generals of the Divisions therein.

Officers holding elections at "Assemblies," shall detail two Officers of the Assembly, who are entitled to vote, as tellers to distribute and collect ballots, and count the votes. General and Staff Officers shall not influence elections.

All elective offices shall be filled by nomination and ballot vote. A majority of the votes cast shall constitute an election. Vacancies shall be filled as in first elections, and for the unexpired term only.

At an election held for Field and General Officers, at an Assembly, by *sealed written proxies*, or jointly, a majority of the Officers entitled to vote should be represented, that the election shall be unquestionably legal.

All supplies whatsoever, except Rituals, will hereafter be furnished direct from Army Headquarters.

All Commissions shall date from the time of their acceptance.

Officers of the grade of Captain and upward, at the expiration of their Commissions, will be allowed to wear their Uniforms; but if they desire to wear the honorable chevron of office past, upon their sleeves, and have their names appear in the roster of retired Officers, they will make application for and obtain retired Commissions.

A majority vote shall determine all questions in every grade organization, and the presiding Officer (if of the command) shall vote as a member of the Body, and in case of a tie vote, shall also give the casting vote.

The Assistant Grand Secretary of the Sovereign Grand Lodge, shall be chief clerk to the Adjutant-General, until otherwise provided by the Military Council.

The Commanders of Departments, Grand Departments, Brigades, Divisions, Army Corps, and General Officers otherwise assigned, will forward to the Deputy Adjutant-General, at Army Headquarters, duplicates of all orders issued by them.

All official communications, of whatsoever nature, intended to reach Army Headquarters, must be forwarded through regular military channels, and other and unofficial communications forwarded direct, must be marked "unofficial," in the heading.

The Ritual, Tactics, Ceremony for Burial of a Chevalier, Ceremony for Laying Corner-stones of Public Edifices, Organic Regulations and general By-Laws for the government of Cantons are published in book and pamphlet form, and are part of the code of laws for Patriarchs Militant.

The following are the three principal Officers, together with the Chiefs of Department Corps : Commander-in-Chief, *ex-officio*, John H. White, Albion, New York; Lieutenant-General and active Commander, John C. Underwood, Covington, Kentucky; Captain-General and Chief of Staff, Franklin Ellis, Troy, Ohio; Adjutant-General, Oliver J. Semmes, Mobile, Alabama; Inspector-General, Francis E. Merriam, Boston, Massachusetts; Quartermaster-General, *ex-officio*, Isaac A. Sheppard, Philadelphia, Pennsylvania; Commissary-General, S. H. Kelsey, Atchison, Kansas; Chief of Equipment, James Pettibone, Cincinnati, Ohio; Surgeon-General, Wm. H. Iszard, Camden, New Jersey; Judge-Advocate-General, John H. Albin, Concord, New Hampshire.

For information concerning the Banners, Uniforms, Jewels, Badges, etc., of the Patriarchs Militant Degree, the reader is referred to the reports of the Lieutenant-General to be found in the Journals of the Sovereign Grand Lodge, 1885, 1886 and 1887, on the specific pages mentioned in the beginning of this chapter.

The Lieutenant-General's last report (a very handsome volume of 262 pages, with an addendum of colored plates of Banners, Flags, Guidons, Pennants, Jewels, Uniforms, etc.), is replete with information relating to the various organizations of the Army, their location, composition and present condition, and the laws and regulations now in force. Among the interesting items furnished are the following :

Cost of Uniforms and Arms, $498,026.85; Cost of Banners, Flags, etc., $12,050.72; Cost of Warrants, Commissions and General Supplies, $16,794.20; Aggregate cost showing the Army's investment, $526,871.77.

General Staff of the Army, Officers, 149 Swords; Strength of the First Army Corps, Officers and Chevaliers, 4,751 Swords; Strength of the Second Army Corps, Officers and Chevaliers, 4,944 Swords; Strength of the Third Army Corps, Officers and Chevaliers, 3,747 Swords; Strength of the Grand Department of the Pacific, Officers and Chevaliers, 894 Swords; Active strength of the Army, 14,336 Swords.

Honorary members of Cantons in First Army Corps, 370; Honorary members of Cantons in Second Army Corps, 405; Honorary members of Cantons in Third Army Corps, 129; Honorary members of Cantons in Grand Department of the Pacific, 19; Total, 923. Entire strength of the Army, Chevaliers, 15,259.

CHAPTER VI.

THE DEGREE OF REBEKAH.

Its History, Development and Beautified Work.

THE natural gallantry of man could not long exclude the better half of mankind from participation in the benefactions of the Order. The teachings and doctrines promulgated in its literature, were and are, essentially and peculiarly suited to the female character. From the greater mysteries of antiquity women were, however, excluded, not because it was believed that they could not keep a secret, but because woman had not obtained her proper position in the family. Her emancipation from the shackles of prejudice and custom was a matter of very slow growth. But when rehabilitated in all her Edenic privileges, she claimed and obtained the right to exercise her energies in every avenue open to man.

From the "Manuel Complet de la Maçonnerie des Dames," it appears that as early as 1775, the Grand Orient of France opened a Lodge in Paris for the reception of women. Similar Lodges were organized throughout Europe, in which the Work was conducted by the sisterhood, assisted by the brethren. In the initiation, the Temptation in Eden, the Building of the Tower of Babel, the Passage of the Israelites through the Wilderness, the Visit of the Queen of Sheba to Solomon, and other biblical subjects were emblematically represented. The work of the evening was generally followed by a banquet or a dance. The Lodges had fanciful and suggestive names, such as: "Knights and Ladies of Joy;" "Ladies of St. John of Jerusalem;" "Companions of Penelope;" "Society of the Chain;" "Perseverance;" "Knights and Nymphs of the Rose," etc. The objects and aims of some of the Lodges were praiseworthy, but in others the motives were of a trivial or merely social nature. In those formed for social purposes or for pleasure, the language used was symbolical and of an amusing nature. The age of admission for Knights was the "age to love;" of Ladies, "the age to please and to be loved." The Lodge was called "Eden," or the "Temple of Love," etc. A glass was called a "lamp," water, "white oil," wine, "red oil;" to fill your glass was "to trim your lamp," etc. The candidate, covered with iron chains, was led about the Lodge, while in the search for "Happiness," and when the Eden of bliss was at length reached, "chains of love," garlands of flowers, replaced the chains of iron.

Lodges thus constituted necessarily failed, after a time, to have any lasting value in the eyes of their members. There was lacking the broad and durable basis for their existence, and the Lodges became mere playthings in the hands of sportive children. It remained for us to build upon a sure and permanent foundation, "to proclaim peace and good will to man, uphold virtue, and restrain the march of vice."

"The Order of Felicity," instituted in Paris in 1742, was divided into the four degrees of Midshipman, Captain, Chief of Squadron and Vice-Admiral; the Emblems and terms were nautical, sailors were its founders, and it excited so much attention, that in 1746 a satire entitled, "The Means of Reaching the Highest Rank in the Navy, without Getting Wet," was published against it. Its field of action was the field of love. A Grand Orient was called "The Offing," the Lodge "The Squadron," and the sisters performed a fictitious voyage to the Island of Felicity, "*sous la voile des freres et pilotées par eux.*"

What is man without his better half, woman? She is as God made her:

> " Fair as morning star, with modesty
> Arrayed, with virtue, grace and perfect love :
>   Eloquent
> Of thoughts and comely words to worship God
> And sing His praise—the giver of all good,
> Light of darksome wilderness : to Time
> As stars to night,
> Whose smiles are hope, whose words are songs,

Whose love the solace, glory and delight
Of man, his boast, his riches, his renown,
When found, sufficient bliss ! when lost, despair !"

Many and earnest efforts were made to bring into communion with the Order the wives of Odd Fellows, but without success until 1850. (*See pages* 64, 65.)

At the session of the Grand Lodge held that year, in Cincinnati, a resolution was introduced by Rep. Smith, of New York, looking to the preparation of a Degree to be conferred upon the wives and daughters of Scarlet Degree members. The resolution was referred to the Legislative Committee. The Grand Encampment of Indiana had, the year before, elected Schuyler Colfax to represent it in the Grand Lodge of the United States. He was full of enthusiasm for the Order, and greatly desired its advancement. He, Larue, of Louisiana, and Kennedy, of New York, composed the Legislative Committee. After the committee had thoroughly considered the resolution referred to them, they could not agree as to the final disposition of the subject. In consequence, two reports were made, the minority report, signed alone by Colfax, who favored the idea with tongue and pen. The battle over the matter, was long and strenuously fought on both sides, but finally resulted in the adoption of the minority report. Colfax, of Indiana; Martin, of Mississippi, and Steele, of Tennessee, were appointed the committee to prepare the Degree. At the next session, held in Baltimore, the committee presented a Degree which was the work of Rep. Colfax. (*See page* 105.)

The opponents of the work fought the matter with all the talent and ability in their possession, but to no purpose, for the report of the committee was adopted by forty-six votes in its favor to thirty-seven against it. The Ritual was at once printed and distributed throughout the jurisdictions, but was not accepted, at the time, by all of them, Maryland and North Carolina failing to authorize their subordinate Lodges to confer it. The Degree was adopted on the 20th of September, 1851, and was declared to be a mere side, or Honorary Degree, for Scarlet members and their wives;

not an integral part of the Work, but optional with Grand Lodges to accept it. It could be rescinded at any time by a majority vote of the Grand Lodge.

In 1852, it was decided that the Annual Password of the Degree should be given by the ladies at the outer door, and that there could be no objection to the Lodge singing any part of the Odes at the time that ladies are introduced into the hall, by the Conductor, for initiation.

In 1854 the Degree was translated into German, and an edition of 500 copies thereof printed, to be sold at the price of the English edition, and the Degree was declared to be a necessary qualification of the Noble Grand of a Subordinate Lodge possessing the Degree.

In 1856 Grand Sire Ellison decided that no pecuniary compensation could be required for conferring the Degree. The reader will perceive that if the legislation extending the privileges was slow, it was sure, and always in the right direction.

In 1858, a Form of Card to be issued by a Subordinate Lodge to a Daughter of Rebekah was prescribed, but it was deemed inexpedient for the Grand Lodge of the U. S. to issue it. (*See Journal, page* 2,929.)

In 1860 the Grand Lodge decided that it is not legal to ballot upon an application to have the Degree conferred on the wives of Scarlet members in good standing, but it must be conferred upon them as a matter of course.

In 1864 the following preamble and resolution were offered, but the Grand Lodge deemed their adoption inexpedient :

Whereas the Degree of Rebekah, in its present status, is a dead letter upon our books, as far as practical benefits are concerned, when, in the opinion of many members of the Order, it might be made of very great service to the fraternity:

Resolved, That the Legislative Committee be requested to inquire into the expediency of providing some means by which ladies in possession of the Degree may form themselves into associations, for the purpose of carrying out more fully the teachings of this Degree, and co-operating with the brethren of this Order, in visiting the sick and relieving suffering humanity.

The ladies were at all times in advance of the Grand Lodge, in their views of the needs and wants of the Degree, and it was owing to their persistent efforts, and not always legal ones, as will be seen, that the Grand Lodge made wider the pathway of progress. Although the legislation, asked for in the above resolution, was not granted, the seed dropped thereby on the wayside, was not lost to them, for it, in time, bore good fruit.

In 1865 Grand Sire Veitch was compelled, by the exigencies of the case, to decide that a Subordinate Lodge could not legally establish a Union Degree of Rebekah Lodge, and hold regular meetings thereof for conferring and working that Degree. Lodges, in some jurisdictions, were, however, doing so, and, as will be seen, continued to do so. The ladies would not be denied active participation and direct interest in the Work. The Grand Sire also decided that Societies of the Degree of Rebekah, composed of ladies in possession of, and holding meetings opened in that Degree; the Regalia worn and the Work used, were irregular, unauthorized, and in contravention with the legislation of the Grand Lodge.

Grand Sire Veitch, in his report in 1866, said:

Notwithstanding the Grand Lodge of the United States has declared that Societies of the Degree of Rebekah, which hold regular meetings, and work in that Degree are illegal, it is believed that they still exist and are in full operation in some of the jurisdictions, and I respectfully recommend additional legislation on the subject, requiring the State Grand Bodies to suppress them within their limits, and prohibit their organization among them. It has come to my knowledge that the law in reference to Union Degree of Rebekah Lodges is totally disregarded in some localities, while in others it is evaded by a number of Lodges contiguous to each other, especially in larger towns and cities, regularly or occasionally, meeting to confer this Degree jointly, on lady candidates who may be present. The instructions accompanying the Work of this Degree seem to contemplate that it is to be conferred on ladies at a special meeting of *the* Lodge in which it has been regularly granted. If, however, the Degree may be conferred in any other Lodge on the presentation of a proper Certificate, and request of the Lodge issuing it, the instructions should more clearly indicate the permission to do so, that all misapprehension in reference thereto may be avoided.

The Legislative Committee, to whom this portion of the Grand Sire's report was referred, submitted a resolution calling the attention of State Grand Lodges to the instructions and laws relating to Union Rebekah Degree Lodges, and concerning communications from various jurisdictions as to the repeal of the Degree of Rebekah, " that the whole subject of repeal await the action of this Grand Body upon the report of a former Special Committee, laid over till next session," which was agreed to.

Grand Sire Sanders saw that something should be done, and suggested, in his report in 1867, the way to allay discontent and breathe into the Degree the breath of life. He said :

> The Degree of Rebekah has been in existence some sixteen years, and the experiment of a Degree of this character has been fully developed. In some jurisdictions the Degree has been conferred on thousands of wives of the brethren, while in others the Degree has never been recognized or received. I think the time has arrived when the Degree should be considered one of the Degrees of our Order—to be universally recognized and conferred upon those entitled to it, or the Degree should be abolished. Experience has taught those who have seen its working, that the Degree is in a crude and imperfect state; not what it should be. While the Work, as given, may be uniform, yet the business matter connected therewith is unsettled, and each State has its own Forms and Regulations for conferring this Degree. I would respectfully suggest, if the Degree is to be continued, that measures should be taken to establish it upon a more permanent basis, with more enlarged powers for doing good; such, for instance, as the organization of regular Degree Lodges to confer this Degree, with a code of laws, which shall be uniform, throughout the jurisdiction of this R. W. Grand Lodge; with all the powers to *elect* their own *officers* and *members ;* but making it the duty of these Lodges to be regularly chartered by the respective Grand Lodges, who shall appoint the Degree Masters for conferring the Degree upon those duly authorized to receive it. With organizations of this character, or of a similar nature, and, perhaps, conferring the Degree on daughters of Scarlet Degree members, over the age of eighteen years, I think much good might be done. Thus some of the objections, now raised against the Degree, removed, and the Degree placed upon a more firm basis, it would become a help to our Subordinate Lodges, and a field where the good and virtuous sisters might meet on common ground, to relieve the sick and distressed members of their *own* Lodges. I trust this matter may receive your careful attention at the present session, as much anxiety is manifest in numerous jurisdictions, as to what will be done with this Degree. They all, I believe, think the Degree may be made more useful and beneficial than at present, and generally hope it may be done.

These words of encouragement, and the unexpected liberality of views, were received everywhere by those interested in the success of the Degree, with pæans of praise and thanksgiving, as they believed them the harbingers of the realization of their hopes so long deferred. Nor were they disappointed; for, at the session of 1868, on motion of Rep. White, of New York, (the present Grand Sire), a Special Committee on the subject, of which Rep. White was chairman, was appointed and reported the following resolutions, which were adopted on Friday, September 25th, 69 members voting in the affirmative, and 28 in the negative:

That the Grand Lodges subordinate to this R. W. Grand Lodge be and they are hereby authorized and empowered to institute Degree Lodges of the Daughters of Rebekah at such places as they may deem proper within their territorial limits, to possess the powers and enjoy the privileges following:

1. To confer the Degree of Rebekah on such Scarlet Degree members and their wives as present a Certificate from a Lodge located in the District designated in the Charter of such Degree Lodge, and also to confer the said Degree on widows of Odd Fellows presenting Certificates from Lodges of which their husbands were members at the time of their decease.

2. To elect and appoint their own officers in the manner prescribed by their By-Laws. The elective officers to consist of a Noble Grand, Vice Grand, Secretary, and Treasurer, and, if so provided in their By-Laws, a Financial Secretary. The appointed officers to consist of a Warden, Conductor, Outside Guardian, Inside Guardian, Right and Left Supporters of the Noble Grand, Right and Left Supporters of the Vice Grand. Any member of the Lodge shall be eligible to any office in the Lodge except that of Noble Grand, which office shall be filled by a Past Grand in good standing in his Lodge, and except Warden, Outside Guardian and Inside Guardian, who shall be Scarlet Degree members. All officers to hold their offices for six months or one year, as prescribed by the Subordinate Grand Lodge.

3. To hold regular and special meetings as provided by the By-Laws.

4. To fix and establish dues, to be paid monthly, quarterly, semi-annually, or annually, as the By-Laws may provide, and to provide by By-Laws when those in arrears for dues shall be dropped from the roll of members. Any brother or sister within the District designated in the Charter may become a member on paying the dues provided by the By-Laws; and any brother may continue such member so long as he remains a member in good standing of his Subordinate Lodge, and pays his dues to the Degree Lodge, and any sister may remain a member so long as her husband is entitled to remain a member, or so long as she remains his widow and pays her dues to the Lodge. All Degree Lodges shall consist of at least ten members, five of each sex, and all in good standing shall participate in the proceedings of the Lodge.

5. To pay and disburse from the funds of the Lodge, for the relief of the sick, the destitute, or the distressed, from time to time, as a majority of the members present shall by vote determine, or as shall be otherwise provided by the By-Laws.

6. To establish such By-Laws and Rules of Order not inconsistent herewith or with the rules, usages, and general regulations of the Order, as they may deem proper, subject, however, to the approval of the Grand Lodge to which they are subordinate.

That the Grand Sire, Deputy Grand Sire, and Grand Corresponding and Recording Secretary be authorized to institute Degree Lodges of the Daughters of Rebekah in any territory under the immediate jurisdiction of this R. W. Grand Lodge, and that such Lodges possess the power and enjoy the privileges of other Rebekah Degree Lodges.

That the widow of an Odd Fellow who had not attained the Scarlet Degree, but who was in good standing at the time of his death, may receive the Degree of Rebekah at the option of the Lodge of which her husband was a member at the time of his death.

That the Grand Corresponding and Recording Secretary be instructed to prepare and cause to be printed Certificates of membership for the Daughters of Rebekah, to be furnished to Lodges at not less than double the cost, and that the sum of $100 be appropriated for that purpose from any money in the treasury not otherwise appropriated.

In 1869, the Regalia to be worn by brethren and sisters in a Rebekah Degree Lodge was prescribed. (*See Journal, pages 4,489, 4,647, and Chapter XI.*)

In 1870, the Grand Lodge refused to continue the membership, in a Rebekah Lodge, of the wife of a member expelled or suspended by his Subordinate Lodge; adopted two Odes for use in the Degree.

In 1871, the Grand Lodge authorized a ballot on an application for membership, a majority vote of all members present to be necessary for an election, except in such jurisdictions as may otherwise provide, and decided that rejected applicants could renew their applications, at such time as the State Grand Lodge determined.

Thus the sweet was mingled with the bitter, but the saccharine application did not soothe to placid rest the ardent spirits of the progressive Daughters. To suffer defeat was but a new incentive to renewed activity. They next sought the exclusive right to confer the Degree in their respective jurisdictions, but to this time the authority has not been granted.

The following resolution was adopted, September 17th, 1872:

That there be added to the Standing Committees of this R. W. Grand Lodge a "Committee on the Degree of Rebekah," to consist of seven members.

In 1873, Lodges were required to report annually, on the 31st of December; Visiting Cards were adopted for the use of sisters of Rebekah Degree Lodges; it was decided that there should be no forfeiture of membership, except by such rules and usages as apply to brothers in Subordinate Lodges; female applicants over eighteen years of age, daughters of Scarlet Degree members in good standing, and daughters of members of the Scarlet Degree who died in good standing, were declared ineligible to membership; an Order of Business was prescribed. (*See Journal, page* 5,915.)

In 1874, Lodges were authorized to grant, by ballot vote of a majority of the members present at a regular meeting, Withdrawal Cards to members who applied therefor, in person or by letter, and were also authorized to admit to membership the holders of such Cards by the same vote required for ordinary admission.

In 1875, the proposition to have public installation of the officers of Degree Lodges of the Daughters of Rebekah was defeated.

In 1876, it was declared that the Charter of a Rebekah Degree Lodge failing to report within thirty days after the time required by law for making the annual report, should be forfeited.

In 1877, the Grand Lodge decided that thereafter the only qualifications for office shall be actual contributing membership, but to be eligible to the office of Noble Grand previous service in the office of Vice Grand in a Rebekah Degree, or Subordinate Lodge, shall be necessary.

In 1878, a Term Password was provided for, and regulations made for the use of the Annual Password; it was decided that a quorum shall consist of seven members, irrespective of sex.

In 1879, it was resolved that Rebekah Degree Lodges shall confer the Degree on those persons only who may apply for membership in such Lodges, unless the Rebekah Degree Lodges shall otherwise provide.

In 1880, Lodges were authorized to admit to membership unmarried daughters, eighteen years of age, of Odd Fellows of the Fifth Degree, whose parents are dead, on proper application.

In 1881, unmarried daughters, eighteen years of age, of deceased Odd Fellows who had not attained the Third or Scarlet Degree, were declared eligible to membership in Rebekah Lodges, on proper application; it was decided that a lady suspended for non-payment of dues, her husband dying while she was under suspension, and she afterwards marrying a man not a member of the Order, could not be reinstated.

In 1882, Lodges were authorized to use the Funeral Ceremony provided by the Grand Lodge for Subordinate Lodges, substituting the word "Sister" where "Brother" occurs. Suitable Jewels for the officers were provided. (*See Chapter XI.*) A Form of Charter for Rebekah Degree Lodges under the immediate jurisdiction of the Sovereign Grand Lodge was adopted; the Degree Work was revised and declared by the Grand Sire, at the next session, to be the only legal Work.

In 1883, a suitable Regalia for the officers of Degree Lodges of the Daughters of Rebekah, was adopted. (*See Journal, page 9,402, and Chapter XI.*)

In 1884, the Grand Lodge authorized the Form of Public Installation printed in the Book of Forms. It also decided that State Grand Bodies had authority to authorize Representatives of Degree Lodges of the Daughters of Rebekah to meet annually to promote the interests of that Branch of the Order, and for social intercourse.

The following Form of Credentials for Representatives is used in Ohio:

This Certifies, that.........................., P. N. G., has been duly elected Delegate from ....Lodge, No........, D. of R., to the State Assembly of..D. of R.

Witness our hands, and the Seal of the Lodge, this .... day of.....................18...   ...., N. G.

[SEAL]   ...., R. S.

In 1885, the Grand Lodge decided that a Daughter of Rebekah is entitled to a Card from the Subordinate Lodge in which she received the Degree, as prescribed on page 2,929, Journal of 1858. The Committee on the Degree of Rebekah reported that they had considered several forms of "Beautified Work," and found in each of them some merit, and on their recommendation a Special Committee was appointed "to present, at the next session of this Grand Lodge, such changes, amendments, alterations, revisions and legislation, as may be necessary to make the Ritual of the Degree Lodges of the Daughters of Rebckah as satisfactory as possible, to the several jurisdictions in which said Lodges are now organized."

In 1886, a Revised Ritual was adopted, " to take effect and be the only anthorized Work for Rebekah Degree Lodges on and after January 1st, 1887." The privilege of membership in the Degree was extended to the mother (a widow) and unmarried stepdaughter of an Odd Fellow, and it was " *Resolved*, That the wife, unmarried daughter, or unmarried sister of an Odd Fellow of the Degree of Truth, who has attained the age of eighteen years, if she be a white woman, may receive the Degree of Rebekah, or be admitted to a Degree Lodge of the Daughters of Rebekah."

In 1887, a Burial Ceremony for a Daughter of Rebekah was adopted. (*See Journal, pages* 10,843–10,845.)

The following is the latest legislation in behalf of the Daughters of Rebekah, and is another step in the path of progress:

Grand Masters of the various State jurisdictions, in which Degree Lodges of the Daughters of Rebekah exist, are authorized to appoint Deputies from among the lady Past Grands of such Lodges, to exercise the duties of installation and such other duties in said Lodges as their office empowers them to do.

Installing officers for the Rebekah Degree Lodges are authorized to fill the various positions in the installations of officers of such Lodges with lady Past Noble Grands.

During the entire existence of the Rebekah Degree, the Grand Lodge of the United States, or, using its new name, the Sovereign Grand Lodge, has always and consistently

occupied a cautious and conservative course. Its legislation in behalf of the Degree has been enacted, only after
thorough conviction of its utility and adaptability for the
purposes intended. If the propositions of the advocates
and friends of the Degree deserved adoption, the Grand
Lodge, however reluctant and hesitating to grant, at the
first demand, the needed boon, never failed, in the end, to
meet the just expectations of the prudent and the conservative.

The progress already made is considerable, as will be
at once apparent, when it is remembered that originally
the wives of Scarlet Degree members were alone authorized
to receive the Degree of Rebekah, and that a lady could
not preside over a Lodge. Numerous restrictions have,
from time to time, been removed, always for the welfare of
the institution. And now that the management of Lodge
matters is surrendered to the ladies, the usefulness of the
Degree will be, no doubt, largely enhanced. Since this
auspicious change, no Branch of the Order has grown more
rapidly or has been more effective for good. With an improved Ritual and the Work beautified, its ardent votaries
may well continue their labors with the happiest auguries
for its assured success. There are now nearly 1,400 Lodges
with more than 67,000 members laboring faithfully for the
success of this Important auxiliary of the Order.

For further information respecting the Degree of
Rebekah, the reader is referred to the Manual.

The following is from the pen of a well-known, earnest
laborer in the cause:

BEAUTIFIED WORK OF THE DEGREE OF REBEKAH.

By Mrs. Louise B. Hall, Evansville, Indiana.

Among the many sources of charity and benevolence, with which the world at present abounds, there is probably none more elevating, more ennobling; none more peculiarly adapted to the nature and temperament of woman; calling into exercise and developing the finer and nobler qualities of her nature, than this Branch of Odd Fellowship, known as the Rebekah Work.

With pride and honor we review this able and successful effort of our lamented Brother and Benefactor, Hon. Schuyler Colfax, through whose untiring energy and magnanimous heart, this Degree was established; thus opening an avenue by which woman was made a participator in the noble duties involved in Odd Fellowship; where she stands side by side with husband, father, brother, in the great duties of man to fellow-man; clinging and dependent, yet hopeful and encouraging, like

> The vigorous oak, with branches long,
> The clinging ivy twines,
> Till both, so firmly knit and strong,
> Their beauteous grace combines.

The principles of Odd Fellowship have a tendency to enlarge and develop the innate benevolence of woman's heart, adapting itself, peculiarly, to her loving and sympathetic nature, flowing out in ready relief to suffering humanity.

While the beautiful instructions of this Degree teach us our duty to each other, they bear equally strong and

binding upon our duties to our fellow creatures. While the
Degree often obligates us to sacrifice, it yields us a grateful
recompense, in its mutually pleasant associations, abundantly
repaying every effort, when the sunshine of home is darkened with the cloud of sorrow and grief.

There are many beauties befitting its mission, which
cannot fail to arrest a reflecting mind. It is pure and exalted in its sentiments, elevating in its instructions, sacred
in its obligations, liberal and generous in its principles,
founded upon, and deduced from, the noblest and purest
characters which adorn the pages of Sacred History. It
portrays the courage, the goodness, the fidelity of true
womanhood; the modesty, worth, and excellence of all those
virtues which combine to make a woman all that is pure,
noble, and good. It harmoniously blends the benevolent
and charitable duties of life with her own domestic and
social relations.

This Degree of Rebekah, which is so beautifully typical
of the mothers of the Bible; the brave and illustrious
women of the olden times; the faithful, noble-hearted wives
and daughters of the ancient Patriarchs, whose courageous
and remarkable careers, stamped them the truest types of
sterling merit; spreads before us an ample field to labor, too,
in works of love and honor. And who than woman, conse-
crating all her intellect and faculties to good and useful
purposes, responds more nobly, cheerfully, and readily to
the call, even though censure and reproach be her ungrate-
ful reward? Her inward nature prompts her ofttimes to
deeds unseen, and unknown only to God and herself. Sig-
nificantly typical too, is the history of the pure, unaffected
life and character of the maiden, Rebekah, whose name it
bears. In fancy, we picture her in her loose, simple, grace-
ful garb of olden times, ministering to the wants of the
stranger; for

> She was Nature's Daughter,
> Endowed by her with grace,
> While Purity and Truth
> Were blended in her face.

REBEKAH AT THE WELL.

Like Rebekah of old, it is still the privilege of "Daughters," to minister, in deeds of kindness, to the wearied traveler and to the stranger, within our gates.   There are many in life, thirsting for the simplest acts of love, strangers to kindness, to charity, to happiness; many whose lives are as barren of refreshing memories, as the trackless desert over which this stranger had just passed; many whose toilsome journeys are never cheered or brightened by a single oasis. Even as the well was a welcome sight to the traveler, and the unaffected hospitality as refreshing and grateful, so the great well of human benevolence is free, liberal, and spacious enough for all mankind; its waters, cool, clear, and abundant.   Let us freely dispense its refreshing draughts to the needy; let us drop our little kindnesses by the wayside of life.

The "Beautified Form" of representing this Work, which has of late years been given additional coloring, greatly enhancing its original beauty, has lent it a new impetus.   It aptly illustrates all those virtues which adorn the female character, and sets forth those admirable qualities which combine to advance, improve, and elevate mankind. The common acceptation of the word "Beautify," is to adorn, ornament, embellish, to transform a plain to an attractive appearance; and the word, in this connection, has been wisely selected; for nothing has so aided in developing its pure and lofty sentiments as the Work, intelligently and creditably rendered in the "Beautified Form."   The characters portrayed are all illustrative of some trait or virtue, which is commendable or admirable in woman.   They are therefore brought before the mind for instruction and imitation, and while effectively impressive in their results, and interspersed with floor movements, significant in their representations, present a charming spectacle, and are a study worthy of the most cultivated intellect.

The Emblems employed to designate this Degree are three of the most speaking, significant, appropriate and strikingly illustrative in their application to every-day life and its duties.

1st. The Bee Hive represents Associated Industry, teaches us constant and untiring diligence in works and labors of love, the good results of united effort and action, and the gratifying reward of industry and perseverance.

2d. The Moon and Seven Stars—indicative of order—the exactness and unerring laws of nature, teach us the necessity of system, order, and regularity in all our duties, both in the Lodge room and out.

3d. The Dove is a lovely type of harmlessness, meekness, innocence, gentleness and purity, so befitting a pure-minded, noble woman; its example prompting us to go forth (like the " Dove,") on our missions of love and mercy, ever bearing our "Olive Branch" of peace.

Even in this limited survey of the Rebekah Work, a studious and reflecting mind will recognize many elevating and purifying influences, which to the memory of its author, will stand as a " Memorial Stone" in the mighty Temple of Odd Fellowship, as long as time exists; and in the hearts of grateful wives, mothers, and daughters, has he erected his own beautiful " Monument of Memory," in bringing to the cause the richest and ripest fruits of a well-stored mind, the rarest gifts of eloquence and brilliant intellect, and in nursing and befriending it with tender care, and with as brave and noble a spirit as God gives to good men. He has passed into the Silent Land, and the white marble which gleams coldly above his lowly resting place, proves to the world and posterity, that his virtues are enshrined in the hearts of the multitude, and the silent tears, those grateful tributes, which price cannot estimate, will glisten and shine as " Stars in the crown of his rejoicing." Lives, such as his, weave their own unfading laurels and build their own beautiful " monument of memory."

Is it more, then, than a fitting tribute to this great and good man, who so calmly laid aside his life's work and passed from our midst, that we revere his memory; that we cherish his virtues, and more than all, that we elevate the work which he has placed in our hands; that we keep its fair name untarnished, its purity unsullied, its beauty unblemished, and that as this " Rising Star " approaches its zenith, it may shine with even more brilliant lustre in the firmament of good works; that its brightness may never grow dim, nor its beauty decline, but that it may, even amid the darkness of night, point to the " Bethlehem of Hope and Love"?

CHAPTER VII.

BIOGRAPHIES.

Thomas Wildey.

THOMAS WILDEY, the "Founder and Father" of American Odd Fellowship, was born in London, England, on the 15th day of January, 1782. At the early age of fourteen, he was indentured an apprentice to learn coach-spring making. After the completion of his indenture, he assiduously followed his vocation in many places throughout his native land, until he left its shores for his new home in Baltimore, where he arrived in September, 1817. In the History of the Order, it has been shown how, when, and under what circumstances he planted the institution of Odd Fellowship in the United States.

He was the first N. G. of Washington Lodge, the first Grand Master of the Grand Lodge of Maryland and of the United States, and the first Grand Sire of the Grand Lodge of the United States, which latter office he filled for eight years. From April 19th, 1819, until 1833, he was in office, and to his zeal, energy, and prudence is due the final success of his undertaking.

In his career he did not escape detraction, and the envy, hatred, and malice of those always ready to malign the successful; but the Order, ever mindful of his services, testified, time and again, its appreciation of his worth, by the presentation of many tokens of their regard and affection. A number of these—Medals, Jewels, Plate, etc.—are now deposited in the Odd Fellows' Library in Baltimore.

In 1835 he was made Traveling Agent of the Grand Lodge of the United States, and, in this capacity, he traveled North, West, and South, establishing and encouraging the Order wherever he went. The pages of the Journals record his unparalleled work in the field of Odd Fellowship. The story of his trials, tribulations, and his final success, is unequaled in interest, even in the domain of fiction. His life is an interesting study, replete with many valuable moral lessons. It is the lot of few men, in any generation, to write their names on the scroll in the temple of fame. The glory and honor of such an achievement, are all the greater in the case of Past Grand Sire Wildey. He was no child of fortune, duly equipped with all the appliances that wealth and a cultivated intellect can supply, to woo and win success. His faith in man's reciprocity of affection inherent in the brotherhood of all, with absolute confidence in the great scheme of Fraternity, to arouse and give exercise to those generally repressed emotions of the soul, Friendship and Love, made his panoply. He ever kept his goal in view, and was never swerved from the path of progress, by the many difficulties, natural and artificial, that appeared before him. The perseverance of the man was equal to his faith, and, in time, he gained a rich and well-deserved reward for his sacrifices and labors.

He died in the City of Baltimore, on the 19th of October, 1861, in the eightieth year of his age, and was buried in Greenmount Cemetery, with all the pomp and honors of the Order, befitting the exalted station and unequaled services of the originator of Odd Fellowship in America.

The late Grand Secretary, James L. Ridgely, wrote his eulogy, which was delivered on the 16th day of September, 1862, in Front Street Theatre, Baltimore, Md. In the Appendix to the Journal of 1862, this truthful and eloquent tribute, fitly commemorating Past Grand Sire Wildey's services in the cause of humanity, may be found. Among the many beautiful references to the lamented dead, none are more true and appropriate than the following :

Although we see him not, with the natural eye, yet he is before us in the vivid memories of the past, in the creations of his genius, in the lustre sparkling from the coronet which wreathes his brow; still lives in the prayers and ministrations which go up from a thousand altars; in the undying deeds of mercy, "which do follow after him;" in the heart of the solaced widow, the relieved brother, and the uplifted orphan ; in the blessings which he scattered broadcast along the slippery paths of life; in the sighs subdued, and the tears wiped away by the spirit of his broad humanity: still lives, and will continue to live, in the comeliness and beauty and moral sublimity of his benefactions to the human family. Every page of the story of Odd Fellowship, from its first feeble glimmerings upon the world, through its eventful progress, amid conflict and trial, obloquy and reproach, until it sweeps across the horizon, scattering every obstacle from its track and crowning the evening of his life and the labors of his youth with imperishable renown, is fragrant with his presence.

On the 26th of April, 1865, the corner-stone of a handsome monument, an offering of the entire brotherhood, was laid in Broadway, Baltimore. It was dedicated on the 20th of September, 1865, with appropriate services, and remains a beautiful memorial of the affection and veneration of the Order for Thomas Wildey, its "Father and Founder."

John Welch.

John Welch was born in Wolverhampton, Staffordshire, England, in November, 1792. At an early age he was apprenticed to the painting and plumbing business. Like Wildey and Boyd, he visited the United States with a view of making it his permanent home, should circumstances prove auspicious. He arrived in Baltimore in May, 1817. Before leaving his native country he was initiated in some Lodge in England, and at the time of his emigration to America was a Past Vice Grand. Wildey and he became companions in 1818, and were in frequent communion, being fellow-countrymen, each having, as yet, a limited circle of acquaintances. It appears that Welch was not, originally, as enthusiastic as Wildey on the subject of organizing a Lodge of Odd Fellows. Having, however, embarked in the enterprise, he gave it special care and earnest attention during its infant state, and, aided by Wildey, Entwisle, and Boyd, brought the tender nursling through all the precarious stages of childhood to vigorous youth. In Chapter I. is told the story of the formation of Washington Lodge. John Welch was its first Vice-Grand, and when, in 1821, the Grand Lodge of Maryland and of the United States was established, he was elected its first Grand Secretary, and held the office until February 22d, 1823, when he was elected

Deputy Grand Master. On the formation of the Grand Lodge of the United States, he was elected Deputy Grand Master, or, as the office was subsequently styled, Deputy Grand Sire. He was Wildey's Mentor and Fidus Achates. Cool and deliberate, he exercised a restraint on his superior officer's impetuosity. His was the calculating head to plan, while the Grand Sire stood ready to execute. He was sober, industrious, a member of the church, had no convivial proclivities, and used whatever influence he possessed, to remove this imperfection from the otherwise fair escutcheon of the Order. His great merit in the work of propagating Odd Fellowship was the dignity and high purposes he gave it, by his education, social position, and unblemished reputation as a model citizen. After the session of 1829 his name no more appears as one of the workers in the growing institution. The ten years of his active and earnest efforts produced such happy results, that, the ship having safely reached the calm waters of prosperity, the weary pilot felt that he could surrender his trust to younger, if untried hands. He died in 1851, mourned by a large circle of friends, acquaintances, and brethren of the Order, who have enshrined him in their temple of honor as a benefactor of the human race.

John Pawson Entwisle.

To the genius of John Pawson Entwisle, the Order is indebted for the chart whereby to steer the ship of Odd Fellowship. Without him, the voyage would have been a fortuitous drifting whither the wind listed. We know that the government of the Order is modeled on that of the United States, but all may not know that to Brother Entwisle was due the present system of Representation. He was the first creature of his own creation, the first Representative-elect to the Grand Lodge of the United States. For one who filled such high positions in the youth of the Order, it is remarkable that so little is known of his personal history. He was born in England, but the time he left his native land and came to America, is lost in the barrenness of the early records. He was educated for the ministry, but at the time of his appearance in Odd Fellowship, he was employed on one of the newspapers of Baltimore City. Unheralded, he comes into view at the preliminary meeting for the organization of the Grand Lodge of Maryland and of the United States, February 7th, 1821, when he was chosen Deputy Grand Master. His literary ability was at once employed in behalf of the Order, for we find that as early as February 22d, 1821, "the intermediate Degrees, called the Covenant and Remembrance," were already in existence, and were the product of his genius and his facile pen. His ability was so well established, that his services were required in a field more congenial to his tastes, and where his literary accomplishments might have full play. February 22d, 1823, he was elected Grand Secretary, and conducted the increasing correspondence of the Grand Lodge with marked success. As a sample of his writing, the reader is referred to the Journal, page 62, where will be found an extract from a letter, prepared by him for the brethren in Boston, regarding the duties and privileges of a Grand Master. At the meeting of the Grand Committee, April 15th, 1824, the action of the committee at a prior meeting, in reference to the organization of the Grand Lodge of the United States, was presented, and the subject referred to a committee consisting of Brothers Wildey, Welch, and Entwisle, to report at the same session. The report was the work of the Grand Secretary, and will be found in the Journal, on page 66. It provided for surrendering the Charter to "the Past Grands of the Grand Lodge of the United States," etc., and was a paper of the greatest importance to the Order. He did not live to see the fruit of his labors, for his death was sudden. The Grand Committee met July 6th, 1824, in special session, to take action relative to his departure. What was done, other than appropriating fifteen dollars to his widow, the record does not disclose. At the session of August 22d, 1823, a resolution was adopted that he should be presented with a medal for his services. This was the first medal voted, but his unexpected demise prevented his receiving it, and the fifteen dollars appropriated to the widow, was the amount intended to be invested in the medal. His career in the Order was short but brilliant, and his death a sad blow to the small and struggling band. Moses like, he saw the promised land, but was not permitted to enter therein.

John Boyd.

John Boyd was born in Lanarkshire, Scotland, in the year 1787. Full of hope and ambition, he sought, in 1817, a home in the New World, where industry and integrity were open avenues to success, if not fortune. Although a common laborer in the mother country, with the characteristic enterprise of his countrymen, it was not long before he had raised himself to a better sphere of labor, each step of progress being merely a starting point for a higher plane, until the fickle goddess, Fortune, crowned his every effort with success, and made him an example of what steady perseverance and devotion to business can accomplish.

The exact date of his admission to Washington Lodge is unknown; it was, however, some time in the year 1819, as he was enrolled as the nineteenth member (in Journal of 1872, page 5570, it is stated seventeenth), and the fourteenth addition to the original five. At the preliminary meeting for organizing the Grand Lodge of Maryland and of the United States, he was chosen Grand Treasurer and Grand Guardian, and was installed into those offices on the 22d of February, 1821. At this meeting, the Golden Rule Degree was conferred upon brothers Boyd, Entwisle, Couth, Welch, and Larkam. On motion of Grand Guardian Boyd, the first recorded expulsion from the Order was made. From his first appearance in the Grand Lodge, he became an active and useful member. November 22d, 1822, he was appointed one of the committee " to settle the books of the Grand Lodge." At the session of February 22d, 1823, he was appointed on the committee to prepare amendments to the Constitution, and on his motion a resolution was adopted to present a medal to Grand Secretary Entwisle for his services. February 22d, 1824, he was appointed proxy Representative for Pennsylvania, and continued in that position until May 1st, 1827. The Patriarchal Degree was conferred upon him September 25th, 1825. He was present at every meeting, except one, from February 7th, 1821, until he was superseded as proxy of Pennsylvania, by the appearance of Representative John Pearce. He assisted in preparing a Form of Visiting Card. At the session of September 5th, 1831, he appeared as the proxy Representative of Delaware, and was one of the petitioners for a Charter for the Grand Encampment of Maryland. The Grand Lodge of Pennsylvania presented him a medal, " a circular tablet of silver neatly enclosed in a frame of the same metal," as described on page 117, Journal. This is the last appearance of his name upon the pages of the Records. Bro. Boyd had no ambition for office, unless the holding of one increased his usefulness. He was of the old school, and cared for no honor higher than the title of Past Grand. As a member of the Grand Lodge, from its organization until 1831, he did much to guide the chariot of progress through the defiles of difficulty and inexperience. His superior financial knowledge was of material aid to the infant Order, but the demands of an extensive business requiring his undivided attention, he was compelled to abate his zeal for Odd Fellowship. His last appearance among the brethren of the Order, was at Front Street Theatre to hear the eulogy on his departed co-worker, Thomas Wildey.

When a competence was acquired he retired to private life, and enjoyed, in the bosom of his family, the rest so justly his due, living in peace, and serenely passing from earth on the 30th day of August, 1871, loved and respected by all who knew him, and venerated as the last relic of the Washington Lodge of 1819.

Augustus Mathiot.

Augustus Mathiot was born in Lancaster, Pennsylvania, August 4th, 1799. His business was that of chair-painting, to which he added cabinet-making, and by industry and enterprise, in time, acquired a competence. He became a member of Washington Lodge in the year 1823, and was the one hundred and seventy-seventh on its roll. The members at this time indulged in convivial customs, and it was through the efforts of Brother Mathiot that Washington Lodge banished liquor from the Lodge room. The practice was not, however, completely eliminated from the Order until the Lodges met in their own Hall on Gay Street. As long as sessions were held in public-houses, it was found impossible to altogether wean the older brethren from the pursuit of pleasure in the old way. To Brother Mathiot, great credit is due for originating the crusade against the universal rule that required refreshments to be supplied at Lodge meetings. More or less odium was cast upon Odd Fellowship on account of its Lodges being located in taverns, and the membership indulging in the flowing bowl. The progress of the Order, after its divorce from this evil, was rapid and astonishing, showing clearly that the impediment to its advancement had been removed. October 16th, 1828, Brother Mathiot was admitted into the Grand Lodge of Maryland; two years thereafter he was elected Deputy Grand Master, and in 1836 became Grand Master. He might have been Grand Master in 1831, except for his refusal to assume the duties of that office on the resignation of the Grand Master. In 1829 he was elected Grand Secretary of the Grand Lodge of the United States, and served until September 3d, 1833. On that day he was unanimously elected Grand Treasurer, and held the office until the installation of his successor, Charles Mowatt, October 9th, 1835. Brother Mathiot was the first American member of the Order to arrive at distinction therein. Whatever defects existed in his early education he greatly repaired by his omnivorous reading and unquenchable thirst for knowledge. He was an ardent, lifelong student, an unwearied searcher for all information that could be found in the books to which he had access, in whose domain he wandered, gathering the posies of thought which he scattered with ready fluency, in his conversations and formal addresses. He was the last of the " Three Odd

Links," a secret association of which Wildey, Boyd, and Couth were the first members. He died on the 12th of July, 1872. His departure was sudden, and unattended by any previous illness or premonition of approaching dissolution.

Richard Marley.

Richard Marley was born in Philadelphia, Pennsylvania, November 12th, 1791. He made Baltimore his home in 1820, and followed his business of shoemaking. He joined Franklin Lodge No. 2 in 1823, and from the time of his initiation, he was a useful, zealous, active member, and was admitted into the Grand Lodge of Maryland October 18th, 1825. His activity in his new sphere of usefulness was unabated, as is evidenced by his election to the office of Grand Warden in February, 1826. In April of the same year he served in the Grand Lodge of the United States, as proxy Representative for New York, and continued to act in this capacity until September 3d, 1832. At the close of his term as Grand Warden, he was elected Deputy Grand Master, and January 18th, 1841, became Grand Master. His success in the Encampment Branch of the Order was equally great. In 1825 he joined Encampment No. 1 ; was a charter member of Salem Encampment No. 2, and was elected Grand Patriarch January 14th, 1839. If he did much for Odd Fellowship, the Order did much for him. July 21st, 1831, the Grand Lodge of Maryland amended its Constitution, providing that it should "open and work exclusively in the Fifth Degree." This determination to admit Scarlet members to the rights and privileges of Past Grands, was exceedingly distasteful to Brother Marley, who thenceforth manifested little interest in the proceedings of the Grand Body, and, with some of his intimate friends in the Order, soon after obtained a Charter from the spurious Grand Lodge of Pennsylvania, and opened a Subordinate Lodge in Baltimore, called " Adam Lodge." In January, 1832, the Grand Lodge adopted a law providing for the suspension or expulsion, if convicted, of "any brother who shall be concerned in organizing, or who shall give countenance and support to, or shall visit any Lodge or Lodges in the State of Maryland, purporting to be Odd Fellows, and not possessing a legal and valid Charter, duly granted and presented by the Grand Lodge of Maryland." Under this law, the Subordinates promptly expelled the members of the Order who were concerned in the spurious Lodge. October 15th, 1835, his Subordinate Lodge was authorized to restore Bro. Marley to membership, and in January, 1836, his name is found in the Journal of the Grand Lodge of Maryland, as a member of the "Joint Standing Committee on Education." It appears that he alone, of all those who violated the laws of the Order, was welcomed back to the shrine of his affections, where he ministered faithfully until summoned from earth. From 1826 to the time of his death, with a few exceptions, he occupied a seat in the Grand Lodge of the United States; was a Representative of the Grand Lodge of Maryland at the time of his decease, and died at his post of duty. He was a devoted, faithful, and untiring laborer in the field of Odd Fellowship, wise in counsel, sound in judgment, and the soul of honor in all his dealings. As a co-laborer of Wildey, he has left his impress upon the pages of the Order's history, an imperishable memorial in the heart of every true Odd Fellow. He died on the 7th day of May, 1869, in the seventy-eighth year of his age.

James L. Ridgely.

James L. Ridgely was born in Baltimore, Maryland, January 27th, 1807. He was graduated from Mount St. Mary's College, Emmittsburg, Md., and selected the law as his profession; was admitted to the Bar in June, 1828; initiated in Columbia Lodge, No. 3, May 27th, 1829; entered the Grand Lodge of Maryland in 1830, and appeared in the Grand Lodge of the United States, September 5th, 1831, as Representative from Maryland. In 1833 he became Grand Secretary of the Grand Lodge of Maryland and in 1834 its Grand Master. In the last named year he was elected a member of the City Council of Baltimore. He took active part in the revision of the Work in 1835, and in the following year was elected Grand Sire, but declined the office. In 1838 he was elected to the Maryland House of Delegates, where he was noted for his ability and attention to his duties. In 1840 he was again elected Grand Sire, and again declined the office, believing that he could be more useful in another portion of the field of labor. He made no mistake in his belief, as the result plainly showed.

The Grand Body, not being able to obtain his services in the capacity of Grand Sire, he was elected Grand Corresponding Secretary, and in 1841, Grand Recording Secretary, which two offices were united in him by a double election September 17th, 1841, when he was styled Grand Corresponding and Recording Secretary. He was now enthroned in the position peculiarly suited to his talents. All the energy he possessed was devoted to the advancement of the Order, whose interests were almost his sole care. He was elected editor of "The Covenant," the official magazine of the Order, which did much to popularize and benefit Odd Fellowship, and he continued in this relation until 1844. His services were so well appreciated in this connection that the Grand Lodge voted him a gold medal. (See page 61.) His devotion to the cause, so earnestly espoused, demanded much of his time, but did not entirely withdraw him from his duties as a citizen. In 1848 he was President of the Board of Education, and, through his exertions, the present system of public schools in Baltimore, was established. In 1849 he was a member of the Convention to prepare a new Constitution for the State of Maryland; in 1864 he was elected Register of Wills for Baltimore County, and held the office for twelve years; he was Collector of Internal Revenue under Presidents Lincoln and Johnson, and was President of the Baltimore County Mutual Fire Insurance Company from 1855 until his death. The labor of his life was, however, in the promotion of the Order, and to this object all the varied and splendid talents of the esteemed brother were devoted.

The brotherhood of man, benevolence, and charity, were the constant themes of his untiring pen. His contributions

to the literature of the Order are immense in volume. As Grand Corresponding and Recording Secretary, he presented at each annual session, from 1840 to 1880, a formal report. His first one will be found in the Journal, pages 336, 337. From that time onward, the reports grew in value and importance; in fact they became the feature of the Grand Lodge Journals.

In the brief space permitted to treat the prolific subject of Brother Ridgely's labors in, and on behalf of, Odd Fellowship, the salient points of his career can alone be touched upon. When he became Grand Corresponding Secretary, in 1840, there were 14 Grand Lodges; 155 Subordinate Lodges; a membership of 11,166 reported; 4 Grand Encampments; 36 Subordinate Encampments; a membership of 463 reported.

To him, and his coadjutors, is due the proud position the Order now holds, in a domain that is boundless, with a mission of charity and love, to fraternize mankind and bring into one harmonious whole all the nations of men that dwell on the face of the earth. His delicate moral sense demanded that the practices and precepts of Odd Fellowship should everywhere be in unison. To effect this end, he labored with all his ability, and not in vain. Not satisfied with the sweet solace of work well done at home, he sought to extend the influence of the Order for good, in England. See his resolution on page 43, and the letter written by the Committee on Correspondence, pages 43, 44. The Past Grand's Charge, the Standard Tract, and voluminous annual reports, will ever remain monuments of his ability. His correspondence, addresses, orations, eulogies, etc., fill up the measure of his greatness. From his election in 1840 to the day of his death, he was the central figure in Odd Fellowship. His last appearance in the Grand Lodge was at the session of 1880, at Toronto.

He was stricken with paralysis December 1st, 1879, and gradually faded away, until the angel of death claimed his own, November 16th, 1881. In 1885, a mourning and disconsolate brotherhood, erected to his memory a handsome monument in Harlem Park, Baltimore, Maryland, on the summit of which is a life-size figure of the deceased, with "his face to the east, the source of light, and the sun in his course, will daily deck his brow with a crown of glory."

Joshua Vansant.

Joshua Vansant was born at Millington, Kent County, Maryland, December 31st, 1803, and with his father removed to Baltimore in 1818, and learned the trade of hatter. He went into business on his own account, and continued therein until 1873, when he was elected Mayor of Baltimore, holding the office two terms, in all, four years. At the expiration of the second term, he was appointed Comptroller of the c   a position that he occupied at the time of his death. His political honors were numerous; he was a member of the House of Delegates of Maryland in 1836, and represented a Maryland district in the 33d Congress. He filled many minor and local offices of trust and honor, with marked ability and sterling fidelity, his thorough business capacity being well understood and fully appreciated by his fellow citizens. His unsullied integrity, pronounced conservatism and phenomenal placidity in the hour of excitement, gained for him a business reputation second to none in the community.

His sobriquet of "Honest Joshua" was richly and deservedly earned. Such was his character and standing as a citizen and a business man. He occupied no less a prominent place in the domain of Odd Fellowship. Initiated in Columbia Lodge, No. 3, at its institution, December 17th, 1823, he was at once appointed Conductor. He soon retired from the Order and did not appear therein again until 1847. His career thereafter, was both rapid and brilliant, for we find him admitted to the Grand Lodge of Maryland July 15th, 1850. An unqualified evidence of his appreciation is shown in his election from the floor to the chair of Grand Master, an unusual occurrence. He was elected Grand Representative to the Grand

Joshua Vansant

Lodge of the United States, July 28th, 1851, and again in 1856, serving in 1851, 1852, 1856, and 1857. In the meantime, in 1852, he was elected Grand Treasurer of the Grand Lodge of the United States, and was regularly re-elected without opposition, holding the office at the time of his death. He was a model Treasurer, punctilious to a fault, and brought to the performance of his duties a wide and varied experience in financial matters, seldom equaled and never exceeded. He died April 8th, 1884, in the 81st year of his age.

CHAPTER VIII.

APPEALS.

IN this chapter reference can be made to the laws of only a few of the one hundred Grand Bodies on the subject of appeals. It is, however, not necessary to produce the laws of every Jurisdiction as, although not uniform in their provisions, they are easily accessible to parties interested.

The Sovereign Grand Lodge has declared that "the right of appeal is sacred, and may be made under any and all circumstances within the mandates of the law applying to the case."

In a SUBORDINATE LODGE OR ENCAMPMENT, a member feeling aggrieved on account of being deprived of benefits he claimed, or believing he has suffered injustice by adverse action of the Subordinate, after trial may appeal to the Grand Body of the Jurisdiction, in accordance with the provisions of such Grand Body, usually embodied in the Constitution of the Subordinate. The appeal may have to go through the District Deputy Grand Master, District Deputy Grand Patriarch, District Grand Committee, or Grand Master, or Grand Patriarch, before it reaches the State Grand Body. A minority may appeal from the action of the majority. An individual, or a majority, cannot appeal from the decision of a Noble Grand or Chief Patriarch, on questions relating to the Work of the Order. If irregularities are supposed to exist, the usual way of reaching the Grand Master, or Grand Patriarch, (who alone are authorized to pass upon such questions in their Jurisdictions,) is by a complaint to the District Deputy.

A stay of proceedings is sometimes provided for, pending appeal, and the status of the party affected is determined by the laws of the State Body. If the laws provide (as is the case in some States) for a "change of venue," the trial of the brother charged, may take place in some other Lodge or Encampment than that in which he holds membership.

APPEALS TO STATE GRAND BODIES.—Each Subordinate Grand Body is at liberty to formulate its own rules and regulations for conducting appeals in its jurisdiction, provided such rules and regulations do not conflict with the general laws of the Order. The Sovereign Grand Lodge has enacted the following:

No appeal to a State Grand Body lies upon the decision of incidental questions during a trial in a Subordinate; an appeal can be taken only after the decision of the entire case by the Subordinate, which is binding until reversed by the Grand Body.

When the laws of a Grand Body limit the time within which an appeal can be taken, such Grand Body cannot disregard its own laws and entertain an appeal after such period has expired. A Grand Body must decide appeals in accordance with its own laws. When the limited time for an appeal has passed without an appeal, the right of appeal is gone and cannot be revived. When the limited time begins to run from the serving of a written notice, by the Secretary or Scribe of the Subordinate, of the action thereof, upon the party interested, such written notice may be waived by the party or his counsel.

In the absence of any local law providing for a stay of proceedings pending an appeal, a Subordinate is bound to obey the mandate of its Grand Body.

In a case where a party has the right to appeal, he may present in writing to his Subordinate his appeal, with all the facts, exceptions, assignments of errors and reference to cases and decisions of the Order; and the Subordinate is bound either to enter the appeal, thus presented, in full on the minutes, or to make an entry of the fact of the taking of the appeal, and direct the filing of the paper; and, in transmitting the appeal to the proper superior tribunal, to accompany it with a certified transcript of all the proceedings and papers in the case.

When an appeal from the decision of a Subordinate is taken to its Grand Body, and a committee is appointed thereby to investigate the case, the Subordinate should be notified of such intended action, so as to have a hearing in the matter.

A Grand Body may reconsider its action on an appeal, provided it be done during the session in which the action was had.

A Grand Body cannot consider an appeal after having, (at a previous session), remanded the case back to the Subordinate, for investigation and further consideration of the subject, and adjourned without a reconsideration of its action.

A State Grand Body cannot reverse the action of a Subordinate without granting a new trial, when its own law authorizes it only to remand the case for a new trial.

The following is the manner of prosecuting appeals prescribed by the Grand Lodges of Maryland, Pennsylvania, New York, New Jersey, Ohio, and Illinois :

MARYLAND.—If a brother appeals from a decision of his Lodge, he must place his appeal with his reasons therefor, in the hands of the Grand Secretary within three months after the decision of the Lodge. The Lodge, within twenty days after the reception of the notice of appeal, shall deliver to the Grand Secretary, under Seal, a certified copy of the charges, minutes of the Committee of Trial, and of all the records relating to the subject matter of the appeal. The Grand Secretary must present the appeal, together with all the papers in the case, to the chairman of the Committee on Grievances. This committee consists of seven Past Grands, elected by the Grand Lodge to serve for one year, no two of whom shall be from the same Lodge. It is the duty of this committee to examine and decide upon all cases of grievance, officially submited to them by the Grand Secretary, as early thereafter as practicable. The trial of the case is *de novo.* They shall notify each party of the result of their examination, and their decision in the case shall be final, unless an appeal is taken by the party interested to the Board of Appeals, within thirty days after being officially notified of the action of the committee ; they shall report to the Grand Lodge at its regular session. The Board of Appeals consists of the Grand Master, Deputy Grand Master, Grand Warden, and six Past Grands, the latter to be selected by the Grand Master, no one of whom shall be a member of the Committee on Grievances, and no two of whom shall be from the same Lodge. They shall consider all appeals from the action of the Committee on Grievances, and decide thereon *from the evidence produced before said committee.* This evidence is obtained from the record of the Committee on Grievances. If neither party appeals from the decision of the Board of Appeals, within thirty days after being notified of such decision, it shall be final. In case of an appeal being taken from the decision of the Board of Appeals, the Board shall submit a report of the case to the Grand Lodge, at its next annual session for its arbitrament. They must also submit to the Grand Lodge, a report of all their decisions. Any five members of the Board constitute a quorum to do business.

PENNSYLVANIA.—In the Grand Lodge of Pennsylvania, there is a Committee on Appeals on Charges against members of Lodges, and a Committee on Appeals for Benefits. If a brother shall consider himself aggrieved by the decision of his Lodge, in relation to charges against him, he may appeal, at any time within three months, by filing with the Grand Secretary his appeal and the reasons therefor. His Lodge shall then, without delay, send, under its Seal, to the Grand Master such appeal, together with certified copies of charges, minutes, and all the records relating to the subject matter of the appeal. The Grand Master shall then refer the same to the Committee on Appeals on Charges, which consists of nine members, three of whom are elected annually to serve for three years. This committee shall hear the parties or their counsel or either of the parties may submit a written statement for the consideration of the committee. The committee shall give to each party to the appeal, at least ten days notice of the time and place for the hearing and determining the case. The hearing shall be confined solely to the specific cause, or causes of complaint, as set forth in the appeal. The committee shall examine the proceedings of the Lodge, the charge or charges, the proceedings of the Committee of Trial and the evidence taken, which shall be reduced to writing, and signed by the witnesses giving the same, and all books and papers submitted to it for examination at the time of trial. No new evidence, except to prove irregularity, informality, or unfairness shall be received by the Appeal Committee. The committee shall write out its decision and submit it to the Grand Master. If he shall approve the same, it shall be final and conclusive, unless an appeal be taken therefrom within three months after the decision of the committee. The appeal shall be confined, however, to matters of law, or of irregularity or improper proceedings of the Appeal Committee. The appeal shall be made by filing with the Grand Master, within the time above mentioned, the appeal and reasons therefor, which appeal, together with the proceedings of the committee shall be presented to the Grand Lodge at its next session. If the notice of the decision of the Grand Master has been received by the Lodge, at least one month before a stated session, the appeal must be presented at said session of the Grand Lodge, but before the appeal can be considered by the Grand Lodge, it must first have been referred to the Committee on the State of the Order, and a report received therefrom, as to whether the grounds of the appeal are proper and legal, and whether the same can be legally considered by the Grand Lodge. The Committee on Appeals for Benefits, consisting of nine members, elected in the same manner as the Committee on Appeals on Charges, have cognizance of appeals for benefits, if it appears that three months have not elapsed from the time the benefits have accrued, or are alleged to have accrued, and the filing of the appeal. If the appellant or his legal representative shall be absent from the State, the time for appeal shall be extended to six months. The manner of proceeding before the committee is the same as before the Committee on Appeals on Charges.

NEW YORK.—Any member intending to appeal from the action of his Lodge, shall, within twenty days thereafter, file with the Secretary a notice of his appeal and of the reasons therefor, upon which the Secretary shall forthwith send the notice, together with a certified copy of charges, reports, and all proceedings relative to the subject matter of the appeal, to the Grand Committee of the District. The Grand Committee will thereupon summon the parties before it, or such sub-committee as it may appoint, and hear the parties, or their counsel and determine the matter of the appeal. Any Lodge, or member, party to an appeal before a District Grand Committee, may appeal from its decision to the Grand Lodge; but such appeal shall be confined exclusively to matters of law or of irregularity, or of unfairness in the proceedings of the Grand Committee. Such appeal shall be made by filing with the District Deputy Grand Master of the District, within twenty days after notice of the decision of the District Grand Committee, a notice of the appeal and the reasons therefor, and thereupon the notice of appeal, together with a copy of the return of the Subordinate Lodge and the proceedings of the Grand Committee, and the decision thereof, shall be forthwith certified by the District Deputy Grand Master and Secretary of the Grand Committee, under Seal, and sent, with the appeal, to the Grand Lodge. The Grand Secretary, on receipt thereof, shall forthwith refer the same to the Committee on Appeals, who shall, if practicable, report thereon at the first session of the Grand Lodge which shall be held thereafter.

NEW JERSEY.—Any member feeling aggrieved by the decision of his Lodge, may appeal to the Grand Lodge, within sixty days after service of notice of said decision, by filing with the Secretary a written notice and the reasons therefor, and also by serving a notice of said appeal upon the Grand Secretary. The Lodge shall, within thirty days after the reception of the notice of appeal, through its Secretary, deliver to the Grand Secretary, under Seal, a certified copy of the minutes of the Committee of Trial, and also of the minutes of the Lodge and papers relating to the subject matter of the appeal. The Grand Secretary shall present the appeal to the Judiciary Committee at its next regular session. The Judiciary Committee consists of seven members, and they meet one week previous to the session of the Grand Lodge. It is their duty to investigate and determine all appeals, from Subordinate Lodges or their members, legally brought before them, and report their action to the Grand Lodge. They may try the case *de novo*. When the appeal is decided by the Grand Lodge, the Grand Secretary shall, within thirty days, notify the Lodge and the appellant, which decision shall be final, unless a further appeal shall be taken to the Sovereign Grand Lodge. In all cases of appeals to the Grand Lodge, the fact of such an appeal shall act as a stay of proceedings; and in all cases appealed to the Sovereign Grand Lodge, the fact of such an appeal shall act as a stay of proceedings, but the decision of the Subordinate shall be final until reversed by the State, or the Sovereign Grand Lodge, as the case may be. When an appeal refers to benefits, the amount in dispute shall be paid by the Subordinate Lodge to the Grand Secretary, to await the final determination of the case.

OHIO.—Any member feeling aggrieved by the decision of his Lodge, may appeal to the District Grand Committee, by filing written notice thereof, with the reasons therefor, with the Lodge, within sixty days after the trial, decision, or action of the Lodge. Upon notice of appeal being filed with the Lodge, it shall furnish a transcript of the record, including the notice of the appeal, duly certified under the Seal of the Lodge, within ten days after demand is made therefor. When said transcript is filed with the District Deputy Grand Master, by the Secretary, the appeal shall be deemed perfected. No appeal will be considered unless perfected within sixty days after the trial, decision, or action of the Lodge. The Past Grands of the several Lodges in any Supervisory District constitute a District Grand Committee, at whose meetings the District Deputy Grand Master, or a Past Grand appointed by him, presides. The District Grand Committee has power to hear and determine, appeals and grievances originating in any Lodge in the District, and also to reverse, vacate, or modify any decision, judgment, or final order made by a Lodge in the District, for errors appearing on the record; provided an exception thereto was taken at the time such errors were committed. Proceedings in such cases shall be by Petition in Error, filed with the District Deputy Grand Master, setting forth the errors complained of, together with a certified transcript of the record of the Lodge; and in cases where the errors complained of do not appear on the record, then a Bill of Exceptions, allowed by the Lodge and signed by the Noble Grand, shall be filed with the petition. When a Petition in Error is filed with the District Deputy Grand Master, he shall at once notify the Lodge of the same, also the time and place of hearing; provided that no Petition in Error shall be heard by the District Grand Committee unless it be filed with the District Deputy Grand Master, within sixty days after the decision, or action of the Lodge. The trial before the District Grand Committee shall be upon both the law and the facts, and shall be a trial *de novo*.

The Subordinate Lodge shall carry out, and perform, the decision and order of the District Grand Committee, which decision shall be final, unless reversed by the Grand Lodge. After the case shall have been decided by the District Grand Committee, if there is a desire to carry the same to the Grand Lodge on error, the party shall file with the Grand Secretary his Petition in Error setting forth the errors complained of, together with so much of the record as may be necessary, properly certified, or a Bill of Exceptions allowed and properly signed. The exception must have been made when the errors complained of were committed. No Petition in Error will be heard unless the same be so filed with the Grand Secretary within one year from the rendition of the decision, or judgment, or making of the order complained of, and no Petition in Error to a Subordinate Lodge shall be filed with the Grand Secretary, except by leave of the Grand Lodge first obtained. An appeal from a decision of a Lodge to the District Grand Committee, or to the Grand Lodge, if perfected, acts as a stay of proceedings. The Committee on Appeals consists of eight members, who take charge of all appeals which may be taken from the decisions of a District Grand Committee, or the Grand Master, during the recess, and investigate the same, and report to the Grand Lodge.

ILLINOIS.—Any member feeling aggrieved by the decision of his Lodge, may appeal to the Grand Lodge, by filing with the Secretary of his Lodge, within three months, after the rendering of the decision of his Lodge, a notice of his appeal with the reasons therefor. The Lodge, under its Seal, must then, without delay, send to the Grand Secretary, the aforesaid notice of appeal, together with certified copies of all minutes, charges, books and papers in possession of the Lodge relating to the subject matter of the appeal. All appeals and grievances received by the Grand Secretary are to be examined by him, for form and sufficiency. If he finds the proceedings or papers informal or incomplete, he must notify the Lodge of such informality or incompleteness, and it is lawful to rectify or amend any informality, or supply any deficiency, upon such notice given, and the papers are then returned to the Grand Secretary. When the proceedings and papers are in form and complete, they must be sent to the Grand Master, whose duty it is to decide such appeals as may be made to him. His decision is final, unless an appeal be taken to the Grand Lodge within one month thereafter; and the Grand Master must then report his decision, with the papers and appeal, to the next session of the Grand Lodge thereafter. The Committee on Appeals report upon all appeals involving mere questions of fact, and the Committee on the Judiciary, upon all appeals involving mere questions of law. Any three members feeling aggrieved by the decision of the Lodge, in a trial, are entitled to an appeal to the Grand Lodge, which appeal must be entered according to the laws and regulations of the Grand

Lodge on the matter of appeals, and, on command of the Grand Lodge, the brother may be tried anew for the same offence.

To the Grand Sire and Sovereign Grand Lodge.—The Grand Sire, during recess, may hear and decide certain appeals. See Constitution, Article IV., Section 1, page 324.

The Constitutional provision of the Sovereign Grand Lodge on the subject of appeals will be found in Article I., Section 4, page 323.

A member or members of a Subordinate Grand Body, may appeal to the Sovereign Grand Lodge without consent, the only condition being that the decision of the Subordinate Grand Body shall stand as final and conclusive until reversed by the Sovereign Grand Lodge.

The appeal that a member or members of a State, District, or Territorial Grand Lodge or Grand Encampment can make, it has been held, "confines such right of appeal to questions affecting the general interests of the entire Order, or to the general interests of the Order in the particular jurisdiction from which the appeal comes, and does not extend it to questions of grievance of individual members, or Lodges."

Individual members of Subordinate Lodges and Encampments, (as well as the Subordinates,) under the immediate jurisdiction of the Sovereign Grand Lodge, may appeal to the Sovereign Grand Lodge.

In all cases of appeal, the Subordinate Grand Body, from whose action any appeal is taken, shall be required to settle definitely, all questions of fact in such appeal, and shall duly certify the same under its Seal, and the signatures of its Executive Officer and Grand Scribe, or Grand Secretary, as the case may be, so that the sole and only business of the Sovereign Grand Lodge shall be to determine the law applicable to the facts thus certified. "The questions of fact required to be settled, may be so done by the Executive Officers and Grand Scribe or Grand Secretary or proper committee of the Grand Body from which the appeal is taken." In the absence of such duly certified facts, the appeal may be returned to have such matters supplied. If the Grand Body shall fail to settle such matters of fact, or the Grand Master or Grand Patriarch and Grand Secretary or Grand Scribe shall fail or neglect to certify them, such failure, or neglect, shall be deemed sufficient reason to reverse the decision of such Grand Body, unless some satisfactory reason shall be given for such neglect or refusal. The statement of facts, in the record of appeal, shall be deemed conclusive, provided both parties to the appeal have been heard, or have had an opportunity to be heard, and the report shall so state. In case of an appeal from the decision of a State Grand Body with its consent, the appellant should bring his appeal and record to the session of the Sovereign Grand Lodge next after the granting of it. On failure to do this, the State Grand Body may determine whether it will renew the permission to take the appeal.

Miscellaneous.—A Grand Master cannot grant an appeal from the action of his Grand Lodge.

With the consent of a State Grand Body, an appeal may be taken from its decision on a hypothetical case.

The Sovereign Grand Lodge will not consider a memorial in relation to the expulsion of a member, pending his appeal to his Grand Body from such expulsion.

When the Sovereign Grand Lodge decides a case at any session, and closes said session, that decision, by the final adjournment, becomes conclusive and binding, and cannot be set aside or annulled at any subsequent session, except in case of gross fraud or mistake which the person in interest must use due diligence to have corrected.

The Sovereign Grand Lodge may reverse the decision of a State Grand Body without granting a new trial.

The Sovereign Grand Lodge will not decide incidental questions which may arise in a case, which, if decided, would not affect the ultimate result.

An appeal to the Sovereign Grand Lodge, gives to the member of the Order under penalty, who is interested therein, no additional privileges, and no different position, from those he enjoys and occupies under the laws of his State Grand Lodge.

Appeals by Subordinates under the immediate jurisdiction of the Sovereign Grand Lodge, or their members, must be presented within twenty days from the action of the Subordinate appealed from, to be forwarded with all the papers, properly certified, to the District Deputy Grand Sire, for transmission to the Grand Secretary of the Sovereign Grand Lodge. Within twenty days after the reception of a notice of appeal to the Sovereign Grand Lodge, the Subordinate, by its Secretary or Scribe, shall deliver to the Grand Secretary, under Seal, a certified copy of the charges, minutes of the Committee of Trial, and also of the records relating to the subject matter of the appeal, and the original testimony taken at the trial, according to the prescribed Form in Constitution for Subordinates. Should the Subordinate fail to make the above return, the Grand Secretary shall notify it of such failure, and direct the return to be made within ten days from the receipt of the notice; and if default be made, he shall report the Subordinate to the Grand Sire as insubordinate. The Grand Secretary shall, within one month after the decision of the appeal, notify the Subordinate and the appellant thereof. The record in appeals from a Subordinate Lodge or Encampment under the immediate jurisdiction of the Sovereign Grand Lodge, need not be printed.

GENERAL REGULATIONS FOR APPEALS TO THE SOVEREIGN GRAND LODGE FROM THE ACTION OF SUBORDINATE GRAND BODIES.

1. Appeals must be filed with the Grand Secretary by the first day of the meeting of the Committee (Wednesday preceding the meeting of the Sovereign Grand Lodge).

2. The appeal must show that the Grand Body appealed from has given its consent to the appellant, except in the case of a suspended or expelled Subordinate that has surrendered its effects, or a minority of the Grand Body.

3. The statement of facts must be certified under the Seal of the Grand Body, and the signatures of the Grand Master and Grand Secretary, or Grand Patriarch and Grand Scribe, as the case may be. The signatures must be written on at least fifteen copies.

4. Appeal papers must be furnished by the appealing parties, printed in

pamphlet form, on a page of the same size as that of the printed Journal of Proceedings of the Sovereign Grand Lodge.   (Type $3\frac{7}{8}$ x $9\frac{3}{8}$ inches.)

5. Appellants must furnish two hundred copies of all appeal papers.

6. Appellants must send with their papers, a certified copy of the Constitution and By-Laws of their Grand Body, of the Constitution for Subordinates, and of the By-Laws of the Subordinate Lodge or Encampment involved in the appeal.

7. Applications to open, rehear, or review decisions of the Sovereign Grand Lodge, in appeal cases, whether by petition, memorial, or otherwise, are subject to the above rules.

CHAPTER IX.

REPORTS, ABBREVIATIONS, ANNIVERSARY AND MEMORIAL DAYS.

ANNUAL returns must be made by each State, District, and Territorial Grand Body to the Sovereign Grand Lodge. Grand Scribes and Grand Secretaries, at the time of making their annual returns to the Grand Secretary of the Sovereign Grand Lodge, must furnish therewith, the post-office addresses of their respective Grand Patriarchs, Grand Scribes, Grand Masters, and Grand Secretaries; also the times and places of the annual sessions of their Grand Bodies. The report should be signed by the Grand Master or Grand Patriarch, and the Grand Secretary or Grand Scribe, in office December thirty-first. Subordinate Lodges and Encampments working under the immediate jurisdiction of the Sovereign Grand Lodge, must transmit annually to the Grand Secretary, reports containing the same information that is required from Grand Lodges and Grand Encampments. Reports of Grand and Subordinate Bodies must be accompanied by the dues in current money. Grand Bodies subordinate to the S. G. L., are required to make such laws and regulations as will enable them to collect from their Subordinates the full returns required by the By-Laws, Article X. (page 332,) and as may be necessary to insure the annual returns to the office of the Grand Secretary of the S. G. L., on or before the first day of April in every year. All term reports which are required to be made to Grand Bodies, by their Subordinates, shall contain, in their own handwriting, the signatures of the elective Officers thereof, and shall be carefully preserved by the Grand Scribes and Grand Secretaries.

The Grand Secretary of the S. G. L. is directed to have blank returns sent to State Grand Lodges, to enable them to make their returns in reference to Rebekah Lodges; and Grand Lodges having Degree Lodges of the Daughters of Rebekah under their jurisdiction, shall require such Lodges to report annually, on the thirty-first of December, the information necessary to complete the returns required by the S. G. L. If any Rebekah Degree Lodge shall, for thirty days after the time by law required for the making of its annual report, neglect to make and forward the same to the proper officer, it shall be the duty of the Grand Master of the jurisdiction to declare the Charter of said Lodge forfeited, and to reclaim the same.

The following Forms of Annual Reports are presented: 1. A Grand Lodge or Grand Encampment Report. 2. The Report of a Subordinate Lodge or Encampment under the immediate jurisdiction of the Sovereign Grand Lodge. (*See Book of Forms for Forms of Reports.*)

ANNUAL REPORT OF THE GRAND LODGE (OR GRAND ENCAMPMENT) OF..................... ....

Commencing January 1, 18..., and ending December 31, 18 .

NUMBER OF LODGES (OR ENCAMPMENTS)		Number of brothers (or Patriarchs) relieved........................ .... Number of widowed families relieved .... Number of brothers (or Patriarchs) buried..............................	
Number of members per last report Add error in last report .... Initiated during the year......... Admitted by Card............... Reinstated.......................		*Amount Paid for the Relief*	Dollars. Cents
		Of brothers (or Patriarchs)... Of widowed families......... For education of orphans.... For burying the dead........ Special relief................	
TOTAL.......................		TOTAL RELIEF...............	
FROM WHICH DEDUCT :		Amount of the Annual Receipts	
Error in last report....... Withdrawn by Card. .... Suspended for cause..... Suspended or dropped for non-payment of dues.. Expelled.................. Deceased.................		Number of weeks' sickness for which benefits were paid..................	
		If the G. Secretary (or G. Scribe) has the information, the following blanks may be filled :	
TOTAL.......................		Current expenses of Subordinates for the year, separate from benefits and charities	
Members December 31, 18		Invested funds of Subordinates..	

IN WITNESS WHEREOF, we have hereunto set our hands and the Seal of the Grand Lodge (or Grand Encampment) of the...........................of.........................
this...........................day of ....in the year one thousand eight hundred and...............................

[SEAL]   ....Grand Master (or Grand Patriarch).
                         ....Grand Secretary (or Grand Scribe).

ANNUAL REPORT OF.................LODGE (OR ENCAMPMENT).............No ....

LOCATED AT.. .
TO THE SOVEREIGN GRAND LODGE OF THE INDEPENDENT ORDER OF ODD FELLOWS,
Commencing January 1, 18...., and ending December 31, 18....

		RECEIPTS.		
Number of members per last report.				
Initiated during the year........ ...				
Admitted by Card			Dollars.	Cents
Reinstated		Initiations............		
		Degrees....		
		Dues......................		
		Deposit of Cards....		
TOTAL...........................		Visiting and Withdrawal Cards		
		TOTAL		
FROM WHICH DEDUCT:				
		AMOUNT PAID FOR RELIEF.		
Withdrawn by Card				
Suspended...................			No.	Amount.
Expelled...........				
Deceased...................		Brothers (or Patriarchs)		Dollars. Cents
		relieved...............		
		Brothers (or Patriarchs) of		
TOTAL....		other Lodges (or En-		
		campments) relieved ...		
Now in membership.... ...		Widowed families re-		
		lieved.................		
		Orphans educated.		
		Brothers (or Patriarchs)		
RANK OF MEMBERS.		buried...		
		Brothers' (or Patriarchs')		
Past Grands (or Past Chief		wives buried...........		
Patriarchs)................		Special relief .... ·		
Third Degree (or Past High		TOTAL paid for relief.......		.
Priests)				
Second Degree (or Royal				
Purple Degree)		Number of weeks' sickness for		
First Degree (or Golden		which benefits were paid..		
Rule Degree).........				
Initiatory (or Patriarchal		Due Sovereign Grand Lodge of the		
Degree)...................		I. O. O. F., *five per cent.* on re-		
		ceipts		
TOTAL...................				

DEGREES CONFERRED.

Initiatory (or Patriarchal Degree)....................

First (or Golden Rule Degree) ....

Second (or Royal Purple Degree) ....

Third Degree ....

TOTAL...................

The attention of Secretaries (or Scribes) is particularly directed to the subjoined:

RESOLVED, That the Grand Secretary be directed to add to the items upon which reports are required to be made to this Grand Lodge, the following item, to-wit: Number of weeks' sickness for which benefits were paid.

RESOLVED, That said Secretary place upon the margin of the form furnished, this note: This information can be easily procured by referring to the Order book of the Lodge or Encampment. For instance, Bro. A. B. has been sick during the year twenty-six weeks, Bro. C. D., ten weeks, Bro. E. F., three weeks. The return is then made thus: Number of weeks' sickness for which benefits were paid, thirty-nine.

There must be annexed to the report, the names of those initiated (or admitted, advanced, and exalted), admitted by Card, reinstated, withdrawn, suspended and cause, expelled and cause, deceased, rejected, and a complete list of the names of members and their rank, with the following appended:

We hereby certify that the foregoing report is correct throughout. In witness whereof, we have hereunto set our hands and the Seal of the Lodge (or Encampment) this................ day of.... ....18....

....N. G. (or C. P.)

[SEAL]   ....Secretary (or Scribe).

ABBREVIATIONS.

A., Annual, Assistant.
A.G.Sec., Assistant Grand Secretary.
A.T.P.W., Annual Traveling Pass Word.
Bro., Brother.
C., Check, Chief, Conductor.
Chap., Chaplain.
C.P., Chief Patriarch.
C.P.W., Check Pass Word
D., Daughter, Degree, Deputy, District.
D.D.G.M., District Deputy Grand Master.
D.D.G.S., District Deputy Grand Sire.
D.G.M., Deputy Grand Master.
D.G.S., Deputy Grand Sire.
D.M., Degree Master.
D.R., Degree of Rebekah, or Daughter of Rebekah.
E., Encampment, Excellent.
F., Fellow, Financial, Friendship.
F.L.T., Friendship, Love and Truth.
F.Scr., Financial Scribe.
G., Golden, Grand, Guard, Guardian, Guide.
G.C., Grand Conductor.
G.Chap., Grand Chaplain.
G.E., Grand Encampment.
G.Guar., Grand Guardian.
G.H., Grand Herald.
G.H.P., Grand High Priest.
G.L Sent., Grand Inside Sentinel.
G.J.W., Grand Junior Warden.
G.L., Grand Lodge.
G.L.U.S., Grand Lodge of the United States.
G.O.Sent., Grand Outside Sentinel.
G.M., Grand Master.
G.Mar., Grand Marshal.
G.Mess., Grand Messenger.
G. of T., Guard of the Tent.
G.P., Grand Patriarch.
G.R., Golden Rule.
G.Rep., Grand Representative.

G.S., Grand Sire.
G.Sec., Grand Secretary.
G.S.W., Grand Senior Warden.
G.T., Grand Treasurer.
Guar., Guardian.
G.W., Grand Warden.
H., Herald, High.
H.P., High Priest.
I., Independent, Inside.
I.G., Inside Guardian.
I.O.O.F., Independent Order of Odd Fellows.
I.Sent., Inside Sentinel.
J., Junior.
J.G.S., Junior Grand Sire.
J.P.G., Junior Past Grand.
J.W., Junior Warden.
L., Left, Lodge, Love.
L.S., Left Supporter.
L.S.N.G., Left Supporter of the Noble Grand.
L.S.S., Left Scene Supporter.
L.S.V.G., Left Supporter of the Vice Grand.
M., Manchester, Master, Militant, Most.
Mar., Marshal.
Mess., Messenger.
M.U., Manchester Unity.
M.W., Most Worthy.
N., Noble.
N.G., Noble Grand.
O., Odd, Official, Order, Outside.
O.F., Odd Fellow.
O.G., Outside Guardian.
O.Sent., Outside Sentinel.
P., Pass Word, Past, Patriarch, Patriarchal, Permanent, Priest, Purple.
P.C.P., Past Chief Patriarch.
P.D.D.G.S., Past District Deputy Grand Sire.
Per., Permanent.
Per.Sec., Permanent Secretary.
P.G., Past Grand.

P.G.M., Past Grand Master.
P.G.P., Past Grand Patriarch.
P.G.Rep., Past Grand Representative.
P.G.S., Past Grand Sire.
P.H.P., Past High Priest.
P.M., Patriarchs Militant.
P.N.G., Past Noble Grand.
P.O., Past Official.
P.P.W., Permanent Pass Word.
P.V.G., Past Vice Grand.
P.W., Pass Word.
R., Rebekah, Recording, Right, Royal, Rule.
Rep., Representative.
R.P., Royal Purple.
R.Sec., Recording Secretary.
R.S.N.G., Right Supporter of the Noble Grand.
R.S.S., Right Scene Supporter.

R.S.V.G., Right Supporter of the Vice Grand.
R.W., Right Worthy.
S., Scene, Senior, Sire, Sovereign, Supporter.
S.A.P.W., Semi-annual Pass Word.
Scr., Scribe.
Sec., Secretary.
Sent., Sentinel.
S.G.L., Sovereign Grand Lodge.
S.S., Scene Supporter.
S.W., Senior Warden.
T., Tent, Term, Traveling, Treasurer, Truth.
T.P.W., Term Pass Word.
U., Uniformed, United, Unity.
U.D.Camp, Uniformed Degree Camp.
V., Vice.
V.G., Vice Grand.
W., Warden, Watch, Word, Worthy.

ANNIVERSARY AND MEMORIAL DAYS.

February 22d, 1824, the Grand Lodge of Maryland and of the United States "ordered, that a recommendation be sent to the Subordinate Lodges in Maryland to have but one general anniversary, and that the time be on the 26th of April." *Journal, page* 64. The Grand Lodge of the United States, considering the above action as merely local in its terms, adopted, September 21st, 1867, the following : " That the 26th of April be, and the same hereby is, established as the Anniversary of the Order, and all Grand Lodges and Grand Encampments are requested to urge their Subordinates to observe the day in some appropriate manner."

The Sovereign Grand Lodge, at the Session of 1886, enacted the following :

Resolved, Whereas, it is not only right and proper, but the very nature, spirit and desire of the Order, demand that a day be set apart in each year on which its members may unite in solemn *Memorial Exercises* in behalf of their honored dead, and it is believed that the most appropriate time for such service would be upon the 20th day of October,* which day is that on which our Past Grand Sire

---

* Past Grand Sire Wildey did not die on the 20th, but on the 19th day of October, 1861.

WILDEY, who, after long years of earnest and successful work in our behalf, was gathered to his fathers; be it, therefore,

Resolved, That the Grand Sire, in conjunction with the Grand Secretary, is hereby instructed to issue a proclamation annually, at least sixty days prior to October 20th, containing the purport of this preamble and resolution, requesting all Subordinate Lodges to assemble on the day above named and engage in appropriate memorial exercises respecting their deceased members, such exercises to be conducted in a manner appropriate to the occasion. Said proclamation shall embrace the names of such officers and members of the Sovereign Grand Lodge, and past officers and members, if any, who died during the term herein named. This resolution to take effect in the year 1887; *provided, however*, that if a different day be more convenient for any Lodge to hold such Memorial Service, such Lodge may select the day.—*Journal, page* 10,517.

The following is a copy of the first proclamation issued under the above direction:

MEMORIAL DAY PROCLAMATION.

SOVEREIGN GRAND LODGE OF THE I. O. O. F.,
OFFICE OF THE GRAND SIRE.

To whom these presents shall come, Greeting:

Pursuant to instructions contained in the resolution of the Sovereign Grand Lodge, adopted at its annual session held at Boston, September, 1886 (*Journal*, 10,517), I, JOHN H. WHITE, Grand Sire, do hereby request all Subordinate Lodges under our jurisdiction to assemble at their respective Lodge-rooms on the 20th day of October, 1887, the anniversary of the death of THOMAS WILDEY, Past Grand Sire, and engage in appropriate memorial exercises respecting their deceased members ; such exercises to be conducted in a manner appropriate to the occasion. Should a different day be more convenient, any lodge is permitted to hold such services on any day such Lodge may select.

Information has been received of the death of the following Past Officers and members of the Sovereign Grand Lodge, since the last annual communication, with date of death, and age, respectively :

(Here the names of the deceased Past Officers and Representatives were stated.)

Done at the city of Columbus, in the State of Ohio, U. S. A., this 15th day of August, 1887, and of our Order the sixty-ninth year.

[Seal.]   JNO. H. WHITE, *Grand Sire.*

Attest : THEO. A. ROSS, *Grand Secretary.*

CHAPTER X.

Manual of the Work and Usages of the Order.

Absence.—The words "temporary absence," as used in the Charge Books, mean absence from the chair merely, but present in the Lodge room or ante-room; while "absence" means not present in the Lodge room or ante-room and nothing more. An officer, during his term, cannot be displaced for non-attendance, if there be no constitutional provision or By-Law on the subject. A Junior Past Grand is not an officer of a Lodge and cannot be fined, as such, for non-attendance at meetings. The penalty for absence varies with the case and the local law. To be entitled to the honors of an office, the incumbent must serve a majority of the nights of the term, excepting when a vacancy is filled, and the majority of the nights served must expire with the end of the term. If excused, on account of sickness, the honors are not forfeited. If an officer elect is not present for installation, and there be no satisfactory reason therefor, the installing officer may order a new election. A Grand Representative, attending the Sovereign Grand Lodge, does not incur any penalty for neglecting his duty in any office he may hold in his State Grand Body. Non-attendance at the funerals of brethren may be punished by fine. State Grand Bodies may determine whether the dead shall be buried by a committee or the whole Lodge. Secretaries and Scribes are generally finable for non-attendance; it is a matter, however, for the local law.

Adjournment.—A Lodge or Encampment cannot hold adjourned meetings. If other than regular meetings are required, they must be held in the manner prescribed by the By-Laws. A motion to adjourn *sine die* is always in order, but the Lodge or Encampment must close in due form.

Advertisement.—Members of the Order must not use any of its Emblems, its Name, Title, Motto, or Initials in connection with any advertisement in the prosecution of any private business. (*See pages* 218, 219.) It is an offense punishable by suspension or expulsion, at the will of the Lodge or Encampment, of the offender. A member of the Order, who publishes a newspaper or periodical in the interests of the Order, is not subject to the above penalty, unless he gives publicity to any of the Signs, or other secrets of the Order in advertisements for private gain.

Amendments to the Constitution and By-Laws of the S. G. L.—See Article XXI., page 329, Rules of Order, 37, page 341, and Article XXX., page 338. If a resolution, in its terms, would alter the Constitution, it must lie over as a proposed amendment. A proposition to amend the Constitution cannot be amended when it comes up for action. A proposed amendment may be indefinitely postponed. An amendment, if not acted upon at the next session after it was proposed, may be acted upon at any succeeding session. If rejected, it can be again proposed and again considered, after the lapse of the proper time. An amendment can be reconsidered at any time during the annual session at which it is adopted, and when adopted it goes into immediate effect. A decision of the Grand Sire, though approved by the S. G. L., cannot set aside a By-Law of the S. G. L. A proposed By-Law must lie on the table for one day, and when it comes up for action it may be amended.

AMENDMENTS TO THE CONSTITUTIONS OF STATE GRAND BODIES.—All amendments to these Constitutions must be submitted to the S. G. L. for approval. Until approved they are inoperative, but when approved they are, at once, in full force. The S. G. L. will not approve a proposed amendment; it must be adopted before presentment for approval. These Constitutions must be amended in the manner prescribed therein. Amendments to the By-Laws of State Grand Bodies do not require the approval of the S. G. L.

AMENDMENTS TO THE CONSTITUTIONS AND BY-LAWS OF SUBORDINATES.— The Constitutions of Subordinates must be amended in the manner prescribed in the Constitutions themselves. State Grand Bodies may require their Subordinates to submit their amended By-Laws for approval. Amendments to the By-Laws of Subordinates under the immediate jurisdiction of the S. G. L., are void and without effect until approved by it.

ANCIENT ODD FELLOW.—An Ancient Odd Fellow is one who has been regularly initiated into the Order and retired therefrom, in good standing, either by taking a Withdrawal Card, or by resignation. If a member resigns, he, at once, becomes an Ancient Odd Fellow, and if he takes a Withdrawal Card, and does not deposit it, he becomes one at the expiration of one year from the date of his Card. He is not entitled to visit a Subordinate Lodge. He may be allowed to renew his membership by deposit of Card in a Lodge at the place of his residence, upon the payment of such fee as the laws of such Lodge require, if he can prove himself in the Work. If he became an Ancient Odd Fellow by written resignation, he may be re-admitted, provided he can pass a satisfactory examination in the Work. If he cannot do so, he can be admitted only by initiation. If his Card has been lost or destroyed, on satisfactory proof thereof, he may be re-admitted, and will be entitled to the rank he can prove himself to have attained.

ARREARS.—Notwithstanding the importance of this subject to the interests of members and Subordinates, it is not as clearly understood as it should be. In the first place, the dues to a Lodge accrue weekly, and only for the convenience of the Lodge are paid at stated periods. (*See Journal* 1848, *page* 1,318.) Generally, Lodges collect their dues quarterly, but no matter when they are collected they *accrue* weekly, and may be charged up to the brethren. It is upon this fundamental proposition that the doctrine of arrears is founded. When it is clearly understood that the dues accrue and are chargeable weekly, all difficulty in interpreting the law of arrears at once disappears. The amount of arrears, as well as the length of time in arrears, requisite to deprive a member of benefits, depends on the local law. (*See page* 289.) Members in arrears for weekly or funeral dues, more than thirteen nights, are not entitled to the Term Password. A brother suspended from membership, by reason of being in arrears, is cut off from all benefits and privileges, and should he die during such suspension, the Lodge incurs no new liability by his decease. A brother who is not entitled to sick benefits, by reason of being in arrears, cannot, during his sickness, by the payment of arrearages, reinstate himself in good standing, so as to be entitled to benefits during that sickness. If a brother is beneficial at the commencement of his sickness or disability, he cannot become in arrears, so as to disqualify him from receiving his benefits during such sickness or disability. (*See page* 141.) If a brother dies while in arrears, through the fault of the Secretary, the Lodge must pay the funeral benefits, if it appears that he would have been beneficial at the time of his death if the Secretary had not been in fault. If a brother is in arrears for more than a year's dues and, while not suspended, pays his dues in full, he is entitled to benefits after the expiration of the probationary period. Members in arrears, if not suspended, are entitled to visitation and care, though not entitled to benefits. (*See page* 268.)

ASSESSMENTS BY THE SOVEREIGN GRAND LODGE.—The Sovereign Grand Lodge may assess, for its own support, the Subordinates, State, District and Territorial Grand Lodges and Grand Encampments under its jurisdiction.

ASSESSMENTS BY STATE GRAND BODIES.—State Grand Bodies may assess their Subordinates to meet deficiencies and to pay their current expenses. They cannot compel the whole or any number of them to adopt an endowment scheme, or assess them to establish a Home for Widows and Orphans, or to support Odd Fellows' Libraries, or for General Relief.

ASSESSMENTS BY SUBORDINATES.—Subordinates may tax their members to be enabled to pay the stipulated weekly benefits to sick members. They cannot assess their members a specific sum to fit up a hall and procure the necessary fixtures.

ATHEISTS are disqualified from becoming members of the Order. (*See page* 238.)

BALLS.—Permission must be obtained to hold Balls where the Regalia of the Order is to be worn. (*See page* 177.) Subordinates under the immediate jurisdiction of the S. G. L. must obtain the desired permission from the Grand Sire.

BEHAVIOR.—All members of the Order are in duty bound, while in their Lodges or Encampments, to be governed in their conduct by the well-known usages and regulations of the Order. In case of their refusal, or neglect so to act, they must atone to the offended law. It is, therefore, proper to prefer charges against them for conduct unbecoming an Odd Fellow. Should they be members of another Lodge or Encampment, their conduct should be reported thereto. Subordinates have, as a requisite to self-protection, the inherent right to protect themselves from disorder, the want of decorum, and violations of the ordinary proprieties of life.

BENEFITS, WEEKLY.—All Subordinates must pay some stipulated weekly benefits. Benefits are a right and not a charity. Neither a Grand Lodge nor a Grand Master can grant a Dispensation to enable a Lodge to suspend the payment of weekly benefits. A member may decline to receive his weekly benefits. (*See page* 267.)

The benefits paid must be continuous and weekly, as long as the beneficiary is entitled to them. The right to benefits cannot be made to depend upon qualifications not recognized by the general law, and in their payment, the Subordinates must be governed by their existing laws. The Subordinates are sovereign as to the amount of such benefits and in the disposition of them. (*See page* 177.) State Grand Bodies may enact uniform Constitutions for their Subordinates, and may fix therein a specific rate of benefits. A Subordinate may provide, in its By-Laws, against paying for a fractional part of a week, or that benefits shall not be paid for the first week's sickness. It is left with the local law to determine as to the payment of a greater amount of benefits to Third Degree members, than to those of a lower Degree; also to determine when the benefits begin; but if there be no legislation on the subject, the Subordinates themselves may determine the matter. Subordinates may, if their law is to that effect, refuse to pay benefits to those members who have received no Degrees, and they may, by law, provide that initiates and members who have not received the Third Degree, are entitled to benefits. A Subordinate under the immediate jurisdiction of the S. G. L., cannot make a By-Law providing that a brother shall not receive benefits until he has been a member six months. After benefits have accrued, a Subordinate cannot reduce the amount, but in the absence of local law, it may reduce the benefits after a certain period of sickness, or after the beneficiary has received a certain amount, such law being applicable to all members alike. The benefits of a member may be reduced, during his sickness, by amendment of the law, without having any reference to any period of sickness, or amount paid, if such amendment is general in its application. A brother suspended from membership, is cut off from all benefits. There is no general law regulating the granting of benefits, and where State Grand Bodies do not prohibit, their Subordinates have the authority to grant benefits to a brother who is more than thirteen weeks in arrears. A member of a Subordinate who is in arrears for weekly or funeral dues, more than thirteen weeks, cannot, if agreeable to the local or Subordinate law, become entitled to benefits until he shall have paid in full, all dues and fines that have accrued against him up to the date of payment; nor then, until the expiration of such probationary period as may also by the laws be provided as a penalty. A Subordinate can charge and collect dues in advance, under penalty of disqualification for benefits, provided it has permission to do so from its Grand Body. When a brother asks for, and is granted, a Withdrawal Card, whether it be taken or not, it relieves the Subordinate from all liability for benefits. Aged and indigent persons are not, *per se*, as a matter of right, entitled to benefits. Lunatics are entitled to such benefits as are given to those who suffer from bodily infirmity. A blind brother is, *prima facie*, entitled to benefits, if he has not, or cannot reasonably obtain an occupation, whereby he can make a living. (*See* SICKNESS.) Subordinates have no right to refuse to pay their members full benefits because they have changed their residence to a place where their health and life are liable to be impaired or endangered ; nor to prohibit them from going wherever their interests or inclination may take them. A Subordinate has no right to refuse to pay benefits to a brother entitled thereto, because he entered an almshouse, or because he is a charge upon the public. A Lodge has no right to initiate a person with a chronic disease, upon the applicant's signing an agreement not to claim benefits in consequence of sickness or disability from such disease.·

FUNERAL BENEFITS AND EXPENSES.—The beneficiaries of a funeral benefit are the widow, orphan, or dependent relatives of the deceased, and dependent relatives are relatives who are members of the family of the deceased and who were dependent upon the deceased for support, at the time of his decease. Legal representatives of an Odd Fellow, are not recognized by the laws of the Order, nor are the personal representatives (executors or administrators) of a deceased brother, because the right of property to the funeral benefits is in the family of the deceased, and not in the brother. It does not begin to exist until after his death, and therefore he cannot dispose of it during his life.

A widow is entitled to funeral benefits where the Lodge is indebted to the brother, her husband, enough to make him beneficial at the time of his death; but she is not entitled to funeral benefits, if the brother, while in arrears so as to deprive him of weekly benefits, is taken sick and pays up his dues during that sickness, from which he dies. Where a member is in arrears so as not to be entitled to benefits, the Lodge is not bound to pay funeral expenses, though incurred. When the laws of a Lodge distinguish between funeral benefits and funeral expenses, the Lodge cannot be required to pay anything on account of the funeral expenses, when a deceased brother has been buried and no such expenses have been incurred by the family. If the expenses were incurred in the burial of the brother, the family is entitled to the amount of the funeral expenses, whether the Lodge authorized the expenditure of all or part of the funeral expenses, or as a Lodge attended the funeral. In the payment of funeral benefits and funeral expenses, the Subordinates are sovereign both as to the amount of such benefits and in the disposition of them. (*See page* 177.) A Lodge cannot refuse to pay funeral benefits to the family of a brother because he committed suicide. If a person becomes a member of the Order by fraud on his part, it shall be legal to investigate and determine the fact of such fraud, even after his death, provided due notice of such intended investigation is given to the representatives, or family of the deceased, claiming benefits. If the fraud be proved, the Subordinate is discharged from all liability from the time the fraud was discovered and proved. A Lodge may be compelled to pay the funerál benefits of a brother whose death was caused by immoral conduct, although the By-Laws provide to the contrary. This is the case where the immoral conduct of the brother was well known to the members of the Lodge, and they suffered the deceased to continue his immoral conduct, until death ensued, without charges preferred against him.

BIBLE.—The Bible is an integral part of Odd Fellowship, and should be present in every Lodge when open for business.

BLIND.—The blind are not eligible to membership. (*See page* 272.) A brother who becomes blind, is, *prima facie*, entitled to benefits; that is, the burden of proof is with the Subordinate, which disputes his claim, to prove to the contrary.

BOOK OF FORMS.—The Book of Forms is published by the S. G. L., and contains so much useful information that every member should have one. The following is the table of contents:

BY-LAWS OF THE SOVEREIGN GRAND LODGE.—See pages 230–238, and AMENDMENTS.

BY-LAWS OF STATE GRAND BODIES.—The By-Laws of State Grand Bodies do not have to be submitted to the S. G. L. for approval, nor can they be repealed by a mere resolution, if another mode of amendment is prescribed.

BY-LAWS OF SUBORDINATES.—Subordinates may make By-Laws for their own government, but when in conflict with the laws of their State Grand Bodies, or of the S. G. L., they give place to the laws of the higher Bodies. State Grand Bodies have absolute control as to requiring their Subordinates to have their By-Laws approved by them. If they must be approved, they are without force and effect until this is done. The S. G. L. will not interfere unless the By-Laws are in conflict with the laws of the Supreme Body. By-Laws must be amended, repealed and modified in the manner prescribed by the By-Laws themselves. State Grand Bodies having the right to approve By-Laws, have, as a necessary concomitant, the right to use their discretion as to adoption or not.

CARDS.—Cards are of four kinds: Visiting, Withdrawal, Wives' or Widows and Daughters' of Rebekah. The Visiting and Withdrawal Cards are issued by Subordinate Lodges, Subordinate Encampments, and Degree Lodges of the Daughters of Rebekah. The Cards for Wives or Widows, and Daughters of Rebekah not members of Degree Lodges of the Daughters of Rebekah, are issued by the Subordinate Lodges alone. The Visiting and Withdrawal Cards and Cards for Wives or Widows are prepared and furnished by the S. G. L., whose Grand Secretary must countersign them. In addition to the counter-sign of the Grand Secretary of the S. G. L., they must be signed by the N. G. and attested by the Secretary of the Lodge issuing the same, or by the C. P. and attested by the Scribe of the Encampment, and be under Seal. All the Cards must be signed by the holders thereof, in the presence of the officer by whom the Annual Password is communicated to the holders. The Visiting and Withdrawal Cards should have stated thereon, the rank and Degree to which the brother or sister has attained in the Branch of the Order from which the Card is obtained. If the recipient be a Grand Representative, or a P. G. Representative, then said rank should be expressed on the Card, whether taken from a Lodge, or Encampment. When the local law requires the prepayment of the Card charge, the officer whose duty it is to issue the Card, has the right to refuse to deliver it until the prepayment is made. State Grand Bodies may prescribe, by law, that all applications for Visiting or Withdrawal Cards, must be in person or in writing.

VISITING CARDS.—Any brother in good standing may obtain a Visiting Card, to be good for a reasonable length of time, expressed on its face.(*See page* 285.) An initiate, or a member who has not received the Third Degree, is entitled to a Visiting Card by which to visit Lodges in the Degree to which he has attained, whether he is entitled to benefits or not. The Card must state whether the holder is entitled to benefits or not, and if he is a non-beneficial member, there should be an endorsement stating the time the brother will become beneficial. Visiting Cards entitle the legitimate holders to visit Lodges, Encampments, or Degree Lodges of the Daughters of Rebekah, as the case may be, until the Cards expire, while without their own jurisdictions. As to visiting in the holder's own jurisdiction, see page 199. These Cards entitle the holders to all the courtesies and beneficial usages of the Order, in case of accident or misfortune. There must be inserted, in the body of the Card, the amount of weekly and funeral benefits allowed by the laws of the Body granting the Card, and said Body is bound for the relief extended. (*See page* 121.) If attentive benefits are allowed, the Secretary or Scribe, as the case may be, must endorse on the Card, the character of the attentive benefits. (*See page* 288.) All Visiting Cards have printed on their backs blanks to be filled by Secretaries or Scribes, recording the date, name and number of the Lodge or Encampment visited by the holders. If the holder of a Visiting Card shall obtain money from a Lodge, Encampment, or Relief Committee, the amount obtained, the date, and the name of the giver, shall be endorsed on the Card and attested by the proper officer. (*See page* 280.)

A Visiting Card is granted, as a matter of course, to a member in good standing. It must be granted at a regular meeting, or by the N. G. and Secretary, or C. P. and Scribe in recess. No ballot is necessary; a formal announcement of application is made, and the presiding officer states that the Card will be granted, if there be no objection. When a member has obtained a Visiting Card he cannot obtain another, until the former one shall have been returned, or until satisfactory proof has been produced that it was lost or destroyed. A Visiting Card cannot be extended by endorsement; a new one must be taken out, if a Card for a longer time is desired. (*See page* 248.) A brother, upon change of residence, can apply for membership in any Lodge or Encampment, by first obtaining and presenting, with his petition, a Visiting Card from the Body in which he holds membership, and then proceeding as described on page 315.

WITHDRAWAL CARDS, also called Clearance, or Final Cards, are granted by the vote of the Subordinate Lodge, Encampment, or Degree Lodge of the Daughters of Rebekah, and by ball ballot. It requires the affirmative vote of a majority of the members present to grant such Cards. (*See page* 183.) The vote by which a Withdrawal Card is granted, cannot be reconsidered or rescinded. An application for a Withdrawal Card, may be withdrawn at any time previous to its being voted on and that, too, without the consent of the Body. If charges be preferred against an applicant for a Card, the vote on granting it should not be taken, until the charges be withdrawn, or a trial has been had upon them. Although an applicant may be in good standing, the Body applied to is not bound to authorize a Card. If a financial officer of a Subordinate refuses or fails to settle his accounts, his Subordinate may refuse to grant him a Card, until his accounts are adjusted and he free himself from all charges. A Card cannot be granted unless there is a quorum of qualified members present. If a Withdrawal Card is lost, without censurable fault, a new Card may be obtained, bearing the same date, from the Body that granted the original one. The face of the new Card must show that it is a duplicate. In the place of a duplicate, the Body may grant a Certificate, under Seal, setting forth the fact of issuing the original. This Certificate may be used as evidence of previous good standing. A Secretary has no right to withhold a Card that has been granted, if the required fee has been paid. If a Grand Scribe, or a Grand Secretary, has in his possession the books of a defunct Encampment or Lodge, he may issue Certificates to the former members, on the payment of such dues as may appear against them. When the books are lost or destroyed, the Grand Master and Grand Secretary, or the Grand Patriarch and Grand Scribe may grant the Certificates, if satisfied as to the good standing of the applicants. (*See page* 172.) A State Grand Body may grant a Withdrawal Card, to enable a member of a defunct Subordinate to join another Subordinate, although the brother is at the time in arrears to such defunct Subordinate. District Deputy Grand Sires have no power to grant Cards to members of defunct Subordinates. A brother holding a Withdrawal Card, desiring to renew his membership in the Order, should deposit it in the Lodge nearest his residence, or should there be several Lodges at equal distances therefrom, he may select either, if the local law does not provide otherwise. A Lodge is not bound to receive a Card on deposit, or to admit the holder to membership. If an application for membership in a Subordinate, by deposit of Card, be made and rejected, the Card must be returned to the applicant, and not mutilated with the endorsement of "rejected" thereon. As to when a Card deposited in a Lodge may be withdrawn, see page 212. Unless there is a local law to the contrary, a brother with a Withdrawal Card, cannot be admitted as a member of a Lodge at a distance, and in another county, whilst residing in the place where his former Lodge is located, without the consent of that Lodge. A member holding a Withdrawal Card, expired or not, may apply for a Charter for a new Lodge. A Withdrawal Card may be annulled, for good cause, which may have existed at the time of its grant, but not known until after delivery, at any time between its granting and its expiration. (*See page* 107.) It can be annulled only during the twelve months of its vitality, but when annulled, it renders it as if it never had been granted, and brings the holder back into his Subordinate. If the Card is annulled, and the holder brought to trial, on charges preferred after the Card is granted, and acquitted, the holder's position in his Subordinate is the same as if the Card had never been granted. The Card may be annulled before charges are preferred. A Card deposited cannot be annulled. State Grand Bodies do not possess the exclusive right to regulate how Withdrawal Cards shall be annulled, but they may enact laws relative thereto, not in conflict with the laws of the S. G. L.

WIVES' AND WIDOWS' CARDS.—Subordinate Lodges may, by a vote of two-thirds of their members voting, grant a Card to the wife or widow of any member who may apply for it, signed by the officers, and countersigned by the recipient on the margin. The Card for a wife shall remain in force not longer than a year, while that granted to a widow shall remain in force as long as she shall remain a widow.

REBEKAH CARDS.—A Card may be granted to a Daughter of Rebekah by the Lodge of which her husband is or was a member.

CERTIFICATES are of various kinds. The more frequently used are the following: Dismissal; for P. O. Degrees; for Degrees in a Degree Lodge; for members of defunct Subordinates; of good standing in Lodge to join an Encampment; for use in place of lost Withdrawal Card; to receive the Degrees away from the location of one's Subordinate. When the law makes it obligatory to grant Dismissal Certificates to brothers suspended for non-payment of dues, it is the duty of the N. G. and Rec. Sec., or C. P. and Scr., upon proper application, in open Subordinate, and payment of the fee, without a vote, to issue such Certificates. A Subordinate cannot refuse a Dismissal Certificate when applied for as above. (*See page* 211.) Dismissal Certificates may be received upon deposit in any Subordinate, but the holder does not possess the privilege of visiting. The holder can apply for a Charter for a new Lodge. (*See page* 312.) The Certificate is sold as other supplies are sold, and at the same rate as Cards. The Certificate must show, upon its face, the highest Degree and rank of the holder. The Certificates to receive the P. O. Degrees, must be furnished without a vote thereon, if the past officers are entitled to them. As to the admission of a Past Grand, or Past Chief Patriarch, into his Grand Body upon a Certificate, see page 132. If the Degrees are conferred by a regular Degree Lodge, the application for them must be made by the brother to his Subordinate Lodge. If they are granted, a Certificate to that effect is given him, which, presented to the Degree Lodge, authorizes it to confer the Degrees. State Grand Bodies are authorized to prepare and issue Certificates to members of suspended or defunct Subordinates, in their respective jurisdictions. These Certificates are to set forth on their face the facts in the case, to be attested by the Grand Secretary, or Grand Scribe, under Seal. Such Certificates, (the S. G. L. not having issued suitable Cards for this purpose), do not require the counter-signature of the Grand Secretary of the S. G. L. They are to be recognized as having the force and effect of *expired* Withdrawal Cards, issued by a Subordinate in good standing. It is the duty of the Secretary of a Lodge to furnish any of its members desiring to enter an Encampment, a Certificate showing their rank and standing in the Lodge. The Lodge which issued a

Withdrawal Card, which has become lost, may issue a Certificate under Seal, reciting the facts of such original issue. The Certificate may be used in lieu of a Card, as evidence of previous good standing. A Certificate authorizing a brother to receive his Degrees away from the location of his Lodge, can be granted only by application to his Lodge at a regular session. Any Lodge, upon the presentation of an authentic Degree Certificate, if the holder is in good standing, should confer the Degrees upon the candidate.

CHAPLAIN.—Subordinate Lodges are not, imperatively, required to have the duties of Chaplain performed in the opening and closing ceremonies, although it is desirable. The performance of the duties of Chaplain, does not constitute him an officer, so as to make him eligible for an elective office. A Grand Lodge may elect its Chaplain. The Junior Past Grand cannot be compelled to perform the duties of Chaplain.

CHARGES, PENAL.—Charges must be certain and definite, clearly setting forth the offense. A copy of them, duly attested, should be furnished the defendant; also a duly attested notice of the time and place of trial. The record should show, by some positive evidence, that a copy of the charges was served on the accused, as well as sufficient notice of the time and place of trial, and that he was summoned to be present at the trial. As to notice of charges to an absconded or concealed brother, see pages 132, 133. Charges may be preferred against a member of another Lodge; one Lodge can report to another Lodge, the unworthy conduct of the holder of a Withdrawal Card from that Lodge. A brother holding an unexpired Withdrawal Card, has the right, during the year the Card extends, to prefer charges, for unworthy conduct, against a member of his Lodge. Private business should not be made subjects for charges. If charges be preferred against the N. G. they are properly placed in the hands of the V. G. to be brought before the Lodge. Charges against the officers of a Grand Lodge, may be indefinitely postponed by that Body. The only effect of undecided, or pending charges against a member, or an officer of a Lodge, is to deprive him from taking a Visiting Card, or where charges relate to the right to benefits, to suspend their payment, until a final decision. In the Sovereign Grand Lodge, an officer or member under impeachment, is debarred the exercise of his office, or the privilege of his membership, but may be heard in his own defense. A member cannot resign from his Lodge, while charges are pending against him, and thus avoid a trial. (SEE OFFENSES, TRIAL.)

CHARTERS.—All State, District and Territorial Grand Bodies, exist by virtue of Charters granted them by the S. G. L. (*See Article* I, *Section* 3, *page* 322.) The manner of obtaining a Charter for a Grand Lodge, or Grand Encampment, will be found described in Articles IV, V, pages 330, 331. The Grand Sire can grant Warrants, during the recess, for Grand and Subordinate Bodies, in places where Grand Bodies do not exist. The Warrants thus granted, remain in force until recalled by the S. G. L. Notwithstanding this, many members of the Order believe that a Warrant is altogether provisional and must be replaced by a formal Charter. Such, however, is not the case, the Warrant is the Charter, and is valid until recalled. When Grand Bodies have forfeited their Charters, they should be reclaimed by the Grand Sire, together with the effects, books and papers belonging to such Bodies.

CHARTERS FOR SUBORDINATE BODIES.—The manner of obtaining a Charter for a Subordinate, in a State, District or Territory where a Grand Body does not exist, will be found described in Articles I, II, page 330. Duplicate Charters issued by the S. G. L. to Subordinates under its immediate jurisdiction, must have subscribed thereto, the names of the Grand Sire and Grand Secretary at the time of issuing the original. A Certificate, signed by the Grand Sire and Grand Secretary, must be attached to the duplicate, setting forth that it is a duplicate Charter, which will have the same effect as an original Charter. If a Subordinate under the jurisdiction of the S. G. L., fails to make its returns for one year, it forfeits its Charter, and, when forfeited, should be reclaimed by the Grand Sire. A D. D. G. Sire has no authority to issue Warrants for Subordinates, or to reclaim their Charters. The Grand Sire alone, can recall, or cause them to be recalled. When a State, District or Territorial Grand Body is instituted, all the Lodges, or Encampments, as the case may be, in the jurisdiction, become subordinate to such Grand Body. As to the Charters under which such Subordinates were organized, see page 301. The manner of obtaining a Charter for a Subordinate under a State, District or Territorial Grand Body is described under "SUBORDINATES." A State Grand Body has the right to refuse to grant a Charter. A duplicate Charter can be granted only when the original has been mutilated or destroyed. The name, in whole, or in part, of any living person, must not be used as the chartered name or title for any Subordinate or Degree Lodge of the Daughters of Rebekah, or a Uniformed Degree Camp. If there be the constitutional number of members, who wish to retain and work under their Charter, the majority of the members cannot surrender it. It is a subject for local legislation whether a Subordinate can retain its Charter and continue to work, after failure, from an exhausted treasury, to pay weekly benefits. A State Grand Body should not, even though there is no law in its Constitution on the subject, deprive any of its Subordinates of their Charters, except for sufficient cause and after trial. If the local law provides that the Charter shall not be forfeited until charges have been preferred, and an opportunity to answer given, then the Grand Body, or the Grand Master, has no right to take the Charter. If a Subordinate Lodge violates the laws of the S. G. L., or those of its own Grand Lodge, and refuses obedience, it may be expelled therefor, and the Grand Master may, during the recess, take possession of the Charter, until the case is tried and determined, by the Grand Lodge, or by the S. G. L., on appeal.

CHARTERS FOR DEGREE LODGES OF THE DAUGHTERS OF REBEKAH.— Seven persons, irrespective of sex, in possession of the Rebekah Degree, may petition for a Charter for a Degree Lodge of the Daughters of Rebekah, if the local law does not provide otherwise. The Grand Sire, Deputy Grand Sire, and Grand Secretary, may institute Degree Lodges of the Daughters of Rebeckah, in any territory under the immediate jurisdiction of the S. G. L. Each State jurisdiction can adopt its own Form of Charter for such Lodges. If a Rebekah Degree Lodge shall, for thirty days after the time by law required to make its annual report, neglect to make and forward it to the proper officer, it shall be the duty of the Grand Master to declare the Charter forfeited and to reclaim it.

CHARTERS OF DEGREE LODGES.—Five members, (unless the local law requires more), of the Degree of Truth, may apply to a State Grand Lodge for a Charter. There is no distinct law for instituting these Lodges.

CHINESE.—The Chinese, and all others not of the pure Caucasian race, are ineligible to membership in the order.

CHARTS.—The Charts that have been designed and published by the S. G. L. are its exclusive private property. The S. G. L. does not prohibit the circulation of Charts, not at present published by it, if they contain no Certificate or Form requiring the signature of an officer of any Lodge or Encampment, Grand or Subordinate. Lodges are prohibited from using Charts not issued by the S. G. L. As to the penalty for unlawfully attaching the Seal to any Chart, see page 193.

COMMITTEES OF THE SOVEREIGN GRAND LODGE.—See Rules of Order, pages 338–344. There is another regular Committee entitled the Sub-Committee on Finance, whose duty it is to examine, within one week prior to the commencement of each session, the books and vouchers of the Grand Secretary and Grand Treasurer. Committeemen, for services rendered, during the recess of the S. G. L., receive each, per day, three dollars, while actually in session, and four cents per mile traveled, by the nearest traveled route, to and from the place of meeting. A salaried officer of the S. G. L. receives no per diem compensation for committee service. Past Grand Sires, who are not Grand Representatives, are not entitled to serve on Committees of the S. G. L. Every Representative, unless excused, must serve on committees.

COMMITTEES OF GRAND AND SUBORDINATE BODIES.—Grand and Subordinate Bodies have also their appropriate committees, but as the number and duties of such committees are left to local legislation, the reader can obtain such information, as he may desire, from the printed Constitutions and By-Laws of the Bodies, in the particular jurisdiction, concerning which the information is sought. A State Grand Body cannot appoint a committee of its own Body, to try a brother of a Subordinate Lodge. It can order the Subordinate to try him. A General Relief Committee, acting independently of the Subordinates, in the jurisdiction where the committee is organized, is considered a voluntary association, and cannot be compelled to adopt, for its government, such Constitution and By-Laws as the State Grand Lodge might propose.

CONFLICT OF LAWS.—The Constitution and Laws of the S. G. L. are supreme, and paramount to the laws of State Grand Bodies, so that the latter, when in conflict, must yield to the former. A Grand Sire's decision does not supersede a By-Law of the S. G. L., although approved by it. Its By-Laws must be changed, or altered, in the manner prescribed by its laws. The Sovereign Grand Lodge has power to direct any Grand Body to remove anything from its Constitution or By-Laws which may be in conflict with the supreme law of the Order, although this very Constitution may have been approved by it. Subordinates are bound to conform to the Constitution and laws ̓adopted by their State Grand Bodies.

CONSOLIDATION.—Grand Bodies are authorized to enact such legislation as shall allow the consolidation of two or more of their Subordinate Lodges, or Encampments, into one Lodge or Encampment.

CONSTITUTIONS.—The Constitution of the S. G. L. will be found on pages 322–330.

CONSTITUTIONS OF STATE GRAND BODIES.—Constitutions of Grand Bodies chartered by the S. G. L. must be approved by it, and when approved, they become, at once, effective. (*See page* 224.) The Grand Sire has not the authority to approve, during the recess, the Constitutions of Subordinate Grand Bodies. When a Grand Body desires to submit its Constitution, or amendments thereto, to the S. G. L. for approval, it is required to present to the Grand Secretary, a complete copy of its Constitution, and all amendments thereto, accompanied with a Certificate from such State Grand Body, attested by its Grand Secretary, or Grand Scribe, and the Seal of the Grand Body attached. (*See page* 149.) All documents without a Seal, when the Body has one, will be returned without having had any consideration. The Constitution of a Grand Body should have its provisions as simple, and as comprehensive as possible, without unnecessary prolixity, and easily understood by any one of ordinary comprehension. A pending amendment to the Constitution or By-Laws of a Grand Body, cannot be amended when under consideration, unless permitted by the local law. A Constitution cannot he so construed by a resolution as to, in effect, amend it. If the Constitution of a Grand Body requires a vote of two-thirds, without further qualification, for the adoption of an amendment thereto, a majority of two-thirds of the votes of the Subordinates present, as a quorum, is sufficient.

CONSTITUTIONS OF SUBORDINATES.—The S. G. L. has prescribed uniform Constitutions for the Subordinates under its immediate jurisdiction. State Grand Bodies have the power to enact uniform Constitutions for their Subordinates. The Constitutions of Subordinate must be approved by their Grand Bodies. The N. G. or C. P. of a Subordinate, has no power to set aside any part of the Constitution of his Subordinate. It can be amended only in the manner prescribed in the instrument itself. Subordinates have no legislative power except to make By-Laws for their own internal government.

CONTEMPT.—The refusal or willful neglect of a member of a Subordinate Body to appear and answer the charges against him, or his willfully absenting himself to avoid the service of summons, or notice to appear and answer, constitutes contempt ; an offense under the laws of Odd Fellowship, and punishable by expulsion from the Order. The brother against whom charges are preferred, although not appearing in person, does not incur the offense of contempt, if he appears before the Trial Committee by counsel.

CONVENTIONS.—A Grand Body may organize a convention for the purpose of devising and reporting a Constitution. It is illegal for Past Grands, as Representatives of their respective Lodges, to hold a convention in which to discuss local grievances and devise the means of obtaining redress therefor. It is the duty of State Grand Bodies to prohibit their Subordinates from holding conventions, without having first obtained their consent, for the purpose of legislating on matters relating to the internal affairs of such Grand Bodies. Subordinates must meet in Convention to petition for a Charter for a Grand Body.

CREDENTIALS.—These are official documents furnished to the Grand Representatives elect, or appointed, to the S. G. L.; to the Representatives of State Grand Bodies; to members in other relations, certifying, under the hands of the proper officers and attested by the Seal of the issuing Body, that the holders thereof have the necessary authority and qualifications to fill, or assume the positions, or to perform the duties mentioned in said Credentials. Grand Representatives, immediately after their election, should obtain such Credentials as are required by law. It is the duty of the Grand Scribe, or Grand Secretary, of the State Grand Body, immediately after the election or appointment of a Grand Representative, to forward to the Grand Secretary of the S. G. L., a duplicate copy of the Grand Representative's Certificate. When the Credentials of a Grand Representative are presented to the S. G. L., they are referred to a committee, whose duty it is to examine their authenticity and also the qualifications of the Representative, who is not regarded as a member until his Credentials have been favorably acted upon, and he himself admitted to a seat in the Grand Body. Until admitted to a seat, and thereby to membership, he has no rights, and cannot wear the Regalia of the office, nor take part in any of the proceedings of the Body. Every representative Body is the judge of the qualifications of its members.

DEAF.—Those, so deaf as to be unable to properly perform the duties and requirements of the Work, should not be admitted into the Order.

DEBATE.—Inasmuch as the laws and Rules of Order of each Body regulate this subject, but few general rules can be given. The following are, however, applicable to all Bodies: The speaker, clothed in proper Regalia, must rise and respectfully address the Chair, and, on being recognized, shall confine himself to the question under consideration, and avoid all personalities. The matter cannot be debated until it is seconded and stated by the Chair. When two or more rise, at the same time, to speak, the Chair shall decide who is entitled to the floor. If a member, while speaking, shall be called to order, he shall take his seat until the question of order is determined, when, if permitted, he may proceed again. During the progress of a ballot, all debate shall be prohibited. A member shall not interrupt another while speaking, unless to explain or to call him to order for words spoken. The following are applicable to the S. G. L.: The elective officers have the power of debating and making motions. The appointed officers, unless Representatives, cannot take part in the proceedings and debates, except when permitted by a majority vote. Past Grand Sires may offer motions and debate. A member is not permitted to speak more than once on the same question, without leave, until every member who chooses to speak shall have spoken. (*See Rules of Order, Chapter II., page* 339.)

DEFORMED PERSONS.—Those persons, whose physical deformity will prevent them from fully complying with the duties and requirements of the Work and laws of the Order, should not be admitted to membership. This is the general principle that should govern, but each individual case should be decided on its merits, and in accordance with the local law, or that of the Subordinate Lodge.

DEFUNCT SUBORDINATES.—The application for the restoration of the Charter of a defunct Subordinate is made to the Body that reclaimed it. The resuscitation of a defunct Subordinate, on the application of only a part of its members who were in good standing at the time of its dissolution, does not restore to membership the remainder of its former members, who were also in good standing when it became defunct. Those who did not join in the application, and who were in good standing as aforesaid, must return to membership in the manner prescribed by the local law. Should a Subordinate, in which an officer or member of the S. G. L. holds membership, become extinct, the seat of such officer or member in the S. G. L. does not become vacated if, within one month thereafter, he shall connect himself, with another like Subordinate. If any assets of a defunct Subordinate come into the possession of a Grand Body, they are liable for any advanced benefits granted by a Subordinate to a member of the defunct Body, and may be legally applied to the extinguishment of such claim. The funds, if not trust funds, and property of defunct Bodies, may, at the option of the Body holding the same, be used for the assistance of the widows and orphans of such defunct Bodies; for assisting needy working Bodies, or for any relief fund in such jurisdiction. A suspended member of a defunct Subordinate may be admitted to membership in a similar Subordinate, upon such terms and evidence, as the proper State Grand Body may prescribe. In case of consolidation, a suspended member of the extinct Subordinate can obtain a Certificate from the Grand Scribe, or Grand Secretary, of his jurisdiction, or a Dismissal Certificate from the Subordinate retaining its Charter in the consolidation, as the local law may prescribe. A brother who has been expelled for crime, from a Subordinate, which subsequently became extinct, can regain membership in the Order, only through the Grand Body to which his Lodge or Encampment was subordinate. As to the names and numbers of defunct Subordinates, see page 293.

DEGREES.—THE GRAND ENCAMPMENT DEGREE.—In 1842 the G. L. U. S. adopted the Work and D*gree for a Grand Encampment, and also appropriate Honorary Degrees for a Past Chief Patriarch and Past High Priest. This action in reference to the Past Official Degrees was repealed in 1844. The Grand Encampment Degree is conferred as a reward for faithful services in a Subordinate Encampment. The Degree may be conferred upon Past Chief Patriarchs, and, if the local law so provides, upon Past High Priests, on the presentation of proper Certificates. A Grand Encampment can work only in the Grand Encampment Degree, and cannot confer the Subordinate Encampment Degrees. Every member of the S. G. L., is entitled to have the Grand Encampment Degree conferred upon him by the Grand Sire. A Grand Representative, who has received the Degree in this manner, cannot claim a seat in the organization of a State Grand Encampment, and the rank and privileges belonging to a Past Chief Patriarch, or a Past High Priest. To be eligible to the office of District Deputy Grand Patriarch, it is not necessary for a] Patriarch to be in possession of the Grand Encampment Degree. The Degree may be conferred on those entitled to receive it, at special sessions held for that purpose, and the provisions for holding such sessions are similar to those applicable to like sessions of Grand Lodges, held for conferring the Grand Lodge Degree. As to conferring this Degree on Past Chief Patriarchs belonging to Subordinates under the immediate jurisdiction of the S. G. L., see page 238.

SUBORDINATE ENCAMPMENT DEGREES.—The Degrees of a Subordinate Encampment are: The Patriarchal, the Golden Rule, and the Royal Purple. The latter is the highest in the Patriarchal Branch of the Order. A brother entering an Encampment receives the Patriarchal Degree, and is then entitled to the Check Password. His membership and his obligation to pay dues, date from this period. The Degrees must be balloted for upon the same evening on which application is made, but the propriety of conferring the Degree on more than one, on the same night, is a matter for local legislation. It is improper to confer an Encampment Degree upon one holding a Withdrawal Card from a Subordinate Lodge, as he has not the necessary qualifications for membership in an Encampment. Applicants for Charters to open Encampments, must be members of the Royal Purple Degree. The possession of the Encampment Degrees is not a requisite for office, or membership, in a State Grand Lodge. When a person has been elected to receive all the Encampment Degrees, and has received the Patriarchal Degree in the Encampment wherein he was elected, any Encampment in the same, or another jurisdiction, may confer on him the other Degrees at the request of his Encampment. A Grand Patriarch may issue a Dispensation, authorizing a more remote Encampment to elevate an applicant to the Patriarchal Degrees, when the only Encampment nearer the residence of the applicant has assented thereto. Where a Subordinate, but no Grand Encampment exists, the District Deputy Grand Sire has the same power, as a Grand Patriarch has, under similar circumstances, to grant Dispensations to brothers wishing to obtain the Degrees out of the jurisdiction. Grand Patriarchs and their Special Deputies, may confer the Degrees upon a sufficient number of Scarlet Degree members, to qualify them to petition for a Charter for an Encampment within their jurisdictio. , at a place where none exists.

THE GRAND LODGE DEGREE.—The Grand Lodge Degree cannot be conferred for a pecuniary consideration, but only as a reward for the faithful performance of the duties of the Noble Grand, and other service in the Subordinate Lodge. The Degree is given, only when a Past Grand becomes a member of the Grand Lodge. A State Grand Lodge is authorized to confer the Degree upon a Past Grand of another State jurisdiction, upon the presentation of a Visiting Card from his Lodge, and also a Certificate executed by the Grand Master and Grand Secretary, under the Seal of the Grand Lodge to whose jurisdiction such Past Grand belongs, that he is eligible and entitled to the same. A Grand Lodge can confer this Degree upon Past Grands belonging to Subordinates under the immediate jurisdiction of the S. G. L., on the presentation of Certificates of the same tenor as above, signed by the Grand Sire and Grand Secretary, and attested by the Seal of the S. G. L. District Deputies cannot confer this Degree. It can be conferred only during the session of the Grand Lodge, and in the room in which the Grand Lodge is assembled, but by special permission, it may be conferred in some contiguous room. Special sessions may be held for conferring this Degree. (*See pages* 259, 260.) A Grand Master has no power to call special sessions for this purpose, until his Grand Lodge has determined whether it will hold such sessions.' Either the Grand Master or the Deputy Grand Master, or the Grand Warden with the Grand Secretary, can hold the session; that is, either one of the first three named, and the Grand Secretary, are sufficient so far as officers are concerned; there must be a quorum of five Past Grands.

SUBORDINATE LODGE DEGREES.—The Past Official Degrees peculiar to the Subordinate Lodge are: Past Secretary, Past Vice Grand, and Past Noble Grand. They are rewards for services in office, and may be conferred at any proper time and place, on those who have earned them, and produced Certificates from the Lodges in which they officiated. Service for a majority of the nights of a term as Secretary, Vice Grand, or Noble Grand, is requisite to entitle one to the Past Official Degree thereto attached. A resignation by the incumbent of either office, at any time previous to the expiration of the term, works a forfeiture of the Past Official Degree. The first N. G. of a new or revived Lodge, who serves to the end of the lawful term, is entitled to receive all the Past Official Degrees, and the Vice Grand of a similar Lodge, and for like service, is entitled to the Degrees of Past Vice Grand and Past Secretary; but to entitle them to such Degrees such Lodge must have been instituted at least fourteen regular meeting nights before the termination of the regular term. State Grand Lodges may cause to be conferred, the Degree of Past Secretary, on any Past Grand in good standing, who has served a lawful term as Vice Grand and Noble Grand. A Certificate for the Past Official Degrees must be furnished to a member entitled thereto, without a vote. A State Grand Lodge may authorize District Deputy Grand Masters to confer the Past Official

Degrees, at any time, upon those duly qualified, or they may direct said Degrees to be conferred in any other manner. The Grand Master of one jurisdiction can confer said Degrees on a qualified Past Grand of another jurisdiction, on the written request of the Grand Master thereof, and they may be conferred upon Past Grands of other jurisdictions, under the circumstances described on page 198. A Vice Grand, who, by any event, fills the chair of the Noble Grand to the end of the term, is not entitled to the Honors of that office, without a previous election thereto. The Degrees of a Subordinate Lodge are: The Initiatory; the First Degree, or Degree of Friendship; the Second Degree, or the Degree of Love; the Third Degree, or the Degree of Truth, which is called, also, the Scarlet Degree. A Subordinate Lodge has, by its Charter, and without the interference of its Grand Lodge, the right to confer these Degrees upon its own members. A Lodge cannot be compelled to send its members to a Degree Lodge to receive the Degrees. No Lodge can confer the Degrees upon a member of any other Lodge, without the consent, under Seal, of the Lodge to which the member belongs. If the Degrees be conferred without such consent, the fees received must be paid to the Lodge whose member received the Degrees. The price of the Degrees is under the control of the several State Grand Lodges. A Certificate to authorize a brother to receive his Degrees away from the location of his own Lodge, can be granted only after the fees have been paid for said Degrees, and by application to his Lodge at a regular session. It is the duty of a Lodge, upon the presentation of a duly authenticated Degree Certificate, if the holder is in good standing, to confer the Degrees upon him. Under such circumstances, he is not required to have a Visiting Card, or the A. T. P. W. The length of time a brother must be a member of the Order before he is entitled to receive the several Degrees, is a matter to be regulated by the local law; so also is the time that must elapse, where a member's application for Degrees has been rejected, before he can again apply. The Degrees are granted by ball ballot, and ballots upon application for any or all the Degrees, must be had when the Lodge is open in the Third Degree. In the absence of local legislation, a separate ballot for each Degree must be had; it is a subject, however, for local legislation whether the ballot shall be separate for each Degree, or for all collectively. Balloting for Degrees must be upon the evening on which the application is made therefor, but there is no law which requires that the Degrees should be conferred at the same session. The time of conferring them is left to the control of the Subordinates, subject to such rules as may be prescribed by local legislation. They may be conferred at other than regular meetings. Grand Lodges may require a separate fee for the Degrees, or may provide that the initiation fee shall include all the Degrees. All the business of the Subordinate Lodges, excepting those under the jurisdiction of the Grand Lodge of the German Empire and the Grand Lodge of Australasia, must be transacted in the Third Degree, or the Degree of Truth. (*See page* 274.) When a Lodge is open in the First Degree, and has concluded the business to be transacted, and desires to open in the Second Degree, the Lodge must close in the First before opening in the Second; the same mode of procedure obtains in all the Degrees. Members who have received the First and Second Degrees under the old Work, are entitled to rank as members of the First Degree of the Revised Work; those who have received the Third and Fourth Degrees of the old Work, are entitled to rank as members of the Second Degree of the Revised Work; those who have received the Fifth Degree of the old Work, are entitled to rank as members of the Third Degree of the Revised Work. As to conferring the three Degrees on five or more initiatory members to qualify them to petition for a Charter for a Lodge, see page 274.

THE REBEKAH DEGREE.—Subordinate Lodges can confer this Degree upon all persons that are qualified by the laws of the Order to receive it. The existence of Degree Lodges of the Daughters of Rebekah, in the same district, cannot prevent Subordinate Lodges from conferring the Degree. If a State Grand Lodge has accepted the Degree, and allowed it to be communicated to its Subordinates, the elective officers thereof must be instructed in the Work of the Degree before installation. Subordinate Lodges cannot require any pecuniary compensation for conferring the Degree. The following are eligible for the Degree: An Odd Fellow of the Degree of Truth, his wife, unmarried daughter, or unmarried sister who has attained the age of eighteen years, if she be a white woman (*see page* 308); the widow of an Odd Fellow who was in good standing at the time of death; an unmarried daughter of an Odd Fellow of the Degree of Truth, who has attained the age of eighteen years, and whose parents are dead (*see page* 267); the unmarried daughters of Odd Fellows who have attained the age of eighteen years (*see page* 274); an unmarried divorced sister of an Odd Fellow of the Degree of Truth; a legally adopted daughter of a member of the Degree of Truth (*see page* 264); the widowed sister of an Odd Fellow of the Degree of Truth; an unmarried half-sister of a brother of the Order, when proposed according to law (*see page* 284); an unmarried step-daughter of an Odd Fellow of the Degree of Truth, if eighteen years of age; the mother (a widow) of an Odd Fellow; the wife of a brother belonging to another jurisdiction, if the proper Certificate is presented. Further information concerning the Rebekah Degree will be found under the title " Degree Lodges of the Daughters of Rebekah."

DEGREE LODGES FOR CONFERRING THE SUBORDINATE LODGE DEGREES.— These Lodges are established for conferring the Subordinate Lodge Degrees, and local legislation determines the qualifications for office in them. No honorary title has been provided for Past Degree Masters. If a Lodge itself does not confer the Degrees upon its members, but prefers to have them conferred by a Degree Lodge, the applicant for the Degrees must obtain from his Lodge a Certificate, (see below,) which, presented to the Degree Lodge, authorizes it to confer the Degrees. The following Form of Certificate may be used:

I. O. O. F.

.... Lodge, No. ...., of ....
.... day of ...., 18....
To .... Degree Lodge, No. ....
This is to certify that Brother ...., is a member of this

Lodge, and has duly applied for the .... Degree (or Degrees), and has been authorized by a ballot of the brethren of the said Degree, (or Degrees), of his Lodge to receive the same.

In testimony whereof, witness our hands and the Seal of our Lodge.

[SEAL.] ...., N. G.

Attest: ...., Secretary.

It is the duty of the Degree Lodge, upon the presentation of a duly authenticated Degree Certificate, if the holder is in good standing, to confer the Degree upon him. The Degree Master cannot refuse to confer a Degree because the candidate cannot prove himself in the Degrees he claims to have received. The management of Degree Lodges is a subject for local legislation.

DEGREE LODGES OF THE DAUGHTERS OF REBEKAH.—For the history of these Lodges the reader is referred to the Chapter on the Rebekah Degree. State Grand Lodges may institute these Lodges at such places, within their jurisdictions, as they may deem proper, and prepare suitable Charters for them. Rebekah Degree Lodges can confer the Degree on those persons only, who apply for membership therein, unless such Lodges shall otherwise provide; but they may confer the Degree upon members of a Subordinate Lodge, or persons qualified to receive the Degree, on the conditions and under the circumstances described on page 280. The Grand Officers may visit such Lodges in their official capacity. They may admit to membership all those who are eligible to receive the Rebekah Degree. A Daughter of Rebekah, who received her degree in her husband's Subordinate Lodge, is not, after his death, and her remarriage to one not a member of the Order, eligible to membership. On the other hand, an unmarried daughter of an Odd Fellow, a member of a Degree Lodge of the Daughters of Rebekah, does not forfeit her membership, or standing in the Lodge, by being married to a man not a member of the Order. They may admit to membership, by the same vote as is required for ordinary admission, the holders of regular Cards, by deposit thereof. They may ballot for membership, and a majority vote of all those present and voting shall be necessary to an election to membership; except the local law provides otherwise. Membership is forfeited according to the rules and usages applicable to brothers in Subordinate Lodges. They elect their own officers. The elective officers are: Noble Grand, Vice Grand, Secretary and Treasurer. They may also elect a Financial Secretary. The appointed officers are: Warden, Conductor, Outside Guardian, Right and Left Supporters of the Noble Grand, Right and Left Supporters of the Vice Grand. To be eligible to the office of N. G., previous service as Vice Grand in a Rebekah Degree, or Subordinate Lodge, is necessary. All the other offices are open to any contributing member in good standing. The term of office is six months, or one year, according to the local law. The meetings, regular and special, are regulated by the By-Laws, which they may make, subject to the approval of the Grand Lodge to which they are subordinate. They may establish, by their By-Laws, the payment of dues, provide, in the same manner, for suspension for non-payment thereof, and disburse their funds for the relief of the sick, the destitute and the distressed. The Grand Sire, Deputy Grand Sire and Grand Secretary of the S. G. L., may institute such

Lodges in any territory under its immediate jurisdiction. All officers must wear the prescribed Regalia. Lodges working under the new Ritual cannot lawfully give that Work before a Subordinate Lodge open in the Degree of Rebekah. The Degree must be conferred in conformity with the requirements of the Ritual. Rebekah Degree Lodge Visiting and Withdrawal Cards, in general, have the same uses and purposes that similar Cards issued by Subordinate Lodges have. Withdrawal Cards may be granted to members who apply therefor, in person or by letter, by a ballot vote of a majority of the members present. A charter is forfeitable for neglecting to make and forward the annual report. *See page* 243.

DIPLOMAS are classed among Supplies, and are furnished by the S. G. L. Those issued to members of the S. G. L., must be attested in the manner that Charters emanating from the S. G. L. are authenticated. See Form of Representative's Diploma, page 51. When issued by Grand or Subordinate Bodies, they must be attested in the same manner that such Bodies now authenticate official documents issued by them. Diplomas are granted by a vote of Grand and Subordinate Bodies, and must be signed, in the first place, by the Grand Secretary of the S. G. L., and by the Grand Master of the State Grand Lodge to which they are delivered. The highest rank of the recipient should be shown in the Diploma. To knowingly publish or circulate any Diploma, purporting to be by authority of the Order, which is not authorized by law, is punishable by expulsion.

DISPENSATIONS.—The laws, general and local, permit Grand Officers to grant to their Subordinates certain privileges when requested in a formal manner, and when the reasons assigned for such requests are satisfactory to the granting powers. The Grand Sire holds the same relation to the Subordinates under the immediate jurisdiction of the S. G. L., that Executive Officers of State Grand Bodies do to their Subordinates. Dispensations are granted for a variety of purposes. By way of illustration, a Grand Master may have, in his jurisdiction, if permitted by local law, the authority to grant the following Dispensations: To confer Degrees on a member without delay; to allow members of the Order to appear in public in Regalia; to allow Lodges to apply to other Lodges for pecuniary assistance; to give entertainments for the benefit of the Order; to allow a Subordinate Lodge to change its place of meeting; to allow a brother to be reinstated after expulsion; to institute Lodges, and authorize them to work as such until the next session of the Grand Lodge; to empower Subordinate Lodges to elect Third Degree members to any office in such Lodges, provided all qualified brothers refuse to serve, etc. A Grand Patriarch can issue a Dispensation for a more remote Encampment to elevate to the Patriarchal Degrees an applicant, the only Encampment nearer the residence of the petitioner having assented thereto. A D. D. G. Master has no power, by Dispensation, to permit a person to be initiated in a Lodge, when there is another Lodge nearer his residence. A D. D. G. Sire may grant a Dispensation, in a State, District or Territory where a Subordinate, but no Grand Encampment exists, to brothers wishing to obtain the Patriarchal

Degrees out of the jurisdiction. The Grand Sire cannot grant a Dispensation to a Grand Body to adjourn to a place other than that provided in its Constitution, or to do anything whatever in conflict with its organic law.

DUES TO THE SOVEREIGN GRAND LODGE.—State, District and Territorial Grand Bodies pay seventy-five dollars per annum for each vote they are entitled to in the S. G. L., and Subordinates under its immediate jurisdiction, five per centum on their receipts. The reports must be accompanied with the dues in current money. All dues for the S. G. L. must be paid to the Grand Secretary, and by him be immediately paid to the Grand Treasurer.

DUES TO STATE GRAND BODIES.—The right of a Grand Body to raise revenue for its legitimate purposes, by assessment on its Subordinates, has been recognized and enforced by the S. G. L. The ratio of membership in the Grand Lodge may form the basis of the assessment which is to come out of the Lodge funds.

DUES TO SUBORDINATE BODIES.—Lodge dues commence at the time of initiation, and Encampment dues at the taking of the Patriarchal Degree. The amount of dues to be paid is a subject for local legislation. If no existing rights are infringed thereby, State Grand Bodies may permit Subordinates to require the payment of dues in advance. Dues accrue weekly, and may be paid in full, or in part, at any time, before suspension. (*See* ARREARS *and pages* 81, 249.) Assessments may become chargeable as dues, when the membership is assessed a certain amount to pay the dependent relatives of a deceased brother the sum stipulated in the laws of the Subordinate. This sum, thus assessed, may be charged, at the end of the quarter, as dues. The dues accruing during suspension for cause, may be remitted, in whole or in part, when application is made for reinstatement. Whether fines are to be considered dues is a question of local law. A Subordinate cannot receive a fixed sum as dues, and by way of consideration therefor, relieve the member paying the same from any further charge for dues during his membership. If dues are paid to the wrong officer, it is optional with the Subordinate whether it accepts the payment thus made. The Lodge or Encampment room is the place to pay the dues. A Subordinate may increase its dues by an amendment to its By-Laws, so that the acceptance of dues in advance, at the old rate, and giving a receipt therefor, specifying the time to which they are paid, does not preclude the Body from collecting the dues accruing from the advanced rate. Money paid for a Degree cannot be appropriated to pay a brother's dues; he cannot demand the money unless the Lodge refuses to confer the Degree, and if not demanded before suspension for non-payment of dues, it is forfeited. If reinstated, his claim thereto is revived. If a member is suspended, obtains a Dismissal Certificate, and is readmitted on said Certificate, the amount due from him at the time of his suspension, cannot be demanded of him. As to dues from members of defunct Subordinates, see page 302.

EFFECTS.—The Grand Sire is required to take possession of the effects of Grand and Subordinate Bodies working under Charters from it, when said

Charters have been forfeited. When a Grand Body is instituted, it is the duty of the Grand Secretary of the S. G. L. to transfer to the proper officers of such Grand Body the Charters, and all the effects, in the possession of the S. G. L. of all defunct or suspended Subordinates in said jurisdiction. Subordinates under State Grand Bodies must surrender their effects, if, from any cause, they fail to continue to work and yield up their Charters. (*See page* 146.) A Subordinate cannot appeal to the S. G. L. without the consent of its Grand Body, until it has surrendered all its effects. A State Grand Body may provide in its Constitution, that the property and effects of a Subordinate, which has surrendered or forfeited its Charter, may be sold and the proceeds added to the Grand Body's funds, if said Subordinate be not reinstated within three years.

ELECTION FOR MEMBERSHIP.—Admission to membership in Subordinates is determined by ballot, but it is left to the local law to decide in what manner members shall be elected, and how many black balls are required to reject. In Subordinates under the immediate jurisdiction of the S. G. L., three black balls reject a candidate, but a majority only of the members present, on ballot, shall be necessary to elect if the application be by Card. If a person is illegally elected, a majority of the Lodge can, previous to the applicant's initiation, order a new ballot, and if a candidate has been elected, but prior to initiation, the Lodge becomes satisfied that he is unworthy, it may annul the election by a majority of two-thirds of the members present. (*See page* 122.)

ELECTION OF OFFICERS.—As to the election of the Officers of the S. G. L. see Chapter II. In the election for these Grand Officers every ticket deposited, whether blank or otherwise, is a vote; and a majority of the whole votes thus polled is necessary to a choice. This rule is applicable to Subordinates where their Constitutions require a majority of the votes cast to elect. If there be but one candidate nominated for a given office, he is not elected, if the number of blank ballots cast exceeds the number of votes given for the candidate. None but those properly qualified for membership in a Grand Body, can be allowed to vote for its officers. When a new election is ordered by a Grand Master, at installation, any member of the Lodge may vote, although a Grand Officer, or acting as such, and clothed in his official Regalia. When the laws of a Lodge provide that on the second ballot the poll shall be between the two candidates having the highest number of votes on the first ballot, all votes cast for other candidates on the second ballot are void. Where the representative system prevails, if an elective Grand Officer fails to be present for installation, the office must be declared vacant and be at once filled by the Representatives, if the law of the jurisdiction so provides. Electioneering circulars and papers of that character, are condemned. It may be provided, by By-Law, that, at the election of officers of a Lodge, the Warden shall distribute and collect the ballots. The ballot box is not required to be in the center of the hall.

ENDOWMENT.—The members of the Order in good standing, in any, several, or all of the Subordinate Grand Jurisdictions, may form themselves in one or more Auxiliary Endowment Benefit Associations, under certain restrictions. (*See page* 259, *and Journal of* 1879, *page* 8,065.) Such Associations may be formed in the Encampment Branch of the Order. A Grand Jurisdiction cannot enforce upon the whole, or any portion of its Subordinates, an endowment scheme, although a majority of said Subordinates vote therefor.

EVIDENCE.—The record in a former trial is conclusive evidence in a subsequent one. Declarations made by dying persons, can be heard in evidence, only after the death of the person making them; the person making them should, at the time, have no hope or expectation of recovery. Such declarations may be rebutted by a voluntary statement of the same person, made to the contrary effect, on a subsequent day. A record of a trial in the courts upon a charge of the violation of the laws of the land is, *prima facie*, proof of the facts appearing therein. Competent evidence may be introduced without regard to the time when such evidence is offered, but the tribunal trying the case should exercise sound discretion as to the introduction of new evidence by either party, after once closing the case on either side. Testimony of events, prior or subsequent to the time of the commission of an alleged offense, if material and relevant, may be received in evidence. The testimony of persons not members of the Order, if absent, and non-resident witnesses, may be used in evidence, when obtained in the manner prescribed by law. (*See page* 142, *and Journal, pages* 2,909, 2,926, 3,537, 3,589.) An *ex parte* statement may be evidence sufficient to place a brother on trial, but it cannot be introduced thereat. If such testimony, as reading newspaper articles, has been used, a new trial will not be granted if it appears that the testimony in the case, exclusive of the *ex parte* matter, was conclusive and plainly required the verdict given. A brother on trial has the right, by himself or counsel, to meet and cross-examine all witnesses. No testimony against him, taken by any committee without notice to him, or in his absence, should be received. A case cannot be postponed to procure the testimony of an absent witness, when the other party to the proceeding admits all that it is assumed can be proved by such absent witness. If the charge is the use of objectionable words, the accused has the right to show the entire sentence, and the connection in which they were used, and to prove the truth of the charge conveyed by them. It is a question for the local law whether, after the report of a trial committee has been made to the Lodge, it can be recommitted with directions to take further evidence. A woman divorced, *a vinculo matrimonii*, may testify against her former husband, but a wife, or a wife divorced, *a mensa et thoro*, cannot testify against her husband, except in the case where he is arraigned upon the charge of inflicting *corporal* injury upon her. The obligation cannot be used in evidence, in a court of law, against a member in his suit against the Lodge. When the testimony is conflicting, and the weight thereof nearly balanced on either side, the S. G. L. will not disturb the judgment of the State Grand Body thereon.

EXPULSION.—Subordinates acting contrary to law, are amenable to such punishment as may be inflicted by their Grand Bodies. When a Subordinate is expelled its functions cease altogether. A member cannot be expelled without a formal trial, on charges preferred, unless he refuses to stand trial, in which case he may be expelled for contempt. Expulsion may be inflicted for the following offenses: Using the Emblems, etc., of the Order in the prosecution of private business, etc.; obtaining admission into the Order by misrepresentation or fraud; introducing a woman of bad repute to an Odd Fellows' festival, with a knowledge of her character; official misconduct, if it be of a nature unbecoming an Odd Fellow; attaching, without authority, to any Chart, Diploma, etc., the Seal of a Grand or Subordinate Body (*see page* 193); writing, printing, exhibiting or using any publication purporting to be the Unwritten Work of the Order, etc. A State Grand Body, or an Encampment, can expel a member from its own Body but not from the Order. A brother expelled from his Grand Lodge ranks, in his Lodge, as a P. G. A member cannot be expelled from the Order on account of being in arrears for dues. An expelled member is out of the Order, and no motion to reconsider the vote of expulsion can be entertained. A Subordinate cannot reinstate an expelled member, without the consent of its Grand Body. A Grand Lodge may confer the power on its Grand Master to grant, during the recess, a petition from a Subordinate to restore an expelled member to said Lodge. The return of an expelled member to the Order, and the form of proceeding, have been left to the local law. If the local law does not prescribe the vote necessary to reinstate an expelled member, the same vote that expelled ought to be required to restore to membership. A member expelled in one jurisdiction, cannot be reinstated in any other, except by the consent of the Lodge expelling. Expulsion by a Lodge severs connection with an Encampment, and a reinstatement by the Lodge does not reinstate in the Encampment. In case of expulsion by an Encampment, prior to expulsion by the Lodge, the Encampment, after the member's reinstatement in the Lodge, and notice thereof, must obtain permission from its Grand Encampment to act upon his application for reinstatement. As to membership in an illegal organization, see page 287.

FEES.—The fee for a Charter for a Grand Body, or a Subordinate working under the immediate jurisdiction of the S. G. L., is thirty dollars, which must accompany the application for the Charter, and will be returned if the Charter is not granted. The fees for Charters of Subordinates under State Grand Bodies are regulated by the local law. Members of a Grand Lodge cannot, on their admission thereto, be charged an entrance fee. The question of the admission of members free of charge, and of remitting initiation fees, belongs to State Grand Bodies; they may admit ministers of the gospel free of charge. Subordinates under the immediate jurisdiction of the S. G. L., cannot admit persons to membership, free of charge. The fee, for reinstatement within one year after suspension for non-payment of dues, is the amount of one year's dues; for reinstatement in a Lodge, after one year's suspension, is the amount charged for an initiate of the same age, or such less sum as the By-Laws may prescribe; but if in an Encampment, the total amount fixed in the By-Laws for the Patriarchal, Golden Rule and Royal Purple Degrees, for a brother of his age, or such less sum as may be fixed by the By-Laws. A member suspended for non-payment of dues, who makes application for a Withdrawal Card for the purpose of uniting with another Subordinate, in the same jurisdiction, may be reinstated and granted a Final Card, at any time within five years from the date of suspension, upon the payment of one year's dues, and the usual price of a Card.

FINES.—Fining members for non-attendance at funerals, is a matter for the legislation of State Grand Bodies. Subordinates under the immediate jurisdiction of the S. G. L. cannot impose fines for non-attendance at meetings. There is no law of the S. G. L. which forbids the imposition of fines by Subordinates for non-attendance. The duties of Chaplain cannot be enforced by fines, nor can a Junior Past Grand be fined, as such, for non-attendance at Lodge meetings. Whether fines are to be considered as dues, is a matter to be determined by the local law. State Grand Bodies have the power to legislate on this subject, to any extent, not in conflict with the supreme law of the S. G. L.

FLAG.—The Odd Fellows' flag was adopted in 1868, and its description slightly amended in 1871; it is used by Subordinates as well as Grand Bodies, and is described as follows: "The flag to be manufactured of white material, either bunting, satin or cotton cloth, as may be selected by those desiring one. The proportions to be eleven-nineteenths of the length for the width. The Emblems to consist of three links, to be placed in the center of the flag, with the letters I. O. O. F., and the name of the State, District or Territory using it, to be painted or wrought in scarlet color, and trimmed with material of the same color. Whenever the flag is to be used by the Encampments, there shall be added two crooks, to be painted or wrought in purple color." The Grand Secretary of the Sovereign Grand Lodge was instructed to procure a flag, of suitable size and proportions as above described, for that Grand Body, to be used for the first time at the celebration of the fiftieth anniversary, on the 26th of April, 1869, and in addition to the Emblems, to add the letters G. L. U. S. The letters S. G. L. are now used. It is the duty of the Grand Secretary to have the S. G. L. flag present, and displayed in some conspicuous place, on all occasions when the S. G. L. shall hold a regular or special session.

FRAUD.—As to any fraudulent misrepresentations of his age by a person seeking admission into either Branch of the Order, see page 177. It shall be legal to investigate and determine the fact of such fraud, even after the death of the alleged guilty person, provided, due notice of such intended investigation is given to the deceased's representatives, or family, claiming benefits from the Lodge or Encampment.

FUNDS.—The funds of Subordinates must not be appropriated for festivals, excursions or other such occasions, even though permission has been obtained from the proper Grand Officers, to hold such festivals, etc., in the name of the Order. They are to be used only for the legitimate objects of the Order. These are: To meet the claims of sick and distressed members, to care for them properly during their illness, to bury the dead, to protect the widow and to educate the orphan. The legitimate purposes of the Order include an appropriation to celebrate the introduction of the Order in America; a donation, as a charity, to a brother in ill-health, not entitled to benefits by the By-Laws, as a matter of right; donations made for the purpose of assisting in the institution of new Subordinates. Funds cannot be appropriated at an informal meeting. The funds must not be loaned without ample security and a reasonable interest, nor can trust funds be diverted from the objects and purposes for which they were intended, as long as they are necessary to be so used. (*See pages* 177, 248.) Subordinates having placed their widows and orphans in an asylum or home, may use their widows' and orphans' funds in defraying the legitimate expenses thereby incurred. (*See page* 316.) For the law governing general relief funds, see page 238. As to the funds of defunct Lodges, see Journal, pages 5,516, 5,546. Subordinates cannot, by a By-Law, pay to a beneficial association assessments on its members, out of its general fund. The funds of a Subordinate must not be appropriated for music at funerals, or to pay the expenses of a supper, or banquet, given on the night of the installation of officers. The S. G. L. does not recognize the appropriation of the funds of a Subordinate for the purpose of entertaining the Officers and Representatives of Grand Bodies, or for the purpose of celebrating the anniversaries of Subordinates, as proper or legitimate. Such appropriations should not be countenanced by State Grand Bodies.

FUNERALS.—Each jurisdiction has the right to determine whether the dead can be buried by a committee of the Lodge, or the whole Lodge. The local law may provide for extending funeral honors to brothers in arrears, against whom no charges of unworthy conduct are pending at the time of their death, but the Lodge cannot, in a body as a Lodge, attend the funeral of a deceased "Ancient Odd Fellow," and conduct the services according to the Ritual of the Order. The Noble Grand may, at his pleasure, open and close the Lodge in regular form, when called to attend the funeral of a brother. It is a matter for the local law whether the prescribed street Uniform shall be worn at a funeral. For Funeral Service and Procession, see Journal, pages 7,381, 7,474, 8,349, 8,461. For Form of Burial Service for a Daughter of Rebekah, see Journal, pages 10,843, 10,982, 11,026, and for Funeral Regalia, see Chapter XI.

GOOD STANDING.—A Grand or Subordinate Body is in good standing, while working under a valid and unreclaimed Charter, and in accordance with the laws of its superior Grand Body. A member in good standing, is one who is an active contributing member in possession and use of all the rights and privileges of full membership, including freedom from any disability by reason of non-payment of dues, or any charge regularly preferred against him, according to the Constitution and By-Laws of his Subordinate. To *acquire* membership in an Encampment, good standing in a Subordinate Lodge is necessary. Such is not always the case to *retain* membership in an Encampment; there are three cases when good standing in a Lodge is not necessary to retain such membership. 1. When a member of an Encampment takes a Withdrawal Card from his Subordinate Lodge, his membership in his Encampment is not affected thereby for a year from the date of the Card. He will be considered in good standing in his Encampment, if he deposits said Card in a Lodge, and becomes a member thereof, at any time within the year the Card has to run, provided, he keeps his dues paid up in his Encampment during that time. 2. A member of an Encampment, who has been suspended by his Lodge, for non-payment of dues, will not be affected thereby, as to his standing in his Encampment, for the term of one year thereafter, provided he shall not rest under any disability during the interim in his Encampment. 3. If an Encampment member's Lodge becomes defunct, and he cannot, by reason of age or infirmity, successfully apply for membership in another Lodge, upon obtaining a Grand Lodge Card from its Grand Secretary, he will be entitled to retain membership in his Encampment upon said Card.

GRAND BODIES.—As to the Sovereign Grand Lodge, the Grand Lodge of the German Empire, and the Grand Lodge of Australasia, see Chapter II.

STATE, DISTRICT AND TERRITORIAL GRAND BODIES—ORGANIZATION.—The reader is referred to Articles IV, and V, pages 330, 331, for much information on the organization of these Bodies. As to the Form for application for a Grand Charter, see page 331. The Grand Sire has power to grant, during the recess, Warrants for Grand Bodies. The traveling and other expenses of the Grand Sire, or instituting officer, must be paid by the Grand Body instituted. When the Warrant is confirmed, the Grand Body is entitled to representation in the S. G. L., and until said confirmation, the dues accruing from Subordinates in the jurisdiction, are payable to the S. G. L.

JURISDICTION AND AUTHORITY.—A Grand Body is supreme for local legislation and appellate jurisdiction within its limits, except as to the reservations made by the S. G. L. As soon as a Grand Body has been chartered, all the Subordinates, within its jurisdiction, become subordinate thereto. The immediate jurisdiction over any territory in which a Grand Lodge does not exist, belongs to the S. G. L. A State Grand Body has the power and authority to act as follows: Elect two Grand Representatives to the S. G. L. if it has more than one thousand members in good standing; and if it has less, to elect but one Representative; elect its Chaplain; admit properly qualified members to witness the Degree Work; enact laws enabling the Subordinates to provide benefits for the aged and infirm, as they may deem proper; provide by constitutional enactment for the erection of Homes for aged and indigent Odd Fellows; make general laws for the government of its Subordinates; enact uniform Constitutions for its Subordinates; establish a representative system; expel a member from its own Body, but not from the Order; postpone indefinitely, or lay on the table, charges preferred against any of its officers for unbecoming conduct; affirm, review, or reverse its former decisions at pleasure; construe its own local law; decide the question of fact as to which candidate for office therein is elected; raise revenue for its legitimate purposes by assessments on its Subordinates; fix the minimum amount to be paid by its Subordinates for benefits, dues, etc., leaving it for them to provide by law for any specific sum above these rates; fix a specific and uniform rate of benefits; permit its Subordinates to require payment of dues in advance, provided such requirement shall not work a forfeiture of any rights now guaranteed by the laws of the S. G. L.; determine when the payment of benefits is to commence; adopt laws regulating the manner in which Final Cards shall be annulled, provided they do not conflict with the legislation and decisions of the S. G. L.; appoint instructors in the Work, so as to insure uniformity throughout the jurisdiction; instruct its Grand Representative as to the mode in which the A. T. P. W. shall be conveyed to the Grand Master or Grand Secretary, whether personally or otherwise; permit Subordinates to hold semi-monthly or monthly meetings; appoint a committee to prepare a statement of facts on an appeal from its action to the S. G. L.; appoint such officers, additional to those required by the law in the Digest, as its wants and convenience may require; permit the use of the names and numbers of extinct Subordinates; authorize the consolidation of two or more Subordinates; refuse to grant a Charter upon application therefor; prohibit processions and balls at which the Regalia, Emblems, etc., of the Order shall be used; pass laws permitting Subordinates in adjacent jurisdictions to initiate or admit to membership persons whose residence, though not actually in said jurisdictions, is nearest to the location of such Subordinates; grant a new trial, if informality, want of fairness, or new testimony be discovered; open and close its meetings with prayer; omit recording such of its proceedings as, in its judgment, should not appear upon the record.

A State Grand Body cannot act as follows : Permit a brother to hold, at the same time, the two offices of Secretary and Treasurer; admit as a member, or Representative, any person, unless he takes and subscribes to the affirmation, page 10,727 of the Journal; examine a brother in the Subordinate Degrees, when a proper Certificate from his Lodge is presented; provide for Subordinates holding a second ballot on application for membership; authorize its Subordinates to expend its funds for any object except the legitimate purposes of the Order; vote in the S. G. L. by its Representative, or Representatives, if in arrears for money due, or if its returns have not been made to the Grand Secretary on or before the first day of June; appoint a committee to enter a Lodge and take its books for examination, and to take testimony concerning certain rumors affecting some of its Subordinates; transfer its legitimate functions to a committee; appoint a committee of its own Body to try a member of a Subordinate Lodge; provide by law that a Noble Grand shall have a seat and vote in said Grand Body; provide a dinner for its members, out of its funds, when its laws are silent on the subject; add to the qualifications for a Grand Officer; assess its Subordinates to establish a home for the Widows and Orphans of deceased Odd Fellows; provide, by its laws, that no person shall be eligible to office therein, until he shall have been a member thereof one year; authorize the imposition of a tax on Subordinates for the establishment or support of Odd Fellows' libraries; enact a law that any three or more Lodges, in any city or town, may, by a majority vote of such Lodges, form themselves into a Board of Relief for transient visiting brethren, and authorize them, by a majority vote, to compel the minority to pay assessments for such relief; change the terms of officers; confer the Grand Degrees for a pecuniary consideration; print any portion of the Work whatever; elect an officer of a Subordinate; make it obligatory upon the members in its jurisdiction to subscribe for and take a paper founded by it, and devoted to the interests of the Order. A State Grand

Lodge transacts its business in the Grand Lodge Degree, but may be opened in the Third Degree, during the installation of officers. Grand Bodies should furnish their officers with the Jewels appertaining to their rank and station. A Grand Body should have a Seal, an impression of which, in wax, should be deposited in the archives of the S. G. L. State Grand Bodies are annually furnished with as many copies of the printed proceedings of the S. G. L., as it has Subordinates working under its jurisdiction, to be distributed among their Subordinates, and one-half of such number for their own use.

GRAND REPRESENTATIVE.—It is the duty of a Grand Representative, on his return to his jurisdiction from a session of the S. G. L., to instruct his Grand Body in the Work of the Order. A Grand Representative has not the right to introduce to a Subordinate Encampment, a visitor whom he knows is not a member of the Patriarchal Branch. For further information, the reader is referred to pages 323, 326, 327, 329, 334.

HONORS OF THE ORDER.—The following are entitled to the Honors of the Order: A Grand Representative, where the laws of his Grand Body provide that he is an elective Grand Officer thereof when visiting a Subordinate officially; Grand Officers after their recognition by the officers of the Subordinate; elective and Past Grand Officers, visiting outside of their jurisdiction, after they have been recognized, and have been introduced, to the presiding officer by name and rank; District Deputy Grand Masters, when visiting Subordinate Lodges for the purpose of installing the officers, or upon other official duty; a D. D. G. Sire, when visiting officially. The same principles apply to the Patriarchal Branch of the Order. A Grand Master, when visiting a Subordinate in his official capacity, must announce himself as Grand Master to make his visit official. The following are not entitled to the Honors: A Past Grand or Past Chief Patriarch who has been appointed to install the officers of a Lodge or Encampment; the officers and members of Subordinates, when visiting, in a body, other Subordinates, and introduced by their own officers.

INCORPORATION.—As to the Act of Incorporation of the S. G. L. see Journal, pages 6,908, 6,909, 8,223, 8,224. Grand Bodies are advised to obtain acts of incorporation in order to be the better able to protect their rights. As to the incorporation of Subordinates and the duties of their Grand Bodies in the premises, see pages 186, 187. The particular form, manner, and proceedings necessary to be observed by Subordinates, to obtain legal incorporation, are questions to be determined under the civil law of each State, etc., and the powers, rights, and privileges to be thereby granted are, so long as they do not interfere with the laws, customs, and usages of the Order, subjects wholly under the direction of the State Grand Bodies and Subordinates, respectively, interested.

INDIANS, half-breeds, and males of mixed blood, are not eligible to membership in the Order. An Indian with a Withdrawal Card, cannot be a petitioner for, nor become a Charter member of a new Lodge. An Indian is not allowed, under any circumstances, to visit a Lodge.

INITIATION.—A candidate for membership in the Order is introduced by the ceremony of Initiation. Certain preliminary steps are required to be taken by the applicant, and by the Lodge, in which he desires membership. The applicant is required to fill up and sign an application, generally furnished him by the brother who proposes him. (*See the Form recommended by the S. G. L., page* 304.) He must also make the following declaration: " I declare upon my honor that I do not hold membership in the Patriarchal Circle, or any successor thereof, by whatever name the same may be known or called." The applicant is required, by our laws, to make a candid statement of his sanitary condition, that the Lodge may know the obligation it assumes. The honesty and sincerity of all, who wish to enter its sacred precincts, are tested at its threshold, because it is a cardinal doctrine of the Order, that we can be Odd Fellows, only while we act like honest men. On the reception of the above application it is referred to a Committee, who are required to make a thorough examination of the character, qualifications, etc., and report, if possible, at the next regular meeting, the result to the Lodge. If the applicant be found worthy, he is balloted for and elected into membership. No rejected person can be proposed again, until after the lapse of the time fixed by the local law. The number of black balls required to reject depends upon the local law. Before, however, he can take his seat in the Lodge, he must pass through certain initiatory forms, and assume certain obligations, which will make him one of the family, and entitle him to its tender care and solicitous attention. He will find his field of labor enlarged, for henceforth his mission is—

> " To meliorate the sorrows of mankind,
> Relieve the poor, the sick, the maim, the blind;
> Lift up the drooping heart; the widow cheer,
> And wipe away the helpless orphan's tear.
> To form of men one wide-spread brotherhood,
> Linked only in the bonds of doing good."

All initiations must take place in the Lodge in which the applicant is elected, and when, after election and in pursuance of notice, he presents himself for initiation, it is improper for the Lodge to examine into his health in the ante-room. Initiations by an expelled or suspended Lodge cannot be legalized by its Grand Lodge. If a person has been illegally or fraudulently elected, a majority of the Lodge, previous to the applicant's initiation, can order a new ballot. After initiation, if the applicant is innocent of any misrepresentation, and the illegality has been confined to the Lodge, he shall be protected in his membership, as if legally initiated; but if he has been guilty of fraud, he may be expelled therefor, after proper trial. If an unworthy person has been admitted to membership, the Lodge cannot go behind his initiation and declare it null and void; he can be expelled, only after a proper trial, upon charges duly preferred and investigated.

INSTALLATION is the formal induction into office. The officers of the S. G. L. are installed at the conclusion of the stated communication at which they are elected and appointed. If not present to be installed, the offices are declared vacant. (*See page* 324.) The obligations of officers can be administered only by those upon whom they have been already conferred. When the officers retire with the Marshal for examination, they address the Chairs. A D. D. G. Sire may appoint a qualified brother to install the officers of Subordinates, during his temporary absence from his jurisdiction. It is the Grand Master's duty to install, or cause to be installed, the officers of Subordinate Lodges. When he visits a Lodge for this purpose, he may take the chair of the Noble Grand. He has no right to refuse, on the regular installation night, to install the officers, without assigning any reason therefor. He is not permitted to arrest the installation ceremony, except objections are raised. The officers elect, having been examined in the ante-room, do not address the Chairs, when they enter for installation. There is no installation by proxy. If an officer elect is not present to be installed, and no satisfactory reason therefor be furnished the installing officer, he may require the Lodge to, at once, elect an officer. When a new election is ordered by the Grand Master, at installation, it is his duty to conduct it. Officers hold their offices until the installation of their successors. Officers of Subordinates will not be installed, unless their reports and moneys due be made or placed in the hands of the proper officer, or are in transit to their proper destination. It is illegal to install the officers of a suspended or expelled Subordinate Lodge. Public installations cannot be held without the authority of the State Grand Body. (*See pages* 147, 191.)

INSTRUCTIONS.—State Grand Bodies have the right to instruct their Representatives in matters pertaining particularly to said Bodies, but the S. G. L. considers the doctrine of instruction in reference to matters of general interest as inexpedient. As to what is necessary to have instructions acted upon by the S. G. L., see page 210. State Grand Bodies are recommended to appoint a qualified brother to annually visit each Subordinate in his District, to give instructions in the Work to preserve uniformity therein. The number of instructors may be increased to four for any jurisdiction. It is the duty of a Grand Representative on his return to his jurisdiction from the session of the S. G. L., to instruct his Grand Body. The Grand Master or Grand Patriarch, of the jurisdiction is required to see that his Subordinates strictly comply with the instructions received by him from the Grand Representative. It is the duty of instituting officers to give to newly instituted Grand or Subordinate Bodies such instructions as the circumstances may require.

INSURANCE COMPANIES.—An Association doing business as an insurance company, under the name of the Order, is illegal, unless it has the sanction of the State Grand Body of the jurisdiction in which it is located. The reader will find references to this subject on pages 243, 312.

LAWS.—A law of the S. G. L. takes effect from the time of its enactment, unless the law itself provides otherwise; or unless it requires District, State or Territorial legislation, to make it effective. All general laws, unless otherwise provided, go into effect on the first day of January after their passage. All laws regulating weekly benefits, apply to both Subordinate Lodges and Encampments. The reader's attention is particularly called to the following important facts: That all laws and decisions, when general in their application, apply to both Lodges and Encampments, although but one of said Bodies may be mentioned therein; the term "Subordinate" does not include a Degree Lodge of the Daughters of Rebekah.

LECTURES.—With permission from the proper authority, lectures and essays, confined exclusively to the subject of Odd Fellowship, may be delivered in Subordinates.

LIBRARIES.—The S. G. L. recommends the establishment of Odd Fellows' Libraries. Although State Grand Bodies cannot tax their Subordinates for their establishment or support, the Subordinates themselves may appropriate their funds for that purpose. (*See pages* 212, 242, 247.)

LIMITATIONS.—State statutes of limitation should not be applied to claims to death benefits, in the tribunals of Odd Fellowship. When a member appeals from a refusal to pay benefits, he is not bound to make demand for the further benefits accruing from the same sickness, pending his appeal, until the determination of the proceedings on the appeal, provided there is no local law requiring that a demand be made for such further benefits; that is, if, by the local law, the time is limited in which to appeal, then, under such law, in all cases of continued sickness or disability, the brother should, within the limited time, make a demand for the benefits due, notwithstanding the pendency of an appeal for benefits claimed for an earlier period of such sickness or disability.

LIQUORS.—The Order teaches the principles of temperance. The S. G. L. cannot prohibit members from engaging in the traffic of intoxicating liquors, without creating a new test for membership in the Order. The legislation upon the use of liquors will be found on pages 177, 233.

LOTTERIES.—Subordinates, and their members, are prohibited from raising funds by lotteries or other such schemes. (*See page* 186.)

LUNATICS are entitled to the same benefits that are given to those suffering from bodily infirmity, and it makes no difference if they are supported and cared for at the public expense. Benefits cannot be withheld from an insane brother, because he has not complied with the law in giving his Subordinate, the usual notice; it may be impossible for him to comply with the requirements of the law.

MANCHESTER UNITY.—There is no communion or agreement for inter-visitation between the Manchester Unity and our Order. Grand or Subordinate Lodges under the jurisdiction of the S. G. L. are empowered to receive into membership by initiation, persons who retain membership in the M. U.; and members of our Order may unite with the Unity, or other lawful associations, without severing their connection therewith.

MANUAL, CUSHING'S.—This Manual was adopted by the S. G. L. for the regulation of its proceedings and debates, and as supplementary to its own Rules of Order.

MEETINGS OF THE SOVEREIGN GRAND LODGE.—The Grand Lodge will hold its sessions in Columbus, Ohio, when not otherwise ordered. As to sessions elsewhere, and time of meeting, see Article XII, page 327.

MEETINGS OF STATE GRAND BODIES.—A State Grand Body can determine, in its Constitution where its sessions shall be held. In the absence of such provision, and where the only designated place of meeting is in its Charter, the place of meeting is alterable at the will of the Grand Body, provided it be done in accordance with the provisions of its Constitution. The S. G. L. cannot give permission to a State Grand Body to meet in a place other than that designated in its Constitution. To change the place, the Grand Body itself, must amend its Constitution. A Grand Master must observe the time fixed by the Constitution of his Grand Lodge for its meetings. A State Grand Body can change its time of meeting, from annual to biennial sessions, by a constitutional amendment to that effect, and may hold special sessions, as often as may be deemed necessary, to give instructions in the Unwritten Work, and to confer the Past Official and Grand Lodge or Encampment Degrees. (*See pages* 259, 264, 267.) A Grand Master has no right to call special sessions to confer Degrees, until his Grand Lodge has determined whether it will hold such sessions.

MEETINGS OF SUBORDINATES.—A Subordinate cannot be compelled, by its State Grand Body, to meet in any particular room against its consent. A Grand Body may, however, interdict its meeting in a place not sufficiently private and free from intrusion. A Subordinate cannot meet out of its jurisdiction, nor can it hold adjourned meetings, but must close its regular sessions in due form. Neither a Grand Body, nor its executive officer, can dispense with the regular meetings of a Subordinate; whenever, however, its regular stated meeting falls upon the National Anniversary, Thanksgiving, or other legally established, or generally recognized holiday, such session may be omitted. The Grand Sire cannot change the meetings of Subordinates under the immediate jurisdiction of the S. G. L., from weekly to semi-monthly.

MEETINGS OF DEGREE LODGES OF THE DAUGHTERS OF REBEKAH.— These Lodges are authorized to hold such regular and special meetings as are provided by their By-Laws.

MEETINGS OF CANTONS.—Cantons must hold at least one regular monthly meeting; they may meet weekly or semi-monthly. (*See page* 445.)

MEMBERSHIP.—Original membership in the Order is obtained by Initiation, which see. One cannot hold membership in more than one Grand, nor in more than one Subordinate Body at the same time. Membership, in a Lodge, commences as provided in the local law; and in an Encampment, when the Patriarchal Degree is received. A brother may regain membership by the following methods: Initiation; deposit of Card or Dismissal Certificate; reinstatement; expiration of definite period of suspension; reversal of conviction, which deprived him of membership, on appeal; upon such terms and evidence as the proper State, District or Territorial Grand Body may prescribe for a member of a defunct Subordinate, which has surrendered its Charter since his suspension; upon the presentation of a Card from the officers of the Grand Lodge, under which a defunct Lodge formerly existed, and from which he withdrew prior to its extinction; if expelled for crime, from a Subordinate, which subsequently became extinct, only through the Grand Body to which his Subordinate belonged; if an expelled member, with the consent of the Grand Lodge, to which his Lodge is Subordinate, or of the Grand Master, by its authority, for his restoration thereto. Membership may be lost in the following ways: By expulsion; taking a Withdrawal Card; resignation; suspension; or suspension or expulsion of a brother's Subordinate. The standing of members in an Encampment, does not affect Lodge membership. A suspended brother is still a member, for some purposes, but he is not a *full* member. A person cannot be admitted into a Subordinate Lodge on an Encampment Card. Honorary membership is not permitted. As to non-affiliated Odd Fellows, see pages 253, 254, 272. Subordinates, if permitted by their Grand Bodies, may receive as non-beneficial members, such members of defunct Subordinates as were in good standing at the time of the extinction of their Subordinates, and who, by reason of their advanced age, are now ineligible to beneficial membership. Citizens of one State cannot become members in another State, without the consent required by Article XVI, Section 3, page 328. (*See page* 136.) State Grand Bodies, whose jurisdictions are adjacent, may permit their Subordinates to initiate or admit to membership, persons, whose residences, although in the contiguous jurisdiction, are nearer the location of such Subordinates than that of similar Bodies in such persons' own jurisdiction, with the consent of the Grand Body, or the Executive of the jurisdiction where the applicants reside, legally authenticated and accompanying the application for initiation or membership. A Subordinate that acts, without the above consent, will forfeit and have to pay, on conviction thereof, to the Grand Body of the adjacent jurisdiction, all initiation and Degree charges received to the date of conviction, from the person admitted to membership by such Subordinate. A temporary resident, a citizen or subject of a foreign power, may be initiated and made a member of a Lodge, with the consent of the Grand Master of the jurisdiction in which he has his permanent residence. As to the admission of an expelled or suspended member into a jurisdiction not his own, see page 329. While sick or disabled and receiving benefits from an Encampment, a brother's membership in his Encampment is not affected by the extinction of his Lodge. (*See page* 229.) A brother, a member of both Subordinates, on the extinction of his Lodge, may under the circumstances, and in the manner described on pages 266, 267, retain his membership in his Encampment. As to application for membership in another Lodge, without first applying for a Withdrawal Card, see page 315. Membership cannot be restricted to persons of a certain age. An application for membership may be withdrawn before the report of the committee thereon, but not subsequently; and if the report is recommitted, it is then too late to withdraw the name of the candidate.

MILEAGE AND PER DIEM.—The mileage and per diem of the officers and members of the S. G. L. are determined by resolution at each annual session.

They are not allowed for Sunday, when the session does not hold over from one week to another. The S. G. L. may pay mileage and per diem to P. G. Sires. Committeemen of the S. G. L., who render service during the recess, are each allowed three dollars per day while actually in session, and four cents per mile traveled to and from the place of meeting, to be computed by the nearest route usually traveled to such place. As to payment of mileage and per diem in cases of contested seats, see page 122. The Junior Past Grand Sire, if present at the sessions of the S. G. L., during the term of his immediate successor, receives mileage and per diem. A State Grand Lodge may provide, by constitutional enactment, that its Past Grand Masters, in good standing, its officers formally installed, and Past Grands, who have been regularly elected as Representatives of Lodges, shall receive, while attending its sessions, mileage and per diem.

NAMES.—The initials I. O. O. F. should be used without the introduction of the word "of" between the two O's. The title and rank of a brother of the Order, should be placed after instead of before his name. "Representative" is the term by which members of the S. G. L. are properly addressed, or referred to, in the debates and proceedings of that Body. There is no such title as "Past Degree Master." As to the use of the name of any person, while living, for the chartered title of a Lodge or Encampment, see page 219. This law applies to Degree Lodges of the Daughters of Rebekah and to Uniformed Degree Camps. A Grand Body may permit the use of the names and numbers of extinct Subordinates, in their jurisdictions.

NURSES.—A Subordinate has the right to expend its funds, not otherwise interdicted, for hiring watchers. As to when, and under what circumstances, a Lodge will be bound to pay for a nurse for a member of the same, see page 275. As to the duty of an Odd Fellow, when away from home, to watch with the sick, see page 316.

ODES are a part of the "Supplies" furnished by the S. G. L., and should have its imprint on them. They are a part of the opening and closing ceremonies, etc., of a Subordinate Lodge.

OFFENSES.—The following are declared offenses against the laws of the Order: Printing and circulating Forms, Ceremonies, or anything that constitutes a source of revenue to the treasury of the S. G. L.; using the Seal of the S. G. L., or of any Grand or Subordinate Body, without authority; circulating illegal Diplomas; obtaining relief by means of a Visiting Card and refusing to pay the same; acquiring the Semi-annual Password improperly and making use thereof to obtain relief; willfully and maliciously making false charges; attempting to defraud the Lodge by claiming benefits, when not entitled thereto; introducing with knowledge of her character, a woman of bad repute to an Odd Fellows festival; contempt. As to the illegal use of Emblems, etc., and holding prohibited membership in secret organizations, see pages 218, 219, 287. "Conduct unbecoming an Odd Fellow," is the general term, and embraces every offense for which a member of the Order is amenable.

Officers of the Sovereign Grand Lodge.—The reader is referred to Article III. page 323. The Assistant Grand Secretary is appointed by the Grand Secretary. In case of the extinction of a Subordinate Body to which an officer or member belongs, the seat of such officer or member shall not be vacated thereby, although such membership was a necessary qualification for said seat; provided, that within one month after such extinction he shall connect himself with a like Subordinate. An officer, or member, taking a Withdrawal Card, preserves his seat, if the Card be immediately deposited in his State Grand Body, accompanying the application for a Charter, or if, on change of residence, the Card be deposited in a Subordinate at his new residence, provided, that until such Subordinate be instituted, and while holding said Card, he can perform no official act. In the election of the Grand Officers, every ticket deposited, whether blank, or otherwise, is a vote; and a majority of all the votes, thus polled, is necessary to a choice. As to serving on committees, see page 302.

Grand Sire.—As to the duties of the Grand Sire the reader is referred to the Constitution, By-Laws and Rules of Order of the S. G. L., Chapter II. He has, during the recess, authority to revive a defunct Subordinate, instituted by a State Grand Body since defunct, and to consent to the removal of Subordinates under the immediate jurisdiction of the S. G. L. The following are some of the things the Grand Sire is not authorized to do: Permit, by Dispensation, or otherwise, a Grand Body, by a unanimous vote, to adjourn to a place other than that provided by its Constitution, or to do anything in violation of its organic law; interfere with the decision of a Grand Master, who has refused to give his consent to a Subordinate of his State to hold a public installation; authorize Royal Purple Degree members to wear aprons at the celebration on the 26th of April, or on any other occasion; authorize Subordinates under the jurisdiction of State Grand Bodies to apply to sister Lodges outside the jurisdiction for pecuniary aid for building Odd Fellows' Halls, or for any other purpose; by his decision, although approved by the S. G. L., supersede a By-Law of the S. G. L.; authorize a Grand Master to communicate the A. T. P. W. to a brother holding a Withdrawal Card, to enable him to visit a Subordinate Lodge; authorize a Lodge under the immediate jurisdiction of the S. G. L., to apply for aid and relief, to Lodges working under a State jurisdiction, without having first obtained the consent of the Grand Master of such jurisdiction, or to change the holding of its meetings from weekly to semi-monthly.

Deputy Grand Sire.—His duties are fully prescribed in the Constitution, By-Laws and Rules of Order of the S. G. L. in Chapter II.

Grand Secretary.—In addition to the duties mentioned in the Constitution, By-Laws and Rules of Order of the S. G. L., the Grand Secretary has many others to perform. He must keep his books and accounts at all times written up and posted; arrange in his tabular statements of receipts, in parallel columns, the amounts, for each specific purpose, received from each Grand Jurisdiction, and Subordinate under the S. G. L.; open an account with each specific appropriation, charging thereto, severally, the amount reported by the Committee on Finance, and placing to the credit of such account all payments made on account thereof. He is also directed to furnish the S. G. L., in his annual report, a full and detailed statement of his accounts, showing the amounts due to it, and a statement of all Grand and Subordinate Bodies that may not have reported; is authorized to close his books on the 20th day of August, in each year, and report the financial operations to and including the day above named; is instructed to send to each Grand Representative to the S. G. L. a blank form, to be filled in by him, with his name in full, his place of birth, profession, place of residence or post-office, the nearest route of travel to the place of meeting of the S. G. L., together with the number of miles to be traveled; the said Representative to return the statement to the Grand Secretary, who must place the same completed form in the hands of the chairman of the Committee on Mileage and Per Diem, one month previous to the meeting of the S. G. L. On application for a Charter for a State Grand Body, the Grand Secretary must inform the Committee on Petitions whether the dues of the Subordinates are all paid. It is his duty, at the opening of every annual session, to place in the hands of the Grand Sire a written statement, showing the name of every Grand Body and its indebtedness to the S. G. L., to be placed by the Grand Sire in the hands of the Committee on Credentials, immediately on the appointment of the committee, so that it may be able to make its report in conformity with the eleventh Article of the By-Laws, page 332. He is to have printed and appended to the proceedings of every session, the post-office addresses and a list of the Grand Patriarchs, Grand Scribes, Grand Masters, Grand Secretaries of the respective Grand Bodies, and the times and places of their annual sessions. He should record, in the Journal of each session, the names of the Past Grand Representatives who may be present and report to him, and mail a copy of the Revised Journal to each P. G. Rep. whose name appears therein. The Seal of the S. G. L. is under his exclusive control; it is only to be used or attached to papers and documents emanating from his office in a legal manner. He may appoint and remove, at his pleasure, an Assistant Grand Secretary, a janitor for his office, and such temporary assistants, clerical and other aid, as may be required for the satisfactory discharge of the duties of his office. The Grand Secretary and his Assistant are especially charged with the preservation and protection of all the property of the Grand Lodge. Before entering on the duties of his office, he is required to execute and deliver to the Grand Sire a bond in the penalty of $10,000, with surety or sureties, to be duly approved.

ASSISTANT GRAND SECRETARY.—He must be a competent book-keeper. He has charge of all supplies furnished by the S. G. L., and is to receive and disburse the same, and is required to perform, generally, such duties as the Grand Secretary may direct. The Assistant Grand Secretary, before entering upon the performance of his duties, must give a bond, with at least two sureties, to the S. G. L., in the sum of $10,000; the bond to be approved by the Grand Secretary.

GRAND TREASURER.—The Grand Treasurer is directed to deposit, in the name of the S. G. L., the funds thereof, as they may be received, in one or more banks of the city or town in which he may reside, where such deposits may be deemed secure. The funds are to be drawn, by his official check, for the payment of only such bills as may be certified by the Grand Secretary. If the Grand Treasurer, in conjunction with such of the Grand Officers with whom he may be able to confer, shall deem such deposits unsafe, he may withdraw them and place the same where they will be secure. He is authorized to close his books on the 20th of August in each year, and report the financial operations to and including that day. His duties, generally, are prescribed in Article VII, page 325. He gives bond for the sum of $10,000.

The duties of Grand Chaplain, Grand Marshal, Grand Guardian, and Grand Messenger are prescribed in Article VIII, page 326, and in the By-Laws and Rules of Order of the S. G. L., Chapter II.

DISTRICT DEPUTY GRAND SIRES.—They are the executive agents of the Grand Sire and Grand Secretary. Their duties, generally, are prescribed in Article XV, page 333. A District Deputy has no power to correct irregularities of Subordinates; he must report them to the Grand Sire, who alone can do so. He has no authority to set aside any illegal action of a Subordinate, on an appeal by an aggrieved brother. He cannot order a new trial, nor direct a Subordinate to prescribe a definite degree of punishment, nor issue Warrants for Subordinates, nor reclaim Charters of Subordinates doing work irregularly. He has no authority to grant Withdrawal Cards to members of defunct Subordinates, nor institute or visit any Uniformed Degree Camp, unless he possesses said Degree. He has the right to act as follows: Introduce visitors into a Subordinate where no Grand Body exists; appoint a qualified brother or brothers to install the officers of Subordinates, during his necessary and temporary absence; grant Dispensations to brothers wishing to obtain the Patriarchal Degrees out of the jurisdiction, as a Grand Patriarch under the same circumstances can, in any State, District, or Territory where a Subordinate Encampment, but no Grand Encampment, exists; grant a Dispensation to a Subordinate under the immediate jurisdiction of the S. G. L. to elect a Scarlet Degree member to fill a vacancy in the office of N. G. or V. G. of a Lodge, when all qualified members refuse to serve. At the expiration of the term which he shall have served, he shall be entitled to be addressed as Past District Deputy Grand Sire, and may wear a Jewel.

OFFICERS OF STATE GRAND BODIES.—The officers of a Grand Encampment are: Grand Patriarch, Grand High Priest, Grand Senior Warden, who are elected; and Grand Sentinel, Outside or Deputy Grand Sentinel, Grand Marshal, who are appointed by the Grand Patriarch. The officers of a State Grand Lodge are: Grand Master, Deputy Grand Master, Grand Warden, Grand Secretary, Grand Treasurer, who are elected; Grand Marshal, Grand Conductor, Grand Guardian, and Grand Herald, who are appointed by the Grand Master. The Grand Chaplain may be either elected or appointed, as the laws of the Grand Lodge may provide. State Grand Bodies may appoint such additional officers as their wants and conveniences require.

GRAND PATRIARCH.—He has powers and duties, as prescribed in the Charge Books of the Order; he has supervisory authority over the jurisdiction of his Grand Encampment. Whether he has power, during the recess of the Grand Encampment, to suspend a Subordinate Encampment is a subject for local law. Unless prevented by constitutional limitation, he has authority to interdict any public display of Emblems or secret working costumes of the Encampment, which, in his judgment, may prove prejudicial to that Branch of the Order. He cannot authorize the removal of a Subordinate Encampment from one town to another, nor suspend the Constitution of any of his Subordinates.

GRAND MASTER.—He has the powers and duties prescribed in the Charge Books of the Order, and performs such duties as are imposed upon him by his Grand Lodge. He is not an independent part of the governing power. During the recess he represents, to some extent, his Grand Lodge. He has no right to refuse to entertain appeals from his decisions to the Grand Lodge, though, in his opinion, an adverse decision might violate the Constitution. He has no power to summarily remove an officer of a Subordinate Lodge. (*See page* 117.) He may vote in his Grand and Subordinate Lodges, at elections for officers, but should not hold office in his Subordinate or in a Degree Lodge. The mode of reaching the Grand Master, to obtain his decision, is a matter for local legislation. When visiting, for installation purposes, he is entitled to take the chair of the N. G., and can do so, as a matter of right, at no other time. His decisions are in full force until reversed by the Grand Lodge. He cannot suspend the action of his Grand Lodge. He is not the law-making power; his functions are ministerial and judicial, not legislative, and he possesses only the powers conferred upon him by the law. When visiting, in his official capacity, he should wear the Regalia and Jewel of his office. Grand Officers are not entitled, *ex officio*, to a vote in their Grand Lodges, but it is competent for local legislation to give them that privilege. If the Grand Lodge is not a representative Body, and all Past Grands are members thereof, and entitled to vote on all questions, the Grand Master is entitled to vote on a call of the yeas and nays, notwithstanding his so doing will produce a tie, and he may then, as Grand Master, be required to give the casting vote.

DISTRICT DEPUTIES.—These are only the executive agents of the Grand Officers they represent, with a general supervisory power in the absence of their principals; they are not required to have the Grand Degrees. They are entitled to the same Honors that are given to the officers they represent, when they visit a Subordinate to install the officers elect, or upon other official duty. They may be removed for neglect, or refusal to perform the duties enjoined upon them by law. They are eligible to office in Subordinates. A District Deputy cannot declare an act of a Subordinate void; he must report the matter to his chief Executive Officer.

OFFICERS OF SUBORDINATE BODIES.—The officers of an Encampment are: Chief Patriarch, High Priest, Senior Warden, Scribe, (Financial Scribe, if the Grand Encampment permit,) Treasurer, Junior Warden, who are elected; Guide,

ODD FELLOWSHIP.

Inside Sentinel, Outside Sentinel, First, Second, Third and Fourth Watches, Four Sentinels of the W., who are appointed by the Chief Patriarch; First and Second Guard of the Tent, who are appointed by the High Priest. The officers of a Subordinate Lodge are : The Noble Grand, Vice Grand, Secretary, Permanent Secretary (if necessary), and Treasurer, who are elected; Warden, Conductor, Outside Guardian, Inside Guardian, Right and Left Supporters of the N. G., Right and Left Scene Supporters, who are appointed by the N. G.; Right and Left Supporters of the V. G., who are appointed by the V. G. The duties of these officers are prescribed by, and contained in, the Charge Books of the Order. The two highest officers of a Lodge and the Chief Patriarch and Senior Warden of an Encampment are entitled to the A. T. P. W., and receive it at the time of their installation, so that they may be able to give it, and superintend the examination of visitors. Officers have no power to use the Seal, unless so ordered by the Subordinate, or in accordance with positive enactments of the Grand Body, under whose jurisdiction it works. They wear the Jewels and Regalia prescribed for them by the laws of the Order. An officer is not suspended from the performance of his duties, during the pendency of charges against him, except so far as those duties may have a relation to the charges, such as the appointing of the committee, in whole or in part, that is to try them, etc. The suspension of an officer for cause, vacates his office, and the suspension of a member by a Lodge, for cause, after conviction, who is an officer in an Encampment, vacates his office in the Encampment. Relatives may hold office, at the same time, in the same Subordinate.

CHIEF PATRIARCH AND NOBLE GRAND.—The N. G. alone, should have the power to call his Lodge together, except in his absence from the city or town, when it is legal for the V. G. to call a special meeting of his Lodge, provided its By-Laws authorize him so to do. A Chief Patriarch, or Noble Grand, cannot refuse to put motions if legitimate. A Noble Grand may deliver the Past Grand's charge. A Chief Patriarch, or Noble Grand, has not the right to admit a member of another Subordinate, in his State jurisdiction, without the Term Password; they may install their successors, in the absence of the proper installing officer, or of all Past Chief Patriarchs or Past Grands; they cannot set aside any part of the Constitution of their respective Subordinates. A Noble Grand, or Vice Grand, of any Lodge, Subordinate or Rebekah, is not obliged to surrender his chair to a team in conferring the Degrees.

SENIOR WARDEN AND VICE GRAND.—In the absence of the C. P., or N. G., it is the duty of the Senior Warden, or Vice Grand, to take the place of his superior officer. (See page 284.) Upon occasions of initiation and grand visitation, the Vice Grand may call to his assistance, and to the chair of the N. G. in his absence, a Past Grand. In the temporary absence of the N. G., or V. G., their seats are occupied by their respective Right Supporters, and in the like absence of the Chief Patriarch, the First Watch takes his chair, and can put motions. The temporary occupant of a chair must wear the Regalia of the chair. In the absence of the C. P., and S. W., the Junior Warden may preside; and in the absence of the High Priest, any Royal Purple member may perform all the duties of his office. In the absence of the N. G. and V. G. any Past Grand may preside. Grand Bodies may authorize Subordinates to enact By-Laws that the V. G. and S. W. may assist in the examination of ballots, and make known the result thereof, so far as to state whether the ballot is favorable or unfavorable, but the C. P. and N. G. must supervise the ballots and declare the result. For further information concerning these two officers, the reader, to avoid repetition, is referred to pages 127, 275, 305, 306.

SCRIBE AND RECORDING SECRETARY.—A brother cannot hold the two offices of Recording Secretary (or Scribe), and Treasurer, at the same time, in any Subordinate. Secretaries are required to keep a register of the members of their respective Lodges, who are Patriarchs of Encampments. (*See page* 258.) For the reciprocal duties of Scribe and Secretary, see page 81. On the reinstatement by a Lodge, of an expelled brother, notice must be given to the brother's Subordinate Encampment. For the Certificate accompanying an application for membership in an Encampment, see page 308. Custom and usage have assigned particular places for the officers of Subordinates. If there is no special legislation to the contrary, such customary places are the proper places. The Warden's position has been declared to be in front, and to the right of the R. S. of the N. G.

PASSWORDS, ANNUAL TRAVELING.—This Password was adopted for the protection of the Order, and is one of the tests by which traveling brothers are proved. (*See Article XXV., page* 336.) It is selected annually by the Grand Sire, and goes into use the first day of January in each year. The Grand Sire communicates it to the Grand Representatives at each session of the S. G. L. If a State's Representative be not present to receive it, the Grand Sire transmits it, through some safe channel, to the proper State authorities; in the case of Subordinates working under the immediate jurisdiction of the S. G. L. he transmits it, through the D. D. G. Sires, to their Noble Grands and Chief Patriarchs. All the officers in possession of it can communicate it only in the discharge of their official duties and to the persons entitled thereto by law. It is the duty of the Grand Representatives to deliver it to the Grand Masters and Grand Patriarchs of the several State Bodies they represent. It is then the duty of these Grand Officers to communicate it to their Grand Secretary and Grand Scribe, and cause it to be communicated to the District Deputies, and such other installing officers as are necessary to assist them in the discharge of their official duties. It is not right for a Grand Representative to give the Word to his Grand Body, during the exemplification of the Unwritten Work. The Grand Sire has no right to authorize a Grand Master to communicate the Word to a brother, holding a Withdrawal Card, to enable him to visit a Subordinate Lodge. (*See page* 171.) If a brother, applying for a Visiting or Withdrawal Card, be absent from the location of his Subordinate, so that he cannot obtain the A. T. P. W. with his Card, in person, it is the duty of the proper officers, upon granting such Card, to transmit the same to the brother, and also send, therewith, a letter, the form of which will be found on page 173. A Noble Grand cannot refuse to confer the Word upon a brother who presents his Traveling Card, with such a letter, except the brother has committed a felony between the date of the letter and its presentation; in such case, he would be justified in declining to give the Word. If the brother holding a With-drawal Card forgets the Word, the N. G. of the Lodge from which he withdrew, may again communicate it to him on the presentation of the Card, within one year from its date. When a brother offers to visit a Subordinate on a Visiting or unexpired Withdrawal Card, or is an applicant for membership therein by deposit of a proper Card, he must prove himself in possession of the Word of the year in which the Card was issued and bears date, but the holder of a Dismissal Certificate, on deposit of the same, is not required to have the A. T. P. W. If a member of a defunct Lodge holds an unexpired Withdrawal Card, the Grand Master of the jurisdiction can give him the Word. When State Grand Officers grant Cards, under the general law, the brother receiving the Card is not en-titled to the A. T. P. W. A brother holding a Withdrawal Card from one State, is entitled to the A. T. P. W. in use at the time, and retains the right to visit, in another State, with the same Word, for a year. A brother should be in pos-session of the A. T. P. W. when depositing a Withdrawal Card in a Lodge to obtain membership. (*See page* 168.) It is the duty of the N. G. to examine him; and should he fail to remember the Word, or should the officers of his Lodge have neglected to impart it to him, or should the Card be an expired one, the brother may be admitted to membership as an Ancient Odd Fellow. The Annual and P. P. W's. of the Degrees are not to be translated into any other language, or spoken other than they are written, spelled and pronounced in the English language. (*See page* 251.)

PASSWORDS—SEMI-ANNUAL, TERM, CHECK, EVENING.—State Grand Lodges have the option to change the Password quarterly, instead of semi-annually, and when the terms of their Subordinates are changed from six months to one year, the Term Password issued by the Grand Master may be used during the whole year, unless his Grand Lodge determines to have two or more *Words* for the term. The Password for the term, is determined by the Grand Master, or Grand Patriarch, for their respective Subordinates. These Grand Officers communicate it to their District Deputies and such other installing officers as may be necessary, who in turn communicate it to the first two officers of the Lodge or Encampment. The Term Password of an Encampment is called the Check Password. A Password for the evening, is determined upon by the Vice Grand, or Senior Warden, each meeting night, and is communicated to the Inside Guardian or Inside Sentinel; and any brother who has retired and wishes to re-enter the same evening, may use this Word, or the explanation of the Pass-word of the current term, for that purpose. The Semi-annual Password will not be furnished to Officers of Subordinates, nor can they be installed, unless the re-ports, returns and moneys, due from such Subordinates to their respective supe-rior jurisdictions, be actually made and placed in the hands of the proper officer, or be actually in transit to the proper destination. A member of an Encamp-ment, who has only received the Patriarchal Degree, is entitled to the Semi-annual (Check) Password. It is competent for a N. G. to give the Semi-annual Pass-word to a brother of another Lodge, in the *same* jurisdiction, at the written re-quest of the N. G. thereof, under the Seal of said Lodge. A member of a Subor-dinate, who is in arrears for weekly or funeral dues more than thirteen weeks, is not entitled to the Term Password. The R. S. of the N. G., temporarily occupying the N. G.'s chair, has no right to authorize a brother to confer the Term Word upon another brother, of the same Lodge, to enable him to visit other Lodges. The Grand Officers of State Grand Bodies, when visiting the Subordinates under their jurisdiction, should give, at the outside door, the same Password that is required of other brothers. After the Subordinate has been informed of the presence, in the ante-room, of the installing officers, no Password should be required of them at the inner door. As to a brother, holding a Visiting Card, visiting in his own jurisdiction, but without Term, or Check Word, see page 199. The N. G. of a Lodge has not the right to admit a member belonging to another Lodge, in his State jurisdiction, without the Term Password; he may admit his own members, until suspended in accordance with the provisions of the Constitution. As to the improper acquisition and use of Password, see page 144.

PASSWORDS OF THE REBEKAH DEGREE.—The Grand Master of a jurisdiction in which Degree Lodges of the Daughters of Rebekah exist, is required to make a Semi-annual Password for such Lodges. (*See page* 260.) The Annual Password is selected by the Grand Sire. It should be given by the ladies at the outer door of the Subordinate Lodge, and in Rebekah Degree Lodges. (*See page* 260.) A brother or sister, not a member of a Rebekah Degree Lodge, is not entitled to the Semi-annual Password, nor can either visit such a Lodge. The Term Password of the Subordinate Lodge, must not be used in a Rebekah Degree Lodge, and only the Passwords of the Rebekah Degree shall be used by both sexes therein. As to the wives of suspended or expelled members, see page 301.

PAST OFFICERS.—Past officers cannot be deprived of their rank, simply because they are not members of Grand Lodges, or Grand Encampments. (*See page* 293.)

PAST GRAND SIRES.—Past Grand Sires are admitted to seats in the S. G. L. As to their privileges, see Article X, page 326. They cannot serve on committees of the S. G. L. The S. G. L. has power to pay them mileage and per diem, when attending its sessions.

PAST GRANDS. PAST CHIEF PATRIARCHS.—A brother must produce satisfactory proof of his rank, to be recognized as a Past Grand. A Past Grand cannot surrender his rights and privileges to any one in the Order; he may fail to use them, but they remain his, as long as he is a member in good standing. These rights are, to a seat in his Grand Lodge, to vote for Grand Officers, and eligibility to office. A Past Grand, who is a member of a Grand Lodge, and in good standing in his Subordinate Lodge, has a right to a seat and a vote in his Grand Lodge, on an election of Grand Officers, although he may not have the Password of the current term. No ballot or vote should be taken upon granting a Past Grand's Certificate. A Past Grand, expelled by his Grand Lodge from membership therein, is entitled to the rank of P. G. in his Subordinate Lodge. A Lodge is bound to give a member P. G. Regalia, who is admitted by Card certifying that he is a P. G., even if he has not the P. O. Degrees. The Certificate that a brother has served a term as N. G., or C. P., is merely *prima facie* evidence of qualification for admission to a Grand Body (*See page* 132.) A Junior Past Grand can be elected Representative to a State Grand Lodge. To become a Junior Past Grand, service as N. G. to the very last moment of the term, is requisite. A Junior Past Grand is not an officer of a Lodge and cannot be fined, as such, for absence from Lodge meetings. A Past Grand cannot be refused admission to his seat in his Grand Lodge, if he presents a proper Certificate of qualification. Grand Encampments consist of all Past Chief Patriarchs and Past High Priests, or, if their Constitutions so determine, of all Past Chief Patriarchs only. Patriarchs who are, or may become members of a Grand Encampment of one State, or jurisdiction, shall be qualified for membership in a Grand Encampment of any other State or jurisdiction. If the Constitution of a State Grand Lodge so provide, Past Grands who are members thereof may be paid mileage and per diem for attendance at its sessions. When the Grand Lodge is a representative Body, Past Grands who are not Representatives, may be deprived of the right of making motions or serving on committees. A Lodge cannot compel the sitting Past Grand to perform the duties of Chaplain, nor fine him for refusal.

PAST HIGH PRIESTS.—A Past High Priest, to become a Past Chief Patriarch, must be elected Chief Patriarch, and serve out his time as such. (See DEGREES, ELECTION and VOTING.)

PETITIONS.—The following Forms of Petitions will be found on the pages mentioned: For membership in a Subordinate Lodge, page 304, and Book of Forms, pages 157, 158; for a Warrant for a Grand Body, page 331; for a Warrant for a Subordinate Body, Book of Forms, pages 142, 143; for the Encampment Degrees to establish an Encampment, Book of Forms, page 141; for aid for a Subordinate Lodge, page 71.

PRAYER.—The S. G. L. is opened and closed with prayer. All Grand and Subordinate Bodies may open and close their meetings with prayer. It is not a part of the Work at initiations. (*See page* 263.) If prayer be used at funerals, the Forms prescribed in the Ceremony in the Book of Forms must be used.

PROCESSIONS.—State Grand Bodies should prohibit all processions in which the Regalia, Emblems, etc., of the Order are used, unless they be authorized by said Grand Bodies, or, in their recess, be permitted by Dispensation of the Grand Master, or Grand Patriarch. The anniversary proclamation of the Grand Sire, is not sufficient authority to appear in public, in Regalia. Permission, as above, must be obtained. Subordinates under the immediate jurisdiction of the S. G. L. must obtain the assent of the Grand Sire. Uniformed Patriarchs will act as escort to such legalized processions of the Order, in which they may elect to take part. A brother holding a Withdrawal Card, has no right to join a procession of the Order, without the consent of the Lodge by which the procession is formed. For the order of precedence, and Forms of Processions, see the Book of Forms, pages 33–53.

PROXY.—Proxies, or alternates, for Grand Representatives of the S. G. L. are not recognized. Past Grands, as Past Grands, cannot vote by proxy. In conventions to organize Grand Bodies, Past Grands, Past Chief Patriarchs, or Past High Priests, cannot be represented by proxies.

QUALIFICATIONS FOR MEMBERSHIP IN THE ORDER.—See Article XVI, Section 2, page 328. Peculiar religious views which do not affect a person's belief in a Supreme Being, the Creator and Preserver of the Universe, cannot disqualify him for membership. (*See page* 92.) The following are ineligible to membership: Indians, half-breeds, Chinese, Polynesians, persons totally deaf, dumb or blind. The race criterion for membership is, that the applicant should be of the pure Caucasian stock. Deformed persons, and those who have lost a limb, may become members, if their condition does not prevent a compliance with the requirements and laws of the Order. (*See page* 175.) Grand or Subordinate Bodies have no authority to change, restrict, or add to the qualifications for membership as prescribed by the Constitution of the S. G. L. It is illegal to provide that a person must be able to read or write, to qualify him for membership.

QUALIFICATIONS FOR MEMBERSHIP IN THE SOVEREIGN GRAND LODGE.— A Grand Representative must have, at the time of his *election*, *all* the qualifications prescribed in Article IX, Section 3, page 326. He must take and subscribe to the affirmation in Journal, page 10,727.

QUALIFICATIONS FOR MEMBERSHIP IN STATE GRAND BODIES.—To obtain membership in a Grand Lodge, a brother must be a Past Grand in good standing, and for membership in a Grand Encampment, he must be a Past Chief Patriarch in good standing, or, if the Constitution of the Grand Body authorizes it, a Past High Priest in good standing.

QUALIFICATIONS FOR MEMBERSHIP IN A SUBORDINATE ENCAMPMENT.— To acquire membership in a Subordinate Encampment, full membership and good standing in a Subordinate Lodge, in good standing, is necessary.

QUALIFICATIONS FOR MEMBERSHIP IN A DEGREE LODGE OF THE DAUGHTERS OF REBEKAH.—See REBEKAH DEGREE, and DEGREE LODGES OF THE DAUGHTERS OF REBEKAH.

QUALIFICATIONS FOR OFFICE IN THE SOVEREIGN GRAND LODGE.—See Article XV, Section 1, page 328.

QUALIFICATIONS FOR OFFICE IN STATE GRAND BODIES.—See above, QUALIFICATIONS FOR MEMBERSHIP IN STATE GRAND BODIES. Past Officers are guaranteed, by ancient usage and the decisions of the S. G. L., the right to hold office in their Grand Bodies, and a provision that a member shall not be eligible to office, until he shall have been a member of his Grand Body one year, is illegal.

QUALIFICATIONS FOR OFFICE IN SUBORDINATE BODIES.—A member must pass the Vice Grand's chair to be made eligible for the office of N. G., except in the first term of a new Lodge, and in case of a vacancy in the office of Noble Grand, when all qualified members refuse to serve, then the Lodge, having first obtained a Dispensation for that purpose, may elect a Scarlet Degree member. Twenty-six nights' service as an inferior officer, other than that of Chaplain, is a sufficient qualification for the chair of the Vice Grand, provided the brother has attained sufficient Degrees, and is otherwise competent. The qualifications of a Chief Patriarch and Senior Warden, are analogous to those of Noble Grand and Vice Grand, respectively. A Grand Encampment may make previous service as a High Priest, a necessary qualification for the office of Chief Patriarch. It is the duty of the elective officers only, of a Subordinate Lodge, to be instructed in the Work of the Degree of Rebekah. All the officers of a Subordinate Lodge, must be in possession of the Degree of Truth, and all the officers of a Subordinate Encampment must have the Royal Purple Degree.

QUALIFICATIONS FOR OFFICE IN DEGREE LODGES OF THE DAUGHTERS OF REBEKAH.—See page 248.

QUORUM.—Representatives from a majority of the whole number of State, District and Territorial Grand Bodies, shall be necessary to form a quorum in the S. G. L. State Grand Bodies are, at present, at liberty to make such number of members a quorum, as they may deem for their best interests. A quorum for Subordinate Lodges, Subordinate Encampments and Uniformed Degree Camps consists of five members; of a Degree Lodge of the Daughters of Rebekah, seven members; of a Canton, nine members.

RANK.—In granting a Visiting, or Withdrawal Card, the highest title to which the brother has attained in the Branch of the Order from which the Card is taken, should be stated thereon, except if the brother be a Representative or a P. G. Representative, then said rank should be expressed on the Card, when taken from either the Subordinate Lodge or Encampment   Rank refers to the highest grade, or title, attained.   Past Grand Representative is not a higher rank than Past Grand Master or Past Chief Patriarch.   A Past Grand Representative is entitled to rank, as such, in every Branch of the Order of which he is a member.   A Representative to the Sovereign Grand Lodge, who was admitted and took his seat therein, is, after resignation therefrom, entitled to wear the Regalia and Jewel of the rank of Past Grand Representative.   A Card stating the rank of a brother, is not conclusive evidence, to entitle him to the privileges such rank confers. (*See page* 187.) The title, or rank of a brother, must be placed after and not before his name. The rank of an Ancient Odd Fellow, in the Lodge to which he may be admitted, will be determined by the Lodge, upon the report of the committee appointed to make the necessary examination.

RECONSIDERATION.—As to the reconsideration of an unfavorable ballot, see page 143. Such reconsideration shall be had within the four meeting nights next succeeding the rejection. The time for a motion to reconsider an unfavorable ballot, is not a subject for local legislation. If a person has been, through fraud or error, elected to membership, a majority of the Lodge can, previous to the applicant's initiation, order a new ballot. The vote by which a Withdrawal Card was authorized, cannot be reconsidered or rescinded. An amendment to the Constitution of the S. G. L. may be reconsidered, at any time, during the annual session at which it is adopted. After the passage of a resolution, by a Grand Lodge, acquitting a brother, who has been charged and expelled by his Subordinate Lodge, it is competent for the Grand Lodge to reconsider such vote, and pass a resolution confirming the decision of his Lodge. In the Sovereign Grand Lodge, any member who has voted in favor of a decision, may move for the reconsideration thereof.

REFRESHMENTS.—All spirituous, vinous and malt liquors shall be excluded from the Lodge rooms and ante-rooms, or halls connected with, or adjoining thereto, under the control of any Subordinate, or Degree Lodge, or Encampment of this Order. Edibles may be used.

REINSTATEMENT—RESTORATION—OF MEMBERS.—A person, who has lost all connection with the Order, desiring to regain membership therein, must apply to the Lodge with which he was formerly connected for reinstatement, or for a Dismissal Certificate, which he may deposit in any Lodge, or Encampment, as the case may be. As to reinstatement after suspension for non-payment of dues, see pages 219, 289. A brother has the right to deposit a Withdrawal Card, on application for membership Should he not have the A. T. P. W., or should the Card be an expired one, he may be admitted as an Ancient Odd Fellow. A Lodge is not bound to reinstate a member suspended for non-payment of dues, nor to admit to membership the holder of a Card. A Subordinate, under the approval of its Grand Lodge, possesses the right to judge of the qualifications of all applicants for admission, or reinstatement to membership, except in cases of definite suspension. The matter of reinstatement, in cases of indefinite suspension for non-payment of dues, is one for the local law to determine. A brother suspended for a definite period of time, as a punishment for some specific offense, upon the expiration of his term of suspension, is *ipso facto* restored to membership, but is responsible for dues during his disability. A member of an Encampment, who is suspended in his Lodge for a definite period, on his restoration to membership therein, is *ipso facto* reinstated in his Encampment, provided he paid his dues in the Encampment during his suspension. The reinstatement of an expelled member in his Lodge, does not restore him to membership in his Encampment. No Subordinate can reinstate an expelled member, of its own motion. (*See Article XVI, Section 4, page* 329.) The consent of the Grand Lodge to which the Lodge is subordinate, or of the Grand Master, by its authority, is absolutely necessary to authorize the restoration. If there is no local law prescribing what vote is necessary to reinstate an expelled member, with the consent of the Grand Body, the same vote that expelled from, ought to be had to restore to membership. A member expelled in one jurisdiction, can be neither legally nor honorably reinstated in another jurisdiction, except with the consent of the Lodge expelling. Notice must be given by the Subordinate Lodge to the Subordinate Encampment, on the reinstatement of an expelled brother. (*See page* 267.) When a brother applies for reinstatement, after suspension for non-payment of dues, and is rejected, the money paid in by him, on his application, must be returned to him, although he is indebted to the Lodge to that amount. If the action of a brother's State Grand Body, on appeal thereto, reverses a decision of his Subordinate, and has the effect of restoring him to membership, he may be reinstated without the consent of his Subordinate. (SEE CARDS, DEFUNCT SUBORDINATES, EXPULSION.)

REINSTATEMENT OF SUBORDINATES.—A Grand Body may permit the use of the names and numbers of its extinct Subordinates. When a Lodge is suspended, or expelled, its functions cease, for all purposes. When the disability is removed, then the Lodge starts again in the exercise of its various functions, as though there had been no interruption. There is a difference between the status of the officers and members of a restored suspended Lodge, and a restored defunct Lodge. In the former case, the officers and members have the same status they had before the suspension, while in the latter case, the members making the application are the only ones restored to their former condition, provided they be present at the organization. The other members in good standing, may resume their membership upon such terms as the local law may prescribe. The application for restoration of a Charter must be made to the State Grand Body to which the Lodge or Encampment was subordinate. The Grand Sire has authority, during the recess of the S. G. L., to revive a defunct Subordinate instituted by a Grand Body which is itself defunct. (SEE CHARTERS, AND DEFUNCT SUBORDINATES.)

REJECTION.—The time that shall intervene, between the rejection of an applicant for membership and a second application of the same person, is a matter for local law; so also is the number of times a person may apply for membership. Applications for membership are determined by ballot, but it is left to State legislation to decide in what manner, and how many black balls are required to reject; but in Subordinates under the immediate jurisdiction of the S. G. L., three black balls reject a candidate. If, however, the application be by Card, for membership in Subordinates under the S. G. L , a majority only, of the members present, on ballot shall be necessary to elect.

RELIEF.—No Lodge or Encampment shall entertain any application for pecuniary aid, unless the same be authorized by the Grand Body, or its principal Grand Officer, of the jurisdiction in which such aid is solicited, and in accordance with the form prescribed for such purposes. (*See page* 70.) The Grand Sire has no power to authorize Subordinates, under the jurisdiction, of State Grand Bodies, to apply to sister Lodges outside the jurisdiction for pecuniary aid. He cannot authorize a Lodge under the sole jurisdiction of the S. G. L. to apply for aid or relief to Lodges working under a State jurisdiction, without having first obtained the consent of the Grand Master of such jurisdiction, so to do. The S. G. L. commends the work of general relief associations, instituted by members of the Order, and recommends the several State jurisdictions to make ample provision for compensating other jurisdictions for expenses paid, and costs incurred, in the relief of brothers in distress, who claim the same under a

Visiting Card, as brothers in good standing. For the law governing general relief funds, see page 238. State Grand Bodies cannot assess their Subordinates for a general relief fund; the contributions to such a fund must be voluntary. As to the formation of Auxiliary Endowment Benefit Associations, see page 259. When a member of the Órder, in possession of a Visiting Card obtains money from a Subordinate, or from a Relief Committee, the amount so obtained must be indorsed upon such Card, with the date, and by what Body furnished, attested by the proper officer. A Grand Lodge cannot be held responsible for relief granted to a member of one of its defunct Subordinates, unless assets, to the amount of the benefits extended, shall have come into the possession of the said Grand Lodge, upon the forfeiture of its Charter by such Subordinate. (SEE BENEFITS AND NURSES.)

RELATIVES.—Persons akin to each other, no matter how close, may hold office, at the same time, in the same Body. The *dependent relatives* of a deceased brother, are those only who are members of his immediate family, and such as were, at his death, dependent upon him for support. (*See page* 315.)

RENOUNCING ODD FELLOWSHIP.—If a brother renounces the Order he thereby forfeits all benefits to which, by law, he may be entitled from the time of his renunciation. If he desire to leave the Order, he should do so in the manner prescribed by law, that is, by resignation, which, at once, severs his membership, or by taking a Withdrawal Card, which, if not deposited within a year, expires. (SEE RESIGNATION.)

RESIGNATION.—A written resignation severs the connection of a brother finally and entirely with the Order, provided that he be in good standing in his Lodge, when he resigns therefrom. A Grand, or other officer, who voluntarily withdraws from the duties of a station, which on their full performance entitles him to the honors thereof, forfeits such honors; but where there is a salary attached to the office, he does not forfeit his right to his portion of the salary for the time served. A member cannot resign from a Lodge while charges are pending against him, and thus avoid a trial.

RULES OF ORDER.—The Rules of Order of the S. G. L. will be found on pages 338-344. The following decisions on questions of order have been adopted by the S. G. L. It is too late to ask for a division of the Grand Lodge after the Chair has declared the resolution adopted. After other business has been introduced, it is too late to appeal. A resolution to discharge a committee, and to refer the same subject to a Special Committee, is not a privileged question, and a motion to lay the whole subject on the table, is in order. A motion for the previous question takes precedence of a motion to refer. A motion to lay on the table is a privileged question, and a motion for the previous question does not take precedence of it. A resolution being under consideration, the Grand Sire, with the sanction of the Grand Lodge, decided that a call for the ayes and noes opens debate, and makes any motion admissible. A proposition which has been rejected, cannot be renewed at the same session. It is not in accordance with parliamentary law, to make a motion to establish a negative of a proposition and the affirmative of another, or, in other words, to move to reject a proposition and adopt another. Debate upon the merits of a subject is not in order, pending a motion to reconsider. When a question has been divided, and the first branch of it adopted, the second branch is open to amendment. A vote adopting an amendment to the Constitution may, at any time during the session at which it was adopted, be reconsidered.

SEAL.—The Seal of the S. G. L. is kept exclusively under the control and in the custody of the Grand Secretary, and is only to be used, or attached to, papers and documents emanating from his office, in a legal manner. Each Grand Lodge and Grand Encampment shall have a Grand Seal, an impression whereof, in wax, shall be sent to the Grand Secretary, and be deposited in the archives of the S. G. L. Seals of Lodges and Encampments, to be authentic, must be printed or impressed upon the paper or instrument they authenticate, and not affixed thereto. The Seal of a Lodge should only be used in transacting the legitimate business of the Lodge. The officers of a Subordinate Lodge or Encampment cannot use the Seal to verify or attest the good standing of any brother of the Lodge, without a formal vote of the Body. The officers are merely the executive agents of these Bodies, and should have no power to use the Seal, unless so ordered by the Subordinates, or in accordance with the positive enactments of the several Grand Bodies under whose jurisdiction they work. The S. G. L. will not recognize a mere printed pamphlet, purporting to be the proceedings of a Grand Body, without any authentication by the Seal or signatures of its Grand Officers. State Grand Bodies must expel members who use Seals without authority. (*See page* 193.) The Seal of a Lodge or Encampment is in the official care of the Secretary of Scribe. (*See pages* 196, 297.)

SICKNESS.—The term "sickness," as used in the Order. implies that state of health which prevents one from attending to his ordinary vocation. One who is not so afflicted as to prevent attendance on ordinary business, though laboring under a peculiar disease which would eventually terminate his life, cannot be regarded at a sick man entitled to benefits. The following decisions of the S. G. L. will assist in elucidating the matter: Lunatics are entitled to the same benefits as are given to those who suffer from bodily infirmity. A brother who, by sickness or accident, has become blind, is *prima facie* entitled to benefits. The burden of proof is on the Lodge to show otherwise. If the By-laws of a Lodge declare that every member rendered incapable, by sickness or accident, of following any business whereby he may obtain a livelihood, shall be entitled, during such sickness or disability, to receive benefits, the admission that the member is able to attend to business of some kind, if it could be found for him, will not justify the Lodge in refusing to pay benefits, unless the Lodge shall further show that the brother was competent to attend to some business, of which he had a knowledge, to pursue successfully. An aged member, wholly unable to do any work on account of paralysis, but who is a director in a bank, who speculates in property, concerning which he gives directions, is entitled to weekly benefits under a law that provides that a member who, through sickness or disability arising from injury, is unable to follow his usual business, or some other occupation whereby he may earn a livelihood, shall be entitled to benefits. A member of the Order, becoming infirm from old age, thereby being incapable of following his usual occupation, is not entitled to weekly benefits, as a right, under a Constitution which provides that every qualified member shall, in case of being disabled by sickness or bodily accident, from following his usual occupation, or otherwise from earning a livelihood, be entitled to receive such weekly benefits as may be fixed by law. A brother who is suffering from a chronic complaint, but is yet able to go to his place of business, superintend it and participate in it to a degree, is *prima facie* not entitled to benefits as a sick brother, but this presumption may be rebutted by positive evidence. When a brother is able, to some extent, to follow his usual occupation, and by that means is capable of procuring the means of subsistence for himself, he is not entitled to benefits, the By-laws of his Lodge providing for benefits, in case of being rendered incapable, by sickness or accident, of providing for his own support. Where the illness, or disability of a brother results from immoral conduct, he is not entitled to benefits. (SEE BENEFITS.)

STAY OF PROCEEDINGS.—In the absence of any local law providing for a stay of proceedings, pending an appeal, a Subordinate is bound to obey the mandate of its superior. State Grand Bodies may provide for a stay, pending an appeal.

SUBORDINATES.—See CHARTERS; Article VIII, Section 7, page 323 ; Article XIV, page 328 ; and Articles I and II, page 330. When a Grand Body has been chartered in a State or Territory, all the Subordinates therein, of that Branch of the Order to which the S. G. L. has issued a Charter, become subordinate to that Grand Body. (*See page* 301.) Any number of brethren, not less than five (in certain sections of some jurisdictions the required number is much greater), holding unexpired Withdrawal Cards, and any additional number holding expired Withdrawal Cards, or Dismissal Certificates, and all possessing the Degree of Truth, may apply to the S. G. L., or the Grand Lodge of a State for a Charter to open a Lodge. Applicants for a Charter to open a Subordinate Encampment must be members of the Royal Purple Degree. Expired Withdrawal Cards may be received on application for a Charter, when the holder is a contributing member of a Subordinate Lodge, but the holder of an unexpired Withdrawal Card from his Lodge, is not a competent petitioner for an Encampment. The mode of organizing a Lodge is as follows : The petition, with the Charter fee (generally thirty dollars), and the Cards of the petitioners must be sent or delivered to the Grand Secretary of the State Grand Lodge, or to the Grand Secretary of the Sovereign Grand Lodge, as the case may be, which officer will present it to the proper Grand Body, if in session, and, if not, to the Grand Master or Grand Sire. The title selected for the Lodge must not be the name of any living person. If the application be favorably received, a Dispensation will be issued for the organization of the Lodge, and in due time a Charter, in substance as follows, will be issued, supposing it to emanate from a State Grand Lodge :

INDEPENDENT ORDER OF ODD FELLOWS.

To All Whom It May Concern :

We,....................., GRAND MASTER OF THE GRAND LODGE OF THE INDEPENDENT ORDER OF ODD FELLOWS OF THE............OF............

Friendship, Love, and Truth.

Know Ye, that the Grand Lodge of...............does hereby Charter and convey to our trusty and well-beloved Brethren.................... and their successors duly and legally elected, the right and privilege to constitute and hold a Lodge in the.... .... of.........., County of........., State of............, to be known and hailed by the title of............... Lodge, No....., and does by these presents confirm the Dispensation issued by the Officers of this Grand Lodge to organize said... .... Lodge, No....., on the ...... day of.........., one thousand eight hundred and.... ....

And we do further Authorize and Empower our said trusty and well-beloved Brethren, and their successors, to admit and make Odd Fellows according to the ancient usages and customs of the Order, and not contrariwise, with full power and authority to hear and determine, all and singular, matters and things relating to the Order within the jurisdiction of said Lodge, according to the Rules and Regulations of the Grand Lodge of............... and the Sovereign Grand Lodge of the I.O. O. F. *Provided always,* that the said above-named Brethren and their succesors, pay due respect to the said Grand Lodges and the ordinances thereof; otherwise this Charter to be of no force or effect.

Given under our hands and the Seal of the Grand Lodge of............. at ...., in the.... .... of............, this............ day of............ ..., one thousand eight hundred and... ...., and of our Order the............... year.

[SEAL.]   ...., Grand Master.
                            ...., Grand Secretary.

If the Dispensation be granted, the Lodge will be organized at the time and place determmed, by the Grand Master, assisted by his Grand Officers, or by some qualified brother deputed to perform this duty. It is necessary to elect the proper officers, who must be examined by the installing officer prior to induction into office, in order that he may be satisfied of their fitness and qualifications. The Lodge is also required to express its satisfaction in the choice it has made for the recipient of each office. It is the further duty of the installing officer to see that the election has been regular in all respects. If, however, objection be made, and its regularity be called in ques tion, for good and sufficient reasons, he will order a new election under his personal supervision. After the installation, he will instruct the officers in their respective duties, and deliver to them their books, papers, etc., and to the Lodge its Warrant, which must always be present in the Lodge during its meetings. If the Grand Lodge of the jurisdiction in question, has a uniform Constitution for its Subordinates, this necessarily becomes that of the new Lodge. If, however, the jurisdiction does not prescribe a Constitution, then the Lodge must adopt one, which must be presented to the Grand Lodge, or the committee appointed by that Body, for approval. Until it receives this approval, it is void and non-operative. The members must sign the Constitution, thereby pledging themselves to obey its provisions and those of the By-Laws, and such amendments and alterations as may, from time to time, be legally made therein.

The Lodge should make such By-Laws as it may require for its internal government, taking care that they are not in conflict with the laws and decisions of its State Grand Body. State Grand Bodies may provide for the approval, by it, of the By-Laws of its Subordinates, and if such approval is required, the By-Laws can have no force and effect until confirmed in accordance with such provisions. The number of brethren required to petition for a Charter varies in jurisdictions and in certain sections of some jurisdictions. The laws of the Grand Lodge of New York provide as follows. On the written application of five or more brothers of the Order praying for a Charter to open a Lodge at a place where there is no Lodge established; or on the application of twenty or more brothers, (five of whom shall have attained the Third Degree), for a Charter to open a Lodge where there are one or more Lodges already established—except in the cities of New York and Brooklyn, where the application of fifty members (thirty of whom shall have attained their Third Degree, and have been members in good standing for at least one year prior to their application) shall be necessary—accompanied by the Charter fee, the Grand Lodge may grant a Warrant. The right of Subordinate Lodges, and Encampments, to re-elect their Officers and prescribe the price for Degrees is under the control of the several State, District and Territorial Grand Bodies. The right to confer the Subordinate Degrees, including the Degree of Rebekah, upon their own members, is guaranteed to Subordinate Lodges by their Charters. Subordinates have control of their financial affairs, and the investment of their funds is a matter for local legislation. A Lodge has the right to refuse attention to documents from another Lodge not attested by its Seal. A Subordinate may act as follows: Adopt By-Laws; expend its funds for the legitimate objects of the Order; allow charges to be brought against a member who has applied for a Dismissal Certificate; donate from its funds to a brother in ill-health, though not entitled to benefits as a matter of right; may open and close its meetings with prayer; be permitted, if working in a foreign language, to dispense with an American copy of its record; appeal with the consent of its Grand Body; petition for aid when authorized by its Grand Body or its principal Grand Officer; consolidate under such rules and regulations as its Grand Body may prescribe. A Subordinate Lodge, not under the jurisdiction of the Grand Lodge of the German Empire, or the Grand Lodge of Australasia, must open and transact all its business in the Third Degree. (*See page* 292.) Subordinates under the immediate jurisdiction of the S. G. L. which fail, for one year, to make their returns, shall forfeit their Charters. Subordinates must conform to the uniform Constitution prescribed for them by their respective Grand Bodies. A Subordinate and its officers, must obey and enforce the laws of the S. G. L. It is the duty of a Lodge, upon the presentation of a duly authenticated Degree Certificate, if the holder is in good standing, to confer the Degrees upon the candidate presenting such Certificate. Members must serve on committees unless excused. Subordinates have no legislative power, except to make By-Laws. They cannot act as follows: Assemble in conventions to legislate upon matters relating to the internal affairs of their Grand Bodies; confer Degrees upon the members of another Body without its consent, given under Seal; resort to any scheme of raffles, lotteries, gift enterprises, or games of hazard or chance to raise money for any purpose of relief or assistance for themselves or for individual members; be compelled to vote brothers their Degrees; change, restrict, or add to the qualifications, prescribed in the Constitution of the S. G. L., for membership; meet out of the jurisdiction of their Grand Bodies, nor initiate candidates residing out of their jurisdiction, without the consent of both Grand Jurisdictions; hold adjourned sessions, but must close their sessions in due form, and if extra sessions are required, they must be called in the manner prescribed by the By-Laws; do business without a quorum; ask advice or counsel from any other quarter than their Grand Bodies; try the members of another Subordinate; vote money or transact business at an informal meeting; be instituted on Sunday; by By-Law, pay to a beneficial association, assessments on their members, out of their general fund. Officers and members entering or retiring must be clothed in proper Regalia and address the Chairs, etc.; the officer in charge of a candidate is not required to address the Chairs. As to the duty of Subordinates to sick or disabled traveling, or sojourning brethren, see page 289. The order of business contained in the Charge Book is not mandatory; a Lodge may regulate the order of business to suit its particular necessities. A brother in good standing, cannot be kept out of his Subordinate or Grand Body while the minutes of the preceding meeting are being read, if he desires to enter and can work his way in. The costumes worn in the G. R. D. cannot be used on public occasions. Subordinates must furnish their officers with the Jewels pertaining to their rank and station, and also suitable Regalia for the members. A lodge is not responsible for funds obtained by a brother who acquires the Semi-annual Password, and by making use thereof obtains relief from a Lodge of which he is not a member. The matter of using the funds to pay for the services of officers, is one for local legislation. Grand Bodies may prescribe, in their Constitutions for Subordinates, that the term of office of Treasurer only, may be one year.

SUNDAY.—Subordinates cannot be instituted on Sunday, nor hold any meeting for work or business, except for funeral purposes on that day. Members cannot be required to attend to committee work on Sunday. Per diem is not allowed to members of the S. G. L. for Sunday, when the session does not hold over from one week to another.

SUPPLIES.—The right to print or publish any portion of the Work of the Order, and the Forms of Charts, Diplomas, Certificates, etc., published by the S. G. L. is its exclusive property. The Grand Secretary is directed to require cash payments, in bankable funds, for all orders for supplies, and if the price of supplies be raised between the receipt of the order therefor and their delivery, (if the order be not accompanied with the cash), the enhanced price must be paid, although no supplies were on hand on the receipt of the Order. Printing or circulating, any forms or ceremonies that constitute a source of revenue to the treasury of the S. G. L., is an offense against its laws. The following is a list of the supplies furnished by the S. G. L., with important information in connection therewith:

	To Grand Bodies.	To Sub-ordinates.
Grand Lodge and Grand Encampment Books, each.........$2	2 00	$....
Subordinate Encampment Institution and Installation Book	2 00	2 50
*Subordinate Encampment Charge Book.....	2 00	2 50
Charter for Subordinate Encampment, Subordinate Lodge, and Degree Lodge Daughters of Rebekah, each	60	...
Subordinate Encampment Chart and Subordinate Lodge Chart, each..	2 00	2 50
Patriarchs Militant Organization, etc., illustrated	50	50
Patriarchs Militant Tactics	1 00	1 00
Patriarchs Militant Degree Ritual (only on order of Lieutenant-General)	....	....
*Subordinate Lodge Institution and Installation Book......	2 00	2 50
Subordinate Lodge Public Installation Book (German)....	2 00	2 50
‖‡†*Subordinate Lodge Ritual...............................	2 00	2 50
Degree Lodge Installation Book.........................	2 00	2 50
*Degree of Rebekah Charge Book.....................	2 00	2 50
*Ritual for Rebekah Degree Lodges, *only*.................	2 00	2 50
*Degree of Rebekah Lodge Institution and Installation Book..	2 00	2 50
‖†*Subordinate and Rebekah Lodge Odes, on Bristol board...	05	08
Encampment Ode Books, with music, paper covers... ...	08	10
Encampment Ode Books, with music, flexible cloth covers	20	25
Anniversary Odes, on card-board.......................	05	08
*Funeral Hymns, with responses, on Bristol board........	05	08
Book of Odes, with music, for Subordinate Lodges, Encampments, and Rebekah Lodges...................	50	60
Visiting and Withdrawal Cards and Dismissal Certificates.	20	25
Visiting and Withdrawal Cards for Rebekah Lodges......	20	25
Card for a Wife or Widow.............................	20	25
Rebekah Certificate, on plate paper, edition of 1885.......	20	25
†*Diploma or Certificate of Membership, on plate paper.....	50	75
Book of Forms, edition of 1888.......................	75	1 00
Bound Journals, twelve volumes (1821-1886), with thirty-two steel engravings of Past Grand Sires, etc., per volume..	1 50	2 00
White's New Digest (to 1884)............................	2 50	3 00
Additions to Digest, 1882-1884—sheets, 25c.; bound, 50c.		
Anniversary Ceremony..................................	20	25
*Funeral Ceremony, of 1874, 1877, 1879, 1880, complete....	20	25
*Burial Ceremony for a Daughter of Rebekah.............	10	15
Question Book, 150 questions, one on page..............	1 00	1 50
Question Book, 600 questions, three on page.............	3 00	3 50
Petition for membership, per 100.......................	50	75

* Published in German language also. ‡ Published in Bohemian language also.
† Published in French language also. ‖ Published in Spanish aud Norwegian languages also.

Resolved, That the Grand Secretary be directed to exact and enforce, in the future, an undeviating compliance with Article 1750 of the Digest of the S. G. L., which requires "cash payments for all orders from State Grand Lodges and State Grand Encampments for Books, Odes, Diplomas, Cards, etc.," and that he permit, in no case, orders for supplies to be filled unless such orders are accompanied by the cash.—*Journal*, 1876, p. 7,002.

Diplomas, Digests, Journals, Book of Forms, Book of Odes. P. M. Organization, Tactics, Anniversary Ceremony and Funeral Ceremony are sold to individuals at the prices charged Subordinates. No other supplies on above list are sold to individuals.

If the order amounts to $50, the articles can be had at the prices charged Grand Bodies.

On an order for Diplomas amounting to $100, a discount of fifteen per cent will be allowed.

☞ *Orders from Grand or Subordinate Bodies must be authenticated by the Seal of the Encampment or Lodge.*

☞ *Lodge and Encampment Rituals, Cards, and Odes will not be sent to any*

Subordinates except those under the immediate jurisdiction of the Sovereign Grand Lodge.

Supplies will be forwarded *by express*, unless other directions are given with the order.

Charts, Odes, Diplomas, Book of Forms, Book of Odes, Charters, P. M. Organization, Tactics, Journals, Digests, Anniversary and Funeral Ceremonies, may be sent by mail at book postage. All other supplies, if sent by mail, will be securely sealed, and will be subject to letter postage.

☞All letters on business with this office should be indorsed " *Official*," and addressed to THEODORE A. Ross, Grand Secretary, P. O. Box 832. Columbus, Ohio.

Checks and P. O. Money Orders should be made payable to the order of THEODORE A. Ross, Grand Secretary.

☞As orders are frequently received for "Rituals," we are left to *guess* whether "Subordinate Lodge Rituals" or "Rituals for Rebekah Degree Lodges" are wanted. Parties ordering are particularly requested to give the titles of supplies, as above, and thus avoid the risk of getting what they do not want. Special care should be taken in ordering "*Degree of Rebekah Charge Book*" and "*Ritual for Rebekah Degree Lodges*," as in several instances orders have been misinterpreted and the wrong books have been sent.

SUSPENSIONS OF SUBORDINATES.—A Grand Master has entire supervision over his Subordinates during vacation, and the right to interfere on all violations of law, and in case of persistent disobedience, may suspend the privileges of a Lodge until the case is tried and determined by the Grand Lodge. Pending an appeal of a Subordinate from its Grand Lodge decision, to the S. G. L., its Grand Lodge may enforce its decisions by demanding the Charter and effects of the Lodge for non-compliance with the decision appealed from. The Suspension of a Lodge takes effect from the time such suspension is published or proclaimed. The suspension of a Lodge suspends its officers and members. As to the effect of the suspension of a Lodge upon its Encampment members, see page 297. Suspensions of members in Subordinates are either for Cause, or for Non-Payment of Dues.

SUSPENSIONS FOR CAUSE, cannot be indefinite, nor for an unreasonable length of time, and should be regulated by the magnitude of the offense, The greatest length of time to which a Subordinate can extend a suspension for cause, is a question to be decided by its legislation on the subject. Ten years suspension is practically an expulsion, and a Lodge ought not to effect, under the name of suspension, what is expulsion. A brother under suspension, of either kind, is still a member of his Lodge, although deprived of certain rights, and is subject to the laws in relation to discipline for unworthy conduct, for which he may be expelled, and should he die during suspension, the Lodge incurs no new liability on account of his decease. A member of an Encampment, who is suspended by his Lodge for a definite period, and who, during such suspension, pays his dues in his Encampment, on his restoration to membership in his Lodge, is *ipso facto* reinstated to membership in his Encampment. An officer or member of the S. G. L., under suspension of either kind, in his Subordinate, is suspended from office or membership, in said Grand Body. Suspension of an officer for cause, vacates the office in the Body in which he is suspended, and the suspension of a member by a Lodge for cause, after conviction, vacates any office he may hold in an Encampment.

SUSPENSIONS FOR NON-PAYMENT OF DUES.—No member can be suspended for non-payment of dues, unless, at the time of his suspension, he shall be indebted to his Subordinate for one year's dues. A brother cannot be suspended for non-payment of dues while his Lodge is indebted to him for benefits, or otherwise, in a sum which, if deducted from the amount against him, would reduce his indebtedness within the limit of liability. The mere fact of a member being over twelve months in arrears, does not constitute him a suspended member. To render him such, his Subordinate must formally declare him to be suspended; it is not necessary to ballot on the suspension, any action whereby the sense of the Body is obtained and made matter of record, is sufficient. Before a member can be suspended for non-payment of dues, he must be notified of the intended action of the Body. (See Membership.)

Terms.—The word term is used in three different ways: A term of a Body; a term of office; the period of service in an office, entitling the incumbent to the Honors of said office. Officers of the S. G. L. are elected biennially. Grand Representatives are chosen for a term of two years, except when elected to fill a vacancy for a part of a term. Grand Lodges and Grand Encampments may elect their officers for a term of one year, or of two years, as their Constitutions may provide; but when they have annual sessions, the officers must be elected for a term of one year. State Grand Bodies may make the terms of office in their Subordinates one year; it is usually six months. A State Grand Body may permit its Subordinates to meet semi-monthly, or monthly. Whatever may be the term of the Subordinate Lodge, its officers must serve twenty-six nights to complete the term that entitles them to the Honors of their offices. If an Encampment meets monthly, instead of semi-monthly, the official term of the officers should be extended to twelve months. The term of a Subordinate ends when the succeeding one begins; that is, on the first meeting in July and January, or April and October. Whenever a Lodge is instituted at least fourteen meeting nights before the time of the termination of the regular term, such period shall constitute a short term which shall end at that time, and the N. G. and V. G., who shall serve during this period, shall be entitled to receive all the Past Official Degrees of the Lodge appertaining to the other and inferior offices not filled by them. The term of office in Degree Lodges of the Daughters of Rebekah is six months, or one year, as prescribed by its Grand Lodge or By-Laws. Neither a Grand Lodge, nor any Body subordinate to the S. G. L., can change the terms of officers. For terms of officers of the Patriarchs Militant Branch of the Order see Chapter V.

Trial.—The S. G. L. and many State Grand Bodies have adopted Codes of Procedure for Trials, for the use of their immediate Subordinates. All trials must be conducted as required by the Code of the jurisdiction. The Code of Procedure adopted by the S. G. L. for the Subordinates under its immediate jurisdiction will be found in the Book of Forms, pages 160–166. A brother cannot be punished by reprimand, suspension (save for non-payment of dues), or expulsion, except by his Subordinate upon charges duly preferred. The general charge is "conduct unbecoming an Odd Fellow," supplemented with a specification or specifications stating the offense, time, place, and such attendant circumstances as will assist in elucidating the case. The charges and specifications are presented and read in the Lodge at a regular session. A Trial Committee is appointed, according to the rules prescribed by the Lodge, to try the case. The brother defendant is furnished with a copy of the charge and specifications, under Seal, and summoned to appear at a fixed time and place for trial. Opportunity is afforded him to procure such testimony as he may require from absent witnesses and those not members of the Order, in the manner prescribed by law. (SEE EVIDENCE.) He may have such witnesses, members of the Order, summoned to testify at the trial as he may require. The manner of conducting the trial depends upon the rules of the Lodge or the local law. The S. G. L. has prescribed some regulations that are universal in their character. The trial of members under charges who have not attained the Third Degree must take place when the Lodge is opened in the highest Degree the member has received, and the Lodge must be specially opened in such Degree for that purpose. On a trial in a Lodge open in the Third Degree, a brother of the First Degree, who preferred the charges, cannot be present. When a Trial Committee report a member guilty, the Lodge cannot dismiss the charges, but must vote " guilty " or " not guilty." When the law fixes the penalty on conviction for a specific offense, it is not necessary for the Trial Committee to recommend a penalty. A member once expelled is out of the Order, and no motion made to reconsider the vote can be entertained. A brother having been tried for an offense against the laws of the Order, by the highest tribunal thereof, and acquitted, that tribunal having adjourned without day, cannot reopen and retry the case, its former action being final and conclusive. Where the accused pleads guilty to the charge, and the local law provides that the vote on the penalty shall " so proceed until some order of punishment is agreed upon," the Lodge must impose some one of the penalties provided by the By-Laws. A member cannot resign while charges are pending against him and thus avoid trial. A Noble Grand cannot be one of a Trial Committee on charges before the Lodge. It is an error to nominate a Trial Committee from the floor of the Lodge, when the By-Laws require such Committee to be appointed by the Noble Grand. A brother may be tried in an Encampment for words, offensive in themselves and evidencing conduct unbecoming an Odd Fellow, although spoken in the Lodge. A suspended member may be arraigned and tried without first being reinstated, but when arraigned for trial, he must be temporarily admitted to the Lodge for the purpose of making his defense. If a Card shall have been granted to an unworthy brother, the Lodge may annul it, taking care to allow the brother a fair and impartial trial. The counsel of the accused, if an Odd Fellow in good standing, and having the requisite Degrees, should be admitted to the Lodge room, although without either the Password or a Card. The time and mode of voting on penalties, after conviction, are regulated by the local law. In the trial of charges, where either party or his counsel does not understand the language in which the proceedings are conducted, such party or counsel cannot be denied the time necessary for the interpretation to him of the proceedings, by interpreters qualified to be present. A Subordinate cannot appoint a committee to investigate rumors regarding the conduct of a brother in good standing, prior to charges being preferred against him, and report to the Subordinate. If a member refuse to stand trial, he cannot be formally tried, and in such case the Lodge may expel for contempt. If the local law so provide, none others than the sitting Past Grand and the advocate of the accused can discuss the question of the guilt or innocence of parties on trial.

There is no such rule in the Order by which the place of trial of a brother may be changed. He must be tried in the Lodge or Encampment where he is a member and where the charges are preferred, except in Subordinate Lodges, under State, District or Territorial Grand Lodges, whose By-Laws' make provision for change of venue. As an Encampment cannot expel from the Order, but only from its own Body, a Subordinate Lodge is the proper tribunal to try all cases of delinquency, when the charge is cognizable under the laws. A Grand Lodge of a State has no power to appoint a committee of the Grand Lodge to try a brother of a Subordinate Lodge. It may order a Subordinate Lodge to try a member, which order the Subordinate must obey. The Sovereign Grand Lodge, a majority consenting thereto, can impeach and try any of its officers and members, and, with the concurrence of two-thirds of the votes cast, expel from office or membership; provided, that a copy of the charges preferred shall have been furnished to the accused at least three days before the trial. During the trial of any impeachment in the S. G. L., the officer or member under impeachment shall be debarred the exercise of his office, or the privilege of his membership, but may be heard in his own defense. (SEE APPEALS, CHARGES, EVIDENCE.)

UNIFORMED DEGREE CAMPS.—In 1882, Grand Encampments were authorized to adopt, or reject, the Uniformed Camp Degree. The only qualification for the Degree was that the applicant should be a R. P. Degree member in good standing. Grand Encampments were empowered to institute Degree Camps, for Uniformed Patriarchs, at such places as they thought proper. For the powers and privileges of such Camps see Journal, pages 9111, 9112, 9115. Uniformed Degree Camps were authorized to appear in Uniform, whenever the Commander or the Body itself so determined, and the members could be compelled to procure Uniforms. Nearly all the Uniformed Degree Camps became merged in the new Degree of Patriarchs Militant. A Uniformed Degree Camp, under command of its officers, and in full Uniform, may visit a Subordinate Lodge, while in session, and when visiting an Encampment, accompanied by either of its first two officers, will be deemed to be in proper Regalia, when clothed in full uniform.

VACANCIES.—Should any elective officer of the S. G. L. fail to appear to be installed, the office must be declared vacant, and the Grand Body will at once proceed to fill the vacancy. The Grand Sire has power to fill all vacancies that may occur during the recess of the Grand Lodge, which are not provided for by the Constitution, such appointment to last until filled by election or otherwise as provided by law. Suspension or expulsion from the Subordinate Lodge or Encampment, in which an officer or member holds membership, vacates his seat in the S. G. L. In case of the extinction of the Representative's Subordinate, see the proviso, page 144. Having taken a Withdrawal Card, he may preserve his seat by complying with the law in this behalf, on page 149. A vacancy in the office of Grand Representative is filled in the manner prescribed by his State Grand Body. As to a vacancy in the offices of Grand Sire and Deputy Grand Sire, see Article IV, pages 324, 325. As to when a State

Grand Body may declare the seat of a Grand Representative vacant, see page 152. The subject of declaring an office vacant, when an installed officer has failed to attend and discharge the duties of the office, is left to the control of State Grand Bodies; and when they have neglected to legislate upon the subject, and its Subordinates are without law thereon, an officer does not vacate his office for non-attendance. (*See page* 127.) If a Noble Grand elect should fail to appear, for some time after the regular period, if the local law provides for vacating an office for non-attendance, the Lodge may regard him as installed and vacate the office.

VISITING.—Members may visit their own Subordinates, although in arrears and without the Term Password, and may do so until suspended or expelled according to law. Members of the Order in one jurisdiction are entitled to admission into the Lodges and Encampments of every other jurisdiction, upon proving themselves according to the established Work of the Order, and the production of a proper Card. Unexpired Visiting and Withdrawal Cards are proper Cards, and Dismissal Certificates and expired Visiting and Withdrawal Cards are not. A member of a suspended or expelled Lodge, has not the right to visit on an unexpired Visiting Card granted prior to such suspension or expulsion. He is suspended from his privileges in the Order and cannot visit an Encampment. Brothers cannot visit Lodges upon Encampment Cards, nor visit Encampments upon Lodge Cards. No brother unintroduced, can visit a Lodge or Encampment out of the State where he resides unless he presents a Card furnished under the signatures of the proper officers and Seal of the Lodge or Encampment of which he is a member, and signed on the margin in his own handwriting, and prove himself in the A. T. P. W., and in the Degree in which the Lodge is open. A Lodge has no right to refuse admission to one having a proper Card and proving himself in the Work. A Uniformed Degree Camp, under command of its officers and in full Uniform, may visit a Subordinate Lodge when in session. Brothers of a lower Degree than the Third are entitled to Visiting Cards, and to visit a Lodge when opened in the particular Degree to which they have attained. An Indian cannot be permitted to visit a Lodge, under any circumstances. A member of an Encampment, who is suspended in his Lodge, cannot visit an Encampment. Visiting and Withdrawal Cards are used also, in Degree Lodges of the Daughters of Rebekah, and to enable a brother of such a Lodge to visit similar Lodges in jurisdictions other than his own, he must present a Card from the Degree Lodge of the Daughters of Rebekah, of which he is a member, the same as a sister of such Lodge. A Lodge or an Encampment, with its officers, can, in a body, visit another Lodge or Encampment outside of its jurisdiction without Cards or the A. T. P. W.; but it is necessary that one of the first two officers in charge, must have the A. T. P. W., and have his Card. Such officer may introduce his accompanying members in the manner provided for the introduction of visitors by elective Grand Officers. A member in good standing of one Grand Encampment, on proof of such membership, is entitled to visit any other Grand Encampment. A Grand Representative instructed in the Grand Encampment Degree at a session of the S. G. L. is not a member of a Grand Encampment, and he cannot visit one. An elective officer of a Grand Lodge or Grand Encampment, is authorized to introduce visiting brothers, having the necessary qualifications, into their respective Subordinate Lodges or Encampments. A Grand Representative may introduce properly qualified visiting brothers into Lodges and Encampments in his jurisdiction. A brother with an unexpired Withdrawal Card, and without the A. T. P. W., may be introduced as above, but the holder of an expired Withdrawal Card cannot be introduced. A District Deputy Grand Master has no right to introduce visitors, but a District Deputy Grand Sire, in jurisdictions where no Grand Body exists, may do so. The Grand Representatives to the S. G. L. of a Grand Encampment have the right to introduce, in any Subordinate Encampment, a brother whom the C. P. of said Encampment does not know to be in good standing in the Order, without said brother giving any Password whatever. The Noble Grand of a Lodge has not the right to admit a member belonging to another Lodge, in the same jurisdiction, without the Term Password, although the time for the installation of the officers of the visitor's Lodge has not yet arrived, and the visitor, for that reason, has not received the Password of the new term. No brother can visit the S. G. L., except upon the voucher of a Representative of his jurisdiction. (*See page* 217.) When a visiting brother presents himself at the door of a Lodge, it is his duty to hand his Card to the Guardian, that it may be placed in possession of the Lodge. If the Lodge be satisfied of its authenticity, a committee of three members shall be appointed, all of whom must have received the Third Degree, to proceed to the ante-room and examine the visiting brother. One member of this committee must be the Noble Grand, Vice Grand, sitting Past Grand, or some brother known to be in possession of the required A. T. P. W., whose special duty it shall be, *first*, to obtain, privately from the visitor, the A. T. P. W. (of the year in which the Card was issued and bears date), it being the visitor's duty to commence by letters. This preliminary being settled, the committee will then proceed to examine the visitor in the Degree in which the Lodge is open. If the Lodge is open in a higher Degree than the brother has attained, he cannot be admitted. (*See page* 147.) His Card should express on its face his rank, so that the honors to which he is entitled, and the Degree, in which he may be proved, may fully appear; if the Card states the holder to be a Past Grand, and he shall not be able to prove himself in the Work of that Degree, from not having received it, the fact, as set forth in the Card, shall be sufficient evidence to entitle him to the privilege such rank confers. A Subordinate Lodge may authorize its Noble Grand to cause brothers visiting by Card to be *examined* prior to the opening of the Lodge, but they cannot be admitted until after the Lodge is open. If the examination of the brother prove satisfactory, he shall be introduced to the Lodge by the examining committee, and is not required to work his way in. A test O. B. N. is no part of the mode of examining visitors, and is not permitted. A brother holding a Withdrawal Card from one State, is entitled to the Annual Traveling Password in use at the time, and retains the right to visit in another State with the same Password, for one year.

VOTING IN SOVEREIGN GRAND LODGE.—A member is not permitted to vote unless in proper Regalia. A Past Grand Sire, or an officer, who is not a

Representative, is not permitted to vote, except the Grand Sire in case of an equal division. The Representative or Representatives of a State Grand Body in arrears for money due the S. G. L., or whose annual report has not been made to the Grand Secretary on or before the first day of June, cannot vote. In voting for Grand Officers a Representative can have but one vote. As to voting by roll-call, see Rule of Order 15, page 340. Voting for officers shall be by ballot. All other voting shall be *viva voce*, or by yeas and nays, and all questions shall be decided by a majority vote, except in cases where a specific majority is required. In voting for officers the S. G. L. refused to adopt the principle of dropping the candidate, on each ballot, having the smallest number of votes. Any member, who has voted in favor of a decision, may move for the reconsideration thereof. A vote adopting an amendment to the Constitution may, at any time during the session at which it was adopted, be reconsidered. A vote to adopt a resolution accompanying the report of a committee does not include the acceptance of the report. A member representing a jurisdiction entitled to two Representatives may, in the temporary or permanent absence of his colleague, cast two votes at all times, except in election for Grand Officers. The Unwritten Work of the Order cannot be amended, or altered, except by a four-fifths vote of the members of the S. G. L. (a four-fifths vote of the members means four-fifths of *all* the members, whether present or absent), and the Written Work of the Order cannot be altered or amended, except with the concurrence of two-thirds of the members of the S. G. L. To alter or amend the Constitution, requires a vote of three-fourths of the members present, on a call of the yeas and nays. A revised Constitution is an amended one, and a resolution construing a constitutional provision is also an amendment, and requires the same formalities to adopt that an amendment of the same effect, would require. The By-Laws may be amended, but not on the day the amendment is offered, by two-thirds of the votes given.

VOTING IN STATE GRAND BODIES.—No peculiar privilege in respect to voting, arises from being an appointed officer, a Past Grand Master, or a Grand Representative. (*See page* 127.) Grand Officers are not entitled, *ex officio*, to a vote in their Grand Lodges, nor are they entitled to vote under the representative system, unless permitted by local legislation. Under the representative system a member may have two votes, one as an officer, and one as a Representative of his Lodge. If the Grand Lodge is not a representative Body, and all the Past Grands in the jurisdiction are members and entitled to vote on all questions, on a call of the yeas and nays, the Grand Master may have two votes, one on the question, and the other, the casting vote on a tie. When the Constitution of a State Grand Lodge determines the number of Representatives a Subordinate Lodge is entitled to send, and that, when a vote by Lodges is taken, each Lodge shall be entitled to as many votes as it can send Representatives, the Representatives present, no matter how few, upon a vote by Lodges, are entitled to cast the entire vote to which the Lodge is entitled, the majority of those present determining what the vote shall be. A Grand Lodge may provide, in its Constitution, that the vote by representation of Lodges may be called upon all questions, except the election of Grand Officers, when such elections take place, originally, in the Grand Lodge. When the Constitution of a Grand Lodge requires a vote of two-thirds to adopt an amendment thereto, but does not declare that it shall be a vote of two-thirds of all the Lodges in the jurisdiction, a majority of two-thirds of the votes of the Lodges present, as a quorum, is sufficient. In an appeal case before a Grand Lodge, in which a Subordinate Lodge is a party, such Lodge should not be permitted to vote, and thus be a juror in its own case. Where a resolution was offered, in a Grand Lodge, that a decision of the Grand Master be sustained, and the vote thereon was a tie, it was held that this was not a reversal of the decision, but simply no expression on the matter. A Grand Lodge has not the right to enact a law permitting Scarlet Degree members, in good standing, to vote for Grand Lodge Officers.

VOTING IN SUBORDINATES.—All voting in a Subordinate Lodge and Degree Lodge is by the voting sign, unless otherwise provided. The following are exceptions: Voting for membership; advancing to Degrees; granting Withdrawal Cards; suspending or expelling members and reinstating them; electing officers; reconsidering a ballot for membership, when the yeas and nays are ordered. On resolutions relative to the death of a brother, a rising vote may be taken, in a Subordinate Lodge, without giving the voting sign. Every brother present in a Subordinate, if qualified to vote, must vote unless excused, or unless he is personally interested in the question under consideration. (*See pages* 217, 233.) A member of a Subordinate in arrears for weekly or funeral dues, more than thirteen weeks, cannot vote. A Grand Master has the right to vote in his own Lodge for officers, membership, and on motions which come before it. When in a Lodge, it requires a majority of the votes cast to elect to office, a candidate to be elected an officer must have a majority of all the votes, including blanks, and if on the second ballot the poll shall be required to be between the two candidates who received the highest numbers of votes on the first ballot, all the votes cast for other candidates are void, and must be excluded from the poll. The election of an officer, in which a disqualified brother voted, cannot be declared void, unless it appears that his vote decided the election. Any member, although a Grand Officer, or acting as such, and clothed in his official Regalia, may vote at a new election ordered by a Grand Master, at installation. Where the law requires a majority of two-thirds of the members *present* to expel, all excused members present, if qualified to vote, must be counted as voting in the negative. The time and mode of voting on penalties, after conviction, are matters of local law. After a ballot and before the ballot-box is examined and the result known, the Noble Grand may order a new ballot on the declaration of a member that he had voted under a mistake and contrary to what he had intended. To grant a Visiting Card, no ballot is necessary, but it must be done formally. The presiding officer may say that "the Card will be granted if there be no objection." Final or Withdrawal Cards are granted only by vote of the Lodge or Encampment, and when once granted, the vote cannot be reconsidered or rescinded. A Diploma cannot be granted, except by a vote of a Grand or Subordinate Body. Applications for membership are determined by ballot. The number of black balls required to reject is a matter for the local law. As to the number required in Subordinates under the immediate jurisdiction of the S. G. L., see page 187. A Lodge cannot adopt a By-Law for the admission of members by Card in any different way from that pointed out by the general law. Its own former members cannot be received in a manner different from that provided for strangers. But one ballot and one reconsideration of the same can be had on application for membership in a Subordinate. Each application for membership by deposit of Card, or otherwise, must be balloted for separately, and a ballot is closed, when it is so declared by the presiding officer. (*See page* 141.) There must be a ballot on an application, whether the report of the committee be favorable or unfavorable. The N. G. or C. P. alone, has the prerogative of deciding the result of a ballot, but a State Grand Body may authorize the V. G., S. W., or other officer to assist in the examination of the ballot for membership and make known the result of his examination. The majority of a Lodge can, previous to an applicant's initiation, order a new ballot, should there be fraud or error in his election. If illegal ballots are cast for membership, by brothers disqualified by the By-Laws, a majority of the Lodge can, previous to initiation, declare the ballot void, if the candidate be elected, but the presiding officer alone cannot do so. If, however, the candidate be rejected, the ballot cannot be declared void. No error, or informality in voting, will reverse any action, unless it may have affected the result. An election of an unworthy person may be declared void, prior to his initiation, by two-thirds of the members present, and if such action be had, nothing remains but to ballot anew. A Lodge cannot compel the N. G. to give the number of black balls cast, in case the applicant is rejected. A brother has the right to vote a secret ball ballot, but has not the right to expose the character of his vote at pleasure. (*See page* 293.) Balloting upon application for membership, and for Degrees, must take place in the Third Degree, and in the absence of local legislation a separate ballot shall be had for each Degree. (*See page* 280.) Balloting for Degrees must be upon the same evening on which the application is made therefor, if the local law does not otherwise provide, but there is no law requiring them to be conferred at the same session. (*See page* 301.) No member shall vote upon any question in which he is interested. (*See pages* 229, 301.) A Lodge is not compelled to vote a brother his Degrees. They must be balloted for, and he must run the risks of the ballot box. A State Grand Encampment can determine whether it is necessary to ballot separately upon conferring each Degree in the Encampment Work.

VOTING IN DEGREE LODGES OF THE DAUGHTERS OF REBEKAH.—The voting in these Lodges is done by "Yes" and "No." These Lodges may ballot on all applications for membership; and as to the vote required, see page 219. Degree Lodges of the Daughters of Rebekah, under the immediate jurisdiction of the S. G. L., require a majority vote of all the members present and voting, to elect to membership.

WIDOWS AND ORPHANS.—There is no law of the Order which prohibits a Subordinate Lodge from appropriating a portion of its Widows and Orphans'

Fund for the purchase or erection of a Home for its widows and orphans. (*See page* 211.) The Widows and Orphans' Fund cannot be appropriated for the relief of aged and infirm members of the Order. The only persons who are the beneficiaries of a funeral benefit are the widow, orphans, or dependent relatives of the deceased. The Widows and Orphans' Fund of a Subordinate Lodge or Encampment is a trust fund. (*See page* 316.) State Grand Bodies have not the power to assess their Subordinates to establish a Home for the Widows and Orphans of deceased Odd Fellows. A Lodge is not relieved from responsibility to care for the orphan children of a deceased member for the reason that they are removed to a distance from the Lodge by their mother, an unworthy woman. A Lodge may grant a Card to a widow of a deceased member, such Card to be signed by the officers and countersigned by the recipient on the margin, and to remain in force as long as she shall remain a widow.

WORK OF THE ORDER.—The Sovereign Grand Lodge regulates and controls the Written and Unwritten Work of the Order. See Article I, Section 5, page 323. As to the right to print or publish the Lectures, Charges, Odes, etc., see page 178. Any violation of this right, by Grand or Subordinate Bodies or individuals, is in opposition to the laws and privileges of said Sovereign Grand Lodge. During the sessions of the Sovereign Body the Books of Diagrams and Secret Work are placed in the hands of the Deputy Grand Sire, for the use and benefit of the Representatives; at all other times they are in the custody of the Grand Secretary, and can be examined only by those entitled, by law, to that privilege. With reference to the Signs, Grips, and Passwords, see page 251. The Revised Work adopted in 1880 is the only legal Work. The Written Work is that furnished to Grand and Subordinate Bodies; the Unwritten Work is found in the Secret Journal and Diagrams in possession of the Sovereign Grand Lodge. The Grand Secretary is required to keep the Journal of all secret sessions, and preserve and keep the evidences of the Unwritten Work, and such alterations as may, from time to time, be made therein. All State, District and Territorial Grand Bodies must enforce upon their Subordinates a strict adherence to the Work of the Order. They shall neither adopt nor use, or suffer to be adopted or used, any other Charges, Lectures, Ceremonies, Forms of Installation or Regalia than those prescribed by the S. G. L. Any member of the Order, upon conviction, will be expelled therefrom, for composing, writing, printing, selling exhibiting, using, having in his possession, or assisting in composing, etc., any publication or writing, or other device purporting to be the Unwritten Work of Odd Fellowship, or any part thereof. (*See page* 204.) The Grand Master or Grand Patriarch is charged with the duty of requiring of Lodges or Encampments, as well as of members a strict compliance with the instructions received by him from the Grand Representative. The Secret Work is communicated to the Subordinates under the immediate jurisdiction of the S. G. L. by the District Deputy Grand Sires. Each Subordinate Lodge is allowed to procure not more than four Charge Books, or Rituals. It is unlawful to take from the Lodge room the Charge Books, or others, containing or relating to the Secret Work of the Order, and members are prohibited from making copies of any portion of the Written or Unwritten Work. The question of dispensing with the use of books in the Work of the Order, is a subject for local law; a Subordinate, however, has the legal right to require proficiency in the Unwritten Work of the last Degree taken, as a condition precedent to a candidate advancing to the next higher Degree. No Lodge room shall be used for conferring any Degrees, or Secret Work not provided for by the existing laws of the Order, under the color of Odd Fellowship. The Odes constitute an integral part of the opening and closing ceremonies of a Subordinate Lodge. Subordinate Grand Bodies may exemplify the Degrees in the presence of all duly qualified members, in good standing, and for that purpose admit them to the floor of said Grand Bodies. The Revised Rebekah Degree Work, adopted at the session of 1882, is the only legal Rebekah Work, and its use, in lieu of the old Work, is mandatory.

CHAPTER XI.

Emblems, Subordinate Lodge.

INITIATORY DEGREE.

THE EYE enveloped in a blaze of light and glory, reminds us that the omniscience of God pierces into every secret of the heart. All our thoughts and actions are to Him revealed, as soon as the one is conceived or the other done, Let us, therefore, so regulate our conduct that we may not fear the scrutinizing eye of any one. Let us always do the right for its own sake more than for the hope of reward or the fear of reproof.

THE THREE LINKS are emblematical of the chain by which we are bound together in Friendship, Love and Truth. We are anchored by them to the steadfast purposes of our covenant, and are cautioned to keep them untarnished and free from rust, as a chain is only as strong as its weakest link.

THE SKULL AND CROSS-BONES remind us of mortality, and warn us to so conduct ourselves here on earth that heaven may be our reward hereafter. We are further taught to decently place in mother earth the mortal remains of our brethren and keep green in our memories an affectionate remembrance of them.

THE SCYTHE reminds us that as the grass falls before the mower's scythe, so we, too, fall before the touch ot Time. We are as the flowers of the field, blooming and bright today, while to-morrow we fall withered and decayed into the bosom of our mother earth.

THE FIRST DEGREE OR THE DEGREE OF FRIENDSHIP.

THE BOW AND ARROWS remind us of David and Jonathan and the covenant made between them. The Bow also recalls to us God's special providence and promise to Noah, that the earth shall never again suffer from a flood. The Arrows direct that we shall pursue our daily tasks and perform our bounden obligations in the straight, direct and narrow path of duty.

THE QUIVER teaches us that there should be a place for everything and everything in its place, in order that we may not waste our precious moments in idle search for things mislaid. Our quiver of usefulness should ever be full, that the willing hand may never fail in the hour of necessity.

THE BUNDLE OF STICKS inculcates the importance of concentrated effort, as expressed in the axiom, " In union there is strength." If we wish to obtain success commensurate with our efforts, we must unitedly and with one mind and purpose, pursue the end for which we strive. Disunion and uncertainty of aims is the most certain source of weakness. They will paralyze the efforts of the strongest and bring to naught the labors of a host. Let us therefore be careful to do nothing calculated to weaken our strength and deprive us of the full measure of our usefulness.

THE SECOND DEGREE OR THE DEGREE OF LOVE.

THE AXE is used by the hardy pioneer, who bravely invades the virgin forests and clears away with unwearied stroke, and unfaltering arm, the encumbering forests, to give place to the labor of the husbandman. It reminds us that we are pioneers in the pathway of life, smoothing the rough places and removing all obstacles to the weak and the faltering.

THE HEART AND HAND teach us that whatsoever the hand finds to do, the heart should go forth in unison, and

EMBLEMS OF THE SUBORDINATE LODGE.

render the task doubly sweet by its savor of affection. The Lord loves a cheerful giver. The work entrusted to us to perform should be one of love, pursued from the promptings of the heart and altogether freed from the taint of mercenary or selfish motives.

THE GLOBE reminds us that the field of our labors is a wide one and co-extensive with the Globe. Until the tear of the sorrow-stricken and oppressed has ceased to flow, and humanity is everywhere swayed in its actions by the divine lessons of peace and good will, our work must continue to occupy our time and thoughts.

THE ARK was the receptacle of the two tables of stone containing the Decalogue, which describes man's duties to God as well as to his neighbor, fellow-man. As the preservation of the Ark was an unceasing object of care to the Israelites, we are reminded by this Emblem to be solicitous for the preservation of our laws, and to ever hold them in such remembrance and respect, that our conduct in the world may bring no reproach upon the brotherhood.

THE SERPENT teaches us that without wisdom to guide and control our actions, we are as a ship without a rudder, at the mercy of the warring winds and angry waves.

This Emblem also reminds us of the brazen serpent erected by Moses to heal the stricken Israelites. God's gifts are a free will offering, without money and without price. Here he gave a life for a look. Let us, then, seek wisdom that our work may be done to the best advantage.

THE THIRD DEGREE OR THE DEGREE OF TRUTH.

TEE SCALES AND SWORD remind us that justice and mercy should be administered without reference to the refined and subtle distinctions of men. Let us weigh well our conduct, and do unto others according to the injunctions of the Golden Rule. Let us consider that the sword of punishment, like that of Damocles, is suspended over our heads, and but awaits the divine fiat to expiate our sins. Temper justice with mercy, but act for the general good.

THE BIBLE is the storehouse from which we draw instructions, and our guide to morality. From this fountain flows forth a healing stream, in whose waters are soothed and mitigated every affliction and every cause of sorrow. It is "a lamp to our feet and a light to our path," and unerringly points the way to reach the promised land, the haven of rest.

THE HOUR GLASS is symbolical of the flight of time. We should therefore improve each passing hour, so that we may enter the great hereafter with life's labor well done. We are reminded that "procrastination is the thief of time," and that constant and persistent labors are bound to result in deserved and merited success.

THE COFFIN reminds us of the inevitable hour when dust shall return to dust and the mortal shall put on immortality. It behooves us to so regulate our lives and conduct here that we may depart hence with a well-founded hope and assurance of eternal happiness. As we know what we are and soon will be, let us make certain that our life's labors are well done, and that our efforts deserve and receive heaven's choicest blessings.

EMBLEMS OF THE ENCAMPMENT.

THE THREE PILLARS are Faith, Hope and Charity. With Faith as our companion we steadfastly pursue our toilsome tasks, confident that our labors will eventually be rewarded. It is a shield for the unprotected, strength to the feeble, and joy to the careworn and weary. Hope is the handmaid of Faith; it cheers the sinking soul in its every hour of deep distress; it borders every cloud with a silver lining, and, at last, conducts with serenity to the portals of death. "It has a throne in every bosom and a shrine in every heart." Charity is the last yet the greatest

EMBLEMS OF THE SUBORDINATE ENCAMPMENTS.

of all. It is the queen, the brightest and best of the virtues. Swayed by its benign influences we can lead the erring to repent, soften every obdurate heart, and reclaim to the paths of rectitude every vicious mind.

THE PATRIARCH'S TENT reminds us of the pilgrimage of the Israelites from Egypt to the promised land. It is emblematic of our own journey through life, and we should profit by the many valuable lessons inculcated in this interesting story. The Patriarch's Tent is symbolical of peace, comfort and hospitality, the prominent characteristics of the shepherds of old. Let us cultivate these virtues that we may enjoy the contentment resulting from their observance.

THE PILGRIM'S SCRIP, SANDALS' AND STAFF. By these Emblems we are reminded that life is a journey, and that our stay here is one of short duration. We are further taught that we should not pursue our way without due preparation for the exigencies of the occasion. We are in duty bound to employ every instrumentality, necessary and likely, to facilitate our work and progress. We must remember that by heedlessness and want of prudence we may commit many a sin of omission as well as commission. Our duty is not fulfilled unless we *do the best we can.*

THE ALTAR OF SACRIFICE reminds us that our selfish purposes and ungenerous impulses must be restrained and sacrificed on the altar of Friendship, Love and Truth. Weak and erring mortals as we are, we need the divine blessing and assistance on our every enterprise. Let our hearts be clean and contrite, and our labors a willing sacrifice for the redemption of humanity.

THE TABLES OF STONE, CROSS AND CRESCENT.—The Tables of Stone remind us of the moral law, by and under which we are bound to regulate all our thoughts and actions. We are taught not to neglect or forget our double duty to God and to our fellow man. The Cross and Crescent teach us toleration. As thought is free, our law eschews all bigotry, and leaves every man at full liberty to worship God according to the dictates of his conscience.

THE ALTAR OF INCENSE reminds us that we owe to the Almighty, praise and thanksgiving for the many blessings we enjoy. Only one possessing a cold and unfeeling heart could withhold a thank-offering to God, for His lavish and unstinted gifts. We receive so much and return so little, that it should be a labor of love to express our gratitude. So, in our intercourse with our brethren, we should, at all times, return our thanks, whenever due, and show our appreciation of any and every act of kindness. To know that our brotherly acts are appreciated, makes the *duty* of doing good a positive *pleasure*. Base ingratitude can never dwell in the generous heart of the true and ardent Odd Fellow.

REGALIA.

THE SOVEREIGN GRAND LODGE.—The Regalia for a Grand Representative, a Past Grand Representative, an Officer or Past Officer, is described in Article XXII., of the By-Laws, pages 335 and 336.

STATE GRAND BODIES.—The Regalia for Grand Officers and Past Grand Officers of Grand Bodies, for Past Grands, Past Chief Patriarchs, Past Grands who are also Past Chief Patriarchs, is described in Article XXII., of the By-Laws, pages 335 and 336. Past High Priests, who are Past Grands, and members of a Grand Encampment, may wear the combined Regalia authorized to be worn by Past Chief Patriarchs. A Past Grand Patriarch may wear a royal purple collar of velvet, not to exceed five inches in width, trimmed with yellow metal lace, fringe and tassels, with crossed crooks and a dove with olive branch, on the face of the collar, and yellow lace and fringe around two-thirds of the length of the neck of the collar.

THE SUBORDINATE LODGE.—See Article XXII., of the By-Laws, page 335.

UNIFORM STREET DRESS, TO BE WORN WHEN IN PUBLIC PROCESSION.

The style of hat, or cap, and dress, shall be left to the jurisdiction of the individual Subordinate Lodges, provided that in each case strict uniformity shall be enjoined and observed. Plain white gloves only shall be worn. A jewel collar two and one-half inches wide (no more nor less) at the widest part, uniting in a point in front, in accordance with pattern, made of light blue silk, Italian cloth, or other material (excepting velvet, which shall not be used), edged with silver lace or braid, one-fourth of an inch wide, and without embroidery, or other ornamentation, of any kind whatever. A medal to be suspended from the collar, of white metal, one and three fourths inches in diameter, having on the obverse side, in raised work, the All-seeing Eye, encircled by rays of light; and on the reverse, also in raised work, the three links of the Order, surrounded by the legend: " IN GOD WE TRUST," " FRIENDSHIP, LOVE AND TRUTH."

Officers and past officers may wear, instead thereof, or in addition thereto, such Jewel or Jewels of the Order as they may be entitled to wear elsewhere, in conformity with the existing relations.

THE SUBORDINATE ENCAMPMENT.—See Article XXII., of the By-Laws, pages 335 and 336.

Patriarchs who have attained the Royal Purple Degree shall wear purple collars or baldrics, trimmed with yellow lace or fringe. The Chief Patriarch, Senior Warden, Junior Warden, Scribe, Treasurer, and Sentinels, a purple collar, trimmed with yellow lace or fringe; High Priest, his robe. For recommendatory Regalia, for all the Patriarchal Degrees, to be used on public occasions, see Journal, pages 7,732–7,733, and for the Uniform of the Patriarchal Branch of the Order, to be worn on public occasions, see Journal of 1874, pages 6,242, 6,317, 6,318; 1883, pages 9,367, 9,455; 1884, pages 9,754, 9,809.

THE DEGREE LODGE OF THE DAUGHTERS OF REBEKAH.—The brethren shall wear the Regalia they are entitled to wear in a Subordinate Lodge. The sisters shall wear a badge or collar of pink and green ribbon, of about an inch in width.

For Noble Grand, the Regalia shall be a collar, not exceeding three inches in width, with pink center and green edges, to be trimmed with silver lace and fringe; Vice Grand, a collar, same width, with green center and pink edges, trimmed with silver lace and fringe; Secretary, a collar, with pink center and green edges, trimmed with silver lace, no fringe; Treasurer, a collar, with green center and pink edges, trimmed with silver lace, no fringe. The collars of all the elective officers to be of the same width, viz., three inches. For Warden, a baldric, not exceeding three and one-half inches in width, to be of pink and green, the upper side to be green and the lower side pink, with a row of silver lace on each edge and through the center, the lowest edge to be trimmed with silver lace and fringe; Conductor, a baldric, same width as Warden's, with one row of silver lace around the inner edge, the upper side to be green and the lower side pink; Inside Guardian, the same as Warden, without fringe; Outside Guardian, the same as Conductor, except that the row of silver lace shall be on the outside, and none in the center; Chaplain, white baldric, with silver lace on each edge, the front to be ornamented with pink roses and green leaves; Supporters to Noble Grand, baldric, pink center and green edges, trimmed with two rows of silver lace; Supporters to Vice Grand, baldric, green center and pink edges, trimmed with two rows of silver lace; Past Grand (sister) collar same as Noble Grand, except that the lace and fringe shall be of gold instead of silver.

THE PATRIARCHS MILITANT UNIFORM will be found described in the Journal, pages 10,124–10,128, and pages 245–262 of the Report of the Lieutenant-General, to the S. G. L., at session of 1885.

THE FUNERAL REGALIA to be worn by all brothers of the Order, when attending the funeral of a deceased brother, shall be as follows:

A black crape rosette, having a center of the color of the highest Degree to which the bearer may have attained, to be worn on the left breast; above it a sprig of evergreen, and below it (if the wearer be an elective or past officer), the Jewel or Jewels which, as such, he may be entitled to wear. The ordinary mourning badge to be worn by brothers in memory of a deceased brother shall be a strip of black crape passed through one button-hole only, of the left lapel of the coat, and tied with a narrow ribbon of the color of the highest Degree to which the bearer may have attained. The several State Grand Encampments and Grand Lodges may, at their discretion, permit the usual Regalia of the Order to be worn at funerals, either in connection with, or as a substitute for, the simple Regalia above described. On such occasions, the Marshal shall wear a black scarf, and bear a baton bound with black crape. The Outside Guardian shall bear a red wand bound with black crape. The Scene Supporters shall bear white wands bound with black crape. The Inside Guardian shall bear the Regalia and Insignia, indicating the rank in the Order of the deceased brother. The Supporters of the Vice Grand shall bear their wands of office, bound with black crape. The Chaplain shall wear a white scarf. The Warden shall bear the axe, bound with black crape. The Conductor shall bear his wand of office, bound with black crape, and the Supporters of the Noble Grand shall each bear their wands of office, bound with black crape.

The prescribed street Uniform may be worn at a funeral of a deceased brother, if the State Grand Jurisdiction shall so determine. It is a matter of local regulation. It is admissible for Odd Fellows to appear in Regalia at the funeral of a Daughter of Rebekah, in case they first obtain permission so to do from the proper Grand Officers of the jurisdiction.

The funds of a Lodge cannot be appropriated to procure street Uniforms. A member of an Encampment, clothed in street Uniform, presenting himself for admission while the Encampment is transacting its ordinary business, shall be treated the same as if he presented himself without such Uniform. It is not necessary for the officers to be clothed in the working Regalia of their office during initiation, but only in the Regalia prescribed for them at initiations, when such Regalia is prescribed. See second paragraph, page 123, also Article XX. of the By-Laws, S. G. L., page 335. A Grand Master when visiting *as such* in his own jurisdiction, should wear the Regalia and Jewel of his office. A Lodge is bound to recognize and give a member a Past Grand's Regalia, who is admitted by Card certifying that he is a P. G., if he has not the P. O. Degrees.

A brother, when he visits his own, or any other Grand or Subordinate Lodge, may wear the Encampment Regalia and Jewel of the highest Degree he has taken. (*See Article XXIV. of the By-Laws, S. G. L., page* 336.) When a Battalion of Uniformed Patriarchs visits an Encampment in a body, accompanied by either of their first two officers, the members thereof shall be deemed to be in proper Regalia when clothed in full Uniform. A Uniformed Degree Camp, under command of its officers, and in full Uniform, may lawfully visit a Subordinate Lodge when in session. The Patriarchs Militant Uniform can be worn by Chevaliers, when visiting Lodges and Encampments. Processions, balls, etc., at which the Regalia, Emblems, etc., shall be used, are not permitted, unless the same be authorized in open Grand Lodge, or, in its recess, by Dispensation of the Grand Master of the State. No brother is entitled to enter or leave the Lodge room unless clothed in Regalia.

JEWELS.

THE SOVEREIGN GRAND LODGE.—The Jewel of the Grand Sire, a Past Grand Sire, a Grand Representative, and a Past Grand Representative, will be found described in Article XXII. of the By-Laws, S. G. L., page 336.

THE STATE GRAND LODGE.—The Jewel for Past Grand Master, is the sun, with hand and heart; Grand Master, sun, with scales of justice impressed or engraved thereon; Deputy Grand Master, a half moon; Grand Warden, crossed gavels; Grand Secretary, crossed pens; Grand Treasurer, crossed keys; Grand Conductor, a Roman sword; Grand Guardian, crossed swords; Grand Marshal, a baton. All of said Jewels shall be of white metal.

THE GRAND ENCAMPMENT.—The Jewel for a Past Grand Patriarch is of yellow metal, two and a half inches in diameter, rim three-eighths inch wide, with double triangle, and rays extending from rim, and the letters P. G. P. in the center of triangle; Grand Patriarch, a double triangle of yellow metal, with a representation of an altar, and crossed crooks in the center; Grand High Priest, same triangle, with representation of the breast plate; Grand Senior Warden, same triangle, with crossed crooks; Grand Junior Warden, same triangle, with single crook; Grand Scribe, same triangle, with crossed pens; Grand Treasurer, same triangle, with crossed keys; Grand Sentinel, same triangle, with crossed swords.

THE SUBORDINATE LODGE.—The Jewel for a Past Grand is a five pointed star; Noble Grand, crossed gavels; Vice Grand, hour glass; Secretary, crossed pens; Treasurer, crossed keys; Warden, crossed axes; Conductor, crossed wands; Supporters of the N. G., a wand, having branching arms, connected by three links, and encompassing a gavel; Supporters of V. G., a wand, arranged same as that of the supporters of the N. G., encompassing an hour glass; Scene Supporters, a wand, arranged in same manner, encompassing a burning torch; Chaplain, a wand, arranged in same manner, encompassing a bible. All of said Jewels shall be of white metal, and be three and a-half inches in length.

THE SUBORDINATE ENCAMPMENT.—The Jewel for elective officers is a single triangle; otherwise as designated for officers of Grand Encampment; Guide, a staff within a triangle; Guard of the Tent; a halberd within a triangle; the

Jewels of both Guards to be alike; Watch, a spear within a triangle; the Jewels of all the Watches to be the same. The Jewels for the officers shall be uniform, in size and style.

THE DEGREE LODGE OF THE DAUGHTERS OF REBEKAH. —The Jewel for a lady Past Noble Grand is a five-pointed star of white metal; Noble Grand, a silver or silver-plated circle, one and a-half inches in diameter, with a representation or figure of "Rebekah at the Well," engraved or stamped thereon on one side, the other side plain, and underneath the figure of Rebekah, the word *Fidelity;* Vice Grand, the same in form and size, with a representation or figures of Ruth and Naomi, and underneath the figures, the word *Industry;* Secretary, the same in form and size, with a representation or figure of a pen, and underneath it, the word *Deborah;* Treasurer, the same in form and size, with a representation or figure of a key, and underneath it, the word *Trust;* Warden, the same in form and size, with a representation or figure of a cross (a bar and axe), and underneath it, the word *Hope;* Conductor, the same in form and size, with a representation or figure of two wands, and underneath it, the word *Safety;* Inside Guardian, the same in form and size, with a representation or figure of a shield, crossed by a spear, and underneath it, the word *Prove;* Outside Guardian, the same in form, size, and similar design, and underneath it, the word *Vigilance.* There is *no prescribed* Jewel for the Financial Secretary.

The law requiring that officers shall wear *Jewels*, it is not a compliance therewith to have them wrought in the Regalia. All officers of Subordinate Lodges and Encampments shall wear the Jewels of their respective offices during the transaction of business. A Past Grand of the R. P. Degree can, and may, wear a Jewel of yellow metal. It is as imperative upon all Grand and Subordinate Lodges and Encampments to furnish the officers of their respective Lodges and Encampments with the Jewels appertaining to their rank and station, as it is for members thereof to be clothed in suitable Regalia.

THE PATRIARCHS MILITANT.—A Jewel may be worn upon the watch-chain or in any appropriate manner, and shall consist of the escutcheons of the Degree, placed with backs together. Upon top center there may be placed a circular tent, or other ornament, with attachment to fasten to chain, and the Norman shield may be placed on golden rays, or the escutcheons may be placed on each side of the golden rays, or a many-pointed star. The three links may be placed on either escutcheon, and "Patriarchs Militant" may be abbreviated P. M. A breast or scarf pin may be made by passing a crook or sword through a raised crown, with Jewels *ad libitum*. Special Jewels for the General Officers of the Army, having distinctive insignia for the various grades of such officers in command of troops, and on the Staff, have been designed, and samples manufactured. Such Jewels are intended for dress and parade occasions, and may be worn on the left breast, at the option of the officer entitled thereto. A Jewel of special design may be worn by General Officers. It shall consist of a breast star, three and one-half inches in outer diameter, after the general pattern of the star of the Legion of Honor of France, with disc of dead gold encircled by a raised wreath of oak and olive branches; the arms of the star shall be of scarlet enamel, bordered with gold, all placed upon a circle of golden rays, and the disc shall bear: For Commander-in-Chief, a raised regal crown of scarlet enamel and gold; Lieutenant-General, a raised helmet of dark enamel and gold over a naked sword, all above the Commander's baton; Major-General commanding troops, the *Pax aut Bellum* escutcheon, in colored enamels, silver and gold; Brigadier commanding troops, a raised crown and lion's paw of scarlet enamel and gold; General Officers upon the Staff, a raised letter "S" (old English) of gold, set with brilliants.

The Jewel, "The Decoration of Chivalry," shall consist of a cross of ancient design, made of white enamel imbedded in a gold frame, having mounted on the face a heart of scarlet enamel, bearing a golden crown; and have engraved upon back the P. M. monogram, and the motto of action,

"*Be just, merciful, honorable, and brave.*" A Chevalier shall wear upon the left breast, the decoration suspended from a gold pin representing radiated rays of light, and when worn by a lady, it shall be fastened at the throat, or be suspended from entwined narrow pink and green silk ribbon around the neck. The Jewel, "The Grand Decoration of Chivalry," shall consist of a cross and heart in a Degree similar to that for "The Decoration of Chivalry." The cross may have diamond settings at the points of the arms, shall be placed over crossed crook and sword, and all mounted upon an eight-pointed gold star of radiated rays; the crook proper shall be of blue enamel or inlaid sapphires on staff of gold, bearing toward butt a raised silver lamb; the grip of the sword shall be scarlet enamel or inlaid rubies, and blade of platinum bearing toward point a raised golden lion; an ornamental regal crown, with scarlet enamel cap, shall be placed upon the upper point of the radiated star; and an engraved monogram and motto on back, the same as upon back of "The Decoration of Chivalry." The Decoration shall be worn upon the left breast, suspended by white and scarlet silk or satin ribbon from a gold pin, representing radiated rays of light and bearing the emblematic three links of black enamel, raised, and (at option) a diamond setting in each link.

Prize Jewels may be made of various designs, the only requirements in construction being, that they shall consist of the Emblems of the Order and Degree, appropriately arranged.

CHAPTER XII.

OF the numerous Branches, or Orders of Odd Fellowship, the Manchester Unity, England, can boast of the greatest number of members. For about twenty-three years, the Order in the United States was closely allied to the Manchester Body which, it may be truthfully asserted, is the parent of American Odd Fellowship, for although Thomas Wildey and his four associates, in 1819, were not Manchester members, the Charter of Washington Lodge, No. 1, came from the Duke of York's Lodge, Preston, England, a Subordinate of the Manchester Unity, and the Grand Annual Movable Committee of 1826, not only confirmed the Warrant, but granted, to the authorities of the Order in America unlimited power " to conduct the business of Odd Fellowship without the interference of any other country." Therefore, though long estranged from the " mother of our youth," it is but natural that we desire some information concerning the birth and the career of our parent.

Intelligent Odd Fellows, in Europe and America, place no reliance upon the old and mythical story that the Order was established in Rome, in the year 79, A. D., by the descendants of the priests and scribes of the Babylonian captivity, who preserved the secret signs of the ancient Order of Naharda, that had been transmitted from century to century, until the conquest of Jerusalem, when Titus Cæsar carried the inhabitants to the city of Rome. It is a pretty romance, the discovery of a plot against the life of the Emperor, his recognition of the loyalty of the members of this secret association, to which he gave the name of " Odd Fellows," and presented them with a Dispensation engraved on a plate of gold, bearing Emblems of the sun, moon, stars, lamb, lion, dove and many other symbols, as a pledge of friendship and appreciation of their fidelity to him, and to their country. It is further said, that the Degree, called in the Ancient Ritual of "The Patriotic Order of Odd Fellows," (1797), "The Royal Arch of Titus, or the Fidelity Degree," was constructed and named in gratitude for the countenance and encouragement of the Emperor. But, as an eminent writer has truthfully said, "however alluring this theory of the origin of Odd Fellowship may be to those who would fain derive everything from a remote antiquity, it is not borne out by history." Nor is the claim that the institution was organized by traveling laborers, or "odd men," any better established, for had this been the case, traces of the Body would have been found in the early history of the Continental laboring Guilds, which we seek for in vain. A careful search of their records fails to furnish any evidence of such a society as "Odd Fellows," of ancient or modern days; therefore, it is concluded that the institution originated about 1745, as will be hereafter explained.

Bro. James Spry, Provincial Corresponding Secretary of the Plymouth District, in his "History of the Order of Odd Fellows, (Manchester Unity)," published in 1866, repudiates "the myths and traditions" referred to, and states the generally accepted theory of the origin of Odd Fellowship, thus: "In the early part of the last century, the writer, Daniel De Foe, mentions the 'Society of Odd Fellows'; and *The Gentleman's Magazine*, in 1745, speaks of the Odd Fellows' Lodge as 'a place where very comfortable and recreative evenings may be spent.'" The objects of these meetings were said to be "the formation of a select society to uphold the dignity of the Sovereign of the Realm; to assist one another in times of misfortune, and to amuse and instruct one another." The presiding officer was styled "Noble Grand," and he was clothed with absolute power to compel obedience to his mandates. One organization paved the way for the formation of others, and in a few years, many Unities of Odd Fellows, derived from the same source, were in existence in England. The scope of these institutions was enlarged and they were adapted to the pleasures and the needs of the membership. While some were content "to meet periodically to eat beefsteaks, tripe, etc., enjoy each other's company, call their officers by high sounding titles, and style themselves Brothers," other organizations were more practical in their operations, and at their weekly meetings, required each member, or visitor, to pay one penny on entering a Lodge. Thus a fund was secured from which to vote a sufficient amount to a needy brother. When the money in the treasury of a Lodge was expended, other Lodges would be called upon for assistance, and it was not an unusual occurrence for an entire Lodge membership to visit a needy Lodge, and hundreds of Odd Fellows went, week after week, to swell the penny collections, until the exhausted treasury was replenished. This was early Odd Fellowship, superseded by the establishment of weekly dues collected by the Warden, who, with axe in hand, at every meeting, called on each member for his offering.

The *Monthly Magazine* of the Manchester Unity, May, 1888, contains drawings of "a solid silver medal, measuring nearly four inches by three, bearing the hall-mark of 1796-7, which was conferred on a Past Secretary of a Grand Independent Lodge of Odd Fellows nearly a century ago." There is no Emblem, Motto, or coat-of-arms, to give a clew to the identity of the Body which had thus rewarded its Secretary. On the obverse of the medal there is engraved a figure of a man, with pen in hand, seated at a writing desk; inkstand with crossed pens, and the words "Past Secretary;" on the reverse, inkstand, pens; the letters T. H., and below them, in a semicircle, "Grand Independent Lodge of Odd Fellows, Duke's Head, Rotherhithe."

About the year 1800 we find mention of the Order as the "Free and Independent," "Original Grand Lodge," etc., and the titles of officers: "Most Noble Odd Fellow," "Deputy Odd Fellow," "Secretary," "Senior Worthy," "Junior Worthy,' "Supporters to the Deputy O. F.," "Usher O. F.," "Keeper O. F."

It is unnecessary, however, to proceed further in this direction. As we read the record, the founders of the Manchester Unity were mature men, who had been originally initiated in the languishing societies of the last century; but who perceived in the principles of Odd Fellowship, the vital germs of a better institution. Secret societies of this character, were the subjects of the closest inspection by the authorities of Great Britain, and members were compelled to conceal their identity with the institution; indeed, on account of the political agitation, many Lodges were closed. In 1813 a convention was held in Manchester, and several Lodges formally seceded from the Union Order, and constituted the nucleus of what is widely known as the " Independent Order of Odd Fellows, Manchester Unity Friendly Society." The brethren at the head of the movement were earnest, active, intelligent men, and at once began operations, by issuing Charters and establishing Lodges throughout the country. The first Lodge was chartered July 21st, 1813, and named " Victoria," No. 1, located at Ashton-under-Lyne. Some accounts state that the Manchester Unity originated in 1809, " a working marble-mason, a member of the Ancient Order of Odd Fellows, belonging to a Lodge in London, who had removed to Manchester," being the prime mover in establishing, (on receiving a Dispensation), " Victory " Lodge, while other writers assert that Robert Naylor, who was Grand Master in 1832-3, was the originator of the Unity. It seems evident, however, that although, the brothers named were, probably, instrumental in establishing Lodges, the *Unity, as a body*, was organized in 1813, principally, perhaps, by Robert Naylor and his associates, who " held convivial meetings periodically, at the ' Rope-maker's Arms', Chapel street, Salford ; drew up a code of rules for self-government, and instituted an awful and absurd ceremonial to be used on the admission of members." It is stated that " the fame of their proceedings induced some members of ' Prince Regent ' Lodge of Odd Fellows to join them, and with this addition they formed themselves into a benefit club, at the ' Robin Hood,' in Church street, Man-

chester, in October, 1810." The name of "Lord Abercrom-
bie Lodge" was assumed and Grand Lodge powers were
exercised, and this, Brother James Spry, Corresponding
Secretary of the Plymouth District, says he is "inclined to
consider the true origin of the Manchester Unity." It is
recorded that in 1814, James Christie was Grand Master;
Benjamin Howarth, Deputy Grand Master; 1815, 1816,
1817 and 1818, John Lloyd, Grand Master; 1816 to 1819,
Thomas Hignett, Corresponding Secretary. If the Body
had a Secretary in 1814 and 1815 his name does not appear
in the record. In the first thirteen years (1814–1826) the
Unity had four Grand Masters, but from 1827 to 1828 there
were no re-elections, the Deputy being chosen Grand
Master. From 1816 to 1888, there were eight Secretaries,
H. Ratcliffe serving from 1849 to 1877. The business of the
Unity is managed by a Body entitled the Grand Annual
Movable Committee, composed of Deputies appointed by
Districts. At the meetings of the A. M. C., the Degrees
for Past Provincial Grand Masters and Past Lodge officers
are conferred, usually on Thursday, or Friday, during the
session. In the 1886 edition of Rules of the A. M. C., we
read:

The A. M. C. shall elect three officers, called the Grand Master, Deputy
Grand Master, Corresponding Secretary, and nine Directors, who, with the
last Past Grand Master shall be the Committee of Management or the Central
Body.

District Branches, to be established by the A. M. C., shall consist of
Branches, called Lodges, established by the Directors under these rules, and
shall be governed by a committee, to be called the "District Committee,"
composed of Deputies appointed by Lodges. Each District Committee shall,
at its annual meeting in December or January, elect, as hereinafter provided
for, a Provincial Grand Master, a Provincial Deputy Grand Master, who, with
the Provincial Corresponding Secretary, and such other members, (if any), as
the rules of the District may direct, shall be the Committee of Management
for such District Branch.

Five Trustees shall be appointed by the A. M. C., and continue in office
during the pleasure of that Body. A banking firm in Manchester shall be
selected by the A. M. C. to act as Treasurer.

Any Branch of this Society, being desirous of seceding, shall first call a
special general meeting, etc.

A general meeting of the Society shall be held annually, commencing at
nine o'clock on Whit-Monday in each year, in a town which shall have been

decided upon, by ballot, at the previous annual meeting. Each District under one thousand members has the privilege of sending one Deputy, and for every additional thousand members, or part thereof, one Deputy. Each Deputy shall be entitled to one vote. Each District to pay the expenses of its own Deputies, the General Society to pay the Officers, cost of rooms, etc. The Corresponding Secretary shall, after election, continue in office during the pleasure of the A. M. C., unless suspended by the Directors. The Corresponding Secretary shall not furnish goods or reply to the correspondence of any person, except through the medium of a District Corresponding Secretary. Any Past Officer, or Permanent Secretary, who has taken the Purple Degree, previous to nomination, and who is a subscribing member of any Lodge in the District, or a District member, shall be eligible for appointment as a Deputy to the A. M. C.

A Lodge, or member, may appeal to the Directors from the action of a District meeting, within three months after the action, the appeal to be in the hands of the Corresponding Secretary of the Order at least eighteen days previous to the meeting of the Directors. Under special circumstances, the Directors may grant a re-hearing, and may hear an appeal within six months. Traveling Cards must, in all cases, bear the Seal of the Examining Officer of the District. Any Lodge, in any year, expending in its management more than its income applicable thereto, and not having a balance to the credit of this fund, shall levy on the members, at equal rates per member, such a sum as shall be sufficient to cover the sum expended beyond the receipts. A member is not entitled to relief more than once from each District he passes through, and travelers are allowed to be relieved only once per day.

There are now 455 Districts. In 1823 there were 98 Deputies at the meeting in Hanley; in 1842, at Wigan, 356; in 1866, at Burton-on-Trent, 230; in 1888, at Gloucester, 470. A District occupies about the same relation to the A. M. C. as a State Grand Lodge to the Sovereign Grand Lodge. From the latest statistics at hand (1886) it is ascertained that the Unity in America consists of the following Districts:

Canadian, 27 Lodges, 914 members; Montreal, 10 Lodges, 788 members; Halifax, 4 Lodges, 206 members; Boston, 16 Lodges, 976 members; Providence, 7 Lodges, 438 members; New York, 1 Lodge, 61 members.

Much of the business of the institution is transacted by the Board of Directors, constituted as heretofore stated. The meetings of this Body are held quarterly, February, April or May, August and November, from six to nine days being devoted to each session. The proceedings, tables, etc., are contained in pamphlets of 100 to 130 octavo pages, issued quarterly, aggregating from 400 to 500 pages per year. All appeals are settled by the Directors and their decision is " final and conclusive, and binding upon all parties concerned, without further power to appeal.

The Journal of November, 1887, shows 19, and February, 1888, shows 9 appeals disposed of. There were 264 general resolutions adopted. In the pamphlets, 92 "proposed new Rules and alterations of Rules," are printed, "to be submitted to the Grand Annual Movable Committee, or Special Meeting of the Order, at Gloucester, on Whit-Monday, May 21st, 1888." The Secretary of a Lodge is fined ten shillings if he fails to send the report of the Lodge to January 1st, to the Corresponding Secretary of the District on or before January 20th, and the Corresponding Secretary of a District is fined ten shillings and six pence if his returns, (including Juvenile Branches), are not made to the Corresponding Secretary of the Order on or before February 1st in each year. Nominations of candidates for Directors, and for the committees to be elected by the A. M. C. are made by the Districts. The following are the committees elected : Sub-Committee ; Relief Committee ; New Districts Committee ; Estimates Committee, each consisting of nine members. The Grand Master, Deputy Grand Master, Corresponding Secretary and Auditors are compensated for attending the A. M. C., and the Directors are allowed mileage and per diem for the quarterly meetings, days of traveling and days in attendance, at £1, 1s. per day. The expenses of the February, 1887, meeting aggregated £140, 2s. 10d.; the May session, £117, 0s. 10d.; the August, £143, 18s. 10d,, and the November session, £135, 4s. 4d.; aggregate for the year, £536, 6s. 10d. The *Magazine* in 1887 yielded a net profit of £80, 6s., after paying all expenses, including the salaries of editors (one, 1 month, £8, 6s. 8d.; one, 6 months, £31, 10s.; and one, time not stated, £44, 14s. 6d.), contributors, four steel portrait-plates, etc. There were 227,236 copies of the *Magazine* sold; an average of 18,936 per month. The Manchester Unity has issued many valuable books and documents, among which the annual " List of the

Lodges," etc., containing the names, numbers, location, etc., of all the Lodges throughout the world, almanac, and other valuable information, a book of about 400 pages, compiled by Thomas Collins, the accomplished Corresponding Secretary of the Order, may be justly termed "invaluable."

The latest information at hand (April, 1888), in a condensed shape, furnishes the following:

Admitted in Great Britain, Ireland and the Channel Islands, 1878, 27,249; 1879, 26,847 ; 1880, 33,536 ; 1881, 34,860 ; 1882, 37,343 ; 1883, 38,501 ; 1884, 38,377 ; 1885, 37,422 ; 1886, 36,418 ; 1887, 37,652. By increase in the Colonies, reinstatement of suspended Lodges, etc., the figures for the ten years are 27,918 ; 27,730 ; 36,166 ; 36,530; 43,971 ; 41,749; 43,959; 40,162 ; 39,938 ; 39,994.

Taking the figures for the year 1887, we find that 1,434 were admitted at the age of 16; 1,659 at 17; 6,110 at 18 ; 3,986 at 19, and the number gradually decreased until the age of 43, when 108 were admitted. At the age of 44, the number was 186. From 1878 to 1886, inclusive, more members were admitted at the age of 18 than any other year, nearly doubling the admissions at 21 years of age. Bro. Thomas Collins, Corresponding Secretary, in his report, said :

It will be observed that during the year 1887, out of 37,652 persons admitted in Great Britain, etc., *by initiation*, 26,974 were under 25 years of age. In 1886, 36,418 ; 1885, 26,188 ; 1884, 27,778 ; 1883, 27,549; 1882, 26,416 ; 1881, 24,839; 1880, 20,828. It must be very gratifying to the members of the Unity to observe such a large increase in the number of young persons admitted during several years past into the Society.

The following is the rate per cent. of admissions in 1887 : Age 16 to 20, 35.02 ; 20 to 25, 36.61 ; 25 to 30, 16.17 ; 30 to 35, 6.99; 35 to 40, 3.45 ; 40 to 45, 1.73.

Similar figures are given for each year from 1881 to 1887, inclusive, but as they do not vary much from the year 1887, it is unnecessary to produce them.

The capital of the institution, that is, the amount of Sick and Funeral Funds of Lodges, and District Management Funds, Widow and Orphan Societies, Past Grands, Grands, Lodges, Juvenile Societies, etc., it may be safely said, amounts to thirty-five million dollars.

The institution is ably and carefully managed, the closest supervision being maintained over all the Lodges, and special care is exercised by the Board of Directors to see that the special funds are sacredly preserved; no Lodge under the jurisdiction of the Unity being permitted to change the relations of the several funds without the special permission of the Directors. It may well be imagined that the care of the interests of 627,594 members is not a light task for any committee, however able the members may be.

There were 908 Juvenile Societies in connection with the Order, January, 1888, with 44,268 members and £48,110 capital. In 1886 there were 560 Lodges, 30,600 members, £31,515 capital. In the *Magazine* we find the following correspondence concerning Juvenile Branches:

In the majority of instances in these old unregistered Lodges, the lowest age for initiation is 8 years, but some, my own Lodge for instance, are as low as 5, and in some cases the member is allowed to continue in the Lodge Juvenile Branch until he is 18 years and 6 months old, but generally speaking, at 18 years their initiation money is paid into the Lodge.

Contributions vary according to age; those joining between 7 and 12 years pay 10*d*. per month and receive 3*s*. per week in sickness, and a funeral donation of £20 at death. The profits each year are equally divided amongst the members and placed to their credit, payable to them on being transferred to an adult Lodge of the Manchester Unity, as soon as convenient after attaining the age of 16 years. This initiation fee is paid for them and they have the option of joining any Lodge they prefer. I quote an example: W. S. joined the Juvenile Lodge in December, 1877, at 7 years of age, and was transferred to an adult Lodge in December, 1886, having been a member just 9 years; the bonus standing to his credit amounting to £2, 5*s*. 5*d*., or 50 per cent. of his contributions. It is optional with the members to receive their bonus in cash, or it is paid into the adult Lodge as contributions.

General Law 26 A, of the Manchester Unity, authorizes a "District Assurance Fund for Children," and some Districts have established it. The "Children of Members' Funeral Fund" is in operation in the Exeter District, by which, in payment of 1*s*. 4*d*. annually, benefits are assured from £1, 10*s*. to £8, according to the age of child on entering and at death.

An engraved "Emblem," and a code of "Model Rules" for Juvenile Societies are among the supplies furnished by the Corresponding Secretary at Manchester.

The Manchester Unity published for many years (from about 1824) a *Quarterly Magazine,* the earliest number accessible being March, 1828, "No. 1, New Series." Since January, 1884, it has been a monthly publication of 32 pages, octavo, and is sold for one penny. The number for June, 1888, is styled " Vol. XIX.—No. 162, New Series—No. 54." It is an interesting and valuable periodical, filled with important correspondence, choice literature, and deals fearlessly with all matters relating to the Order. The January, April, July and October issues are embellished with fine steel engravings of Past Grand Masters and other prominent members of the Unity. The number for January, 1887, contains the likeness and biography of James John Stockall, Grand Master from 1886 to 1887, (whose name must be familiar to the readers of the Journals of 1886 and 1887, of the Sovereign Grand Lodge). We quote the following :

We have been greatly delighted with reading copies of correspondence which have passed between the Grand Master of the Manchester Unity and brethren of the American Order ; still further have we been delighted by the revelations conveyed in that correspondence, showing that distance cannot sunder the true fraternity of manhood prevailing in the Anglo-Saxon race and in the heart's unity of Odd Fellowship. (*See Journal of S. G. Lodge,* 1886, *pages* 10,266-10,269). If from out of this there may spring a truer fraternization, we shall indeed be more than gratified. And as the present is, or should be, a time for the development of the principles of universal brotherhood, let us, with all humility, invoke the blessing of the Great Architect of the Universe on the good cause we have at heart, and reserving for future discussion the questions of detail, whilst we join the angel song of " Peace on Earth, Good Will Towards Men," breathe forth alike to all good Odd Fellows, "where'er dispersed o'er land or water," the best of all wishes, that of A HAPPY NEW YEAR.

It appears that there is an agitation in favor of removing the " Headquarters " of the Order from Manchester, articles in the August and September (1887) numbers of the *Magazine*, decidedly favoring the measure. One writer, (in the September publication), asserts that there were only 120 members in Manchester, and the official returns for 1886 showing 4 Lodges, 134 members, apparently justify the statement. Although the date of the District is 1814, the Lodges are rated as instituted : No. 252, in 1827, members 68 ; No. 456, in 1831, members 9 ; No. 1012, in 1844, members 24 ; No. 1358, in 1838, members 33. The writer referred to, said :

On reading the report of the proceedings of the Dover A. M. C., I notice that the question was mooted of moving the headquarters of the Order from Manchester to some more central position, and, considering the condition of the Order in Manchester, one need not be surprised at the question being raised. Is it not remarkable that whilst the Order is making such rapid progress in other places, the town in which it originated, and from which it takes its name, should contain so few members, which are decreasing each year? Are there no means by which this can be remedied, and the otherwise inevitable extinction of the Order there be averted? It cannot be expected that young men will join the existing old and decaying Lodges, but surely, in a large city like Manchester, with a little effort and energy on the part of leading members, there should be no difficulty in opening new Lodges, based on the present graduated tables of contributions and benefits, which would, in a few years, be the means of re-establishing the Order there on a firm footing.

The space allotted for this Chapter, will not permit further notice of what an enthusiastic writer describes as " an enormous Body which overshadows the minor societies of Odd Fellows throughout the world, having its ramifications everywhere, and now accepted as the best and most authoritative association of the kind anywhere known." The assertions are broad and certainly comprehensive, but with due deference to the opinions expressed, it may be suggested that the author of such fulsome praise possessed very limited knowledge of the operations of the Order under the jurisdiction of the Sovereign Grand Lodge.

The strength of the Order of Odd Fellows in the entire world, as nearly as can be ascertained, is as follows :

		LODGES.	MEMBERS.
1.	Sovereign Grand Lodge	8,413	574,975
2.	Manchester Unity	4,375	627,594
3.	Grand United Order	1,305	81,610
4.	Nottingham Ancient Imperial Order	984	37,025
5.	Ancient Noble Order	410	27,374
6.	British United Order	153	9,261
7.	Derby Midland United Order	63	3,613
8.	Improved Independent Order	163	9,829
9.	National Independent Order	603	47,718
10.	Kent Unity	40	1,776
11.	Norfolk and Norwich Unity	58	5,087
12.	Albion Order	31	4,786
*	Ten Minor Orders, (as below), say	176	14,000
	Totals	16,774	1,444,648

*Leeds United Order; Economical Order; Enrolled Order; Ancient True Order; Kingston Unity; Auxiliary Order; Staffordshire Order; West Bromwich Order; Wolverhampton Order; Handsworth Order.

CHAPTER XIII.

THE AIMS AND ATTAINMENTS OF ODD FELLOWSHIP.

BY H. L. STILLSON, Past Grand Master of Vermont.

IN the evening of the nineteenth century, an age of marvellous progress and wonderful development, this "History and Manual" is written, delineating the principles upon which our grand Order is founded, noting its growth, and eulogizing its attainments.

Amid what surroundings has Odd Fellowship been nurtured? Within what sphere has it grown great?

Glance at the advances made in the arts and sciences, and in every department of knowledge! Survey the century's progress! Man has literally chained the powers of Nature and attached them to his conquering chariot wheels; nay, more, he has made the very lightnings move the wheels, and light his pathway. Electricity carries the voice long distances; the telegraph, bridging oceans and seas, as well as threading the land with its net-work, conveys intelligence from the one extreme to the other, fairly out-flying swift-winged Time. Untiring research has brought to light the buried remains and monuments of a remote antiquity, and, by means of the inscriptions thereon, the history of civilizations and peoples long ago perished and forgotten has been restored. The buried dead of the East tell anew the story of their lives, their hopes and fears, their motives of action, their death, their expectation of future existence, from thirty to fifty centuries subsequent to the deposit of their embalmed bodies in what was supposed by them to be an eternal sleep. Inventive genius has well-nigh belted the earth with bands of iron, superseding the spreading sail, and, in this manner, utilizing the power of steam, dictates the movements of the people and their diversified commerce, "The desert buds and blossoms as the rose!"

Fraught with achievements like these, our own proud country, leading the van in this mighty conquest of peace, towers aloft as the greatest Republic, the most beneficent government, on which the sun has ever smiled. Among her co-laborers, deserving of mention, are the "Fatherland," and that other Great Empire upon whose domain the sun does not go down.

In this "land of the free and home of the brave," and amid such surroundings, fostered by the enlightened civilization which produced them, the republic of the Independent Order of Odd Fellows arose.

Odd Fellowship, as known by the American Order, therefore, is not a descent from antiquity. Its methods, its growth, its inspiration are of the century that gave it birth: the elevation of Man to a state of freedom and equality, becoming more and more the actuating motive of all civilized nations, crystallized as Universal Brotherhood in our Ritual, is not a creation of the fraternities of antiquity. They taught not the doctrine, which we dare to believe, " He has made of one blood all nations of men, to dwell on the face of the earth."

That is, men are indeed of one heart and one mind, and might enjoy all things, if they would, in common. This is the promise. And the growth of our Order is the assured discovery that this good news is true. It is an acknowledgment of how joyful and pleasant a thing it is for brethren to dwell together in unity.

To conform to its history the Order's development in three great lines will be presented:

(A) The original plan, the Lodge System (including the Encampment Branch);

(B) A continuation of it, incorporating the Degree of Rebekah (or the union of Odd Fellows and their families);

(C) Both of these, associated with the Patriarchs Militant, sworn to protect and perpetuate the whole, by peaceful means, if possible, by the drawn sword, if necessary: Friendship, Love, Truth; *Justitia Universalis; Pax aut Bellum.*

(A) The earliest of the three epochs suggests at once

the fundamental principle of our association, the *fraternity* which the Fathers of the Order denominated the foundation-stone of our institution. Upon its solid basis the super-structure was to rise; destined safely to repose, as long as time itself should endure.

This presupposed Love in its fullest sense, embracing not only what man owed to his brother, but what he believed himself to owe to a Higher Power, and compre-hended those primary principles of right and wrong, which are of general, if not of absolutely universal, acceptance. Upon this broad platform men of diverse positions in religious, social, and political life might be brought to coöperate, without regard to birth or worldly circumstances.

An associate of Love, the central link, and forming the first in the chain, is the Covenant of Friendship. The fun-damental qualities of true friendship are constancy and fidelity. Where constancy is wanting there can be no fidelity, which is the other basis of friendship. The first of the Order's "Three Links," therefore, presumed entire confidence.

Its practice was to be the antithesis of the world's motives, where so many recognized no personality but their own, and deprecated the selfishness which enforced the assertion that all things exist for pleasure or convenience. Odd Fellows were taught to be unselfish, and to consider everywhere, in the Order and in their lives, to the extent of their ability, the claims, upon their sympathy and charity, of dependent beings like themselves.

Self must be sacrificed in the presence of these manifold demands upon them — hence, we very early find incorpo-rated into the primary statutes, a system of weekly dues, and systematic relief: the obligatory payment of stated weekly benefits to the sick; funeral benefits, assuring the decent sepulture of the brother's body; optional benefits, that the "Great Command" should always be within the scope of the Order's known duty: "Visit the Sick, Relieve the Dis-tressed, Bury the Dead, and Educate the Orphan." This special characteristic of the practice of Friendship, prompted

by Love, and upheld by Truth, inheres solely in Odd Fellowship. Whatever others may do, the Order's mission is
to enable brethren to assist each other, by mutual counsels,
and united financial efforts, in the multiplied struggles and
trials common to human existence.

In this way the law of sacrifice became the axiom of
the Order's inner life. Thus, following the rule of the
Divine and natural economy, it "inherited the promises."
With the development of the system, this tenet was
expanded and "Moses, the Law-giver," became our ensam-
ple of unselfishness without a parallel; the adopted son of
royalty, learned in the wisdom of Egypt's golden age and
civilization, he forsook them all — princely associations,
station, power, becoming an outcast, bearing the rod of
fidelity, which is perpetuated as one of the twin tokens of
Odd Fellowship. The other token, "Rainbow of Promise,"
symbolizes the victory attained by Moses when he was led
forth from his abasement to his glorious reward, and
unknown burial by the hand of God.

Such is the figure, typical of the lot of the brother who
is "Faithful to his vows, and fraternal to his fellow-man."

It may be asked : Why emphasize the self-denial of
Moses, and, afterwards, an exhibition of Abraham's faith in
the Almighty, in the Ritual of the Order ?

The answer is implied by the third link in "our mystic
chain "—Truth. The discovery and recognition of the
Brotherhood of Man foreshadowed the higher article of
belief — the Fatherhood of God.

Our Creator is Jehovah because He is the Eternal Father:
one important attribute of fatherhood, Love, is the free gift
of self for others, which delights in opening the treasures of
life for another's welfare and happiness, so that this acknowledged, Odd Fellowship, by the examples quoted, stands
well defined as an Order based upon an enduring foundation. This harmonized, and perfected into a sublime one-
ness, the precept and practice of the three-fold graces of the
immortal motto : Friendship, Love, Truth.

Through our early literature runs the thread of an

appeal to antiquity, as if the theory of a modern society was not the thought in the minds of Odd Fellows. There is so much witchery attached to ancient ruins, and such a solemn awe surrounds temples erected by hands long since crumbled to dust, that many were impressed with the belief that a traditional descent, traced from some remote age, would give to the struggling Order some new harbinger of hope, or impart an alchemistic "elixir of life." But this theory obtained few followers and was soon abandoned. Nevertheless, the research of to-day presents interesting evidence that each era of the world's progress has probably fostered fraternities tending to make the governments thereof more beneficent.

In Egypt's "Book of the Dead," written two thousand years before Abraham was born (according to a late chronology), and of recent translation, occurs a passage, interesting in this connection, because of its correspondence with Odd Fellowship's "Great Commission," viz:

"He hath given bread to the hungry, water to the thirsty, clothes to the naked; he hath given a boat to the shipwrecked; he hath made due offerings to the gods, and paid due rites to the departed."

This was possibly a portion of the ritualistic lesson by which Moses was initiated into the royal family; and when presented before the golden throne, in that supreme moment of earthly exaltion, he was also enjoined: "Mind thee of the day when thou, too, shalt start for that [dead] land."

The convivial practices of our early brethren had a counterpart in these ancient mysteries, for, at the conclusion of the elaborate ceremonial, as well as at various stages of its progress, covering days and weeks of time, refreshments, with wine and other accessories, were consumed, the culmination of which may possibly be paralleled by a reference to Persian life, at the court in Shushan, during the reign of Ahasuerus, the Xerxes of ancient history.

During the first decades of our Order, these recently discovered facts, if known, would have afforded an inex-

haustible mine of resource for those advocating the legend
of a traceable connection, or affinity, with antiquity.

(B) The second epoch, with its enlarged privileges,
follows from the very nature of our history. The Order
was moving onward from victory to victory, but it was not
best "for man to be alone," and the Degree of Rebekah, in
1851, was added to the complement of degrees.

This result might have been foreseen. Odd Fellowship
comprehending all that had been claimed, and aiming to
establish a universal dominion over the minds and hearts of
its members, seeking to redeem man from selfishness and
raise humanity above the subtle influences that debase it, to
a plane, where, with united front, the great hand-to-hand
battle with evil must be fought, found that its ranks should
include all those, who, in any way, stood in need of its
offices.

The family, no less than the fraternity, destined to
endure suffering and misery, sickness and death, is, also,
entitled to human sympathy. The Order's weapons, forged
in Heaven, may as well be wielded by the hand of woman
as by man. The wife, the widowed mother, the sister, the
daughter, are equally competent to rejoice in the triumph
of Friendship over selfishness, Love over hatred, Truth over
falsehood, as her natural protector and chevalier.

(C) The transition to the third epoch, in 1885, though
natural and logical, was long delayed. The preliminary
strife was necessary to prepare for its advent. It was a
growth rather than a new creation.

The great Order of Odd Fellowship had thrown itself
as a solid mass into the cause of justice, mercy, and upright-
ness. Through similar efforts — recording many a failure,
and, anon, girded with the might of some prevailing conquests, with only dim hints and glimpses remaining of the
long and traditional strife by which, through slow and patient struggles — man has evolved himself from the savage
state, found time and strength to study and comprehend the
larger issues, in which lay the beginnings of government

and growth of society, of which the family is the unit, and has wrought out the fact of this century's civilization.

This impulse, with its fixed intent, came to us from out of the dark heart of the mysterious East.

The Order, also, arose from that source, began its benign work for humanity, and had assumed almost colossal proportions (during the two periods named), by a like conflict.

Reasoning from analogy, our Order, in pursuance of its great mission to teach and propagate the doctrine of the Universal Brotherhood of Man, a mission hardly begun, and only to be ended with the dawn of the millennial day, must be fully equipped for the long and portentous struggle.

The impulse must be given direction; the organization must be complete. With woman a component of Odd Fellowship, knightly courtesy, the glory of the race, must likewise be incorporated. The Patriarchs Militant furnished the "cap-stone," and "crowned the fabric."

An Odd Fellow of the "Grandest Degree," in another sense, is sworn to protect the maiden, the wife, the widow, the orphan, in their rights; and "to permit no extortion," if preventable; "to support those who are weak, and powerless; to administer justice to the advancement of honor, and the suppression of vice."

Without arrogating to himself higher social functions than ought to be held by all good men, the Chevalier bows in acknowledgment of the peculiar graces which adorn and endear woman, even in her minutest charms, and reverences the beauty of soul of which her outward form is the interpreter.

The Daughter of Rebekah is enthroned queen in our mystic temple, and her more than twenty thousand Chevaliers, and rapidly increasing army of Patriarchs Militant, will ever demand that she be accorded the tender homage due the exalted character of her sex, and that her image, bearing the spiritual loveliness attributed to sweet and saintly Madonnas, be forever enshrined in the hearts and affections of men.

Actuated by motives and governed by principles like these, the Three Branches of Odd Fellowship, like a mighty host, comprehensive in its organization and work, are moving onward to record a more noble history.

The rising sun of this century had gotten himself well up from his golden bed in the East, the region of promise, before his beams could warm and cheer the one Lodge and its five humble members.

These hardy pioneers were sheltered from the storm with little better than a cabin built of drift-wood, rudely thrown together, through the cracks and crevices of which the rays of light shone in, as if the sun himself hastened to become their day-spring. Cheered by these tokens of heavenly benediction the five Patriarchs raised aloft the colors of the Order, held the staff with firm hands while the favoring breeze unfolded the primitive flag upon which was inscribed the motto : Friendship, Love, Truth, proclaiming the Fatherhood of God and the Brotherhood of Man.

The sun at the century's meridian warmed into new life the Order thus established. Few of the Early Fathers lived to see that auspicious day, however, but the test of the tree was the fruit thereof.

The Lodge of five had grown, in 1850, to an army of 174, 637, gathered into 2,354 Lodges; then dispensing for relief, annually, the large sum of $483,404.15, divided as follows : Relief of brothers, $347,450.59; widowed families, $42,410.33 ; education of the orphan, $7,348.44; burying the dead, $68,056.71 ; other assistance rendered, $18,138.08.

And now, with the gold, and blue, and purple, gathering in the West, as the century's sun declines amid its billowy light, while the evening shadows grow apace, *there*, in its well-defined lines, stands the mystic temple of Odd Fellowship, known and respected of all men.

The rude cabin of the morning, assuming the proportions of a symmetrical building at noon, has, with the progress of the age, become the stately temple of the evening, with its gorgeous decorations, where the perpetual incense of tender ministries of mercy rises from its holy altars, and around whose shrines gather, annually, more than half a million brethren, and from the portals of which were disbursed in 1886, the munificent sum of $2,227,324.50, out of a total revenue of $5,659,772.37.

To give a fuller expression of this munificence, as well as to indicate, in a more forcible manner, the results of our continued occupation of cities, towns, villages, and the acquisition of new fields of labor abroad, all of which make possible this great prosperity, reference is here made to a table, in another place, showing " The Progress of the Order from the Year 1840 to 1886, inclusive," and exclusive of Australasia and Germany ; also to the following statistical summaries. The first gives the condition of the Order, December 31, 1886, in these terms :

Sovereign Grand Lodge	1
Independent Grand Lodges (German Empire and Australasia)	2
Subordinate Grand Encampments	47
Subordinate Encampments	2,016
Subordinate Grand Lodges	65
Subordinate Lodges	8,334
Encampment members	100,223
Lodge members	547,856

Those not of us, while they have not failed to note the enlarging of our resources, and the value to the body politic of our extended and extending benevolence, little realize the wonderful volume of attainments shown by the second table, giving, as far as information can be obtained, the statistics of the Order from the year 1830 to December 31, 1886, as follows :

Initiations in Subordinate Lodges	1,460,459
Members relieved	1,265,268
Widowed families relieved	163,573
Members deceased	124,060
Total relief	$43,589,061.87
Total receipts	115,014,145.25

Men are surprised whenever the princely sum paid for relief is mentioned, and especially are they lost in wonder when told that the enormous sum of $43,589,061.87, is exclusive of Relief Associations and all auxiliary means — that it represents the aggregate disbursed within the Order's inner doors (taking into account the impediments overcome, and the contumely encountered during many of the earlier years).

The law of sacrifice is shown even in financial matters. These vast accumulations came not from the rich, who of their abundance bestowed charity. They came from the man of moderate means, the hardy yeoman, the humble mechanic, the worker in all classes, who, loving his brethren, gave a few cents weekly.

The record, glorious as it is, does not represent all the Order has done, or is doing. To know this the inner life must be investigated : the nightly ministrations followed through the thousands, and tens of thousands, of quiet channels ; the silent watches beside the sick and the dying,

" While stars their sleepless vigil kept."

The care for, and burial of, the dead ; the widening avenues of relief in the increasing auxiliary ways of rendering assistance, adding (to the sums noted above) during the past few years, $9,533,679.55 ; and now nearly $1,500,000, annually (and rapidly augmenting), paid to the widows and orphans of Odd Fellows by the several voluntary Relief Associations connected with Odd Fellowship.

The many other methods, kindred in their character, should also be regarded : libraries, schools, homes for the aged and indigent, orphan asylums, committees for general relief and employment, systems of lectures and public instruction, and savings banks — all these are powerful bonds of union.

From the " Odd Fellows Female Collegiate Institute," at Rogersville, Tenn., in 1854, followed by the " Martha Washington College," at Abington, Va., in 1855, both institutions projected for the education of the orphaned daughters of Odd Fellows, down to 1870 and 1871, when "schools, asylums, libraries, and like institutions," had so multiplied these auxiliaries that the *Grand Sires considered them of sufficient

---

* E. D. Farnsworth, Fred D. Stuart.

importance to enumerate their worth, and the Sovereign Grand Body acknowledged their value and recommended fostering care, to our own day when homes and other charitable institutions exist in many Grand Jurisdictions, and are planned in nearly all the others, have these optional means of aiding the Order in its grand work increased.

In 1870, it was recorded of the first home of the Independent Order: " It is now thirty-nine years since Maryland entered upon the education of the orphan." The " Home " beneficence! who can compute its aggregate value and comfort to the aged and infirm, from the Grand Jurisdiction of Pennsylvania, with its Philadelphia institution and $60,000 assets, to the latest one projected, or established?

Many of these attainments are due to our great and noble principles, but to our policy of administration, following closely that of the government of the United States, combined with the self-sacrificing labors of a devoted membership, is the world indebted for the boon of Odd Fellowship.

These brethren watch the sunset as its colors deepen in the West; they view with honest pride their temple of Odd Fellowship, upon which the century's sun is soon to set. Diamonds, emeralds, pearls, rubies, precious stones, are not brighter than the jewels of sacrifice, of noble and unselfish deeds performed for humanity, which sparkle in the waning light; these grace the walls as well as deck the inner shrines, and symbolize drops of refreshment from the · River of Everlasting Life.

The site of our temple is a goodly heritage. Underlying the grand moral structure, and forming its foundation, rests the immutable rock Fraternity, an essential and fundamental Truth which cannot be shaken by the wars and convulsions of earth.

Upon this base securely rest the four corner-stones, and above it rise the walls, composed of the same fraternal material. These corner-stones bear the " Great Commission," viz : " We Command you to Visit the Sick, Relieve the Distressed, Bury the Dead, and Educate the Orphan."

The walls are laid with millions of minute stones, jewels every one, firmly cemented together, representing in their individuality the mites contributed in response to the Order's calls — myriads, in number, like the sands of the sea, in their combination a glorious building !

Who laid these foundations ? Brothers cast in the stern mold of unsullied integrity. The Fathers possessed minds superior to fear, to selfish interests; governed in all things by the principles of rectitude and sterling worth, they were the same in prosperity or adversity ; neither by pleasure melted into effeminacy, nor by distress sunk into dejection, their persevering efforts fairly compelled men to recognize the Order, and assured its ultimate eminence in their sight, as they swept down the avenue of time and disappeared through the gate of death.

The outer walls are decked with the "jewels of sacrifice," and the floor is tiled with like material. The divisions of this golden pavement are, each, a memorial of the noble and honored successors, as well as of the founders, of this superb structure ; its roof is the floor of Heaven.

Three spires arise, Friendship, Love, Truth, standards by which the Order is judged of men ; they are, therefore, raised aloft in their sight : Friendship, the motive ; Love, to nerve and urge us on ; Truth, to bear the Odd Fellows' flag and the Patriarchs Militant's banner on high.

The threshold has engraved upon it the Golden Rule precept of "Toleration," corollary of the inscription, "Brotherhood of Man," above the door.

Inside the edifice, underneath a glowing arch, bearing the words, "Fatherhood of God," approached by eight burnished Degree steps (and these steps represented upon the inner walls by priceless paintings), is our High Altar, in the rear of which stand the figures *Pax aut Bellum.* The golden shield adorning the altar frontal, below the jewelled crown, bears the chivalric motto : *Justitia Universalis.* In the presence of the Angel of Peace, War has sheathed the sword.

Four steps upward from the floor is a platform with Scarlet coverings, outlining a resting place.

Upon the left side of this, and rising one pace therefrom, rests a shining side-altar, Evangel of the Order.

Around this shrine gather loved forms. What a soft and holy grace floats about their presence, calms us when they are near, draws us closer and closer, and speaks of peace, purity, and every lovely thing ; how gentle the waving of their hands; how hopeful the deep sympathies in their eyes and hearts; how tender, gracious, and unselfish are all their doings ; how full and rich the sound of their voices ; how bright and cheering their coming; how sad their final departure ; and if sorrow or distress assail us, how confidingly we turn to them, and willingly resign ourselves to their undoubted delicacy of touch; how persuasive are they in all their goodness — what Odd Fellow does not, with the Chevalier, bow before Rebekah's throne !

We are in the company, let us say, of men and women like ourselves; separately in part, and again together, we participate in ancestral rites made classic by time ; while, with united voice, we rehearse the grand and solemn litanies which are destined to float like sweet refrains for æons and æons.

The processions come and go within this temple like those of the ages. Their mission is to instruct, advance, exalt ; and, last but not least, to fulfil the "second tie" in Odd Fellowship's "Great Command." As one after another pauses before the symbolic pictures on the walls it is discovered that these paintings are a part and parcel of the building — each pointing to the skies; each inculcating, in a most impressive manner, some tenet of the Order, by which the brother, if faithful to his obligations, must be governed. Whether it is the neophyte, sitting at the feet of "Age and Experience," learning the lesson and symbolism of the burial of an Odd Fellow in the passing procession clothed in dark robes, marching with solemn tread ; or, anon, studiously regarding the representation of the "Covenant of Friendship ;" the journey, memorable for its parable of Brotherly Love, the very bond of unity, teaching the "first tie" in a most practical manner; or, again, the Truth of the Priestly Order, which "Consecrates the whole and leads to victory," the way to the "resting place," with its Scarlet decorations, is the "rule of life" for a majority of the brethren.

Should the forms be decked with waving plumes and armed with flashing steel, the unerring paintings will show that the fatigues of the Patriarch's life have been overcome, its faith accepted; the lesson of Toleration, and the Golden Rule, learned; the "Journey of Life" accomplished in symbol, and the soldierly armor of the Order put on. Whatever the station or the dress, the same peculiar light, rays from the Eternal Throne, greets their coming:

> "Hark! the sound of holy voices,
> Chanting o'er the crystal sea."

These are the one hundred, twenty and four thousand and sixty, gladly welcoming (in ever increasing numbers) to his reward the faithful member of the Order, while his surviving brethren, remembering only his virtues, tenderly lay his body at rest in "Mother Earth."

Our temple is completed; our work is its defence. The Odd Fellow fights not for himself alone, but also for his brothers and sisters. The morning is sure to follow the night of trial; suffering and sickness shall flee away, and if faithful to vows the dawn will find each and every one clothed in the robes of eternal youth.

When the Angel of the Morning shall take his station to behold the rise of the twentieth century's sun, the vigil beginning, in similitude, just before

> "The winged chorus of the sky
> Chirrup their matins!"

His vision shall be that of a man upon a mountain; the valley enveloped in a thick darkness, for the moment, from which even the light of twinkling stars has fled away; the black clouds rolling in waves before the first rays of light like the troubled sea; a shudder passes over the watcher, and he turns his eyes toward the source of light and promise. The picture in the eastern skies is enrapturing by contrast; billows of silver and golden light herald the near approach of the orb of day, painting the scene from horizon to zenith, beyond the power of man to imitate, until the full splendor bursts over the valley, chasing away the last lingering shadow of the night, bathing the landscape in the glory of yellow light ; then shall the radiance of the coming century's sun adorn and gild the temple of Odd Fellowship, and the benison of Heaven shall rest upon it forever.

CHAPTER XIV.

A TABLE FOR NEW YORK,

Showing the Progress of the Order from 1824 to 1886,
Inclusive.

Year.	No of. Lodges.	No. of Members.	Total Relief.	Relief per Member.	Total Receipts.	Receipts per Member.
1824	1	*	*	*	*	*
1825	3	*	*	*	*	*
1826	3	*	*	*	*	*
1827	4	*	*	*	*	*
1828	6	*	*	*	*	*
1829–30	7	*	*	*	*	*
1831	4	*	*	*	*	*
1832	6	*	*	*	*	*
1833	6	*	*	*	*	*
1834	9	348	*	*	$1,623	$4.66
1835	10	529	*	*	3,142	5.93
1836	13	754	*	*	4,162	5.51
1837	*	*	*	*	*	*
1888	10	752	$1,306	$1.72	2,909	3.86
1839	14	1,132	1,318	1.16	6,285	5.55
1840	28	2,477	4,578	1.84	16,259	6.56

Showing the Progress of the Order from 1824 to 1886, Inclusive.

Year.	No. of Lodges.	No. of Members.	Total Relief.	Relief per Member.	Total Receipts.	Receipts per Member.
1841	42	6,624	$10,843	$1.63	$46,710	$7.02
1842	62	8,763	24,842	2.83	59,495	6.78
1843	81	10,001	31,016	3.10	64,708	6.47
1844	113	12,496	35,275	2.82	86,700	6.93
1845	161	16,498	50,358	3.05	123,850	7.50
1846	239	23,745	64,031	2.69	197,462	8.31
1847	309	30,296	86,196	2.84	232,980	7.69
†1848	351	34,370	103,760	3.01	228,231	6.64
1849	216	39,440	106,635	2.70	258,945	6.56
1850	540	42,701	142,701	3.34	290,819	6.79
1851	603	45,436	121,257	2.66	303,104	6.67
1852	641	45,003	122,747	2.72	282,329	6.27
1853	656	39,997	117,322	2.93	236,747	5.91
1854	649	39,613	94,040	2.37	239,412	6.04
1855	653	33,343	93,880	2.81	197,485	5.92
1856	644	29,258	69,522	2.37	156,560	5.35
1857	635	23,661	60,016	2.53	118,229	4.99
1858	623	20,258	58,595	2.89	114,788	5.66
1859	611	18,915	48,461	2.56	101,625	5.37
1860	611	15,799	46,196	2.92	95,235	6.02
1861	610	13,734	47,932	3.49	90,118	6.56
1862	603	12,320	44,051	3.57	82,250	6.67
1863	600	11,711	40,048	3.59	81,281	6.94
1864	*	11,983	39,245	3.27	86,849	7.24
1865	213	12,672	43,617	3.44	96,094	7.58
1866	‡100	14,028	37,049	2.64	79,767	5.68
1867	195	14,817	40,033	2.70	100,752	6.79
1868	196	16,271	50,442	2.10	142,086	8.73
1869	210	17,950	51,663	2.87	162,488	9.05
1870	245	20,732	50,413	2.43	186,925	9.01
1871	306	26,826	115,721	4.31	354,783	13.22
1872	339	33,140	133,563	4.03	414,069	12.49
1873	368	35,665	126,394	3.54	341,277	9.59
1874	410	38,429	136,758	3.55	342,989	8.90
1875	441	39,943	147,746	3.69	345,337	8.64
1876	454	39,626	151,684	3.82	333,762	8.42
1877	466	38,632	150,407	3.89	329,744	8.53
1878	470	38,160	162,721	4.26	327,969	8.59
1879	481	48,618	153,781	3.16	318,149	6.54
1880	487	38,428	152,867	3.97	322,977	8.40
1881	488	39,312	162,550	4.13	324,451	8.25
1882	499	40,838	171,744	4.25	366,695	8.97
1883	485	41,864	184,967	4.41	372,309	8.89
1884	486	42,277	190,974	4.51	377,306	8.92
1885	496	42,406	197,402	4.65	387,546	9.11
1886	514	44,191	201,492	4.55	401,982	9.09
			$4,480,109		$10,239,149	

* No Report.
† Northern and Southern New York.
‡ Only the Lodges in Southern New York

A TABLE FOR MARYLAND,

Showing the Progress of the Order from 1830 to 1886, Inclusive.

Year.	No. of Lodges.	No. of Members.	Total Relief.	Relief per Member.	Total Receipts.	Receipts per Member.
1830	5	709	*	*	*	*
1831	12	1,500	*	*	*	*
1832	19	1,520	*	*	$10,822	$7.12
1833	21	1,781	$2,125	$1.19	3,968	2.22
1834	17	1,434	2,194	1.53	7,976	5.56
1835	19	1,455	2,744	1.88	5,821	4.00
1836	21	1,329	2,839	2.13	6,544	4.92
1837	22	1,475	2,786	1.88	2,397	1.62
1838	23	1,603	2,787	1.10	6,684	4.16
1839	24	1,752	3,219	1.83	7,743	4.41
1840	26	1,663	2,709	1.62	9,016	5.42
1841	28	2,119	4,552	2.14	18,250	8.61
1842	24	2,337	6,336	2.71	13,227	5.65
1843	25	2,669	7,886	2.96	13,264	4.96
1844	29	3,115	8,392	2.69	16,343	5.25
1845	26	4,065	8,898	2.18	23,265	5.71
1846	32	5,285	15,973	3.02	31,083	5.88
1847	41	6,197	36,311	5.85	44,239	7.13
1848	46	7,570	14,469	1.91	56,841	7.50
1849	66	8,592	33,984	3.95	65,582	7.63
1850	62	9,614	39,157	4.07	70,426	7.32
1851	70	10,787	53,560	4.96	82,425	7.64
1852	70	11,433	58,809	5.14	80,721	7.07
1853	77	12,259	58,985	4.81	89,284	7.22
1854	80	13,070	59,371	4.54	93,388	7.14
1855	82	13,332	72,607	5.44	91,203	6.91
1856	83	12,906	60,701	4.70	87,195	6.75
1857	85	13,146	60,310	4 58	87,176	6.63
1858	90	12,360	59,039	4.77	89,676	7.25
1859	90	12,300	58,340	4.74	103,514	8.41
1860	90	12,128	57,156	4.71	88,986	7.34
1861	91	11,929	59,254	4.96	98,419	8.25
1862	91	11,199	59,063	5.27	85,789	7.66
1863	83	11,058	54,876	4.96	74,748	6.76
1864	83	10,306	61,797	5.99	84,763	8.22
1865	80	10,782	63,009	5.84	93,588	8.70
1866	78	11,446	64,595	5.67	107,376	9.38
1867	82	12,237	61,155	5.00	104,908	8.57
1868	86	13,025	62,776	4 81	118,149	9.07
1869	89	13,427	65,242	4 85	117,810	8.77
1870	93	13,715	73,222	5.33	116,850	8.52
1871	99	13,682	130,376	9.45	189,052	13.81
1872	100	13,386	89,031	6.65	133,167	9.94
1873	101	13,529	70,972	5.24	132,585	9 80
1874	103	13,138	83,529	6.35	124,557	9 48
1875	105	12,663	79,979	6.31	110,983	8.76
1876	105	12,118	79,329	6.54	98,829	8.15
1877	104	11,037	84,073	7.22	98,152	8.43
1878	104	11,320	73,833	6.52	99,273	8.77
1879	105	12,020	73,075	6.07	97,090	8.07
1880	105	10,924	71,030	6.50	94,587	8.65
1881	105	10,785	61,353	5.68	87,349	8.08
1882	106	10,513	67,753	6.44	89,215	8.48
1883	104	10,078	62,539	6.25	83,077	8.24
1884	104	9,692	58,132	6.00	69,457	7.16
1885	106	9,381	52,874	5.63	73,250	7.81
1886	107	9,052	50,584	5.58	75,127	8.30
			$2,609,690		$3,965,102	

* No Report.
The Relief for the years 1833–1837, inclusive, was taken from the Journal of the Grand Lodge of Maryland.

A TABLE FOR MASSACHUSETTS,

Showing the Progress of the Order from 1842 to 1886, Inclusive.

Year.	No. of Lodges	No. of Members.	Total Relief.	Relief per Member.	Total Receipts.	Receipts per Member.
1842	7	310	$188	$0.60	$2,056	$6.63
1843	14	1,489	1,498	1.00	13,077	8.78
1844	40	4,298	4,889	1.13	41,956	9.76
1845	78	8,254	15,509	1.87	86,269	10.45
1846	114	11,836	29,513	2.49	104,239	8.80
1847	119	12,613	37,704	2.99	75,329	5.17
1848	124	12,256	33,571	2.73	63,043	5.14
1849	130	11,881	31,914	2.68	57,761	4.86
1850	128	11,031	29,839	2.70	56,198	5.09
1851	128	9,701	26,270	2.70	48,541	5.00
1852	121	8,952	26,190	2.92	43,093	4.81
1853	111	8,066	23,233	2.81	37,855	4.69
1854	103	7,585	22,915	3.02	38,228	5.04
1855	94	6,958	18,550	2.66	32,281	4.63
1856	86	6,238	17,770	2.84	17,942	2.87
1857	75	5,661	16,161	2.84	27,529	4.86
1858	71	5,313	14,728	2.77	25,902	4.87
1859	67	4,859	14,785	3.04	19,787	4.07
1860	60	4,602	13,131	2.85	26,215	5.69
1861	60	4,521	11,409	2.52	23,906	5.28
1862	58	4,308	15,572	3.61	20,989	4.87
1863	58	4,312	17,053	3.95	24,830	5.75
1864	58	4,482	16,937	3.77	30,249	6.74
1865	58	4,998	19,669	3.93	36,991	7.40
1866	59	5,706	26,308	4.61	51,757	9.07
1867	59	6,671	29,540	4.43	55,903	8.38
1868	64	7,971	17,982	2.25	69,060	8.66
1869	70	9,491	19,726	2.07	89,513	9.43
1870	76	10,819	23,040	2.12	101,942	9.42
1871	95	13,682	47,078	3.44	157,241	11.52
1872	100	15,650	38,627	2.46	152,903	9.07
1873	105	17,459	41,878	2.39	184,602	10.57
1874	118	19,262	48,687	2.52	182,832	9.49
1875	128	20,972	56,612	2.69	201,886	9.62
1876	134	21,685	57,975	2.67	179,078	8.25
1877	140	22,520	64,511	2.86	191,916	8.52
1878	150	23,218	64,594	2.70	197,870	8.53
1879	155	23,869	68,447	2.86	197,766	8.28
1880	156	24,965	67,324	2.85	211,751	8.48
1881	159	26,147	76,213	2.83	231,292	8.84
1882	164	27,483	80,211	2.91	252,614	9.19
1883	167	28,799	87,299	3.10	274,295	9.52
1884	172	30,115	94,198	3.12	264,390	8.77
1885	175	31,218	104,499	3.34	272,878	8.74
1886	179	32,759	111,072	3.39	303,586	9.26
			$1,684,821		$4,779,341	

A TABLE FOR PENNSYLVANIA,

Showing the Progress of the Order from 1827 to 1886, Inclusive.

Year.	No. of Lodges.	No. of Members.	Total Relief.	Relief per Member.	Total Receipts.	Receipts per Member.
1827	4	*	*	*	*	*
1828	6	568	*	*	*	*
1829	13	1,009	*	*	$5,812	$5.76
1830	33	2,247	*	*	12,905	5.74
1831	38	2,753	*	*	15,822	5.74
1832	50	3,603	*	*	21,348	5.92
1833	52	3,872	*	*	16,259	4.19
1834	48	3,881	*	*	13,922	3.63
1835	42	3,293	*	*	12,434	3.77
1836	50	3,106	*	*	12,883	4.14
1837	51	3,085	*	*	13,375	4.33
1838	40	2,665	*	*	11,527	4.32
1839	40	3,180	*	*	13,594	4.27
1840	45	3,194	*	*	13,698	4.22
1841	47	3,618	*	*	15,391	4.25
1842	53	4,403	*	*	20,522	4.66
1843	62	5,116	$8,862	$1.73	26,417	5.16
1844	72	5,935	9,483	1.59	29,562	4.98
1845	97	8,786	14,857	1.69	36,769	4.18
1846	182	15,629	25,049	1.60	95,893	6.11
1847	253	23,105	42,915	1.85	139,789	6.05
1848	308	29,093	67,642	2.32	173,311	5.95
1849	363	33,268	83,044	2.49	172,757	5.19
1850	398	38,193	94,927	2.43	204,268	5.34
1851	445	42,394	102,767	2.42	221,595	5.23
1852	460	44,237	119,649	2.70	220,964	4.77
1853	470	44,122	91,381	2.07	173,255	3.92
1854	496	46,588	114,508	2.45	244,719	5.25
1855	505	46,117	130,461	2.83	227,935	4.94
1856	508	43,114	119,767	2.77	221,624	5.11
1857	517	46,375	113,223	2.44	237,867	5.10
1858	508	44,119	112,051	2.53	204,483	4.63
1859	511	42,542	110,577	2.59	225,966	5.31
1860	504	41,769	104,999	2.51	239,926	5.74
1861	503	41,099	118,746	2.88	166,550	4.05
1862	483	38,564	110,305	2.86	206,523	5.35
1863	477	37,646	116,227	3.08	232,601	6.12
1864	467	39,548	132,163	3.34	261,567	6.61
1865	475	43,993	147,343	3.34	321,949	7.31
1866	474	51,798	160,518	3.09	393,400	7.59
1867	498	59,183	190,080	3.21	456,871	7.71
1868	526	66,235	206,116	3.14	523,290	7.90
1869	549	69,970	225,703	3.22	522,979	7.47
1870	601	75,565	250,777	3.31	630,799	8.34
1871	664	80,153	276,501	3.44	670,718	8.36
1872	754	91,213	397,311	4.35	795,617	8.72
1873	800	95,197	363,591	3.81	898,302	9.43
1874	844	96,844	378,858	3.91	814,940	8.41

A TABLE FOR PENNSYLVANIA.—*Continued*.

Showing the Progress of the Order from 1827 to 1886, Inclusive.

Year.	No. of Lodges.	No. of Members.	Total Relief.	Relief per Member.	Total Receipts.	Receipts per Member.
1875	878	94,892	$385,548	$4.07	$798,111	$8.41
1876	894	91,738	379,266	4.13	764,825	8.33
1877	899	85,361	365,566	4.28	711,209	8.33
1878	905	80,118	343,725	4.28	663,761	8.28
1879	905	76,369	345,854	4.52	647,990	8.48
1880	898	76,476	343,237	4.48	686,940	8.98
1881	894	77,134	357,680	4.59	710,231	9.12
1882	895	80,389	371,578	4.62	779,235	9.69
1883	904	80,504	379,531	4.71	760,452	9.44
1884	911	81,317	393,935	4.84	750,357	9.22
1885	914	80,824	422,124	5.22	747,660	9.24
1886	932	81,480	406,960	4.99	759,602	9.31
			$9,035,405		$18,763,361	

* No Report.

A TABLE FOR THE DISTRICT OF COLUMBIA,
Showing the Progress of the Order from 1830 to 1886,
Inclusive.

Year.	No. of Lodges.	No. of Members.	Total Relief.	Relief per Member.	Total Receipts.	Receipts per Member.
1830	4	80	*	*	$395	$4.94
1831	5	99	*	*	482	4.87
1832	4	130	*	*	538	4.14
1833	3	*	*	*	*	*
1834	3	*	*	*	1,409	*
1835	3	114	*	*	408	3.58
1836	3	104	*	*	561	5.39
1837	3	115	*	*	513	4.45
1838	3	113	*	*	685	6.06
1839	5	209	$377	$1.80	1,391	6.66
1840	6	367	570	1.55	3,179	8.66
1841	7	465	*	*	2,624	5.64
1842	7	631	1,965	3.11	4,762	7.78
1843	9	719	2,874	7.05	3,942	5.42
1844	10	866	2,523	2.82	5,526	6.37
1845	11	1,111	3,016	2.71	7,720	7.04
1846	14	1,399	3,068	2.19	9,006	6.44
1847	13	1,634	3,762	2.30	8,551	5.23
1848	13	1,307	2,933	2.24	6,617	5.06
1849	13	1,216	3,842	3.15	6,972	6.56
1850	13	1,160	3,206	2.76	6,962	6.00
1851	13	1,195	3,811	3.20	6,940	5.86
1852	13	1,283	3,817	2.98	7,813	6.09
1853	13	1,279	3,832	3.00	7,457	5.83
1854	13	1,339	4,170	2.86	7,632	5.70
1855	13	1,363	5,331	3.91	8,876	6.51
1856	13	1,370	4,936	3.60	7,711	5.63
1857	13	1,311	4,534	3.46	7,807	5.10
1858	13	1,355	4,054	2.99	9,107	6.72
1859	13	1,397	4,665	3.34	9,408	6.73
1860	13	1,371	4,860	3.54	9,057	6.60
1861	13	1,329	3,862	2.90	7,806	5.87
1862	10	1,270	5,200	4.09	8,478	6.60
1863	13	1,404	5,063	3.60	12,449	8.81
1864	13	1,676	7,446	4.44	14,355	8.57
1865	13	1,998	6,537	3.27	18,966	9.49
1866	13	2,156	8,805	4.08	21,901	10.16
1867	13	2,321	11,067	4.77	23,841	10.27
1868	13	2,412	11,249	4.67	23,008	9.54
1869	13	2,348	11,335	4.83	19,918	8.48
1870	13	2,327	11,220	4.82	19,121	8.22
1871	13	2,389	18,710	7.83	33,484	14.00
1872	13	2,227	15,209	6.82	27,082	12.16
1873	13	2,197	14,533	6.62	25,483	11.60
1874	13	2,167	10,220	4.71	22,004	10.15
1875	13	2,056	13,099	6.37	23,947	11.16
1876	13	1,952	12,792	6.55	21,869	11.20
1877	14	1,892	11,274	5.95	21,128	11.16
1878	14	1,791	9,344	5.22	19,075	11.21
1879	14	1,894	8,224	4.34	17,931	9.47
1880	15	1,926	9,472	4.92	19,709	10.23
1881	15	1,854	11,308	6.09	20,691	11.16
1882	15	1,830	9,643	5.27	18,405	10.05
1883	15	1,814	9,378	5.17	19,995	11.02
1884	15	1,811	11,568	6.39	17,215	9.51
1885	15	1,862	10,517	5.64	21,662	11.63
1886	15	1,620	9,499	5.86	18,815	11.61
			$338,720		$672,389	

*No Report.

A TABLE FOR DELAWARE,
Showing the Progress of the Order from 1833 to 1886, Inclusive.

Year.	No. of Lodges.	No. of Members.	Total Relief.	Relief per Member.	Total Receipts.	Receipts per Member.
1833	4	125	*	*	*	*
1834	5	*	*	*	*	*
1835	5	151	*	*	$776	$5.13
1836	4	*	*	*	*	*
1837	*	*	*	*	*	*
1838	*	*	*	*	*	*
1839	*	*	*	*	*	*
1840	*	*	*	*	*	*
1841	3	45	*	*	239	5.31
1842	3	102	*	*	583	5.71
1843	5	129	*	*	905	7.01
1844	4	200	*	*	1,223	6.11
1845	5	286	*	*	2,175	7.50
1846	6	447	$456	$1.02	2,738	6.12
1847	11	692	799	1.15	4,150	5.99
1848	16	1,037	2,570	2.47	6,923	6.67
1849	21	1,447	2,378	1.64	12,363	8.54
1850	23	1,566	3,386	2.16	8,804	5.62
1851	24	1,744	1,929	1.10	8,804	5.04
1852	23	1,803	3,227	1.78	8,804	4.88
1853	23	1,975	4,886	2.47	17,195	8.70
1854	24	2,102	5,236	2.49	*	*
1855	24	2,164	5,842	2.70	11,231	5.19
1856	25	2,085	5,763	2.76	9,673	4.63
1857	26	2,059	4,919	2.38	8,212	4.00
1858	26	1,968	3,560	1.80	*	*
1859	28	1,923	3,607	1.87	9,415	4.89
1860	28	1,939	3,864	1.99	11,242	5.79
1861	27	1,862	2,125	1.14	7,897	4.24
1862	27	1,742	3,260	1.87	8,243	4.73
1863	27	1,682	3,481	2.06	6,946	4.12
1864	27	1,712	4,969	2.90	9,615	5.61
1865	28	1,889	4,953	2.62	11,601	6.14
1866	29	2,189	5,996	2.73	13,198	6.02
1867	29	2,438	7.281	2.98	13,850	5.68
1868	30	2,551	7,637	2.99	14,115	5.52
1869	30	2,603	6,847	2.63	14,451	5.55
1870	31	2,654	6,510	2.45	14,817	5.58
1871	31	2,542	5,968	2.34	15,612	6.14
1872	32	2,676	10,478	3.91	15,379	5.74
1873	32	2,681	10,522	3.92	14,904	5.55
1874	33	2,593	12,534	4.83	18,150	7.00
1875	33	2,644	13,895	5.24	29,113	11.01
1876	33	2,537	10,603	4.17	26,523	10.45
1877	32	2,318	10,721	4.62	24,182	10.43
1878	32	2,284	11,215	4.91	23,265	10.18
1879	33	2,268	9,863	4.34	45,348	20.00
1880	33	2,361	4,799	2.03	13,365	5.66
1881	33	2,458	16,261	6.61	46,303	18.83
1882	32	2,548	12,691	4.98	31,172	12.23
1883	32	2,518	15,388	6.11	34,608	13.74
1884	32	2,531	16,061	6.34	37,792	14.93
1885	32	2,434	17,278	7.09	31,586	12.97
1886	32	2,431	14.285	5.87	31,520	12.96
			$297,843		$679,010	

* No Report.

A TABLE FOR OHIO,

Showing the Progress of the Order from 1832 to 1886, Inclusive.

Year.	No. of Lodges.	No. of Members.	Total Relief.	Relief per Member.	Total Receipts.	Receipts per Member.
1832	3	350	*	*	$200	$0.57
1833	5	391	*	*	1,533	3.90
1834	5	536	*	*	1,837	3.29
1835	5	736	*	*	3,818	5.19
1836	5	693	*	*	3,759	5.42
1837	6	786	*	*	3,623	4.61
1838	6	853	*	*	4,845	5.68
1839	*	*	*	*	*	*
1840	7	1,166	*	*	911	7.81
1841	10	1,241	$1,497	$1.20	7,154	5.76
1842	10	1,311	1,738	1.32	7,173	5.40
1843	16	1,563	1,674	1.07	7,635	4.88
1844	26	1,869	2,297	1.23	10,839	5.80
1845	34	2,551	4,206	1.65	17,283	6.78
1846	65	4,058	6,333	1.57	32,316	7.96
1847	87	6,373	20,681	3.25	75,839	11.90
1848	111	8,067	18,881	2.34	62,388	7.73
1849	133	9,546	22,677	2.38	66,115	6.93
1850	159	11,039	30,966	2.81	77,671	7.04
1851	185	12,644	27,315	2.16	86,405	6.83
1852	202	14,320	33,457	2.34	92,092	6.43
1853	225	16,197	35,151	2.16	105,701	6.53
1854	255	18,214	40,667	2.23	118,921	6.53
1855	290	18,972	48,171	2.54	115,607	6.09
1856	294	20,653	45,929	2.22	120,702	5.84
1857	311	21,271	30,758	1.45	131,119	6.16
1858	329	22,119	38,360	1.73	116,571	5.27
1859	339	22,229	39,866	1.79	117,130	5.27
1860	347	22,332	34,850	1.56	112,663	5.04
1861	350	21,103	30,728	1.41	106,516	5.00
1862	351	20,626	35,726	1.73	82,978	4.02
1863	342	19,480	41,015	2.10	92,240	4.73
1864	331	19,879	46,912	2.36	105,170	5.29
1865	325	20,212	52,117	2.58	118,817	5.88
1866	324	22,649	50,973	2.30	146,116	6.45
1867	336	25,659	60,521	2.36	163,659	6.38
1868	353	28,810	61,865	2.15	188,756	6.55
1869	363	30,718	62,091	2.02	218,622	7.12
1870	393	32,986	71,684	2.17	249,613	7.57
1871	461	37,678	111,890	2.97	298,667	7.92
1872	500	40,315	101,666	2.52	319,534	7.92
1873	523	42,598	113,066	2.65	319,791	7.51
1874	561	44,343	107,011	2.41	329,272	7.42
1875	580	45,393	116,251	2.56	358,861	7.90
1876	622	44,981	116,743	2.59	322,134	7.16
1877	629	43,758	114,369	2.61	318,415	7.27
1878	629	43,095	115,050	2.67	306,513	7.10
1879	640	42,065	116,666	2.77	315,713	7.50
1880	642	44,572	113,708	2.55	323,436	7.26
1881	647	46,133	129,218	2.80	356,027	7.70
1882	657	48,080	123,714	2.58	384,250	8.00
1883	659	48,621	139,630	2.87	389,357	8.01
1884	666	48,781	154,754	3.17	417,985	8.51
1885	670	48,545	157,615	3.04	402,439	8.29
1886	676	49,267	148,200	3.08	440,305	8.96
			$2,953,057		$8,528,352	

* No Report.

A TABLE FOR LOUISIANA,

Showing the Progress of the Order from 1832 to 1886, Inclusive.

Year.	No. of Lodges.	No. of Members.	Total Relief.	Relief per Member.	Total Receipts.	Receipts per Member.
1832	1	127	*	*	$1,784	$14.04
1833	1	*	*	*	*	*
1834	2	*	*	*	*	*
1835	2	*	*	*	*	*
1836	2	98	*	*	2,333	23.77
1837	2	109	*	*	1,964	18.01
1838	2	176	$414	$2.35	2,070	*
1839	2	198	*	*	4,273	21.58
1840	*	*	*	*	*	*
1841	2	146	*	*	*	*
1842	2	92	443	4.82	1,179	12.82
1843	3	109	177	1.62	1,381	12.67
1844	4	112	*	*	1,561	13.93
1845	6	216	*	*	3,060	14.35
1846	9	456	779	1.71	9,264	20.32
1847	14	1,040	1,893	1.82	18,264	17.56
1848	22	1,594	6,409	4.02	27,734	11.13
1849	23	1,819	8,115	4.46	28,598	15.69
1850	28	2,131	9,586	4.50	35,281	16.55
1851	30	2,435	10,282	4.22	34,595	14.21
1852	32	2,763	11,069	4.01	38,946	14.06
1853	33	2,914	14,739	4.27	45,529	15.62
1854	34	2,863	19,273	6.70	43,851	15.32
1855	35	2,845	16,616	6.05	41,879	14.72
1856	35	2,719	13,382	4.92	34,483	12.68
1857	35	2,560	11,650	4.55	34,576	13.50
1858	32	2,420	12,242	5.05	33,152	13.70
1859	36	2,401	15,236	6.35	35,079	14.61
1860	34	2,337	11,681	4.96	31,185	13.34
1861	*	*	*	*	*	*
1862	*	*	*	*	*	*
1863	*	*	*	*	*	*
1864	*	*	*	*	*	*
1865	33	1,535	7,108	4.66	18,160	11.85
1866	32	1,607	6,965	4.34	26,900	16.74
1867	31	1,722	9,662	5.61	29,412	17.08
1868	31	1,671	12,255	7.33	25,255	15.20
1869	31	1,717	8,264	4.81	23,527	13.70
1870	30	1,700	7,816	4.60	24,485	14.40
1871	33	1,713	16,007	9.34	37,673	21.95
1872	32	1,659	9,699	5.85	24,376	14.69
1873	30	1,417	10,610	7.49	17,695	12.49
1874	24	1,079	4,746	4.40	15,281	14.16
1875	25	1,026	4,588	4.47	11,837	11.64
1876	25	1,086	5,270	4.85	15,742	14.50
1877	25	1,090	5,540	5.08	14,410	13.22
1878	26	1,051	5,293	5.03	13,413	12.76
1879	26	1,055	4,930	4.67	12,497	11.88
1880	25	1,036	4,761	4.60	11,892	11.48
1881	26	1,066	4,344	4.08	13,915	13.05
1882	26	940	3,532	3.76	11,980	12.70
1883	26	885	3,361	3.80	11,022	12.45
1884	24	794	4,434	5.58	9,031	11.39
1885	24	726	3,259	4.49	9,218	12.70
1886	20	751	4,247	5.65	10,267	13.67
			$266,697		$858,159	

*No Report.

A TABLE FOR NEW JERSEY,

Showing the Progress of the Order from 1833 to 1886, Inclusive.

Year.	No. of Lodges.	No. of Members.	Total Relief.	Relief per Member.	Total Receipts.	Receipts per Member..
1833	3	51	*	*	$206	$4.04
1834	5	209	*	*	1,144	5.47
1835	5	181	*	*	577	3.18
1836	5	144	*	*	607	4.90
1837	6	116	*	*	462	3.98
1838	5	141	*	*	624	4.42
1839	3	163	*	*	581	3.60
1840	3	219	*	*	645	2.94
1841	2	184	$392	$2.13	678	3.68
1842	10	749	586	78	3,591	4.79
1843	18	1,301	1,869	1.44	10,774	8.28
1844	25	1,955	2,976	1 52	9,898	5.06
1845	29	1,792	2,877	1,605	12,410	6.94
1846	40	3,438	6,656	1.93	24,703	7.18
1847	63	4,768	11,024	2.31	35,698	7.48
1848	80	6,177	12,155	1.96	44.453	7.19
1849	90	7,138	16,767	2.34	45,586	6.38
1850	100	7,776	21,038	2.70	49,285	6 33
1851	103	7,808	19,691	2.52	48,387	6.19
1852	107	7,844	21,594	2.75	44,501	5.67
1853	108	7,349	18,973	2.58	43,100	5.86
1854	108	7,003	19,161	2.73	41,816	5.97
1855	106	6,790	18,492	2.72	38,027	5.60
1856	107	5,914	14,458	2.44	35,143	5.94
1857	107	5,302	13,484	2.54	33,159	6.25
1858	103	5,068	11,285	2.22	27,736	5.47
1859	98	4,583	11,306	2.46	28,695	6.26
1860	86	4,864	11,862	2.43	29,387	6.04
1861	86	4,866	13,571	2.78	24,718	5.07
1862	85	4,523	12,023	2.65	28,049	6.20
1863	84	4,490	14,297	3.18	30,203	6.72
1864	74	4,147	13,187	3.17	27,045	6.52
1865	72	5,022	15,983	3.18	41,896	8.34
1866	78	5,837	14,484	2.48	39,344	6.74
1867	75	6,986	19,786	2 83	61,315	8.77
1868	82	8,162	24,824	3.04	71,659	8.77
1869	97	9,623	27,913	2.90	88,675	9.21
1870	108	11,069	32,520	2.93	103,724	9.37
1871	137	13,344	34,366	2.57	103,357	7.74
1872	143	14,484	55,231	3.81	147,392	10.10
1873	150	15,251	63,458	4.16	154,357	10.12
1874	158	15,427	62,579	4.05	155,531	10.08
1875	167	15,428	68,003	4.40	150,006	9.72
1876	168	14,740	68,314	4.63	141,206	9.57
1877	169	14,054	68,080	4.84	140,461	9.99
1878	175	13,721	63,669	4.64	86,822	6.32
1879	176	13,761	59,308	4.30	210,191	15.27
1880	178	14,167	58,655	4.14	222,098	15.67
1881	182	14,884	70,206	4.71	160,594	10.78
1882	187	15,892	71,642	4.50	179,080	11.26
1883	197	16,682	79,067	4.73	181,288	10.86
1884	201	17,515	83,258	4.75	194,850	11.12
1885	200	17,747	90,417	5.09	201,212	11.33
1886	206	18,775	96,843	5.15	213,591	11.37
			$1,508,330		$3,770,562	

* No Report.

A TABLE FOR KENTUCKY,

Showing the Progress of the Order from 1836 to 1886, Inclusive.

Year.	No. of Lodges.	No. of Members.	Total Relief.	Relief per Member.	Total Receipts.	Receipts per Member.
1836	4	279	*	*	$3,875	$18.89
1837	5	340	*	*	2,669	7.85
1838	5	397	*	*	3,485	8.78
1839	5	367	*	*	3,868	10.54
1840	5	387	$190	$0.49	3,569	9.22
1841	7	472	839	1.78	4,414	9.35
1842	12	577	1,635	2.83	5,386	9.34
1843	14	653	1,370	2.09	5,117	7.84
1844	17	688	1,070	1.56	5,757	8.37
1845	19	796	2,054	2.58	7,744	9.73
1846	23	1,073	3,050	2.84	10,196	9.50
1847	33	1,619	3,500	2.16	15,978	9.87
1848	50	2,435	7,083	2.98	31,515	12.94
1849	56	2,921	14,251	4.89	26,871	9.20
1850	66	3,338	9,222	2.76	30,840	9.00
1851	80	3,862	9,465	2.45	34,483	8.93
1852	89	4,111	9,653	2.35	33,798	8.22
1853	101	4,544	10,762	2.37	39,688	8.73
1854	110	5,152	13,260	2.57	46,320	9.00
1855	122	5,556	13,158	2.37	41,948	8.75
1856	119	5,235	14,022	2.70	38,438	7.24
1857	123	4,852	8,829	1.82	32,327	6.67
1858	116	4,676	9,649	2.06	30,147	6.45
1859	112	4,941	11,877	2.40	36,834	7.45
1860	113	5,151	11,479	2.23	31,449	6.11
1861	111	4,432	9,254	2.09	24,888	5.62
1862	110	3,890	9,850	2.50	18,767	4.82
1863	110	3,463	11,160	3.22	23,942	6.91
1864	104	3,472	12,056	3.47	31,637	9.11
1865	102	4,424	14,776	3.34	43,048	9.74
1866	108	5,161	15,237	2.95	54,974	10.65
1867	113	5,926	18,020	3.04	52,448	8.85
1868	123	6,344	18,163	2.86	55,930	8.97
1869	125	6,714	20,731	3.09	55,545	8.27
1870	138	7,678	22,285	2.89	66,250	8.63
1871	160	8,560	38,638	4.52	93,254	10.89
1872	174	9,096	28,830	3.19	59,413	6.59
1873	192	9,873	34,891	3.74	67,336	6.81
1874	205	10,301	28,570	2.77	73,505	7.14
1875	214	10,424	33,641	3.51	65,232	6.26
1876	216	10,028	32,061	3.20	54,034	5.38
1877	214	9,800	29,093	2.97	51,055	5.21
1878	210	9,077	29,828	3.18	49,526	5.46
1879	206	12,299	26,793	2.17	40,407	3.29
1880	203	8,774	25,258	2.88	32,925	3.75
1881	185	8,760	27,267	3.10	28,200	3.21
1882	189	6,998	29,580	4.23	35,074	5.01
1883	186	6,832	25,282	3.70	48,653	7.14
1884	189	6,909	24,413	3.53	35,071	5.08
1885	179	6,907	23,666	3.43	35,458	5.13
1886	168	6,948	25,095	3.61	38,021	5.47
			$257,512		$1,826,541	

* No Report.

A TABLE FOR INDIANA,

Showing the Progress of the Order from 1839 to 1886, Inclusive.

Year.	No. of Lodges.	No. of Members.	Total Relief.	Relief per Member.	Total Receipts.	Receipts per Member.
1839	4	208	*	*	$2,235	$10.75
1840	17	*	*	. *	*	*
1841	&	398	*	*	2,468	6.20
1842	9	413	*	*	2,006	4.86
1843	10	395	$937	$2.37	3,401	6.59
1844	14	516	1,015	1.95	4,479	8.68
1845	21	697	*	*	6,906	9.91
1846	33	848	1,282	1.51	13,244	15.51
1847	45	1,594	3,264	2.05	19,978	12.53
1848	60	2,273	5,179	2.28	26,157	11.07
1849	66	2,836	*	*	31,203	11.00
1850	82	3,670	8,380	2.27	37,973	10.35
1851	94	4,397	12,074	2.75	53,603	12.19
1852	115	5,119	13,300	2.60	*	*
1853	134	6,147	15,828	2.57	107,114	17.42
1854	148	7,085	16,963	2.39	122,093	11.23
1855	166	7,696	22,047	2.87	*	*
1856	172	8,282	21,109	2.55	83,277	10.06
1857	188	7,306	10,969	1.50	90,000	12.32
1858	189	8,683	15,990	1.84	193,105	22.24
1859	194	8,785	19,025	2.16	221,172	25.18
1860	303	8,965	18,282	2.03	71,484	7.97
1861	207	8,786	20,722	2.35	67,708	7.71
1862	201	8,328	17,529	2.10	58,171	6.98
1863	195	7,939	20,474	2.58	67,478	8.50
1864	195	8,040	11,976	1.49	35,938	4.47
1865	204	9,730	34,289	3.52	121,696	12.50
1866	225	11,283	35,716	3.16`	117,203	10.40
1867	248	13,066	33,839	2.58	127,959	9.80
1868	273	14,737	36,035	2.45	146,443	9.94
1869	298	15,970	36,937	2.31	116,711	7.31
1870	320	17,823	41,958	2.35	177,439	9.95
1871	350	20,219	78,556	3.88	281,927	13.94
1872	383	21,797	59,261	2.42	202,281	9.85
1873	419	23,190	61,010	2.36	228,987	9.87
1874	496	24,730	66,248	2.68	245,837	9.94
1875	502	26,732	79,950	2.99	266,537	9.97
1876	515	26,404	76,007	2.50	235,552	8.92
1877	518	25,146	74,512	2.96	218,616	8.69
1878	529	24,302	72,111	2.97	213,366	8.78
1879	536	37,728	75,836	2.01	224.706	5.96
1880	537	25,341	69,837	2 75	218,905	8.63
1881	543	25,859	80,151	3.09	273,257	10.57
1882	544	26,196	77,954	2.98	259,176	9.89
1883	549	25,561	86,496	3.38	235,934	9.23
1884	551	25,370	90,551	3.57	234,076	9.23
1885	547	24,915	88,240	3.54	253,939	10.15
1886	552	26,270	89,783	3.41	263,810	10.04
			$1,701,622		$5,985,570	

*No Report.

A TABLE FOR VIRGINIA,

Showing the Progress of the Order from 1838 to 1886, Inclusive.

Year.	No. of Lodges.	No. of Members.	Total Relief.	Relief per Member.	Total Receipts.	Receipts per Member.
1838	13	825	*	*	$7,976	$9.67
1839	17	1,232	*	*	8,987	7.29
1840	*	*	*	*	*	*
1841	19	525	*	*	9,451	18.00
1842	20	1,551	$2,486	$1.60	7,312	4.71
1843	22	1,546	3,689	2.39	*	*
1844	24	1,606	4,152	2.59	8,469	5.27
1845	22	1,546	*	*	6,728	4.35
1846	31	1,980	4,024	2.03	12,956	6.54
1847	47	2,917	5,598	1.92	21,976	7.54
1848	65	4,127	9,580	2.32	47,046	11.40
1849	77	4,896	11,096	2.27	31,207	6.37
1850	92	5,640	14,283	2.53	35,286	6.26
1851	100	6,280	13,709	2.18	35,975	5.73
1352	105	6,696	14,671	2.21	33,793	5.05
1853	111	6,913	16,633	2.41	33,060	4.78
1854	113	7,003	17,715	2.53	32,742	4.68
1855	113	6,820	18,251	2.68	29,990	4.40
1856	110	6,483	22,701	3.50	28,622	4.41
1857	112	6,021	16,118	2.68	25,563	4.24
1858	99	5,619	12,157	2.16	23,910	4.25
1859	89	5,478	12,230	2.23	23,971	4.37
1860	89	5,217	13,430	2.57	25,134	4.82
1861	*	*	*	*	*	*
1862	*	*	*	*	*	*
1863	*	*	*	*	*	*
1864	*	*	*	*	*	*
1865	*	*	*	*	*	*
1866	35	2,418	2,456	1.02	*	*
1867	36	2,605	10,713	4.11	*	*
1868	37	2,711	9,890	3.65	14,823	5.47
1869	40	2,712	8,796	3.24	16,429	6.06
1870	43	2,563	10,254	4.00	15,613	6.09
1871	39	2,896	17,826	6.16	29,511	10.19
1872	40	3,060	8,572	2.80	12,064	3.94
1873	42	3,226	14,909	4.62	22,447	6.91
1874	45	3,221	15,110	4.69	21,338	6.62
1875	49	3,272	16,202	4.95	24,726	7.55
1876	48	3,192	21,424	6.71	32,986	10.33
1877	49	2,945	14,702	4.99	27,975	9.50
1878	48	2,832	13,933	4.92	25,024	8.84
1879	47	3,826	12,936	3.38	26,417	6.90
1880	47	2,973	15,213	5.12	29,014	9.76
1881	51	2,960	16,265	5.49	26,427	8.93
1882	51	2,858	14,190	4.96	28,074	9.83
1883	52	3,176	14,209	4.41	34,305	10.80
1884	53	3,302	13,809	4.18	35,588	10.78
1885	51	3,340	15,408	4.64	30,592	9.16
1886	55	3,416	15,796	4.62	29,280	8.58
			$495,136		$972,797	

* No Report.

A TABLE FOR MISSISSIPPI,

Showing the Progress of the Order from 1838 to 1886, Inclusive.

Year.	No. of Lodges.	No. of Members.	Total Relief.	Relief per Member.	Total Receipts.	Receipts per Member.
1838	3	227	*	*	$1,916	$8.44
1839	4	261	*	*	3,778	14.47
1840	*	358	*	*	6,287	17.56
1841	*	*	*	*	*	*
1842	6	394	*	*	3,538	8.98
1843	8	367	$350	$0.95	5,165	14.07
1844	9	414	921	2.22	4,781	11.55
1845	12	489	1,731	3.54	5,840	11.94
1846	15	606	960	1.58	7,036	11.61
1847	22	879	1,585	1.80	13,734	15.62
1848	33	1,306	2,490	1.91	18,906	14.48
1849	36	1,443	4,712	3.26	18,070	12.52
1850	41	1,513	2,844	1.88	17,100	11.30
1851	44	1,634	2,365	1.45	17,661	10.81
1852	45	1,661	2,233	1.34	15,133	9.11
1853	46	1,636	-1,817	1.11	13,591	8.31
1854	47	1,683	3,654	2.17	15,321	9.10
1855	54	1,808	2,432	1.34	18,332	10.14
1856	55	1,854	3,495	1.89	14,161	7.64
1857	55	1,832	3,650	1.99	13,917	7.59
1858	50	1,630	1,705	1.05	13,197	8.09
1859	57	1,675	1,800	1.07	12,597	7.52
1860	59	1,710	2,210	1.29	14,128	8.26
1861	*	*	*	*	*	*
1862	*	*	*	*	*	*
1863	*	*	*	*	*	*
1864	*	*	*	*	*	*
1865	*	*	*	*	*	*
1866	53	1,337	488	.36	7,466	5.58
1867	*	*	*	*	*	*
1868	37	1,268	1,414	1.12	7,338	5.78
1869	41	1,318	1,338	1.02	7,895	5.91
1870	46	1,482	1,614	1.09	11,133	7.51
1871	41	1,634	2,898	1.78	19,595	11.99
1872	45	1,835	4,009	2.18	17,646	9.62
1873	47	1,817	3,641	2.00	15,150	8.34
1874	52	1,825	2,773	1.52	14,845	8.13
1875	54	1,764	2,437	1.38	11,603	6.57
1876	46	1,577	2,312	1.47	10,565	6.70
1877	45	1,546	1,698	1.10	10,633	6.88
1878	42	1,577	3,173	2.01	9,650	6.12
1879	34	1,435	3,903	2.72	10,855	7.56
1880	36	1,243	2,151	1.73	12,420	9.99
1881	36	1,237	4,217	3.41	10,159	8.21
1882	30	1,203	2,458	2.04	8,576	7.13
1883	31	1,146	2,402	2.10	7,570	6.61
1884	31	1,201	2,657	2.21	7,968	6.63
1885	28	966	2,137	2.21	5,978	6.19
1886	28	956	2,492	2.61	6,925	7.24
			$91,166		$468,158	

* No Report.

A TABLE FOR MISSOURI,

Showing the Progress of the Order from 1839 to 1886, Inclusive.

Year.	No. of Lodges.	No. of Members.	Total Relief.	Relief per Member.	Total Receipts.	Receipts per Member.
1839	2	261	*	*	*	*
1840	4	*	*	*	*	*
1841	4	226	*	*	$2,208	$9.77
1842	5	326	$617	$1.89	4,399	13.49
1843	6	345	531	1.54	2,965	8.59
1844	10	401	900	2.24	4,649	11.59
1845	13	578	2,204	3.81	6,383	11.04
1846	17	755	1,868	2.47	7,985	10.58
1847	24	1,068	2,501	1.41	12,244	11.46
1848	33	1,525	3,891	2.54	17,089	11.21
1849	40	1,932	6,002	3.11	21,437	11.10
1850	41	2,093	8,606	4.11	23,589	11.27
1851	45	2,278	9,367	4.11	20,132	8.84
1852	54	2,442	9,279	3.80	23,574	9.65
1853	59	2,720	8,770	3.23	28,275	10.40
1854	70	3,080	9,342	3.03	30,149	9.79
1855	81	3,365	10,118	3.01	31,332	9.31
1856	92	3,790	9,629	2.54	32,680	8.62
1857	102	4,262	15,381	3.61	37,066	8.70
1858	112	4,641	9,935	2.14	39,148	8.44
1859	122	4,824	9,765	2.03	43,432	9.00
1860	130	4,918	6,809	1.39	42,709	8.71
1861	136	4,880	16,401	3.36	46,381	9.51
1862	119	3,111	9,995	3.21	18,035	5.80
1863	96	2,430	8,934	3.43	16,908	6.96
1864	78	2,623	9,882	3.77	22,504	8.58
1865	78	3,015	11,608	3.85	28,387	9.41
1866	91	4,052	13,936	3.44	38,564	9.53
1867	112	5,029	18,648	3.71	46,787	9.21
1868	137	6,176	18,229	2.95	58,415	9.46
1869	156	7,483	20,373	2.72	68,416	9.14
1870	185	8,897	24,162	2.72	83,181	9.35
1871	234	10,723	27,493	2.56	86,329	8.05
1872	250	11,188	31,335	2.80	88,668	7.92
1873	274	11,940	34,892	2.92	94,763	7.94
1874	285	12,615	36,205	2.87	80,346	6.37
1875	296	12,302	35,388	2.88	91,472	7.43
1876	315	12,691	36,315	2.86	89,695	7.07
1877	323	13,057	38,148	2.92	92,560	7.01
1878	324	12,900	43,592	3.38	81,069	6.28
1879	326	13,475	38,847	2.88	73,368	5.44
1880	339	14,575	44,073	3.02	104,287	7.29
1881	351	15,569	46,518	2.99	104,136	6.75
1882	372	16,114	44,046	2.73	119,686	7.43
1883	392	16,418	51,962	3.16	112,755	6.87
1884	379	16,364	54,115	3.31	101,379	6.20
1885	373	15,002	38,266	2.55	68,943	4.60
1886	376	15,154	50,924	3.36	93,353	6.16
			$929,602		$2,341,832	

* No Report.

A TABLE FOR ILLINOIS,

Showing the Progress of the Order from 1839 to 1886, Inclusive.

Year.	No. of Lodges.	No. of Members.	Total Relief.	Relief per Member.	Total Receipts.	Receipts per Member.
1839	5	97	*	*	$805	$8.29
1840	2	*	*	*	*	*
1841	*	*	*	*	*	*
1842	8	143	*	*	1,101	7.67
1843	8	199	$237	1.19	1,007	*
1844	*	*	*	*	*	*
1845	9	223	*	*	930	4.17
1846	16	690	778	1.12	6,792	9.84
1847	26	1,004	1,871	1.86	7,854	7.82
1848	40	1,720	2,396	1.39	15,652	9.10
1849	56	2,518	3,072	1.22	18,529	7.35
1850	76	3,291	5,532	1.68	25,393	7.71
1851	94	4,035	4,031	.99	29,409	7.28
1852	114	4,787	6,630	1.38	34,185	7.14
1853	129	5,205	7,880	1.88	37,793	7.26
1854	158	6,676	8,768	1.31	50,333	7.53
1855	184	8,308	11,430	1.37	59,090	7.11
1856	210	9,882	9,584	.97	69,986	7.11
1857	321	11,044	11,651	1.05	77,007	6.97
1858	254	10,549	13,837	1.31	66,434	6.29
1859	270	10,562	13,520	1.28	56,614	5.36
1860	273	9,810	12,092	1.23	56,448	5.75
1861	267	8,031	8,373	1.04	44,057	5.48
1862	237	6,248	7,237	1.15	33,856	5.41
1863	237	6,836	7,649	1.11	43,629	6.88
1864	246	7,390	10,415	1.40	53,810	7.28
1865	261	8,553	12,638	1.47	63,621	7.43
1866	246	10,512	14,855	1.36	86,277	8.20
1867	249	12,191	16,486	1.35	95,132	7.80
1868	286	14,407	19,277	1.33	121,832	8.45
1869	318	15,040	19,560	1.30	121,972	8.10
1870	351	16,887	23,461	1.39	148,889	8.81
1871	395	19,287	51,513	2.67	250,171	12.97
1872	431	21,797	39,812	1.82	192,509	8.88
1873	466	23,352	46,536	1.99	202,574	8.67
1874	496	25,195	42,222	1.67	226,070	8.97
1875	535	26,686	53,239	1.99	218,708	8.19
1876	560	26,812	50,242	1.87	219,807	8.19
1877	583	26,042	51,522	1.97	215,506	8.27
1878	581	25,459	56,618	2.22	207,558	8.15
1879	588	25,932	57,791	2.22	224,002	8.64
1880	595	28,008	69,873	2.49	218,905	7.81
1881	601	30,529	69,790	2.28	289,108	9.46
1882	625	32,045	71,789	2.24	306,891	9.57
1883	646	32,347	82,570	2.55	286,900	8.86
1884	664	32,101	81,943	2.55	274,726	8.55
1885	663	31,352	83,367	2.65	274,901	8.76
1886	669	31,806	105,396	3.81	364,340	11.45
			$1,266,983		$5,401,113	

* No Report.

A TABLE FOR CONNECTICUT,

Showing the Progress of the Order from 1841 to 1886, Inclusive.

Year.	No. of Lodges.	No. of Members.	Total Relief.	Relief per Member.	Total Receipts.	Receipts per Member.
1841	5	389	$430	$1.26	$1,770	$5.22
1842	6	756	1,242	1.64	6,435	8.51
1843	12	1,245	1,727	1.38	8,987	7.84
1844	13	1,836	3,597	1.96	13,190	7.78
1845	22	2,587	5,336	2.06	17,255	6.66
1846	33	3,321	8,475	2.55	24,934	7.59
1847	50	4,650	10,269	2.20	33,056	7.11
1848	55	5,517	12,728	2.30	34,339	6.22
1849	68	5,945	14,024	2.35	32,559	5.47
1850	71	5,878	15,115	2.57	35,235	5.99
1851	72	6,143	13,309	2.16	34,655	5.64
1852	71	5,411	13,500	2.49	27,959	5.14
1853	68	4,865	10,377	2.13	28,819	5.92
1854	62	4,374	5,592	1.27	15,071	3.44
1855	65	3,136	6,333	2.01	17,933	5.71
1856	51	2,964	7,046	2.37	17,683	5.96
1857	46	2,414	6,978	2.88	14,743	6.10
1858	44	1,774	6,981	3.93	14,019	7.90
1859	32	1,900	6,227	3.27	12,946	6.81
1860	50	1,493	5,279	3.53	11,846	7.93
1861	23	1,494	4,645	3.10	10,474	7.01
1862	23	1,441	4,495	3.11	9,995	6.93
1863	20	1,303	5,023	3.85	10,175	7.80
1864	20	1,308	5,050	3.86	10,678	8.16
1865	19	1,362	4,890	3.59	11,319	8.30
1866	19	1,655	5,817	3.51	14,132	8.53
1867	19	1,895	4,612	2.43	17,967	9.48
1868	20	2,178	3,520	1.61	21,830	10.02
1869	23	2,521	6,006	2.38	29,724	11.79
1870	25	2,877	4,645	1.61	15,621	5.42
1871	27	3,268	10,769	3.29	32,101	9.82
1872	34	3,980	10,945	2.75	41,664	10.46
1873	37	4,547	13,586	2.98	50,066	11.01
1874	41	4,966	16,140	3.25	54,180	10.91
1875	46	5,574	19,243	3.45	59,537	10.66
1876	49	5,930	18,974	3.20	57,402	9.69
1877	50	6,257	22,863	3.65	60,725	9.70
1878	52	6,675	27,497	4.11	65,405	9.79
1879	52	6,961	27,341	3.92	67,743	9.73
1880	54	7,279	28,296	3.85	73,149	10.04
1881	53	7,657	30,301	3.95	69,734	9.10
1882	54	8,140	33,188	4.07	77,472	9.51
1883	57	8,768	35,856	4.08	85,032	9.69
1884	57	9,128	37,201	4.07	83,893	9.15
1885	57	9,385	36,971	3.93	83,387	8.89
1886	59	10,107	39,471	3.95	94,441	9.34
			$602,910		$1,611,280	

A TABLE FOR TEXAS,

Showing the Progress of the Order from 1841 to 1886, Inclusive.

Year.	No. of Lodges.	No. of Members.	Total Relief.	Relief per Member.	Total Receipts.	Receipts per Member.
1841	3	69	*	*	$1,117	$16.18
1842	3	*	*	*	*	*
1843	3	68	*	*	*	*
1844	*	*	*	*	*	*
1845	2	59	*	*	229	3.87
1846	3	76	$118	$1.55	805	10.69
1847	3	106	299	2.82	1,498	14.08
1848	3	132	701	5.31	1,589	12.03
1849	4	139	669	4.83	2,838	20.45
1850	12	184	221	1.20	1,268	6.89
1851	13	382	716	1.87	6,664	17.44
1852	23	613	1,223	1.99	9,076	14.82
1853	33	879	1,224	1.39	10,957	12.44
1854	40	1,276	2,125	1.66	14,966	11.73
1855	51	1,695	1,336	.78	18,420	10.86
1856	58	1,571	1,590	1.01	13,340	8.42
1857	61	1,858	1,931	1.04	12,357	6.65
1858	65	2,400	2,793	1.16	16,720	6.96
1859	74	2,749	6,569	2.60	26,459	9.69
1860	75	3,045	5,198	1.70	28,787	9.45
1861	*	*	*	*	*	*
1862	*	*	*	*	*	*
1863	*	*	*	*	*	*
1864	*	*	*	*	*	*
1865	*	*	*	*	*	*
1866	16	924	1,343	1.45	3,804	4.11
1867	27	1,340	2,563	1.91	8,996	6.71
1868	53	1,177	2,911	2.47	11,719	9.96
1869	56	1,330	2,145	1.61	17,779	13.36
1870	64	2,152	3,673	1.75	12,802	5.94
1871	88	3,282	7,043	2.14	48,608	14.81
1872	104	3,937	6,941	1.76	64,846	16.47
1873	152	4,650	11,177	2.40	45,300	9.74
1874	168	5,061	8,229	1.62	60,087	11.86
1875	165	5,173	9,393	1.81	57,640	11.14
1876	173	4,749	9,067	1.92	50,622	10.66
1877	172	4,687	8,713	1.86	54,756	11.68
1878	157	4,562	8,389	1.83	46,059	10.09
1879	152	4,255	7,147	1.68	43,290	10.17
1880	143	4,508	7,886	1.75	82,204	18.23
1881	161	5,044	9,937	1.97	74,899	14.84
1882	169	4,995	11,670	2.33	87,710	17.56
1883	173	5,145	13,400	2.60	78,111	15.18
1884	164	5,196	12,844	2.46	85,830	16.50
1885	165	4,558	12,079	2.65	65,104	14.28
1886	170	4,450	11,184	2.51	80,148	18.00
			$194,447		$1,247,349	

* No Report.

A TABLE FOR TENNESSEE,

Showing the Progress of the Order from 1841 to 1886, Inclusive.

Year.	No. of Lodges.	No. of Members.	Total Relief.	Relief per Member.	Total Receipts.	Receipts per Member.
1841	2	106	*	*	$775	$7.31
1842	4	200	$253	$1.27	2,663	13.32
1843	6	286	179	.63	3,275	11.45
1844	6	326	*	*	3,175	9.74
1845	9	471	906	1.92	574	1.22
1846	20	810	806	1.00	11,332	13.99
1847	27	1,300	2,507	1.93	17,108	13.
1848	38	1,871	3,149	1.68	21,278	11.16
1849	50	2,205	4,373	2.00	21,843	9.37
1850	60	2,152	3,093	1.44	19,749	9.91
1851	70	2,595	3,481	1.34	23,397	9.13
1852	76	2,746	4,030	1.47	18,386	6.02
1853	78	3,053	5,746	1.88	24,309	7.69
1854	78	*	*	*	*	*96
1855	78	*	*	*	*	*
1856	94	5,100	1,290	.25	22,474	4.41
1857	100	3,279	4,237	1.29	21,596	6.60
1858	106	2,874	5,950	2.07	18,850	5.56
1859	106	2,592	3,727	1.44	17,405	6.71
1860	96	2,700	4,437	1.64	18,879	6.99
1861	*	*	*	*	*	*
1862	65	1,938	4,286	2.21	9,858	5.09
1863	*	1,370	2,186	1.59	5,914	4.32
1864	16	868	5,223	6.02	12,718	14.65
1865	25	1,037	2,815	2.71	6,623	6.38
1866	48	1,243	2,341	1.88	7,977	6.42
1867	66	2,635	5,614	2.13	16,844	6.39
1868	83	3,329	6,226	1.87	23,689	7.12
1869	95	3,450	4,171	1.21	29,942	8.68
1870	97	3,524	7,374	2.09	33,658	9.55
1871	116	4,309	14,446	3.35	63,974	14.74
1872	120	3,937	11,547	2.93	40,270	12.77
1873	130	4,589	15,999	3.49	50,303	10.96
1874	142	4,684	11,390	2.43	42,000	8.95
1875	145	4,323	12,813	2.96	35,451	8.20
1876	146	4,138	11,892	2.87	31,452	7.60
1877	147	3,683	12,415	3.37	27,790	7.55
1878	149	3,347	19,766	5.91	30,243	9.04
1879	147	2,928	14,009	4.78	22,864	7.81
1880	139	3,152	11,463	3.64	29,752	9.44
1881	120	3,207	12,835	4.00	24,371	7.60
1882	120	3,198	12,354	3.87	23,928	7.49
1883	122	3,236	11,477	3 55	25,414	7.85
1884	122	3,361	11,320	3.37	29,864	8.89
1885	124	3,347	12,679	3.78	26,713	7.98
1886	125	3,420	10,551	3.08	25,371	7.42
			$295,356		$944,051	

*No Report.

A TABLE FOR SOUTH CAROLINA,

Showing the Progress of the Order from 1841 to 1886, Inclusive.

Year.	No. of Lodges.	No. of Members.	Total Relief.	Relief per Member.	Total Receipts.	Receipts per Member.
1841	2	161	*	*	$1,440	$8.94
1842	5	731	$585	$0.80	9,523	13.03
1843	8	1,116	1,342	1.20	11,490	10.30
1844	9	1,431	2,351	1.64	13,210	9.23
1845	11	1,505	3,654	2.43	13,510	8.98
1846	11	1,531	3,809	2.49	12,027	8.85
1847	14	1,566	5,715	3.65	14,018	7.95
1848	17	1,689	· 6,444	3.81	13,429,	9.95
1849	18	1,662	6,462	3.89	15,290	7.20
1850	20	1,848	5,325	2.88	15,936	8.62
1851	19	1,861	6,495	3.49	14,117	7.59
1852	20	1,884	6,710	3.56	14,192	7.53
1853	28	1,928	7,161	3.71	14,514	7.53
1854	24	2,000	7,239	3.62	16,549	8.23
1855	24	1,871	9,000	4.81	9,047	4.84
1856	25	1,696	12,100	7.13	17,125	10.10
1857	25	1,742	6,759	3.88	14,958	8.59
1858	25	1,641	7,175	4.37	7,175	4.37
1859	22	1,610	6,098	3.79	11,166	6.94
1860	19	1,569	6,832	4.35	10,483	6.68
1861	*	*	*	*	*	*
1862	*	*	*	*	*	*
1863	*	*	*	*	*	*
1864	*	*	*	*	*	*
1865	18	*	*	*	*	*
1866	18	1,002	1,328	1.32	6,787	6.77
1867	18	959	*	*	6,779	7.07
1868	18	926	*	*	4,204	4.54
1869	11	786	*	*	3,768	4.79
1870	10	701	1,041	1.49	3,553	5.07
1871	12	763	3,183	4.17	2,758	3.65
1872	12	827	*	*	*	*
1873	16	904	2,471	2.73	7,495	8.29
1874	16	957	1,540	1.61	5,245	5.48
1875	15	807	1,435	1.78	5,183	6.42
1876	15	663	726	1.10	3,255	4.91
1877	15	612	1,118	1.83	3,209	5.24
1878	15	585	797	1.36	2,268	3.88
1879	15	388	872	2.25	2,822	7.27
1880	16	427	886	2.07	2,810	6.58
1881	16	408	887	2.17	3,120	7.65
1882	16	526	938	1.78	3,633	6.91
1883	16	536	532	.99	2,524	4.71
1884	15	570	*	*	219	.38
1885	16	581	1,023	1.76	2,324	4.00
1886	16	611	1,180	1.93	2,670	4.37
			$131,208		$323,852	

* No Report.

A TABLE FOR ALABAMA,

Showing the Progress of the Order from 1842 to 1886, Inclusive.

Year.	No. of Lodges.	No. of Members.	Total Relief.	Relief per Member.	Total Receipts.	Receipts per Member.
1842	2	106	$274	$2.58	$4,232	$39.92
1843	3	119	441	3.70	2,141	17.90
1844	4	112	644	5.75	1,636	14.60
1845	9	553	300	.54	6,332	11.45
1846	9	568	893	1.57	9,540	16.79
1847	18	856	1,829	2.13	12,608	14.72
1848	28	1,146	2,545	2.22	13,353	11.65
1849	32	1,371	3,406	2.48	14,201	10.35
1850	37	1,529	3,455	2.25	15,642	10.23
1851	40	1,675	2,560	1.52	18,742	11.18
1852	46	1,569	3,612	2.30	17,856	11.38
1853	48	1,555	4,170	2.68	16,485	10.60
1854	49	1,556	4,224	2.71	17,453	11.21
1855	49	1,555	4,686	3.01	17,452	11.22
1856	49	*	*	*	*	*
1857	35	1,046	2,650	2.53	11,545	11.03
1858	31	1,079	3,089	2.86	10,968	10.16
1859	32	1,108	3,724	3.36	12,038	10.86
1860	31	976	2,767	2.83	8,909	9.12
1861	*	*	*	*	*	*
1862	*	*	*	*	*	*
1863	*	*	*	*	*	*
1864	*	*	*	*	*	*
1865	*	*	*	*	*	*
1866	14	583	1,891	3.24	5,247	9.00
1867	25	730	3,282	4 49	9,545	13.06
1868	24	725	2,748	3.79	*	*
1869	28	820	2,607	3.18	8,935	10.89
1870	29	1,002	2,160	2.15	8,935	8.91
1871	30	1,117	3,123	2.79	9,510	8.51
1872	29	1,025	3,418	3.33	10,917	10.65
1873	31	1,119	3,505	3.13	10,365	9.26
1874	33	1,157	2,246	1.94	9,510	8.21
1875	35	1,118	1,911	1.70	9,352	8.36
1876	38	1,183	1,932	1.63	8,336	7.04
1877	36	1,101	2,324	2.11	8,093	7.35
1878	36	1,095	3,031	2.76	8,264	8.46
1879	37	1,074	2,785	2.59	6,947	6.46
1880	36	1,156	1,445	1.25	7,525	6.51
1881	37	1,192	2,289	1.92	7,670	6.43
1882	37	1,232	2,251	1.82	7,365	5.97
1883	35	1,236	2,133	1.72	7,002	5.64
1884	37	1,356	2,350	1.73	9,385	6.92
1885	35	1,441	3,264	2.26	7,677	5.32
1886	33	1,507	3,504	2.32	9,580	6.35
			$99,368		$381,393	

* No Report.

A TABLE FOR NORTH CAROLINA,

Showing the Progress of the Order from 1843 to 1886, Inclusive.

Year.	No. of Lodges.	No. of Members.	Total Relief.	Relief per Member.	Total Receipts.	Receipts per Member.
1843	3	159	*	*	$463	$2.91
1844	*	*	*	*	*	*
1845	4	324	$453	1.39	2,591	8.00
1846	7	450	806	1.79	4,365	9.70
1847	13	761	749	.98	7,143	9.39
1848	18	1,022	1,005	.98	8,346	8.17
1849	26	955	1,463	1.53	7,673	8.03
1850	*	*	*	*	*	*
1851	39	1,512	1,892	1.25	11,925	7.89
1352	39	1,639	2,329	1.42	14,156	8.64
1853	40	1,760	2,692	1.53	12,933	7.34
1854	45	1,849	2,941	1.60	13,393	7.24
1855	48	1,842	2,286	1.24	1,800	.98
1856	51	1,473	1,593	1.08	7,606	5.16
1857	43	1,310	1,919	1.46	8,253	6.30
1858	46	1,178	1,633	1.39	6,969	5.91
1859	47	1,180	1,433	1.21	6,883	5.83
1860	32	1,026	1,352	1.32	6,300	6.14
1861	*	*	*	*	*	*
1862	*	*	*	*	*	*
1863	*	*	*	*	*	*
1864	*	*	*	*	*	*
1865	*	*	*	*	*	*
1866	11	547	84	.15	116	.21
1867	20	582	212	.36	2,611	4.49
1868	22	654	641	.98	2,316	3.54
1869	23	636	693	1.09	2,412	3.79
1870	23	731	420	.57	3,661	5.01
1871	16	907	887	.98	7,694	8.48
1872	16	666	757	1.14	5,234	7.86
1873	27	1,022	2,067	2.02	7,968	7.79
1874	47	1,556	1,572	1.01	11,086	7.12
1875	52	1,762	1,837	1.04	11,815	6.71
1876	58	1,784	1,624	.91	10,543	5.91
1877	60	1,713	1,119	.65	8,900	5.20
1878	54	1,583	1,233	.78	7,958	5.03
1879	50	1,566	1,492	.95	7,528	4.81
1880	43	1,539	1,534	1.00	9,746	6.33
1881	39	1,529	1,572	1.03	6,500	4.25
1882	38	1,083	1,447	1.34	7,242	6.69
1883	40	1,107	1,825	1.65	7,547	6.82
1884	42	1,194	1,425	1:19	7,818	6.55
1885	41	1,208	1,803	1.49	8,262	6.84
1886	36	1,169	1,986	1.70	8,099	6.93
			$50,776		$265,855	

* No Report.

A TABLE FOR GEORGIA,

Showing the Progress of the Order from 1844 to 1886, Inclusive.

Year.	No. of Lodges.	No. of Members.	Total Relief.	Relief per Member.	Total Receipts.	Receipts per Member.
1844	8	909	$720	$0.79	$8,657	$9.52
1845	10	1,108	2,438	2.20	10,272	9.27
1846	11	1,447	2,677	1.85	13,729	9.48
1847	17	1,632	3,275	2.00	14,942	9.15
1848	27	1,860	4,077	2.19	17,374	9.34
1849	32	1,941	3,145	1.62	16,723	8.61
1850	37	1,831	3,984	2.17	16,184	8.83
1851	42	1,743	4,068	2.33	13,879	7.96
1852	42	*	*	*	*	*
1853	44	1,709	5,188	3.03	12,432	7.27
1854	44	1,546	3,468	2.24	9,591	6.20
1855	41	1,368	3,435	2.51	7,824	5.71
1856	39	913	2,344	2.56	5,263	5.76
1857	21	1,150	1,886	1.64	7,478	6.49
1858	21	1,041	2,669	2.56	6,387	6.13
1859	23	1,015	2,732	2.69	6,931	6.82
1860	16	1,066	3,180	2.98	6,925	6.49
1861	*	*	*	*	*	*
1862	*	*	*	*	*	*
1863	*	*	*	*	*	*
1864	*	*	*	*	*	*
1865	13	1,072	2,315	2.15	7,018	6.54
1866	13	1,087	2,636	2.51	6,017	5.53
1867	14	992	3,135	3.16	7,462	7.52
1868	16	1,008	3,173	2.88	8,390	7.64
1869	19	1,258	3,768	2.99	10,676	8.48
1870	22	1,400	3,326	2.37	11,756	8.39
1871	32	1,742	8,448	4.84	20,501	11.76
1872	35	2,033	5,117	2.51	16,144	7.94
1873	37	2,125	4,951	2.32	15,468	7.27
1874	41	2,078	4,471	2.15	13,955	6.71
1875	47	2,106	3,849	1.82	15,017	7.13
1876	48	2,043	6,074	2.97	12,922	6.32
1877	48	1,963	5,510	2.80	11,549	5.88
1878	42	1,964	4,856	2.47	12,733	6.48
1879	44	2,031	5,397	2.65	13,171	6.48
1880	45	2,093	4,650	2.22	12,567	6.00
1881	41	2,000	5,442	2.72	13,107	6.55
1882	40	1,937	4,820	2.48	13,776	7.11
1883	42	1,908	5,455	2.85	12,328	6.46
1884	44	1,912	6,016	3.14	13,097	6.84
1885	47	1,958	5,756	2.93	13,285	6.78
1886	49	2,038	5,500	2.69	13,977	6.85
			$153,951		$449,507	

*No Report.

637

A TABLE FOR MAINE,

Showing the Progress of the Order from 1845 to 1886, Inclusive.

Year.	No. of Lodges	No. of Members.	Total Relief.	Relief per Member.	Total Receipts.	Receipts per Member.
1845	30	3,435	$4,255	$1.23	$29,477	$8.58
1846	40	4,789	7,304	1.52	30,130	6.08
1847	49	5,348	10,593	1.98	27,289	5.10
1848	53	5,611	11,928	2.12	27,671	4.93
1849	58	5,886	10,830	1.84	22,329	3.79
1850	59	5,088	9,736	1.91	20,372	3.98
1851	61	4,492	8,406	1.89	13,132	2.92
1852	55	4,280	5,231	1.22	7,554	1.78
1853	56	2,644	3,258	1.23	9,029	3.41
1854	47	3,343	4,109	1.23	8,822	2.63
1855	46	2,906	5,025	1.73	6,658	2.29
1856	46	2,406	3,532	1.47	5,410	2.24
1857	30	1,537	3,903	2.58	5,426	3.53
1858	29	1,307	2,567	1.96	3,711	2.83
1859	24	1,203	2,965	2.46	4,193	3.48
1860	24	1,187	3,152	2.65	4,611	2.88
1861	23	1,210	2,759	2.27	5,000	4.13
1862	24	1,171	3,016	2.57	4,870	4.15
1863	22	1,237	3,167	2.56	5,793	4.60
1864	22	1,225	3,022	2.46	7,314	5.96
1865	19	1,180	3,010	2.55	5,248	4.48
1866	20	1,207	4,847	4.01	7,754	6.42
1867	20	1,452	3,342	2.30	*	*
1868	21	1,705	4,455	2.61	11,959	7.01
1869	20	2,109	4,720	2.24	14,191	6.72
1870	21	2,271	7,222	3.18	16,325	7.18
1871	23	2,767	11,749	4.24	29,862	10.79
1872	27	3,503	8,300	2.37	27,177	7.72
1873	32	4,291	11,750	2.74	36,050	8.40
1874	42	5,473	16,078	2.94	50,805	2.28
1875	52	6,721	21,250	3.16	64,040	9.52
1876	54	7,606	23,507	3.09	59,226	7.77
1877	62	8,658	26,717	3.08	75,139	8.66
1878	65	9,265	28,549	3.08	60,189	6.61
1879	68	9,743	31,186	3.20	69,739	7.15
1880	71	10,327	30,520	2.95	74,489	7.21
1881	82	11,245	34,571	3.08	85,112	7.56
1882	94	12,608	34,928	2.77	96,980	7.85
1883	102	13,861	42,563	3.07	116,756	8.27
1884	105	14,656	46,907	3.20	107,062	7.37
1885	110	15,220	47,021	3 09	109,274	7.18
1886	112	16,041	48,487	3.02	114,295	7.12
			$600,437		$1,451,163	

* No Report.

A TABLE FOR RHODE ISLAND,

Showing the Progress of the Order from 1845 to 1886, Inclusive.

Year.	No. of Lodges.	No. of Members.	Total Relief.	Relief per Member.	Total Receipts.	Receipts per Member.
1845	9	1,055	$694	$0.65	$1,126	$1.06
1846	13	1,674	3,656	2.18	14,078	8.41
1847	13	1,743	*	*	3,905	2.18
1848	13	1,628	, 6,520	4.04	5,410	3.32
1849	13	1,537	4,680	3.04	*	*
1850	13	1,474	4,248	2.88	9,768	6.62
1851	15	1,322	3,014	2.27	7,657	5.79
1852	15	1,297	3,841	2.96	7,880	6.07
1853	15	1,233	5,620	4.55	8,399	6.89
1854	14	1,132	3,709	3.27	6,418	5.66
1855	14	1,045	3,217	3.07	*	*
1856	16	953	3,038	3.18	5,492	5.78
1857	14	888	3,410	3.84	5,026	5.66
1858	14	773	4,338	5.74	4,132	5.34
1859	14	729	2,153	2.95	4,602	6.31
1860	16	694	2,063	2.97	3,984	5.65
1861	13	671	2,944	4.38	3,168	4.72
1862	13	605	1,783	2.94	2,951	4.87
1863	13	560	1,606	2.86	3,360	6.00
1864	12	539	1,037	1.92	3,525	6.55
1865	11	534	1,279	2.39	5,080	9.51
1866	11	606	1,634	2.69	6,347	10.47
1867	11	644	1,944	3.01	6,432	9.98
1868	11	830 .	1,269	1.52	9,508	11.45
1869	12	1,090	2,975	2.72	12,351	11.33
1870	15	1,694	4,402	2.59	23,981	14.14
1871	20	2,463	6,840	2.77	89,218	15.92
1872	30	3,762	5,933	1.57	50,933	13.53
1873	33	4,489	8,097	1.80	55,255	12.30
1874	38	5,091	12,980	2.54	62,985	12.35
1875	39	5,413	18,602	3.43	66,840	12.34
1876	40	5,419	18,717	3.45	58,457	10.78
1877	42	5,276	20,165	3.82	63,149	11.96
1878	42	5,101	17,824	3.49	68,443	13.41
1879	42	4,888	19,840	4.05	48,266	9.87
1880	42	4,714	18,562	3.93	53,905	11.43
1881	43	4,756	20,519	4.31	56,215	11.81
1882	43	4,862	21,559	4.43	58,888	12.11
1883	43	5,100	24,965	4.89	71,007	13.93
1884	43	5,223	26,905	5.15	63,178	12.09
1885	43	5,292	26,219	4.95	61,274	11.57
1886	45	5,539	29,752	5.37	71,379	12.88
			$372,553		$1,114,274	

* No Report.

A TABLE FOR NEW HAMPSHIRE,

Showing the Progress of the Order from 1844 to 1886, Inclusive.

Year.	No. of Lodges.	No. of Members.	Total Relief.	Relief per Member.	Total Receipts.	Receipts per Member.
1844	*	*	*	*	*	*
1845	11	1,142	$692	$0.61	$10,953	$9.59
1846	19	1,812	3,743	2.07	8,541	4.71
1847	19	1,980	4,406	2.23	5,641	2.85
1848	23	2,191	5,930	2.71	5,464	2.49
1849	29	2,400	5,250	2.19	5,346	2.23
1850	34	2,545	4,342	1.71	4,479	1.76
1851	37	2,403	5,012	2.09	3,947	1.64
1852	39	2,570	5,347	2.08	4,178	1.63
1853	39	2,488	4,324	1.77	2,111	.87
1854	39	2,240	3,417	1.52	2,642	1.18
1855	38	2,034	3,004	1.48	8,621	4.24
1856	36	2,243	3,712	1.65	*	*
1857	28	1,927	3,134	1.63	*	*
1858	28	1,827	3,326	1.82	1,477	.81
1859	25	1,730	2,945	1.70	1,826	1.06
1860	23	1,641	3,096	1.88	*	*
1861	22	1,658	3,690	2.23	2,118	1.28
1862	22	1,676	3,495	2.09	2,060	1.23
1863	19	1,696	3,681	2.17	2,598	1.53
1864	22	1,851	4,831	2.61	9,117	4.92
1865	22	2,055	4,386	2.13	10,363	5.04
1866	20	2,303	5,015	2.18	13,882	6.03
1867	21	2,600	5,883	2.26	16,685	6.42
1868	25	3,034	5,506	1.81	19,322	6.37
1869	29	3,552	7,922	2.23	25,177	7.09
1870	29	3,869	8,859	2.29	24,273	6.27
1871	33	4,215	18,109	4.30	36,155	8.53
1872	36	4,692	12,391	2.64	31,506	6.71
1873	37	5,087	12,820	2.52	33,643	6.61
1874	41	5,646	14,814	2.62	39,511	7.00
1875	44	6,184	15,525	2.51	44,090	7.13
1876	49	6,642	17,142	2.58	43,697	6.58
1877	53	7,033	17,342	2.47	48,318	6.87
1878	58	7,370	17,852	2.42	50,867	6.90
1879	62	7,705	18,758	2.44	52,056	6.76
1880	64	7,970	18,089	2.27	53,990	6.77
1881	67	8,284	22,453	2.71	57,675	6.97
1882	67	8,501	22,738	2.67	62,337	7.33
1883	69	8,722	24,080	2.76	59,167	6.78
1884	69	8,986	26,739	2.97	67,662	7.53
1885	70	9,195	26,409	2.87	61,900	6.73
1886	73	9,483	30,191	2.18	65,260	6.88
			$430,400		$998,655	

*No Report.

A TABLE FOR MICHIGAN,

Showing the Progress of the Order from 1845 to 1886, Inclusive.

Year.	No. of Lodges.	No. of Members.	Total Relief.	Relief per Member.	Total Receipts.	Receipts per Member.
1845	9	628	$105	$0.16	$5,280	$8.40
1846	15	992	1,028	1.04	7,622	7.41
1847	24	1,557	2,692	1.73	11,966	7.68
1848	36	2,305	3,650	1.58	17,819	7.73
1849	43	2,743	3,839	1.40	15,849	5.77
1850	49	2,974	4,785	1.69	18,622	6.26
1851	56	3,223	5,433	1.68	18,810	5.83
1852	58	3,289	5,532	1.68	16,580	5.04
1853	61	3,247	4,557	1.40	18,143	5.58
1854	64	2,847	2,949	1.26	13,953	5.95
1855	62	2,257	4,711	2.08	11,658	5.16
1856	57	2,521	1,933	.76	10,130	4.02
1857	44	1,869	1,823	.97	9,264	4.95
1858	39	1,291	1,368	1.06	5,479	4.24
1859	35	1,443	1,212	.84	7,236	5.01
1860	62	1,686	1,138	.67	4,453	2.64
1861	63	1,663	1,738	1.04	1,698	1.02
1862	65	1,820	843	.46	7,862	4.92
1863	50	2,125	1,710	.80	8,954	4.21
1864	50	2,428	2,213	.91	13,112	5.40
1865	50	2,869	2,856	.82	15,061	5.25
1866	60	3,562	3,377	.92	20,703	5.81
1867	71	4,434	2,248	.50	24,240	5.46
1868	79	5,175	4,062	.78	33,449	6.46
1869	98	6,193	3,518	.56	36,414	5.87
1870	107	7,207	4,588	.63	41,749	5.79
1871	147	8,557	6,735	.78	54,621	6.38
1872	174	10,124	10,396	1.02	68,185	6.72
1873 ·	187	11,482	9,899	.86	72,111	6.28
1874	225	12,136	14,139	1.16	79,508	6 55
1875	248	12,935	14,550	1.12	86,689	6.70
1876	262	13,451	15,609	1.16	78,723	6.67
1877	285	13,148	13,929	1.06	71,738	5.46
1878	296	13,191	16,143	1.22	68,592	4.23
1879	303	13,341	14,909	1.11	75,411	5.61
1880	313	14,120	15,589	1.10	79,492	5.63
1881	319	14,832	17,752	1.23	87,125	5.87
1882	332	15,923	17,999	1.13	100,216	6.29
1883	344	16,574	22,074	1.33	102,011	6.15
1884	347	17,183	21,419	1.24	91,710	5.33
1885	357	17,224	19,381	1.12	88,953	5.16
1886	367	17,302	22,321	1.29	90,328	5.22
			$326,757		$1,691,519	

A TABLE FOR WISCONSIN,

Showing the Progress of the Order from 1847 to 1886, Inclusive.

Year.	No. of Lodges.	No. of Members.	Total Relief.	Relief per Member.	Total Receipts.	Receipts per Member.
1847	14	699	$126	$0.18	$5,680	$8.12
1848	27	1,224	1,099	.89	5,173	4.22
1849	36	1,665	1,027	.66	11,138	6.68
1850	49	2,287	2,689	1.13	15,303	6.73
1851	53	2,621	4,439	1.69	15,132	5.77
1852	58	2,774	3,128	1.13	15,490	5.59
1853	62	2,490	2,529	1.02	11,241	4.51
1854	66	2,700	2,085	.77	13,225	4.87
1855	83	3,033	1,571	.51	14,565	4.80
1856	89	3,207	1,541	.48	11,450	3.57
1857	93	2,262	3,221	1.42	9,998	4.43
1858	65	2,303	1,134	.49	7,126	3.09
1859	61	2,099	901	.43	8,532	4.07
1860	61	1,722	845	.49	7,590	4.41
1861	61	1,832	467	.25	6,463	3.52
1862	56	1,948	853	.44	5,804	2.98
1863	52	1,631	869	.53	6,592	4.05
1864	53	1,901	2,332	1.23	9,861	5.19
1865	51	1,811	2,369	1.31	7,798	4.31
1866	52	2,381	1,157	.49	13,891	5.83
1867	64	3,215	3,007	.94	20,941	6.51
1868	94	4,317	2,673	.62	25,874	5.99
1869	110	5,778	5,212	.90	41,705	7.22
1870	135	6,848	6,954	1.02	45,451	6.64
1871	175	8,365	12,349	1.48	76,022	9.09
1872	186	9,758	8,746	.90	38,948	3.99
1873	205	10,628	14,195	1.34	68,516	6.45
1874	220	12,051	14,664	1.13	81,687	6.78
1875	231	13,039	26,161	2.01	83,993	6.44
1876	239	13,487	22,172	1.73	86,867	6.44
1877	251	13,492	23,986	1.77	84,864	6.25
1878	264	13,890	22,441	1.62	91,113	6.56
1879	266	14,142	20,456	1.45	92,042	6.51
1880	273	14,476	24,104	1.67	92,100	6.36
1881	283	15,121	28,659	1.90	104,393	6.90
1882	288	15,399	23,297	1.51	115,069	7.47
1883	294	15,672	24,611	1.57	106,144	6.77
1884	296	15,825	26,549	1.68	106,989	6.76
1885	301	15,594	25,318	1.62	124,392	7.98
1886	300	14,983	22,998	1.53	98,290	6.56
			$392,934		$1,786,952	

A TABLE FOR VERMONT,

Showing the Progress of the Order from 1848 to 1886, Inclusive.

Year.	No. of Lodges.	No. of Members.	Total Relief.	Relief per Member.	Total Receipts.	Receipts per Member.
1848	13	695	$1,458	$2.10	$2,535	$3.65
1849	15	841	1,512	1.80	5,785	6.88
1850	20	971	2,689	2.76	6,046	6.23
1851	22	1,030	1,689	1.64	4,232	4.21
1852	24	1,140	1,362	1.19	6,073	5.30
1853	26	1,127	2,329	2.07	5,270	4.66
1854	25	1,008	1,524	1.51	4,382	4.35
1855	25	1,020	1,466	1.44	3,592	3.53
1856	22	786	890	1.13	3,294	4.19
1857	20	678	557	.82	1,840	2.71
1858	14	431	689	1.60	1,513	3.51
1859	12	306	177	.57	1,255	4.10
1860	11	271	199	.73	969	3.57
1861	*	*	*	*	*	*
1862	*	*	*	*	*	*
1863	4	141	180	1.28	74	.52
1864	5	152	136	.89	66	.43
1865	5	*	408	*	*	*
1866	5	195	*	*	883	4.52
1867	4	235	*	*	1,113	4.73
1868	5	239	*	*	119	.50
1869	11	421	590	1.40	2,045	4.86
1870	12	551	588	1.06	3,727	6.76
1871	15	741	809	1.09	5,865	7.91
1872	16	907	605	.67	4,993	5.50
1873	16	1,010	576	.57	4,960	4.71
1874	16	1,092	891	.82	5,648	5.17
1875	18	1,231	1,316	1.07	6,092	4.95
1876	17	1,282	1,665	1.30	6,087	4.75
1877	18	1,246	1,448	1.16	6,913	5.54
1878	20	1,269	1,192	.94	6,021	4.78
1879	21	2,222	1,493	.67	6,472	2.91
1880	23	1,464	1,537	1.05	8,387	5.73
1881	26	1,649	2,202	1.33	10,196	6.18
1882	27	1,736	1,786	1.03	10,620	6.12
1883	29	1,897	2,560	1.35	10,927	5.76
1884	29	1,960	2,682	1.37	10,860	5.54
1885	30	2,008	2,586	1.28	10,893	5.42
1886	31	2,101	3,040	1.44	12,645	6.02
			$44,831		$182,392	

* No Report.

A TABLE FOR IOWA,

Showing the Progress of the Order from 1849 to 1886, Inclusive.

Year.	No. of Lodges.	No. of Members.	Total Relief.	Relief per Member.	Total Receipts.	Receipts per Member.
1849	24	746	$472	$.51	$7,586	$10.16
1850	28	946	1,184	1.19	7,936	8.38
1851	30	1,066	1,337	1.25	3,916	3.67
1852	40	1,378	2,645	1.91	*	*
1853	48	1,648	1,478	.89	11,994	7.27
1854	55	1,979	1,813	.91	13,212	6.67
1855	74	2,637	2,907	1.10	18,597	7.05
1856	92	3,726	2,382	.63	23,437	6.29
1857	106	4,401	3,194	.72	30,223	6.86
1858	117	4,453	3,253	.73	25,969	5.83
1859	118	3,711	2,582	.69	19,671	5.30
1860	114	3,756	2,923	.77	18,793	5.00
1861	109	3,274	2,206	.67	14,849	4.53
1862	104	2,776	1,931	.69	11,912	4.29
1863	92	2,865	2,828	.98	15,041	5.24
1864	84	3,098	3,212	1.03	17,711	5.71
1865	89	3,602	3,462	.96	23,064	6.40
1866	96	4,597	4,593	.99	30,551	6.64
1867	109	5,679	5,268	.92	33,987	5.98
1868	122	6,544	6,832	1.04	40,895	6.24
1869	133	7,517	7,090	.94	44,730	5.98
1870	103	8,606	7,493	.87	55,035	6.39
1871	199	9,858	11,417	1.15	85,510	8.67
1872	221	11,161	9,503	.85	68,311	6.12
1873	237	12,830	14,936	1.16	81,707	6.35
1874	271	14,441	17,294	1.19	90,915	6.29
1875	303	16,328	20,663	1.26	100,324	6.14
1876	324	17,476	20,454	1.11	97,244	5.55
1877	336	17,917	22,682	1.26	90,653	5.05
1878	351	17,812	27,535	1.54	86,190	4.83
1879	356	25,872	26,642	1.03	88,017	3.40
1880	376	19,161	25,805	1.34	100,261	5.23
1881	392	20,364	31,750	1.55	114,525	5.62
1882	407	21,678	33,118	1.52	131,081	6.04
1883	428	21,912	34,793	1.58	120,672	5.50
1884	454	22,156	36,078	1.62	110,987	5.00
1885	460	21,717	34,897	1.60	106,925	4.92
1886	465	21,461	35,282	1.64	116,847	5.44
			$473,884		$2,059,278	

* No Report.

A TABLE FOR ARKANSAS,

Showing the Progress of the Order from 1850 to 1886, Inclusive.

Year.	No. of Lodges.	No. of Members.	Total Relief.	Relief per Member.	Total Receipts.	Receipts per Member.
1850	6	197	$108	$0.55	*	*
1851	6	280	138	0.49	*	*
1852	6	*	*	*	*	*
1853	*	*	*	*	*	*
1854	6	*	*	*	*	*
1855	12	415	*	*	$388	$0.94
1856	13	392	*	*	2,816	7.18
1857	14	418	*	*	2,711	6.49
1858	*	*	*	*	*	*
1859	16	549	357	0.65	4,991	9.09
1860	17	750	503	0.67	5,783	7.71
1861	*	*	*	*	*	*
1862	*	*	*	*	*	*
1863	*	*	*	*	*	*
1864	*	*	*	*	*	*
1865	*	*	*	*	*	*
1866	9	258	159	0.62	382	1.48
1867	11	390	853	2.19	572	1.47
1868	17	610	611	1.00	704	1.16
1869	19	671	905	1.33	703	1.04
1870	20	790	1,383	1.75	840	1.06
1871	33	1,227	1,804	1.47	14,956	12.19
1872	40	1,389	1,795	1.29	16,641	11.98
1873	43	1,483	2,579	1.74	13,984	9.36
1874	43	1,430	2,057	1.44	10,949	7.66
1875	49	1,465	1,934	1.32	12,998	8.87
1876	56	1,487	1,783	1.20	11,400	7.67
1877	63	1,533	1,765	1.15	9,864	6.43
1878	60	1,593	2,993	1.88	11,618	7.29
1879	58	1,568	1,834	1.17	9,669	6.17
1880	58	1,603	2,206	1.38	11,883	7.41
1881	63	1,777	2,563	1.45	13,957	7.86
1882	61	1,715	2,640	1.53	11,480	6.69
1883	64	1,688	2,020	1.20	10,149	6.01
1884	66	1,776	2,430	1.37	10,419	5.87
1885	61	1,722	2,616	1.51	9,847	5.73
1886	65	1,592	1,858	1.17	9,246	5.81
			$39,894		$192,450	

*No Report.

A TABLE FOR FLORIDA,

Showing the Progress of the Order from 1851 to 1886, Inclusive.

Year	No. of Lodges.	No. of Members.	Total Relief.	Relief per Member.	Total Receipts.	Receipts per Member.
1851	7	264	$ 77	*	$1,161	$4.39
1852	7	*	*	*	*	*
1853	7	242	468	$1.93	2,164	8.94
1854	8	317	979	3.08	3,616	11.40
1855	9	312	902	2.89	3,103	9.94
1856	9	308	853	2.76	2,182	7.08
1857	9	253	864	3.41	1,960	7.74
1858	9	250	279	1.11	1,784	7.13
1859	9	247	290 ·	1.17	1,629	6.59
1860	9	229	470	2.05	1,796	7.84
1861	*	*	*	*	*	*
1862	*	*	*	*	*	*
1863	*	*	*	*	*	*
1864	*	*	*	*	*	*
1865	*	*	*	*	*	*
1866	5	100	*	*	*	*
1867	5	120	368	3.06	1,179	9.82
1868	5	148	194	1.31	804	5.43
1869	4	85	169	1.98	205	2.41
1870	3	133	144	1.08	231	1.73
1871	5	129	439	3.40	1,820	14.10
1872	5	205	277	1.35	1,959	9.55
1873	7	253	659	2.60	2,442	9.65
1874	7	230	437	1.90	2,434	10.58
1875	8	284	439	1.54	2,910	10.24
1876	10	318	239	.75	3,058	9.61
1877	11	338	449	1.32	3,281	9.70
1878	11	380	1,071	2.81	4,185	11.01
1879	11	600	891	1.48	3,840	6.40
1880	13	374	1,034	2.76	3,705	9.90
1881	14	451	916	2.03	5,063	11.22
1882	12	416	1,522	3.65	5,884	14.14
1883	13	420	2,342	5.57	4,674	11.12
1884	15	467	1,362	2.91	5,328	11.40
1885	19	557	1,763	3.16	6,648	11.93
1886	20	555	1,562	2.81	4,785	8.62
			$21,459		$83,830	

*No Report.

A TABLE FOR CALIFORNIA,

Showing the Progress of the Order from 1852 to 1886, Inclusive.

Year.	No. of Lodges.	No. of Members.	Total Relief.	Relief per Member.	Total Receipts.	Receipts per Member.
1852	6	*	*	*	*	*
1853	13	571	*	*	$1,863	$3.26
1854	28	1,393	$5,311	$3.81	51,305	36.83
1855	42	1,940	7,988	4.11	57,100	29.43
1856	59	2,514	15,743	6.26	69,904	27.80
1857	70	2,936	8,886	3.02	76,682	22.71
1858	76	3,523	13,110	3.72	91,762	26.04
1859	88	4,475	19,355	4.32	112,273	25.08
1860	98	5,091	20,412	4.00	121,125	23.79
1861	101	5,636	23,538	4.17	133,020	23.60
1862	108	5,597	27,932	5.00	129,764	23.18
1863	118	6,100	34,634	5.67	159,944	26.22
1864	125	6,925	39,485	5.70	182,284	26.32
1865	128	6,876	43,454	6.31	166,151	24.16
1866	127	7,559	49,318	6.52	199,967	26.45
1867	133	8,444	55,041	6.51	211,796	25.08
1868	141	10,053	73,937	7.35	239,592	23.83
1869	152	11,748	86,346	7.35	283,159	24.12
1870	171	13,093	100,602	7.68	298,884	22.82
1871	188	14,747	104,285	7.07	306,789	20.80
1872	206	16,277	168,814	10.37	511,714	31.43
1873	219	17,484	127,761	7.30	366,267	20.94
1874	217	18,007	126,580	7.02	357,449	19.85
1875	228	19,342	146,799	7.58	419,411	21.68
1876	238	20,201	149,187	7.38	436,118	21.58
1877	248	20,729	160,254	7.73	458,888	22.13
1878	264	21,203	182,927	8.62	448,181	21.13
1879	271	21,346	171,740	8.04	452,213	21.18
1880	271	21,468	172,898	8.05	456,812	21.27
1881	274	21,858	174,683	7.99	462,930	21.17
1882	287	22,248	183,181	8.23	448,040	20.13
1883	293	22,754	187,455	8.23	464,234	20.40
1884	296	23,447	195,749	8.34	451,815	19.26
1885	298	24,078	210,708	8.75	468,983	19.47
1886	303	24,375	206,101	8.45	468,022	19.20
			$3,294,214		$9,564,441	

*No Report.

A TABLE FOR THE LOWER PROVINCES,

Showing the Progress of the Order from 1856 to 1886, Inclusive.

Year.	No. of Lodges.	No. of Members.	Total Relief.	Relief per Member.	Total Receipts.	Receipts per Member.
1856	4	130	$80	$0.62	$711	$5.47
1857	3	129	159	1.23	563	4.36
1858	3	121	96	.79	482	3.98
1859	4	156	134	.87	900	5.77
1860	5	205	150	.73	1,200	3.85
1861	4	200	*	*	90	.45
1862	4	171	*	*	*	*
1863	*	*	*	*	*	*
1864	*	*	*	*	*	*
1865	*	*	*	*	*	*
1866	3	154	*	*	40	.26
1867	3	206	353	1.71	1,096	6.40
1868	3	242	260	1.07	897	3.70
1869	3	213	250	1.17	870	4.08
1870	6	280	219	.78	1,449	5.17
1871	8	462	510	1.10	3,725	8.06
1872	8	563	499	.88	2,717	4.82
1873	12	856	1,037	1.21	4,809	5.60
1874	16	1,169	1,139	.97	8,733	7.47
1875	22	1,513	1,480	.98	9,132	6.03
1876	23	1,629	1,585	.97	8,891	5.45
1877	25	1,871	1,888	1.00	10,928	5.84
1878	29	2,166	3,451	1.59	13,155	6.07
1879	33	3,219	2,488	.77	11,514	3.57
1880	35	2,229	2,533	1.13	12,734	5.70
1881	36	2,332	2,855	1.22	12,739	5.46
1882	38	2,355	3,480	1.43	15,928	6.76
1883	39	2,374	3,002	1.26	14,095	5.51
1884	42	2,389	2,793	1.17	13,280	5.56
1885	40	2,275	2,695	1.19	12,749	5.60
1886	40	2,303	2,758	1.19	12,591	5.46
			$31,944		$176,018	

* No Report.

A TABLE FOR OREGON,

Showing the Progress of the Order from 1858 to 1886, Inclusive.

Year.	No. of Lodges.	No. of Members.	Total Relief.	Relief per Member.	Total Receipts.	Receipts per Member.
1858	7	240	*	*	$4,872	$20.30
1859	7	*	*	*	*	*
1860	7	318	$260	$0.81	4,299	13.52
1861	9	315	*	*	5,128	16.27
1862	10	350	*	*	3,592	10.26
1863	11	380	*	*	4,400	11.58
1864	13	465	*	*	8,270	17.78
1865	13	649	1,106	1.70	14,735	22.70
1866	17	726	2,215	3.05	16,500	22.72
1867	21	977	2,001	2.05	21,000	21.48
1868	26	1,114	2,558	2.30	26,000	23.31
1869	31	1,375	2,527	1.84	30,212	21.97
1870	37	1,635	3,847	2.35	37,366	22.85
1871	45	1,955	10,042	5.14	77,684	39.74
1872	53	2,244	4,241	1.89	45,908	20.46
1873	60	2,401	10,802	4.49	45,030	18.75
1874	61	2,590	12,461	4.81	46,801	18.07
1875	65	2,803	14,612	5.21	55,354	19.74
1876	72	2,891	11,774	4.07	58,142	20.11
1877	72	2,961	13,577	4.59	54,599	18.44
1878	71	2,868	14,097	4.91	51,888	18.09
1879	72	3,471	15,638	4.51	50,267	14.48
1880	72	3,029	14,330	4.73	54,197	17.89
1881	75	3,201	12,764	3.99	53,677	16.76
1882	75	3,447	13,700	3.97	58,482	16.97
1883	72	3,397	14,609	4.30	57,497	16.92
1884	75	3,490	14,635	4.19	48,772	13.97
1885	75	3,442	14,791	4.29	53,777	15.62
1886	82	3,560	18,837	5.29	59,836	16.80
			$225,424		$1,048,285	

* No Report.

A TABLE FOR MINNESOTA,

Showing the Progress of the Order from 1856 to 1886, Inclusive.

Year.	No. of Lodges.	No. of Members.	Total Relief.	Relief per Member.	Total Receipts.	Receipts per Member.
1856	7	254	$51	$0.20	$776	$3.06
1857	7	624	152	.24	2,424	3.88
1858	8	355	177	.50	2,150	6.06
1859	9	334	156	.46	2,385	7.14
1860	9	330	314	.95	1,852	5.61
1861	9	334	172	.52	1,562	4.67
1862	9	275	117	.43	1,209	4.76
1863	8	276	180	.65	1,796	6.47
1864	7	289	189	.65	1,892	6.55
1865	8	310	388	1.25	2,132	6.88
1866	8	365	377	1.03	2,951	8.05
1867	12	492	654	1.33	5,282	10.63
1868	16	754	678	.90	7,959	10.56
1869	20	1,033	865	.84	11,219	10.86
1870	20	1,162	911	.78	11,090	9.54
1871	28	1,463	2,215	1.51	20,223	13.82
1872	31	1,697	2,232	1.32	16,027	9.44
1873	36	2,086	2,102	1.01	21,419	10.27
1874	41	2,234	2,880	1.29	20,780	9.30
1875	44	2,401	3,669	1.53	22,458	9.35
1876	50	2,598	4,377	1.68	26,004	10.01
1877	55	3,007	4,093	1.36	28,283	9.41
1878	60	3,184	5,300	1.66	28,473	8.94
1879	65	4,532	4,880	1.07	30,699	6.78
1880	73	3,936	4,715	1.20	36,719	9.33
1881	78	4,245	8,470	2.00	41,429	9.32
1882	86	5,052	8,672	1.72	55,007	10.89
1883	89	5,549	11,187	2.02	57,030	10.28
1884	92	5,840	11,717	2.01	49,717	8.41
1885	103	6,037	11,526	1.91	53,244	8.82
1886	107	6,471	11,048	1.71	60,699	9.38
			$104,458		$624,830	

A TABLE FOR KANSAS,

Showing the Progress of the Order from 1858 to 1886, Inclusive.

1858	5	174	*	*	$1,580	$9.08
1859	10	333	*	*	3,738	11.23
1860	11	370	$250	$0.68	3,377	9.13
1861	13	403	156	.38	2,543	6.31
1862	10	652	436	.67	2,271	3.48
1863	8	346	421	1.22	3,128	9.04
1864	8	384	570	1.48	2,727	7.10
1865	9	422	645	1.53	3,827	9.07

* No Report.

A TABLE FOR KANSAS—*Continued.*

Year.	No. of Lodges.	No. of Members.	Total Relief.	Relief per Member.	Total Receipts.	Receipts per Member.
1866	16	771	937	1.22	8,152	10.57
1867	25	1,211	1,716	1.42	11,461	9.46
1868	31	1,556	1,906	1.22	13,795	8.86
1869	43	2,029	1,492	.73	18,232	8.99
1870	54	2,673	3,050	1.14	22,086	8.26
1871	84	3,489	5,463	1.57	29,368	8.42
1872	99	4,094	6,043	1.48	33,314	8.14
1873	104	4,823	6,349	1.31	35,717	7.41
1874	120	4,530	4,767	1.05	35,882	7.92
1875	127	4,664	8,394	1.80	34,408	7.37
1876	130	4,968	7,579	1.52	36,262	7.30
1877	134	5,064	8,068	1.59	36,062	7.12
1878	144	5,635	9,801	1.74	41,798	7.42
1879	161	6,690	12,171	1.82	46,866	7.01
1880	167	7,202	11,352	1.58	59,911	8.32
1881	188	8,141	13,648	1.68	68,356	8.40
1882	194	9,007	15,584	1.73	77,624	8.62
1883	220	9,839	17,964	1.83	86,217	8.76
1884	231	10,956	17,864	1.63	93,955	8.58
1885	258	11,964	20,713	1.73	103,845	8.68
1886	305	12,885	24,969	1.94	115,789	8.99
			$202,308		$1,032,291	

A TABLE FOR NEBRASKA,

Showing the Progress of the Order from 1858 to 1886, Inclusive.

Year.	No. of Lodges.	No. of Members.	Total Relief.	Relief per Member.	Total Receipts.	Receipts per Member.
1858	5	*	*	*	*	*
1859	6	204	$44	$0.22	$950	$4.66
1860	5	158	34	.22	389	2.46
1861	5	133	90	.68	400	3.00
1862	4	122	175	1.44	788	6.46
1863	5	178	122	.68	847	4.76
1864	6	231	137	.59	1,652	7.15
1865	7	306	242	.79	2,322	7.59
1866	7	364	348	.96	2,028	5.57
1867	8	399	432	1.08	2,582	6.47
1868	9	478	457	.96	3,807	7.96
1869	10	569	868	1.52	6,955	12.22
1870	19	754	694	.92	9,940	13.18
1871	30	1,112	2,148	1.93	18,754	16.86
1872	44	1,292	1,377	1.07	13,636	10.55
1873	42	1,626	2,001	1.23	16,754	10.30
1874	52	2,065	1,270	.62	19,765	9.57
1875	55	2,196	2,237	1.02	20,450	9.31
1876	62	2,345	2,242	.96	19,870	8.47
1877	65	2,437	2,884	1.18	20,334	8.34

* No Report.

A TABLE FOR NEBRASKA—*Continued*.

Year.	No. of Lodges.	No. of Members.	Total Relief.	Relief per Member.	Total Receipts.	Receipts per Member.
1878	69	2,566	2,983	1.16	19,012	7.41
1879	74	3,734	2,907	.78	22,697	6.07
1880	85	3,285	3,033	.92	29,541	8.99
1881	90	3,659	2,587	.71	31,547	8.62
1882	100	4,256	3,428	.81	50,391	11.84
1883	108	4,592	4,115	.89	50,746	11.05
1884	126	4,960	5,768	1.16	38,986	7.86
1885	132	5,160	5,529	1.07	46,401	8.99
1886	136	5,610	5,332	.95	47,092	8.39
			$53,484		$498,636	

A TABLE FOR WEST VIRGINIA,

Showing the Progress of the Order from 1866 to 1886, Inclusive.

Year.	No. of Lodges.	No. of Members.	Total Relief.	Relief per Member.	Total Receipts.	Receipts per Member.
1866	27	$1,610	$1,916	$1.19	$6,421	$3.99
1867	34	2,061	4,321	2.10	16,337	7.93
1868	41	2,617	4,792	1.83	20,835	7.96
1869	43	3,093	6,918	2.24	20,737	6.70
1870	48	3,460	8,293	2.40	21,555	6.23
1871	62	3,779	16,398	4.34	47,462	12.56
1872	64	4,177	11,385	2.73	29,445	7.05
1873	69	4,404	14,137	3.21	28,934	6.57
1874	72	4,484	13,565	3.05	31,199	6.96
1875	78	4,490	13,162	2.93	34,761	7.74
1876	81	4,426	13,345	3.02	34,950	7.90
1877	84	4,283	8,121	1.90	27,110	6.33
1878	85	4,033	10,603	2.63	23,478	5.82
1879	80	5,118	10,871	2.13	16,180	3.16
1880	81	4,027	11,636	1.89	22,791	5.66
1881	87	4,084	11,777	2.86	30,148	7.38
1882	87	4,294	15,330	3.57	28,777	6.70
1883	79	3,866	14,177	3.67	34,609	8.95
1884	79	3,868	14,847	4.10	36,518	9.44
1885	80	3,729	14,919	4.00	34,506	9.25
1886	80	3,629	13,265	3.66	33,611	9.26
			$233,780		$580,376	

A TABLE FOR NEVADA,

Showing the Progress of the Order from 1867 to 1886, Inclusive.

Year.	No. of Lodges.	No. of Members.	Total Relief.	Relief per Member.	Total Receipts.	Receipts per Member.
1867	13	792	$4,936	$6.23	$14,698	$18.56
1868	13	955	5,650	5.92	31,259	32.73
1869	16	1,100	12,170	11.06	21,071	19.16
1870	18	1,282	8,624	6.73	10,131	7.90
1871	21	1,335	9,160	6.86	34,419	25.78
1872	24	1,664	14,407	8.66	46,168	27.75
1873	27	1,974	14,426	7.31	56,272	28 51
1874	25	1,943	12,262	6.31	55,535	28.58
1875	27	2,028	14,162	6.98	59,137	29.16
1876	27	2,045	12,509	6.12	49,313	24.11
1877	28	1,975	14,334	7.26	53,999	27.34
1878	29	2,003	14,025	7.00	58,159	29.04
1879	30	2,003	18,038	9.01	55,514	27.72
1880	30	1,924	14,568	7.56	48,068	24.98
1881	30	1,865	13,841	7.42	49,630	26.61
1882	29	1,748	13,904	7.95	38,124	22.38
1883	28	1,648	11,618	6.05	37,903	23.00
1884	27	1,584	14,976	9.45	31,569	19.93
1885	26	1,483	10,919	7.36	28,276	19.07
1886	26	1,433	12,134	8.47	27,183	18.97
			$246,663		$806,428	

A TABLE FOR COLORADO,

Showing the Progress of the Order from 1868 to 1886, Inclusive.

1868	5	282	$260	$0.92	$5,484	$19.45
1869	11	485	437	.90	10,610	21.88
1870	13	554	437	.78	10,131	18.29
1871	17	797	2,469	3.98	22,560	28.30
1872	20	905	1,954	2.16	15,185	16.78
1873	16	872	2,377	2.73	15,267	17.51
1874	19	918	2,276	2.48	14,302	15.58
1875	23	1,069	2,321	2.17	15,906	14.88
1876	27	1,215	3,407	2.80	16,863	13.88
1877	28	1,263	2,763	2.19	17,001	13.46
1878	30	1,378	3,459	2.51	17,701	12.84
1879	32	2,358	3,868	1.64	21,717	9.21
1880	38	2,030	5,791	2.85	25,783	12.70
1881	41	2,375	6,080	2.56	31,107	13.10
1882	48	2,772	6,651	2.40	38,948	14.05
1883	53	2,992	8,133	2.72	37,820	12.64
1884	58	3,138	8,502	2.71	31,499	10.04
1885	59	3,338	13,312	3.99	29,540	8.85
1886	60	3,448	13,868	4.02	37,070	10.75
			$88,365		$414,494	

A TABLE FOR ONTARIO,

Showing the Progress of the Order from 1868 to 1886, Inclusive.

Year.	No. of Lodges.	No. of Members.	Total Relief.	Relief per Member.	Total Receipts.	Receipts per Member.
1868	17	1,480	$2,145	$1.45	$9,948	$6.72
1869	20	1,762	2,548	1.45	13,281	7.54
1870	30	2,392	3,290	1.37	18,611	7.78
1871	57	4,115	7,074	1.72	44,852	10.90
1872	71	5,649	8,767	1.55	25,299	4.48
1873	89	7,525	12,082	1.61	62,284	8.27
1874	121	9,236	15,342	1.66	86,606	9.37
1875	148	10,633	18,098	1.70	99,745	9.38
1876	164	11,738	20,663	1.76	101,976	8.69
1877	178	12,348	22,144	1.79	110,675	8.96
1878	180	12,434	23,118	1.86	104,374	8.39
1879	184	13,744	23,926	1.74	108,946	7.56
1880	189	12,314	27,410	1.41	105,835	8.59
1881	192	13,074	32,055	2.45	120,983	9.25
1882	202	13,861	33,903	2.45	141,475	10.21
1883	203	14,174	38,994	2.75	129,847	9.15
1884	203	14,330	41,225	2.88	129,833	9.06
1885	208	14,506	45,150	3.11	129,102	8.89
1886	210	14,856	47,017	3.16	135,951	9.15
			$424,951		$1,674,623	

A TABLE FOR BRITISH COLUMBIA,

Showing the Progress of the Order from 1874 to 1886, Inclusive.

Year.	No. of Lodges.	No. of Members.	Total Relief.	Relief per Member.	Total Receipts.	Receipts per Member.
1874	5	408	$2,228	$5.46	$7,959	$19.50
1875	5	459	3,500	7.62	9,986	21.75
1876	5	492	3,302	6.71	10,716	21.78
1877	5	500	3,338	6.67	10,775	21.55
1878	5	496	4,297	8.66	10,873	21.92
1879	5	509	4,147	8.14	10,166	19.97
1880	5	499	3,866	7.74	9,229	18.69
1881	5	468	4,061	8.67	8,590	18.36
1882	6	466	4,096	8.78	9,070	19.47
1883	6	500	4,711	9.42	10,842	21.08
1884	6	546	5,823	10.66	11,391	20.84
1885	6	614	5,773	9.40	13,972	22.75
1886	7	700	6,545	9.35	13,621	19.45
			$55,687		$137,190	

A TABLE FOR MONTANA,

Showing the Progress of the Order from 1874 to 1886, Inclusive.

Year.	No. of Lodges.	No. of Members.	Total Relief.	Relief per Member.	Total Receipts.	Receipts per Member.
1874	5	171	$220	$1.29	$2,040	$11.93
1875	7	210	611	2.91	4,608	21.94
1876	8	256	604	2.36	4,959	19.37
1877	8	274	789	2.88	4,506	16.44
1878	10	327	1,188	3.63	5,209	15.93
1879	11	446	1,662	3.73	6,270	14.05
1880	11	428	1,533	3.57	7,777	18.17
1881	11	458	1,480	3.22	7,409	16.18
1882	13	538	1,631	3.03	8,867	16.48
1883	15	689	2,919	4.24	12,512	18.16
1884	17	723	2,641	3.65	10,848	15.00
1885	21	822	3,215	3.91	14,106	17.16
1886	22	1,060	3,111	2.93	19,894	18.77
			$21,604		$109,005	

A TABLE FOR SWITZERLAND,

Showing the Progress of the Order from 1874 to 1886, Inclusive.

Year.	No. of Lodges.	No. of Members.	Total Relief.	Relief per Member.	Total Receipts.	Receipts per Member.
1874	4	147	$109	$0.74	$1,425	$9.69
1875	4	178	133	.74	1,515	8.51
1876	7	236	302	1.28	1,865	7.90
1877	8	282	319	1.13	2,837	10.06
1878	8	294	439	1.49	2,770	9.42
1879	8	273	403	1.47	2,466	9.03
1880	8	241	451	1.87	2,082	8.64
1881	8	241	*	*	*	*
† 1882	7	204	1,003	4.91	3,007	14.74
1883	7	190	661	3.47	1,186	6.24
1884	7	188˙	487	2.59	1,688	8.98
1885	5	170	1,310	7.70	1,450	8.53
1886	5	179	715	3.99	1,379	7.70
			$6,332		$23,670	

* No Report.   † Report for two years

A TABLE FOR UTAH,

Showing the Progress of the Order from 1874 to 1886, Inclusive.

Year.	No. of Lodges.	No. of Members.	Total Relief.	Relief per Member.	Total Receipts.	Receipts per Member.
1874	5	268	$473	$1.76	$6,060	$26.41
1875	5	282	828	2.93	6,215	22.04
1876	5	296	542	1.83	6,677	22.55
1877	6	322	1,514	4.70	6,913	21.78
1878	6	335	1,793	5.35	7,102	21.18
1879	6	513	924	1.80	6,409	12.49
1880	6	325	1,237	3.84	5,152	15.88
1881	6	342	1,703	4.98	6,601	19.30
1882	6	333	1,917	5.75	8,512	25.56
1883	9	522	3,005	5.75	12,087	23.15
1884	8	506	2,560	5.05	11,724	23.17
1885	8	493	1,297	2.63	9,935	20.15
1886	8	498	1,496	3.00	9,202	18.47
			$19,289		$102,589	

A TABLE FOR WYOMING,

Showing the Progress of the Order from 1873 to 1886, Inclusive.

Year.	No. of Lodges.	No. of Members.	Total Relief.	Relief per Member.	Total Receipts.	Receipts per Member.
1874	8	331	$755	$2.28	$5,952	$11.93
1875	9	404	710	1.73	6,541	16.19
1876	9	418	1,024	2.45	5,565	13.30
1877	9	375	961	2.56	5,126	13.66
1878	9	339	695	2.05	5,124	15.11
1879	9	335	1,036	3.09	4,385	13.08
1880	10	405	1,149	2.83	5,487	13.54
1881	10	464	780	1.69	6,960	15.00
1882	10	477	1,254	2.62	6,253	13.10
1883	10	446	1,506	3.35	6,192	13.87
1884	12	484	1,477	3.05	7,172	14.81
1885	12	495	2,101	4.24	6,145	12.21
1886	12	504	2,303	4.56	5,651	11.01
			$15,751		$76,553	

A TABLE FOR CHILE,

Showing the Progress of the Order from 1875 to 1886, Inclusive.

Year.	No. of Lodges.	No. of Members.	Total Relief.	Relief per Member.	Total Receipts.	Receipts per Member.
1875	7	320	$340	$1.06	$11,290	$35.29
1876	8	399	524	1.31	11,504	28.83
1877	8	*	*	*	*	*
1878	8	*	*	*	*	*
†1879	7	333	6,320	18.98	25,402	76.28
1880	5	266	1,699	6.39	4,830	18.16
1881	5	267	1,262	4.73	5,213	19.52
1882	5	269	2,562	9.52	5,276	19.61
1883	6	283	1,775	6.27	6,353	22.44
1884	6	289	1,446	5.00	4,960	17.16
1885	7	296	2,044	6.90	5,885	19.88
1886	5	263	712	2.70	4,045	15.38
			$18,684		$84,758	

* No Report.   † Report for three years, 1877, 1878, and 1879.

A TABLE FOR DAKOTA,

Showing the Progress of the Order from 1875 to 1886, Inclusive.

Year.	No. of Lodges.	No. of Members.	Total Relief.	Relief per Member.	Total Receipts.	Receipts per Member.
1875	7	252	$157	$0.62	$2,451	$9.72
1876	11	315	351	1.11	3,271	10.38
1877	13	426	1,552	3.64	4,886	11.47
1878	15	507	862	1.70	6,363	12.51
1879	17	841	942	1.12	8,803	10.57
1880	26	952	1,041	1.09	10,912	11.46
1881	32	1,241	1,546	1.24	15,147	12.21
1882	38	1,564	2,524	1.63	23,000	14.70
1883	56	2,122	3,234	1.52	28,214	13.24
1884	66	2,485	3,580	1.44	35,964	14.47
1885	79	2,955	4,675	1.51	37,996	12.86
1886	87	3,462	4,868	1.41	44,749	12.92
			$25,332		$221,756	

A TABLE FOR QUEBEC,

Showing the Progress of the Order from 1878 to 1886, Inclusive.

Year.	No. of Lodges.	No. of Members.	Total Relief.	Relief per Member.	Total Receipts.	Receipts per Member.
1878	8	544	$271	$0.50	$1,051	$1.93
1879	11	870	1,141	1.31	4,254	4.89
1880	13	720	982	1.36	5,342	7.42
1881	13	734	1,778	2.42	5,058	6.89
1882	13	763	1,493	1.95	5,710	7.48
1883	14	795	1,789	2.25	6,139	7.72
1884	12	732	1,758	2.40	6,299	8.60
1885	13	739	2,306	3.12	6,117	8.28
1886	13	773	2,022	2.62	5,596	7.24
			$13,540		$45,566	

A TABLE FOR WASHINGTON,

Showing the Progress of the Order from 1878 to 1886, Inclusive.

Year.	No. of Lodges.	No. of Members.	Total Relief.	Relief per Member.	Total Receipts.	Receipts per Member.
1878	14	478	$841	$1.76	$8,074	$16.68
1879	16	677	1,908	2.80	9,204	13.59
1880	17	621	2,433	3.92	12,220	19.68
1881	22	886	2,790	3.15	24,395	27.65
1882	25	1,117	4,278	3.83	26,004	23.28
1883	26	1,248	4,600	3.69	34,970	28.02
1884	32	1,463	4,799	3.28	36,418	24.90
1885	38	1,609	5,329	3.31	32,574	20.24
1886	44	1,808	7,360	4.08	40,183	22.23
			$34,338		$224,042	

A TABLE FOR MANITOBA,

Showing the Progress of the Order from 1883 to 1886, Inclusive.

Year.	No. of Lodges.	No. of Members.	Total Relief.	Relief per Member.	Total Receipts.	Receipts per Member.
1883	8	495	$57	$0.11	$932	$1.88
1884	11	628	758	1.20	8,163	13.00
1885	11	720	1,268	1.76	8,677	12.05
1886	13	1,005	2,163	2.15	12,184	12.12
			$4,246		$29,956	

A TABLE FOR IDAHO,

Showing the Progress of the Order from 1883 to 1886, Inclusive.

Year.	No. of Lodges.	No. of Members.	Total Relief.	Relief per Member.	Total Receipts.	Receipts per Member.
1883	9	305	$919	$3.01	*	*
1884	10	316	1,675	5.30	$3,501	$11.08
1885	13	435	1,379	3.16	8,680	19.95
1886	17	547	1,417	2.59	10,617	19.40
			$5,390		$22,798	

*No Report.

A TABLE FOR DENMARK,

Showing the Progress of the Order from 1884 to 1886, Inclusive.

Year.	No. of Lodges.	No. of Members.	Total Relief.	Relief per Member.	Total Receipts.	Receipts per Member.
1884	17	1,585	$2,627	$1.66	$25,262	$15.92
1885	20	1,900	5,810 •	3.05	31,904	16.79
1886	21	1,923	6,377	3.31	22,500	11.70
			$14,814		$79,666	

A TABLE FOR ARIZONA,

Showing the Progress of the Order from 1884 to 1886, Inclusive.

Year.	No. of Lodges.	No. of Members.	Total Relief.	Relief per Member.	Total Receipts.	Receipts per Member.
1884	6	319	$1,134	$3.55	$6,867	$21.52
1885	6	315	2,011	6.38	8,470	26.88
1886	6	326	1,741	5.34	7,657	23.48
			$4,886	·	$22,994	

THE PROGRESS OF THE ORDER FROM THE YEAR 1840 TO 1886, INCLUSIVE.

(Australasia and Germany are not included.)

Year	Grand Lodges	Subordinate Lodges	Rebekah Degree Lodges	Grand Encampm'ts	Subordinate Encampm'ts	Lodge Members	Encampment Members	Relief by Lodges	Relief by Encampments	Relief by Rebekah L's	Revenue of Lodges	Revenue of Encampments	Revenue of Rebekah L's	Total Relief	Total Revenue
1840	14	155		4	36	11,166	*463	*$8,044			*$59,299	*$2,868		$8,044	$62,187
1841	18	199		5	34	17,854	834	*18,552	+		*115,878	*4,986		18,552	120,776
1842	20	265		5	61	24,160	*2,097	*43,436	+		*163,719	*12,963		43,496	175,982
1843	21	352		9	73	30,048	2,434	*66,863	+		*191,635	*18,751		66,863	205,396
1844	26	457		10	*102	40,288	*3,536	*72,114	+		*283,133	*20,664		72,114	308,797
1845	27	688		10	146	61,858	6,847	*155,361	*$5,526		*455,977	*37,977		130,887	498,954
1846	30	932		15	273	90,768	9,409	*197,317			*708,205	*53,999		197,817	762,204
1847	31	1392			300	118,961	13,704	*302,243	*967		888,605	82,164		310,210	970,769
1848	33	*1713		23	388	122,697	16,916	*306,446	*20,797		*673,418	*86,024		327,243	961,437
1849	32	1727		25	*409	139,242	17,113	365,557	*26,161		*886,175	*92,378		391,718	987,008
1850	31	*2354		27	499	174,687	19,722	*453,404	*31,438		1,217,417	*90,883		514,842	1,300,795
1851	32	2647		27	*524	189,512	21,080	*450,161	31,044		1,219,685	*96,562		511,205	1,316,227
1852	33	*2729		28	508	193,298	21,409	*614,722	*36,670		1,164,331	*92,824		651,392	1,257,155
1853	33	2941		29	541	193,030	21,771	491,822	*90,927		1,209,229	*95,617		522,249	1,304,846
1854	34	3129		29	613	190,197	23,062	499,527	37,504		1,384,985	*118,524		536,031	1,453,480
1855	35	3318		30	613	*200,000	23,081	545,415	39,061		*1,147,134	*96,607		584,476	1,243,741
1856	37	3397		30	630	193,614	23,749	492,798	*37,898		*1,180,825	*102,984		530,072	1,283,109
1857	37	3505		30	612	188,712	22,756	488,412	*34,040		*1,188,211	*92,970		472,463	1,298,787
1858	39	3390		30	*651	176,700	23,319	440,259	*38,670		*1,223,685	*94,040		476,929	1,383,848
1859	39	3485		30	641	177,711	23,448	440,960	*36,710		*1,116,081	*110,157		477,670	1,325,818
1860	39	3547		30	671	173,818	23,674	*470,739	*41,546		*1,163,407	*109,787		531,285	1,270,904
1861	39	*2035		30	*553	149,289	20,572	*470,086	*40,388		*900,981	*107,497		510,474	984,121
1862	39	*3608		30	557	137,286	18,328	*379,964	*36,597		*849,907	*53,140		416,561	980,087
1863	39	*2750		30	*512	133,280	17,908	*397,740	*40,418		*989,657	*80,920		438,158	1,094,778
1864	39	*2118		30	466	187,623	19,234	*415,461	*43,989		*1,040,169	*112,660		454,480	1,161,839
1865	40	*2441		30	*470	153,594	21,682	*507,957	*49,810		*1,302,969	*127,103		557,767	1,430,092
1866	39	2650		30	587	189,128	27,598	*550,288	*58,664		*1,574,028	*165,639		603,952	1,389,067

THE PROGRESS OF THE ORDER FROM THE YEAR 1840 TO 1886, INCLUSIVE.

(Australasia and Germany are not included.)

Continued.

Year	Grand Lodges	Subordinate Lodges	Rebekah Degree Lodges	Grand Encampments	Subordinate Encampments	Lodge Members	Encampment Members	Relief by Lodges	Relief by Encampments	Relief by Rebekah L's	Revenue of Lodges	Revenue of Encampments	Revenue of Rebekah L's	Total Relief	Total Revenue
1867	40	*2860		31	$697	*214,561	*34,842	*$180,384	*$66,295		$1,804,234	*$215,877		$694,650	$2,020,111
1868	41	3195		31	795	245,096	*43,478	*695,618	70,488		2,110,952	*252,345		766,056	2,363,297
1869	41	3473		31	900	268,608	49,443	*700,430	*81,807		2,347,047	*283,244		842,237	2,630,318
1870	41	3867		31	1059	298,387	56,388	*859,907	*92,216		2,724,419	335,240		952,123	3,090,659
1871	41	4292		33	1198	327,577	63,293	977,561	114,534		2,950,101	350,908		1,092,095	3,310,009
1872	46	5045	168	38	1398	385,097	73,963	1,342,890	160,560	$517	3,828,310	462,891	$6,640	1,504,057	4,297,841
1873	48	5468	512	38	1512	414,815	80,131	1,335,037	150,787	3,550	3,989,794	478,469	15,738	1,490,275	4,494,101
1874	48	5987	632	38	1634	438,701	88,692	1,374,743	159,350	4,543	4,006,331	466,670	98,664	1,538,635	4,511,665
1875	48	6395	879	39	1756	454,089	87,450	1,510,854	180,909	7,045	4,193,666	488,482	32,155	1,698,869	4,714,242
1876	48	6678	640	39	1806	456,135	87,785	1,507,649	173,151	4,685	4,008,983	453,035	29,323	1,689,488	4,489,872
1877	50	6975	770	39	1835	448,019	84,787	1,516,242	181,482	5,542	3,961,901	431,828	21,853	1,705,207	4,423,052
1878	50	7067	734	39	1863	442,291	82,408	1,553,727	177,181	9,498	3,814,127	415,834	30,925	1,740,406	4,260,097
1879	50	7172	856	40	1842	440,763	79,512	1,539,623	170,296	4,946	3,970,630	382,100	28,485	1,714,805	4,391,215
1880	50	7306	899	41	1857	456,942	79,498	1,582,930	167,343	4,816	4,191,464	364,804	32,578	1,695,970	4,618,847
1881	54	7514	995	41	1864	475,948	80,643	1,657,419	168,257	6,496	4,416,375	407,484	31,018	1,831,171	4,854,877
1882	54	7708	1066	43	1906	493,996	85,110	1,704,291	166,807	11,346	4,755,702	441,885	48,359	1,862,444	5,245,946
1883	54	7845	1182	44	1934	505,871	90,882	1,819,328	183,931	12,573	4,804,716	495,027	58,396	2,015,838	5,300,041
1884	54	7956	1247	44	1947	516,290	94,257	1,901,474	197,593	12,020	4,786,586	480,978	56,493	2,111,987	5,274,306
1885	54			44		517,310	94,376	1,960,418	205,620	14,444	4,761,112	473,652	71,925	2,180,902	5,309,689
1886	54	8109	1848	44	1996	580,300	97,773	2,002,419	208,015	16,261	5,079,689	496,308	83,034	2,297,885	5,659,772
								$87,807,973	$8,801,966	$118,031	$100,770,832	$10,387,058	$598,146	$41,728,471	$111,756,036

* Incomplete Reports.   † No Report,

JURISDICTIONS COMPARED—LODGES.

Jurisdictions.	No. of Lodges.	No. of Members.	Av. No. Mem's to a Lodge.
Alabama	33	1,507	46
Arizona	6	326	54
Arkansas	65	1,592	24
British Columbia, Canada	7	700	100
California	303	24,375	80
Chile	5	263	53
Colorado	60	3,448	57
Connecticut	59	10,107	171
Dakota	87	3,462	40
Delaware	32	2,431	76
Denmark	21	1,923	92
District of Columbia	15	1,620	108
Florida	20	555	27
Georgia	49	2,038	43
Idaho	17	547	32
Illinois	669	31,806	48
Indiana	552	26,270	48
Iowa	465	21,461	48
Kansas	305	12,885	42
Kentucky	168	6,948	41
Louisiana	20	751	38
Lower Provinces, B. N. A	40	2,303	58
Maine	112	16,041	143
Manitoba, Canada	13	1,005	93
Maryland	107	9,052	84
Massachusetts	179	32,759	183
Michigan	367	17,302	47
Minnesota	107	6,471	60
Mississippi	28	956	34
Missouri	376	15,154	40
Montana	22	1,060	48
Nebraska	136	5,610	41
Nevada	26	1,433	55
New Hampshire	73	9,483	130
New Jersey	206	18,775	91
New York	514	44,191	86
North Carolina	36	1,169	33
Ohio	676	49,267	73
Ontario, Canada	210	14,856	71
Oregon	82	3,560	43
Pennsylvania	932	81,480	87
Quebec, Canada	13	773	59
Rhode Island	45	5,539	122
South Carolina	16	611	38
Switzerland	5	179	36
Tennesee	125	3,420	27
Texas	170	4,450	26
Utah	8	498	62
Vermont	31	2,101	70
Virginia	55	3,416	62
Washington	44	1,808	41
West Virginia	80	3,629	45
Wisconsin	300	14,983	50
Wyoming	12	504	42
Alberta, Canada	1	51	51
Cuba	6	329	55
Indian Territory	5	257	51
Mexico	2	91	45
Netherlands, Europe	2	102	51
New Mexico	8	307	87
Peru, South America	3	138	46
Sandwich Islands	2	172	86
		530,300	

JURISDICTIONS COMPARED—ENCAMPMENTS.

Jurisdictions.	No. of Encampments.	No. of Members.	Average No. of Members to an Encampment.
Alabama	7	186	27
Arkansas	4	91	23
California	74	4,641	63
Colorado	25	850	34
Connecticut	22	2,614	119
Dakota	21	598	28
Delaware	9	358	40
District of Columbia	4	460	115
Florida	7	122	17
Georgia	10	422	42
Illinois	174	5,733	33
Indiana	131	5,958	45
Iowa	120	4,039	34
Kansas	67	2,121	32
Kentucky	36	1,561	43
Louisiana	5	135	27
Maine	45	4,292	95
Maryland	26	1,278	49
Massachusetts	56	7,809	157
Michigan	97	2,954	27
Minnesota	28	1,208	50
Mississippi	12	245	20
Missouri	78	2,217	28
Montana	7	234	33
Nebraska	22	639	29
Nevada	9	364	40
New Hampshire	29	2,689	93
New Jersey	51	2,686	53
New York	95	5,839	61
North Carolina	10	210	21
Ohio	187	10,926	58
Ontario, Canada	64	3,032	47
Oregon	20	671	33
Pennsylvania	204	12,674	62
Rhode Island	18	1,735	91
South Carolina	4	52	13
Tennessee	18	352	20
Texas	40	790	20
Vermont	12	605	50
Virginia	14	469	33
Washington	11	326	30
West Virginia	21	607	29
Wisconsin	71	1,858	22
Wyoming	6	146	24
Arizona	1	26	26
British Columbia, Canada	2	47	23
Denmark, Europe	4	401	100
Idaho	1	37	37
Indian Territory	2	75	37
Lower Provinces, B. N. A	5	148	30
Manitoba, Canada	3	127	42
New Mexico	4	78	19
Peru, South America	1	43	43
Sandwich Islands	1	42	42
		97,820	

JURISDICTIONS COMPARED—DEGREE LODGES OF THE DAUGHTERS OF REBEKAH.

Jurisdictions.	No. of Lodges.	No. of Members.		Total Membership.	Average No. of Members to a Lodge.
		Brothers.	Sisters.		
Alabama............	6	292	262	554	92
Arizona.........	2	30	18	48	24
Arkansas...........	11	119	82	201	18
California.	89	2,719	2,950	5,669	64
Colorado...........	4	81	60	141	35
Connecticut	16	671	768	1,439	90
Dakota.............	3	74	55	129	43
Delaware.......... ..	1	33	42	75	75
Denmark...........	1	49	53	102	102
District of Columbia	2	55	59	114	57
Georgia....	2	57	51	108	54
Idaho.............	3	68	45	113	38
Illinois.............	91	2,266	2,363	4,629	51
Indiana....,........	233	2,457	3,007	5,464	24
Iowa.............	80	1,942	1,906	3,848	48
Kansas.............	82	2,025	1,321	3,346	41
Kentucky...........	22	396	410	806	37
Louisiana...........	2	37	25	62	31
Lower Prov., B.N.A.	2	52	81	133	66
Maine	23	1,159	1,275	2,434	106
Massachusetts......	50	3,277	3,408	6,685	134
Michigan...........	98	1,764	1,634	3,398	35
Missouri...........	31	571	518	1,089	35
Montana........ ...	1	64	37	101	101
Nebraska...........	27	249	238	487	18
Nevada.........	3	55	80	135	45
New Hampshire.....	30	1,762	1,814	3,576	119
New Jersey........	17	699	568	1,267	75
New York..........	76	2,969	3,015	5,984	79
Ohio..............	120	3,435	3,784	7,219	60
Oregon.............	13	191	187	378	29
Pennsylvania	78	975	1,163	2,138	27
Rhode Island.......	18	800	724	1,524	85
Tennessee..	5	81	60	141	28
Texas	3	35	36	71	24
Vermont...........	8	450	341	791	98
Washington.........	7	191	136	327	47
West Virginia.......	7	110	164	274	39
Wisconsin.........	75	954	1,139	2,093	28
Wyoming..	3	65	57	122	41
		33,279	33,936	67,215	

CHAPTER XV.

ODES SET TO MUSIC.

MARCH. E♭.

Bro. W. F. Hascall.

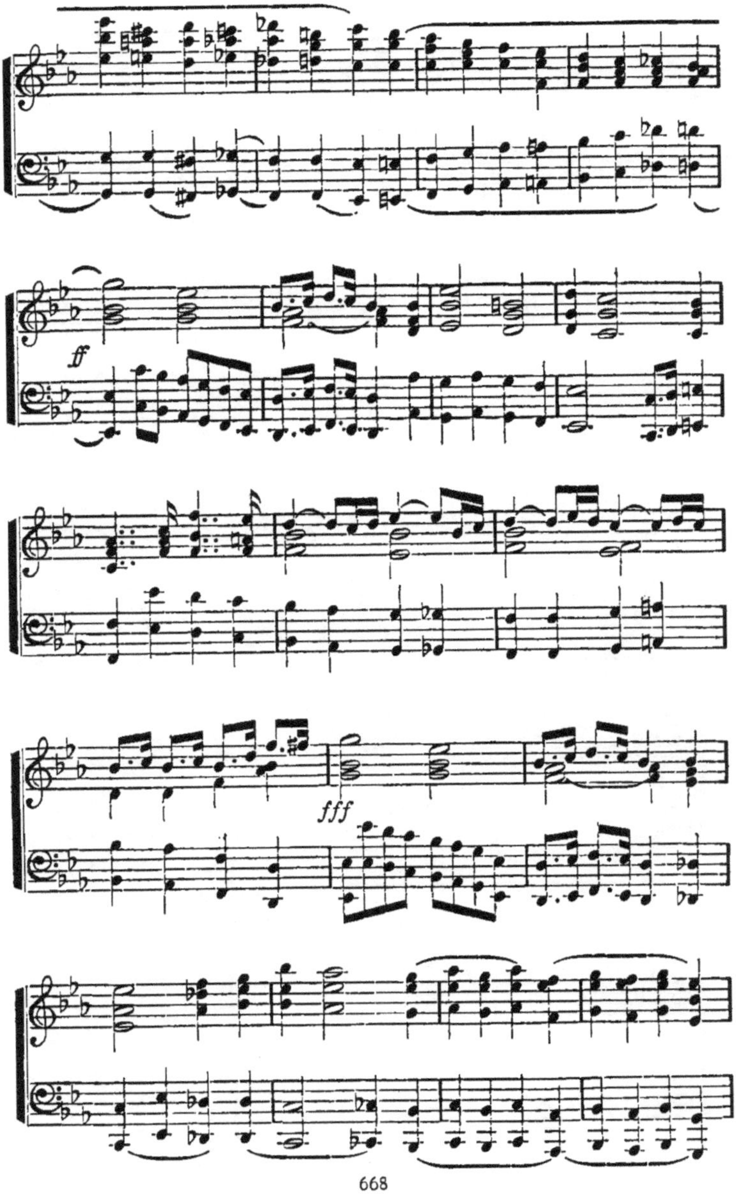
ff
fff

MARCH.—Concluded.

Fine.

TRIO.

p

mf

f *ff*

D.C. ⊕

CHARITY.

Words by D. C. COLESWORTHY.

W. F. HASCALL.

p 1. When to the bosom warmly press'd, We take some wanderer home, Who sought in vain a place of rest, Too fee-ble now to roam— We but o - bey the voice that speaks, From Him that rules the skies: "He who his neighbor's wel - fare seeks, Shall to my kingdom rise."

2. O, blest are they that never turn,
   A brother from the door—
   In every face a friend discern,
   Though feeble, sick and poor;
   And with the hand, wide-spread, receive
   And nurture him with care;
   Such souls a crown of glory weave,
   In paradise to wear.

ODE.

WALTER H. LEWIS.

With feeling,

1. Hail! Hail! Hail! Hail to thee, ho - ly Char - i - ty, Thy
2. Hail! Hail! Hail! Hail to thee, glo-rious Friendship hail! Thy

birth - place is the skies; Thy dwell - ing is the ten - der heart, Thy
birth - place is the heart; Thy mas - ter hand who wrought the link, Wills

language—tear - ful eyes. Thine at - tributes beam in the smile, That J
that it should not part. In un - ion strong our or - der stands, The

like morn's sunlight glow, To soothe the furrowed brow of care, And
haven of th' oppressed, Then Friendship, hail, and Char - i - ty, Light

1st Ending.

heal the bos - om's woe.

2d Ending.

of the hu - man breast.

GLEE.

W. F. Hascall.

O, what pleasure 'tis to meet, With friends so blythe and jol-ly, Who all de-light to drive a-way, The gloom of mel-an-cho-ly, Then let us throw all care a-side, Let's mer-ry be and mel-low, May Friendship, Love, and Truth a-bide, With ev-ery true Odd Fellow.

2. True friendship is a treasure great,
    As such may we regard it;
  May discord ne'er our Lodge intrude,
    Nor anything retard it.
  But let the song and toast go round,
    Let every heart be mellow,
  And may our motto still be found
    In every true Odd Fellow.

NOTE.—The first line in second verse is sung like the sixth line in the first verse, as regards joining the words to the music.

672

TABLE ODE.

W. F. HASCALL.

Allegro.

f 1. Here a-round this fes-tal ta-ble, Let thine influence *Friendship*, fall.

Bind-ing, by a un-ion sta-ble, All to each, and each to all!

Not a-lone, mid hours of glad-ness, O'er us be thy wings outspread,

Guide us, in our scenes of sadness, By the sick, the grieved, the dead.

2. Here, too, *Love*, at this our meeting,
    Come and warm each brother's breast;
Here, let quickened pulses beating,
    Show thy power, o'er all, confessed.
Seldom have so many brothers,
    Met around one board before
Draw each heart to all the others,
    F'er they part to meet no more.

3. *Truth*, may'st thou, too, hover o'er us,
    Teach each lip, and warm each heart;
Never, with thy light before us
    Can we from the path depart.
By this triple bond united,
    Brothers, we may stand secure;
May it ne'er be scorned or slighted,
    But remain firm, bright, and pure.

* Last verse loud.

LOVE.

Caroline F. Orne.

W. F. Hascall.

p 1. A voice from the o - pen-ing flowers,.... A voice from the dim old woods, A tone from the murmuring streams, A shout from the sounding floods. A whis-pering 'mid the leaves,...... Light from the sphere a - bove,........ And the voi - ces of the flow - ers, the woods, and stream, Speak ev - er - more of love.

2. The song of the summer bird,
    With its music glad and free ;
The restless, wandering wind,
    And the ever flowing sea.
All voice of one delight,
    Round us and above,
Pour out to the Highest evermore,
    One anthem strain of love.

3. Oh, that high and holy power
    Should fill every human heart,
Never, by thought, or word, or deed,
    From its spirit should we depart.
First should our heart be given
    To God who reigns above,
And it must follow, as light the sun
    Our neighbor we must love.

✱ Ties 2d verse. † Ties 3d verse.

674

FUNERAL ODE.

W. F. HASCALL.

1. The things we love, they pass a - way, With all the hopes that round them
2. 'Tis true that time may bring a - gain, The birds, the flow'rs, the breath of

cling, The cheer - ful birds, the fra - grant flowers, The
spring; Wak - en the sum - mer's my - riad charms, And

gen - tle smile and breath of Spring. The Sum - mer's bright - er,
o'er our path her beau - ties fling;— While au - tumn's fruits, and

warm - er joy, The fruits of au - tumn, win - ter's mirth, Per -
win - ter's joys, Fol - low suc - ces - sive - ly her train; Yet

- ish, and pass like bub - bles light, With the same hour that saw their birth.
nev - er, nev - er, may the friends Who fade and fall re - vive a - gain.

3. Ah, no—they sleep while seasons change,
   And fast recede the long, long years—
We may not rouse them—'tis in vain,
   From feelings fast spring up the tears.
Sad, sad, 'tis ever to behold
   Life's cherished objects swift decay;
But there's no sorrow keen as that
   We feel, when loved one's pass away.

CHAPTER XVI.

A LEXICON

Of a Few Proper Names in the Old and New Testaments,
and of Common Latin Words in Frequent Use.

Aaron, lofty, mountainous.
Ab'ba, father.
A'dah, assembly.
A'gur, stranger.
A'in, fountain.
Al'lon, oak.
A'mos, weighty.
A'nak, collar.
A'ner, affliction.
An'te, before.
Ar, awakening.
A'rad, dragon.
A'sia, muddy.
As'tra, stars.
A'ven, riches.

Ba'rak, thunder.
Be'dad, friendship.
Be'er, well.
Be'rith, covenant
Be'sor, glad news.
Be'tah, confidence.
Beu'lah, married.
Be'zek, lightning.
Bil'dad, old friendship.
Boz'rah, distress.
Brev'is, short.

Cain, possession.
Ca'lah, good opportunity.
Ca'leb, basket.
Car'mel, harvest.
Car'pus, fruit.
Cas'tor, beaver.
Ce'phas, stone.
Che'sed, destroyer.
Chlo'e, green herb.
Clau'da, broken voice.
Clau'dia, lame.
Cle'ment, merciful.

Co'pia, plenty.
Cus'tos, keeper.

Da'gon, fish.
Dam'aris, little woman
Da'ra, generation.
Da'vid, beloved.
Deb'orah, bee.
De'dan, friendship.
De'mas, popular.
Di'nah, judgment.
Do'eg, fisherman.
Do'than, the law.
Du'mah, silence.
Du'ra, habitation.
Dux, leader.

E'bed, servant.
E'den, delight.
E'dom, red.
Eg'lah, chariot.
E'lam, virgin.
El'dad, beloved of God.
E'lim, strong.
E'lon, grove.
Eph'ron, dust.
Eras'tus, lovely.
Es'se, to be.
Es'ther, hidden.
E'than, strong.
Eu'nice, good victory.
Eve, living.
E'zel, going abroad.
Ez'ra, helper.

Fe'lix, happy.
Fes'tus, joyful.
Feli'citer, happily.
Fides, faith.
Fortuna'tus, prosperous.

Gad, band.
Gath, press.
Ga'za, strong.
Ge'ra, pilgrimage.
Gil'gal, revolution.
Go'mer, consumer.
Go'shen, approaching.
Go'zen, pasture.
Grex, flock.
Gur, dwelling.

Ha'dad, joy.
Ha'gar, stranger.
Ha'mul, merciful.
Ha'nun, gracious.
Ha'rod, astonishment.
He'bron, friendship.
He'lam, trouble.
Hel'bon, milk.
Her'mon, destruction.
Ho'bah, love.
Ho'red, desert.
Hul, infirmity.
Hur, liberty.

Ib'har, election.
Id'do, praise.
I'jon, fountain.
Im'lah, plentitude.
In'dia, praise.
I'ra, spoil.
I'saac, laughter.
Ish'bak, forsaken.
Ith'iel, God with me.
I'vah, iniquity.

Jab'bok, dissipation.
Ja'besh, confusion.
Ja'bez, sorrow.
Ja'cob, the heel.
Ja'sher, righteous.
Je'rah, the moon.
Jes'se, my present.
Jo'ab, voluntary.
John, the mercy of the Lord.
Jo'nah, dove.
Jop'pa, beauty.
Jo'seph, increase.
Ju'lia, downy.
Jus'tus, upright.

Ka'desh, holiness.
Ke'da, blackness.
Ke'naz, lamentation.
Kish'ron, perfuming.
Kit'tim, coloring.
Ko'hath, obedience.

La'ban, white.
La'el, to God.
Lah'mi, my head.

La'ish, lion.
Le'ah, weary.
Le'hi, jawbone.
Lex, law.
Li'nus, nets.
Lo'is, better.
Lu'cas, luminous.
Lux, light.
Luz, separation.

Mah'lon, infirmity,
Mal'chus, kingdom.
Mam'mon, riches.
Mam're, rebellious.
Ma'on, house.
Ma'ra, bitter.
Mi'cah, poor.
Mil'cah, queen.
Mil'lo, fullness.
Mir'iam, exalted.
Miz'pah, sentinel.
Mos, custom
Mo'ses, from the water.
My'ra, weep.

Na'dab, prince.
Nag'ge, brightness.
Na'hum, comforter.
Na'in, beauty.
Na'omi, agreeable.
Na'pish, the soul.
Ne'mo, no one.
Ni'ger, black.
Nim'rod, rebellious.
Ni'san, banner.
No'ah, repose.
Nod, vagabond.
Nun, durable.

O'bed, servant.
Oc'ran, disturber.
O'hel, brightness.
O'mar, bitter.
Om'ri, sheaf of corn.
O'nus, burden.
O'phir, ashes.
O'reb, raven.

Pal'ti, deliverance.
Pa'phos, very hot.
Pa'ran, beauty.
Par'bar, gate of the temple.
Pash'ur, whiteness.
Path'ros, mouthful of dew.
Pat'mos, mortal.
Paul'us, worker.
Pax, peace.
Pe'leg, division.
Pe'ter, rock.
Phal'lu, hidden.
Phe'be, pure.

Phi'col, perfection.
Phil'ip, lover of horses.
Phle'gon, burning.
Phu'rah, that grows.
Pi'non, gem.
Pis'gah, fortress.
Pol'lux, boxer.
Pon'tus, the sea.
Pris'ca, ancient.
Pu'dens, shamefaced.
Pul, destruction

Quar'tus, the fourth.
Quid, why?
Qui'ver, a receptacle.
Quo'rum, of whom

Rab'bah, powerful
Ra'chab, proud.
Ra'chel, sheep.
Ra'gan, neighbor.
Res, a thing.
Re'sin, bridle.
Re'zon, secret.
Rho'da, rose.
Rim'mon, exalted.
Riz'pah, extension.
Ro'gel, foot.
Ro'man, powerful.
Ros, dew.
Ru'fus, red.
Ru'mah, rejected.
Rus, country.
Ruth, satisfied.

Sa'doc, just.
Sa'lah, mission.
Sa'lem, peace.
Sal'mon, peaceable.
Sa'mos, full of gravel
Sam'son, his son.
Sa'rah, princess of the multitude.
Sar'gon, snares.
Sa'ruch, branch.
Sa'tan, adversary.
Saul, destroyer.
Se'ba, drunkard.
Se'bat, sceptre.
Se'gub, fortified.
Se'lah, rock.
Sem'per, always.
Se'rah, the morning.
Sha'lim, fox.
Sham'gar, stranger.
Sha'mir, prison.
Sha'ron, his plain.
She'ba, repose.
Shem, renown.
She'nir, lantern.
She'va, vanity.
Shi'loh, the apostle.

Shu'ah, meditation.
Shu'shan, lily.
Sib'mah, captivity.
Si'don, hunting.
Si'hon, conclusion.
Si'las, three.
Si'van, thorn.
Sod'om, their lime.
Spes, hope.
Ste'phen, crown.
Susan'na, lily.

Tab'bath, goodness.
Ta'bor, choice.
Tad'mor, palm tree.
Ta'mar, palm tree.
Tar'sus, winged.
Te'bah, murder.
Te'kel, weight.
Te'ma, admiration.
Thom'as, twin.
Thum'min, perfection.
Tek'vah, congregation.
Ti'mon, honorable.
Tir'zah, benevolent.
Ti'tus, honorable.
Tob, goodness.
To'la, scarlet.
To'phet, drum.
Tu'bal, the earth.
Tu'tor, protector.

U'cal, power.
U'lam, the porch.
Ul'la, leaf.
Un'ni, afflicted.
Uz'zah, strength.

Vash'ni, second.
Vash'ti, thread.
Ver, spring.
Voph'si, fragment.
Vox, voice.

Za'bad, dowry.
Zab'di, portion.
Za'dok, just.
Za'rah, brightness.
Ze'bul, habitation.
Ze'nas, living.
Zer, perplexity.
Zi'don, venison.
Zil'lah, shadow.
Zim'ran, song.
Zi'on, monument.
Ziph, mouthful.
Zip'por, crown.
Ziz, lock of hair.
Zo'bar, army.
Zo'na, girdle.
Zo'rah, leprosy.

INDEX.

688   INDEX.